THE CRITICAL NEXUS

AMS Studies in Music

JANN PASLER, *General Editor*

Editorial Board

Conceptualizing Music:
Cognitive Structure, Theory, and Analysis
Lawrence Zbikowski

Inventing the Business of Opera:
The Impresario and His World in Seventeenth-Century Venice
Beth L. Glixon and Jonathan Glixon

Lateness and Brahms:
Music and Culture in the Twilight of Viennese Liberalism
Margaret Notley

The Critical Nexus:
Tone-System, Mode, and Notation in Early Medieval Music
Charles M. Atkinson

Music, Criticism, and the Challenge of History:
Shaping Modern Musical Thought in Late Nineteenth-Century Vienna
Kevin C. Karnes

Jewish Music and Modernity
Philip V. Bohlman

Changing the Score:
Arias, Prima Donnas, and the Authority of Performance
Hilary Poriss

Rasa:
Affect and Intuition in Javanese Musical Aesthetics
Marc Benamou

Josquin's Rome:
Hearing and Composing in the Sistine Chapel
Jesse Rodin

Details of Consequence:
Ornament, Music, and Art in Paris
Gurminder Kaur Bhogal

Sounding Authentic:
The Rural Miniature and Musical Modernism
Joshua S. Walden

Brahms Among Friends:
Listening, Performance, and the Rhetoric of Allusion
Paul Berry

The Critical Nexus

Tone-System, Mode, and Notation
in Early Medieval Music

Charles M. Atkinson

OXFORD
UNIVERSITY PRESS

OXFORD
UNIVERSITY PRESS

Oxford University Press is a department of the University of Oxford.
It furthers the University's objective of excellence in research, scholarship,
and education by publishing worldwide.

Oxford   New York

Auckland   Cape Town   Dar es Salaam   Hong Kong   Karachi
Kuala Lumpur   Madrid   Melbourne   Mexico City   Nairobi
New Delhi   Shanghai   Taipei   Toronto

With offices in

Argentina   Austria   Brazil   Chile   Czech Republic   France   Greece
Guatemala   Hungary   Italy   Japan   Poland   Portugal   Singapore
South Korea   Switzerland   Thailand   Turkey   Ukraine   Vietnam

Oxford is a registered trade mark of Oxford University Press
in the UK and certain other countries.

Published in the United States of America by
Oxford University Press
198 Madison Avenue, New York, NY 10016

Library of Congress Cataloging-in-Publication Data
Atkinson, Charles M. (Charles Mercer), 1941–
The critical nexus: tone-system, mode, and notation in early medieval music / Charles M. Atkinson
p. cm. — (AMS studies in music)
Includes bibliographical references and index.
ISBN 978-0-19-514888-6 (hardcover); 978-0-19-027399-6 (paperback);
1. Music theory—History—500–1400.
2. Music theory—To 500—Influence. I. Title.
ML174.A85 2008
781.2'63—dc22   2007011368

The manufacturer's authorised representative in the EU for product safety is
Oxford University Press España S.A. of Parque Empresarial San Fernando de Henares,
Avenida de Castilla, 2 – 28830 Madrid (www.oup.es/en or product.safety@oup.com).
OUP España S.A. also acts as importer into Spain of products made by the manufacturer.

In memoriam Fritz Reckow

The original impetus for this study came from my friend Fritz Reckow (1940–1998), who invited me to participate in a symposium in Kiel in 1985. Held under the co-sponsorship of the Universität Kiel and the Schleswig-Holsteinische Landesbibliothek, the symposium dealt with the creation of a European musical culture in the Middle Ages ("Die Formung einer europäischen musikalischen Kultur im Mittelalter"). My presentation at the symposium was originally titled "On the Formation of a Medieval Theory of Mode." As I continued to work on the topic, with a view toward publishing the essay in the conference report, I realized that the substance of my study encompassed far more than the original title conveyed. That realization notwithstanding, and given the restrictions of page limits and deadlines, the version I submitted for publication was essentially the paper I had presented at the symposium. Unfortunately, the proceedings of the original symposium had not been published at the time of Fritz's untimely death on August 30, 1998, and the plan for publishing the proceedings had to be abandoned. I hope that publishing this essay in its expanded form may serve to complete one small part of Fritz Reckow's legacy to the fields of musicology and medieval studies.

ACKNOWLEDGMENTS

As its title intends to suggest, this is a book with a broad scope but a narrow focus. It is simultaneously both an attempt to provide a satisfactory answer to a specific question and a compendium of much of my work during the past three decades. Although its immediate impetus was the invitation from Fritz Reckow to participate in the 1985 Kiel symposium mentioned in the dedication, its roots ultimately extend back to a paper I wrote on the *parapteres* for a seminar on medieval theory with Calvin Bower at the University of North Carolina. As one might expect of a work with such a long gestation period, this one owes much to many. I cannot possibly name all the people and institutions that have played a role in its realization, but I should like to name at least a few.

The person who was present at the inception of this work, and who continues to be a source of information and inspiration to me, is Calvin Bower. His insights inform this study in ways too numerous to catalogue, but they are especially important to the sections on Boethius in chapter 1 and on the *Alia musica* in chapter 5.

I owe a debt of a special kind to Leo Treitler. His work on the advent of musical notation in the West has been of seminal importance for me, as it has for many others. Beyond that, though, his interest in the subject of this book and his reading and commenting on parts of the manuscript itself have made it a far better work than it would otherwise have been.

This study has profited additionally from intensive discussions with colleagues in the United States and Europe, who have afforded me the opportunity to present my work on this topic in seminars and colloquia at various stages of its development. The present study took its initial shape in a seminar I presented at Harvard University in 1984, at the invitation of David Hughes. I was able to present more fully developed versions in seminars at the University of North Carolina, where I had the honor of being a guest professor in the spring of 1987, and at the Graduate Center of the City University of New York in 1994, upon the invitation of Raymond Erickson. The work took something close to its present form in Paris in 2001, thanks to Marie-Noël Colette's having arranged for me to present it as a course at the École Pratique des Hautes Études of the Sorbonne. Her searching questions and observations as we translated the text into French were of great help in clarifying a number of issues, especially those concerning notation. The seminars and colloquia I was subsequently asked to present by Susan Patrick (University of New Mexico), Wulf Arlt (Universität Basel), and Andreas Haug (Universität Erlangen-Nürnberg) likewise contributed substantially to giving the work its present shape and substance. My profound thanks go to these friends and colleagues and to their students.

Of course, the people who have been most immediately involved in this work are my colleagues and students in musicology at Ohio State University. Arved Ashby, Daniel Avorgbedor, Graeme Boone, Burdette Green, Herbert Livingston (deceased), Martha Maas, Margarita Mazo, Lois Rosow, and Udo Will have been constant sources of inspiration and encouragement. I have been fortunate to have had a number of fine students in the various courses and seminars I offered on topics related to this study. Two of them, Cynthia Cyrus and Jane Warburton, contributed directly to this work by writing excellent papers on the *Alia musica* and on species theory, respectively. I take special pleasure in acknowledging their contributions here.

The following institutions provided support for this work in different ways, for which I am extremely grateful: The Ohio State University and its libraries; Bamberg, Staatsbibliothek; Bern, Burgerbibliothek; Besançon, Bibliothèque Municipale; Brussels, Bibliothèque Royale; Düsseldorf, Universitäts- und Landesbibliothek; Erlangen, Universitätsbibliothek; Karlsruhe, Badische Landesbibliothek; Leiden, Universiteitsbibliotheek; London, The British Library; Munich, Bayerische Staatsbibliothek; Orléans, Bibliothèque Municipale; Oxford, Bodleian Library; Paris, Bibliothèque nationale de France; Reims, Bibliothèque Municipale; Rochester, Sibley Music Library, Eastman School of Music of the University of Rochester; and St. Gall, Stiftsbibliothek. I should especially like to acknowledge the Österreichische Nationalbibliothek in Vienna for its permission to reproduce on the cover of this book the picture of Guido d'Arezzo and Bishop Theodaldus that appears on folio 35v of the manuscript cpv 51 in their collection.

The excursus on Aurelian and the Paleofrankish script in Chapter 3 is drawn from my article, "*De accentibus toni*," which appeared in *Essays on Medieval Music in Honor of David G. Hughes*. I wish to thank the Department of Music of Harvard University, publisher of the volume, and its editor, Graeme Boone, for their permission to republish that material here.

A special acknowledgment is due the National Endowment for the Humanities, whose fellowship for the academic year 2003/04 enabled me to complete this book and prepare the final manuscript.

I cannot close this section of acknowledgments without expressing my deep gratitude to the members of the Publications Committee of the American Musicological Society, who serve as the editorial board for the AMS Studies in Music. I am especially grateful to the two readers who reviewed the final manuscript for the Publications Committee. They raised questions about various parts of the study and made a number of valuable comments and suggestions. I have tried to respond to their questions and incorporate their suggestions in every case, but, should mistakes or shortcomings still remain, I accept full responsibility for them.

I should especially like to thank the series editor for this volume, Lawrence Bernstein, not only for his wonderful editorial work but also for his unflagging support in seeing the book through to publication.

Finally, I must express my profound gratitude to my family, Gretchen, Karen, and David, for their constant encouragement despite the fact that they so often had to compete with a manuscript, a book, or an article for my attention. This project would not have been possible without their support.

CONTENTS

Note on Abbreviations and Nomenclature for Pitch   xiii

Prologue   3

1. The Heritage of Antiquity   6

PART I. THE EIGHTH AND NINTH CENTURIES

2. The Reception of Ancient Texts in the Carolingian Era   49
3. The Heritage of the Church   85

PART II. THE SYNTHESIS OF ANCIENT GREEK THEORY
AND MEDIEVAL PRACTICE

4. Hucbald of St. Amand and Regino of Prüm   149

5. *Alia musica*   171

6. Pseudo-Bernelinus, Bern of Reichenau, Pseudo-Odo,
and Guido d'Arezzo   202

Epilogue   234

Bibliography   259
Index of Chants and Manuscripts   292
General Index   297

NOTE ON ABBREVIATIONS AND
NOMENCLATURE FOR PITCH

ABBREVIATIONS

General bibliographical abbreviations are explicated at the beginning of the bibliography. Throughout the text, manuscripts are cited by the city of their current provenance and the numeric part of their call number (or a portion thereof). More complete citations are given in the list of manuscripts in the bibliography.

PITCH

Letter names are used to identify pitches. Gamma (Γ) is equivalent to the G on the first line of the staff in bass clef. A represents the note a second above that; a the note an octave higher; and aa the note yet another octave higher.

THE CRITICAL NEXUS

PROLOGUE

In the sixth chapter of his *Dialogus de musica* (ca. 1000 A.D.), the anonymous author usually known as Pseudo-Odo of Cluny tries to explain to his student the effect that the placement of tones and semitones in a chant has on the determination of its mode. He gives as examples several chants that were difficult to classify, along with various solutions to the problems they present, and he concludes his discussion as follows.

> From this it is understood that the musician who lightly and presumptuously emends many melodies is ignorant unless he first goes through all the modes to determine whether the melody may perhaps not stand in one or another, nor should he care as much for its similarity to other melodies as for its fidelity to the rules. But if it conforms to no mode, let it be emended according to the one with which it least disagrees. This also should be observed: that the emended melody either sound better or depart little from its previous likeness.[1]

This statement raises a number of interesting questions, but perhaps the most fundamental for a modern-day reader is why the melodies of these chants, represented as having been divinely inspired,[2] should have had to be "emended" at all!

Providing the answer to that and to several other questions raised by Pseudo-Odo's statement will be the task of this study. As will become apparent, the prob-

---

1. "Ex quo comprehenditur, quia imperitus musicus est, qui facile ac praesumptuose plures cantus emendat, nisi prius per omnes modos investigaverit, si forsitan in aliquo stare possit; nec magnopere de similitudine aliorum cantuum, sed de regulari veritate curet. Quodsi nulli tono placet, secundum eum tonum emendetur, in quo minus dissonat. Atque hoc observari debet, ut emendatus cantus aut decentius sonet, aut a priori similitudine parum discrepet" (GS 1: 256–57; transl. in McKinnon, *The Early Christian Period and the Latin Middle Ages*, 96). As just one hint of the kinds of questions to be treated here, one might note that Pseudo-Odo uses two different Latin words, *tonus* and *modus*, for what McKinnon appropriately translates as "mode."

2. One of the most enduring images of the divine origin of the chant is that of the Holy Spirit in the form of a dove, perched on the shoulder of Gregory the Great and singing the chants into his ear (see Matt. 3: 16–17). On the history of this image and some of its implications for the subject under investigation here, see Treitler, "Homer and Gregory."

lem addressed by Pseudo-Odo concerns a complex of issues in the areas of tone-system or scale, mode or tone, and musical notation. Obviously, each of these topics is vast in its own right, each has been investigated extensively, and each still deserves further studies of its own.[3] Rather than examining tone-system, mode, and notation as separate entities, however, I shall, in this book, treat them as interwoven with each other, as a web or nexus, so to speak.[4] For the sake of clarity, each will be discussed separately at various points, but the reader should bear in mind their inherent interconnectedness.

As far as possible, the sources will be allowed to speak for themselves.[5] There will, however, be no attempt to account for the evidence brought forth by every theorist or in every manuscript. Instead, the focus will be on those sources that appear to offer the most telling treatment of the topics under consideration. The organization of this book's narrative will be chronological for the most part, although, of course, the testimony of contemporaneous witnesses will have to be presented sequentially, rather than simultaneously.

We shall begin in chapter 1 with an examination of the concepts of tone-system, mode, and notation that were a legacy to the Middle Ages from Antiquity. The

3. Among the studies that proved to be of seminal importance for my own work in these areas are Brambach, *Das Tonsystem und die Tonarten des christlichen Abendlandes im Mittelalter;* Jacobsthal, *Die chromatische Alteration im liturgischen Gesang der abendländischen Kirche;* and Markovits, *Das Tonsystem der abendländischen Musik im frühen Mittelalter.* On the subject of tone-system, I cite especially Sachs, *Mensura fistularum;* and Sachs, "Musikalische Elementarlehre im Mittelalter." Important contributions on the subject of mode include Gombosi, "Studien zur Tonartenlehre des frühen Mittelalters"; Huglo, *Les Tonaires,* along with many other articles by the same author; Powers, "Mode," *NG;* and Ferarri-Barassi, "I modi ecclesiastici." Finally, on the early history of notation, see Stäblein, *Schriftbild der einstimmigen Musik;* and various articles by Leo Treitler, but particularly his studies "The Early History of Music Writing in the West" and "Reading and Singing: On the Genesis of Occidental Music-Writing." See also a number of studies by Kenneth Levy now brought together in *Gregorian Chant and the Carolingians;* but note especially "On the Origin of Neumes."

Perhaps the single most important primary source for all three of these aspects of this study is Boethius's *De institutione musica.* The penetrating insights of Boethius's translator and interpreter, Calvin Bower (in *Boethius: Fundamentals of Music* and other studies) have informed this work from its very inception.

4. It would be disingenuous of me not to acknowledge that several of my own essays have formed the foundation for this study. The most directly related are "Parapter" (in *HmT*); "'Harmonia' and the 'Modi, quos abusive tonos dicimus'"; "From 'Vitium' to 'Tonus acquisitus'"; "*De accentibus toni oritur nota quae dicitur neuma*"; "Modus" (in *HmT*); and "Das Tonsystem des Chorals im Spiegel mittelalterlicher Musiktraktate."

I should also like to acknowledge that some of the issues I treat here have been explored quite effectively by Marie-Elizabeth Duchez in several of her articles listed in the bibliography. Unfortunately, I was unable to consult her dissertation, "*Imago mundi*, naissance de la théorie musicale occidentale dans les commentaires carolingiens de Martianus Capella," which she had announced in earlier publications. I hope, in any event, that my own work may prove to be a worthwhile complement to hers.

5. I realize that, strictly speaking, this is impossible. The sources are written in Latin and Greek, which means that, at the very least, they must be translated, and hence interpreted, at some level. The order of presentation of the witnesses and of their testimony also constitute a component of the narrative that must be guided, rather than simply expressed. These factors notwithstanding, the principle set forth here—that of attempting to allow the evidence of the sources to resonate directly—is one I have attempted to maintain throughout the course of this work.

next two chapters form a pair that spans the eighth and ninth centuries. Chapter 2 will consider the ways ancient texts treating these topics were received and taught in the Carolingian era, and chapter 3 will proceed to examine the traditions and practices of the Christian church and some of the early attempts to develop a rational system of classification for its music. In the next section of the book—its last three chapters—I shall examine the ways various components of ancient Greek theory were grafted onto medieval practice and were themselves modified, leading to a theory of both tone-system and mode, and a concomitant system of notation, that is uniquely medieval. Chapter 4 addresses the writings of Hucbald of St. Amand and Regino of Prüm; chapter 5 the *Alia musica;* and chapter 6 the relevant contributions of Pseudo-Bernelinus, Bern of Reichenau, Pseudo-Odo, and Guido d'Arezzo. In the epilogue, I examine some of the difficulties that arose from this synthesis, concluding with an exploration of some of the ways theory moves to accommodate practice in the later Middle Ages. We shall see that what resulted from this accommodation was a theory of tone-system and mode that would remain viable until it was supplanted by Glareanus's theory of twelve modes in the sixteenth century.

CHAPTER ONE

THE HERITAGE OF ANTIQUITY

Interim parabantur exsequiae . . . cum subito raptus in spiritu ad tribunal iudicis pertrahor, . . .
interrogatus condicionem Christianum me esse respondi. et ille, qui residebat: "mentiris," ait,
"Ciceronianus es, non Christianus; ubi thesaurus tuus, ibi et cor tuum."

—Jerome, letter to Eustochius

It has often been said that Western European intellectual life in the Middle Ages rested on two bases—the heritage of Antiquity and the traditions and practices of the Christian church. The bifurcate nature of medieval intellectual history is, to my mind, nowhere better exemplified than in the formation of a theory of melodic classification into tones or modes and the concomitant establishment of a tone-system or scalar matrix for medieval music. Whereas in some areas the two main sources of influence stood in conflict with each other (as the words of Jerome above suggest),[1] the formation of a theory of both mode and tone-system in the medieval Latin West represents not so much a conflict as a construct of ideas from both Antiquity and the Christian church. Let us begin, then, with a brief look at two fundamental aspects of ancient Greek music that are particularly relevant to this study, and then turn our attention to the ways the knowledge of Greek music was transmitted to the Middle Ages.

A number of excellent studies have reminded us recently that ancient Greece had a long, rich musical tradition that extended from pre-Homeric times (ca. ninth century B.C.E.) up to the fifth century C.E. and beyond.[2] A serious problem in gain-

---

1. Sancti Hieronymi Epistula XXII: 30, 3, *Sancti Eusebii Hieronymi epistulae*, ed. Hilberg, 1: 190. In Mierow's translation (cited below), the passage reads: "Meanwhile, preparations for my funeral were being made. . . . Suddenly I was caught up in the spirit and dragged before the tribunal of the Judge. . . . Upon being asked my status, I replied that I was a Christian. And He who sat upon the judgment seat said: 'Thou liest. Thou art a Ciceronian, not a Christian. Where thy treasure is, there is thy heart also'" (Matt. 6:21). *The Letters of St. Jerome*, transl. Mierow, 1: 166. This letter is addressed "ad Eustochium" and was probably written in 384.

2. I refer, in particular, to the works of Mathiesen (*Apollo's Lyre*, as well as his introductory "Greece,"

ing an overview of this tradition is that there are only about thirty surviving examples of actual Greek music; most of those are mere fragments on stone or pa-
pyrus, and fairly late.[3] What we do have in relative abundance are (1) depictions of
musicians and music-making in works of plastic art, such as vase paintings;[4] (2) references to music in literary and philosophical writings, such as those of Homer
(e.g., *Iliad, Odyssey*), Plato (e.g., *Laws, Republic, Timaeus*), and Aristotle (e.g., *Politics,
Metaphysics, De anima*);[5] and (3) a relatively small group of technical works that treat
music as a manifestation of harmonic and acoustic theories.[6]

One of the features of ancient Greek music that will prove to be especially important for the subject under investigation here is the integral relationship between the disciplines of music and grammar. As Frieder Zaminer points out, the
discipline of μουσική [Lat. *musica*] originally included poetry, music, and dance,
but it was then subdivided into poetry and music.[7] He says that at the time of Plato
and Aristotle the discipline of grammar (γραμματική) included the theory of
speech-sounds (vowels, consonants, etc.) and letters, as well as prosody. With the
latter, however, it extended into the areas of meter, rhythm, and melody,[8] and whoever taught it could with equal validity be designated γραμματικός (grammarian)
or μουσικός (musician).[9] To the knowledge of the μουσικός also belonged, as
Plato expressly mentions in *Philebos,*[10] the knowledge of the varying qualities,
number, and names of the intervals (διαστήματα). With the increasing specializa-
tion in the fourth–third centuries B.C.E., the areas designated μουσική and γραμματική gradually moved apart, although they are united in works such as Aristides
Quintilianus's *De musica* (late third–early fourth centuries C.E.), [11] Augustine's *De*

---

pt. 1, "Ancient," in *NG 2*, 10: 327–48); West (*Ancient Greek Music*); Anderson (*Music and Musicians in Ancient Greece*); and Barker (*Greek Musical Writings*). Earlier studies of equal moment include: Winnington-
Ingram ("Greece, Ancient," in *NG*, 7: 659–72); and Henderson ("Ancient Greek Music," *NOHM*, 1:
336–403). Many additional studies might be mentioned. In *Apollo's Lyre* (13–16), Mathiesen provides a
concise survey of recent scholarship that is complemented by a comprehensive bibliography (669–783).
Although there is archaeological evidence for ancient Greek music as early as 2700 B.C.E., Mathiesen
adopts the so-called Archaic Period (eighth–sixth centuries B.C.E.) as his terminus a quo, and the fifth
century C.E., marked by the fall of Rome and the collapse of the Western empire, as a reasonable terminus ante quem (*Apollo's Lyre*, 17–18).

  3. These are collected, edited, and transcribed in Pöhlmann, ed., *Denkmäler altgriechischer Musik*.
  4. On the importance of the three categories named here, see Barker, *Greek Musical Writings*, 1: 1–2.
For further information and bibliography on ancient Greek music and musical instruments in the plastic arts, see 1: 4–17; Maas and Snyder, *Stringed Instruments of Ancient Greece;* and Wegner, *Griechenland*.
  5. A selection of these has been translated into English in Barker, *Greek Musical Writings*, vol. 1; and
Mathiesen, *Greek Views of Music*.
  6. The most important of these are translated in Barker, *Greek Musical Writings*, vol. 2; and Mathiesen,
Greek Views of Music.
  7. Zaminer, "Über Grammatica und Musica," 255–57. See also Laum, *Das Alexandrinische Akzentuationssystem*, esp. 21–26, 103–9, 119–25. On the broader Greek concept of music, μουσική, see Mathiesen,
Apollo's Lyre, 6–7.
  8. See Plato, *Hippias maior*, 285d; Aristotle, *Poetica*, 1456b–1459a.
  9. See Quintilian, *Institutio oratoria*, 1: 10, 17–22.
  10. See *Philebos*, 55e–56c.
  11. On the date of Aristides' treatise, see Mathiesen, *Aristides Quintilianus on Music*, 14; Barker, *Greek*

musica libri sex (ca. 387–89),[12] and Martianus Capella's *De nuptiis Philologiae et Mercurii* (ca. 437 C.E.).[13]

Ancient Greek music was important to the Middle Ages not only, however, because of its relationship with grammar. Even more important was the role of music as another discipline within the liberal arts, namely harmonics. This was the discipline that provided the system of nomenclature, principles, and procedures through which the abstract concept of ἁρμονία [Lat. *harmonia*]—the "well-fittedness" of things, the "divine ordering of the universe"—could be discussed.[14] As a harmonic discipline, music was grouped among the mathematical arts, those that treated of number in its various manifestations: arithmetic (number as static quantity), geometry (number in static spatial relationships), music (number as quantity in motion), and astronomy (number in moving spatial relationships).[15]

Based solidly on the disciplines of grammar and mathematics, the theoretical foundation on which the Middle Ages could construct its own theories of tone-system, mode, and notation was thus rather substantial. Indeed, virtually every Greek writer on harmonics included a treatment of the theory of tone-system and mode, the latter most often designated with the terms τόνος [Lat. *tonus*] or τρόπος [*Lat. tropus*].[16] Several of these writings became the subjects of translations or commentaries by Roman authors, thereby making them available to medieval Europeans in a language they could understand.[17] In his study of the transmission of ancient music theory to the Latin West, Michael Bernhard provides a list of Roman writers who treat of music, along with a description of their influence on the Middle Ages, as measured by manuscript transmission and citation by later writers (a summary of his conclusions appears in table 1.1).[18]

Musical Writings, 2: 392; and Winnington-Ingram, ed., *Aristidis Quintiliani: De musica libri tres*, xxiii–xxiv. Both Mathiesen and Barker provide characterizations of the treatise itself.

12. See Finaert and Thonnard, eds., *De musica libri sex*.

13. See note 19 below for bibliography and information on the dating of this work.

14. On ἁρμονία, see Mathiesen, "Problems of Terminology in Ancient Greek Theory: ΑΡΜΟΝΙΑ." Mathiesen points out that the meanings of ἁρμονία, ἁρμονική (harmonics), and related terms shift somewhat between writers of the Hellenic period (e.g., Plato, Aristotle, Aristoxenus, and Pseudo-Plutarch), and those of the later, Greco-Roman tradition (e.g., Alypius, Cleonides, and Gaudentios).

15. On the importance of number as a key to the understanding of the universe, see Barker, *Greek Musical Writings*, 2: 28–29; and Burkert, *Weisheit und Wissenschaft*, 14–45 and 348–64. As both writers make clear, this view was one associated most closely with Pythagoras and the so-called Pythagorean School.

16. Tone-system and mode are two of the seven categories of harmonics set forth by Aristoxenos, who wrote in the late fourth century B.C.E. (*Elementa harmonica*, Book II, secs. 35–38): genera (γένη), intervals (διαστήματα), notes (φθόγγοι), tone-systems (συστήματα), modes (τόνοι), modulation (μετάβολη), and melic composition (μελοποιία). (See da Rios, ed., *Aristoxeni Elementa harmonica*, 44–48.) On the terms τόνος and τρόπος themselves and their ranges of meaning in Greek Antiquity, see in particular the entries for them in Michaelides, *The Music of Ancient Greece*. See also the discussion of the *tonoi* in Barker, *Greek Musical Writings*, 2: 17–27, and Atkinson, "Tonos/tonus."

17. Knowledge of Greek in the medieval Latin West was not widespread, but it did not die out entirely. For an excellent study of the topic see Berschin, *Griechisch-Lateinisches Mittelalter*, transl. Frakes, *Greek Letters and the Latin Middle Ages*. On the subject of ancient Latin translations from Greek originals, see, in particular, Wille, *Musica romana*, 406–42; 594–715; and Manitius, *Geschichte der lateinischen Literatur im Mittelalter*, 1: 1–36.

18. Bernhard, "Überlieferung und Fortleben der antiken lateinischen Musiktheorie im Mittelalter."

TABLE 1.1.   Treatises from Roman Antiquity that deal with music (from Bernhard, "Überlieferung und Fortleben der antiken lateinischen Musiktheorie im Mittelalter," 7–35)

1. Vitruvius, *De architectura* (ca. 27 B.C.E.). Disseminated in 55 MSS, but had little impact on the Middle Ages.

2. Quintilianus, *Institutio oratoria*. (2nd c., C.E.). Virtually unknown in the Middle Ages.

3. Censorinus, *De die natali* (238 C.E.) and Fragmentum Censorini. 3 MSS from the early Middle Ages (one in 8th-c MS., Cologne 166; and a number from the 15th and 16th cc. The *Musica enchiriadis* (9th c.) cites this, probably from the Cologne MS.

4. Calcidius, translation of and commentary on Plato's *Timaeus* (4th c. C.E.). Disseminated in ca. 150 MSS, but exerted very little influence on medieval musical writing. *Musica enchiriadis* (9th c.) begins with Calcidius's definition of *vox* (cf. *Timaeus a Calcidio translatus*, XLIV [ed.. Waszink, 92]).

5. Augustine, *De musica* (387–89 C.E.). Transmitted widely in MSS. Consists of 6 books, treating music as part of metrics. John Scottus (d. 877) cites it for *numerus*, but it does not become truly important until the 12th-13th cc. Its definition of music, *Musica est scientia bene modulandi* (probably from Varro), finds its way into Cassiodorus, thence into the Middle Ages.

6. Macrobius, Commentary on Cicero's *Somnium scipionis* (ca. 400 C.E.). Disseminated in ca. 230 MSS. Transmitted astronomical, mathematical, musical, and cosmological knowledge of Antiquity into the Middle Ages. Especially important as a source for harmonic theory, but reception in musical circles begins fairly late: 12th c. and later.

7. Favonius Eulogius. Preserved in 1 MS. Another commentary on Cicero's *Somnium scipionis*, perhaps originating before Macrobius's.

8. Martianus Capella, *De nuptiis Philologiae et Mercurii* (before 439 C.E.). Transmitted in 241 MSS. Very important school text from the 9th c. and later, with important commentaries by 9th-c. figures such as John Scottus Eriugena and Remigius of Auxerre, but with surprisingly little resonance in writings dealing specifically with music. (Hucbald for names of notes; Regino of Prüm for numbering of planets; *Dulce ingenium* for designations of notes, intervals; Engelbert of Admont cites it with Remigius's commentary). Its 9th book., "De Armonia," is drawn in part from Quintilianus, *De musica*.

9. Fulgentius, *Mitologiae* (5th–6th cc. C.E.). Disseminated in a reasonably large number of MSS. Important as a source for the study of ancient poets. Its version of the Orpheus legend is the one used by John Scottus and Remigius of Auxerre in their commentaries on Martianus Capella, and by the *Musica enchiriadis* and Regino of Prüm.

10. Boethius (ca. 480–524 C.E.), *De institutione musica libri V* (ca. 500). Preserved in more MSS than almost any other music treatise except Guido's *Micrologus*.

11. Cassiodorus, *Institutiones* (after 540 C.E.). Treatment of music in the second book. Quite widespread in the Middle Ages. Mynors lists 109 MSS and states that he has not tried to enumerate those mentioned in medieval library catalogues from the continent.

12. Isidore of Seville, *Etymologiae* (ca. 627–36 C.E.). Chapters on music in the third book. Quite widely disseminated in the Middle Ages. Lindsay's edition is based on 35 MSS.

As one can see (table 1.1), there are relatively few authors whose treatises transmit ancient Greek harmonic theories to the Middle Ages, and only two who present those theories in a manner that could be considered extensive: Martianus Capella, whose *De nuptiis Philologiae et Mercurii*[19] became one of the favorite handbooks on the liberal arts among medieval readers, and Anicius Manlius Severinus Boethius, whose *De institutione musica* and *De arithmetica* became the prime sources for Greek harmonic theory in the Middle Ages.[20] Because Boethius provides the more complete theory of the two, his treatment of mode and tone-system will better serve as the starting point for our investigation.

Boethius follows in the tradition of several of the Greek treatises on harmonics (especially that of Ptolemy, which he translates in part),[21] in that he restricts himself to "musica . . . quae in quibusdam constituta est instrumentis," that is to say, music that is "constituted," "arranged or disposed," or "fixed" in instruments such as the kithara, tibia, organ, and bells, and whose principles can be demonstrated on the monochord.[22] For Boethius, as for his Greek predecessors, this type of music is preferred not only because it embodies the principles of *harmonia* found in all music[23]

Bernhard traces the influence of ancient Latin writers on music on medieval music theory, from Vitruvius (*De architectura*, before 27 B.C.E.) through Isidore of Seville (*Etymologiae*, 627–36 C.E.). His method is to examine the transmission of their works in manuscript sources and citations of them by later writers. He mentions (10), for example, that although Vitruvius's work was well known in the Middle Ages, having been preserved in fifty-five manuscripts, the music-theoretical portion of *De architectura* had no impact on the medieval world.

19. Edited most recently by Willis, *Martianus Capella*; it is available in English translation in Stahl, *Martianus Capella and the Seven Liberal Arts*. The treatise has been dated as early as ca. 410–39 C.E. and as late as the 470s–480s. The earlier dating was suggested initially by Cappuyns, "Martianus Capella," and has been adopted more recently by both Bernhard, "Überlieferung und Fortleben der antiken lateinischen Musiktheorie im Mittelalter," 20; and Grebe, "Die Musiktheorie des Martianus Capella," 23. Shanzer opts for the later date in *Martianus Capella's De nuptiis Philologiae et Mercurii, Book 1*, 28.

20. For modern editions of *De arithmetica* and *De musica*, see Friedlein, ed., *Anicii Manlii Torquati Severini Boetii: De institutione arithmetica libri duo; De institutione musica libri quinque*. *De arithmetica* has been translated into English by Masi in *Boethian Number Theory*; for an English translation of *De musica*, see Bower, *Boethius: Fundamentals of Music*. Both treatises were written ca. 500 C.E. (see Bower, *Fundamentals*, xix–xx; Bernhard, "Überlieferung und Fortleben der antiken lateinischen Musiktheorie im Mittelalter," 24–31). The medieval glosses on Boethius's *De musica* are edited in Bernhard and Bower, eds., *Glossa maior in institutionem musicam Boethii*.

21. On the relationship of Boethius's *De musica* to Ptolemy, see Bower, *Boethius: Fundamentals*, xxvi, xxviii–xxix; Bower, "Boethius and Nichomachus," 5, 28–38, 41–45; Pizzani, "Studi sulle fonti del 'De institutione Musica' di Boezio," 126–36, 139–56; and Gushee, "Questions of Genre in Medieval Treatises on Music," 376–82. Both Bower and Pizzani agree that Book V of Boethius is a paraphrased translation of Ptolemy. While Pizzani believes that the last chapters of Book IV are also translated (albeit poorly) from Ptolemy, Bower maintains that a translation of Nichomachus's now-lost *Fundamentals of Music* served as the basis for all of the first four books. It should be pointed out that all of the material from Boethius presented in this study is drawn from Books I–IV. That Nichomachus might have provided the model for Boethius is important, because Boethius's treatment of tone-system differs in approach from that of Ptolemy. In substance, however, the two are very closely related.

22. Boethius, *De musica*, Book I, chap. 2 (ed. Friedlein, 189). For the monochord division, see *De musica*, Book IV, chaps. 5–12 (ed. Friedlein, 314–35); as well as Meyer, *Mensura monochordi*, xxvi–xxix; Adkins, "The Theory and Practice of the Monochord," 95–108; and Wantzloeben, *Das Monochord*, 35–40.

23. Boethius defines *harmonia* as follows: "Est enim armonia plurimorum adunatio et dissidentium

but also—and more important—because it makes possible the precise definition and determination of these principles governing music as the expression of abstract, proportionate, quantitative relationships.[24]

Using these proportionate relationships, Boethius ultimately derives the Pythagorean consonances (diatessaron, diapente, octave) and the remaining notes of the Greater and Lesser Perfect systems in all three genera of their constituent tetrachords: diatonic (ST-T-T, reading upward in pitch), chromatic (ST-ST-m3), and enharmonic (1/4T, 1/4T, M3).[25] Boethius's diagrams for deriving species and explicating the modes, however, use the diatonic genus only (possibly because the proportions for determining the chromatic and enharmonic genera made use of large numbers). As a result, and perhaps also because its division of tonal space was perceived to be closest to that of the chant repertoire to which it was eventually applied, the diatonic genus was the one taken over from Boethius into the medieval theoretical tradition.[26]

The two ancient Greek tone-systems presented by Boethius may be described as shown in examples 1.1–2. The Greater Perfect System (ex. 1.1), referred to by Boethius as the bis-diapason system,[27] consists of two pairs of conjunct tetrachords, separated in the middle by a point of disjunction between the mese and paramese. This results in a two-octave scale of fifteen notes that may be represented as A-a^1 in modern pitch nomenclature.[28] The Lesser Perfect System (ex. 1.2), which Boe-

---

consensio" ("Harmonia is the uniting of the many and the agreement of the disagreeing"); De arithmetica, Book II, chap. 32; ed. Friedlein, 126. When not otherwise indicated, the translations in this study are my own.

24. On the relationship between instruments and the quantitative theory found in Boethius, see Reckow, "Organum-Begriff und frühe Mehrstimmigkeit," 56–62.

25. In Book IV, chaps. 6–12 of De musica (ed. Friedlein, 318–35; Bower, Boethius: Fundamentals, 131–46). Boethius presents an arithmetic division of the monochord in all three genera, using numbers that parallel those used by Aristides Quintilianus (Book III, chap. 2, ed. Winnington-Ingram, 97; cf. Mathiesen, Aristides Quintilianus on Music, 162; Barker, Greek Musical Writings, 2: 497–98).

26. Accordingly, the following discussion will treat only the diatonic genus. Boethius's own motivation—or that of his Greek source—for focusing on the diatonic genus in his diagrams for species and the modes may have been that, by his day, the diatonic was the genus most commonly in use. Aristides Quintilianus (fourth century C.E.?), for example, says: "Of these [genera], the diatonic is the more natural, for it is singable by everyone, even by those altogether uneducated. The color is the more artistic, for it is sung only by men of education; and the enharmonic is the more precise, for it has gained approval by those most distinguished in music; but for the multitude, it is impossible" (De musica Book I, chap. 9, ed. Winnington-Ingram, 16; transl. Mathiesen, Aristides Quintilianus on Music, 84; cf. Barker, Greek Musical Writings, 2: 418).

27. De institutione musica, Book IV, chap. 15 (ed. Friedlein, 341–42; Bower, Boethius: Fundamentals, 153). This two-octave system is called the "perfect" or "complete system" (systema teleion) by Ptolemy (Harmonika, Book II, chap. 4, ed. Düring, 50–51), in contrast to systems of smaller ambitus, such as the diapason, the diapason-plus-diatessaron, or the diapason-plus-diapente, which do not contain all the possible species of octave. (Further on this matter, see ex. 1.7 and the associated discussion.) For the sake of clarity, I shall maintain the traditional designations for the Greater and Lesser Perfect Systems as found, for example, in Cleonides, Harmonica introductio (ed. Jan, Musici scriptores graeci, 199–201; Solomon, "Cleonides," 136–37; Mathiesen, Greek Views of Music, 43–44). On the systemic nomenclature in Greek music treatises, see Barker, Greek Musical Writings, 2: 11–17.

28. I shall use the words "note" or "pitch" to designate what Boethius refers to as either chorda (lit.

EXAMPLE 1.1.   The Ancient Greek Greater Perfect System, as presented in Boethius, *De institutione musica*, Book I, chap. 20 (ed. Friedlein, 212; Bower, *Boethius: Fundamentals*, 39)

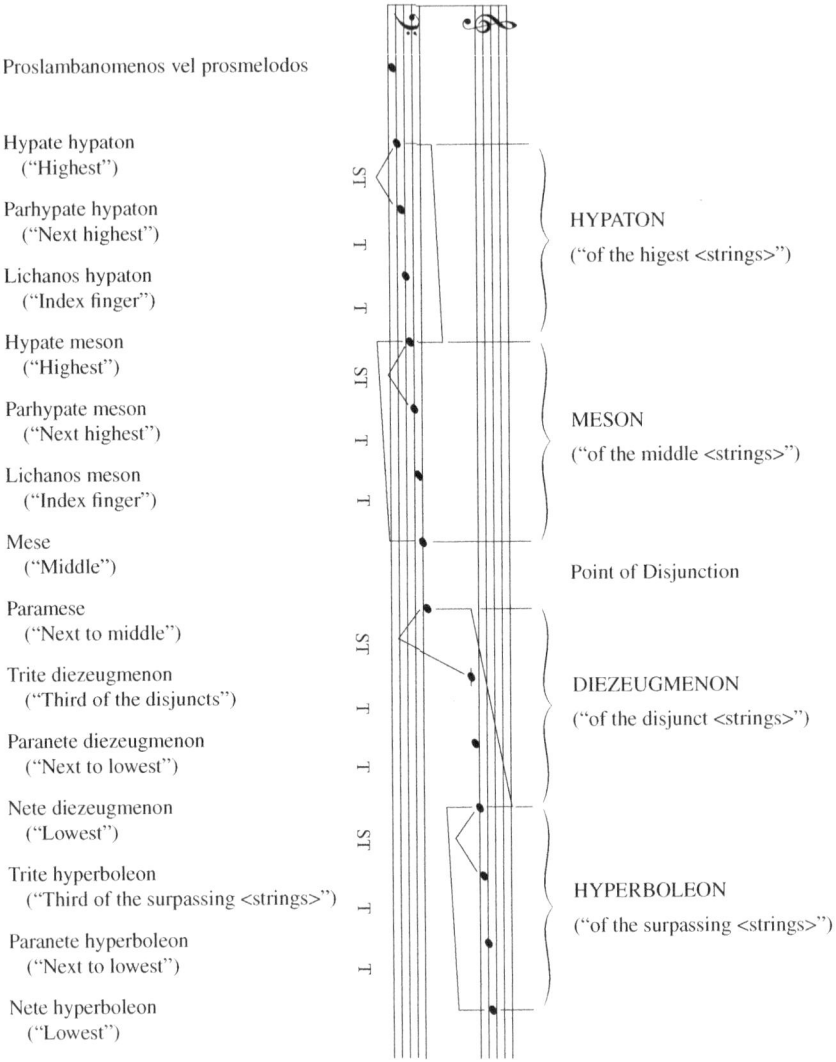

Proslambanomenos vel prosmelodos

Hypate hypaton
("Highest")

Parhypate hypaton
("Next highest")   HYPATON
                                                           ("of the higest <strings>")
Lichanos hypaton
("Index finger")

Hypate meson
("Highest")

Parhypate meson
("Next highest")   MESON
                                                           ("of the middle <strings>")
Lichanos meson
("Index finger")

Mese
("Middle")   Point of Disjunction

Paramese
("Next to middle")

Trite diezeugmenon
("Third of the disjuncts")   DIEZEUGMENON
                                                           ("of the disjunct <strings>")
Paranete diezeugmenon
("Next to lowest")

Nete diezeugmenon
("Lowest")

Trite hyperboleon
("Third of the surpassing <strings>")   HYPERBOLEON
                                                           ("of the surpassing <strings>")
Paranete hyperboleon
("Next to lowest")

Nete hyperboleon
("Lowest")

thius refers to as the diapason-plus-diatessaron or synemmenon system,[29] consists exclusively of conjunct tetrachords, joining the synemmenon tetrachord to the hypaton and meson tetrachords at the mese.

"string") or *vox* ("voice," "pitch"). *Nota* ("graphic sign"), Boethius's term for the notational symbols of the notes, I shall either leave in Latin or translate as "graphic sign" or "notational symbol." I do this because the semantic field of "note" in English includes the meanings of both pitch and graphic symbol.

29. *De institutione musica*, Book IV, chap. 15 (ed. Friedlein, 342; Bower, *Boethius: Fundamentals*, 153).

EXAMPLE 1.2.   The Ancient Greek Lesser Perfect System, as presented in Boethius, *De institutione musica*, Book I, chap. 20 (ed. Friedlein, 210; Bower, *Boethius: Fundamentals*, 37)

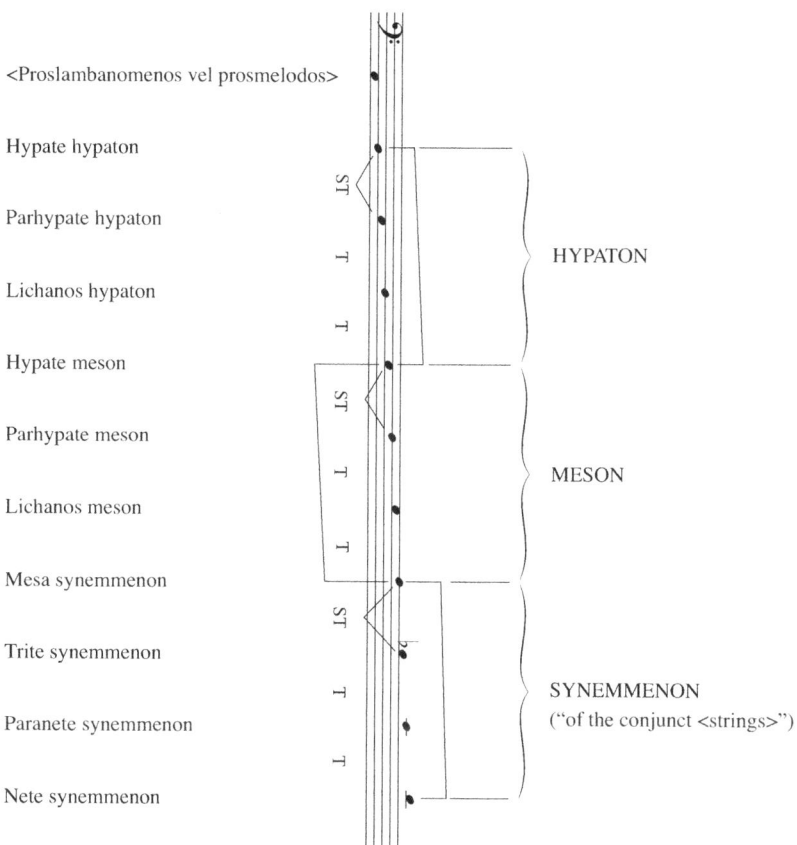

This system has three note names not in the Greater Perfect System, namely the trite, nete, and paranete synemmenon; in terms of pitches; however, it has only one degree that differs from the two-octave system, the trite synemmenon ($b♭$). It is thus usually represented as an additional tetrachord in the Greater Perfect System, which results in a combined eighteen-note system, referred to by several Greek writers as the *ametabolon systema* or Immutable System.[30] This can also be repre-

Ptolemy also refers to this system either as the diapason-plus-diatessaron or "conjunct system" (*systema synemmenon; Harmonika*, Book II, chap. 4, ed. Düring, 50–51, and Book II, chap. 6, ed. Düring, 54).

30. This system carries no designation in Boethius, but it is called *ametabolon systema* by later Greek writers including Thrasyllus (d. 36 C.E.), as quoted in Theon of Smyrna (fl. 115–40 C.E.), *Expositio rervm mathematicarvm ad legendvm Platonem vtilivm* ("Exposition of the Mathematics Useful for Reading Plato"), ed. Hiller, p. 90, l. 22–p. 93, l. 9; Cleonides (second century C.E.?), in his *Harmonica introductio* (sec. 10; Jan, *Scriptores*, p. 201, ll. 8–11; Solomon, "Cleonides," p. 137) and Bacchius Geron (fourth century C.E. or later) in his *Introductio artis musicae* (Jan, *Scriptores*, p. 308, l. 3).

EXAMPLE 1.3.   The Ancient Greek Immutable System, as presented in
Boethius, *De institutione musica*, Book I, chap. 22 (ed. Friedlein, 215–16;
Bower, *Boethius: Fundamentals*, 44)

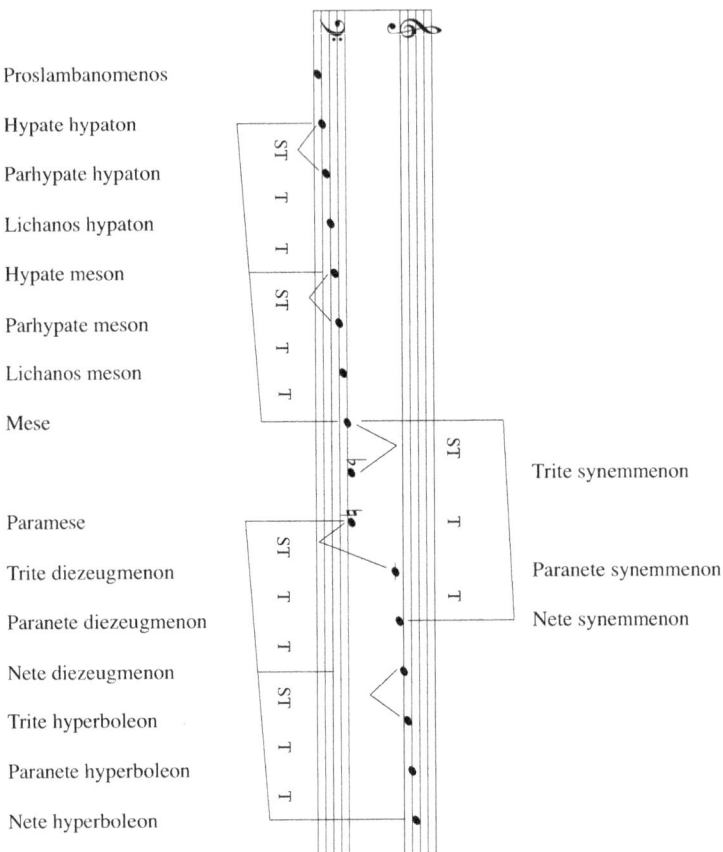

sented as a fifteen-note system with one alternative pitch, the trite synemmenon
(ex. 1.3). As we shall see, Boethius utilizes the latter method in one of the most famous diagrams of the treatise, that in Book IV, chap. 16, which presents the eight
modes (see ex. 1.8 later).

As is apparent in the discussion and examples just cited, Boethius uses the ancient Greek names (e.g., mese, paramese, synemmenon) to designate both individual pitches and tetrachords. This nomenclature is based on the position of these
notes as strings on an instrument, the kithara, not on their positions relative to each
other within acoustic space. Hence, the system is presented "upside down" with reference to pitch. The hypate hypaton, the "highest of the high" tetrachord, has that
name because it occupies the highest position on the kithara and, accordingly, appears at the top of the diagrams of the system; its pitch is actually the lowest. The
nete hyperboleon ("lowest of the 'surpassing'" tetrachord) is at the bottom of the

EXAMPLE 1.4.   Boethius's first tone-system for
the determination of species, from *De institutione
musica*, Book IV, chap. 14 (ed. Friedlein, 341;
Bower, *Boethius: Fundamentals*, 152)

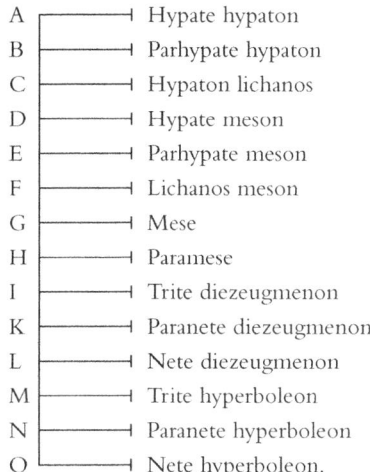

A	Hypate hypaton
B	Parhypate hypaton
C	Hypaton lichanos
D	Hypate meson
E	Parhypate meson
F	Lichanos meson
G	Mese
H	Paramese
I	Trite diezeugmenon
K	Paranete diezeugmenon
L	Nete diezeugmenon
M	Trite hyperboleon
N	Paranete hyperboleon
O	Nete hyperboleon.

system, even though it is the highest pitch (cf. ex. 1.1).[31] In addition to this nomenclature, however, Boethius also attaches Latin letter names to the degrees of the system for the purposes of dividing the monochord (Book IV, chaps. 5–11) and deriving the species of consonances (Book IV, chap. 14). For the latter, he uses two
different letter arrays, one presenting fourteen notes beginning with the hypate hypaton as "A" and extending from A to O (ex. 1.4), the other presenting fifteen degrees lettered A to P, but without designation of string names (see ex. 1.9 later).[32]
These letters have sometimes been referred to as a kind of musical notation.[33] They
are best not characterized in this way, however, but viewed, rather, as convenient
designators of mathematic or geometric points, as in a Euclidean proof.[34]

31. It is clear from Boethius's discussion of tone-system that he was well aware of the distinction between the "physical" or "instrumental" nomenclature for the strings and the acoustic basis for their func-
tioning. As is represented by the orientation of the diagrams in Bower's translation, the tone-system is
set out vertically in the manuscripts, with the lowest pitch, the proslambanomenos, at the top and the
highest, the nete hyperboleon, at the bottom. The diagrams therefore project a visual image of the physical, not the acoustic, nomenclature for the strings. See, for example, the diagrams in Book I, chap. 20
(ed. Friedlein, 205–12; Bower, *Boethius: Fundamentals*, 29–39) and Book IV, chaps. 4 and 14 (ed. Friedlein,
312–14, 341; Bower, *Boethius: Fundamentals*, 127, 152).
32. Boethius, *De musica*, Book IV, chap. 17 (ed. Friedlein, 347; Bower, *Boethius: Fundamentals*, 159).
33. See, for example, Vogel, "Die Entstehung der Kirchentonarten."
34. This point was made by Hans Schmid in the discussion following Vogel's presentation ("Die
Entstehung der Kirchentonarten") at the 1962 meeting of the Gesellschaft für Musikforschung. As
Schmid pointed out, the letters used by Boethius for designating species do not correspond to those used
in dividing the monochord, and in the monochord divisions themselves, the assignment of letters to
notes varies according to genus. Cf. Bernhard, "Traditionen im mittelalterlichen Tonsystem," 11–12.

Boethius does provide a discussion and diagram of actual Greek musical notation; he does so in his fourth book, in preparation for the derivation of species and the explication of the modes that appear at the end of that book. The relevant chapter (chap. 3) is titled *Musicarum notarum per graecas ac latinas litteras nuncupatio* (The naming of musical notes in Greek and Latin scholarship). As this title suggests, the pitches are named in Greek, but they are now also given their equivalent names in Latin.[35] More important: Boethius provides in this chapter the Alypian notational signs both for singing and for the playing of instruments in all three genera in the Lydian mode (ex. 1.5).[36]

These signs are constructed of the letters of the Greek alphabet, modified and manipulated in various ways, as may be seen, for example, in the following quotation from the Bower translation of *De musica*: "Proslambanomenos, which can be called *adquisitus* [added]; an incomplete zeta and a tau lying on its side: ⨑. Hypate hypaton, which is the *principalis principalium* [principal of the principal tetrachord]; a backward gamma and a normal gamma: ⌐⌐."[37] Once the notational signs for the pitches have been introduced, Boethius can assign actual pitch content to them by converting the proportional ratios they represent into sound. His tool for doing this is the monochord.[38]

The division of the monochord itself is one of the most crucial components of Boethius's treatise, since it provided the means by which the mathematical theory of consonances and systems could be demonstrated precisely and translated into actual sound.[39] Two different divisions are presented—the first, a fairly straightforward, geometric one in the diatonic genus, which is presented in example 1.6; the second, a more complicated, arithmetic one in all three genera.[40]

The manuscript transmission for both divisions is problematic. The first is incomplete; the second is marred by a number of inconsistencies and omissions.[41] As

To Bernhard's remarks I would add that Boethius uses letters in this way throughout the treatise, not just for the division of the monochord and for the determination of species in Book IV. A classic case may be found in Book III, chap. 1, Boethius's proof that the tone cannot be divided into two equal parts.

35. The English translation of the title from chap. 3 is from Bower, *Boethius: Fundamentals,* 122. Note that Boethius's term for the graphic signs of musical notation is *nota*, the standard Latin term for such signs in Antiquity and the early Middle Ages. As Bower points out (122), the Latin names for the pitches closely parallel those given in Martianus Capella, *De nuptiis*, Book IX, sec. 931.

36. Boethius, *De musica*, Book IV, chap. 3 (ed. Friedlein, 308–14; Bower, *Boethius: Fundamentals,* 122–27). For the Alypian signs themselves, see the edition of Alypius's *Eisagoge* in Jan, ed., *Musici scriptores graeci,* 367–406. Other sources for the Greek notational symbols are Gaudentius, *Harmonica introductio* (ed., Jan, *Musici scriptores graeci* , 319–56; transl. Mathiesen, *Greek Views of Music*, 66–85); and the Bellermann Anonymous III (ed. Najock, *Anonyma de musica scripta Bellermanniana*, 19–21).

37. Bower, *Boethius: Fundamentals,* 123. The diagram on p. 127 of Bower's translation offers a more accurate rendering of the signs than that in Friedlein's edition, 312–14.

38. Since there is no standard length for the monochord, the sounding pitches produced by dividing it are relative, not absolute.

39. See Sachs, "Musikalische Elementarlehre im Mittelalter," 152–61; and Sachs, *Mensura fistularum*, 2: 132–34, 144–46.

40. Boethius, *De musica*, Book IV, chaps. 5–12 (ed. Friedlein, 314–35). See Sachs, "Musikalische Elementarlehre im Mittelalter," 152–54; and Sachs, *Mensura fistularum*, 2: 132–43. See also Bower, *Boethius: Fundamentals,* 126–46.

41. For discussion of these divisions, see Bower, *Boethius: Fundamentals,* 126, 130.

EXAMPLE 1.5.   The Alypian notes for the pitches of the combined Greater and Lesser Perfect System in all three genera in the Lydian mode (from Boethius, *De institutione musica*, Book IV, chap. 4 (ed. Friedlein, 312–14; Bower, *Boethius: Fundamentals*, 127 — reprinted from Bower)

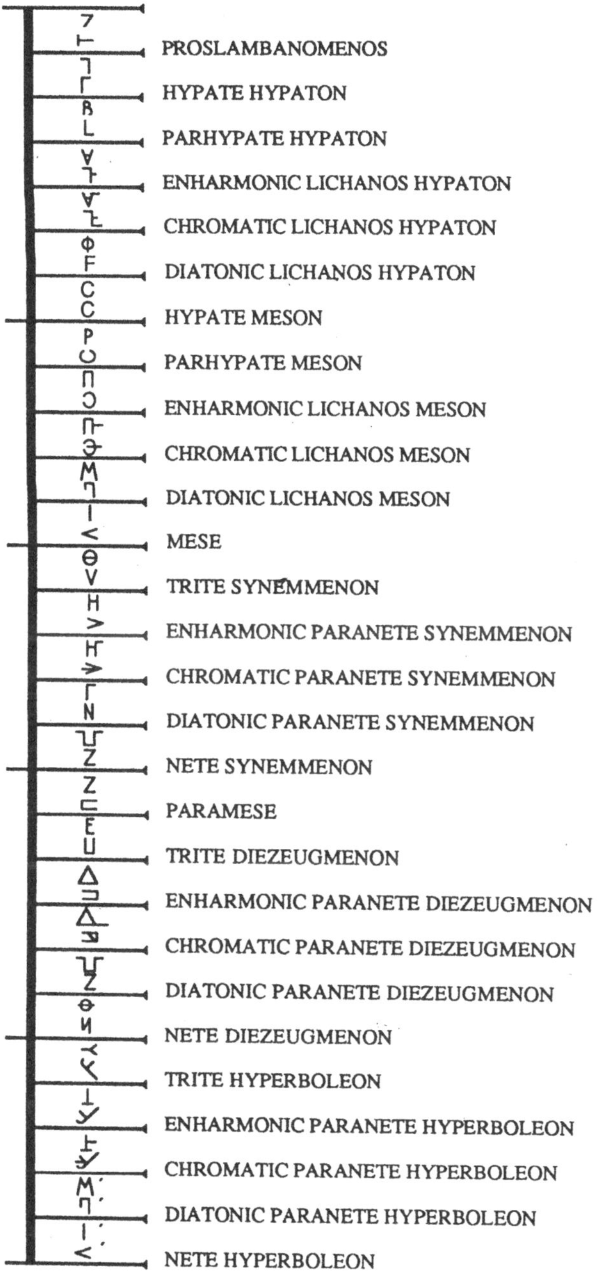

PROSLAMBANOMENOS

HYPATE HYPATON

PARHYPATE HYPATON

ENHARMONIC LICHANOS HYPATON

CHROMATIC LICHANOS HYPATON

DIATONIC LICHANOS HYPATON

HYPATE MESON

PARHYPATE MESON

ENHARMONIC LICHANOS MESON

CHROMATIC LICHANOS MESON

DIATONIC LICHANOS MESON

MESE

TRITE SYNEMMENON

ENHARMONIC PARANETE SYNEMMENON

CHROMATIC PARANETE SYNEMMENON

DIATONIC PARANETE SYNEMMENON

NETE SYNEMMENON

PARAMESE

TRITE DIEZEUGMENON

ENHARMONIC PARANETE DIEZEUGMENON

CHROMATIC PARANETE DIEZEUGMENON

DIATONIC PARANETE DIEZEUGMENON

NETE DIEZEUGMENON

TRITE HYPERBOLEON

ENHARMONIC PARANETE HYPERBOLEON

CHROMATIC PARANETE HYPERBOLEON

DIATONIC PARANETE HYPERBOLEON

NETE HYPERBOLEON

EXAMPLE 1.6.   Geometric division of the monochord in the diatonic genus, from Boethius, *De institutione musica*, Book IV, chap. 5 (ed. Friedlein, 314–18; Bower, *Boethius: Fundamentals*, 126–31)★

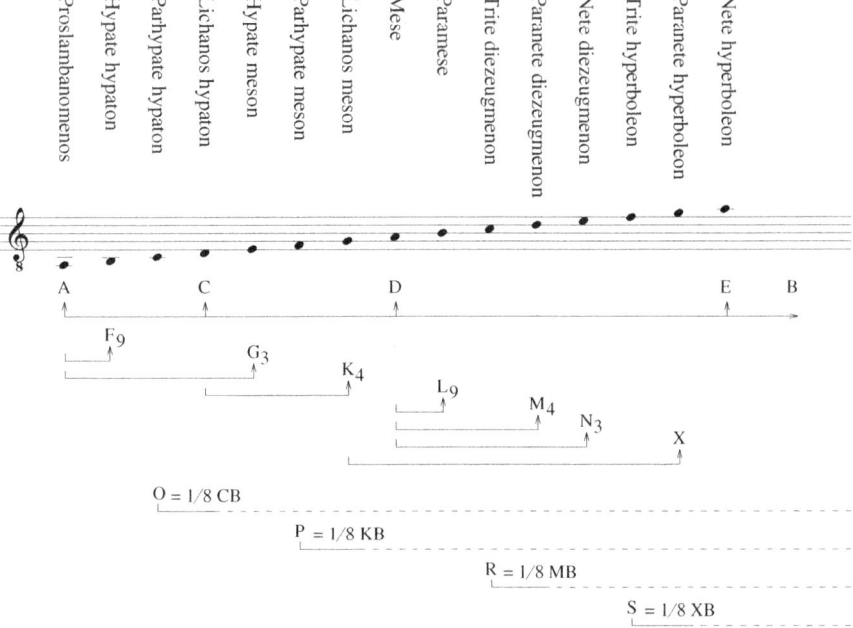

★ The steps indicated by dotted lines, which are necessary to complete the division, have been supplied from Bower, *Boethius: Fundamental*. 130–31.

mentioned above, the diatonic division is the one that had the greatest resonance in the Middle Ages. In it (ex. 1.6), the string, AB, is first divided into four equal sections, which locates the proslambanomenos, the lichanos hypaton, the mese, and the nete hyperboleon. Then the string is shortened by a ninth part, yielding the hypate hypaton. Following this, it is shortened by a third to yield the hypate meson. In subsequent steps, it is divided into proportionate segments (thirds, fourths, ninths) to yield the paramese, nete synemmenon, nete diezeugmenon, and paranete hyperboleon. Although the steps necessary to derive the parhypatai and tritai are not present in this division, these degrees could be located by adding eighth parts to the points already set out.[42] For the Middle Ages, however, the procedural model this monochord division provided was its most important feature. Later writers would devise any number of variants on Boethius's original scheme.[43]

42. See Bower, *Boethius: Fundamentals*, 130–31; Bower, "The Transmission of Ancient Music Theory into the Middle Ages"; and Sachs, "Musikalische Elementarlehre im Mittelalter," 154 n. 185.

43. For discussion of these variants, see Markovits, *Das Tonsystem der abendländischen Musik im frühen Mittelalter*, 37–42; Meyer, *Mensura monochordi*, xxvi–xxxvii; Smits van Waesberghe, *De musico-paedagogico et theoretico Guidone*, 156–72, nos. 1–37; and Adkins, "The Theory and Practice of the Monochord," 108–37.

EXAMPLE 1.7.   Boethius's first enumeration of species of the diapason, *De institutione musica*, Book IV, chap. 14 (ed. Friedlein, 339; Bower, *Boethius: Fundamentals*, 150)

Order	Succession of intervals in Starting pitch to termination pitch		diatonic genus
1st	O-G	(nete hyperboleon to mese)	T-T-ST-T-T-ST-T
2nd	N-F	(paranete hyperboleon to lichanos meson)	T-ST-T-T-ST-T-T
3rd	M-E	(trite hyperboleon to parhypate meson)	ST-T-T-ST-T-T-T
4th	L-D	(nete diezeugmenon to hypate meson)	T-T-ST-T-T-T-ST
5th	K-C	(paranete diezeugmenon to lichanos hypaton)	T-ST-T-T-T-ST-T
6th	I-B	(trite diezeugmenon to parhypate hypaton)	ST-T-T-T-ST-T-T
7th	H-A	(paramese to hypate hypaton)	T-T-T-ST-T-T-ST

With the monochord division in all three genera complete, the tone-system itself can be divided into species, that is, the pattern of intervals in a given genus between any two pitches of the scale that are consonant with each other.[44] Boethius first sets out a fourteen-note scale, assigning letters in succession to each of the pitches, starting with A for the hypate hypaton and extending to O for the nete hyperboleon (see ex. 1.4). After enumerating the three species of diatessaron, followed by the four species of diapente, he situates the seven species of diapason as shown in example 1.7.[45] Boethius provides a second enumeration of the species of diapason following this, but it is the first one that will prove central to the determination of mode.[46]

In the fourth book of *De musica,* after dividing the monochord, and after demonstrating the species of diatessaron, diapente, and diapason in the diatonic genus by means of Latin letter names, Boethius provides a technical description of the "modi, quos eosdem tropos vel tonos nominant" (Book IV, chap. 15). Although *modus* and *tonus* are discussed here in detail, this is by no means their first appearance in the treatise. *Modus,* for example, appears in the first chapter of Book I: "This is especially true of the sense of hearing, whose power can apprehend sounds in such a way that it not only makes a judgment concerning them and recognizes their differences, but often may be delighted by them, if they be sweet and well-ordered modes [*modi*],

44. Boethius's own definition of species reads: "Species autem est quaedam positio propriam habens formam secundum unumquodque genus in uniuscuiusque proportionis consonantiam facientis terminis constituta" ("A species is a particular segment of notes in one of the genera with a unique pattern of intervals; the segment is arranged within the terms of some ratio yielding a consonance"); ed. Friedlein, 337–38; Bower, *Boethius: Fundamentals,* 148.

45. The passage from Boethius on which ex. 1.7 is based reads "Prima ab eo, quod est .O., ad .G., secunda ab eo, quod est .N., ad .F., tertia ab eo, quod est .M., ad .E., quarta ab eo, quod est .L., ad .D., quinta ab eo, quod est .K., ad .C., sexta ab eo, quod est .I., ad .B., septima ab eo, quod est .H., ad .A." (ed. Friedlein, 339).

46. On the determination of species in Boethius, see Bower, *Boethius: Fundamentals,* 148–52. Bower employs a different set of Latin letters from those given in Friedlein's edition.

or distressed if they strike the sense as unordered or incoherent."[47] Indeed, much of the remainder of the first chapter deals with the special character of the modes.

From this passage and from subsequent appearances of *modus* in *De musica,* it becomes clear that Boethius is using the Latin term *modus* to refer to what the Greek theorists designate as τόνος (Lat. *tonus*) or τρόπος (Lat. *tropus*) in the sense of τρόπος συστηματικός (*tropos systēmatikos:* "systemic trope").[48] Boethius's term *modus* itself is almost certainly a translation into Latin of the Greek τρόπος.[49] This assumption is corroborated by the fact that Boethius uses the Latin cognate *tropus* in only one place in his treatise, namely the passage cited above, from Book IV, chap. 15.[50]

Boethius's first use of the term *tonus* also appears in Book I, chap. 16: "If a pitch should be higher or lower than another pitch by a duple [proportion], the diapason consonance arises; if a pitch be higher or lower than another pitch by a sesquialter proportion, or a sesquitertia, or a sesquioctave, it produces the consonance diapente, diatessaron, or tone."[51] He then addresses the question of whether or not the two parts that result from the division of a tone can be equal, offering the following brief demonstration.

> Moreover, a tone cannot be divided into two equal parts; the reason for this will be clear later. For now it suffices to know that a tone is never divided into two equal parts. So that this may be easily verified, let there be the sesquioctave proportion 8 to 9. No mean number falls naturally between these. Therefore, let us multiply these by 2. $2 \times 8 = 16$; $2 \times 9 = 18$. One number falls naturally between 16 and 18, which is of course 17. Disposed in order, they are 16, 17, 18. Sixteen in relation to 18 holds the sesquioctave proportion, and thus the tone. But the mean number 17 does not divide this proportion into equal parts. For compared to 16, it contains within itself the total—16, plus its sixteenth part—that is, one unit. If to this number 17 the third number, 18, is compared, it will contain all of it plus its seventeenth part. Therefore, 17 does not surpass the smaller number and is not surpassed by the larger number by the same parts. The smaller part is one-seventeenth, the larger, one-sixteenth. But both of these are called semitones, not because these mean semitones are of equal size, but because it is customary for that to be called "semi-" which does not amount to a whole. But between these, one semitone is called major, the other minor.[52]

47. "Idem quoque de ceteris sensibilibus dici potest, maximeque de arbitrio aurium, quarum vis ita sonos captat, ut non modo de his iudicium capiat differentiasque cognoscat, verum etiam delectetur saepius, si dulces coaptatique modi sint, angatur vero, si dissipati atque incohaerentes feriant sensum" (ed. Friedlein, 179).

48. Τρόπος συστηματικός is the term used by Aristides Quintilianus in his discussion of the τόνοι in Book I, chap. 10, of his *De musica.* See Winnington-Ingram, ed., *Aristidis Quintiliani,* 20.

49. See Chailley, ed., *Alia musica,* 29; and Bower, "Boethius' *The Principles of Music*," 276 n. 45; and Bower, "The Modes of Boethius," 253.

50. See Bernhard, *Wortkonkordanz zu Anicius Manlius Severinus Boethius, "De institutione musica."*

51. "XVI. Nam si vox voce duplo sit acuta vel gravis, diapason consonantia fiet, si vox voce sesqualtera proportione sit vel sesquitertia vel sesquioctave acutior graviorque, diapente vel diatessaron vel tonum consonantiam reddet" (ed. Friedlein, 201–2).

52. "Rursus tonus in aequa dividi non potest, cur autem, posterius liquebit; nunc hoc tantum nosse sufficiat, quod nunquam tonus in gemina aequa dividitur. Atque ut id facillime conprobetur, sit sesquioctava proportio .VIII. et .VIIII. Horum nullus naturaliter medius numerus incidet. Hos igitur binario multiplicemus, fiuntque bis.VIII. XVI., bis.VIIII. XVIII. Inter .XVI. autem ac .XVIII. unus numerus natu-

This is the brief demonstration! A more complete proof follows in Book III, chaps. 1 and 2.[53]

Significant in Boethius's treatment of the division of the tone is that *tonus* is described therein as an intervallic magnitude expressed by the proportion 9:8. This usage corresponds to one of the four Greek meanings of τόνος as a constitutive element of harmonics, namely as a διάστημα (Lat. *diastēma:* interval) or μέγεθος φωνῆς (*megethos phōnēs:* magnitude of sound).[54] Greek theory had also used the term τόνος to mean "pitch" (τάσις; Lat. *tasis*) or "musical sound" (φθόγγος; Lat. *phthonggos* or *phthongus*), but Boethius consistently employs *vox* and *sonus,* respectively, to express those meanings. The fourth meaning of τόνος for the Greeks was described by them variously as τόπος τῆς φωνῆς (*topos tēs phōnēs:* "position of the sound" or "position of the voice"; often translated "region of the voice") or τρόπος ("trope")—most easily expressed in English as "transposition scale"—the individual τόνοι being assigned the names of Greek peoples, Lydian, Phrygian, and so on.[55] For this meaning of τόνος, Boethius reserves the term *modus.* It is important to note that when he describes the *modi* in detail (Book IV, chap. 15), Boethius uses *tonus* consistently in its meaning as the intervallic magnitude expressed by the proportion 9:8.

Boethius opens his discussion of the modes in chapter 15 of Book IV with the well-known lines quoted in part earlier: "Therefore, out of the species of the diapason consonance arise those things which are called modes, which they also name tropes or tones."[56] He then goes on to describe the latter: "Tropes are systems that differ according to highness or lowness throughout entire sequences of pitches. A system is, as it were, an entire collection of pitches, brought together within the framework of a consonance such as the diapason, diapason-plus-diatessaron, or the bis-diapason."[57] After a brief description of the diapason, the diapason-plus-

---

raliter intercidit, qui est scilicet .XVII. Qui disponantur in ordinem. XVI. XVII. XVIII. Igitur .XVI. ac .XVIII. collati sesquioctavam retinent proportionem atque idcirco tonum. Sed hanc proportionem .XVII. numerus medius non in aequalia partitur. Comparatus enim ad .XVI. habet in se totum .XVI. et eius sextam decimam partem, scilicet unitatem. Si vero ad eum, id est ad .XVII., tertius .XVIII. numerus comparetur, habet eum totum et eius septimam decimam partem; non igitur isdem partibus et minorem superat et a maiore superatur. Et est minor pars septima decima, maior sexta decima. Sed utraque semitonia nuncupantur, non quod omnino semitonia ex aequo sint media, sed quod semum dici solet, quod ad integritatem usque non pervenit. Sed inter haec unum maius semitonium nuncupatur, aliud minus" (ed. Friedlein, 202–3).

53. Ed. Friedlein, 268–73; Bower, *Boethius: Fundamentals,* 88–92.

54. On the four meanings of τόνος in harmonic theory, see Cleonides, *Harmonic Introduction,* sec. 12: "'Tonos' is used in four senses: as note, interval, position of the voice, and pitch" (Mathiesen, *Greek Views of Music,* 44).

55. See the entries on διάστημα, τάσις, φθόγγος, and τρόπος in Michaelides, *The Music of Ancient Greece.*

56. "Ex diapason igitur consonantiae speciebus existunt, qui appellantur modi, quos eosdem tropos vel tonos nominant" (ed. Friedlein, 341).

57. "Sunt autem tropi constitutiones in totis vocum ordinibus vel gravitate vel acumine differentes. Constitutio vero est plenum veluti modulationis corpus ex consonantiarum coniunctione consistens quale est vel diapason vel diapason et diatessaron vel bis diapason" (ed. Friedlein, 341). The translation is Bower's (*Boethius: Fundamentals,* 153).

diatessaron, and the bis-diapason systems,[58] Boethius provides an exposition of the modes that is a model of clarity:

> Therefore, if one should make these entire systems higher or lower according to the species of the diapason consonance discussed above, then one would make the seven modes, whose names are these: Hypodorian, Hypophrygian, Hypolydian, Dorian, Phrygian, Lydian, Mixolydian. Their arrangement proceeds as follows. Let there be a disposition of pitches in the diatonic genus from the proslambanomenos to the nete hyperbolaion. Let this be the Hypodorian mode. Therefore, if one should raise the proslambanomenos higher by one tone [interval!] and diminish the hypate hypaton by this same tone, and make the others higher by a tone, the entire disposition will appear higher than it was before it received the transposition of a tone. This entire, transposed system will be the Hypophrygian mode. And if the pitches in the Hypophrygian receive the transposition of a tone, the Hypolydian modulation is born. And if one should raise the Hypolydian by a semitone, it will make the Dorian.[59]

As if he were not content even with a prose description as clear as this one, Boethius goes on to provide two diagrams by way of illustration. The second of them appears in example 1.8. In describing the species of octave, Boethius had given as his first species that extending down from the nete hyperboleon (O) to the mese (G), yielding the descending sequence of T-T-ST-T-T-ST-T.[60] As a glance at example 1.8 will show, this becomes the species of the first mode, the Hypodorian.

The second species of octave had been demonstrated as that lying between the paranete hyperboleon (N) and the lichanos meson (F), which yields the descending sequence T-ST-T-T-ST-T-T. The third species had been marked from the trite hyperboleon (M) to the parhypate meson (E), yielding ST-T-T-ST-T-T-T in descending order. These two species become those for the second and third modes (Hypophrygian and Hypolydian), as one can see most easily in example 1.8 by reading down from the thetic nete hyperboleon to the mese in the columns for the Hypophrygian and Hypolydian modes, respectively.[61] This process, carried on through the remaining modes, does indeed show how the modes, tropes, or tones arise "out of the species of the diapason consonance."

---

58. See notes 27 and 29 above. As mentioned in note 29, Boethius also refers to the diapason-plus-diatessaron system as the "synemmenon system."

59. "Has igitur constitutiones si quis totas faciat acutiores, vel in gravius totas remittat secundum supradictas diapason consonantiae species, efficiet modos .VII., quorum nomina sunt haec: hypodorius, hypophrygius, hypolydius, dorius, phrygius, lydius, mixolydius. Horum vero sic ordo procedit. Sit in diatonica genere vocum ordo dispositus a proslambanomeno in neten hyperboleon atque hic sit hypodorius modus. Si quis igitur proslambanomenon in acumen intendat tono hypatenque hypaton eodem tono adtenuet ceterasque omnes tono faciat acutiores, acutior totus ordo proveniet, quam fuit priusquam toni susciperet intentionem. Erit igitur tota constitutio acutior effecta hypophrygius modus. Quod si in hypophrygio toni rursus intentionem voces acceperint, hypolydii modulatio nascetur. At si hypolydium quis semitonio intendat, dorium faciet" (ed. Friedlein, 342).

60. See ex. 1.7.

61. The "thetic" names are those that designate the notes according to their positions in the Greater Perfect System in its fundamental placement, in this case in the Hypodorian mode. (This contrasts with the "dynamic" nomenclature, which names the notes according to their functions in the various transpositions of the system—the modes, tropes, or tones. The mese (indicated by the letter M in ex. 1.8), for

EXAMPLE 1.8. "Wing" diagram of the modes using combined Greater and Lesser Perfect Systems, from Boethius, *De institutione musica*, Book IV, chap. 16 (ed. Friedlein, 343, addenda; Bower, *Boethius: Fundamentals*, 156—reprinted from Bower)

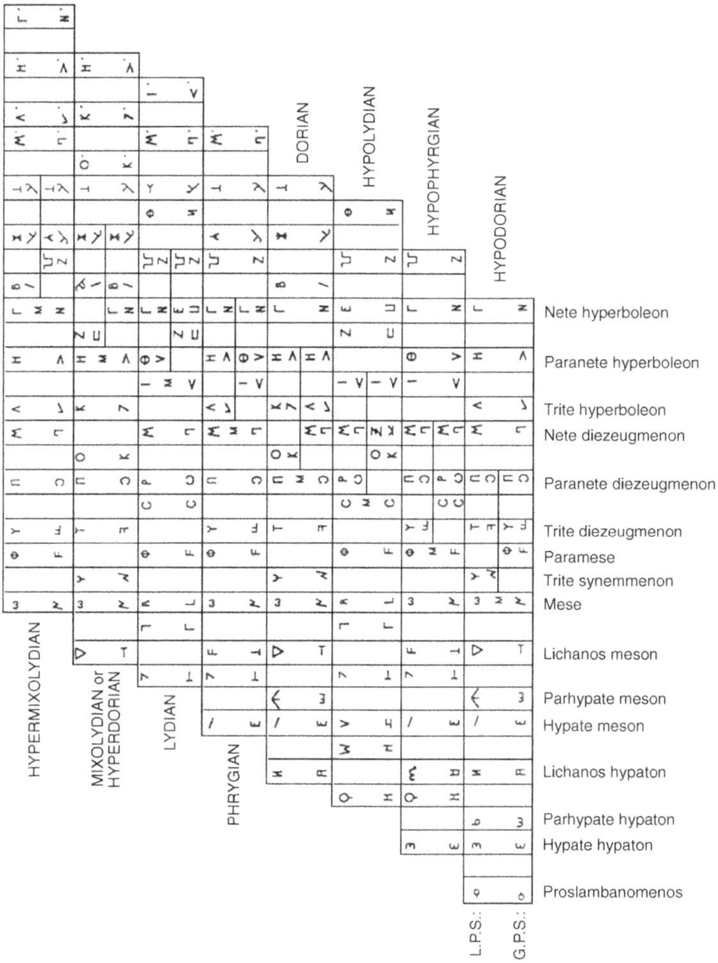

Mode labels (columns): DORIAN, HYPOLYDIAN, HYPOPHRYGIAN, HYPODORIAN, HYPERMIXOLYDIAN, MIXOLYDIAN or HYPERDORIAN, LYDIAN, PHRYGIAN

Note labels (rows, right side):
- Nete hyperboleon
- Paranete hyperboleon
- Trite hyperboleon
- Nete diezeugmenon
- Paranete diezeugmenon
- Trite diezeugmenon
- Paramese
- Trite synemmenon
- Mese
- Lichanos meson
- Parhypate meson
- Hypate meson
- Lichanos hypaton
- Parhypate hypaton
- Hypate hypaton
- Proslambanomenos

L.P.S.: G.P.S.:

Although Boethius's treatment of the modes for the most part follows the principles outlined in Ptolemy's *Harmonics*, Boethius differs significantly from Ptolemy with respect to the number of the modes (ex. 1.9).[62]

example, maintains its position at the midpoint of the scale in any mode, but its thetic position will change according to the transposition. In the Hypophrygian mode, for example, it will occupy the thetic position of the paramese. The species identifying that same mode extends from the dynamic paranete hyperboleon to the lichanos meson, which correspond to the thetic nete hyperboleon and mese, respectively.) Ptolemy, in Book II, chap. 5 of the *Harmonika*, makes the distinction between thetic and dynamic nomenclature. See Barker, *Greek Musical Writings*, 2: 325–26.

62. Boethius, *De musica*, Book IV, chap. 17 (ed. Friedlein, 347). The source for this diagram is prob-

EXAMPLE 1.9.   Diagram of the Greater Perfect System to demonstrate the position of the eighth mode, Hypermixolydian, by means of species (*De institutione musica*, Book IV, chap. 17; ed. Friedlein, 347; transl. from Bower, *Boethius: Fundamentals*, 159–60). N.B.: the letter J in the diagram on p. 159 of Bower's text should be omitted.

A   B   C   D   E   F   G   H   I   K   L   M   N   O   P

Diapason igitur consonantiam servat .A. ad id, quod est .H. Octo enim vocibus continetur. Primam igitur diximus esse speciem diapason eam, quae est .AH., secundam vero .BI. tertiam .CK. quartam .DL. quintam .EM. sextam .FN. septimam .GO. Relinquitur igitur extra .HP., quae ut totus ordo inpleretur, adiecta est. Atque hic est octavus modus, quem Ptolomaeus superadnexuit.

Translation: A to H holds a consonance of a diapason, for it is joined together by eight pitches. Thus, we have said that the first species of diapason is AH, the second BI, the third CK, the fourth DL, the fifth EM, the sixth FN, and the seventh GO. There still remains then HP, which has been added so that the whole series might be filled out. This then is the eighth mode, which Ptolemy incorporated at the top.

Ptolemy had accepted only seven τόνοι, corresponding to the seven discrete species of octave that could be set out between the fixed pitches nete hyperboleon and hypate hypaton. Boethius, however, adds an eighth mode, the Hypermixolydian, which, he claims, Ptolemy added "at the top."[63] The method Boethius uses for demonstrating this seems at first a bit confusing. As shown in example 1.9, he sets out horizontally a series of fifteen letters extending from A to P, but without indication of pitch. Although one might assume that the series of letters A–O given in

---

ably Ptolemy, *Harmonika*, Book II, chap. 3 (see ed. Düring, 49–50), which Boethius modified by adding the proslambanomenos. Neither Ptolemy nor Boethius provides pitch names, and the diagram itself is presented horizontally in both treatises, thereby making it somewhat difficult for a reader to determine, literally, "which end is up." It is clear in Ptolemy, however, that A represents nete hyperboleon and O hypate hypaton; hence P must designate the proslambanomenos.

  63. Boethius, *De musica*, Book IV, chap. 17 (Bower, *Boethius: Fundamentals*, 159–60). Ptolemy's discussion of the number of τόνοι may be found in Book II, chaps. 8–10 of the *Harmonika* (Barker, *Greek Musical Writings*, 2: 333–38). He implies that there are other theorists who wish to augment the number of modes to eight or more but does not accept the expanded number. Even though he dismissed the possibility of an eighth mode, Ptolemy is credited with this addition by several later writers, among them both Boethius and Manuel Bryennius (*Harmonika*, Book I, chap. 8, ed. Jonkers, 116–21). Bower (*Boethius: Fundamentals*, 159–60) suggests that Boethius or his source cites Ptolemy not so much for the addition of an eighth mode as for the fact that it is placed "at the top." The discrepancy between Ptolemy and Boethius here and in other parts of Book IV, chaps. 14–17 of *De musica* is one bit of evidence that leads Bower to conclude that the direct source for these chapters contain was not Ptolemy but Nichomachus. On this and the following discussion of Boethius's modal theory see Bower, *Boethius: Fundamentals*, 148–61; Bower, "Boethius and Nichomachus," 27–37; Bower, "The Modes of Boethius"; Pizzani, "Studi sulle fonti del 'De institutione Musica' di Boezio," 128–37; and Kunz, "Die Tonartenlehre des Boethius."

Book IV, chapter 14 (see exs. 1.4 and 1.7) has simply been shifted one pitch lower, placing A on the proslambanomenos, Boethius actually follows Ptolemy in starting the series from the nete hyperboleon (i.e., A). Hence, the first species here, AH, corresponds to OG, the first species of octave named in Book IV, chapter 14, extending from the nete hyperboleon to the mese. This species had originally been the one that identified the Hypodorian mode. After having set out the octave species in succession as AH, BI, CK, DL, EM, FN, and GO, Boethius concludes: "There still remains then HP [mese to proslambanomenos], which has been added so that the whole series might be filled out. This then is the eighth mode, which Ptolemy incorporated at the top."

As comparison with example 1.8 will make clear, the octave species of the Hypermixolydian and the Hypodorian modes are the same, but the dynamic mese (H) of this eighth mode is situated on the thetic nete hyperboleon, and the dynamic proslambanomenos (P) on the thetic mese of the Greater Perfect System. As a result, the Hypermixolydian is an octave higher in pitch than the Hypodorian.[64] If the array in example 1.9 were rotated 90°, so that the proslambanomenos could occupy its normal position at the upper end of the system, the relative position of the species HP would at least explain the last part of Boethius's statement that Ptolemy had added the eighth mode "at the top."

Despite the fact that Boethius departed from his Greek model in numbering the modes, his *De musica* offered the most comprehensive and detailed treatment of them available to the Middle Ages.[65] This begins to become apparent when one examines the corresponding section—Book IX, "De harmonia,"—of Martianus Capella's *De nuptiis Philologiae et Mercurii,* a work dating from the fifth century c.e.[66] Martianus, too, treats music as one of the liberal arts, but in a much broader way than does Boethius. Taking over the principal categories of the technical side of music from his primary source, Aristides Quintilianus's Περὶ μουσικῆς (Lat. *De musica*), Martianus ostensibly considers music under three aspects: harmonics, rhythmics, and metrics.[67] He draws only on parts of Book I of Aristides' work, combined with material from other authors, and, even when discussing the same topics as Aristides, his approach is not always the same.[68] Hence, Martianus's treatment of harmonic theory is rather confusing, even when considered from an organizational

---

64. The material from Book IV, chap. 14 of *De musica* appears in Friedlein's edition, 341. Cf. Ptolemy, *Harmonika,* Book II, chap. 10, ed. Düring, 63; and Barker, *Greek Musical Writings,* 2: 336): "The one that was to be at an octave above this last *tonos* [the Hypodorian], and so was the same as it, they entitled Hypermixolydian."

65. See Bower, "The Transmission of Ancient Music Theory into the Middle Ages."

66. See note 19 above for bibliographical citations on the treatise and its date. For the results of recent work on Book IX, see the new edition, translation, and commentary by Cristante, *Martiani Capellae De nuptiis Philologiae et Mercurii Liber IX.*

67. In fact, Martianus discusses only the first two of these.

68. See Stahl, *Martianus Capella,* 1: 53. The part of Martianus's "De harmonia" based on Aristides—that starting with sec. 936—is preceded by a shorter one consisting of a general introduction and a superficial treatment of subjects that Martianus treats more fully later. Commenting on this introductory portion of *De nuptiis,* Sabine Grebe ("Die Musiktheorie des Martianus Capella," 56) postulates that secs. 921–29, and perhaps even secs. 930–35, are from Varro's *Disciplinarum libri IX.*

perspective.[69] Nonetheless, his work gave the Middle Ages an important additional source of information about ancient Greek views on music in general and *tonus* or *tropus* in particular.[70]

Like Boethius, Martianus first describes *tonus* as an interval: "A whole tone is an interval [*spatium*] of a certain magnitude that is encompassed between two mutually different sounds."[71] This is later modified to read: "A tone is a magnitude of space, which is called *tonus* because it was the first pitch [*uox*] that was stretched across this space."[72] These definitions of *tonus* are quite close to Aristides' generic definition of διάστημα as pertaining to music: "An interval [διάστημα] is a magnitude of sound [μέγεθος φωνῆς] circumscribed by two pitches [φθόγγοι]."[73] Martianus does not say that the tone cannot be divided into two equal halves; in fact, he says "A semitone is so called because it holds half a tone."[74] He offers no mathematical demonstration of the precise magnitude of either the tone or semitone.

Boethius and Martianus differ in yet another respect, for Martianus treats *tonus* as the equivalent of *sonus:* "'Tone' [*tonus*] is often called 'sound' [*sonus*]. There are for each and every trope eighteen sounds, of which the first is called 'proslambanomenos' by the Greeks, 'adquisitus' by the Romans, etc."[75] Martianus goes on (in sec. 931) to list the eighteen *soni* for the combined Greater and Lesser Perfect systems in ascending order of pitch; Aristides had given twenty-eight φθόγγοι, the fifteen pitches of the double-octave system in all three genera.[76] Other Greek writers, such as Cleonides and Alypius, give eighteen in each genus, including the synemmenon tetrachord.[77] The ambiguity of the referent of *sonus* in Martianus is clarified when he returns in section 939 to *sonus* as the first of the seven subjects of harmonics: "We call sounds *phthongi;* but the term *phthongus* is applied to a particle of modulated

69. Indeed, Stahl, *Martianus Capella and the Seven Liberal Arts* (1: 53), characterizes the two different sections of Martianus's Book IX, "De harmonia," as "discrepant and repetitious."

70. Concerning the impact of Martianus Capella on medieval theory, see Bernhard, "Überlieferung und Fortleben der antiken lateinischen Musiktheorie im Mittelalter," 20–22. Leonardi, "I Codici di Marziano Capella," catalogues the 241 extant manuscript copies of the work; Lutz, "Martianus Capella," in *CTC*, describes medieval commentaries on it.

71. "Verum tonus est spatium cum legitima quantitate, qui ex duobus sonis diuersis inter se inuicem continetur" (*De nuptiis*, sec. 930; ed. Cristante, 132; ed. Willis, 356–57).

72. "Tonus est spatii magnitudo qui ideo tonus dictus quia per hoc spatium ante omnes prima uox quae fuerit extenditur" (sec. 960; ed. Cristante, 150; ed. Willis, 370). As Stahl points out (*Martianus Capella and the Seven Liberal Arts*, 2: 370), *tonus* is from the Greek τείνω, "to stretch."

73. Winnington-Ingram, ed., *Aristidis Quintiliani: De musica libri tres,* 10. Cf. Mathiesen, *Aristides Quintilianus on Music,* 80; and Barker, *Greek Musical Writings,* 2: 410.

74. "Hemitonium dicitur quod toni medium tenet" (sec. 930; ed. Cristante, 132; ed. Willis, 357).

75. "Tonus igitur idem plerumque appellatur et sonus: uerum soni sunt per singulos quosque ac per omnes tropos numero duodeuiginti, quorum primus dicitur apud Graecos προσλαμβανόμενος, apud Romanos uero, quia eadem uoce nos uti summus Iuppiter statuit, idem dicitur adquisitus" (sec. 931; ed. Cristante, 134; ed. Willis, 357).

76. Winnington-Ingram, ed., *Aristidis Quintiliani: De musica libri tres,* 7; Mathiesen, *Aristides Quintilianus on Music,* 77; Barker, *Greek Musical Writings,* 2: 406–7.

77. Ed. Jan, *Musici scriptores graeci,* 179–207 (Cleonides) and 367–406 (Alypius). Cleonides' "Harmonic Introduction" is translated in Mathiesen, *Greek Views of Music,* 35–46, based on the text in Solomon, "Cleonides," 114–44. As mentioned in note 30 above, Cleonides refers to the eighteen-note array as the Immutable System.

voice produced on a single *intentio* [lit.: stretching (of a string)]. *Intentio,* which is what we call *tasis,* is that in which pitch consists and sound continues."[78] He then says that there are twenty-eight *soni,* which he had named earlier. In fact, he had not, but his enumeration of twenty-eight sounds here at least brings him back into line with Aristides.[79]

Once the *soni* have been named in a tone-system, Martianus is prepared to name the species, which he actually calls "systemata" ("scales"). (He does not do so, however, until sec. 954, following his treatment of intervals.) In his words:

> Now we should explain what a system is. A system is a range of pitch that consists of many intervals and that can receive many types of division, which I shall skip over in silence because I treated the same topic in the section on *diastemata* [intervals]. There are eight absolute and perfect systems. The first is the one constructed from the *adquisitus,* which is what we call the proslambanomenos, to the *media,* which is what we call the mese. The second extends from the *principalis principalium* [the hypate hypaton] to the *paramese;* the third is joined from the *subprincipalis principalium* [parhypate hypaton] to the *tertia divisarum* [trite diezeugmenon]; the fourth, from the *extenta principalium* [hypate hypaton] to the *divisarum diatonus* [paranete diezeugmenon]; the fifth progresses from the *principalis mediarum* [hypate meson] to the *nete divisarum* [nete diezeugmenon]; the sixth is drawn from the *subprincipalis mediarum* [parhypate meson] to the *tertia excellentium* [trite hyperboleon]; the seventh from the *extenta mediarum* [lichanos meson] to the *diatonus excellentium* [paranete hyperboleon]; the eighth, from the *media* [mese] to the *ultima excellentium* [nete hyperboleon].[80]

There are several important differences between Martianus and Boethius with regard to their methods of describing species and the ways these species are employed. The most obvious difference—and it is not inconsequential—is that Martianus names them *systemata,* not *species.* Another immediate difference is that Martianus does not use letters to demarcate the boundary pitches of the species, as does Boethius, but rather refers to them by their names in thetic instrumental nomenclature. Whereas Boethius's first description of species started at the highest pitch, the nete hyperboleon, and went down in pitch, or "up" on the instrument, Martianus's starts with the proslambanomenos and goes up in pitch, or "down" on the instrument.[81] Martianus also provides an eighth octave species, which would facilitate the adding of an eighth mode "at the top," as Boethius would later do, but he himself makes no statement as to the relationship between species and mode. His sequence of intervals for the eighth species, moreover, is from the mese to the nete hyperboleon (T-ST-T-T-ST-T-T), not from the mese to the proslambanomenos, H-P (T-T-ST-T-T-ST-T), as given by Boethius. In yet another difference from Boethius, Martianus's description of systems does not make clear their intervallic content. It would thus be quite difficult to determine how the species actually differ from each other in sound; this in turn would make it virtually impossible to distinguish the modes or *tropi* from each other.

This difficulty becomes acute when one looks at Martianus's treatment of the modes, which he calls *tropi,* in section 935. Although he later provides eight different species of octave (in sec. 954) and enumerates both eighteen and twenty-eight *soni* (in secs. 931 and 939, respectively), Martianus disposes these *soni* in fifteen *tropi* and explains their relationships to each other. Section 935 reads as follows in William Stahl's 1971 translation.

> [1] There are fifteen *tropi* [octave species]: five principal ones, and a pair of *tropi* attached to each of them. There is the Lydian, with which the hypolydian and the hyperlydian are conjoined; the Ionian· with which the hypoionian and the hyperionian are conjoined; the Aeolian, and with it the hypoaeolian and the hyperaeolian; the Phrygian, and with it the hypophrygian and the hyperphrygian; and the Dorian, with the hypodorian and the hyperdorian.
> [2] A certain compatibility or kinship exists among these *tropi,* drawing them to each other, as in the case of the kinship between the hypodorian and the hypophrygian, or between the hypoionian and the hypoaeolian. Likewise there is a compatible relationship between the hypophrygian and the hypolydian. These are the only pairs that are joined together. [3] The middle tone [*media*] of the lower *tropus* becomes the proslambanomenos of the higher *tropus.*[82]

Perhaps the most important point to make concerning this passage is that Martianus does not give his readers the means for determining precisely what the tropes

---

This description of *systemata* seems to owe more to Aristoxenos (Book I, secs. 16–17) than to Aristides (Book I, chap. 8). In Barker's translation, Aristoxenos says "a *systema* is to be understood as something put together from more than one interval," and then adds "it is obvious that *systemata* can differ in magnitude" (Barker, *Greek Musical Writings,* 2: 136–37). Aristides says "a *systema* is that which is constituted out of more than two intervals," but he then defines them not according to their "magnitude," but rather by saying that "some systemata are tetrachords, . . . some pentachords, and others octochords" (Barker, *Greek Musical Writings,* 414; Mathiesen, *Aristides Quintilianus on Music,* 82–83). I have translated Martianus's term *magnitudo vocis* (Gr.: μέγεθος φωνῆς, lit. "magnitude of pitch") as "range of pitch." The phrase "ex multis modis" here is clearly to be translated as "of many intervals" (see Atkinson, "Modus," *HmT,* sec. IV. (III). As will be shown, this definition would prove problematic to medieval commentators, at least in part because it is not provided until *after* Martianus has named the fifteen *tropi* and described their positions relative to each other.

81. This can be visualized most easily by situating the successive species on the Greater Perfect System, as set out in ex. 1.4.

82. Stahl, *Martianus Capella and the Seven Liberal Arts,* 2: 362. I have provided numbers for the sentences as they appear in the Latin text.

are. (Stahl's glossing the term *tropi* with "octave species" is symptomatic of the difficulties later readers would face. Martianus posits fifteen tropes but provides only
eight species of octave with which to distinguish them.) As one sees in the text
quoted, Martianus says that there are five principal tropes—Lydian, Ionian, Aeolian,
Phrygian, and Dorian—to which the forms "hypo" and "hyper" have been attached—Lydian with its Hypolydian and Hyperlydian, Ionian with its Hypoionian
and Hyperionian, and so on. He suggests, in the second paragraph, that these tropes
are related by way of "a certain compatibility" or "a certain friendly concord"
(*quaedam amica concordia*) between them, "drawing them to each other." The examples he cites are Hypodorian and Hypophrygian, Hypoionian and Hypoaeolian,
and Hypophrygian and Hypolydian. He then corrects a possible misinterpretation
by saying that these three pairs are the only ones so related, adding that the characteristic linking them together is that "the middle tone [the *media*, i.e., the mese] of
the lower tropus becomes the proslambanomenos of the higher one."

The chief problem here, and one that would create difficulties for both medieval
and modern readers of the text, is that Martianus's attempt to clarify the relationships between the tropes in the second paragraph makes no sense. As anyone familiar with Boethius's "wing diagram" of the modes will recognize (see ex. 1.8), the
mese of the Hypodorian is equivalent not to the proslambanomenos of the Hypophrygian, but rather to the lichanos meson in that mode; the proslambanomenos
of the Hypophrygian is equivalent to the hypate hypaton of the Hypodorian.

The reader might suspect an error in translation, but Stahl's reading is supported
not only by the edition on which he based his translation—that by Adolf Dick with
addenda by Jean Préaux—but by all other modern editions as well, from Eyssenhardt's (1866) to Willis's (1983).[83] The same is true of the lemmata drawn from this
passage and glossed by John Scottus Eriugena and Remigius of Auxerre, as Cora
Lutz makes clear in her editions of their commentaries on *De nuptiis*.[84]

If the modern editions of both the treatise and its commentaries are accurate indicators, section 935 of *De nuptiis Philologiae et Mercurii* created great difficulty for
Carolingian scribes and commentators. The chief questions this situation raises for
us are as follows.

• What should the text of this section actually be?

---

83. The editions referred to here are Eyssenhardt, ed., *De nuptiis Philologiae et Mercurii* (1866); Dick,
ed., *Martianus Capella* (1925); Dick, ed., with addenda by J. Préaux, *De nuptiis Philologiae et Mercurii* (1978);
and Willis, ed., *Martianus Capella* (1983). The text of the passage, as it appears on pp. 359–60 in the edition by Willis, reads as follows: [1] Tropi vero sunt quindecim, sed principales quinque, quibus bini co-
haerent: id est Lydius, cui adhaerent Hypolydius et Hyperlydius; secundus Iastius, cui sociatur Hypoiastius et Hyperiastius; item Aeolius cum Hypoaeolio et Hyperaeolio; quartus Phrygius cum duobus
Hypophrygio et Hyperphrygio; quintus Dorius cum Hypodorio et Hyperdorio. [2] verum inter hos tropos est quaedam amica concordia, qua sibi invicem germanescunt, ut inter Hypodorium et Hypophrygium, et item inter Hypoiastium et Hypoaeolium; item conveniens aptaque responsio inter Hypophrygium et Hypolydium, qui tamquam duplices copulantur. [3] mediae vero graviorum troporum his, qui
acutiores sunt, προσλαμβανόμεναι fiunt.

84. Lutz, ed., *Iohannis Scotti Annotationes in Marcianum;* and *Remigii Autissiodorensis Commentum in
Martianum Capella.* See also her entries on these commentators in *CTC*, 2 (1971): 367–70 (Remigius)
and 371 (John).

- To what source or sources can one trace the text as it stands in modern editions of both Martianus's treatise and Carolingian commentaries on it?
- What effect did the incorrect text have on medieval commentators' understanding of the ancient Greek *tropi* as presented by Martianus Capella?

Our task would be a relatively simple one were it possible to consult a truly authoritative source for this passage. Unfortunately, scholars have not been able to identify such a source—either in Greek or Latin—for section 935 of Martianus's treatise.[85] As indicated earlier, however, the model for most of Book IX of *De nuptiis*—from section 936 onward—is Aristides' *De musica*.[86]

In the tenth chapter of the first book, Aristides sets out the names of fifteen *tonoi* or scalar tropes—thirteen attributed to Aristoxenos, with an additional two added by the "moderns." Following the putative Aristoxenian order, Aristides begins with the Hypodorian.[87] His order is Hypodorian, Hypoiastian, Hypophrygian, Hypoaeolian, Hypolydian, Dorian, Iastian, Phrygian, Aeolian, Lydian, Hyperdorian, Mixolydian or Hyperiastian, and Hypermixolydian or Hyperphrygian. He concludes this list by naming the Hyperaeolian and the Hyperlydian added by the "younger theorists" so that "each tonos might have a low, medial, and high pitch."[88]

Following this listing of the tones or tropes, Aristides describes their positions relative to each other in acoustic space. In the translation by Thomas Mathiesen: "Each of the tonoi will exceed the former by a semitone if we choose to begin from the lowest, or will be lesser by a semitone if we make a beginning from the highest pitch. Their *proslambanomenoi* comprise, as I said, an octave and a tone." (Mathiesen provides a graphic display showing these relationships—ex. 1.10 here.)[89] The diagram makes it readily apparent that the proslambanomenos of the Hyperlydian, the highest mode, would lie an octave and a tone higher than that of the lowest mode, the Hypodorian. Neither Aristides' description nor Mathiesen's diagram, however, makes clear the "friendly concord" posited by Martianus, in which the mese of the Hypodorian, for example, would become the proslambanomenos of the Hypophrygian.

Perhaps realizing that matters such as these are not always immediately apparent to the reader, Aristides then provides a further explanation of the derivation of the fifteen tropes, using his own diagrams to illustrate them. Continuing with Mathiesen's translation:

---

85. As mentioned, Grebe ("Die Musiktheorie des Martianus Capella," 56), postulated that secs. 921–29, and perhaps also secs. 931–35 of *De nuptiis*, are drawn from Varro's *Disciplinarum libri IX*. As evidence for this assertion, Grebe cites parallels between Varro's work and Censorinus, *De die natali*. In the case of sec. 935, however, the discussion is moot because Varro's *Disciplinae* is lost, and the music chapters of Censorinus's *De die natali* do not offer direct parallels with the theory presented in this part of Martianus's work.

86. For a modern edition of the treatise, see Winnington-Ingram, ed., *Aristidis Quintiliani: De musica libri tres;* translations are available in Mathiesen, *Aristides Quintilianus on Music;* and Barker, *Greek Musical Writings,* 2: 392–535.

87. Mathiesen, *Aristides Quintilianus on Music,* 86–87; Barker, *Greek Musical Writings,* 2: 421. For the Greek text, see Winnington-Ingram, ed., *Aristidis Quintiliani: De musica libri tres,* 20–21.

88. Mathiesen, *Aristides Quintilianus on Music,* 86–87; Barker, *Greek Musical Writings,* 2: 422. Barker translates: "so that each *tonos* might possess depth, intermediacy, and height."

89. Mathiesen, *Aristides Quintilianus on Music,* 86–87; diagram p. 87.

AMPLE 1.10.   Description of the relative positions of the *tonoi* or *tropoi systematikoi* in Aristides Quintilianus, *De musica* (Mathiesen, *Aristides Quintilianus on Music*, 87)

Aristoxenus		Proslambanomenos		"Younger theorists"
		g		Hyperlydian
		f♯		Hyperaeolian
Hyperphrygian (or Hypermixolydian)		f		
High and low Mixolydian	⎡ Hyperiastian ⎣ Hyperdorian	e e♭		
High and low Lydian	⎡ Lydian ⎣ Aeolian	d c♯		
High and low Phrygian	⎡ Phrygian ⎣ Iastian Dorian	c B B♭	octave and a tone	
High and low Hypolydian	⎡ Hypolydian ⎣ Hypoaeolian	A G♯		
High and low Hypophrygian	⎡ Hypophrygian ⎣ Hypoiastian Hypodorian	G F♯ F		

Having made a beginning of the deepest of the modes [the Hypodorian], we ascend again by a semitone and prescribe the *proslambanomenos* of the next mode; and by placing together the sequential notes by the same excesses, we fill out the number of the fifteen modes. Given below are the display of the letters by semitone, the display by tone, and then the modes derived from these. . . . The diagram of the modes is akin to a wing, explaining the excesses which the tonoi have one to another.[90]

As Aristides promises, the diagrams by semitone and tone then follow (ex. 1.11).[91] But nowhere to be found is a diagram of the modes whose appearance is "akin to a wing," similar to that in Boethius. Had Aristides cast his diagram in this manner, it would most probably have looked like the following wing diagram based on the tables in Alypius's Εἰσαγωγὴ μουσική (*Introduction to Music*), as we see in example 1.12.[92] By means of this table, one can readily determine the correct readings for section 935 in Martianus.

In the table, the dynamic proslambanomenos of each trope is enclosed within brackets and the mese for each within parentheses. As one can see, there are only three tropes whose proslambanomenoi correspond to the mesai of those below them: the Hyperphrygian, the Hyperaeolian, and the Hyperlydian, which are

90. Ibid.

91. Winnington-Ingram, ed., *Aristidis Quintiliani: De musica libri tres*, 24–27.

92. For the wing diagram in Alypius see the insert in Jan, *Musici scriptores graeci*, 367–406, where it is keyed to his edition of the treatise itself.

EXAMPLE 1.11. Display of the letters by semitone and by tone from Aristides Quintilianus, *De musica* (reprinted from Mathiesen, *Aristides Quintilianus on Music*, 90)

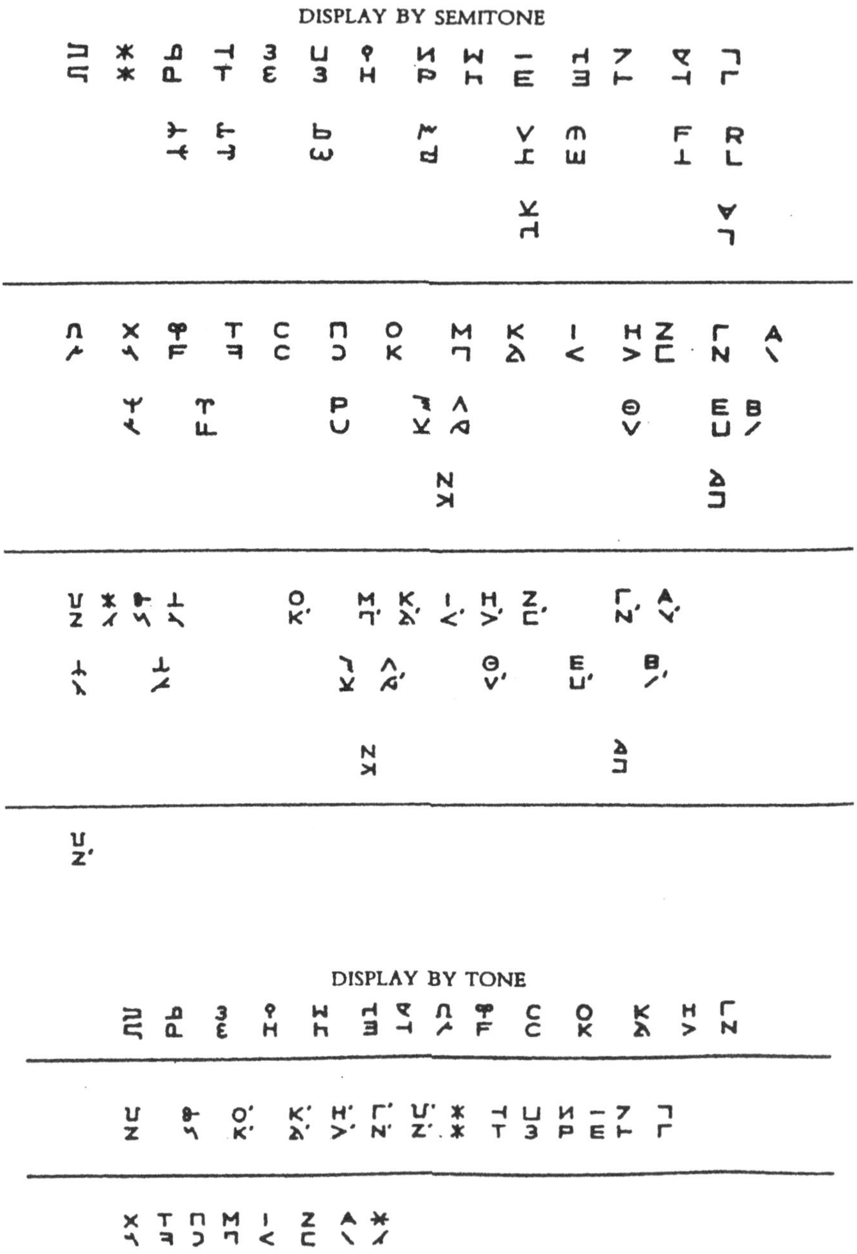

DISPLAY BY SEMITONE

DISPLAY BY TONE

EXAMPLE 1.12. "Wing Diagram" of fifteen modes (reprinted with additions from Mathiesen, *Aristides Quintilianus on Music*, 23)

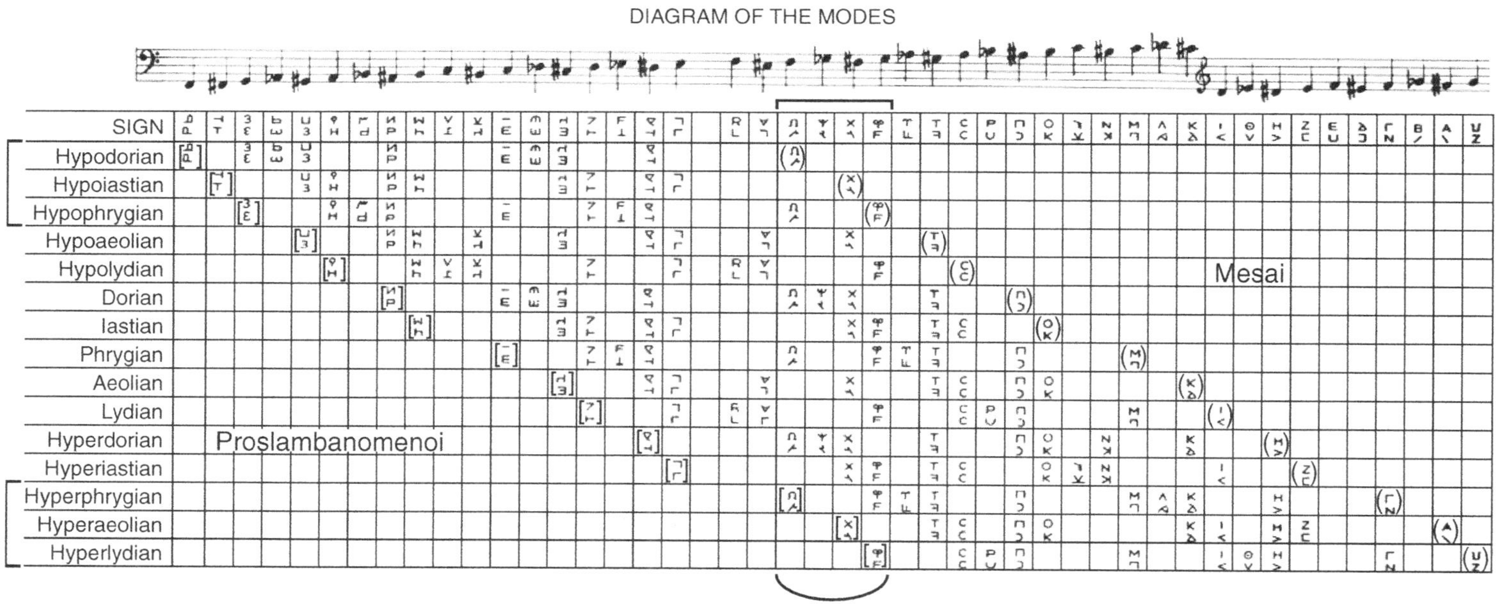

DIAGRAM OF THE MODES

33

joined, respectively, with the Hypodorian, the Hypoiastian, and the Hypophrygian. One can also see quite readily why the pairings given earlier—namely, Hypodorian and Hypophrygian, Hypoiastian and Hypoaeolian, and Hypophrygian and Hypolydian—are confusing. The proslambanomenoi of these modes are distant from each other by the interval of a tone in each case, placing the proslambanomenos of the upper member of each pair on the same pitch as the hypate hypaton—not the mese—of its lower neighbor. As we all know, neighbors are not always friends, and they certainly are not here!

Sentences 2 and 3 of section 935 of Martianus can now be emended to read as follows.

> [2] uerum inter hos tropos est quaedam amica concordia, qua sibi inuicem germani sunt, ut inter ὑποδώριον et ὑπερφρύγιον et item inter ὑποιάστιον et ὑπεραιόλιον item conueniens aptaque responsio inter ὑποφρύγιον et ὑπερλύδιον qui tantum duplices copulantur. [3] mediae uero grauiorum troporum his, qui acutiores sunt, προσλαμβανόμεναι fiunt.

> [2] Truly, among these tropes there is a certain friendly concord, by which they are related to each other as siblings: namely, between the Hypodorian and the Hyperphrygian, the Hypoiastian and the Hyperaeolian; further, there is a fitting and proper relationship between the Hypophrygian and the Hyperlydian, which are likewise joined together as doubles. [3] The mesai of the lower tropes become the proslambanomenoi of those which are higher.

Ironically, the emendation I propose here was first suggested in 1875 by François Gevaert, in his *Histoire et théorie de la musique dans l'antiquité*.[93] It was broached again in 1967 by Günther Wille, in his *Musica romana*,[94] and most recently by Lucio Cristante in 1987, in his study of the ninth book of *De nuptiis*.[95] A correct reading of this passage was thus available to all the modern editors and translators of *De nuptiis*, except Eyssenhardt. The editors can hardly be considered blameworthy, however, for only two of the twenty-two manuscripts consulted by Dick and Willis have the passage copied correctly.[96] I believe that there is a reason for these difficulties.

Figure 1.1 reproduces section 935 as it appears in a twelfth-century manuscript of *De nuptiis*, Paris 14753, folio 146.[97] In this source, the names of the tropes are copied in a mixture of Latin and Greek when they are first set out (see ll. 1–4 in fig. 1.1). When the pairs of "friends" are presented, however, they are written exclusively in Greek (see ll. 5–8). All this, written in beautiful script, happens to be incorrect. Not only does the scribe have the wrong readings for the three pairs, with the prefix "hypo" for all of them, but also he has inserted an extra pair for good measure, which I have underlined in figure 1.1—and it is the only one that is correct ("Hypophrigion" and "Hyperlidion"). (Obviously, the paradox of an error-ridden essay produced beautifully on a laser printer has roots that extend a long way back.)

93. Gevaert, *Histoire et théorie de la musique de l'antiquité*, 1: 225.

94. Wille, *Musica romana*, 645 n. 460.

95. Cristante, ed., *Martiani Capellae De nuptiis Philologiae et Mercurii: Liber IX*, 293–95.

96. The two manuscripts that transmit the correct reading of the passage are Bamberg 39 and Karlsruhe 73.

97. For information on this manuscript and its contents, see Leonardi, "I Codici di Marziano Capella," 34 (1960): 444–45.

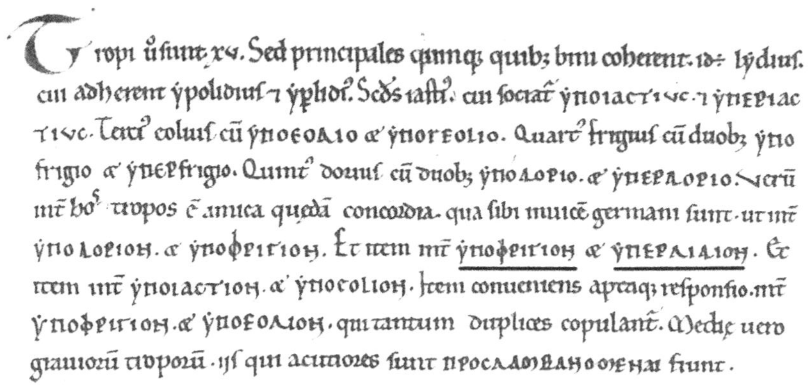

Ty ropi ūsunt̄ xu. Sed principales qſnnq; quib; bmi cohⸯerent.19= lydiuſ.
cui adhⸯerent ypolidiuſ ꝉ yphoꝰ. Sⷯedꝰs iaſtiꝰ cui socrat̄ ynoiacriuc. ꝉ ynⷧeⷯⷡiac
riuc. Iⷧⷧⷶⷶⷶⷶⷶ coluiſ cū ynoⷠeoꝛio a' ynoⷠeolio. Quar̄ friguſ cū duob; yno
frigio a' ynⷧⷶⷡfrigio. Quint̄ dⷬouiuſ cū duob; ynoꝛⷶoⷡio. a' ynⷧⷶⷡⷡⷶⷡⷛⷩorio Ncrū
mē boꝰ tropos ꝯamica qⷷeda concoꝛdia. qua ſibi muicē germani ſunt.ut mē
ynoꝛⷶⷡⷛⷩioꝶ. a' ynoⷠeirioꝶ. Et ncrm mē ynoⷠeirioꝶ a' ynⷧⷶⷡⷶⷶⷶioꝶ. Et
ncrm mē ynoiacrioꝶ. a' ynoⷠoꝛioꝶ. Item cōueniens apcaq; reſponſio.mē
ynoⷠeirioꝶ.a' ynoⷠeoꝛioꝶ. qui rantum dupliceſ copulant̄. Medie uero
grauioꝛu ciⷭoꝛu .ꝛꝛſ qui acutioreſ ſunt πⷤⷭoⷴⷧⷶⷠoⷭⷣⷶⷠoⷤⷩⷶⷶ frunt.

FIGURE I.I.   Martianus Capella, *De nuptiis Philologiae et Mercurii,* sec. 935, in Paris 14753, fol. 146 (reproduced with the permission of the Bibliothèque nationale de France)

Figure 1.2 shows a manuscript whose scribe copied section 935 correctly: Bamberg 39, a book dating from the ninth or tenth century.[98] Here again, the fifteen trope names are set out in a mixture of Latin and Greek, but the names of the three pairs of related tropes are copied exclusively in Greek. It is clear from the corrections that the scribe had some trouble with this passage, but he did get it right. Interestingly, this manuscript was among the sources Willis consulted (his Source B), but he ignored its readings for this passage.

Willis's Source A, London 2685, also dates from the ninth century (fig. 1.3).[99] It, too, displays a mixture of Latin and Greek for the fifteen *tropi* and exclusively Greek for the three pairs of *amici*. A closer look at these "friends," though, leads to questions as to the reliability of this manuscript. Its first pair consists of the "Hypioarioum" and the "Hyperirtioum"; the second pair links the "Hypoastioum" and the "Hypereolyoum." Rather than presenting the normal three pairs of *amici,* this scribe omits the last pair completely.

Paris 8670 (fig. 1.4), which Bernard Bischoff dates to the ninth century, originally had the incorrect readings as well.[100] But a later hand—ostensibly of a person who knew Greek—effaced the originals and wrote in new Greek names (see ll. 3–5). The corrector got the first two pairs right—but then he wrote "Hypolydium" rather than the proper "Hyperlydium."[101]

The four sources discussed so far were unglossed. Bern 56b (from which a folio is reproduced in fig. 1.5) dates from the tenth century and has glosses by Remigius

98. Leonardi, "I Codici di Marziano Capella," 6–7.

99. Leonardi, "I Codici di Marziano Capella," 77–78.

100. Bischoff's opinon as to the date and provenance of the manuscript is presented in Leonardi, "I Codici di Marziano Capella," 437.

101. Had this manuscript been copied at St. Gall, I might have thought the corrector was one of the "Hellenic brothers" I had to criticize for their faulty knowledge of Greek, in an article several years ago (Atkinson, "The *Doxa,* the *Pisteuo,* and the *ellinici fratres"*), but it was actually copied at Corbie, according to Bischoff.

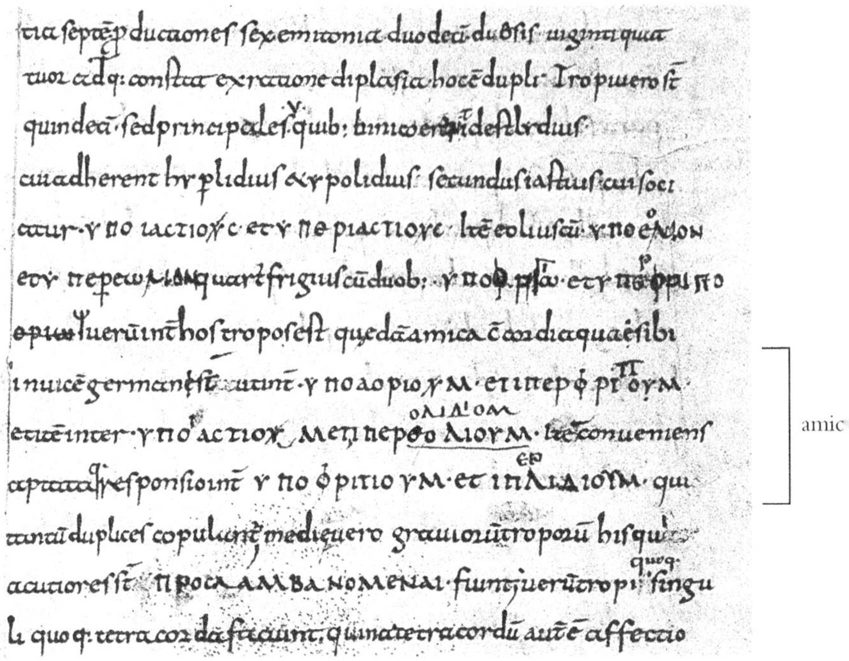

amic

FIGURE 1.2.   Martianus Capella, *De nuptiis Philologiae et Mercurii*, sec. 935, in Bamberg 39, fol. 214 (reproduced with the permission of the Staatsbibliothek Bamberg)

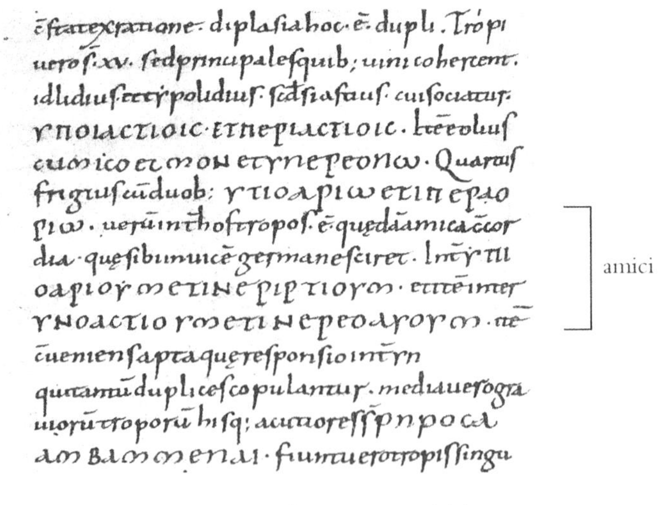

amici

FIGURE 1.3.   Martianus Capella, *De nuptiis Philologiae et Mercurii*, sec. 935, in London 2685, fol. 98v (reproduced with the permission of the British Library)

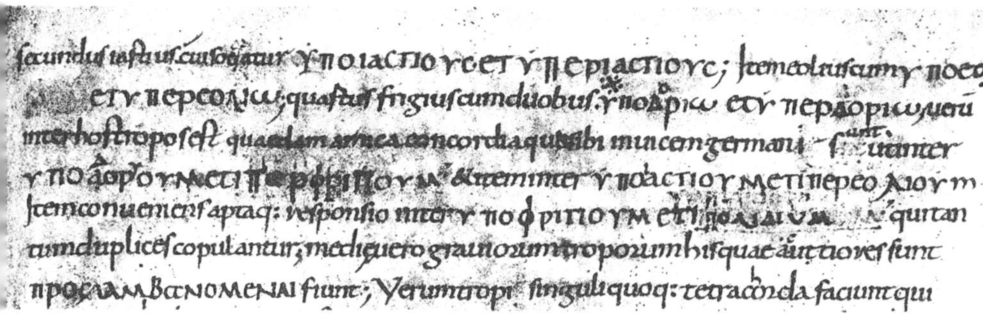

FIGURE 1.4.   Martianus Capella, *De nuptiis Philologiae et Mercurii*, sec. 935, in Paris 8670, fol. 115 (reproduced with the permission of the Bibliothèque nationale de France)

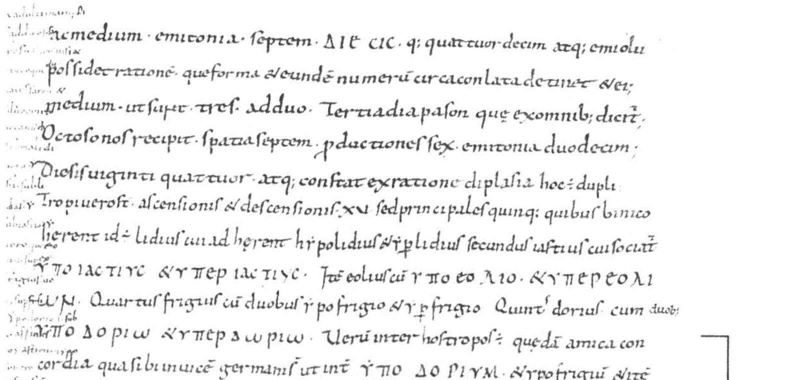

FIGURE 1.5.   Martianus Capella, *De nuptiis Philologiae et Mercurii*, sec. 935, with glosses by Remigius of Auxerre, in Bern 56b, fol. 173v (reproduced with the permission of the Burgerbibliothek Bern)

of Auxerre.[102] This manuscript exhibits the scribal features already found in the other examples, with the names of all fifteen tropes copied in Latin and Greek and the names of the three pairs of concordant tropes copied in Greek. Here again, though, the names of the paired tropes are not correct. (I can testify that this is true of all the glossed sources I have seen.) This means that the commentators faced a doubly difficult task. First, the names of the fifteen tropes themselves are Greek, not Latin, and they are consistently written either in Greek characters or in transliteration. Second, the names of the three pairs of concordant tropes appear almost exclusively in Greek characters. Although we can no longer hold that "The Middle Ages knew no Greek," it is probably true that the average scribe did not.[103]

One of the main commentators on *De nuptiis*, however, was John Scottus Eriugena, a writer with a first-rate mind whose Greek was excellent. Yet even he would have been hard-pressed to make the necessary emendations in section 935. For one thing, there is no wing diagram of the tropes or modes in Martianus Capella, just as there was none in Aristides Quintilianus. Moreover, Aristides had at least provided a good verbal description of the way the tropes were related to each other—saying that each would exceed the preceding one by a semitone if one started from the lowest pitch. Martianus gives no such description. The commentators were therefore left to their own devices. Their attempts to make sense out of nonsense tell us something important about the ways they understood the concept of "mode." Indeed, those attempts will be a subject of prime interest in the next chapter.

The difficulties and lack of clarity that characterize their treatment by Martianus Capella notwithstanding, the fifteen *tropi* or *toni* enumerated in *De nuptiis Philologiae et Mercurii* are also taken over by Cassiodorus in his *Institutiones*,[104] and by Isidore of Seville in his *Etymologiae*.[105] Whereas Martianus had not described the positions of the tropes relative to each other in acoustic space, Cassiodorus goes to great lengths to specify these relationships. Indeed, he takes two pages in modern translation to say what Aristides had said in a single sentence: "Each of the *tonoi* will exceed the former by a semitone if we choose to begin from the lowest, or will be lesser by a semitone if we make a beginning from the highest pitch."[106]

---

102. See Leonardi, "I Codici di Marziano Capella," 11; and Lutz, ed., *Remigii Autissiodorensis Commentum in Martianum Capellam;* and Lutz, "Martianus Capella," *CTC*, 2 (1971): 372–75.

103. For an excellent survey of the Greek the Middle Ages did know, see Berschin, *Griechisch-Lateinisches Mittelalter,* transl. Frakes: *Greek Letters and the Latin Middle Ages.* On the study of Greek at St. Gall, see Kaczynski, *Greek in the Carolingian Age.*

104. Ed. Mynors, *Cassiodori Senatoris Institutiones,* Book II, chap. 5; "De musica" appears on pp. 142–50 of Mynors's edition; it is also printed in *GS* 1: 15–19. For an English translation, see McKinnon, *The Early Christian Period and the Latin Middle Ages,* 33–38. On the impact of Cassiodorus on medieval theory, see Bernhard, "Überlieferung und Fortleben der antiken lateinischen Musiktheorie im Mittelalter," 31–33.

105. Ed. Lindsay, *Isidori Hispalensis.* Book III, chaps. 15–23; the chapters dealing with music are also printed in *GS* 1: 20–25. They appear in English translation in McKinnon, *The Early Christian Period and the Latin Middle Ages,* 39–45. As regards Isidore's impact on medieval music theory, see Bernhard, "Überlieferung und Fortleben der antiken lateinischen Musiktheorie im Mittelalter," 33–35; and Huglo, "Die Musica Isidori."

106. Winnington-Ingram, ed., *Aristidis Quintiliani: De musica libri tres,* 20–21; Mathiesen, *Aristides Quintilianus on Music,* 86–87; Barker, *Greek Musical Writings,* 2: 421. The passage in question in Cassio-

Finally, both Cassiodorus and Isidore use the Latin cognate *tonus*—not *modus*—as the designation for the Greek τόνος.[107] Combining lexical elements from two earlier authors, Cassiodorus provides a definition of the term that was to become one of the most widespread in the Middle Ages:"Tonus est totius constitutionis armonicae differentia et quantitas, quae in vocis accentu sive tenore consistit."[108] This is actually a conflation and slight modification of two different descriptions of *tonus,* one of which is given by the Greek author on harmonics Gaudentios, the other by the fourth-century Latin grammarian Donatus.[109] Gaudentios's definition of *tonus* reads:

Τόνος μέν διαστήματος μέγεθος καὶ συστημάτων δὲ διαφορά.[110]

"Tonos is a size of interval and a difference of systems."

Donatus describes *tonus* as follows.

Tonos alii accentus, alii tenores nominant.

"Some people name tones 'accents,' others 'inflections.'"[111]

In constructing his own definition, Cassiodorus, or his Latin source, omits Gaudentios's reference to "interval," which results in a definition that begins (following Gaudentios) "*Tonus* is a size and difference of the entire harmonic system" and continues (after Donatus) "which consists in the accent or inflection of the voice." Isidore modifies this definition slightly: "Tonus est acuta enunciatio vocis. Est enim harmoniae differentia & quantitas, quae in vocis accentu vel tenore consistit" ("*Tonus* is the raised enunciation of the voice. It is the difference and size of the *harmonia,* which consists in the accent or inflection of the voice").[112]

---

dorus, which begins at McKinnon, *The Early Christian Period and the Latin Middle Ages,* 36, says the Hypodorian *tonus* is the lowest of all, and "The Hypoiastian exceeds the Hypodorian by a semitone." It concludes (37–38) with the statement "The Hyperlydian, the newest and highest of all, exceeds the Hyperaeolian by a semitone, the Hyperphrygian by a tone, the Hyperiastian by a tone and a half, the Hyperdorian by two tones, the Lydian by two tones and a half, that is, by the consonance diatessaron, the Aeolian by three tones, the Phrygian by three tones and a half, that is, by the consonance diapente, the Iastian by four tones, the Dorian by four tones and a half, the Hypolydian by five tones, the Hypoaeolian by five tones and a half, the Hypophrygian by six tones, that is, by the consonance diapason, the Hypoiastian by six tones and a half, the Hypodorian by seven tones."

107. Martianus rarely uses the term *modus* in reference to the transposition scales, preferring instead either *tropus* or *tonus.* His primary Greek source, Aristides Quintilianus, employs both τόνος and τρόπος συστηματικός.

108. Ed. Mynors, 145; GS 1: 17.

109. As those familiar with Cassiodorus's work will know, Donatus is the source for his chapter on grammar, and the first author he mentions in his discussion of music is Gaudentios, translated into Latin by Mutianus: "Gaudentius quidam, de musica scribens . . . [quem] vir disertissimus Mutinanus transtulit in Latinum" (*Cassiodori Senatoris Institutiones,* Book II, chap. V, sec. 1, ed. Mynors, 142).

110. *Gaudentii Isagoge,* chap. 3 (Jan, ed., *Musici scriptores graeci,* 330). The work is translated in Mathiesen, *Greek Views of Music,* 66–85.

111. The definition appears in chap. 5 of the *Ars [maior] Donati* (ed. Holtz, *Donat et la tradition de l'enseignement grammatical,* 609).

112. Ed. Lindsay, *Isidori Hispalensis,* Book III, chap. 20, sec. 7; GS 1: 22. Note that Isidore omits Cassiodorus's word *constitutionis,* his Latin rendering of Gaudentios's συστημάτων, "of systems." Given that Cassiodorus had already omitted Gaudentios's word διαστήματος (*diastematos*), "of interval," the

His definition created problems for at least one medieval author, Aurelian of Réôme.[113]

The *toni* that both Cassiodorus and Isidore refer to in the passages just cited are the ancient Greek transposition scales, as the sentence that follows in each author's presentation makes clear. Cassiodorus writes: "Toni sunt quindecim: Hypodorius, Dorius, Hyperdorius; Hypoiastius, Iastius, Hyperiastius" ("There are fifteen *toni*: Hypodorius, Dorius," etc.).[114] Isidore renders: "[Tonus est acuta enunciatio vocis] cuius genera in XV. partibus musici diviserunt, ex quibus hyperlydius novissimus & acutissimus, hypodorius omnium gravissimus est" (["*Tònus* is the raised enunciation of the voice] whose genera musicians have divided into fifteen parts, of which the Hyperlydian is the newest and highest, the Hypodorian the lowest of all").[115] There is, however, another type of *tonus* discussed by Cassiodorus and Isidore, and by Martianus Capella as well, that would also have an important impact on medieval music.

The *tonus* in question is one Cassiodorus alludes to in his definition of the term itself: *tonus* as an element of grammar. As mentioned, Cassiodorus conflates two significantly different conceptions in constructing his own definition of *tonus* in music. He draws one from the discipline of harmonics, the other from that of grammar. Cassiodorus had actually treated grammar in a chapter of its own earlier in the *Institutiones*.[116] That chapter is in fact a précis of Donatus's *Ars maior*. Hence, we must look first to Donatus in order to gain an idea of the grammatical concept of *tonus* in Antiquity that would be transmitted to the Middle Ages.

Donatus discusses *tonus* in the fifth of the six chapters of Book I of his *Ars maior*.[117] Following the opening chapter on articulate versus inarticulate speech— with inarticulate being defined as that which cannot be written down using letters—the next five chapters provide a syntactic description of Latin, proceeding from the smallest element, the letter, up to the sentence or period.[118] (Larger divisions, such as paragraphs or sections of a speech, would be treated in discussions of rhetoric and logic.) Two chapters, *De pedibus* and *De tonis,* are devoted to the treatment of whole words, while the final chapter takes up the sentence and its subdivisions by colon and comma.

---

meaning of Isidore's definition, which I have translated fairly literally, is rather opaque. McKinnon reads Isidore as follows: "Key (*tonus*) is a raised enunciation of the pitch. It is the categorization and ranking of the *harmoniae* according to the intonation or level of the voice" (McKinnon, *The Early Christian Period and the Latin Middle Ages*, 41). McKinnon's reading certainly makes more sense to the modern reader than my more literal rendering, but it may also make more sense than the original Latin did to its readers.

113. See chap. 3, ex. 3.3, and the discussion associated with it.

114. Ed. Mynors, 145; GS 1: 17.

115. Ed. Lindsay, Book III, chap. 20, sec. 7; GS 1: 22.

116. Ed. Mynors, 94–96.

117. *Ars [maior] Donati*, ed. Holtz, *Donat et la tradition de l'enseignement grammatical.* The beginning of this chapter may be found as text 2.1 here.

118. The chapters in question are (1) *De voce;* (2) *De littera;* (3) *De syllaba;* (4) *De pedibus;* (5) *De tonis;* and (6) *De posituris.* Holtz, *Donat et la tradition de l'enseignement grammatical*, 58–62, points out that the organization of this book of the *Ars maior* is based on principles set forth in Melampous, a commentator on the grammar of Dionysios of Thrace, and is quite close to the Τέχνη περὶ φωνῆς of Diogenes of Babylonia.

The chapters most relevant here are the final two, *De tonis* and *De posituris*. The very first sentence of the fifth chapter establishes a direct connection with music: "Tonos alii accentus, alii tenores nominant" ("Some call tones 'accents,' others 'inflections' [*tenores*]").[119] This is, of course, the phrase that begins Cassiodorus's definition of *tonus* in the chapter headed "De musica" in his *Institutiones*. Although it echoes a passage in Quintilian, this description goes back ultimately to the Greek grammarians, for whom *tonos* (from the verb τείνω "to stretch") is the standard term for vocal inflection and the most important element of prosody.[120] The direct lineage of the description from the Greek is demonstrable: two of its terms, *tonus* and *tenor*, have Greek roots, and *accentus* is a translation of the Greek προσῳδία (*prosodia*).[121]

Donatus lists three principal types of accents—acute, grave, and circumflex. He then contrasts Greek usage with Latin, saying, for example, that the acute accent can appear in any of three syllabic positions within a word in Greek, but in only two positions in Latin.[122] He also mentions that the grave accent can be placed in the same word with either an acute or circumflex accent, but says that this trait is not reciprocal—that is, acute and circumflex accents may not appear together in the same word. After setting out the rules for placement of accents within words, Donatus finally tells us what the accents actually are: "An acute accent is a *nota* [a graphic sign] ascending toward the right in oblique motion: /; a grave accent is a *nota* descending toward the right from above: \; a circumflex accent is a *nota* made from acute and grave: ^."[123] He then goes on to describe the *notae* used for long and short syllables—a long line drawn from left to right and a short, curved stroke, respectively—followed by the hyphen, diastole, and apostrophe. Donatus closes the

119. *Ars [maior] Donati*, Book I, chap. 5 (ed. Holtz, 609–10). This connection is established most directly by the word *tonos*, in Latin the accusative plural of *tonus* (Gr. τόνος). As Scott Fisher has shown ("*Tonos* and Its Relatives"), the term *tonus*, in its early history, had multiple meanings, not only in the field of music but also in the fields of hunting, mechanics, and furniture-building, to name only a few. By about 300 B.C.E., however, it was firmly in place as a technical term in the vocabularies of both music and philosophy (p. 1). Fisher goes on to point out that "while τόνος takes on a variety of meanings over time, the word found its way early on into contexts having to do with music, and it never lost that musical connection" (p. 2). As will be shown, the terms *accentus* and *tenores* in the first sentence of Donatus's *Ars maior*, Book I, chap. 5, also have strong musical connections. (See "Accentus," *LmL*, 2: cols. 20–23; and Hoffmann-Axthelm, "Tenor," *HmT*.)

120. See Marcus Fabius Quintilianus, *Institutio oratoria libri XII*, ed. Radermacher, Book I, chap. 5, sec. 22. For examples of the Greek usage, see *Dionysii Thracis Ars grammatica et Scholia in Dionysii Thracis Artem grammaticam*, ed. Uhlig, *Grammatici Graeci*, vol. 1, nos. 1 and 3.

121. On the Greek origins of Cassiodorus's definition of *tonus*, see the discussion of Isidore and Martianus on pp. 42–44 below, as well as Hoffmann-Axthelm, "Tenor," in *HmT*.

122. "Acutus cum in Graecis dictionibus tria loca teneat, ultimum, paenultimum et antepaenultimum, apud Latinos paenultimum et antepaenultimum tenet, ultimum numquam. Circumflexus autem, quotlibet syllabarum sit dictio, non tenebit nisi paenultimum locum. Gravis poni in eadem dictione vel cum acuto vel cum circumflexo potest, et hoc illi non est comune cum ceteris" (Holtz, *Donat et la tradition de l'enseignement grammatical*, 609). Holtz goes on to say that Donatus's word *dictio* is his equivalent of λέξις (Lat. *lexis*) in Diogenes and is used to signify a word as a sounding and written entity, apart from its meaning (62).

123. "Acutus accentus est nota per obliquum ascendens in dexteram partem /, gravis nota a summo in dexteram partem descendens \, circumflexus nota de acuto et gravi facta ^" (ed. Holtz, 610).

chapter with examples of the *dasia* and the *psile,* which signify the addition or absence of the *aspiratus,* the letter *H* in Latin.[124] In the final chapter of Book I of the *Ars maior,* Donatus discusses the *positurae* or punctuation signs: a high point placed at the end of a sentence or distinction; a low-level point placed at the end of a subdistinction or comma, where not much of the sentence is left; and a midlevel point for a medial distinction or colon, where enough of the sentence is left that it might require a new breath.[125]

In keeping with the systematic character of the six chapters of Book I of the *Ars maior,* Donatus's treatment of the accents and *positurae* in the last two of these chapters provides a complete set of notational signs to convey graphically the inflection and articulation of a text, from individual syllables to phrases to the totality of a complete sentence. With regard to the accent signs themselves, it is perhaps significant that Donatus does not define them in terms of their pitch inflections, but rather in terms of their appearance as graphic signs. His use of the term *nota* for these signs is completely in keeping with the use of that word in late Antiquity as a notational sign for various linguistic purposes, and even for music.[126] As noted, Boethius uses the same term when he presents the Alypian notation in his *De musica.*[127]

Even though Donatus himself does not describe the *toni* or accents in terms of their pitch inflections, ninth-century commentators such as Murethach and Sedulius Scottus do.[128] But they derive their own descriptions from two intervening sources—Isidore of Seville and Martianus Capella. As Louis Holtz has pointed out, the sections on grammar in Isidore's *Etymologiae* incorporate and expand on Donatus's work.[129] This is readily apparent from Isidore's treatment of *accentus* and

124. "Longus linea a sinistra in dexteram partam aequaliter ducta —, breuis uirgula similiter iacens, sed panda atque contractior ◡, hyfen uirgula subiecta uersui: hac nota subter posita duo uerba, cum ita res exigit, copulamus, ut *ante_tulit gressum* et *Turnus ut ante_uolans.* Huic contraria est diastole, dextera pars [quaedam] circuli ad imam litteram adposita: hac nota male cohaerentia discernuntur, ut est *ereptae, uirginis ira* et *uiridique in litore conspicitur, sus.* Apostrophos circuli item pars dextera, sed ad summam litteram adposita: hac nota deesse ostendimus parti orationis ultimam uocalem, cuius consonans remanet, ut est *tanton' me crimine dignum duxisti?* Ceterum dasian ⊦ et psilen ⊣ apud latinos H littera uocali addita uel detracta significat" (ed. Holtz, 610–11).

125. "DE POSITVRIS. Tres sunt <omnino> positurae vel distinctiones quas θέσεις Graeci vocant, distinctio, subdistinctio, media distinctio. Distinctio est, ubi finitur plena sententia: huius punctum ad summam litteram ponimus. Subdistinctio est, ubi non multum superest de sententia, quod tamen necessario separatum mox inferendum sit; huius punctum ad imam litteram ponimus. Media distinctio est, ubi fere tantum de sententia superest, quantum iam diximus, cum tamen respirandum sit: huius punctum ad mediam litteram ponimus. In lectione tota sententia periodos dicitur, cuius partes sunt cola et commata" (ed. Holtz, 612). It should be pointed out that many manuscripts do not have a separate title for this chapter; hence, they discuss not only prosodic accents but also the punctuation signs under the chapter heading "De tonis."

126. See the extensive discussion of this matter in Sullivan, "Grammar and Harmony," 186–231.

127. Boethius, *De institutione musica,* Book IV, chap. 3: "Musicarum *notarum* per graecas ac latinas litteras nuncupatio." See also notes 35 and 36 above and the associated discussion in the text.

128. See Murethach, *In Donati Artem maiorem,* ed. Holtz, 37–45; Sedulius Scottus, *In Donati Artem maiorem,* ed. Löfstedt, 40–41; and an anonymous commentary on Donatus, the *Ars Lavreshamensis* (ed. Löfstedt, 177–78). For bibliographic information on these and other commentaries see Holtz, "Sur trois commentaires irlandais de l'*Art majeur* de Donat au IXe siècle"; and Holtz, *Donat et la tradition de l'enseignement grammatical,* 438–41.

129. Holtz, *Donat et la tradition de l'enseignement grammatical,* 250, 432.

positura. He begins by providing an etymology for the term "accent": "Accent, which is called *prosodia* in Greek, takes its name from the Greek. For πρός in Greek is *ad* in Latin, ᾠδή in Greek is the Latin *cantus*—hence the Latin *ad-cantus* or *accentus*.[130] He then echoes Donatus in saying that the Latins have other names for accent, "For they call accents both tones and tenors, because here the sound rises and falls."[131] The way the sound "rises and falls" is then described:

> The acute accent is so called because it elevates and lifts up a syllable; the grave is so called because it depresses and pushes it down. It is thus the opposite of the acute. The circumflex is so called because it consists of the acute and grave. Beginning from the acute, it ends in the grave, and thus a circumflex is made because it both ascends and descends [*ascendit et descendit*].[132]

The next section follows Donatus in demonstrating the placement of accents in words of varying numbers of syllables and quantities. This discussion is in turn followed by treatments of the graphic signs for the accents (*De figuris accentuum*) and of the punctuation marks (*De posituris*). In comparing Isidore's discussion of the latter two topics with Donatus, one finds that Isidore does little but add the Greek names for the accents and provide an expanded treatment of the *positurae.*

The close parallels between Donatus and Isidore become all the more obvious when one compares the two authors with Martianus Capella. In Book III of his *De nuptiis Philologiae et Mercurii,* Martianus provides an extensive treatment of prosodic accents. In the main, it follows the precepts we have already seen in both Donatus and Isidore, but it differs from both of those authors in some rather important details.

Some of these differences occur at the very outset of Martianus's discussion of the accents.[133] He says:

> Every single syllable is either grave, acute, or circumflex; and just as there is no utterance without a vowel, so, too, there is none without an accent. As some assert, accent is the soul of utterance and the seedbed of music [*seminarium musices*], because every melody is composed of elevation or depression of the voice. Thus *accentus* is called *ad-cantus*—"for the purpose of song"—so to speak.[134]

The section that follows this, which discusses the placement of the accents within words, is interesting primarily because Martianus uses two different Latin

---

130. "DE ACCENTIBVS. Accentus, qui Graece prosodia dicitur [ex Graeco nomen accepit]. Nam Graece πρός, Latine 'ad,' ᾠδή Graece, Latine 'cantus' est." Isidore, *Etymologiae* (ed. Lindsay, Book I, chap. 18).

131. "Nam accentus et tonos et tenores dicunt, quia ibi sonus crescit et desinit" (Isidore, *Etymologiae,* ed. Lindsay, Book I, chap. 18). Isidore's terms "crescit et desinit" could mean "increases and ends." I have chosen to translate them somewhat freely, "rises and falls," in consideration of the context.

132. "Acutus accentus dictus, quod acuat et erigat syllabam, gravis, quod deprimat et deponat. Est enim contrarius acuto. Circumflexus, quia de acuto et gravi constat. Incipiens enim ab acuto in gravem desinit, atque ita dum ascendit et descendit, circumflexus efficitur" (Isidore, *Etymologiae,* ed. Lindsay, Book I, chap. 18).

133. The beginning of Martianus Capella's treatment of accent may be found as text 2.2 here.

134. "Unaquaeque enim syllaba aut gravis est aut acuta aut circumflexa: et ut nulla vox sine vocali est, ita sine accentu nulla. et est accentus, ut quidam putaverunt, anima vocis et seminarium musices, quod

terms synonymously with "circumflex": *inflexus* and, simply, *flexus.* Like any good writer, Martianus was conscious of the need for *variatio sermonum,* but, strikingly, he applied this rhetorical device only to the circumflex.

A bit further on in his discussion of *toni* or accents, Martianus offers a view that contrasts rather markedly with those of Donatus and Isidore.[135] Both had said that the grave accent could be placed in a single word together with one of the other accents, but that it could not appear with both of the others. In addressing this matter, Martianus first describes the *notae* for the acute, grave, and "inflexus" accents, characterizing the "inflexus" as a sigma facing downward. He goes on to suggest that the accents could also be called *fastigia, toni,* or *soni* in Latin and *prosodiae* in Greek. Then, however, Martianus says that "It should be known that all three accents can occur together in one word, as is the case in *Argiletum.*"[136] Thus, according to Martianus at least, the inflections of all syllables of a word could be represented by way of the accent signs, irrespective of whether those signs were acute, grave, or circumflex.

Our account of the discussions of the *toni* or prosodic accents in Donatus, Isidore, and Martianus Capella, reveals that:

- Acute, grave, and circumflex were the principal accents, the circumflex also being called "flexus" or "inflexus" by Martianus.
- The accents were graphic signs, *notae,* used to represent the vocal inflections of a text.
- The inflections themselves are described as "ascending," "descending," or a combination of both (not merely "high" or "low").
- The accents were applied over individual syllables of words, and, according to Martianus, every syllable could carry an accent;
- In conjunction with the system of *positurae,* the accents provided a cohesive system for the graphic representation of the melodic inflections and articulations of a complete text, from syllable to sentence.
- In some manuscripts, the entire repertoire of graphic signs for both prosodic accents and *positurae* are referred to as *toni* or "accents."

What may well be the most remarkable feature of the theory of accent as it was being transmitted in treatises such as those we have been discussing is the fact that, by the end of the fourth century C.E., if not earlier, the accent in spoken Latin was one of stress, rather than pitch.[137] The evidence for this comes primarily from the

---

omnis modulatio ex fastigiis vocum gavitateque componitur, ideoque accentus quasi adcantus dictus est" (Willis, ed., *Martianus Capella,* 71). The word "adcantus" could also be translated "toward song."

135. This section of Martianus Capella's treatment of accent may be found as text 2.3 here.

136. "Acutus accentus notatur virgula a sinistra parte in dexteram ascendente, gravis autem a sinistra parte ad dexteram descendens, inflexi signum est sigma super ipsas litteras devexum. accentus partim fastigia vocamus, quod litterarum capitibus apponantur, partim cacumina, tonos vel sonos. Graeci prosodias. sciendum etiam uni vocabulo accidere omnes tres accentus posse, ut est *Argiletum*" (ed. Willis, 74). On this passage, see Atkinson, "Glosses on Music and Grammar and the Advent of Music Writing in the West."

137. This view is presented most succinctly in Allen, *Vox Latina,* 83: "There is little disagreement that the prehistoric accent of Latin was a stress accent, and that this fell on the first syllable of the word."

behavior of the language itself, in which one finds many examples of reduction or suppression of vowels following accented syllables, indicating "unmistakably" the presence of a stress accent (this according to Lindsay).[138] Corroborating evidence comes from a few later grammarians, such as Servius and Pompeius (both fifth century C.E.), who say "Accentus in ea syllaba est quae plus sonat."[139] As a perusal of Keil's *Grammatici Latini* reveals, however, most of the Latin grammarians, from Varro and Quintilian through Donatus and Priscian, describe accents in terms of pitch inflection, translating them from the Greek προσῳδία (*prosodia*) with its ὀξεῖα, βαρεῖα, and περισπωμένη (Lat. *acutus, gravis, circumflexus*).[140] These become in Latin the prosodic accents acute, grave, and circumflex. As noted, these accents were treated by Latin grammarians in the same way their Greek counterparts were, despite fundamental differences between the two languages.[141] Indeed, such a scholar as W. S. Allen sees proof in the slavish application of Greek terms and principles to the Latin language that Latin accent was not characterized by pitch inflection. In Allen's view, "The very similarity of the Latin statements to those which apply to Greek is . . . an embarrassment rather than a support to the idea of a pitch accent for Latin."[142] Supporting this view even further is the fact that apart from treatises on grammar, graphic evidence of prosodic accents is almost completely absent from written Latin texts in either Antiquity or the Middle Ages.[143]

(See also Allen, *Accent and Rhythm*, 151–53) According to Serbat, *Les Structures du Latin*, 41, "Ce qui est sûr, c'est qu'au iv⁰ siècle p.C. l'accent latin était (ou était devenu) un accent d'intensité, comme le prouvent plusieurs témoignages concordants." For an account of earlier scholarship on this topic see Lindsay, *The Latin Language*, 148–217.

138. Lindsay, *The Latin Language* , 150. Lindsay's example of reduction of the unaccented vowel is *ábigo*, as compared with the Greek ἀπάγω; examples of syncope or suppression of syllables following the accent include *objurgo* from *objúrigo* and *caldus* from *cálidus*.

139. See Marius Servius Honoratus, *Commentarius in artem Donati*, ed. Keil, *Grammatici Latini*, 4: 426; and Pompeius, *Commentum artis Donati*, ed. Keil, *Grammatici Latini*, 5: 127. The collected statements of the Roman grammarians on accent may be found in Schoell, "De Accentu linguae Latinae."

140. See Allen, *Vox Latina*, 84; and Lindsay, *The Latin Language*, 152–53.

141. See Bielitz, *Die Neumen*, 83–99. In discussing differences between the treatment of the prosodic accents in the Latin West and in Byzantium following the Theodosian reform (fifth century), Bielitz says: "Im Gegensatz dazu [i.e., to the Byzantine usage], übernahm der Westen das geschlossene, und vom praktisch-grammatischem Gebrauch kaum berührte System der antiken grammatischen Akzente. Im Westen war keine Reform der Akzente notwendig, da man sie für die lateinische Sprache sowieso nicht brauchte; d. h. si wurden als System tradiert aber nicht als angewendetes, notwendiges Zeichensystem" (83). As to *why* Latin grammarians would have continued to describe accents in terms of pitch, rather than stress, Lindsay (*The Latin Language*, 151–52) offers two hypotheses. His first is that the Roman grammarians were not as conscious of a difference between stress and pitch accent as speakers of English might be, because their own stress accent was not as strongly marked as is that in English. Second, he postulates that by the time the Roman grammarians were writing their handbooks, the nature of Greek accent was changing from pitch to stress. Hence, both Greek and Latin grammarians were continuing to write about pitch accents at a time when such accents were no longer in use in either language.

142. Allen, *Vox Latina*, 84.

143. I cannot pretend to have examined carefully each of the plates of the 1,811 manuscripts described in Lowe, *Codices Latini antiquiores*, but the negative results of the cursory search I did make of these facsimiles are much in line with Sir Edward Maunde Thompson's statement that "Accents were seldom used by Latin scribes" (*An Introduction to Greek and Latin Paleography*, 64). There is an abundance of evidence for stress accents in written Latin texts, as Leonard Boyle pointed out in a plenary address

As noted, the treatises on grammar by Donatus, Isidore, and Martianus Capella are among those that describe accents characterized by inflection of pitch, that is, as prosodic. Yet, as will be shown in the next chapters, at the very time these treatises were being taught and commented on (i.e., in the ninth and tenth centuries), the Latin language itself had already been characterized for at least half a millennium by the use of stress—and not prosodic—accent.

This chapter began by setting out the bifurcation between the heritage of Antiquity and the traditions and practices of the Christian church. In addition, a "bifurcation" of a different sort has been discussed, that between harmonic theory and grammar. It is important to keep in mind, however, that both were a part of the discipline of music in Antiquity.[144] Both dealt with principles governing the organization of sound (φωνή, vox, sonus), but in ways specific to each.[145] Topics such as tone-system and mode, whose principles could be demonstrated on precisely measurable instruments, belonged properly within the purview of harmonics. In this discipline, pitches were precisely determined by way of mathematical ratios. They were given names according to their positions on an instrument, the kithara, and could also be notated using combinations and modifications of Greek letters. The same pitches could be translated into sound by means of the monochord, using Greek musical notation or Latin letters to demarcate division points, as in Boethius. Using the tuned scales thus set out, one could derive the "modes, which they also name tropes or tones," whether seven (Ptolemy), eight (Boethius), thirteen (Aristoxenos), or fifteen (Martianus Capella, Cassiodorus, Isidore of Seville). But none of this described the flow of sounds (voces, soni) in succession; that type of description lay properly in the domain of grammar. Grammatical organization started with the definition of sound (de voce), then proceeded from the smallest element, the letter, through syllables and feet up to the sentence or period. Punctuation, the distinction between long and short syllables, the presence or absence of an initial aspirate, and the pitch-inflection of the voice on individual syllables could all be represented by means of graphic signs—the toni or accents.

Clearly, the principles of both harmonic theory and grammar played a complementary role in the discipline of music in Greek and Roman Antiquity. Given this conception of music, it should not be surprising that a concept such as tonus should have drawn elements from both grammar and harmonics. As will become apparent, both of these disciplines proved influential in shaping the development of a medieval tone-system, a theory of mode, and a method of notation for the plainchant of the Western church.

---

to the Kalamazoo Congress on Medieval Studies in 1998 (published as "Vox paginae": An Oral Dimension of Texts). He talked about the "scoring" of manuscripts for reading aloud, that is, the indication of the accented syllables in words in which the accent might not fall naturally. He said the graphic indication of accent is usually a small apostrophe or tick, and never a sign that could be construed as an acute, grave, or circumflex accent. In addition to the work just cited, see also Boyle, "Tonic Accent, Codicology, and Literacy"; and Boyle, "The Friars and Reading in Public." For a treatment of stress accent in a work from the eleventh century, see Kneepkens and Reijnders, eds., Magister Siguinis "Ars lectoria."

144. See the discussion of the work by Zaminer, "Über Grammatica und Musica," at note 7 above.

145. For a discussion of vox and sonus in Roman and Carolingian treatises on grammar and music, see Sullivan, "Grammar and Harmony," 44–64, 146–79.

PART I

THE EIGHTH AND NINTH CENTURIES

THE RECEPTION OF ANCIENT TEXTS
IN THE CAROLINGIAN ERA

As noted at the end of chapter 1, the spectrum of meaning for *tonus* in Antiquity was broad and varied. Both the term and concept, along with related ideas of tone-system, mode, and notation, were transmitted into the medieval Latin West in manuscripts of Boethius, Martianus Capella, Cassiodorus, Isidore of Seville, Donatus, and others copied during the eighth and ninth centuries and beyond. Moreover, these terms and concepts received substantial explication and amplification in Carolingian commentaries on the ancient sources. The primary locus for both the dissemination of the ancient texts and the commentaries on them was the Carolingian school.[1]

Two capitularies issued by Charlemagne document the importance he attached to the founding of schools and give us information as to their functions. The first of these is the *Admonitio generalis* issued by Charlemagne to the Frankish clergy in 789.[2] In chapter 72, this document states that in every monastery and diocese there should be schools for teaching boys to read, and it implies that they should be given instruction in "Psalms, written characters, chants, calculation, and grammar" (*psalmos, notas, cantus, compotum, grammaticam*).[3] It goes on to emphasize the necessity of hav-

1. Among the many works that treat of this topic, see, in particular, Alberi, "Alcuin, the Aachen Palace School of Charlemagne, and the Carolingian Renaissance"; Brunhölzl, "Der Bildungsauftrag der Hofschule"; Bullough, *Carolingian Renewal;* Contreni, *The Cathedral School of Laon;* Contreni, "Inharmonious Harmony: Education in the Carolingian World"; Contreni, "The Carolingian Renaissance: Education and Literary Culture"; DeJong, "From *Scolastici* to *Scioli*"; Glauche, *Schullektüre im Mittelalter;* Hildebrandt, *The External School in Carolingian Society;* Holtz, "L'École d'Auxerre"; Iogna-Prat et al., eds., "*L'École carolingienne d'Auxerre*"; Jeauneau, "Les Écoles de Laon et d'Auxerre au IXe siècle"; Laistner, *Thought and Letters in Western Europe;* Möller, "Zur Frage der musikgeschichtlichen Bedeutung der Akademie Karls des Grossen"; Ochsenbein, "Die St. Galler Klosterschule"; and Riché, *Écoles et enseignement dans le haut moyen âge.*

2. Boretius, ed., *Admonitio generalis* 789, pp. 52–62. On Alcuin's possible role in the conception of this capitulary, see Möller, "Institutionen, Musikleben, Musiktheorie," 136–40.

3. "Et ut scolae legentium puerorum fiant. Psalmos, notas, cantus, compotum, grammaticam per singula monasteria vel episcopia et libros catholicos bene emendate [thus in three MSS; *emendent* in one; *emendatos* in ten others]; quia saepe, dum bene aliqui [*aliquid* in three MSS] Deum rogare cupiunt, sed

ing accurate texts of religious works, making the statement that "catholic books"—presumably Bibles, psalters, and liturgical books—should be carefully emended. The importance of these books in the spiritual life of a monastery or congregation is underscored by the statement that "all too often men desire to ask some grace of God aright but ask it ill, because the books are faulty." Hence, young clerks should not be allowed to corrupt these texts, "either in reading aloud or in copying," and the making of new copies of books such as the evangelium, psalter, or missal should be done by a grown man working with due care, not by a boy.[4]

The second Carolingian document to urge the formation of schools is the capitulary *De litteris colendis,* issued around 795.[5] It offers an eloquent rationale for teaching:

> It has seemed to us and to our faithful councilors that it would be of great profit and sovereign utility that the bishoprics and monasteries of which Christ has deigned to entrust us the government should not be content with a regular and devout life, but should undertake the task of teaching those who have received from God the capacity to learn. . . . Doubtless good works are better than great knowledge, but without knowledge it is impossible to do good.[6]

As even this brief excerpt suggests, the scope of teaching advocated in *De litteris colendis* is broader than that in the *Admonitio generalis.* Here, the door is opened to virtually all of antique learning, with a more complete understanding of the Bible as the primary goal:

---

per inemendatos libros male rogant. Et pueros vestros non sinite eos legendo vel scribendo corrumpere; et si opus est euangelium, psalterium et missale scribere, perfectae aetatis homines scribant cum omni diligentia" (Boretius, ed., *Admonitio generalis,* 60). There may be a problem here with the text. Strictly translated, the beginning of the second sentence of the text should read "Emend well the Psalms, notes, chants, calculation, grammar through the individual monasteries or bishoperics and catholic books"—a reading that has troubled several scholars, myself included. Contreni ("The Carolingian Renaissance: Education and Literary Culture," 726) makes a tacit emendation of his own, combining the first two sentences. In his translation, the first part reads "Let there be schools for boys, teaching the reading of Psalms, Tironian notes, chant, reckoning and grammar," which has the advantage of capturing the broader sense of the Latin verb *lego legi lectum.* Although it has been taken as early evidence for musical notation (for example, in Levy, "Charlemagne's Archetype," 11–12; and Levy, "From Aural to Notational," 13) or as a reference to Tironian notes, as in Contreni's translation here, the word *notas* in the principal manuscript of the *Admonitio* is qualified by a gloss connecting it with the *notarius,* a secretary, implying that the boys should also be taught how to write (see Hiley, *Western Plainchant,* 364). For a somewhat different reading of this passage see Grier, "Adémar de Chabannes," 63–65.

4. The translations into English here are from Ganshof, "Alcuin's Revision of the Bible," 29.

5. Boretius, ed., *Karoli epistola de litteris colendis* (780–800), 78–79. See Wallach, *Alcuin and Charlemagne,* 202–4. Wallach thinks that it was written ca. 794–800 and that its chief author was Alcuin. Treitler, in "Reading and Singing: On the Genesis of Occidental Music-Writing," 135, dates it ca. 795. On the *Epistola,* its date and author, see also Bullough, "*Europae Pater,*" 101–2. The document was initially addressed to Baugulf, Abbot of Fulda, but was later issued as a circular letter under the title *De litteris colendis.*

6. "Notum igitur sit Deo placitae devotioni vestrae, quia nos una cum fidelibus nostris consideravimus utile esse, ut episcopia et monasteria nobis Christo propitio ad gubernandum commissa praeter regularis vitae ordinem atque sanctae religionis conversationem etiam in litterarum meditationibus eis qui donante Domino discere possunt secundum uniuscuiusque capacitatem docendi studium debeant impendere. . . . Quamvis enim melius sit bene facere quam nosse, prius tamen est nosse quam facere" (Boretius, ed., *Karoli epistola de litteris colendis,* 79). Translation from Treitler, "Reading and Singing: On the Genesis of Occidental Music-Writing," 135.

We urge you not only not to neglect the study of [ancient] literature, but indeed to learn it eagerly, with humble and devout attention to God, so that you may be able to penetrate more easily and correctly the mysteries of the divine scriptures. Since figures of speech, tropes, and the like may be found within the sacred pages, there can be no doubt that anyone reading them can more quickly understand them spiritually to the extent to which he has first been fully instructed in the mastery of [nonspiritual] literature.[7]

With an exhortation such as this, it is hardly any wonder that Carolingian schoolmasters would ultimately seize the opportunity to teach sophisticated ancient works, such as the last book of Martianus Capella's *De nuptiis Philologiae et Mercurii* and Boethius's *De institutione musica*. But first their students had to learn the basics, and the most basic discipline of all was learning to read and write according to the rules of grammar. Indeed, there was an immediate and pressing need for precisely these skills, not only in the ecclesiastical realm, but perhaps even more so in the governmental domain.

Upon his ascent to the Frankish throne in 771, Charlemagne had become the ruler of an empire that was increasing in size and importance, and would become even larger and more influential during his reign. New techniques of administration were required and indeed were forthcoming. One of the administrative techniques Charlemagne adopted is of special interest here. Under his rule, the administration of both secular and ecclesiastical affairs became increasingly dependent on written documents, especially in the period after 800.[8] As Ganshof has pointed out, "Whatever the field, Charlemagne attached great importance to setting things down in writing."[9] His administrators obviously needed to know how to read and write— and they needed to know how to do those things well. One Carolingian author reports that Charlemagne "devoted just as much ardor to abolishing imperfections of language as he devoted to vanquishing his enemies on the field of battle."[10]

As Ganshof and others have shown, the ability to read and write was a skill that

---

7. "Hortamur vos litterarum studia non solum non negligere, verum etiam humillima et Deo placita intentione ad hoc certatim discere, ut facilius et rectius divinarum scripturarum mysteria valeatis penetrare. Cum autem in sacris paginis schemata, tropi et caetera his similia inserta inveniantur, nulli dubium est, quod ea unusquisque legens tanto citius spiritualiter intellegit, quanto prius in litterarum magisterio plenius instructus fuerit" (Boretius, ed., *Karoli epistola de litteris colendis,* 79). On this document, see in particular Glauche, *Schullektüre im Mittelalter,* 17; and Contreni, "The Carolingian Renaissance," 726, among, and in addition to, the works cited in the preceding notes. Glauche feels that this passage is a call for the study of not just literature (*litterae*), but the liberal arts in general.

8. Ganshof, "The Use of the Written Word in Charlemagne's Administration," 125–26. Ganshof remarks that from about the middle of the seventh century until the time of Pippin III, "the only use for written records seems to have been to furnish proof of individual rights, or to assist in such proof." He continues: "So far as we can judge from the sources, the use of the written word for administrative purposes started to revive under Pippin III, though only to a very modest extent. . . . When we come to the reign of Charlemagne we find a change in the situation. The number of sources to enlighten us about administrative records becomes more plentiful; and, although more numerous for the period after the imperial coronation, they are spread over the entire reign. This abundance of documentation is novel and revealing."

9. Ganshof, "The Use of the Written Word in Charlemagne's Administration," 126.

10. *MGH, Poetae latini aevi carolini* 1: 89–90. Cited after Riché, *Écoles et enseignement dans le haut moyen âge,* 112.

was not in great supply in the Frankish kingdom in the mid- to late eighth century.[11] Thus, Charlemagne had to create an educational system that could provide
trained administrators in both sacred and secular realms. In order to do that, he
brought to his court some of the most gifted men of the day—Paulinus of Aquileia,
Peter of Pisa, and Theodulf of Orléans among them—and in 782 convinced Alcuin
of York to take over the direction of the palace school and to assist him in imple-
menting a program of educational reform.[12]

Although a description of Alcuin's program does not survive, its structure is
reflected in the educational program he established at St. Martin of Tours. The
school at Tours had one division for Bible study, a second one for the liberal arts,
and a third devoted specifically to grammar.[13] From this design and from the preface to Alcuin's treatise on grammar, one can deduce that the ultimate and highest
goal of instruction was the study of the Bible, but one progressed to that through
study of the liberal arts.[14] And the first of these—in both a literal and a figurative
sense—was grammar. Beyond the most fundamental types of elementary instruction, such as the learning of reading and writing and the memorization of certain
liturgical texts,[15] grammar was the one liberal art we can reasonably assume everyone was expected to study.[16] As we know, moreover, from the testimony of Alcuin's

11. Ganshof, "The Use of the Writtten Word in Charlemagne's Administration," 135. See also Laistner, *Thought and Letters in Western Europe*, 191–92; and Dyer, "The Monastic Origins of Western Music
Theory," esp. 210–11.

12. On this, see Brunhölzl, "Der Bildungsauftrag der Hofschule"; Laistner, *Thought and Letters in
Western Europe*, 192–99; and DeJong, "From *Scolastici* to *Scioli*."

13. Brunhölzl, "Der Bildungsauftrag der Hofschule," 30. In a letter to Charlemagne from late 796 or
early 797 (Alcuini epistola 121, ed. Dümmler, in *MGH, Epistolarum* IV, *Karolini Aevi*, 2: 176–78). Alcuin
says "Ego vero Flaccus vester secundum exhortationem et bonam voluntatem vestram aliis per tecta
sancti Martini sanctarum mella scripturarum ministrare satago; alios vetere antiquarum disciplinarum
mero inaebriare studeo; alios grammaticae subtilitatis enutrire pomis incipiam." In another letter, an unknown bishop (Arno?) tells Alcuin that he should oversee instruction and names grammar, reading, and
study of the Bible as subjects (Alcuini epistola 161 in *MGH, Epistolarum* IV, *Karolini aevi* 2: 260). In Brunhölzl's view, such witnesses tell us that Alcuin's poem 26 also depicts the court school itself.

14. Brunhölzl, "Der Bildungsauftrag der Hofschule," 33–44. The preface to Alcuin's treatise on
grammar is the *Disputatio de vera philosophia*. For its text, see Migne, ed., *PL* 101: cols. 849–54. In the *Disputatio*, Alcuin's students ask him to explain the stages leading up to philosophy. He responds by quoting
the Bible: "Wisdom hath builded her house, she hath hewn out her seven pillars" (Prov. 9:1). The seven
pillars are to be understood not just as the seven Gifts of the Holy Spirit, but also as the seven liberal arts.
See Migne, ed., *PL* 101: cols. 853–54. On Alcuin as a teacher, see Duckett, *Alcuin, Friend of Charlemagne*,
109–17. That the program of instruction begun under Charlemagne continued under Louis the Pious is
suggested by Hrabanus Maurus's *De institutione clericorum libri tres* of 816–19 (ed. Zimpel; see especially
Zimpel's introduction and Book III of the treatise, which is a virtual school curriculum for the clergy).

15. The texts in question here are the Pater noster, the Credo, and the Psalms. See Bischoff, "Elementarunterricht und Probationes Pennae," 9–20; or the expanded form of this article in Bischoff, *Mittelalterliche Studien*, 1: 74–87; and Brunhölzl, "Der Bildungsauftrag der Hofschule," 39.

16. See Riché, *Écoles et enseignement dans le haut moyen âge*, 111–12; and Brunhölzl, *Geschichte der
lateinischen Literatur des Mittelalters* I, 246–47. Brunhölzl characterizes grammar as the "Grundlage aller
Wissenschaften" and continues: "Es ist dabei von sekundärer Bedeutung, daß man in der Praxis von den
artes liberales zunächst fast nur die Fächer des Triviums—Grammatik, Dialektik, Rhetorik—pflegte,
unter denen wiederum die Grammatik den weitaus größten Raum einnahm, während die Einbeziehung
der rechnenden Disziplinen des Quadriviums—Arithmetik, Geometrie, Musik und Astronomie—in

own treatise on grammar, along with ninth-century library catalogues and editions and commentaries by many Carolingian authors, the chief authority for grammar was Donatus.[17] The saying "Every schoolboy had his Donatus" was no less true in the Carolingian period than in late Antiquity. It should come as no surprise, then, that among the texts discussed in chapter 1, one of the first to be copied and commented on in the Carolingian era was the *Ars grammatica* of Donatus, along with the section on grammar in one of the other "standardized textbooks" for the Carolingians, Martianus Capella's *De nuptiis Philologiae et Mercurii*.[18]

In a series of articles published during the 1970s and 1980s, Marie-Elizabeth Duchez posited three stages in the reception of ancient texts and their assimilation into musical discourse by scholars in the Carolingian era.[19] The first of these stages begins in the later eighth century, with the reception of and commentary on texts on grammar, such as those of Donatus, Martianus Capella, and Isidore of Seville. The second stage is ushered in by commentaries on Book IX (*De harmonia*) of Martianus Capella's *De nuptiis Philologiae et Mercurii*. And a third stage is marked by the reception of Boethius's *De institutione musica*.[20] As will be shown, and as Mariken Teeuwen

---

nennenswertem Umfang erst etwa seit der Mitte des 9. Jahrhunderts und auch da allmählich und an den verschiedenen Schulen in sehr vershiedenem Maße erfolgte."

17. See Alcuin, *Grammatica*, PL 101, cols. 854–902. Donatus is cited early in the treatise (col. 855c: "Ut reor, in Donato legimus") and several times subsequently. See Brunhölzl, "Der Bildungsauftrag der Hofschule," 39. For listings of Donatus in ninth-century library catalogues, see Lehmann, *Mittelalterliche Bibliothekskataloge Deutschlands und der Schweiz*, in particular the catalogues from St. Gall and Reichenau. For a listing of the most important extant manuscripts, as well as a discussion of medieval editions of and commentaries on Donatus, see Holtz, *Donat et la tradition de l'enseignement grammatical*, 354–421 (manuscripts) and 438–41 (Carolingian editions and commentaries).

18. On this point as it pertains to instruction in music, see Huglo, "Le Développement du vocabulaire de l'*Ars musica*, 131–51. The principal sources for the present discussion are ninth- and tenth-century glossed manuscripts for the *Ars maior* of Donatus and *De nuptiis Philologiae et Mercurii* of Martianus Capella. In addition, I have drawn on the editions of ninth-century glosses and commentaries as follows: (1) on Donatus—those of Murethach, ca. 825–40 (ed. Holtz), Sedulius Scottus, ca. 840–50 (ed. Löfstedt), and the *Ars Laureshamensis*, late ninth to early tenth century (ed. Löfstedt); and (2) on Martianus Capella—those of Pseudo-Martin of Laon/Pseudo-Dunchad, ca. 830–40 (ed. Lutz), John Scottus Eriugena, ca. 847–50 (ed. Lutz), and Remigius of Auxerre, ca. 900 (ed. Lutz).

The edition of the *Ars grammatica* of Donatus Ortigraphus, ca. 850–900, by John Chittenden, was also consulted, but it is actually an independent work, rather than a commentary on Donatus. Manuscript sources for Donatus are listed and described in Holtz, *Donat et la tradition de l'enseignement grammatical*, 354–423; those for Martianus Capella can be found in Leonardi, "I Codici di Marziano Capella." I have also consulted a number of early manuscripts of the *Etymologiae* of Isidore of Seville: Bern 101, Bern 36, Leiden 74, Leiden 82, Leiden 122, Munich 6250, Munich 6275; Paris 7583–85, Paris 7670, Paris 7671; Reims 426, St. Gall 231, and St. Gall 237. I found these manuscripts, however, much less rich in glosses than those for Donatus and Martianus.

19. Duchez, "Des neumes à la portée"; Duchez, "Description grammaticale et description arithmétique des phénomènes musicaux"; Duchez, "La Représentation de la musique"; and Duchez, "La Représentation spatio-verticale du caractère musical."

20. In her dissertation on the *ars musica* in ninth-century commentaries on Martianus Capella, Mariken Teeuwen points out that the oldest layer of glosses to both Martianus Capella's *De nuptiis* and Boethius's *De musica* can be dated to the second third of the ninth century (Teeuwen, *Harmony and the Music of the Spheres*, 162–83). As pointed out by Holtz (*Donat et la tradition de l'enseignement grammatical*, 320–26), the transmission and glossing of Donatus's *Ars grammatica* begins even earlier in the century.

has also pointed out,[21] the tradition of glossing the texts on harmonic theory in the works of Martianus and Boethius seems to begin at about the same time for both writers. Nonetheless, I have organized the following discussion along the lines set out by Duchez, primarily because there are relatively few ninth-century glosses on Boethius for the topics under discussion here.[22] Because of its centrality to this study, I begin with glosses on *tonus* as a grammatical concept in Donatus and Martianus Capella, and I shall treat it later as a component of harmonic theory in Martianus Capella and Boethius.

One may gain a good sense of the flavor of Carolingian commentaries on Donatus from two such glosses on the opening sentence of chapter 5 of his *Ars maior*. (For Donatus's text see text 2.1 here, and for the commentaries see examples 2.1 and 2.2. In these examples, the base text appears in normal type, interlinear glosses in italics within hairpin brackets, and marginal glosses in italics within square brackets.)

In example 2.1, the commentator expands the meaning of *tonus* with the phrase "id est sonus. Whence thunder is called 'tonitruum,' because its *sound* can create fear."[23] In the next sentence, he specifies that the grave accent is a tone that "lowers and makes more weighty." Gloss II, example 2.2, takes Donatus's words directly into the realm of music. Its author says that *tonos* comes from *tonando*, "sounding out loudly,"[24] then adds the phrase *quasi ad cantus,* "as if in singing" or "for the purpose of song, so to speak."[25] Sound likewise plays a role in his explanation of the term *tenores,* which are so called from *tenendo,* because they *hold the sound* in one syllable.[26] Indeed, for this commentator, the accents can be called either "tones" or "sounds," as the last sentence in the example makes clear.

Whereas the emphasis in these first two glosses is on the meanings of words, and on sound and the inflection of the voice, the gloss in example 2.3, from the ninth-century manuscript Paris 13025, draws attention to the graphic signs conveying those inflections.[27] Although the signs themselves, the *notae,* have not yet been introduced

21. Teeuwen, *Harmony and the Music of the Spheres,* 162–83, esp. 182–83.

22. According to Leonardi's catalogue ("I Codici di Marziano Capella"), there are forty-nine manuscripts of *De nuptiis* dating from the ninth century, almost all of them with glosses. By comparison, there are only eleven manuscripts of *De institutione musica* from the same period, only six of which were glossed in the ninth century (see Teeuwen, *Harmony and the Music of the Spheres,* 182; Bower, "Die Wechselwirkung von philosophia, mathematica und musica," 164–68; and Bernhard and Bower, eds., *Glossa maior in institutionem Boethii,* 1: xli–xliii and lxxiv–lxxv).

23. See Löfstedt, ed., Sedulius Scottus, *In Donati Artem maiorem,* 40: "Tonus est sonus, id est uox."

24. The three Irish commentaries, Murethach, Sedulius Scottus, and the *Ars Lavreshamensis,* all preserve virtually the same reading of the sentence "Toni igitur dicuntur a tonando, id est sonando, eo quod illa syllaba, quae accentu regitur, plus sonet in dictione"—offered here as it appears in Holtz, ed., Murethach, *In Donati Artem maiorem,* 37. On the relationships among these three commentaries—especially close between Murethach and the *Ars Lavreshamensis*—see Holtz, "Sur trois commentaires irlandais," 67; he postulates that all three are based on a single anterior source.

25. See Murethach, *In Donati Artem maiorem,* 37: "Accentus uero dicitur quasi adcantus, eo quod sit iuxta cantum sicut aduerbium iuxta uerbum"; *Ars Lavreshamensis,* 177: "Accentus itaque dicitur quasi adcantus, eo quod iuxta cantum sit, sicut aduerbium dicitur, eo quod sit aduerbium."

26. See Murethach, *In Donati Artem maiorem,* 37: "Tenores dicuntur, eo quod naturalem sonum in syllabis seruent"; *Ars Lavreshamensis,* 178: "Tenores denique dicuntur, eo quo naturalem sonum in syllabis seruent."

27. Description in Holtz, *Donat et la tradition de l'enseignement grammatical,* 371–74.

TEXT 2.1.   Donatus, *Ars Maior*, Book I, chap. 5 (Holtz, ed., *Donat et la tradition de l'enseignement grammatical*)

DE TONIS: Tonos alii accentus, alii tenores nominant. Toni igitur tres sunt, acutus, gravis, circumflexus. Acutus cum in Graecis dictionibus tria loca teneat, ultimum, paenultimum et antepaenultimum, apud Latinos paenultimum et antepaenultimum tenet, ultimum numquam. Circumflexus autem, quotlibet syllabarum sit dictio, non tenebit nisi paenultimum locum. Gravis poni in eadem dictione vel cum acuto vel cum circumflexo potest, et hoc illi non est comune cum ceteris. . . . In trisyllabis et tetrasyllabis et deinceps, si paenultima correpta fuerit, acuemus antepaenultimam, ut Tullius Hostilius; si paenultima positione longa fuerit, ipsa acuetur et antepaenultima graui accentu pronuntiabitur, ut Catullus, Metellus.

Acutus accentus est nota per obliquum ascendens in dexteram partem /, gravis nota a summo in dexteram partem descendens \, circumflexus nota de acuto et gravi facta ^.

EXAMPLE 2.1.   Donatus Gloss I (Paris 7490, fol. 44v)

DE TONIS: Tonos alii accentus, alii tenores nominant.
[(Tonus) *id est sonus; unde tonitruum dicitur. quod sonus eius terreat*]
toni igitur tres sunt; acutus, gravis *deprimens tonus gravans*, circumflexus.

EXAMPLE 2.2.   Donatus, Gloss II (Paris 1620, fol. 28)

DE TONIS. Tonos <*a tonando. quasi ad cantus*> alii accentus alii tenores nominant
<*tenores a tenendo eoquod teneant sonum in una syllaba*>. Toni <*soni*> tres sunt, acutus, gravis, circumflexus.

EXAMPLE 2.3.   Donatus Gloss III (Paris 13025, fol. 27v)

---

si paenultima positione longa fuerit, ipsa acuetur et antepaenultima gravi accentu pronuntiabitur, ut cåtéllus, mèténllus.

EXAMPLE 2.4.   Donatus Gloss IV (Paris 13025, fol. 58v (after "De posituris")

INTEREST DE ACCENTU. *Accentus quid est? Accentus est, qui grece prosodia dicitur. accentus quasi a[d]cantus. accentus habet acutum / et gravem \ seu circumflexum*

---

in the running text of the treatise, the glossator places them over the syllables of *catellus* and *metellus*. I have included them here because one finds them in many manuscripts of the *Ars maior,* even ones that have few glosses. As these sources suggest, the commentators were apparently intrigued by the idea that every syllable could carry an accent, but that only one syllable would typically receive an acute or circumflex.

The fourth gloss (ex. 2.4) reinforces the connection with song noted in Gloss II, but it also establishes a further link with yet another glossing tradition, that for the treatise of Martianus Capella (in this case, perhaps, by way of Isidore of Seville).[28]

After posing the question "What is accent?" the glossator answers "*Accentus* is that which is called *prosodia* in Greek." He then goes on to say "*accentus* is *ad cantus* ['toward' or 'for the purpose of' song], so to speak." As we shall see, the phrase "qui grece prosodia dicitur" is drawn almost verbatim from Martianus, as indeed is the phrase "accentus quasi ad cantus."[29]

The influence of both Martianus Capella and Isidore of Seville is even more clearly manifested in the commentaries on Donatus by Murethach of Auxerre and, following him, those of Sedulius Scottus and the Lorsch grammar (ex. 2.5).[30]

Murethach and the Lorsch commentator explain the word *accentus* by drawing a parallel with *adverbium: accentus* is called "quasi adcantus" because it is related to *cantus* in the same way that *adverbium* is related to *verbum*. While *cantus* is the sound in the pronunciation of a syllable, *accentus* represents the elevation or depression of the voice. Sedulius shares the derivation of *accentus* from *adcantus* with his two compatriots, but then explains that *adcantus,* hence *accentus,* is itself the Latin equivalent of the Greek προσῳδία.

All three Irish commentators provide a definition of *tenores* similar to the one noted in example 2.2: *tenores* are so called because they hold the natural sound in syllables; they are called "tenores" because any part (of a word) that is performed without them appears disconnected, like a people without a leader.

---

28. Donatus Gloss IV derives the word *accentus* itself from the Greek προσῳδία ("Accentus est, qui grece prosodia dicitur. accentus quasi acantus"). Both Sedulius Scottus and the Lorsch commentator make a similar connection. Sedulius comments: "Dictus autem accentus quasi adcantus, quod sit 'iuxta cantum'; est enim compositum ex ad et cantus, quod Grece sonat prosodia: πρός 'ad,' ᾠδή 'cantus'" (*In Donati Artem maiorem,* 40). The related passage from the Lorsch commentator reads: "Accentus autem qui Grece prosodias dicitur quasi adcantus, eo quod ex Greco nomen accepit. Nam Grece πρός Latine ad, oden Grece Latine cantus dicitur" (*Ars Lavreshamensis,* 177).

The connection of accent with *prosodia* may be read in the following excerpts from a number of writers: (1) Martianus Capella—"nunc de fastigio uideamus, qui locus apud Graecos περὶ προσῳδιῶν appellatur" (*De nuptiis Philologiae et Mercurii,* Book III, ed. Dick, with addenda by Préaux, 98); (2) Marius Servius Honoratus—"Accentus dictus est quasi adcantus secundum Graecos, qui προσῳδίαν vocant. nam apud Graecos πρός dicitur ad, cantus vero ᾠδή vocatur" (*Commentarius in Artem Donati,* ed. Keil, *Grammatici Latini,* 4: 426); and (3) Sergius—"dictus autem accentus est quasi adcantus iuxta Graeci nominis interpretationem, quod prosodia dicitur Latine adcantus" (*Explanationes Artis Donati,* ed. Keil, *Grammatici Latini,* 4: 482). The wording in Donatus Gloss IV, however, is much closer to that in Isidore of Seville's *Etymologiae:* "Accentus, qui Graece prosodia dicitur [ex Graeco nomen accepit]. Nam Graece πρός Latine 'ad,' ᾠδή Graece, Latine 'cantus' est" (*Isidori hispalensis Etymologiarum sive Originum Libri XX,* ed. Lindsay, 1: xviii).

29. The phrase "quasi ad cantus" also appears in Donatus Gloss II, discussed above, but there not as a gloss on *accentus,* but on *tonus*.

30. See the bibliography and discussion in notes 24 and 28 here.

A	B	C
		Accentus est anima uocis acuendi, grauandi siue circumflectendi libera. Nam sicut corpus humanum sine anima subsistere nequit, ita nullum potest esse uerbum sine accentu.
Accentus uero dicitur quasi adcantus, eo quod sit iuxta cantum, sicut aduerbium iuxta verbum. Sed sciendum, quod cantus est in syllaba sonus pronuntiationis accentus uero elevatio uel depressio uocis ut 'arma.' Tenores dicuntur, eo quod naturalem sonum in syllabis seruent;	Accentus itaque dicitur quasi adcantus, . . . iuxta cantum sit, sicut adverbium iuxta verbum. . . . dicendum, quod cantus est In syllabis sonus pronuntiationis accentus uero elevatio uel depressio uocis. Tenores denique dicuntur, eo quod naturalem sonum in syllabis seruent.	Dictus autem accentus quasi adcantus, quod sit 'iuxta cantum'; Est enim compositum ex ad et cantus, quod Grece sonat prosodia: πρός 'ad', ᾠδή 'cantus'. Tenor a tenendo dicitur eo quod ibi sonus teneatur uerbi in rectitu-dine naturali.
qui ideo uocantur tenores,	Qui ideo uocantur tenores,	Qui ideo tenores dicuntur, quasi vigores, . . .
quia omnis pars sine istis prolata tenoribus dissoluta uidetur sicut populus sine princeps.	quia omnis pars sine istis prolata tenoribus dissoluta uidetur sicut populus sine princeps.	Omnis <enim> pars sine tenoribus prolata dissoluta uidetur.

TONI IGITVR TRES SUNT, ACVTVS GRAVIS CIRCUMFLEXUS.

A	B	C
Acutus dicitur, eo quod acuat et erigat syllabam;	Acutus dicitur, quod acuat et erigat syllabam,	Dictus uero acutus accentus eo quod acuat et erigat syllabam; et ideo erectus et eleuatus dicitur.
grauis uero, eo quod inclinet et deprimat; circumflexus,	grauis uero, eo quod inclinet et deprimat; circumflexus autem,	Gravis . . . , eo quod inclinet et deprimat . . . Circumflexus . . .
eo quod erigat et inclinet.	Eo quod erigat et inclinet.	qui constat de acuto et graui; incipiens enim de acuto in grauem desinit, atque dum ascendit et descendit, cirumflexus (id est circumcuruus) efficitur.

The last sentence in example 2.5, which explains that there are three *toni,* is drawn almost verbatim from Isidore of Seville.[31] Following Isidore, Murethach says: "The acute accent is so called because it elevates and lifts up a syllable; the grave is so called because it depresses and moves it downward; the circumflex is so called because it both elevates and moves it downward."

As clearly as these passages indicate the influence of Martianus Capella on the glosses to Donatus, arguably the clearest evidence of all is offered by the first sentence of Sedulius's treatment of accent (see ex. 2.5, top of the righthand column). As comparison with lines 3–6 of text 2.2 will show, this sentence is drawn from Martianus's treatment of accent, but with some interpretative alterations. Martianus says "accent is the soul of utterance [*vox*] and the seed-bed of music [*seminarium musices*]," continuing "just as there is no utterance without a vowel, so too there is none without an accent." (In the latter part of Martianus's statement on accent, *vox,* translated as "utterance," actually implies "syllable.") Omitting the reference to *seminarium musices,* Sedulius says "Accent is the free soul of utterance [*anima vocis*]," then adds "elevating, lowering, or 'circumflecting' it." Then, focusing on one of the phrases in Martianus's description that is richest in its implications, Sedulius says "just as the human body cannot exist without a soul, so too, no *word* [*verbum*] can be without an accent." Martianus had said implicitly that no *syllable* could be without an accent—a crucial deviation from Classical accent theory.[32] Sedulius therefore tries to correct what he perceived as a mistake in Martianus's treatment of accent, bringing it back under the Classical rules of grammar—he is, after all, writing a commentary on Donatus—and thereby emphasizing the verbal use of accent. As we shall see, other commentators would use these phrases to reinforce the connection between grammar and music.

Let us now turn to the passage on *tonus* or accent that served as the model for Sedulius—the beginning of the treatment of accent in Book III of *De nuptiis Philogiae et Mercurii* by Martianus Capella (see text 2.2 and exx. 2.6 and 2.7). Perhaps because it was a more comprehensive treatise than that of Donatus, encompassing all the liberal arts, Martianus's work received some of the most interesting and illuminating glosses of all. The quality and character of its glosses may also be attributed to its having made a direct connection between prosodic accents and music. We can see this in text 2.2, the introduction to Martianus's treatment of prosodic accents, *de fastigio.*

On introducing this topic, Martianus says that it is called in Greek περὶ προσῳδιῶν (Lat. *De prosodia*), and that it is divided into three aspects. He continues, saying:

> Every single syllable is either grave, acute or circumflex; and just as there is no utterance [again *vox,* here meaning "syllable"] without a vowel, so, too, there is none without an accent. As some assert, accent is the soul of utterance and the seed-bed of music [*seminarium musices*], because every melody is composed of elevation or depression of the voice. Thus accentus is called "ad-cantus"—"for the purpose of song"—so to speak.[33]

31. See the discussion of Isidore in chapter 1 here, pp. 42–43.
32. See the discussion of this passage in text 2.2.
33. On this passage, see Bielitz, *Die Neumen in Otfrids Evangelien-Harmonie,* 100–103.

TEXT 2.2.   Martianus Capella, *De nuptiis Philologiae et Mercurii*, Book III, secs.268–69 (ed. Willis, 71)

Hactenus de iuncturis; nunc de fastigio videamus. qui locus apud Graecos περὶ προσῳδιῶν appellatur. hic in tria discernitur: unaquaeque enim syllaba aut gravis est aut acuta aut circumflexa; et ut nulla vox sine vocali est, ita sine accentu nulla. et est accentus, ut quidam putaverunt, anima vocis et seminarium musices, quod omnis modulatio ex fastigiis vocum gravitateque componitur, ideoque accentus quasi adcantus dictus est. omnis igitur vox Latina simplex sive composita habet unum sonum aut acutum aut circumflexum; duos autem acutos aut inflexos habere numquam potest, graves vero saepe.

EXAMPLE 2.6.   Martianus Gloss I (Leiden 88, fol. 41)

Hactenus de iuncturis; nunc de fastigio <*id est accentu*> videamus. qui locus apud grecos. περὶ προσῳδιῶν. <*de accentibus*> appellatur . . . et est accentus ut quidam putaverunt anima <*id est vivificatio*> vocis et seminarium <*origo vel exordium*> <*gentivus grecus:*> musices <*id est modulationis. eo*>quod omnis modulatio ex fastigiis <*elevatione*> vocum gravitateque componitur. Ideoque accentus quasi ad cantus dictus est. Omnis igitur vox latina simplex sive composita habet unum sonum <*accentum*> aut acutum aut circumflexum. Duos autem acutos aut inflexos habere nunquam potest, graves <*scilicet plures*> vero saepe <*scilicet potest habere*>.

EXAMPLE 2.7.   Martianus Gloss II (Leiden 36, fol. 27v)

Hactenus de iuncturis; nunc de fastigio videamus. qui locus apud Graecos peri prosodion <*de accentibus*> appellatur.

[*Pros. grece* ~~cantus~~ *ad. Ode. cantus. Inde accentus. ad prosodion grece dicitur. Hinc et exo*<*r*>*dion initium cantilene dicitur & praecentor exo*<*r*>*diarius appellatur.*] . . .

et est accentus <*diffinitio vocis*>, ut quidam putaverunt, anima vocis <*origo*> et seminarium musices, quod <*eoquod*> omnis modulatio ex fastigiis <*elevationis*> vocum gravitateque componitur.

EXAMPLE 2.8.   Martianus Gloss III (Leiden 48, fol. 22v)

Hactenus de iuncturis; nunc de fastigio videamus. qui locus apud Graecos peri prosodion <*id est de accentibus*> appellatur. hic <*locus*> in tria discernitur: unaquaeque enim syllaba aut gravis est aut acuta aut circumflexa; et ut nulla vox sine vocali est, ita sine accentu nulla. et est accentus, ut quidam oputaverunt, anima <*pulcritudo*> vocis et seminarium musices <*matheries musices: id est, musicae artis*>.

[*Tonus id est cantus id est emissio vocis. accentus autem exaltatio vel depositio eius unde accentus quasi ad cantus dicitur.*]

As one might expect of a passage that has at least one phrase of Greek, along with several Latin words and phrases whose meanings were not entirely obvious, this passage inspired a lively response from medieval commentators. A typical example is that given in Martianus Gloss I (ex. 2.6), from Leiden 88.[34] The commentator explains virtually every problematic word, starting with *fastigium* and περὶ προσῳδιῶν —"accentus" and "de accentibus," respectively—and concludes with two glosses devoted to the idea that several grave accents can occur in a single word. Particularly important are his glosses on the phrase *seminarium musices: seminarium* is "origin" or "beginning"; *musices* is explained as a Greek genitive, meaning "of modulation."[35]

A later glossator, whose work is seen in example 2.7, Martianus Gloss II, from the tenth-century manuscript Leiden 36, goes even further in relating the phrase περὶ προσῳδιῶν to music.[36] In a rather extensive marginal gloss, he explains that *pros* in Greek is "ad" in Latin, and that *ode* is "cantus," whence *accentus* is called "prosodion" in Greek. He then tries to demonstrate his erudition by providing a parallel example: "From this it follows that the beginning of a chant is called the 'exordium,' and the precentor an 'exordiarius.'"[37] The only problem here is that instead of *exordium* and *exordiarius,* the anonymous commentator actually wrote "exodium" and "exodiarius"—*exodium* being a staged piece of comic description, and an *exodiarius* a player in the *exodium.* Assuming that the commentator's Latin was better than his Greek, his references to the *initium cantilene* and to the *precentor* certainly make clear the musical referent of this gloss.

The musical implications of this section of Martianus are underscored even further by a passage from Leiden 48,[38] a commentary formerly attributed to Martin of Laon (ex. 2.8, Martianus Gloss III).[39] In the sentence beginning "et est accentus," the anonymous commentator glosses the word *anima* (soul) with "pulcritudo" (pulchritude or beauty); *seminarium musices* becomes for him the "materies musices, id est musicae artis"—"the very stuff or substance of music, that is, of the musical art." He concludes with a marginal commentary on the theory of accent introduced by Donatus's term *tonus:* "Tonus, that is cantus, which is the projection of the voice.

---

34. Description and bibliography in Leonardi, "I Codici di Marziano Capella," 62–63; and Teeuwen, *Harmony and the Music of the Spheres,* 117–26 and plate 4.

35. I thank Leofranc Holford-Strevens for sharing with me his reading of this passage.

36. Description and bibliography in Leonardi, "I Codici di Marziano Capella," 61–62; and Teeuwen, *Harmony and the Music of the Spheres,* 135–40 and plate 7.

37. *Hinc et exo<r>dion initium cantilene dicitur & praecentor exo<r>diarius appellatur.*

38. Description and bibliography in Leonardi, "I Codici di Marziano Capella," 67–68; and in Teeuwen, *Harmony and the Music of the Spheres,* 88–98 and plate 1.

39. See Leonardi, "I Codici di Marziano Capella," 13–14; Lutz, "Martinus Laudunensis," *CTC, 2* (1971): 370–71; Contreni, "A Note on the Attribution of a Martianus Capella Commentary to Martinus Laudunensis," in addenda to *CTC, 3* (1976): 451–52; Préaux, "Le Commentaire de Martin de Laon sur l'oeuvre de Martianus Capella"; and Teeuwen, *Harmony and the Music of the Spheres,* 33–41, 148–50, but 88–98 for the description and bibliography of Leiden 48. Both Contreni and Teeuwen express strong reservations as to the putative authorship of Martin. Teeuwen (148–50) hypothesizes that the commentary, which she refers to as "anonymous," may have been the product of a group of scholars associated with the courts of Louis the Pious (reg. 813/14–840) and Charles the Bald (reg. 840–77). I refer here to the earlier attribution to Martin of Laon primarily because Leonardi, following Préaux ("Le Commentaire de Martin de Laon sur l'oeuvre de Martianus Capella"), Lutz, and others, employs that designation in his manuscript descriptions.

TEXT 2.3.   Martianus Capella, *De nuptiis Philologiae et Mercurii*, Book III, sec. 273 (ed. Willis, 74)

---

acutus accentus notatur virgula a sinistra parte in dexteram ascendente, gravis autem a sinistra parte ad dexteram descendens, inflexi signum est sigma super ipsas litteras devexum. accentus partim fastigia vocamus, quod litterarum capitibus apponantur, partim cacumina, tonos vel sonos, Graeci prosodias. sciendum etiam uni vocabulo accidere omnes tres accentus posse, ut est Argiletum.

Accent is its elevation or deposition; whence accent is called 'ad cantus,' 'for the purpose of song,' so to speak." In this passage, it is hard to tell whether music or grammar is the primary referent, so complete is the interweaving of elements from the two disciplines.

Our final excerpt from Martianus on grammar, text 2.3, begins by describing the graphic signs for notating prosodic accents, signs Donatus calls *notae* (as we saw in text 2.1): "An acute accent is notated as a virgula ascending from left to right; a grave [is notated as a virgula] descending from left to right; the sign of the circumflex [*inflexus*] is a sigma facing downward over its respective syllable."

Unlike the sources for Donatus, however, those for Martianus do not present the *notae* themselves in the running text. Indeed, in a number of the best manuscripts, they do not appear at all.[40] This is so, for example, in Bamberg 39, the B source for the editions of both Dick and Willis (fig. 2.1). It is also the case for the manuscript that was the A source for Dick's edition, Bern 56b (fig. 2.2).[41] As one can see here, a later hand has added the *notae* for the accents in the margins.

Apart from the presence or absence of the accent signs, however, there is a more substantive feature that distinguishes Martianus's text from that of Donatus. Donatus had said that the grave accent could be placed in a single word together with one of the other accents, but that it could not appear with both of the others. However, after describing the *notae* for the acute, grave, and "inflexus" accents, as noted, Martianus says: "It should be known that all three accents can occur together in one word, as is the case in *Argiletum*."[42] Thus, according to Martianus, at least, the inflections of all syllables of a word could be represented via the accent signs, irrespective of whether those signs were acute, grave, or circumflex. With all three accents over

---

40. Given the clarity of the description, inserting the *notae* themselves may have been considered superfluous. It is interesting that Martianus does provide descriptions of the vocal inflections represented by the *notae*, descriptions Donatus had not provided—presumably because the inflections and the signs representing them were considered to be inextricably linked together. On these relationships and their implications for the rise of musical notation, see Duchez, "Description grammaticale et description arithmétique des phénomènes musicaux," 561–79, esp. 563–76; Duchez, "Des neumes à la portée," 22–65, esp. 25–30; and Bielitz, *Die Neumen in Otfrids Evangelien-Harmonie,* 1–7, 79–132, 148–55.

41. On these manuscripts, see Dick, ed., *Martianus Capella*; Dick, ed., with addenda by Préaux, *De nuptiis Philologiae et Mercurii*; Willis, ed., *Martianus Capella*.

42. From text 2.3: "sciendum etiam uni vocabulo accidere omnes tres accentus posse, ut est Argiletum."

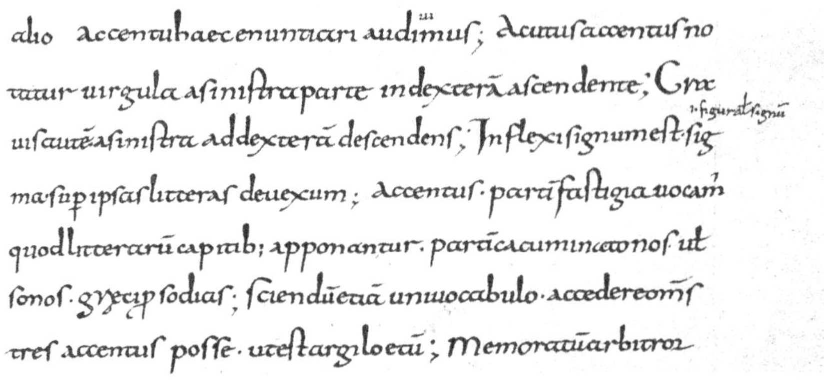

FIGURE 2.1.   Martianus Capella, *De nuptiis Philologiae et Mercurii*, sec. 273 in Bamberg 39, fol. 47 (reproduced with the permission of the Staaatsbibliothek Bamberg)

its syllables, the word *Argiletum* thus encapsulates a significant change in the theory of prosodic accents.

Unfortunately, Martianus did not say which accents should go over which syllables in *Argiletum*. Perhaps because the scribes were not comfortable enough with the rules of prosody to place them correctly, most texts contain no accents at all over the word—either in the original hand or in that of a glossator. In fact, rather than commenting on the position of the accents in *Argiletum*, several commentators explain the meaning of the word itself. Typical is a line that appears at the end of Martianus Gloss IV (ex. 2.9): Argiletum "ubi argila est vel mors argi," "where the *argilla* [clay] is or *mors argi*—'death of Argos.'" Remigius of Auxerre would later gloss *Argiloetum* as "locus ubi sepultus est Argus occisus ab Evandro," "the place where Argus was buried upon being killed by Evander."[43]

43. Paris 8674, fol. 37v: "Argiloetum, id est locus ubi sepultus est Argus occisus ab Evandro, volens abstrahere regnum eius." This is from Lutz's "B" family of manuscripts containing Remigius's commentary; hence it does not appear in her edition, *Remigii Autissiodorensis Commentum in Martianum Capellam*. The word "Argiletum" and the source of Remigius's gloss is Virgil's *Aeneid*, Book VIII, ll. 345–46: "nec non et sacri monstrat nemus Argileti / testaturque locum et letum docet hospitis Argi" ("he [Evander] shows the wood of sacred Argiletum, and calls the place to witness and tells of the death of Argus, his guest"). According to Fordyce, ed., *P. Vergili Maronis Aeneidos libri VII–VIII with a Commentary*, 243, "the Argiletum lay in the low ground south of the Quirinal: in historical times it was a trading quarter, where Cicero owned shops (Att. xii. 32.3) and Martial's bookseller had his premises (i. 3. I). The name clearly meant 'clay-pits' (from *argilla*: a parallel formation to *arboretum, quercetum, dumetum*), but popular etymology interpreted it as *Argi-letum* and invented an *aition* for it in the story of an Argus who was Evander's guest and was killed by Evanders's people for seeking to dethrone his host. Varro, *De lingua latina*, v. 157, impartially offers both the true explanation and the invention." The line in Varro is: "Argiletum sunt qui scripserunt ab Argo La<ri>saeo, quod is huc venerit ibique sit sepultus, alii ab argilla, quod ibi id genus terrae sit" ("The Argiletum, according to some writers, was named from Argus of Larisa, because he came to this place and was buried there; according to others, from the argilla 'clay,' because this kind of earth is found at this place"). *Varro, on the Latin Language*, transl. Kent, 148–49.

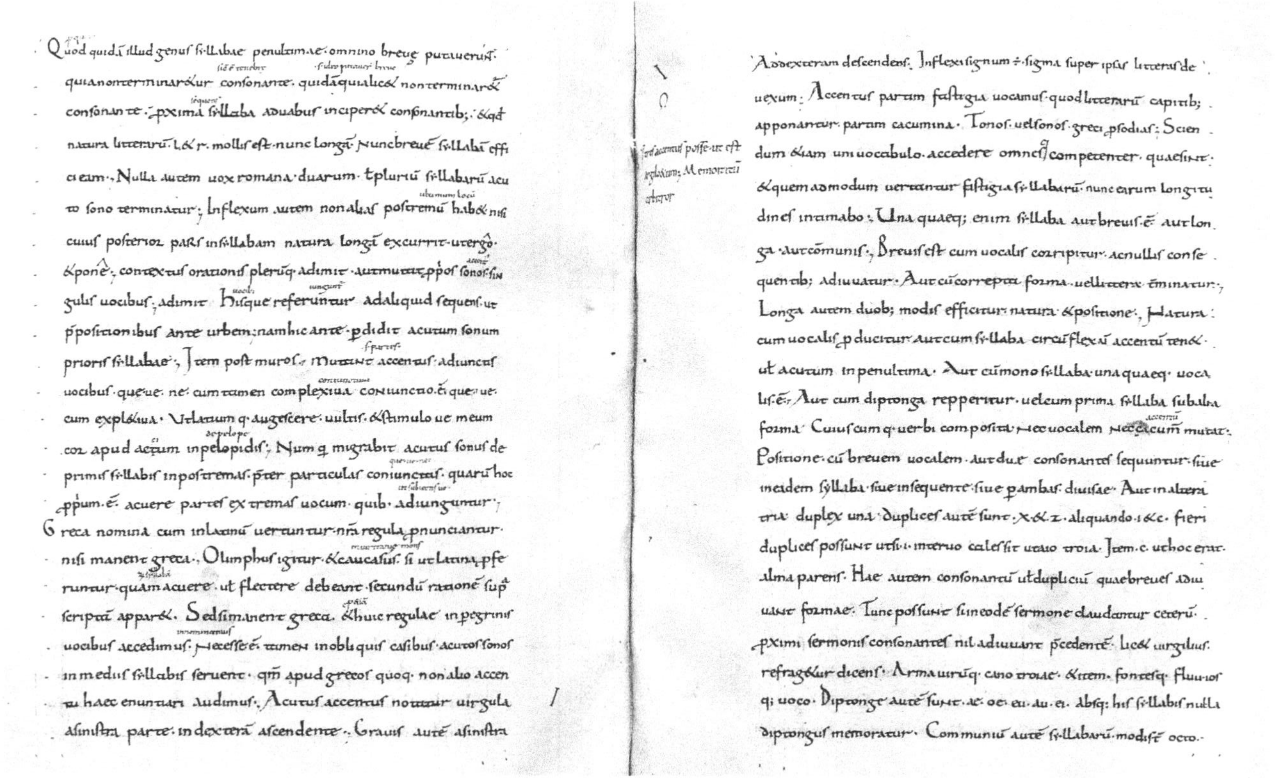

FIGURE 2.2. Martianus Capella, *De nuptiis Philologiae et Mercurii*, sec. 273 in Bern 56b, fol. 49v–50 (reproduced with the permission of the Burgerbibliothek Bern)

EXAMPLE 2.9.   Martianus Gloss IV (Leiden 36, fol. 29)

---

acutus accentus [**/**] notatur virgula a sinistra parte in dexteram ascendente, gravis [****] autem a sinistra parte ad dexteram descendens, inflexi signum est sigma super ipsas litteras devexum [**∧**] accentus partim fastigia vocamus

[*Tunc vocantur fastigia cum apponuntur litteris. Cum vero elevantur cacumina.*]

quod litterarum capitibus apponantur, partim cacumina, tonos vel sonos, Graeci <*vocant*> prosodias. sciendum etiam uni vocabulo accidere omnes tres accentus posse, ut est Argiletum <*ubi argila est vel mors argi*>.

The lexical and prosodic difficulties of *Argiletum* notwithstanding, a few glossators deal directly with the main point of Martianus's text, namely the proper inflection of *Argiletum* and the placement of all three accent signs to convey it. The text of one such gloss appears as example 2.10: Martianus Gloss V, taken from Paris 8669.[44] The commentator has added the accent signs over *Argiloetum*—incorrectly, as it turns out. Since the penultimate is long, with a circumflex accent, the antepenultimate should receive a grave; the first syllable, long by position, should then receive an acute. As one can see, that is not the case here. But at least he tried!

Example 2.10.   Martianus Gloss V (Paris 8669, fol. 25v)

Sciendum etiam uni vocabulo accidere omnes tres accentus posse, ut est argíloetùm.

Yet another glossator takes a different route in order to show that each of the syllables in *Argiletum* can carry an accent. Figure 2.3 is from the manuscript Paris 14754, a late eleventh- or early twelfth-century source from northern France.[45] At the beginning of section 273, the glossator adds the graphic signs for the accents—the *notae*—just as we have seen them in several other sources. Rather than placing these accent signs over *Argiletum,* however, he illustrates the inflection of the word by writing neumes over the syllables that do not already carry an accent. (The circumflex seems to be in the original hand.) Granted, all the neumes are *pedes,* and thus should represent acute accents, but the glossator seems to have been interested in showing that there can be an accent on every syllable, a reasonably logical illustration of Martianus's statement.

Whatever his motivation, and regardless of his knowledge of the rules of prosody, the important fact for us is that this glossator presents the "*notae* that are called neumes" as equivalent to the *notae* for the prosodic accents.[46] We should not be sur-

---

44. Description in Leonardi, "I Codici di Marziano Capella," 436–37.

45. Description in Leonardi, "I Codici di Marziano Capella," 444–45.

46. This phrase is based on the words of the anonymous Vatican scribe in the passage "De accentibus toni oritur nota quae dicitur neuma" (ed. Wagner, "Un piccolo trattato," 482). The pluralization is mine.

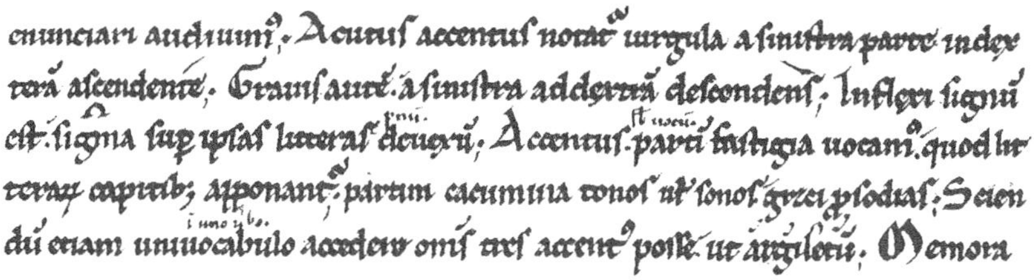

FIGURE 2.3.   Martianus Capella, *De nuptiis Philologiae et Mercurii*, sec. 273 in Paris 14754, fol. 121 (reproduced with the permission of the Bibliothèque nationale de France)

prised that neither he nor the person responsible for Gloss V could place the accents correctly. After all, graphic signs for prosodic accents as a component of actual linguistic usage had long since disappeared in Latin—if indeed they had ever been used at all. That meant that those very signs, and a fully developed theory to explain their use, were available to the Carolingians as a partial foundation for notating the melodic inflections of Latin texts that were not spoken, but sung.[47] We shall consider the implications of this in chapter 3.

———————

Let us now return to the domain of music as a harmonic discipline and examine how it was handled by the Carolingian commentators, starting with the treatment of tone-system, species, and mode in Book IX, *De harmonia,* of *De nuptiis Philologiae et Mercurii* by Martianus Capella. As was shown earlier, the organization of Book IX and various features of its treatment—not to mention problems in its manuscript transmission—made it rather difficult to comprehend. That difficulty is perhaps reflected in the relative paucity of commentary on the topics with which this study is concerned. For example, when Martianus sets out the notes of the tone-system in section 931 of his work, John Scottus has nothing to add, and Remigius only a little more. Remigius does say of the proslambanomenos, however, that "this string is the lowest of all, and placed outside the others."[48] The anonymous glosses of Pseudo-Martin of Laon generally content themselves with clarifying the number of the notes (eighteen, of which there are fifteen in each trope),[49] or the names of the strings (e.g., proslambanomenos, i.e., "added." According to Boethius, the proslambanomenos is called the "prosmelodos").[50] In one place, however, they do provide

47. See Bielitz, *Die Neumen in Otfrids Evangelien-Harmonie,* xiv; 211 n. 8; and the following quotation at 79–80: "Die neue, 'musikalische' Verwendung der Prosodie- bzw. Akzent-Zeichen, die ja aus der antiken-griechischen Tradition stammten, im Westen, zu einer Zeit, in der Griechisch-Kenntnisse etwa so verbreitet waren wie heute, war möglich, weil die lateinischen Grammatiker das System in seiner Gesamtheit weitergegeben haben, auch wenn es für die eigene Sprach nicht ganz passen konnte und auch in seiner Subtilität unnötig war." See also the articles by Duchez cited in note 19 here.

48. "PROSLAMBANOMENOS haec chorda gravissima est omnium extra alias posita" (Lutz, ed., *Commentum in Martianum Capellam,* 331).

49. 357.11: "Generaliter xviii sunt soni et unusquisque . . . et tropus xv" (Teeuwen, *Harmony and the Music of the Spheres,* 492).

50. 357.14: "PROCLAMBANOMENOC i. adquisita; secundum Boetium prosmelodos dicitur proslambanomenos" (Teeuwen, *Harmony and the Music of the Spheres,* 492).

some musically relevant information. The gloss for the eighth string, or μέση (here transliterated MECH), says that up to the *mese* the sounds are low (*graves*); from the *mese* onward they are high (*acuti*).[51] Martianus himself had provided no such information.

Two of the core manuscripts for the commentary of Pseudo-Martin, Leiden 48 and Besançon 594, both dating from the ninth century, have a rather extensive comment in the margin opposite section 932 of Martianus's text.[52] The text itself reads as follows.

> Hi sunt igitur soni, qui modulationem aptè & cum ratione componunt. Constat autem omnis modulatio ex grauitate soni uel acumine. Grauitas dicitur quae modi quadam emissione mollescit; Acumen ueró, quod in aciem tenuatam gracilis et erectae modulationis extenditur.[53]

> These, therefore, are the sounds with which melody (*modulatio*) is aptly and rationally composed. Every melody consists of depth or height of sound. That which is called depth soothes by a certain relaxation of the mode; height is that which is projected in the sharp compression of a high, thin melody.[54]

The marginal commentary makes the following observation (Ex. 2.11).[55]

EXAMPLE 2.11.   Martianus Gloss VI (Besançon 594, fol. 78)

> [*Primo* <facis> *materiam in animo simul cum grauitate aut etiam cum acumine. Ergo si libet tibi, ut ex grauioribus tropis alterum formes, praeparandum est opus aut fistula aut fidibus et caetera, aut etiam voce, similiter fide acutis.*]

51. 357.19: "OCTAVUS MECH Usque mece sunt grave[s] soni, a mece autem acuti sunt soni" (Teeuwen, *Harmony and the Music of the Spheres*, 493).

52. For description and bibliography of Leiden 48, see Leonardi, "I Codici di Marziano Capella," 13–14; Lutz, "Martinus Laudunensis," *CTC*, 2 (1971): 370–71; Contreni, Addenda to *CTC*, 3 (1976): 451–52; and Teeuwen, *Harmony and the Music of the Spheres*, 88–98. Teeuwen provides description and bibliography of Besançon 594, 98–103. Leiden 48 was written ca. 850, probably in Auxerre, according to the sources listed in Teeuwen (88–89). Besançon 594 dates from the third quarter of the ninth century and was apparently copied at the abbey of Saint-Claude in Saint Oyan (98–99).

53. Martianus Capella, *De nuptiis Philologiae et Mercurii*, Book IX, sec. 932, in *Antiquae musicae auctores septem Graece et Latine*, ed. Marcus Meibom, 2: 180. I use Meibom here because his text for this section of the treatise is the same as that found in the two manuscripts. Related to this and the following discussion, consider the gloss on Boethius, *De institutione musica*, Book I, chap. 8, which presents the definition of *sonus*, as it appears in the eleventh-century manuscript Paris 16201: "*Sonus casus vocis* dicitur, i. exitus vel emissio vel processio de gravi in acutum, vel de acuta in gravem, vel talis vocis terminatio, que sit apta melo" (Bernhard and Bower, eds., *Glossa maior in institutionem Boethii*, 1: 164, Gloss 3 on Book I, chap. 8). See chapter 3 here, note 100.

54. Stahl translates the last two sentences as follows: "Moreover, all musical movement (*modulatio*) consists of lower- or higher-pitched tones. A low pitch has a soothing effect because of the slackening of its sound; a high pitch, on the other hand, is due to the tightening and raising of the music to a thin and shrill sound" (Stahl, *Martianus Capella and the Seven Liberal Arts*, 2: 361).

55. The Latin text is a modified version of that in Teeuwen, *Harmony and the Music of the Spheres*, 304–5, 315, and in her edition, 496 (lemma 359.9). My translation, however, is rather different from hers, as the following note and the text associated with it explain.

First <you compose> the (melodic) material in your mind, with both depth and height. Thus, if you wish to form another (melody?) from the lower tropes—if the work has to be prepared for an organ or stringed instrument, et cetera, or even for the voice—you must likewise form it for the stringed instrument from the higher tropes.

What the glossator seems to say in this reading is that if one adapts a melody to instruments or composes a new melody, one must employ both low and high pitches.[56] This reading is supported, or at least not contradicted, by the glosses of both John Scottus and Remigius on section 932. John simply explains the words *mollescit* ("dulcescit," "sweetens"); *acumen* ("altitude," "height"); *in atiem* ("in acumen vocis," "in the sharpness of the voice"); and *erectae* ("acute," "high").[57] Remigius glosses the crucial sentences of the text as follows (ex. 2.12):

EXAMPLE 2.12.   Martianus Gloss VII, from the Commentary of Remigius of Auxerre (Lutz, ed., *Remigii Autissiodorensis Commentum in Martianum Capellam*. 2: 332)

> CONSTAT AUTEM OMNIS MODULATIO EX GRAUITATE SONI id est ex inaequalibus, VEL ACUMINE. Omnis modulatio ex inaequalibus constat. Si enim aliter fuerit, iam non erit modulatio. GRAVITAS DICITUR QUAE MODI id est soni QUADAM EMISSIONE id est descensione, REMISSIONE vel productione MOLLESCIT dulcescit, remittitur.

"EVERY MELODY CONSISTS OF DEPTH OR HEIGHT OF SOUND, that is, of unequal [varying] sounds.[58] If it were not so, it would not be a melody. DEPTH SOOTHES, sweetens, lowers, BY A CERTAIN RELAXATION, that is, descent, lowering or stretching out OF THE MODE, that is, of the sound."

Remigius interprets the word *modus* in the lemma as "sound," not "trope," and he makes no reference to a melodic adaptation or new composition such as that found in the anonymous commentary.

56. Teeuwen associates this commentary with sec. 935, the section in which Martianus discusses the tropes. In accord with this, her translation is as follows: "First <you compose> the (melodic) material in your mind, at the same time for both the high region and the low region. Thus, if it pleases you to form a different (melody) out of the lower modes—the work has to be adapted for a flute or stringed instrument etcetera, or even for the human voice,—then <you can make> the same (melody) for a high string." If Teeuwen's interpretation and translation are correct, this comment might possibly be one of the earliest references to two-part parallel organum. My translation results from my assumption that the comment is on sec. 932, and that *modus* in Martianus's text (as given here) is taken as an alternate for *sonus*—rather than *tropus*—as it appears in the reading of the same commentary in Paris 8671. Unfortunately, there is no cue in either Leiden 48 or Besançon 594 to indicate the section of the main text to which this comment pertains. Moreover, nothing like it appears in the commentaries of John Scottus Eriugena and Remigius of Auxerre for either sec. 932 or 935. The comment must remain a tantalizing mystery for the present.

57. Ed. Lutz, *Iohannis Scotti Annotationes*, 206. I have emended her reading of "MOLLESCAT dulcescat" to "MOLLESCIT dulcescit" following the readings of both Dick and Willis, as well as her own of Remigius (see ex. 2.12).

58. On equal and unequal sounds as necessary components of melody, see the gloss on Boethius, *De institutione musica*, Book I, chap. 3, that appears in two manuscripts from Einsiedeln dating from the tenth century, Einsiedeln 298 and Einsiedeln 358. For the lemma "QUOCIRCA SONI QUOQUE PARTIM SUNT AEQUALES, PARTIM VERO SUNT INAEQUALITATE DISTANTES" ("Therefore, some sounds are also equal, while

The situation regarding glosses to Martianus's treatment of species (*systema*, in his usage) is similar to that regarding the scale.[59] John Scottus offers only one gloss, explaining that *modis* in Martianus's definition of *systema* should be interpreted as "sonis": (SYSTEMA EST MAGNITUDO UOCIS EX MULTIS MODIS id est sonis CONSTANS). Both Pseudo-Martin of Laon and Remigius of Auxerre add more, but they are rather perfunctory, offering only explanations of individual words, names of strings, and so on, without truly clarifying the essential nature of the eight species as differing arrays of intervals—for example, "Remigius: SYSTEMA EST MAGNITUDO UOCIS id est magnum intervallum, EX MULTIS MODIS id est sonis, vel ex V et III vel ex pluribus, CONSTANS" ("A SYSTEM IS A RANGE OF PITCH, that is, a large interval, CONSISTING OF MANY MODI, that is, sounds, either eight or more").[60]

When we turn to Martianus's presentation of the tropes or modes, in section 935 of *De nuptiis Philologiae et Mercurii*, we are confronted with some of the most fasci-

---

others stand at an interval from each other by virtue of an inequality"), they offer the following gloss (see Bernhard and Bower, eds., *Glossa maior in institutionem Boethii*, 1: 125, Gloss 150 on Book I, chap. 3):

equales soni	inequales
	‑ ‑
‑	
Astiterunt reges	terre et

(Antiphona I ad Matutinum in Feria VI. in Parasceve; *CAO* 3, 1506. "Astiterunt" is recited on G, "terre et" on b♭, G, and F).

This gloss may actually have had its source in *De harmonica institutione* (ca. 885–99) by Hucbald of St. Amand (ca. 850–930), one of whose earliest sources is the manuscript Einsiedeln 169. Hucbald begins his treatise with the statement "Whoever wishes to be introduced to the elements of music, who seeks, even provisionally, to acquire an understanding of melody, should pay special attention to the quality or position of each of the sounds," and he then specifies that "one should note first which sounds are equal and consistently alike, and which are unequal, differing from each other by various intervals" ("Ad mvsicae initiamenta qvemlibet ingredi cvpientiem, qvi aliqvam scilicet interim cantilenarvm percipere intellegentiam qverit, qvalitatem sive positionem quarumcumque uocum diligenter aduertere oportebit. Et primo, quae sunt aequales uoces atque uniformiter sibi consimiles; quae deinde inaequales et quibusdam spatiis a se discrepantes"); Chartier, ed., *L'Oeuvre musicale d'Hucbald*, 136; GS 1: 104a; Traub, ed., "Hucbald von Saint-Amand," 24; Babb and Palisca, eds., *Hucbald, Guido, and John on Music*, 13. Significantly, *Astiterunt reges* is the chant Hucbald uses to illustrate equal sounds. Of the unequal sounds, Hucbald says that they are called "disjunct," and he specifies that they exist as nine degrees of intervals, ranging in size from the semitone up to the major sixth ("Inaequalium vero sonorum qui disiuncti dicuntur, diuersae species offeruntur . . . quae paruissimo quodam exorsa, gradatimque per singulos, ampliatione adiecta, usque ad nouem modorum crementa consurgunt"; Chartier, ed., *L'Oeuvre musicale d'Hucbald*, 140; GS 1: 105a; Traub, ed., "Hucbald von Saint-Amand," 26; Babb and Palisca, eds., *Hucbald Guido, and John on Music*, 16.

59. As a reminder, this section begins as follows: "systema est magnitudo uocis ex multis modis constans, quod licet multa diuisionum genera recipiat . . . sunt autem absoluta et perfecta systemata numero octo: et primum est, quod ab adquisito, quem προσλαμβανόμενον dicimus, ad mediam, quam μέσην diximus, omne conficitur; secundum, quod a principali principalium in παράμεσον usque tenditur" (*Martianus Capella*, ed. Willis, 367). ("A system is a range of pitch that consists of many intervals and that can receive many types of divisions. . . . There are eight absolute and perfect systems. The first is the one constructed from the *adquisitus*, which is what we call the proslambanomenos, to the *media*, which is what we call the mese. The second extends from the *principalis principalium* [the hypate hypaton] to the *paramese*, etc.")

60. *Commentum in Martianum Capellam*, ed. Lutz, 344.

EXAMPLE 2.13.   Martianus Gloss VIII (Besançon 594, fol. 78)

Tropi <.*i. modi*> vero sunt xv, sed principales <*sunt v.*> quibus bini coherent.
<.*i. superior & inferior*> Lydius cui adherent [y]polidius <.*i. sub qui gravius sonat*> &
hyperlydius. super [etc.]. . . .

Verum inter hos tropos <*modos*> est quidam amica concordia. item conveniens aptaque
responsio inter ὑποφρίγιυμ & ὑπολίδιουμ, qui tantum duplices <.*i. ypofrigius*> copulantur. Media vero graviorum trophorum his <*tropis*> qui acutiores sunt προσλαμβανόμεναι <*i. in grauissimis*> fiunt.

---

nating glosses on his work. As shown in figure 1.5, the manuscript Bern 56b, dating
from the tenth century, contains glosses by Remigius of Auxerre.[61] We noticed that
it preserves the names of all fifteen tropes mentioned by Martianus, copied in a mixture of Latin and Greek, with the names of the three pairs of *amici* in Greek. As I
suggested was true of all the glossed sources I have seen, these names are incorrect,
leaving the Carolingian commentators to their own devices in their attempts to
make sense out of nonsense.

Given the difficulties presented by Martianus's description of the *tropi* in section
935 of *De nuptiis,* it should come as no surprise that many of the glossed manuscripts
have no glosses for this section of the treatise. Of the ones that do, many simply provide explanations for Greek words or phrases, or clarifications of syntax. A good example is that appearing in example 2.13, which is from the commentary of Pseudo-
Martin of Laon, as it appears in Besançon 594.[62] As one can see, this commentator
glosses Martianus's Greek word *tropi* with the Latin "modi"—"modes"—and explains that *hypo* means "sub, that which sounds lower," and that the prefix *hyper* has
the Latin equivalent "super" ("above"). In the last sentence ("Media vero graviorum . . ."), he clarifies the antecedent of *his* as "tropis" and explains that the *proslambanomenoi* to which Martianus refers are those in the lower tropes of each pair, those
"in gravissimis."

With the next example, we turn to the commentary attributed to John Scottus
Eriugena.[63] As one might expect from one of the great minds of the ninth century,

---

61. See Leonardi, "I Codici di Marziano Capella," 11; Lutz, ed., *Commentum in Martianum Capellam;*
and Lutz, "Martianus Capella," *CTC,* 2 (1971): 372–76 (Remigius) and 371 (John).

62. See Leonardi, "I Codici di Marziano Capella," 13–14; Lutz, "Martinus Laudunensis," *CTC,* 2
(1971): 370–71; Contreni, Addenda to *CTC,* 3 (1975): 451–52; and Teeuwen, *Harmony and the Music of the
Spheres,* 98–103 for description of Besançon 594. As mentioned in note 39 here, for compelling reasons,
Teeuwen prefers not to assign the name of a single author to these glosses, referring to them instead
simply as "anonymous."

63. See Leonardi, "I Codici di Marziano Capella," 62–63; and Lutz in *CTC,* 2 (1971): 371. Lutz's edition of John's commentary, *Annotationes in Marcianum,* was based on only one manuscript, Paris 12960.
Her own subsequent work, along with that of others, has identified four additional sources for John's
commentary: Oxford 2.19 (see Labowsky, "A New Version of Scottus Eriugena's Commentary"), Bern
331, Paris 8675, Vienna 3222, and Leiden 88. Of these, only the Oxford manuscript contains commentary on all nine books; the Bern, Paris, and Vienna sources contain Books VI–IX; the Leiden manuscript
has John's glosses only on Book IX.

EXAMPLE 2.14.   Martianus Gloss IX, from the Commentary attributed to Johannes
Scottus Eriugena (Leiden 88, fol. 174)

Verum inter hos tropos est quaedam amica concordia. qua sibi invicem germani sunt.
<*quinque in gravitate, quinque in acumine, quinque in temperato sono.*> ut inter ὑποδόριον
& ἱποφρίγιον. et item inter ὑποιάςτιον & ἱπολίδιον; item conveniens aptaque responsio <*convenientia*> inter ὑποφρίγιον & ὑποεόλιον qui tantum duplices* copulantur. [In margine: *acutior enim duplo superat graviorem. Tòno* (lege: *Tonus*) *quippe ad
emitonium sonat. est autem tonus duplum emitonii.*]

Mediae vero graviorum troporum his qui auctiores <*vel acutiores*> sunt προςλαμβανό-
μεναι fiunt <*vicem proslambanomenes cordae obtinent.*>

John goes beyond Martin in his glosses on this passage. Example 2.14 presents these
glosses as they appear in Leiden 88, a ninth-century source from Reims that, according to Jean Préaux and others, preserves John's commentary on Book IX in his
own hand.[64] As one can see in example 2.14, John chooses to gloss the phrase DU-
PLICES COPULANTUR, seizing on the word *duplices* as a reference to the interval between one mode and another. He explains that the higher (trope) lies above the
lower one by a duple proportion, as in the relationship between a semitone and a
tone, since a tone is two times a semitone. (Martianus had earlier said, in sec. 930,
that a semitone was half a tone.)[65] The proportional relationship of 2:1 as the interval of a tone is not what Martianus was referring to as a "quaedam amica concordia," but it is a relationship that accurately describes the pairs of concordant tropes
as they are named in most of the manuscripts: Hypodorian and Hypophrygian, Hypoiastian and Hypoaeolian, and Hypophrygian and Hypolydian.

As was made clear in example 1.8, the proslambanomenos of the Hypophrygian
mode lies a whole tone above that of the Hypodorian. The same is true of the Hypoaeolian in relation to the Hypoiastian and of the Hypolydian in relation to the
Hypophrygian. Thus, John was quite correct, insofar as the proslambanomenoi are
concerned; but his explanation does not take account of the mesai, or "middle
tones" (see ex. 1.8). Martianus had said that the "middle tones of the lower tropes
become the proslambanomenoi of the higher ones"—a statement John rephrases,
suggesting that "the middle strings hold the function of the proslambanomenos"
(see ex. 2.14).[66]

---

64. See Leonardi, "I Codici di Marziano Capella," 62–63. The question of what part of the glosses
in Leiden 88 is actually in John's hand is complicated, as is demonstrated in Leonardi's essay "Glosse eriugeniane a Marziano Capella in un codice leidense," 173–79. He points out (173 n. 4) that it was Préaux
who first raised this question in his article "Le Commentaire de Martin de Laon," 439 n. 1, and again in
"Deux manuscrits gantois de Martianus Capella," 19. Leonardi himself had come to the same conclusion independently, and he was supported in his opinion by Bernhard Bischoff (see Leonardi, "I Codici
di Marziano Capella," 63). On this issue, see also Bishop, "Autographa of John the Scot" 90, 92; and
Schrimpf, "Zur Frage der Authentizität unserer Texte von Johannes Scottus' Annotationes in Martianum," 132.

65. In Martianus's words: "hemitonium dicitur, quod toni medium tenet" (*De nuptiis*, ed. Willis, 357).

66. I have adopted Teeuwen's translation of *vicem* as "function."

EXAMPLE 2.15.   Martianus Gloss X, from the Commentary of Remigius of Auxerre (Lutz, ed., *Remigii autissiodorensis commentum in Martianum Capellam*, 2: 333–34)

Verum inter hos tropos id est xv, est quaedam amica concordia qua sibi invicem germani sunt id est convenientes. Nam *quinque in gravitate, quinque in acumine, et quinque in temperato sunt [sono:* Paris 14754], ut inter ΥΠΟΔWΡΙΟΝ et ΥΠΟΦΡΙΓΙΟΝ et item inter ΥΠΟΙΑCΤΙΟΝ et ΥΠΟΛΥΔΙΟΝ. item conveniens aptaque responsio *id est convenientia,* inter ΥΠΟΦΡΥΓΙΟΝ et ΥΠΟΑΙΟΛΙΟΝ, qui tantum duplices copulantur. *Acutior enim duplo superat graviorem. Tonus quippe ad hemitonium sonat. Est autem tonus duplum hemitonii.*

Mediae vero scilicet chordae, graviorum troporum his id est ad illos, qui acutiores sunt. ΠΡΟCΛΑΜΒΑΝΟΜΕΝΑΙ fiunt *id est vicem proslambanomenes chordae obtinent.* Non solum proslambanomenai fiunt in gravissimis sed etiam in acutis tropis graves fiunt, sed tamen non sic graves in acutis sicut in gravissimis. Verbi gratia, si quis dixerit mihi quomodo resonari debet ultima chorda ad primam in tetrachordo, dicetur sub epitriti ratione.

If John had interpreted the proportion 2:1 as an octave, rather than a tone, he might have hit upon the modal relationships Martianus intended and might have emended the text accordingly. But he did not interpret the proportion as an octave.[67] Nor did the slightly later commentator Remigius of Auxerre (ex. 2.15). For the most part, Remigius simply expands and elaborates on the glosses of John Scottus, which I have given in italics in example 2.15. After repeating John's comment that the higher trope lies above the lower by a duple proportion, as in tone to semitone, Remigius suggests that the proslambanomenoi are the lowest notes in both the lower and higher tropes, saying nothing at all about the middle notes. He then provides his own supporting illustration drawn from Pythagorean mathematics, commenting that the outer strings of a tetrachord are related via the epitritus proportion, 4:3. Remigius's quasi-Pythagorean "legitimization" of the proportional relationship of 2:1 as a tone, along with his relating the paired proslambanomenoi to each other, rather than to the mesai of their concordant modes, would only help cement the false relationships preserved in the manuscripts.

Oddly enough, there was in a certain part of the glossed manuscript tradition for *De nuptiis Philologiae et Mercurii* something that might have helped John, at least, find the solution to the problems presented by section 935. I refer to the diagram in figure 2.4. Clearly derived from Boethius's wing diagram of the modes, this diagram appears in some seven ninth- and tenth-century manuscripts of *De nuptiis,* including two that contain the glosses of Pseudo-Martin of Laon.[68] The diagram presents the fifteen modes of Martianus opposite the first fifteen of the twenty-eight

---

67. This is all the more surprising because elsewhere (in the *Annotationes*) John clearly acknowledges the 2:1 proportion as the interval of an octave ("si extremi soni sibi invicem ex dupla proportione iungantur, ut sunt duo ad unum, diapason armoniam, quae in simplicibus simphoniis maxima est effitiunt"). See Lutz's edition of the *Annotations* after Paris 12960, esp. the extensive commentary to p. 10, l. 11.

68. A preliminary list of these manuscripts appears in Meyer, "Métaphore instumentale et présenta-

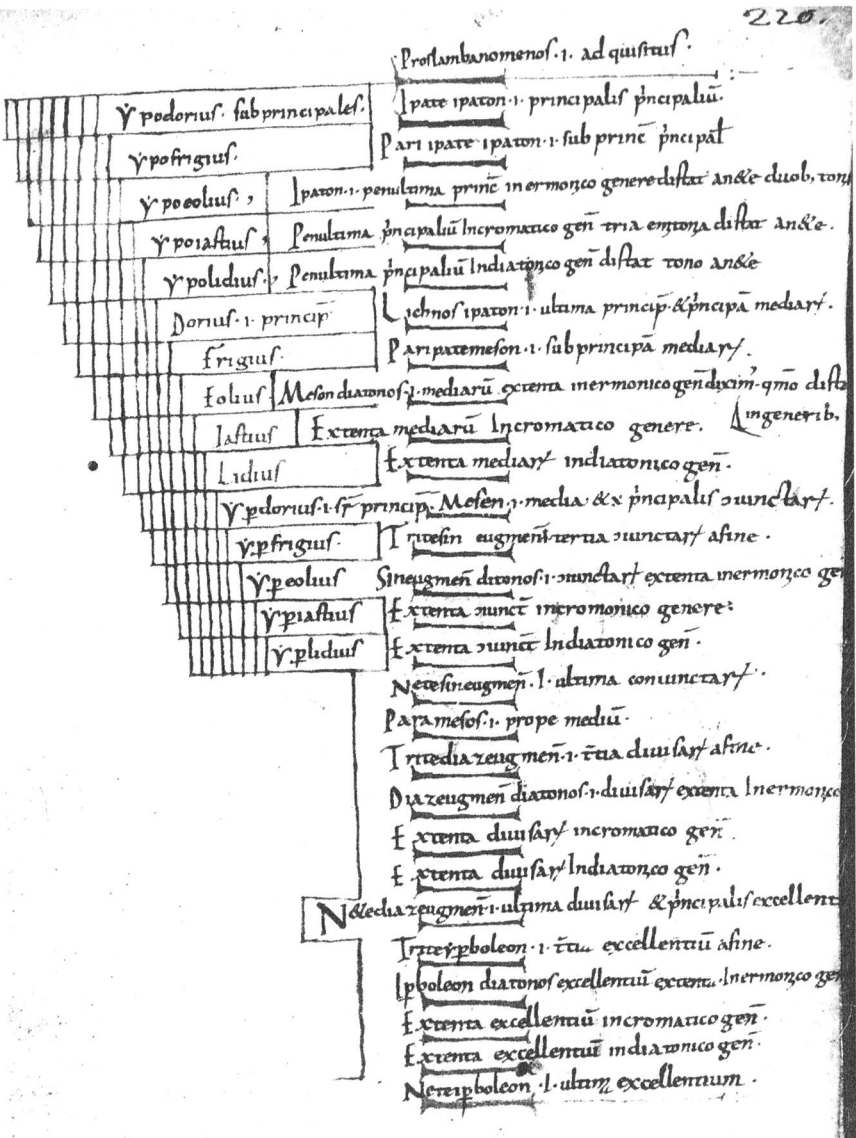

FIGURE 2.4.   "Wing diagram" of the fifteen tropes of Martianus Capella, *De nuptiis Philologiae et Mercurii*, in Munich 14729, fol. 220 (reproduced with the permission of the Bayerische Staatsbibliothek)

notes of the combined Greater and Lesser Perfect Systems in all three genera; it was apparently intended to clarify section 935 of *De nuptiis,* as the text accompanying it in several sources makes clear:

> Mese ypodorii est adquisita [proslambanomenos] eolii. Mese ypofrigii, adquisita iastii. Mese ypoeolii, adquisita lidii. Mese ypoiastii, adquisita yperdorii. Mese ypolidii, adquisita yperfrigii. Mese dorii, adquisita ypereolii. Mese frigii, adquisita yperiastii. Mese eolii. adquisita yperlidii.[69]

> The mese of the Hypodorian is the *adquisita* [proslambanomenos] of the Aeolian. The mese of the Hypophrygian is the *adquisita* of the Iastian. The mese of the Hypoaeolian is the *adquisita* of the Lydian. The mese of the Hypoiastian is the *adquisita* of the Hyperdorian. The mese of the Hypolydian is the *adquisita* of the Hyperphrygian. The mese of the Dorian is the *adquisita* of the Hyperaeolian. The mese of the Phrygian is the *adquisita* of the Hyperiastinan. The mese of the Aeolian is the *adquisita* of the Hyperlydian.

The pairs mentioned in this gloss text, however, are no more correct than the incorrect pairs given in other glossed sources. (The mese of the Hypodorian is not the proslambanomenos of the Aeolian, nor is the mese of the Hypophrygian the proslambanomenos of the Iastian, etc.) If the originator of this diagram had had access to a fifteen-mode wing diagram such as that given in example 1.12,[70] the problem would almost certainly have been solved—especially had that person been John Scottus. As we have seen, however, those ideal circumstances did not obtain, and the problem of the incorrect pairings persisted.

Indeed, neither John's nor Remigius's glosses convey an adequate picture of the ancient Greek modes as presented by Martianus Capella.[71] As they stand, though, the glosses of both writers are consonant with a different kind of modal relationship—one that had begun to be discussed in theoretical writings contemporaneous with the glossators I have been discussing. Here I refer to the medieval theory of the church tones or modes first presented in works such as the mid-ninth-century *Musica enchiriadis* and the slightly later treatises of Hucbald and the *Alia musica.*[72]

In these works, as we shall see in the following chapters, the modes are presented as differing segments or species of a scale, not as successive transpositions of a single scale in three different genera, as was the case with the ancient Greek τόνοι. The classic presentation of this type of modal theory is that found in the principal trea-

---

tion du système acoustique"; a more complete list and discussion appears in Teeuwen, *Harmony and the Music of the Spheres,* 310–13.

69. From Teeuwen, *Harmony and the Music of the Spheres,* 311.

70. Easily accessible modern transcriptions of the fifteen-mode wing diagram from Alypius's *Introductio musica* may be found in Mathiesen, *Aristides Quintilianus on Music,* 23; and Barker, *Greek Musical Writings,* 2: 428–29.

71. This is a statement with which James Willis would concur; see "Martianus und die mittelalterliche Schulbildung." As we have seen, however, the medieval commentators were severely handicapped in their attempts to elucidate Martianus's text by the faulty state of the text itself in most of its manuscript copies.

72. See Powers, "Mode," *NG* 12: 376–450; Atkinson, "Modus," *HmT* 24, esp. sec. III (1), 14–18; and Meyer, "Die Tonartenlehre im Mittelalter," esp. 146–54.

EXAMPLE 2.16a.   Presentation of *modi* in the Principal Treatise of *Alia musica* (ed. Chailley, 107, §15)

---

a) Erit ergo primus modus omnium gravissimus videlicet hypodorius ex prima specie diapason, et terminatur eo qui meses dicitur, medio nervo. b) Secundum modum hypophrygium secunda species diapason efficit, quae in paramesen finitur. c) Tertium modum hypolydium tertia species diapason determinat in eum quem vocant triten diezeugmenon nervum. c) Quartum modum dorium quarta species diapason reddit, quae finit in paranete diezeugmenon. e) Quintus modus phrygius quinta specie diapason finitur, cui nete diezeugmenon nervus est ultimus. f) Sextum nihilominus modum lydium sexta species diapason exerit, cui trite hyperbolaeon est finis. g) Septimum quoque modum mixolydium septima species diapason informat, quam paranete hyperbolaeon determinat.

EXAMPLE 2.16b.   Greater Perfect System in letter notation, from Paris 7211 and Paris 7212 (ed. Chailley, 180–81). The segmentation into *modi* follows the *Alia musica* (ed. Chailley, 107, § 15).

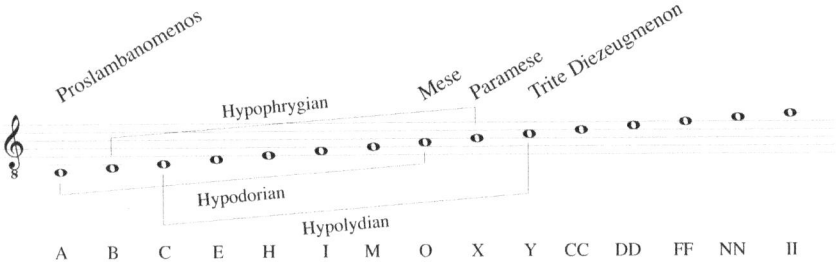

tise of the *Alia musica* (see ex. 2.16a).[73] Its author says that the first mode, the Hypodorian, is of the first species of octave, and it ends on the mese; the second mode, the Hypophrygian, is of the second species of octave, and it ends on the paramese; the third, the Hypomixolydian, is of the third octave species, and it ends on the trite diezeugmenon, and so on.

The reader will have noticed in example 2.16b that I have given the Greater Perfect System, or diatonic scale, as set out in letter notation in two of the manuscripts of the *Alia musica*, Paris 7212 and Paris 7211, sources dating from the eleventh and twelfth centuries, respectively.[74] There was a special reason for doing this. The same letter notation accompanies the diatonic scale as it is set out in the tenth-century

---

73. Chailley, ed., *Alia musica,* 107, §15. See also Chailley's commentary in the chapter "L'*Alia* et les modes," 28–56, esp. 47–50; and the discussion in chapter 5 here, pp. 187–88.

74. On these manuscripts, see Chailley, ed., *Alia musica,* 64–65; Smits van Waesberghe, ed., *Guidonis Aretini Micrologus, CSM* 4, 48 (Paris 7211); and Smits van Waesberghe, ed., *The Theory of Music, RISM* B III[1], 101–5 (Paris 7212), 105–6 (Paris 7211).

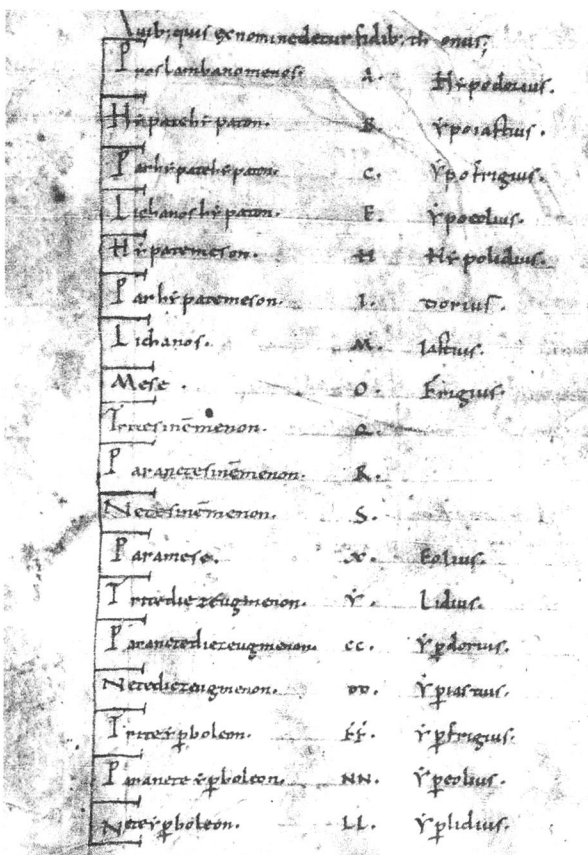

FIGURE 2.5.   Equation of fifteen tropes with fifteen of the
eighteen notes of the ancient Greek Immutable System,
expressed in letter notation, in Paris 8674, fol. 111v
(reproduced with the permission of the Bibliothèque
nationale de France)

manuscript Paris 8674, folio 111v—where it immediately follows Remigius's commentary on Martianus Capella (see fig. 2.5).[75]
    The scale is set out in this manuscript just as it is in Boethius, with the lowest
sounding note (proslambanomenos) at the top. The reader will note that opposite
the fifteen notes of the scale, with both their ancient Greek names and the Latin
letter notation, the scribe has written the names of the fifteen tropes or modes as
they are given in Martianus. The modes and the note names do not correspond;
Martianus had not given enough information to make that possible. It is clear, however, that whoever conceived this diagram was trying to comprehend Martianus's

75. See Lutz, ed., *Commentum in Martianum Capellam*, 51; and *CTC*, 2 (1971): 373. The diagram is
copied in a hand that is contemporaneous with that of the commentary itself.

modes on the basis of the modes he himself knew: namely, the eight church modes linked with octave species resulting from successive segmentations of the Greater Perfect System or diatonic scale.[76] I suspect that that may have been what John Scottus and the other ninth-century glossators were trying to do as well. If so, their misunderstanding of the ancient Greek τόνοι or τρόποι, as presented by Martianus, was a harbinger of *Alia musica*'s misunderstanding of the ancient Greek modes, as presented by Boethius. We shall return to this topic in chapter 5.

Let us now move from commentaries on the Greek *tropi,* as presented in section 935 of Martianus Capella, to commentaries on *tonus* as an aspect of harmonic theory, as opposed to grammar, in that work and in Boethius's *De institutione musica.* As we shall see, *tonus* is treated in these works not so much as the mere equivalent of *sonus* or pitch; rather, it is presented as an interval in "vertical," harmonic space and, together with the Phythagorean consonances, considered one of the building blocks of all music. The term *tonus,* in this sense, is the subject of the following glosses on *De nuptiis Philologiae et Mercurii,* now from Book IX. Examples 2.17–19 are drawn from commentaries by Pseudo-Martin of Laon, John Scottus Eriugena, and Remigius of Auxerre, respectively, on Martianus's definition of the tone and semitone, which is presented in example 2.17: "A whole tone is an interval [*spatium*] of a prescribed magnitude that is encompassed between two mutually different sounds. A hemitonium is so called because it holds half a tone."

The anonymous glosses attributed to Pseudo-Martin of Laon exhibit a variety of explanations, underscoring Mariken Teeuwen's point that they do not represent a unified tradition. Those in Leiden 36 explain that *tonus* is "where the duple is," continuing "from string to string" as an explanation of *spatium.* (This may be the source of the enigmatic explanation we encountered earlier in John Scottus's commentary on section 935 of Martianus. There, the tone was defined as a duple proportion, or twice the hemitonium; see ex. 2.14.) The sources differ as well in their explanation of *cum legitima quantitate.* Besançon 594 and Leiden 48 read "with a rational magnitude" or "measure," respectively. Leiden 48 adds that the measure in question is the "epogdous, eight plus one," a relationship that is also suggested in Paris 8671.

As befits a scholar who knew Greek, or perhaps one who knew the gloss in Leiden 48, John Scottus (ex. 2.18) explains that the "prescribed magnitude" (*legitima quantitate*) in Martianus is that of the *epogdous,* the Greek designation for the proportion 8:9. He underscores the importance of the 9:8 tone by saying "thus *tonus* in music is just as 8 to 9 in arithmetic, a prescribed magnitude that is the ratio of the epogdous, which measures all music." In making this statement, John may have been influenced by his probable source, Boethius's *De arithmetica.* In Book II, chapter 54, Boethius says that the epogdous ratio is called *tonus* in music "quae omnium musicorum sonorum mensura communis est"—"which is the measure common to all musical sounds."[77] John's gloss on line 494.17 (see ex. 2.18) specifies that the two "mutually different sounds" differ in that one is low, the other higher. He concludes by saying that the semitone is the division of the tone by its median part, presum-

---

EXAMPLE 2.17.   Martianus Gloss XI, on *tonus* in sec. 930 (ed. Willis) or p. 494, ll. 15–18 (ed. Dick)

930: verum tonus est spatium cum legitima quantitate, qui ex duobus sonis diversis
       inter se invicem continetur. hemitonium dicitur, quod toni medium tenet.
Pseudo-Martin of Laon (ed. Teeuwen, *Harmony and the Music of the Spheres,* 489–90)
494.15: VERUM TONUS EST ubi dupla *Leb* (= Leiden 36)
494.16: SPATIUM a corda ad cordam *Leb Par,* ad] in *Par* (= Paris 8671)
494.16: CUM LEGITIMA QUANTITATE rationabili magnitudine *Be* (= Besançon
      594)
   cum rationabili mensura *La* (= Leiden 48)
   Hoc est epogdous: una et octa (Leiden 48)

EXAMPLE 2.18.   Martianus Gloss XII, on *tonus* in sec. 930 (ed. Willis) or p. 494, ll. 16–18 (ed. Dick). See the text above.

John Scottus (ed. Lutz, *Johannis Scotti Annotationes in Marcianum*):
494.16: LEGITIMA cum epogdoo QUI tonus
494.16: LEGITIMAM QUANTITATEM octava parte. Nam tonus in musica epogdous
      est in arithmetica et ita tonus est in musica sicut VIII ad VIIII, in arithmetica
      legitima quantitas est ratio epogdoi quae totam metitur musicam.
494.17: DIVERSIS id est gravi et acuto. EMITONIUM id est divisio toni sequitur.
494.18: MEDIUM id est mediam partem toni

EXAMPLE 2.19.   Martianus Gloss XIII, on *tonus* in sec. 930 (ed. Willis) or p. 494, l. 15 (ed. Dick). See the text above.

Remigius of Auxerre (ed. Lutz, *Commentum in Martianum Capellam*):
494.15: VERUM TONUS EST SPATIUM Grece sisthema, Latine spatium inter
      chordam et chordam CUM LEGITIMA QUANTITATE, id est cum ratione
      epogdoi, id est superoctavi. LEGITIMA QUANTITATE id est octava parte;
      nam tonus in musica epogdous est arithmetica, et ita tonus est in musica sicut
      octo ad novem in arithmetica. Legitima quantitas est ratio epogdoi, quae totam
      metitur musicam. Qui scilicet TONUS EX DUOBUS SONIS, id est ex
      duabus chordis, DIVERSIS INTER SE INVICEM CONTINETUR id est
      ut gravior unus, acutior alter sit. Verbia gratia, "Tunc praecepit eos omnes."
494.17: HEMITONIUM DICITUR QUOD TONI MEDIUM TENET id est
      mediam partem toni, licet in duo aequa non possit umquam dividi.

ably yielding two equal halves. Although other parts of John's commentary demonstrate that he did, in fact, know Boethius's *De musica*—indeed, Duchez suspects that
he may have been the "premier lecteur" of the treatise—John does not adopt the
Boethian stipulation that the tone cannot be divided into two equal halves.[78]

Example 2.19 offers the glosses by Remigius of Auxerre. After getting off to a bit
of a shaky start by equating the Latin *spatium* with the Greek term *systema* or scale,
he simply expands and elaborates the material already given by John Scottus. There
are two innovations, however. First, at the end of his glosses on the nature of the
whole tone, Remigius cites an example from the realm of practical music, the antiphon "Tunc praecepit eos omnes," from Lauds, *In inventione Sanctae Crucis.* Second,
in glossing the lemma "hemitonium . . . toni medium tenet," Remigius first follows
John with the phrase "that is, the half part of a tone." But he then qualifies this, saying "it cannot ever be divided into two equal halves." Even if he did not understand
systema, Remigius *had* apparently read Boethius.

Turning from Boethius in glosses on Martianus Capella to glosses on Boethius's
De musica itself, we are aided substantially by the fine new edition of the *Glossa maior*
by Michael Bernhard and Calvin Bower. In two recent articles, Bower has made the
point that the earliest layer of glosses on *De institutione musica,* which he dates around
800 to 830, represents a coming to grips with the subtleties of the text itself as a document of ancient Greek harmonic theory.[79] He points out that there is an "obsession
with discrete pitch," with the Pythagorean consonances being examined in detail
and—as one can see in example 2.20—the 9:8 tone being presented as the building
block, the *communis omnium mensura,* for all intervals.[80] To this I would add that just
as Boethius finds his way into glosses on Martianus Capella, so, too, does Martianus
find his way into glosses on Boethius, as examples 2.21 and 2.22 clearly reveal.

The Pythagorean/Boethian notion that the tone cannot be divided into two equal
parts is, as one might expect, the subject of some comment in the *Glossa maior.* One
wonders in some cases, though, whether the earliest glossators fully understood the
mathematical proofs of this. In Book I, chapter 16, for example, in which Boethius
provides the first, short proof that the tone cannot be divided equally, the ninth-

---

78. For the argument on behalf of a close relationship between John's commentary and Boethius,
see Duchez, "Jean Scot Érigène, premier lecteur du 'De institutione musica' de Boèce?" One of her
prime pieces of evidence is John's gloss on the lemma IN UNAM SPECIEM, on p. 60, l. 11 of Dick's
edition. To this phrase John adds: "hoc est in unam mundi imaginem . . . tota musica in una imagine de-
scribitur per *tonos* et *tropos* caeterosque *modos* et horum singula super notatos numeros et litteras et notas"
(emphasis added). Duchez relates this gloss to Boethius's wing diagram of the "modi, quos eosdem tropi
vel toni nominant."

79. Bower dates the earliest layer of glosses to ca. 800–830 ("Die Wechselwirkung von *philosophia,
mathematica* und *musica*," 168). Yet the earliest surviving glossed manuscripts date from no earlier than the
mid- to late ninth century (Bernhard and Bower, eds., *Glossa maior in institutionem Boethii,* 1: xlii–xliii).
Since none of the three earliest sources is copied from another, Bower and Bernhard postulate the existence of an earlier exemplar or group of manuscripts—now lost—dating from the early years of the ninth
century. It should be recalled that Teeuwen (*Harmony and the Music of the Spheres*) feels that the glossing
traditions on harmonics within *De nuptiis Philologiae et Mercurii* and for *De institutione musica* begin at
about the same time (see notes 20–22 here and the accompanying discussion). She places the onset of
these traditions a bit later, in the second third of the ninth century.

80. See ex. 2.18 and the related discussion.

EXAMPLE 2.20.   Boethius Gloss I,7,2 on *tonus*, in *De institutione musica*, Book I, chap. 7 (ed. Bernhard and Bower, *Glossa maior in institutionem musicam Boethii*, 1: 160)

Boethius's text (ed. Friedlein, 194,20): AUT IN DUPLICI AUT IN TRIPLICI AUT IN QUADRUPLA AUT IN SESQUALTERA AUT IN SESQUITERTIA PROPORTIONE

Gloss I,7,2: In omnibus his latet epogdous, i. sesquioctava proportio, [quod est tonus,] ideoque specialiter inter symphonias non connumeratur; ex ea namque ceterae componuntur. Est enim communis omnium mensura.

All but the bracketed text appears in the ninth-century manuscripts Paris 7200; Paris 13908; and Orléans 293B.

quod est tonus appears in the eleventh-century manuscripts Munich 6361; Munich 18478; and Paris 10275.

(Cf. *De arithmetica*, 2: 54: "VIII vero et VIIII ipsi contra se medii considerati epogdoum iungunt, qui in musico modulamine tonus vocatur, quae omnium musicorum sonorum mensura communis est" ed. Friedlein, 171–72.

EXAMPLE 2.21.   Boethius Gloss I,8,32 on *tonus*, in *De institutione musica*, Book I, chap. 8, (ed. Bernhard and Bower, *Glossa maior in institutionem musicam Boethii*, 1: 167)

Boethius's text (ed. Friedlein, 195,6): INTERVALLUM VERO EST

Gloss I,8,32: Felix Capella: "Tonus est spatium cum legitima quantitate, qui diversis inter se sonis conficitur."

Sources: Paris 7200; Paris 13908; and Orléans 293B

EXAMPLE 2.22.   Boethius Gloss I,16,57, on *tonus*, in *De institutione musica*, Book I, chap. 16 (ed. Bernhard and Bower, *Glossa maior in institutionem musicam Boethii*, 1: 233)

Boethius's text (ed. Friedlein, 202,26): RETINENT SESQUIOCTAVAM PROPORTIONEM

Gloss I,16,57: Est enim sesquioctava proportio tonus, i. legitimum spatium inter chordam et chordam.

Sources: Paris 7200 (in the second and fifth hands; the latter scribe actually wrote in the eleventh century, basing his work on Orléans 293B

Cf. Gloss I,8,32 in Ex. 2.21 above; and Martianus Capella, *De nuptiis Philologiae et Mercurii*, Book. 9, sec. 930.

EXAMPLE 2.23.   Boethius Gloss I,16,83 on major and minor semitones, in *De institutione musica*, Book I, chap. 16 (ed. Bernhard and Bower, *Glossa maior in institutionem musicam Boethii*, 1: 236)

Boethius's text (ed. Friedlein, 203,7): ET EST MINOR PARS SEPTIMA DECIMA;
    MAIOR SEXTA DECIMA:
Gloss I,16,83: plus est habere XVI^mam partem alicuius rei quam XVII^mam
The gloss appears in Munich 14272 (first early hand); Paris 7200 (fifth later hand); Paris
    7297; Rome 1005; and Rome 1638 (second later hand). The earliest of these is
    a tenth-century manuscript.
XVI^mam] XVII: Autun 46; London 15; Milan 128; Munich 14272; Orléans 293B
XVII^mam] XVIII: Autun 46; London 15; Milan 128; Munich 14272; Orléans 293B; Paris
    7297; Rome 1005; Rome 1638 (second later hand). Of these, Orléans is the
    earliest (ninth century).

---

century glossator of Orléans 293B responds to the phrase "the smaller part is one-seventeenth, the larger part one-sixteenth," by saying "To have the seventeenth part of something is more than the eighteenth part" (ex. 2.23). Later glossators modify this to read "For anything to have the sixteenth part is more than the seventeenth part."

When one looks at the designations for the two semitones (ex. 2.24), one again wonders how completely the ninth-century glossator of Orléans 293B understood what he was reading. He glosses the phrase "the larger part one-sixteenth" correctly as that which is called "apotome." He explains that the smaller part, however, "is called the comma," which is incorrect.[81] Given that in the very next sentence Boethius himself says "Both of these are called semitones" ("Sed utraque semitonia nuncupantur"), one cannot but wonder how well the glossator of Orléans 293B was comprehending this passage.

The early glosses on tone-system in the *Glossa maior* are quite similar in character to those found in glossed manuscripts of Martianus Capella.[82] They typically explain the Greek names of the strings or their positions relative to each other within the various diagrams. For example, the Hyperboleon (tetrachord) is explained by the Orléans glossator as "superexcellens" and as "excellens" by the second glossator of Paris 13908.[83] Three of the earliest sources of the *Glossa maior*, along with many later ones, offer the following gloss by way of explaining the number of strings in the tone-systems of the various genera, together with that of the number of different names in Book I, chapter 22 (ex. 2.25): The gloss transmitted in most manuscripts correctly says that there will be twenty-eight different string names. This is so because there are eighteen strings in each genus—diatonic, chromatic, and enharmonic—and all have five strings that are different in individual tetrachords. If

---

81. The comma is the difference in size between the major and minor semitones or between six whole tones and an octave. It is defined for the first time in Book II, chap. 31, where it is found in the ratio 524,288:531,441.

82. See notes 48–51 here and the discussion connected with them.

83. See Bernhard and Bower, eds., *Glossa maior in institutionem Boethii*, 1: 280, glosses 226–27 on Book I, chap. 20.

EXAMPLE 2.24.   Boethius Glosses I,16,84 and I,16,87 on major and minor semitones, in *De institutione musica*, Book I, chap. 16 (ed. Bernhard and Bower, *Glossa maior in institutionem musicam Boethii*, 1: 236)

Boethius's text (ed. Friedlein, 203,7): MINOR PARS
Gloss I,16,84: quae vocatur comma
Sources: Orléans 293B; Paris 7297; Rome 1638 (second later hand). Orléans 293B is a
        ninth-century manuscript; the others (or the relevant portions of them) stem
        from the tenth century.
Boethius's text (ed. Friedlein, 203,7): MAIOR SEXTA DECIMA
Gloss I,16,87: et vocatur apotome
Sources: Autun 46; London 15; Munich 14272; Orléans 293B; Paris 7200 (fifth
        later hand); Paris 7297; Rome 1005; Rome 1638 (second later hand).
        Orléans 293B is a ninth-century source; the others are from the 10th or 11th
        centuries.

---

one adds the five that are different in the chromatic and the five that are different in the enharmonic to the eighteen in the diatonic, the total comes to twenty-eight.

As important as such an observation is, however, it does not explain exactly what the pitch layout of the tone-system is, nor does it explicate the species of consonances that will be necessary in order to explain the modes. Moreover, although the glossators could explain the long Greek string names, they had not yet been given the system of Greek letter notation that they could conceivably use as a musical shorthand for notating melodies. That information is given only in Book IV, chap-

---

EXAMPLE 2.25.   Boethius Gloss I,22,130a on the number of similar and dissimilar strings, in *De institutione musica*, Book I, chap. 22 (ed. Bernhard and Bower, *Glossa maior in institutionem musicam Boethii*, 1: 307)

Boethius's text (ed. Friedlein, 215, 7): SI NERVI SIMILES IN OMNIBUS CUM EIS,
        QUI SUNT DISSIMILES, COLLIGANTUR, FIANT SIMUL OMNES
        OCTO ET VIGINTI.
Gloss I,16,22 and 130a: Nam cum sint X et VIII et in diatonico et in chromatico et in
        enarmonio, reliquae similes sunt exceptis V, quae sunt in singulis tetrachordis
        dissimiles. Ipsae ergo de chromatico et enarmonico V et V sumptae ad XVIII
        adiiciuntur et fiunt XXVIII.
Sources: Leipzig 1493; Munich 6361; Munich 18478; Munich 18480 (second early
        hand); Orléans 293B; Paris 2664; Paris 7297; Paris 13908 (second early hand);
        Rome 1638 (first early hand); SchaVhausen 108; and Vienna 2269. The ninth-
        century sources are Orléans 293B, Paris 13908, and Rome 1638; the rest are
        from the tenth century.

For critical apparatus, see Bernhard and Bower, *Glossa maior in institutionem musicam
        Boethii*, 1: 307.

---

ters 3–18, those dealing with the naming of the notes, the division of the mono-chord, the species of consonance, and the modes.

Given the importance of Book IV for Boethius's treatise in general and for this study in particular, it is all the more unfortunate that only one of the ninth-century sources, Paris 13908, offers commentary on the chapters of this book. Even worse, the final gatherings of this manuscript have been lost, leaving commentary only through Book IV, chapter 11, with nothing for the remainder of Book IV and all of Book V. Still, the glosses that do appear in this manuscript offer convincing testi-mony that the second glossator of Paris 13908 did, in fact, understand the text on which he was commenting.

Bernhard and Bower point out that the chapters on Greek notation (chaps. 3 and 4) receive very few glosses altogether, and that most of these are glosses specifically on individual words, as opposed to sentences or concepts.[84] For example, with re-spect to the phrase explaining that the upper row of notational symbols will be for the text, that is, for the words ("notulae dictionis, id est verborum"), the second glossator of Paris 13908, along with others, adds that these *notulae* are the "names of the strings" (*nomina cordarum*).[85] In the chapters on the division of the monochord (chaps. 5–11), the glosses also generally address individual words, although occasion-ally sentences are considered in these glosses as well.

In several instances, however, we find notable examples of the second Paris glos-sator's acumen and understanding of the text, for example, in Book IV, chapter 6, "Partition of the monochord of the netai hyperboleon through three genera" (ex. 2.26). In Paris 13908, the text scribe wrote the numbers for the proslambanomenos, mese, and nete hyperboleon in Greek alphanumeric notation.[86] The second Paris glossator explains these signs quite adequately: "Theta with a stroke over it equals 9,000; without the stroke, it signifies 9. Likewise Delta with stroke signifies 4,000; without the stroke, 4. In the same manner, Beta with stroke is 2,000; without the stroke, 2." Oddly enough, he does not explain that CIS (ΣΙϛ) is the Greek number 216, XH 608, or ΤΔ 304, but he apparently thought that they would be self-explanatory, or perhaps he did not quite understand them himself. Nonetheless, in an age in which knowledge of Greek was not widespread, this glossator clearly knew more about that language than did the average scribe.[87] Bower points out that this notation was not understood by subsequent scribes and thus dropped out of the textual tradition.[88]

Unfortunately, examples of uncommon understanding such as this one only tan-talize us, making us wonder, for example, what the glossator in question might have had to say about species and the modes. As mentioned earlier, however, Paris 13908

84. *Glossa maior in institutionem Boethii,* 1: lx.

85. *Glossa maior in institutionem Boethii,* 3: 216, gloss 37 on Book IIII, chap. 3.

86. See the edition by Friedlein, 319; and Bower, *Boethius: Fundamentals,* 132 n. 52.

87. On the knowledge of Greek in the period under discussion, see the studies by Berschin, *Griechisch-Lateinisches Mittelalter,* transl. Frakes: *Greek Letters and the Latin Middle Ages,* and Kaczynski, *Greek in the Carolingian Age.*

88. If, indeed, it belonged there at all. Bower feels that the Greek notation "obviously does not be-long with this second division of the monochord" (*Boethius: Fundamentals,* 132 n. 52).

EXAMPLE 2.26.   Boethius Gloss IIII,6,31 explaining the meaning of the stroke in the Greek alphanumeric numbering scheme, in *De institutione musica*, Book IV, chap. 6 (ed. Bernhard and Bower, *Glossa maior in institutionem musicam Boethii*, 3: 238)

Boethius's text (ed. Friedlein, 319, critical apparatus; emended after Bower, *Boethius: Fundamentals*, 132, n. 52):

Proslamb[anomenos]	Mese	Nete
ϴ CIS	ᴀ XH	฿ TᴧΔ
·VIIII·CCXVI·	·IIII·DCVIII·	·II·CCCIIII·

Gloss IIII,6,31: ϴ cum virgula $\overline{VIIII}$, sine autem virgula IX significat. Similiter ᴀ cum virgula $\overline{IIII}$, sine virgula IIII. Tali modo ฿ virgulatum $\overline{II}$, sine virgula II.

Source: Paris 13908 (second early hand)

---

breaks off after chapter 11, which leaves us without a single surviving ninth-century gloss on Boethius's treatment of either the species of consonances (in chap. 14) or the modes (in chaps. 15–17). We know that the content of these chapters was available in several ninth-century manuscripts of Boethius's treatise, and that it was being studied and probably taught by masters such as John Scottus Eriugena. Without any glosses, however, it is difficult to know just how these chapters were taught or how well they were understood.

Although there is no ninth-century manuscript containing glosses on Boethius's treatment of the ancient Greek *tonoi* at the end of Book IV of his work, there is a gloss in a ninth-century source outside the tradition of the *Glossa maior* that bears on the topic of this study. This is the gloss preserved in Munich 14523, which is reproduced in example 2.27.[89] Commenting on Boethius's "wing diagram" of the modes or tones, this glossator says "The beginning of the *Autentus protus* starts on the parhypate meson in the diatonic genus in the diapente proportion." He continues his description by suggesting that it then descends by semitone to the hypate meson, then by tone to the lychanos hypaton, following which it returns to the hypate meson. It moves back to the lychanos hypaton by tone, and then descends to the proslambanomenos by two tones and a semitone. Following this the glossator gives a similar description of the *plagis proti*. (I have rendered his descriptions of both in Pseudo-Odonian letter notation at the bottom of example 2.27.)

Clearly, this gloss has nothing to do with the ancient Greek *tonoi* as described in Boethius. For our purposes, however, it is important: first because of the terminology it employs—*Autentus proti* and *plagis proti*, terms we have not seen before—and second because it describes these terms by means of melodic incipits. Both of these factors are important components of a new theory of *tonus* in the Carolingian era, that of the so-called church tones or modes. That theory and the ways by which it

---

89.   The same text appears in the upper margin of fol. 178 in Munich 14272—there as a gloss to the *Alia musica*. See Chailley, ed., *Alia musica*, 210–11.

EXAMPLE 2.27.   Commentary in the ninth-century manuscript, Munich, 14523 on Boethius's "Wing diagram" illustrating "Modi, quos eosdem tropos vel tonos nominant" (ed. Bernhard and Bower, *Glossa maior in institutionem musicam Boethii*, 3: 365–66)

Boethius's diagram appears as *Descriptio II*, inserted between pp. 342 and 343 in Friedlein. It may also be seen as Fig. D21 in Bower, *Boethius: Fundamentals of Music*, 156.

The Gloss in Munich 14523: HYPERMIXOLYDIUS . . . (D21): *Autenti proti* primitus incipit in parhypate meson genere diatoni diapente proportione. Deinde in hypate meson descendit transito semitonio. Deinde in lychanos hypaton tono transit, post hoc iterum redit tono in hypate meson. Deinde remigrat iterum in lychanos hypaton per tonum et inde se deflectit in proslambanomenos duobus tonis et dimidio. *Plagis proti* incipit ubi autenti desinit, i. in proslambanomenos, et inde cadit tono inferius. Ex hinc iterum surgit in proslambanomenos et vadit inde in lychanos hypaton chromatico genere. Post hoc transit in proximum hemitonium ad hypate meson a lychanos hypaton eiusdem generis, i. chromatici, tono distans, et exinde redit iterum ad lychanos hypaton chromatice, et inde flectens in proslambanomenos desinit (emphasis added).

Translated into pitches (but ignoring the chromatic genus), this becomes:

Protus autentus: F E D E D A

Plagis proti: A G A D E D A

---

came into existence will be the principal burden of the narrative in the next chapter, whose subject is the theory and practice of music in the church during the Carolingian period.

What I hope to have demonstrated in this chapter is that the terms and concepts from the works of Boethius, Martianus Capella, Cassiodorus, Isidore of Seville, and Donatus that I discussed under the rubric of "the heritage of antiquity" were likewise important as objects of study during the Carolingian era. Starting with manuscripts from the first part of the ninth century, we observed that Carolingian schoolmasters, such as John Scottus Eriugena and Remigius of Auxerre made concentrated attempts to understand and explain such concepts as *tonus, tropus, accentus,* and *seminarium musices.* They grappled with them, moreover, on their own terms, that is, as they had been understood in Antiquity. At the same time, their commentaries could not help but reflect—and in turn influence—the milieu in which they were written and the directions in which musical thought was heading. As we shall discover in the next chapter, both the grammatical theory of accent, as represented here by Donatus, and the harmonic theory of the "modes," which they also call "tones" or "tropes" after Boethius, would be important ingredients in the musical ferment of the Carolingian period and beyond.

CHAPTER THREE

THE HERITAGE OF THE CHURCH

A great irony in the series of developments that led ultimately to a medieval theory of mode and tone-system is that one of the most important of those developments had nothing to do with either ancient or medieval conceptions of *tonus, tropus,* or *modus*—or, for that matter, with anything else that has been discussed thus far in this study. The development in question is the translation of the Roman liturgy into Francia and the concomitant suppression of the Gallican rite. That suppression began in 754 with the Masses said by Pope Stephen II (752–57) at the court of Pepin III (751–68) and at other Frankish churches. It was, for the most part, brought to completion under Charlemagne (768–814).[1]

As a result of the imposition of the new rite, Frankish singers had to learn and perform Roman chant, and they had to do this in the early years without the aid of musical notation.[2] As we know from writers such as John the Deacon and Notker

---

The material in the excursus beginning on p. 106. is drawn from my article "*De accentibus toni.*"

1. On the *translatio* and its consequences, see, in particular, Netzer, *L'Introduction de la messe romaine en France sous les Carolingiens;* Klauser, "Die liturgischen Austauschbeziehungen"; the following studies by Helmut Hucke: "Die Einführung des Gregorianischen Gesangs im Frankeneich," "Die Entstehung der Überlieferung von einer musikalischen Tätigkeit Gregors des Grossen," "Die Herkunft der Kirchentonarten und die fränkische Überlieferung des gregorianischen Gesangs," "Karolingische Renaissance und Gregorianischer Gesang"; and by Cyrille Vogel: "Les Échanges liturgiques entre Rome et les pays francs jusqu'à l'époque de Charlemagne," "La Réforme cultuelle sous Pépin le Bref et sous Charlemagne," and "La Réforme liturgique sous Charlemagne." See also Huglo, "Römisch-fränkische Liturgie"; Stäblein, "Der altrömische Gesang," 66*–75*, 140*–145*; McKitterick, *The Frankish Church and the Carolingian Reforms, 789–895,* 115–54; and Walter, *Grundlagen der Musik des Mittelalters,* 7–16. A concise survey of this literature is available in Hiley, *Western Plainchant,* 514–18.

2. The earliest extant books recording a cycle of proper chants for the Roman rite in musical notation date from ca. 900 (Jeffery, "The Oldest Sources of the *Graduale*," 318). Scholars have posited several earlier dates as possible *termini a quo* for the introduction of such books into the Frankish kingdom. After careful marshalling of the available evidence, Kenneth Levy postulated a date of ca. 800 for the production of a neumed archetype in Francia ("Charlemagne's Archetype of Gregorian Chant," "A Carolingian Visual Model," and "From Aural to Notational: The Gregorian *Antiphonale Missarum*"). He dates the origins of musical notation itself to the late eighth century and situates this development in the Frankish kingdom, not in Rome ("A Carolingian Visual Model," 245–52). It must be pointed out, however, that the earliest surviving sources for the gradual (eighth–ninth centuries; ed. in Hesbert,

Balbulus, the latter task was not easy.[3] The Frankish response to the challenge of learning a different liturgy and music manifested itself in various ways. The writing of the *ordines romani* and *expositiones missae,* the importation and local production of sacramentaries and graduals, and the various Carolingian treatises on music can all be seen as logical outgrowths of this development.[4]

One of the most immediate needs of the Franks was a method of classification that would enable them to gain control over a vast repertoire of chant. The earliest response to this need was the tonary, whose main practical function was that of classifying chants (primarily antiphons) sung with verses in such a way that there might be a "euphonious" connection between the end of the antiphon and the beginning of the psalm verse, and between the end of the psalm verse and the beginning of the antiphon.[5]

Antiphonale missarum sextuplex), as well as the earliest tonaries (those of St. Riquier and Metz, from the eighth to the mid–ninth centuries, respectively), contain no musical notation and make no provision for it (see the discussion that follows). Paris 17436, ed. in Hesbert, *Antiphonale missarum sextuplex,* does contain some neumes added after the initial copying of the manuscript. See Hesbert, *Antiphonale missarum sextuplex,* xix, table 5. Dom Hourlier, "Le Domaine de la notation messine," 111, dates these additions to the tenth century. With these chronological considerations in mind, Helmut Hucke postulates an origin for the neumes in the later ninth century (see Hucke, "Der Übergang von mündlicher zu schriftlicher Musiküberlieferung im Mittelalter," "Towards a New Historical View of Gregorian Chant," "Die Anfänge der abendländischen Notenschrift," and "Gregorianische Fragen"). See also McKitterick's review of Levy's *Carolingian Chant and the Carolingians.*

3. Both of these authors wrote in the later ninth or early tenth centuries. The relevant passages from John's "Life of Gregory the Great" and the "Life of the Emperor Charles the Great" that have been attributed to Notker, albeit with less than absolute certainty, have recently been translated by James McKinnon in *The Early Christian Period and the Latin Middle Ages,* 68–73. John says that while the "Germans and Gauls" were able "to learn and repeatedly to relearn" the Roman chant, "they were by no means able to maintain it without distortion, as much because of their carelessness (for they mixed in with the Gregorian some of their own) as because of their native brutishness." The Latin for this passage is "Huius modulationis dulcedinem inter alias Europae gentes Germani seu Galli discere crebroque rediscere insigniter potuerunt, incorruptam vero tam levitate animi, quia nonnulla de proprio Gregorianis cantibus miscuerunt, quam feritate quoque naturali servare minime potuerunt" (*PL* 75: col. 90). On this passage and its context, see also Berschin, *Biographie und Epochenstil in lateinischen Mittelalter,* 377–78; Walter, *Grundlagen der Musik des Mittelalters,* 53–54; and Haas, *Mündliche Überlieferung und altrömischer Choral,* 138–45.

4. See the studies cited in chapter 2 here, note 1. The *ordines romani,* Frankish descriptions of the Roman liturgy, are available in modern edition in Andrieu, *Les Ordines romani.* The standard introduction to the Frankish commentaries on the Mass, such as Amalarius's *Expositio totius missae,* is Wilmart, "Expositio missae." On the sacramentaries, see Delisle, *Mémoire sur d'anciens sacramentaires;* the earliest graduals are edited in Hesbert, *Antiphonale missarum sextuplex.* Hiley (*Western Plainchant,* 287–373) provides a useful introduction to the various types of liturgical books and to the origins of musical notation.

5. On the tonary, its function, and its sources, see Huglo, *Les Tonaires,* and "Tonary"; Merkley, *Italian Tonaries;* and Merkley, *Modal Assignment in Northern Tonaries;* Hiley, *Western Plainchant,* 325–35; and Hankeln, "Tonar." Huglo makes an important distinction between "didactic" tonaries, such as the late eighth-century tonary from St. Riquier (Paris 13159), and "practical" tonaries, such as that from Metz (Metz 351), which dates from before 869, or that attributed to Regino of Prüm, which dates from the late ninth or early tenth centuries. For editions of the latter three tonaries, see, respectively, Huglo, "Un tonaire de graduel"; and Huglo, *Les Tonaires,* 26–28 (St. Riquier); Lipphardt, ed., *Der karolingische Tonar von Metz* (Metz); and *CS* 2: 3–73 (Regino of Prüm). Further on the tonary from Metz, see Huglo, "Un Troisième Témoin du tonaire carolingien"; and Merkley, *Modal Assignment in Northern Tonaries,* 13–22. (Merkley, 23–25, prefers the designations "small" and "large" to Huglo's "didactic" and "practical.") As is typical of didactic tonaries, the St. Riquier manuscript "demonstrates" each *tonus* by citing representative an-

The method followed in the earliest tonaries employs eight categories, called *toni*. Of these, four are primary, labeled with the Greek ordinal numbers *protus, deuterus, tritus,* and *tetrardus* (first, second, third, and fourth), with two subcategories of each, labeled *authentus* or *autentus* and *plagis* (authentic and plagal).[6] Each of the eight categories is typically identified by an intonation formula (NONANOEANE, NOEANE, etc.).[7] Along with each of these go one or more *differentiae,* often indicated over the words *saeculorum Amen.*[8] Within each tonal category and differentia, chants are listed in order of the liturgical year, beginning in Advent.[9]

---

tiphonal and responsorial chants that belong to it. Practical tonaries, such as those of Metz and Regino, on the other hand, provide comprehensive lists of psalmodically based chants in each *tonus,* subdivided according to the cadences (differentiae) of the psalm tone sung for each, classified by genre (Introit, Communion, etc.), and ordered sequentially according to the position of each chant during the liturgical year. The description given here is based on the usage of the tonaries from St. Riquier, Metz, and that of Regino of Prüm, as well as the verbal tonary in Aurelianus Reomensis, *Musica disciplina* (ed. Gushee, *CSM* 21) and the *Commemoratio brevis* (ed. Bailey; and Schmid, *Musica et scolica enchiriadis,* 157–78). My use of the word "euphonious" to describe the desired character of the connections between psalm verse and antiphon comes from the tenth-century (?) treatise *De tonis* in Rome 235, fol. 39v, ed. Wagner, "Un piccolo trattato."

6. On these terms, see Huglo, "Comparaison de la terminologie modale en orient et en occident," and "Le Développement du vocabulaire de l'*Ars musica*," and the discussion below. It should be pointed out that the spelling of the terms themselves is quite fluid.

7. On the intonation formulas, see Strunk, "Intonations and Signatures"; Raasted, *Intonation Formulas and Modal Signatures;* Kunz, "Ursprung und textliche Bedeutung der Tonartensilben Noeane, Noeagis"; Bailey, *The Intonation Formulas of Western Chant;* Huglo, "L'Introduction en occident des formules byzantines d'intonation"; Huglo, "Les Formules d'intonations 'noeane noeagis' en orient et en occident"; and Brockett, "Noeane and Neuma." Although they do not appear in the St. Riquier tonary, the intonation formulas are used in other early sources described here. According to the testimony of Aurelian of Réôme, these formulas are Byzantine in origin. (Raasted, *Intonation Formulas and Modal Signatures,* 43–44, 66, 78–84, offers several possibilities as to the way the formulas, also called ἠχήματα (*ēchēmata*), were performed in the Byzantine rite. At the most practical level, they were probably sung by the soloist at the beginning of a chant intended to be sung by the choir in order to establish the starting tone and serve as a guide to the position of the semitones in the following melody.) In some sources, e.g., the *Commemoratio brevis* and Regino's tonary, the intonation formulas are given melodic suffixes in the form of melismas traversing the same tonal space as the formulas themselves. In addition to, or in place of, the intonation formulas, tonaries from the tenth century and later often add a more extended mnemonic verse for each of the eight tonal categories: *Primum quaerite regnum dei* ("First seek the kingdom of God"), *Secundum autem simile est huic* ("Moreover, the second is similar to this"), *Tertia dies est quod haec facta sunt* ("It is the third day that these things were done"), etc.

8. The term *differentia* (also called *diffinitio, divisio,* etc.) typically appears as a designation for subcategories within a *tonus;* its concrete manifestation is the variable termination of a psalm tone that provides for a smooth transition back to the beginning of the following antiphon. (As noted in Brussels 2750/65, "Divisio autem dicitur differentia quae fit in versu in novissima syllaba ut decens & rata fiat consonantia.") Since the final return of the antiphon is always preceded by the lesser Doxology (*Gloria Patri, et Filio, et Spiritui Sancto: Sicut erat in principio, et nunc, et semper, et in saecula saeculorum. Amen*), the melody of the differentia is always sung to the words *saeculorum Amen.* Those words or their sequence of vowels, EUOUAE, thus provided a practical cueing device for the melody of the differentia. Inasmuch as the differentiae are inextricably linked to the practice of psalmody, they constitute a fixed element in practical tonaries, but not in their didactic equivalents. For more on the function of the differentia, see, among others, Huglo, "Tonary"; Stäblein, "Psalm, B"; Brockett, "*Saeculorum Amen* and *Differentia*"; and Hiley, *Western Plainchant,* 326–27.

9. *Ecce nomen domini,* the first Office antiphon under the first differentia of the Protus authentic, is

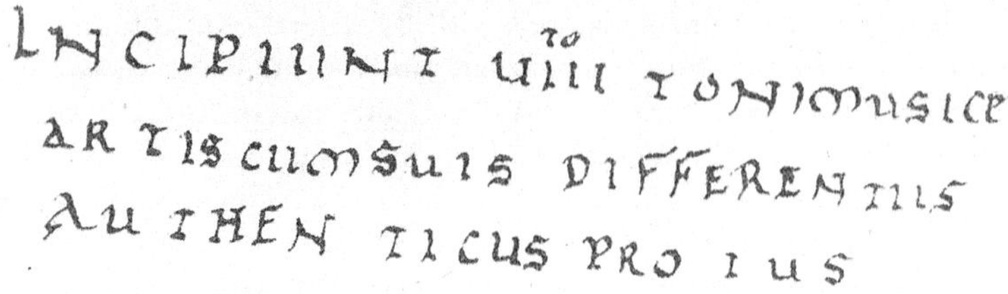

FIGURE 3.1A.   The title of the tonary of Regino of Prüm (Brussels 2750/65, fol. 45v; reproduced from *CS* 2: 3)

The earliest tonaries, those from St. Riquier and Metz, have no musical notation and were not copied so as to leave room for its later addition.[10] Let us therefore use as an example the later, notated tonary attributed to Regino of Prüm. Figures 3.1a and 3.1b present the introductory title and beginning of this tonary—the first differentia for Office antiphons of the Protus authentic—as it appears in Brussels 2750/65, folio 45v–46.[11] Figure 3.1c, from folio 58v of the same source, presents two differentiae and the beginning of a third for the Introit antiphons in Protus authentic.

In order to gain an idea of how the process works, let us consider the Introit antiphons and their differentiae as they are depicted in figure 3.1c. Example 3.1 presents reconstructions of the three differentiae given in the tonary, together with the incipits of the Introits with which they would have been sung.[12]

---

the antiphon for the Magnificat of First Vespers of the first Sunday in Advent; that is, it is sung at Vespers the Saturday evening before. It should be pointed out that a number of later tonaries list antiphons in alphabetical, rather than liturgical, order within each category.

10. See, for example, the facsimiles from Metz 351 in Lipphardt, ed., *Der karolingische Tonar von Metz*, 1 and 2.

11. *CS* 2: 4–5. The manuscript, which has been dated to the tenth to thirteenth centuries, is described in *RISM* B III¹: 53–54. Huglo, *Les Tonaires*, 73–74, points out that the photolithography in *CS* 2 is not an adequate representation of the manuscript, and that the transcription of its text contains many errors. Note that a later hand has added in the upper lefthand margin the incipit "Primum querite regnum Dei," the mnemonic verse for Protus authentic. Merkley, *Modal Assignment in Northern Tonaries*, 77, questions the attribution to Regino. It must be said, however, that in certain ways this tonary is in closer agreement with the *Epistola* of Regino than is the tonary in Leipzig 169, the primary source for the version of the *Epistola* edited by Gerbert (*GS* 1: 230–47) and Bernhard (*Clavis Gerberti*, 39–73).

12. I have chosen these partly because they exhibit a close correlation with the Metz tonary. The four Introits in each of the first two differentiae in Regino's tonary are the same ones that are listed first under the two differentiae given in Metz, except that the order of the differentiae themselves is reversed. The Introits *Gaudeamus omnes, Suscepimus Deus, Rorate caeli,* and *Inclina Domine* appear in the first differentia in Metz, whose second differentia begins with the Introits *Gaudete in Domino, Etenim sederunt, Statuit ei Dominus,* and *Exsurge quare.* Metz does not have a third differentia for Protus authentic; its second continues with the Introits *Misereris omnium* and *Lex Domini inreprehensibilis . . . Meditatio cordis mei.* Regino's tonary assigns the latter to a third, "superior" (higher) differentia. In the discussion that follows, I shall use Pseudo-Odonian pitch nomenclature (Γ A B C D E F G a b h c d e f g aa) for the sake of convenience.

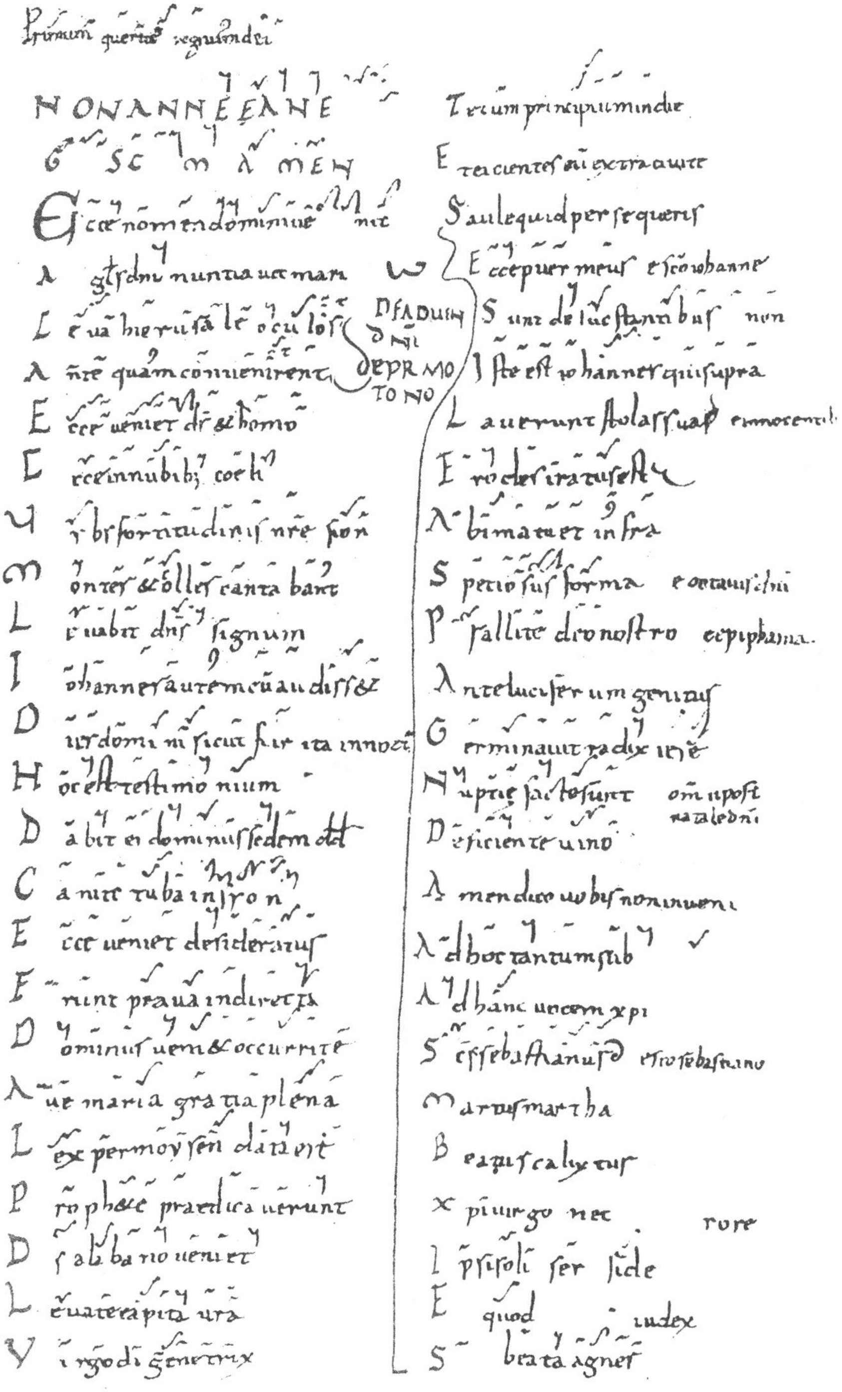

FIGURE 3.1B.   The beginning of the tonary of Regino of Prüm (Brussels 2750/65, fol. 45v–46; reproduced from *CS* 2: 5)

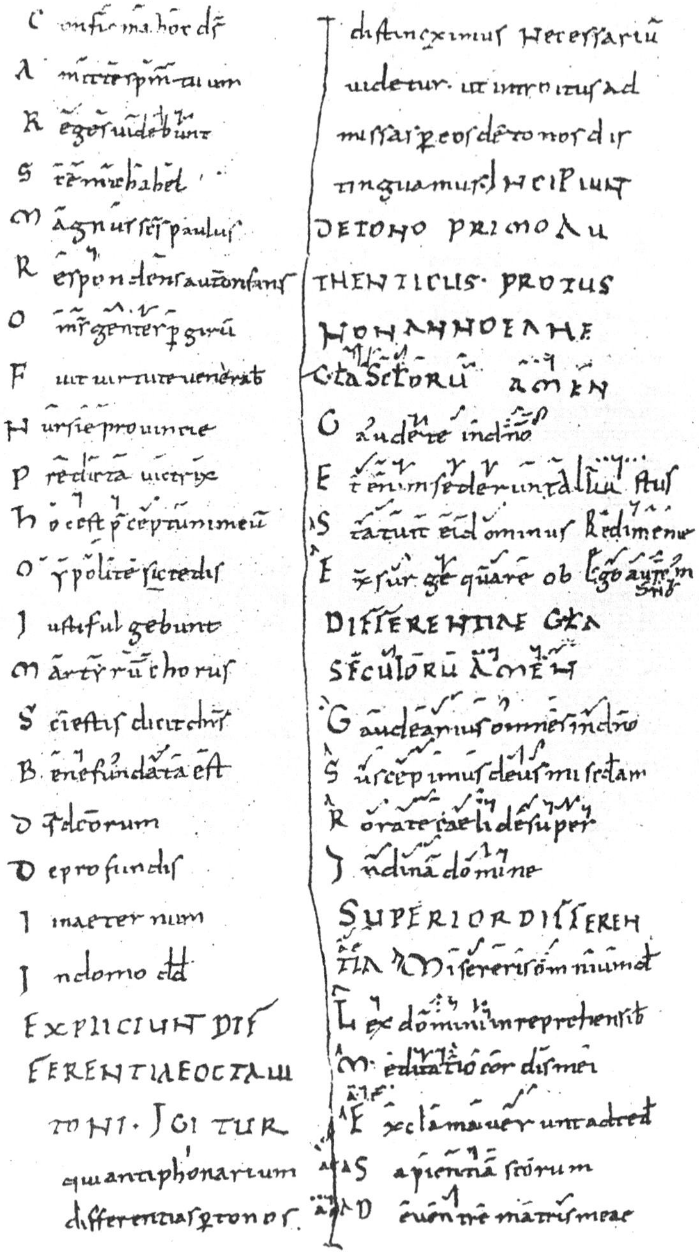

FIGURE 3.1C.   The first two differentiae and the beginning of a third for Introits in Protus authentic in the tonary of Regino of Prüm (Brussels 2750/65, fol. 58v; reproduced from CS 2: 55)

EXAMPLE 3.1.   Reconstruction of differentiae for Protus authentic and the incipits of their respective Introits in the tonary of Regino of Prüm (Brussels 2750/65, fol. 58v; reproduced from CS 2: 55).★

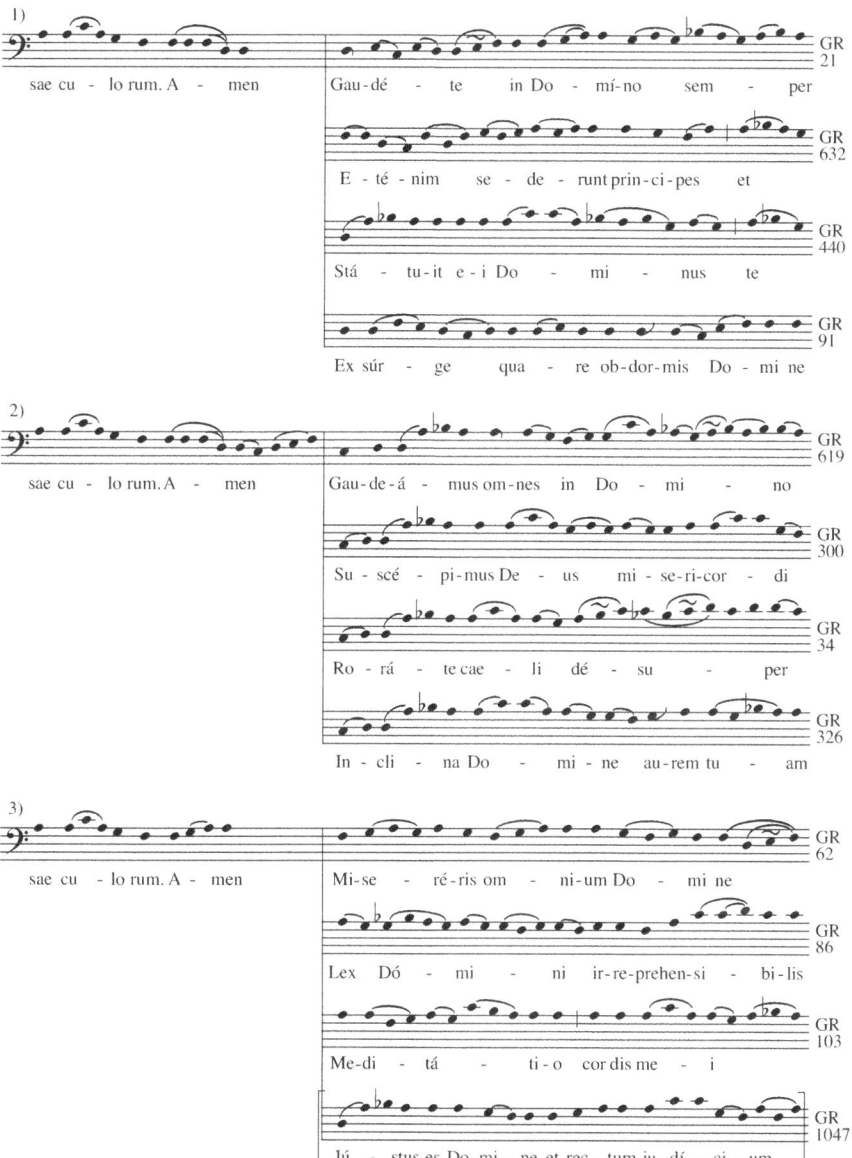

★The differentiae have been reconstructed as follows: the first from Frutolf of Michaelberg, *Breviarium de musica et Tonarius* (ed.Vivell, 125); the second and third from Paris 10508, fol. 151v, following the notation in Brussels 2750/65. The Introits themselves are taken from the *Graduale Romanum*.

One notices first that the only part of the *saeculorum Amen* melody that changes from one differentia to the next is that over *Amen*. The opening section, and hence the psalm tone itself, remains the same. Regarding the melodies of the Introits, one is struck immediately by the uniformity of the opening phrases of those sung under the second differentia. These consistently begin on *C,* with an immediate step up to *D,* followed by the distinctive move *D-a-b*ᵇ on the first accented syllable. Although not so immediately evident in the Introits of the other two categories, there is, in each case, at least one melodic gesture linking them. Three of the four incipits under the first differentia are marked by their focus on the minor third *D-F* within the first phrase. The shared trait of the pieces sung with the "superior" differentia, apart from their relatively "high" tessitura centered on *a,* would appear to be the prominence of the filled-in major third *F-G-a* or *a-G-F* in the opening phrase of each, echoing the preceding *Amen*. An apparent exception, the Introit *Statuit ei,* would seem to belong under the second differentia. The reason for its not having been placed there, however, must be that it starts immediately on *D.* That is, it lacks the initial upward step *C-D* that characterizes the incipits of the second differentia, and that is prepared by the conclusion of that differentia itself, *D-C D-E-F.*

The principle at work here is what Peter Wagner called the *Anpassungsgesetz* ("rule of accommodation"), the idea that when two melodies stand in succession, the first must be accommodated to the second via appropriate treatment of its ending.[13] The incipits of melodies assigned to a given differentia may be linked by their focus on a specific interval or melodic gesture, or they may all share the same melodic ductus. In practical terms, this means that a large number of melodies can be placed into a relatively small number of classifications—the divisions, in this instance, being the variable differentiae that are integral to the eight tonal categories and their respective psalm tones or verses.

This principle is not new. François-Auguste Gevaert discovered it at least as early as the late nineteenth century.[14] By comparing the melodies of over thirteen hundred Office antiphons assigned to the eight *toni* and their thirty-six differentiae in Regino's tonary, Gevaert was able to reduce the number of different melodies used in these antiphons to a corpus of forty-seven *thèmes*. More recently, Paul Merkley has discussed a ninth- or tenth-century manuscript in which there are incipits for thirty-nine different antiphons, arrayed under the eight intonation formulas (NONA-NOEANE, NOEAIS, etc.).[15] On comparing these antiphons to Gevaert's *thèmes,* Merkley came to the conclusion that these thirty-nine melodies represented distinct thematic families, families that could be systematized via the eight *toni* given in tonaries. He makes the following statement about them.

> One aspect of the history of tonaries can be regarded, overall, as the struggle of musicians to find clear, systematic ways of categorizing chant. This struggle is reflected . . . in the tonaries of Regino, Guido and Berno. . . .
> There is, however, another aspect of the history of tonaries that we tend to overlook

---

13. See Wagner, *Gregorianische Formenlehre,* 78–79, 129–34.

14. Gevaert, *La Mélopée antique dans les chants de l'église latine.* See esp. chap. 5, sec. 1: *Nomes ou thèmes mélodiques,* 123–32. Cf. Hiley, *Western Plainchant,* 90–91.

15. Merkley, "Tonaries and Melodic Families of Antiphons," a study of the tonary in Paris 4995. This

because of our concentration on the evolution of modal theory. Many tonaries reflect the thematic conception of the Gregorian repertoire. As we turn our attention from large, formal tonaries to those lacking many formal characteristics, we find that the smallest, least formal sources are the ones most closely indicative of the thematic conception, and these point clearly to a pre-notational practice of chant dependent on a small group of melodic themes.[16]

Tonaries provided a framework for melodic classification based on the practice of psalmody, a constant in the daily life of every medieval monk. By taking advantage of the thematic organization of psalmodic chant, the early tonaries provided a method of classification that could operate within a notationless musical culture and that could enable Carolingian singers to gain control over a large repertoire of plainchant. A more efficient and appropriate initial response to the challenge of learning Roman chant can hardly be imagined.

Yet another Frankish response to that challenge came in the form of the various music manuals that were written in the ninth through the eleventh centuries. These manuals provide important evidence of the conjoining of ideas and practices from several sources that finally was to result both in a tone-system and in a theory of mode for medieval music.

The earliest of the extant Carolingian music manuals seems to be the *Musica disciplina* of Aurelian of Réôme, perhaps written as early as 840–49, but possibly dating from after 877.[17] In the preface to his treatise, Aurelian relates that he had been asked by his monastic brethren to write about certain "paradigms of melody" that are called *toni* or *tenores*.[18] As this phrase suggests, the main body of the work (chaps.

---

tonary exhibits only text incipits, with no musical notation. It contains no tonal designations (e.g., Protus autentus or plagis) or indications of differentiae (or *saeculorum Amen* formulas).

16. Merkley, "Tonaries and Melodic Families of Antiphons," 22. Further evidence for the importance of this thematic conception in the performance of chant before the advent of notation can be found in the automelic-prosomoiac chants of the Byzantine repertoire and in the collection of hymns ascribed to Ephraim of Syria (d. 373). On the *automela* (generative melodies) and *prosomoia* (imitations) in the Byzantine repertoire, see Levy, "Plainchant before Neumes," esp. 196–97. On the role of model melodies in the work of Ephraim, see Haas, "Modus als Skala—Modus als Modellmelodie," 28–32. Haas points out that Ephraim's collection contains twelve hymn cycles, each consisting of between four and eighty-seven hymns. These are sung to a collection of approximately fifty melodic models.

17. Ed. in *GS* 1: 27–63, and by Gushee in his dissertation ("The *Musica disciplina* of Aurelian of Réôme") and in *CSM* 21 (see Bernhard, ed., *Clavis Gerberti*, 10–11). The work has been translated into English by Ponte, "Aureliani Reomensis Musica disciplina." Other studies devoted specifically to the *Musica disciplina* include Waeltner, "Die 'Musica disciplina' des Aurelianus Reomensis"; Waeltner, "Die Methode terminologischer Untersuchungen frühmittelalterlicher Musiktraktate"; Raasted, "The 'laetantis adverbia' of Aurelian's Greek Informant"; and Haggh, "Aurelian's Library." The earlier date for the treatise is that advanced by Gushee, "The *Musica disciplina* of Aurelian of Réôme," 1: 36, and in *CSM* 21, 16. The possible later date is advanced in Bernhard, "Textkritisches zu Aurelianus Reomensis," 60–61. In a presentation at the conference "Musiktheorie im Mittelalter," held in Munich, 23–27 July 2000, Barbara Haggh presented convincing evidence that the earliest manuscript of the *Musica disciplina*, Valenciennes 148, contains a revised version of the treatise completed ca. 859–61. She dates the manuscript ca. 875–85. Haggh's argument is published in a Polish translation by Katarzyna Naliwajek: "Traktat 'Musica disciplina' Aureliana Reomensis. Proweniencja i datowanie," *Muzyka: Kwartalnik Instytutu Sztuki Polskiej Academii Nauk* 45 (2000): 25–79 (English summary, 78–79).

18. "Rogatus a fratribus ut super quibusdam regulis modulationum quas tonos seu tenores appel-

8–19) is essentially a tonary in prose form, but its introductory chapters are a fascinating *cento*, with pieces stitched together from several earlier sources combined with Aurelian's (?) own additions.

A particularly telling example of this may be found in the second chapter of the *Musica disciplina*, "Concerning its name [*Musica*] and inventors, and how the forms of numbers may have been found."[19] Following Boethius's *Musica*, Book I, chapter 10, almost verbatim, it relates the story of Pythagoras using the four hammers to produce the intervals of the octave, diatessaron, diapente, and tone.[20] After the introduction of the proportions for each interval, however, Aurelian inserts an illustration of each of these, namely, an Introit drawn from the repertory of plainchant, the ductus of each of which does indeed manifest the interval in question (ex. 3.2).

As he says, the octave may be found in *Inclina Domine* "and all that are found in the first *tonus*," the diatessaron in *Confessio et pulchritudo* "and all those that are entered in the autentus deuterus *tonus*," the diapente in *Circumdederunt me* "and others that are found in the autentus tritus," and the tone in *Puer natus est nobis* "and all that are ascribed to the norms of the autentus tetrardus."

Clearly, the process of fusing Greek harmonic theory with medieval chant had now begun. Three of the four chants listed in this passage later form the kernel of the "First Quidam" in *Alia musica*.[21] The connection with Boethius is cemented by the fact that three tenth-century manuscripts of *De institutione musica* include Aurelian's examples, and even his descriptive vocabulary, as glosses to the presentation of the ratios of the Pythagorean consonances in Book I, chapter 10 of Boethius's work.[22] The same glosses also appear in two eleventh-century manuscripts of Regino of Prüm's *Epistola de harmonica institutione* at the corresponding passage, likewise drawn from Boethius and introducing the Pythagorean consonances.[23]

Particularly important here, though, is Aurelian's choice of nomenclature in classifying the examples drawn from plainchant: each of the pieces exemplifies a specific

---

lant . . . praescriberem sermonem" (ed. Gushee, *CSM* 21, 53). The Latin *regulae modulationum* is difficult to render in English. *Regula* means a "rule," "ruler," or "standard"; *modulatio* can signify "measure," "singing," or "melody," among other things. "Paradigms of melody" is the translation of the phrase given in Ponte, "Aureliani Reomensis *Musica disciplina*," Book II, chap. 4. In any event, it is the equation of *tonus* and *tenor* that is most germane here, recalling, as it does, definitions of *tonus* and *accentus* given by Donatus and Isidore, respectively. On the terms *tonus* and *tenor* in Aurelian, see Waeltner, "Die Methode terminologischer Untersuchungen frühmittelalterlicher Musiktraktate."

19. "De nomine et inventoribus eius, et quomodo forme numerorum invente fuerint" (ed. Gushee, *CSM* 21, 61).

20. Ed. Gushee, *CSM* 21, 62–63.

21. See Chailley, ed., *Alia musica*, 85–97.

22. See Bernhard and Bower, eds., *Glossa maior in institutionem Boethii*, 1: l–lvi and 199–201 (Glosses 143, 146, 151, and 153 on Book I, chap. 10). The manuscripts in question are Chicago F. 9, Paris 7297, and Rome 1638. Bower and Bernhard feel that the passage in Aurelian originated as four glosses to Boethius's *De musica* that were then incorporated into the running text of Aurelian. This would certainly seem logical, given that this section of Aurelian's work is stitched together from several earlier sources, drawing particularly heavily from Boethius's *De arithmetica*. The chief argument against this view is the fact that the earliest manuscript of the *Musica disciplina*, Valenciennes 148, almost certainly dates from the ninth century. See note 17 here.

23. See Bernhard, ed., *Clavis Gerberti*, 39–73, and specifically the critical apparatus on 57–58. The manuscripts in question are Montpellier 159 and Metz 494.

EXAMPLE 3.2.   Aurelianus Reomensis, *Musica disciplina*, chap. 2 (ed. Gushee, *CSM* 21, 32; emphasis added). Aurelian's additions to Boethius are indented. Since the examples in the treatise are not notated, the notated versions are taken from the *Graduale Romanum*.

Hi igitur mallei qui .XII. et .VI. ponderibus vergebant diapason in duplo consonantiam concinebant

ut hic:

Antiphona *Inclina Domine aurem tuam,*

et omnia quae *in primo* inveniuntur *tono.*

Malleus .XII. ponderum ad malleum .VIIII. et malleus .VIII. ad malleum .VI. ponderum, secundum epitritam proportionem, diatessaron consonantiam perficiebant.

Adest exemplum:

Antiphona *Confessio et pulchritudo,*

et cuncta que *in tono autenti deuteri* conscribuntur.

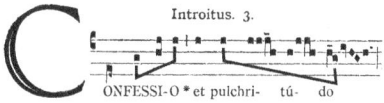

.VIIII. vero ponderum ad .VI., et .XII. ad .VIII., diapente consonantiam permiscebant,

veluti hic:

Antiphona *Circumdederunt me,*

et cetera que *in autentu trito* inveniuntur.

.VIIII. vero ad .VIII. in sesquioctava proportione resonabat tonum,

iuxta illud:

Antiphona *Puer natus est nobis,*

et omnia quae *autenti tetrardi* adscribuntur norme.

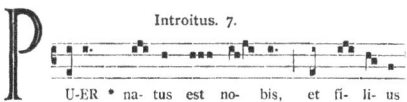

Etenim *sunt iiii toni, scilicet autentus protus, autentus deuterus, autentus tritus, autentus tetrardus, qui geminati ex se viii reddere videntur, quos quidam latus, quidam autem discipulos nuncupant.* Quod ut evidentius appareat, si volueris segregare a magistro discipulum, (id est, ab autentu proto plagis proti) et coniungere cum aliquo altero tono, non vales. Similiter et de ceteris intellegendum est tonis, quia semper origo inferioris a superiori initium ducit.

tonus, of which there are four principal ones: autentus protus, deuterus, tritus, and tetrardus. As the passage at the bottom of example 3.2 makes clear, there are also four secondary ones, called *plagi,* which some call *latus* or *discipuli,* that are integrally related to their authentic counterparts.[24] This is, of course, the same nomenclature as that encountered in tonaries.

Aurelian's first actual definition of *tonus* appears in the fifth chapter of his work: "Tonus est acuta enuntiatio vocis. Est enim armoniae differentia et quantitas, que in vocis accentu et tenore consistit."[25] This definition is drawn directly from chapter 6 of Isidore's *Etymologiae,* as is, in fact, the entire passage that follows it. In the section of Isidore's work that serves as a model, there are thirteen descriptions of "qualities of the voice" following the names of the highest and lowest tones (ex. 3.3). Aurelian apparently took them all to be aspects or "modes" of *tonus,* describing as *modi,* in this sense, not only hyperlydian but also "inflexion of the voice" (*inflexio vocis*), "sweet voices" (*suaves voces*), "a harsh voice" (*aspera vox*), "a blind voice" (*caeca vox*), "a flexible voice" (*vinnola vox*), and "the perfect voice" (*perfecta vox*).

What might at first seem to be a more satisfactory treatment of *tonus* appears in the sixth chapter of Aurelian's work. Nonetheless, after a slightly confused paragraph, in which Aurelian has the fifteenth sound exceeding the first by eight (whole) tones,[26] Aurelian provides a listing of the fifteen Greek *tonoi* drawn from Cassiodorus.[27] Both this and the preceding discussion suggest that Aurelian's understanding of the ancient Greek *tonoi* ranges from minimal to nonexistent. In any event, it plays no role in the treatment of *tonus* in the central part of his treatise.

The main body of Aurelian's work begins with a chapter titled "On the Eight *Toni,*" itself a glossed version of an earlier, independent tract attributed to Alcuin.[28] Its definition of *tonus* is taken over from Cassiodorus: "Difinitur autem ita: tonus est totius constitutionis armonice differentia, et quantitas quae in vocis accentu sive tenore consistit."[29] Echoing the nomenclature of tonaries and of his own classification of chants in the second chapter of his work, Aurelian names four primary cat-

---

24. I translate: "And thus there are four *toni,* autentus protus, autentus deuterus, autentus tritus, and autentus tetrardus, which appear to render eight by creating doubles of themselves, which some call 'auxiliaries' and others call 'disciples.' It should be rather obvious that should you wish to separate the 'disciple' from its 'master' (that is, the plagis protus from the autentus protus) and join it to some other *tonus,* it will not be valid. The same should likewise be understood concerning the other *toni,* because the source of the inferior always takes its beginning from the superior."

25. Ed. Gushee, *CSM* 21, 69. See chapter 1 here, notes 107–13 , and the associated discussion.

26. "Quo autem ordine sonitus quindecim efficiant ac simphonias sex et tonos viii, hinc contemplare licebit cum inspexeris acute quantum singuli se superent, quousque altitudinem ultimi conscendant: ita ut singuli sese emitonio, id est medio tono, superent, quousque quintadecima primum octo tonis precedat" (ed. Gushee, *CSM* 21, 75).

27. Ed. Gushee, *CSM* 21, 75–76, from Cassiodorus, *Institutiones,* Book II, chap. 5. See the discussion at notes 102–4 and 106 in chapter 1 here.

28. On this, see Gushee, "The *Musica disciplina* of Aurelian of Réôme," 1: 138–54; Gushee, "Questions of Genre in Medieval Treatises on Music," 388; Gushee, in *CSM* 21, 40–41; and Möller, "Zur Frage der musikgeschichtlichen Bedeutung der Akademie Karls des Grossen,"272–85; Möller, "*De octo tonibus:* Ein europäisch-amerikanisches Verwirrspiel und seine Klärung," esp. 700–708.

29. Ed. Gushee, *CSM* 21, 78. See the discussion at notes 107–13 in chapter 1 here.

EXAMPLE 3.3.   Two types of *toni* and thirteen types of voice in Isidore and Aurelian

Isidore	Aurelian
Tonus est acuta enuntiatio vocis. Est enim harmoniae differentia et quantitas, quae in vocis accentu vel tenore consistit: cuius genera in quindecim partibus musici dividerunt, ex quibus	*Tonus* est acuta enuntiatio vocis. Est enim armoniae differentia et quantitas, que in vocis accentu et tenore consistit. Genera autem eius in quindecim partibus musici diviserunt, . . . Primus tamen vocum est modus
hyperlydius novissimus et acutissimus, *hypodorius* omnium gravissimus. Cantus est *inflexio* vocis, nam sonus directus est; praecedit autem sonus cantum. *Arsis* est vocis elevatio, hoc est initium.	*yperlidius,* qui est novissimus et acutissimus. *Yppodorius* secundus, ipse est omnium gravissimus cantus. Tercius modus est [aequa] *inflexio* vocis, nam sonus directus est. Precedit autem sonus cantum. Quartus est *arsis,* id est vocis elevatio, hoc est initium. Quintus tesis, est enim
Thesis vocis positio, hoc est finis.	*tesis* positio, hoc est finis. Sextus modus est, ubi insunt voces suaves.
Suaves voces sunt subtiles et spissae, clarae atque acutae. *Perspicuae* voces sunt, quae longius protrahuntur, ita ut omnem inpleant continuo locum, sicut clangor tubarum.	*Suaves* autem sunt voces subtiles et spisse, clare atque acute. Septimus ubi *perspicue* voces quae longius protrahuntur ita ut omnem impleant contiguum locum sicut tuba. Octavus est ubi
Subtiles voces sunt, quibus non est spiritus, qualis est infantium, vel mulierum, vel aegrotantium, sicut in nervis. Quae enim subtilissimae cordae sunt, subtiles ac tenues sonos emittunt. *Pingues* sunt voces, quando spiritus multus simul egreditur, sicut virorum. *Acuta* vox tenuis, alta, sicut in cordis videmus. *Dura* vox est, quae violenter emittit sonos, sicut tonitruum, sicut incudis sonos, quotiens in durum malleus percutitur ferrum.	*subtiles* voces sunt, ut infantium vel nervorum. Nonus, *pinguis,* ut virorum. Decimus, ubi *acuta* est vox, tenuis, alta, sicut in cordis. Undecimus, ubi *dura* est vox, quae violenter emittitur, ut mallei in incûde. Duodecimus est modus, ubi aspera est vox.
Aspera vox est rauca, et quae dispergitur per minutos et indissimiles pulsus.	*Aspera* autem vox est rauca et quae dispergitur per minutos et indissimiles sonos. Terciusdecimus est . . . ubi vox caeca consistit.
Caeca vox est, quae,mox emissa fuerit, conticescit, atque suffocata nequaquam longius producitur, sicut est in fictilibus. *Vinnola* est vox mollis atque flexibilis. Et vinnola dicta a vinno, hoc est cincinno molliter flexo. *Perfecta* autem vox est alta, suavis et clara: alta, ut in sublime sufficiat; clara, ut aures adinpleat; suavis, ut animos audientium blandiat. Si ex his aliquid defuerit, vox perfecta non est.	*C[a]eca* vox dicitur que cum emissa fuerit, conticescit. Quartusdecimus modus ubi *vinnola* vox est. Vinnola autem est flexibilis vox. Vinnola vero dicitur a vinno, id est cincinno molliter flexo. Quintusdecimus est . . . *perfecta* vox. *Perfecta* autem est vox alta, suavis et clara. Si aliquid ex his defuerit, vox perfecta non erit.
Isidori Hispalensis episcopi Etymologiarum sive originum liber III.xv (ed. Lindsay), fol. K7v–K8.	*CSM* 21, 69–70.

egories—protus, deuterus, tritus, and tetrarchus—each of which is subdivided into authentic and plagal. Instead of describing the characteristics of the tones themselves, as Boethius had done, Aurelian simply explains their Greek names for his Latin audience.[30] At the same time, there is at least one passage here that may provide a bit of "technical" information about the tones. Aurelian says "That four of them are called authentic is attributed to their special sound [*praecipuus sonus*], because a certain guidance and instruction is offered by them to the other four. Whence the first are higher, the second lower."[31] This is reinforced a few lines later when he says that the plagal *toni* are called inferior "because their sound is perceived as lower than the higher ones."[32]

A bit more substantive information about the tones comes at the end of the same chapter. Here we learn that the *toni* have to do with the performance of antiphonal chant: "There were several singers who asserted that there were certain antiphons that could be fitted to none of these paradigms."[33] We also learn that the Greeks were considered the "inventors" of the tones, and that Charlemagne had ordered the number of the tones to be augmented by four.[34] These four are described by means of words associated with intonation formulas (ANANNO, NOEANE, etc.) in the tonaries. This is made clear in the following chapter, in which the Greek whom Aurelian asked to explain them says that these formulas have no intrinsic meaning, but do contain the *modulationem tonorum* ("melody of the tones").[35]

The remainder of the principal part of Aurelian's handbook is a verbal tonary, treating verse chants and their characteristics. The "tone is set" in chapter 10, where one discovers that the category *autentus protus* has several subcategories or *varietates*. In Aurelian's words: "The first authentic has numerous varieties. It contains three varieties for the Introits."[36] (It should be recalled that the tonary ascribed to Regino

---

30. Ed. Gushee, *CSM* 21, 79. He explains *protus*, for example, by saying that it means "first," which is why the first martyrs are called protomartyrs; *tetrarchus* is so called because it is fourth in order. He continues: "Four is called *tetra* by the Greeks, whence the name of God [θεός] is a *tetragrammaton* because it is said to be written with four letters."

31. "Nam quod quattuor eorum autentici vocantur ad *precipuum eorum sonum* refertur, eo quod aliis iiii quasi quidam ducatus et magisterium ab eis prebeatur. Unde et primi altiores, secundi inferiores" (ed. Gushee, *CSM* 21, 78; emphasis added).

32. "[Plagi autem dicuntur] inferiores quia sonus eorum pressior quam superiorum deprehenditur" (ed. Gushee, *CSM* 21, 79).

33. "Extitere etenim nonnulli cantores qui quasdam esse antiphonas quae nulle earum regulae possent aptari asseruerunt" (ed. Gushee, *CSM* 21, 82) The term *regula*, here translated as "paradigm," was used earlier in the same chapter to explain *tonus*: "Est autem *tonus* minima pars musicae, regula tamen" (78).

34. Continuing the passage quoted in the preceding note, "unde pius augustus avus vester Carolus paterque totius orbis iiii augere iussit quorum hic vocabula subter tenentur inserta: ANANNO NOEANE NONANNOEANE NOEANE. Et quia gloriabantur Greci suo se ingenio octo indeptos esse tonos, maluit ille duodenarium adimplere numerum" (ed. Gushee, *CSM* 21, 82). On these extra *toni*, see Atkinson, "The *Parapteres*: *Nothi* or Not?"

35. "Etenim quendam interrogavi Grecum: 'In Latina quid interpretarentur lingua?' Respondit se nihil interpretari sed esse apud eos letantis adverbia . . . estque *tonorum* in se continens *modulationem*" (ed. Gushee, *CSM* 21, 84; emphasis added). Jørgen Raasted has delved further into the question of Aurelian and the intonation formulas in "The 'laetantis adverbia' of Aurelian's Greek Informant." He believes it likely that Aurelian's informant was indeed a Greek (esp. 56–58).

36. "Autentus protus plures habet varietates. Denique introitum varietates insemet continet tres"

likewise has three subcategories for Introits in Protus authentic, which it calls "differentiae.") According to Aurelian, these subcategories are present in order to facilitate the joining of the end of the verse to the beginning of the antiphon:

> The second [variety] is this: the antiphon *Iustus es, Domine,* the end of whose verse is elevated so that it can be joined to the beginning of the antiphon. The third is this: the antiphon *Suscepimus Deus,* in which the last syllable of the verse makes delays [that are] a little longer than in the first and second, and the pitch is raised so that it can be fitted to the beginning of the introit.[37]

Aurelian's description shows that the differences between "varieties" result in different final cadences in the psalm tone—that is, in the differentia or *saeculorum Amen*—characteristic of each. The crucial role played by the differentia is reinforced in the Valenciennes manuscript of Aurelian's treatise, in which a later hand has added the melody for the incipit and differentia of the psalm tone immediately above *Gaudete in Domino.* It appears, truncated, in the right margin opposite *Suscepimus Deus.* Most important: the melody is written in Paleofrankish neumes ( ).[38] As is made clear later in the same chapter, the impetus for assigning an antiphon to a certain "variety" comes from its opening melodic gesture:

> The first, then, receives the end of the verse directly in itself for this reason: because it both begins the verse straight, and the voice does not wind through tortuous curves, and because the *tonus* is found on the third syllable, that is, on "-te" in *Gaudete.* But in the second, the last syllable of the verse is elevated for this reason: because the *tonus* is on the first syllable, that is, on "Ius-" in *Iustus es, Domine.* But in the third, the last syllable is raised higher and is allowed to have longer delays for this reason: because the completed *tonus* is found on the second syllable, . . . that is, on "-ce-" in *Suscepimus Deus.* Therefore, not undeservedly is the end of the verse prolonged, and it is carried higher.[39]

As this passage indicates, and as may also be seen in example 3.4, the crucial factor for determining *tonus,* and hence the "variety" of the tone, is the opening melodic formula of the antiphon.

(ed. Gushee, *CSM* 21, 85). The translation is that in Ponte, "Aureliani Reomensis *Musica disciplina,*" 2: 70. On Aurelian's use of the designation *varietates,* see Waeltner, "Die Methode terminologischer Untersuchungen frühmittelalterlicher Musiktraktate," 53–54.

37. "Secunda haec: Antiphona Iustus es Domine, cuius versiculi finis in altum elevatur ut queat ipsius initio iungi. Tertia haec: Antiphona Suscepimus Deus, in qua ultima versiculi pars diuscule moras agit quam in primo et secundo, extolliturque vox in sublime ut capiti possit aptari introitui (ed. Gushee, *CSM* 21, 85; transl. Ponte, "Aureliani Reomensis *Musica disciplina,*" 2: 74–76).

38. Valenciennes 148, fol. 72. These entries are reproduced in Gushee's edition in *CSM* 21, 165, as plt. I, nos. 3 and 5, respectively. It would appear from plt. I, no. 5 that the end of the differentia for *Suscepimus Deus* was cut off in the process of trimming the manuscript. See *CSM* 21, 27.

39. "Primus siquidem in se idcirco directe finis versuum recipit, quia et in directum incoat, nec vox sinuosos decurrit per anfractus, atque in tertia tonus invenitur sillaba scilicet in TE, ut 'Gaudete.' In secundo vero ideo sursum pars ultima sublimatur, quia tonus in prima adest sillaba, id est in IUS, ut 'Iustus es, Domine.' In [tertio] vero idcirco altius finis erigitur morasque habere diutius patitur, quoniam perfectus tonus in secunda repperitur sillaba, . . . hoc est in CE, ut 'Suscepimus Deus.' Ideoque non inmerito longe finis protrahitur versiculi altiusque profertur" (ed. Gushee, *CSM* 21, 86).

EXAMPLE 3.4.   Incipits of the Introits *Gaudete in Domino* (*GR* 21), *Suscepimus Deus* (*GR* 300), and *Iustus es Domine* (*GR* 1047), with their respective differentiae from Paris 10508, fol. 151v, as given in Ponte, "Aureliani Reomensis *Musica disciplina*," 3: 51–53

Since the *tonus* in *Gaudete in Domino* is projected by the minor third ascent *D-F* on the syllable "-te," the *Amen* in the *saeculorum Amen* anticipates that melodic gesture via a drop from the tristopha on *F* down to *D*, the opening note of both the antiphon itself and the syllable "-te."[40] The *tonus* in the Introit *Iustus es,* according to Aurelian, is given by the upward leap from *D* to *a*, followed by a move to the upper accessory before returning to *a* for the syllable "-stus." In some tonaries, such as Metz 351, *Iustus es* receives the same differentia as *Gaudete in Domino,* with a descent from *a* down to *D* by way of an intervening tristropha on *F*. In others, however, such as Paris 10508, the "Amen" concludes on *a* ("the last syllable of the verse is elevated," as Aurelian puts it), thereby providing an appropriate preparation for the immediate return to *a* at the beginning of the antiphon.[41] As noted, *Suscepimus Deus,* the representative of Aurelian's third category, is one of a highly unified group of four Introits sung under the first differentia in Metz 351 and under the second in Brussels 2750/65.[42] The hallmark of this group is an opening step of *C-D* followed by an upward leap of a fifth with upper-neighbor suffix (*D-a-b♭*) on the first accented syllable. Aurelian says of the differentia for this variety that it "makes delays a little while longer than in the first and second, and the pitch is raised up so that it can be fitted to the beginning of the Introit." Indeed, as one compares the three dif-

---

40. As was the case in ex. 3.2, both the music in ex. 3.4 and the nomenclature used in describing them in the text are modern. Neither diastematic notation nor the pitch nomenclature I am using for ease of discussion had yet come into existence in Aurelian's time. In "Aureliani Reomensis *Musica disciplina*," 3: 51–54, Ponte provides transcriptions of both differentiae and incipits for *Gaudete in Domino, Suscepimus Deus,* and *Iustus es* from several later medieval sources, including those reproduced in ex. 3.4.

41. See Ponte, "Aureliani Reomensis *Musica disciplina*," 3: 53.

42. See the discussion of Figure 3.1 and Example 3.1.

ferentiae in example 3.4, one notices that the "Amen" for this one is somewhat longer than those for the other two, and that its melody is indeed "raised up," first moving down to *C,* then stepwise back up to *F.*

As the reader will by now have grasped, Aurelian's treatment of the varieties of the Protus authentic provides confirmation of Wagner's *Anpassungsgesetz* and its implications, as explored above in conjunction with Regino's tonary.[43] Indeed, the Introits exemplifying Aurelian's three different *varietates* are likewise classified under three discrete differentiae in Brussels 2750/65. As a comparison of example 3.4 with example 3.1 reveals, *Gaudete in Domino* appears with the first differentia and *Suscepimus Deus* with the second in Brussels 2750/65. Although it is not included in example 3.1, *Iustus es, Domine* is classified under the "superior" differentia in the tonary ascribed to Regino.[44] Hence, there is virtually complete congruence between Aurelian's classifications of Introits in the Protus authentic and those of Regino.

In the discussion of tonaries at the beginning of this chapter, I concluded that they provided a "method of classification that could operate within a notationless musical culture and that could enable Carolingian singers to gain control over a large repertoire of plainchant." Much the same could be—and has been—said about Aurelian's treatise.[45] At the same time, one chapter of the treatise makes several references to notation; the earliest manuscript of the work, Valenciennes 148, contains at least two examples of musical notation that may be contemporaneous with the copying of the text, two further instances in which space was left for notation, and five more entries of notation in the so-called Paleofrankish script.[46] What, then, is the nature of musical notation as witnessed by Aurelian's treatise?[47]

The specific references to notation in Aurelian's *Musica disciplina* appear in chapter 19 of the treatise, "Patterns for discerning the density, sparsity, height, and depth of the verses of all the *toni,*"[48] which is primarily a description of the psalm tones for antiphons, Introits, and Responsories. The word Aurelian uses to refer to nota-

43. See pp. 92–93 above.

44. See *CS* 2: 56–57. Although several of the Introits under the heading *Superior differentia* are followed by a notated *Amen* that would actually place them in the first differentia, *Iustus es* is not among them.

45. Consider, for example, Treitler's statement that "Aurelian certainly knew the chant tradition as an oral tradition, and he wrote his treatise with the presumptions, habits, and expectations that implies. . . . The *Musica disciplina* is a treatise for singers in an oral tradition. It is the first and last of its kind" ("Reading and Singing: On the Genesis of Occidental Music-Writing," 161).

46. See Gushee's list and description in *CSM* 21, 27; facsimile reproductions of these, as well as examples of musical notation in later manuscripts, appear on 165–67, in plts. I–III. On the Paleofrankish script, see Handschin, "Eine alte Neumenschrift"; Handschin, "Zu 'Eine alte Neumenschrift'"; Jammers, "Die Paläofränkische Neumenschrift"; Hourlier and Huglo, "La Notation paléofranque"; Stäblein, *Schriftbild der einstimmigen Musik,* 26–29, 106–8; Corbin, *Die Neumen,* 3: 75–81; and Atkinson, "De accentibus toni."

47. This question has been raised most recently by Levy in "Aurelian's Use of Neumes." See also the discussion in Gushee, "The *Musica disciplina* of Aurelian of Réôme," 1: 244–62.

48. "Norme qualiter versuum spissitudo raritas celsitudo profunditasque discernatur omnium tonorum" (ed. Gushee, *CSM* 21, 118).

tion is *nota*—"graphic sign" or "mark"—the same term used in Antiquity for a graphic sign representing a musical sound.[49] Occurring altogether twelve times in this chapter, the term *nota* appears most frequently in formulations such as "notarum formula" or "figura notarum." Such is the case with its first occurrence in the chapter, with the intonation formula for Protus authentic:

En figura melodie sicut subiecta *notarum* demonstrat formula:
(This is the shape of the melody, just as the formula *of the notes* below demonstrates):
NONAN NOEANE[50]

Unfortunately, no actual *notae* are provided for this passage either in the Valenciennes manuscript or in most of the other sources for the treatise.[51] Indeed, the sources provide no *notae* at all for most of the passages in which the text clearly refers to them. It would therefore be a mistake, I believe, to assume that any of the surviving sources—Valenciennes 148 included—preserves the *notae* that Aurelian actually intended.

Fortunately, Aurelian's text does give some clues as to the appearance of these *notae*. In a number of instances, Aurelian describes, syllable by syllable, the chants he uses to illustrate specific points. For example, immediately following the "formula notarum" for the intonation formula of the Protus authentic (NONAN NOEANE given above), he introduces a detailed description of the psalm tone for this *tonus* by saying "In accord with the hearing of the singer and visual inspection of the notes, precisely by these same ones, the *tonus* is perceived to produce a connection, however subtle, at the beginning of the verses of antiphons and Introits."[52] He then describes the psalm tone itself (see ex. 3.5), saying that it has an "acute accent" on the second syllable, if that syllable is a dactyl or short, and on the fourth syllable, if that syllable is long.[53] Aurelian goes on to say that the eighth syllable "will be circumflexed" (*circumflectetur*), and that the ninth "will be made acute."[54] The twelfth syllable "will be

49. See notes 35–36 and 127 in chapter 1 here and the associated discussion. See also Bautier-Regnier, "A propos des sens de *neuma* et de *nota*," for a discussion of these terms in treatises of the ninth through the twelfth centuries.

50. I have corrected *subiectum* to *subiecta* following the reading in Oxford 212. For a different reading, see Bautier-Regnier, "A propos des sens de *neuma* et de *nota*," 8.

51. The sole exception is the twelfth-century manuscript Paris 7211, fol. 134v–144, which provides Aquitanian neumes for most of the examples requiring notation.

52. "Hisdem denique tonus in incoatione versuum antiphonarum ac introituum secundum speculationis auditum et inspectionem notarum pervidetur quantulamcumque habere connexionem" (ed. Gushee, *CSM* 21, 119).

53. "Secunda *acuto* enunciabitur *accentu*, videlicet '-ri-.' Ea tamen ratione, si dactilus fuerit, vel quelibet correpta syllaba; . . . Quarta post haec, hoc est: 'Pa-,' si producta fuerit veluti haec eadem syllaba quae positione producitur, in ea *acutus* accendetur vocis *accentus*" (ed. Gushee, *CSM* 21, 119; emphasis added).

54. "Octava vero, hoc est '-li,' *circumflectetur*. Nona *acuetur*, id est '-o'" (Gushee, *CSM* 21, 119; emphasis added).

wound around" (*circumvolvetur*),[55] and the fifteenth will receive a threefold percussion of the voice.[56]

The language in use here is, of course, that of the grammarians' treatment of prosodic accents, discussed in chapter 1.[57] Aurelian's use of it should come as no surprise, given his projection at the outset of his work that he was going to discuss *toni seu tenores*. The same equation had earlier been made by Donatus in his *Ars maior* ("Tonos alii accentus, alii tenores nominant") and by Isidore of Seville in his *Etymologiae* ("Nam accentus et tonos et tenores dicunt"), both in conjunction with their respective treatments of prosodic accents.[58] We should also recall, however, that these *accentus, toni,* and *tenores* were not merely inflections of the voice. They were also *notae*—the graphic signs representing these inflections. Given that Aurelian quotes Isidore of Seville rather extensively, one must assume that Aurelian was familiar with accent both as vocal inflection and as graphic sign. The question remains: does Aurelian's use of accents as *notae* correspond ontologically to any kind of musical reality? The answer, I believe, must be yes.

Let us look at three examples, the first being the psalm tone for the Protus authentic already described (ex. 3.5). Example 3.5 presents two versions of the *Gloria patri* for the Protus authentic: a modern one from the *Graduale Romanum* and, in parallel with it, a version that supplies prosodic accents in the places specified by Aurelian. Although Aurelian's version and the modern one differ in details, it is nonetheless clear that the melodic gesture to which he refers when he specifies an acute accent is an upward ascent of two notes; the gesture referred to as *circumflexio* or *circumvolutio* is an ascent and descent of three notes. These melodic inflections are the same ones prescribed for the prosodic accents in Classical sources.

The next example (ex. 3.6) presents parallel passages from two Great Responsories, *Erue a framea* and *De ore leonis libera me*. Aurelian says of *Erue a framea* that "the melody that is made on the tenth syllable, that is, 'a-,' is borne around slowly and with a long curve ("melodia quae fit in decima syllaba, videlicet 'a-,' tractim prolixoque amfractu, . . . circumfertur").[59] Of the parallel passage in *De ore leonis* ("-ra" of the phrase *libera me*), he says: "The arrangement of the sound is not carried out thus with a *circumflex* but is shortened" ("non tam *circumflexe* protraitur vocis concentus, sed corripitur").[60] As one can tell from comparing the two chants in

---

55. Here and elsewhere in the treatise, Aurelian uses the verbs *circumvolvo* and *circumflecto* and the nouns *circumvolutio* and *circumflexio* interchangeably, with all four terms referring to a three-note melodic gesture that both ascends and descends, insofar as one can determine. See the articles on these terms in the *Mittellateinisches Wörterbuch*. Cf. Martianus's use of *variatio sermonum* with respect to the circumflex accent, as discussed in chapter 1 here, pp. 43–44.

56. "Duodecima, hoc est '-ri-,' circumvolvetur. . . . Quintadecima vero, videlicet 'Sanc-,' terna gratulabitur vocis percussione" (ed. Gushee, *CSM* 21, 119). My paraphrase is based on the translation by Ponte, "Aureliani Reomensis *Musica disciplina*," 2: 156–58. See Bielitz, *Musik und Grammatik*, 116.

57. See pp. 40–46 above. See also McKitterick's review of Levy, *Carolingian Chant and the Carolingians*, 289.

58. See pp. 41–43 above. As noted there, both Cassiodorus and Isidore use variants of these phrases in their definitions of the *toni* in their respective treatments of music.

59. Ed. Gushee, *CSM* 21, 122; transl. from Ponte, "Aureliani Reomensis *Musica disciplina*," 2: 166.

60. Ed. Gushee, *CSM* 21, 122 (emphasis added).

EXAMPLE 3.5.   *Gloria patri* for Protus authentic in the *Graduale Romanum,* and as described in Aurelian of Réôme, *Musica disciplina,* chap. 19 (*CSM* 21, 119)

En figura melodie, sicut subiectum notarum demonstrat formula:

NONAN   NOEANE.

Hisdem denique tonus in incoatione versuum antiphonarum ac introituum secundum speculationis auditum et inspectionem notarum pervidetur quantulamcumque habere connexionem

Igitur in reciprocatione introituum, si versus eiusdem XVI in se continuerit syllabas, ut est: 'Gloria patri et filio et spiritui sancto,' mediocriter prima initiabitur syllaba id est 'Glo-,' et secunda acuto enunciabitur accentu, videlicet '-ri-.' Ea tamen ratione, si dactilus fuerit vel quelibet correpta syllaba; sin autem producta fuerit, tunc circumflexione gaudebit.

Tercia vero, scilicet '-a,' suspensa tenebitur voce. Quarta post haec, hoc est: 'Pa-,' si producta fuerit, veluti haec eadem syllaba, quae positione producitur, in ea acutus accendetur vocis accentus.

Quinta autem, sexta ac septima, vicelicet he: '-tri et Fi-,' gravi tenebuntur tenore. Octava vero, hoc est '-li,' circumflectetur. Nona acuetur, id est '-o.'

Decima et undecima, scilicet he 'et Spi-' graviter pronunciabuntur, [ac] duodecima, hoc est '-ri-,' circumvolvetur. Tercia autem decima atque quarta decima, id est '-tu-' et '-i,' in imis deponentur.

Quintadecima vero, videlicet 'Sanc-,' terna gratulabitur vocis percussione. Sane sextadecima syllaba, scilicet '-to,' sive prima fuerit, secundave seu tertia divisio iuxta normam superius insitam eorum erit distributio divisionum; sin alias uberior fuerit versus, interpolatio ilico fiet modulationis iuxta congeriem litterarum, ut hic:

[*GR* Version:]

example 3.6, the syllable "-ra" of *libera me* in *De ore leonis* is indeed "shortened," concluding with a punctum on *D,* rather than with the pitches *D-E-D* of the parallel passage in *Erue a framea.* Had those three "avoided" pitches been present in *De ore leonis,* they could certainly have been represented graphically by the *nota* for a circumflex accent—just as Aurelian says.

A final example provides further confirmation of the link between prosodic accents and the musical gestures of the chants Aurelian uses as examples (ex. 3.7). Aurelian cites *In ecclesiis benedicite Deum* in order to illustrate an unusual feature of the Responsories of the Deuterus plagal. He says of it that "on the third syllable before the end of the verse, that same syllable, that is '-le-,' is wound around [*circumvolvitur*]

EXAMPLE 3.6.   Parallel passages from *Erue a framea* and *De ore leonis libera me*: St. Gall 390–91, 167 (*Pal. mus.* 2: 1); Lucca 601, fol. 171 (Pal. mus., 9), and Worcester 160, fol. 108 (*Pal. mus.,* 12); together with Aurelian's "avoided" version with circumflex accent (*CSM* 21, 121–22)

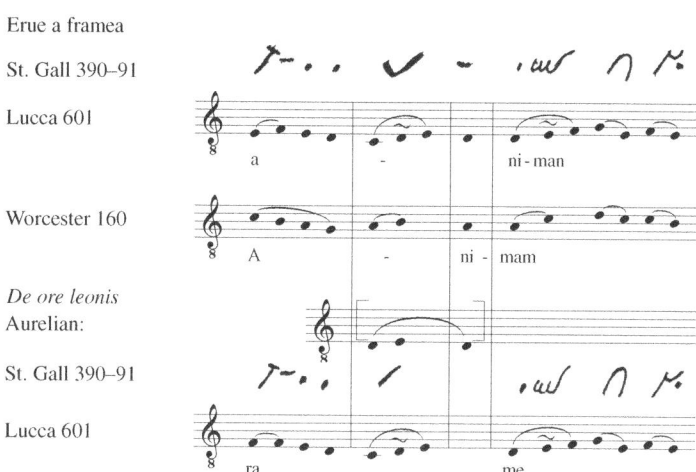

Erue a framea

St. Gall 390–91

Lucca 601

De ore leonis
Aurelian:

St. Gall 390–91

Lucca 601

at the third iteration in this way, with the figure of the notes: *alle—luia.*"[61] As one can see in the example, the syllable "-le-" is sung to a melisma of some twelve notes in modern transcription, set out in three "iterations" marked by melodic peaks on *a*. The third iteration is a three-note ascent and descent, *g-a-g,* represented by a torculus in all the manuscripts I have consulted. It is particularly unfortunate that no manuscript preserves Aurelian's notation for this passage. Had its *notae* been provided, the third iteration would almost certainly have been represented via the circumflex accent I have provided in the musical example.

As suggested, there has long been debate about the language of Aurelian's treatise. Should it be understood as referring to musical notation or not, and, if so, what might the nature of that notation have been?[62] Handschin felt that in his use of terms drawn from the discipline of grammar (*accentus acutus, circumflexio, circumvolutio,* etc.) Aurelian was, in fact, referring to neumatic notation, specifically that of the Paleofrankish script that has been entered ex post facto into Valenciennes 148.[63] Ernst Ludwig Waeltner, on the other hand, disagreed, saying "Contrary to the general assumption, these terms should not be viewed as names for neumes. Rather, the terms employed by Aurelian describe directly the movement of the voice in chant."[64] As I see it, the question itself is in a certain sense moot. The melodic ges-

61. "In tertia syllaba ante finem versus, eadem videlicet syllaba '-le-,' terna circumvolvitur iteratione hoc modo, cum notarum figura: alle luia" (ed. Gushee, *CSM* 21, 123).

62. See Corbin, *Die Neumen,* 3: 18; Treitler, "Reading and Singing: On the Genesis of Occidental Music-Writing," 152; and Levy, "Aurelian's Use of Neumes," 187–94.

63. Handschin, "Eine alte Neumenschrift," 69–71.

64. "Entgegen der allgemeinen Annahme sind diese Termini nicht als Namen für Neumen anzusehen. Die von Aurelian verwendeten Termini beschreiben vielmehr unmittelbar die Bewegung der

EXAMPLE 3.7.   "Alleluia" from *In ecclesiis benedicite Deum*: Worcester 160, fol. 143 (*Pal. mus.*, 12), Lucca 601, fol. 238 (Pal. mus., 9), and St. Gall 390–91, 251 (*Pal. mus.* 2: 1)

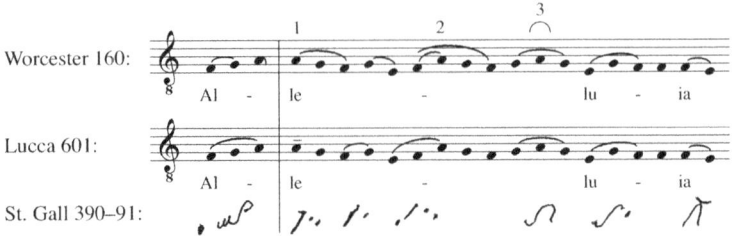

tures in the chants Aurelian cites and the terminology he uses to describe them are congruent with the inflections of the voice and their graphic representation under the system of prosodic accents. Given that the *notae* for the accents cannot be separated from their character as vocal inflections in Classical sources, it can hardly be argued that they should be so separated here.[65]

EXCURSUS: AURELIAN AND THE
PALEOFRANKISH SCRIPT

The argument set forth in the preceding paragraphs leads logically to another question: was there any kind of musical notation in broader use in the ninth century that corresponded to the prosodic accents Aurelian discusses? As the reader will have deduced from the discussion above, the answer to this question must be affirmative. Jacques Handschin began his article "Eine alte Neumenschrift" with a detailed examination of the terminology Aurelian uses and a consideration of the varying opinions about it held by scholars such as Peter Wagner and Ewald Jammers.[66] He determined, as I have here, that the *acutus accentus* mentioned by Aurelian corresponded to a two-note inflectional ascent, and the *circumflexio* or *circumvolutio* to a three-note ascent and descent.[67] In response to the implied question as to whether

Stimme im Gesang" (Waeltner, "Die 'Musica disciplina' des Aurelianus Reomensis," 294). See his "Die Methode terminologischer Untersuchung frühmittelaltlicher Musiktraktate," 50.

65. On this point, see Atkinson, "*De accentibus toni*," a part of which appears below. In that article, I take issue with the long-held "accent theory" of notation, which posited that the *acutus accentus* became the virga of neumatic notation, the *gravis* a punctum, and the *circumflex* a clivis. I attempt to demonstrate, rather, that there is actually a direct correspondence between the acute, grave, and circumflex accents of Classical prosody and the podatus, clivis, and torculus of the musical notation known as the Paleofrankish script. Given that correspondence, the appearance of five examples of the Paleofrankish script in the text of the *Musica disciplina* in Valenciennes 148 may be seen as particularly telling, but it is not, ipso facto, evidence that that notation is immanent to the treatise itself. (For a readily accessible statement of the "accent theory," see that by Peter Bohn as quoted in Treitler, "Reading and Singing: On the Genesis of Occidental Music-Writing," 181; and in my "*De accentibus toni*," 29.)

66. Cf. Wagner, *Einführung in die gregorianischen Melodien*, vol. 2, *Neumenkunde*, 104–8; and Jammers, *Der gregorianische Rhythmus*, 53, 168.

67. Aurelian does not use the term "gravis" at all in chap. 19; the one occurrence of the term that

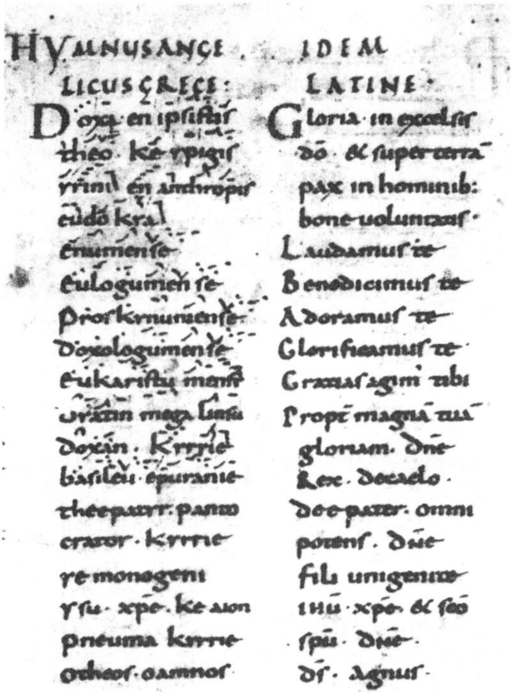

FIGURE 3.2. *Doxa in ipsistis theo* in Paris 2291, fol. 16 (reproduced with the permission of the Bibliothèque nationale de France)

Aurelian's descriptions had any relationship to neumatic notation, Handschin said "we certainly do not need to speak of such a type of neumatic notation in the abstract, because it is documented with examples."[68] The examples he cited were those from the later entries into Valenciennes 148 and, perhaps most important, the notation that appears in the setting of the *Doxa in ipsistis theo* in Paris 2291, which dates from 875 or 876.[69] It appears in figure 3.2. The neumatic script in question is

might refer to a *nota* is in chap. 4. With reference to the antiphon *Exclamaverunt ad te Domine,* he says that the syllable "Ex-" has a *gravis accentus.* As given in the *Graduale Romanum,* the Introit *Exclamaverunt ad te Domine* begins with a single note on F for "Ex-," followed by the pitches C and D for the syllables "clama." One cannot but suspect, however, that the version Aurelian was familiar with had a two-note descent on the first syllable.

68. "Indessen brauchen wir von einer solchen Art Neumenschrift durchaus nicht nur in abstracto zu sprechen, denn sie ist durch Beispiele belegt" (Handschin, "Eine alte Neumenschrift," 71).

69. Deshusses, "Encore les sacramentaires de Saint-Amand," 310–12. This is a postscript to his article "Chronologie des grands sacramentaires de Saint-Amand." In it, he is concerned with the three latest of the St. Amand sacramentaries: Reims 213, Paris 2291, and Stockholm 136. Deshusses had originally proposed a date of "vers 871" for Paris 2291. In his "postscript," he sets the date of that manuscript at between Christmas of 875 and October of 877 (most likely between 875 and 876), and he dates Stockholm 136 between 876 and 877. The basis for Deshusses's revised chronology is that the word "rex" has been crossed out and the word "imperator" substituted for it in both of these manuscripts. Charles the Bald was crowned emperor on Christmas Day, 875, and he died in October, 877. Further on the St. Amand sacramentaries and the Greek pieces they contain, see Atkinson, "Zur Entstehung und Überlieferung der 'Missa graeca,'" 141–43; "O amnos tu theu," 27–28; "The Doxa, the Pisteuo, and the *ellinici fratres,*" 93–94; and "Further Thoughts on the Origin of the *Missa graeca,*" 83–88, and figs. 1–15.

one of the oldest types of practical musical notation, the so-called Paleofrankish script.[70]

By comparing this setting of the *Doxa* with that in thirteen other manuscripts, Handschin was able to establish a close connection between the Paleofrankish neumes in Paris 2291 and what he believed were the "neumes" Aurelian described with designations such as *acutus accentus* and *circumflexio* or *circumvolutio*.[71] Handschin found that the oblique upward stroke answering the grammarians' descriptions of an acute accent stands for an ascending two-note melodic gesture. (Examples of it may be seen in fig. 3.2: in l. 2 over the "-e-" in *theo;* in l. 3 over the "y-" in *yrini;* and over the "-o-" in *anthropis.* It may also be seen in ll. 5–9 over the syllable "-men" in the phrase *enumen se, eulogumen se, proskynumen se, doxologumen se eukaristumen sy.*) The oblique downward stroke corresponding to the grammarians' description of the grave accent represents a descending two-note gesture. (For examples, see fig. 3.2 at the beginning of l. 2 and over the syllable "-men" in ll. 5–9.) Finally, in figure 3.2, lines 10 and 11, the note that looks like a letter *C* facing downward—a downward sigma as Martianus Capella would have described it—corresponds to a torculus, consisting of a three-note ascent and descent.[72]

Handschin had discovered that the Paleofrankish script incorporated the signs for prosodic accents, but he then proceeded to deny that these signs had anything to do with the accents! There were two reasons for this. First, his understanding of the relationship between accents and neumes was based on what I have called the "accent theory" of musical notation, and not on a reading of the ancient grammatical treatises themselves or their Carolingian commentaries.[73] The fact that the acute, grave, and circumflex signs in the notation in Paris 2291 did not correspond to virga, punctum, and clivis as postulated by the "accent theory" of notation, which had long since attained the status of accepted wisdom by the musicological community, led Handschin to conclude that those signs could not have been derived from prosodic accents. (At one point, he does ask whether the grammarians might not have understood the acute accent as an ascent, rather than a high tone, but he carries this no further.)[74] The second kind of evidence against any putative role for accents in the Paleofrankish script came from a different characteristic of this script itself—namely, its heighting.

As can be seen in example 3.8, in which the neumatic settings of the *Doxa* in

70. I use the term "practical" to imply a kind of notation that was used primarily for recording graphically the melodic gestures of a performed musical repertoire—in this case plainchant—and that could be employed as a guide to performance, whether actually used during the course of performance or not. Conversely, I would rely on the terms "theoretical" or "pedagogical" to refer to a type of notation employed primarily to demonstrate or teach theoretical precepts. Obviously, there can be some overlap between these two categories.

71. Handschin, "Eine alte Neumenschrift," 69–73, 78–79.

72. Handschin, "Eine alte Neumenschrift," 72–78.

73. Atkinson, "*De accentibus toni*," 29–42.

74. Handschin, "Eine alte Neumenschrift," 79. In his words: "Man könnte übrigens fragen, ob nicht schon die Grammatiker beim 'Acutus' manchmal an Aufstieg statt an Hochton gedacht haben." On the next page, he raises further doubts about the "accent theory" when he says "Man mag immerhin den letzteren Typus weiterhin als 'Akzent-neumen' bezeichnen (dies unter der *nicht ganz zutreffenden Voraussetzung, dass der Acutus immer nur den Hochton und nicht die steigende Folge bezeichnet hat*")—emphasis added.

EXAMPLE 3.8.   *Doxa in ipsistis theo* in Paris 2291, fol. 16 (A), and in Paris 1118, fols. 67v–68v (B)

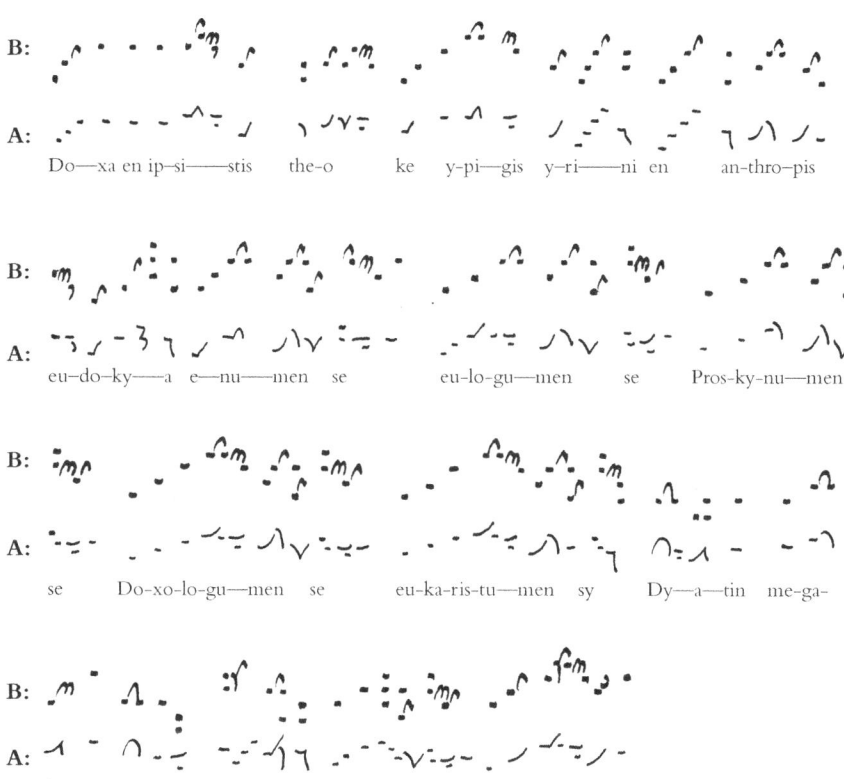

Paris 2291 and Paris 1118 are compared, the neumes in Paris 2291 are rather carefully heighted so as to convey the fundamental shape of the melody. Handschin went so far as to say that the Paleofrankish script had "diastematic character."[75] It is not diastematic—it does not indicate all intervals, including half and whole steps, unequivocally—but the script is certainly a good example of what Leo Treitler has called "iconic" notation.[76] In any event, the relatively good heighting of the neumes in Paris 2291 led Handschin to the following conclusion: "The principle of this neumatic script is clear. The higher or lower position on the parchment corresponds to pitch-level; insofar as a rising or falling line is used, it serves to link such positions, but it is not itself a notational character. Therefore no *virga = accentus acutus* in the sense of the grammarians."[77]

75. Handschin, "Eine alte Neumenschrift," 74.

76. See Treitler, "Reading and Singing: On the Genesis of Occidental Music-Writing"; and his earlier article "The Early History of Music Writing in the West," where this concept was presented for the first time.

77. Handschin, "Eine alte Neumenschrift," 78–79: "Das Prinzip dieser Neumenschrift ist klar: dem

Unfortunately, Handschin had apparently not studied many other examples of the Paleofrankish script.[78] Had he been able to do so, he would have realized that most of them are not as carefully heighted as is the *Doxa* in Paris 2291.[79] One such example is figure 3.3. This is the setting of the Introit *Ad te levavi* as it appears in the sacramentary Düsseldorf D. 1. The sacramentary itself dates from the ninth century; the Paleofrankish neumes were probably entered in the tenth century.[80] I have provided a synoptic, diplomatic transcription of *Ad te levavi* from several early manuscripts in example 3.9.

A comparison of figure 3.3 and example 3.9 quickly reveals that the script in Düsseldorf D. 1 cannot be described as being "carefully heighted." If it were, the ascent on "le-" of *levavi* would be larger than that on "an-" of *animam,* to cite only one example. Heightedness, not to mention diastematy, is clearly not the persistent, commanding feature of this notation. If one compares the various scripts in example 3.9 from the perspective of accent, however, a different picture emerges. Wherever the Paleofrankish setting has an oblique upward stroke—the sign for an acute accent—the other manuscripts have a podatus (e.g., over the syllables "le-" of *levavi,* and "an-" and "-mam" of *animam*). Whenever it has a descending oblique stroke—the sign for a grave accent—the other sources have a clivis (e.g., over the syllables "me-" in *meus,* "e-" in *erubescam,* "-de-" of *irrideant,* and "me-" in *mei*). Wherever it has a downward *C* or sigma—the circumflex—the other manuscripts have a torculus (e.g., over the syllables "-que" of *neque,* "-ri-" of *irrideant,* "ex-" and "-tant" of *expectant*).

The significance of the "accent" signs in Düsseldorf D. 1 is thus precisely the same as it was in Paris 2291—they represent two-note ascending and descending gestures and the three-note ascent/descent, respectively. They do not represent the virga, punctum, and clivis postulated by the accent theory—and they do not serve as links between positions on a diastematic matrix as Handschin supposed. Instead, they are employed in both manuscripts in a fashion completely consistent with the descriptions of the prosodic accents in ancient grammatical treatises and in their

---

Tonhöhen-Grad entspricht der höhere oder tiefere Ort auf dem Pergament; sofern die (aufsteigende oder absteigende) Linie verwendet wird, dient sie dazu, solche Orte zu verbinden, sie ist aber nicht an sich ein Tonzeichen. Also keine Virga = accentus acutus im Sinne der Grammatiker." This sentence is quoted by Walter (*Grundlagen der Musik des Mittelalters,* 26), who classifies the Paleofrankish script as a "demonstration notation."

78. Handschin also discusses in detail the examples of the Paleofrankish script entered into Aurelian's *Musica disciplina* in Valenciennes 148, as well as the isolated examples of the script in Valenciennes 107, 294, 337, and 399. For a listing of the sources for the Paleofrankish script, see Hourlier and Huglo, "Notation paléofranque," 216. Of these, Handschin had apparently not consulted Boulogne-sur-Mer 666; Douai 6 and 246; Düsseldorf D. 1, D. 2, and D. 3; Leiden 28; and Paris 1618, 2717, 7972, 15614, 17305, and 17306.

79. On this matter, see Corbin, *Die Neumen,* 3: 77; Arlt, "Anschaulichkeit und analytischer Charakter," 36–41; and Saulnier, "La Mise par écrit par repertoire romano-franc." Saulnier suggests the isolation of two Paleofrankish scripts, the second of which (as shown here) is similar in its features to other early scripts notated *in campo aperto.*

80. On this setting, see Stäblein, *Schriftbild der einstimmigen Musik,* 106–7; Jammers, *Die Essener Neumenhandschriften,* 25–27 and plts. 5–7; Jammers, "Die Paläofränkische Neumenschrift" ["The Paleofrankish Notation"] and Hourlier and Huglo, "Notation paléofranque," 216.

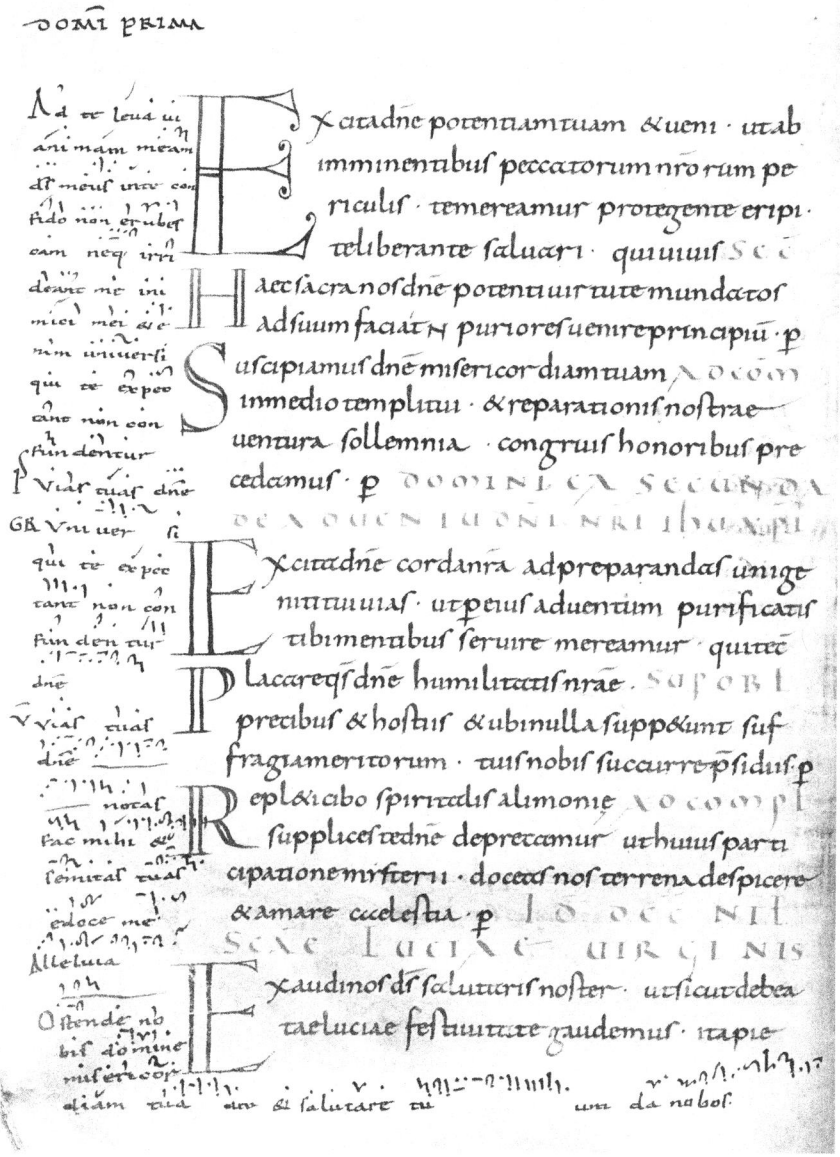

FIGURE 3.3.   *Ad te levavi* in Paleofrankish script from Düsseldorf D 1, fol. 126v
(reproduced with the permission of the Universitäts- und Landesbibliothek Düsseldorf)

Carolingian commentaries. What conclusions may be drawn from this as it pertains
to Aurelian? It follows from what has just been demonstrated that the melodic gestures referred to by the terms *acutus accentus* and *circumflexio* or *circumvolutio* in the
Musica disciplina and represented by the graphic signs of the Paleofrankish script in
manuscripts such as Paris 2291 and Düsseldorf D. 1 are one and the same.

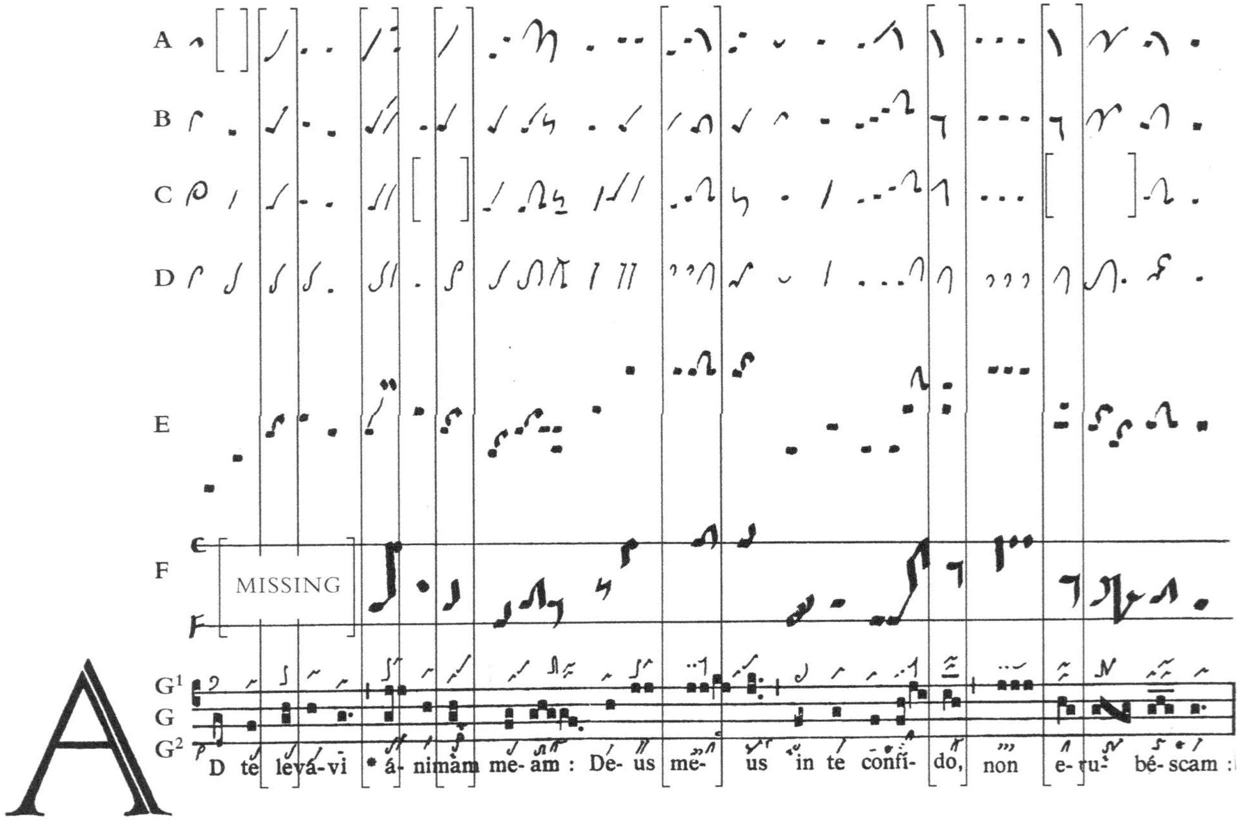

A

B

C

D

E

F MISSING

G¹

G

G²

D te levá-vi • á-nimam me-am : De- us me- us in te confi- do, non e- ru- bé-scam :

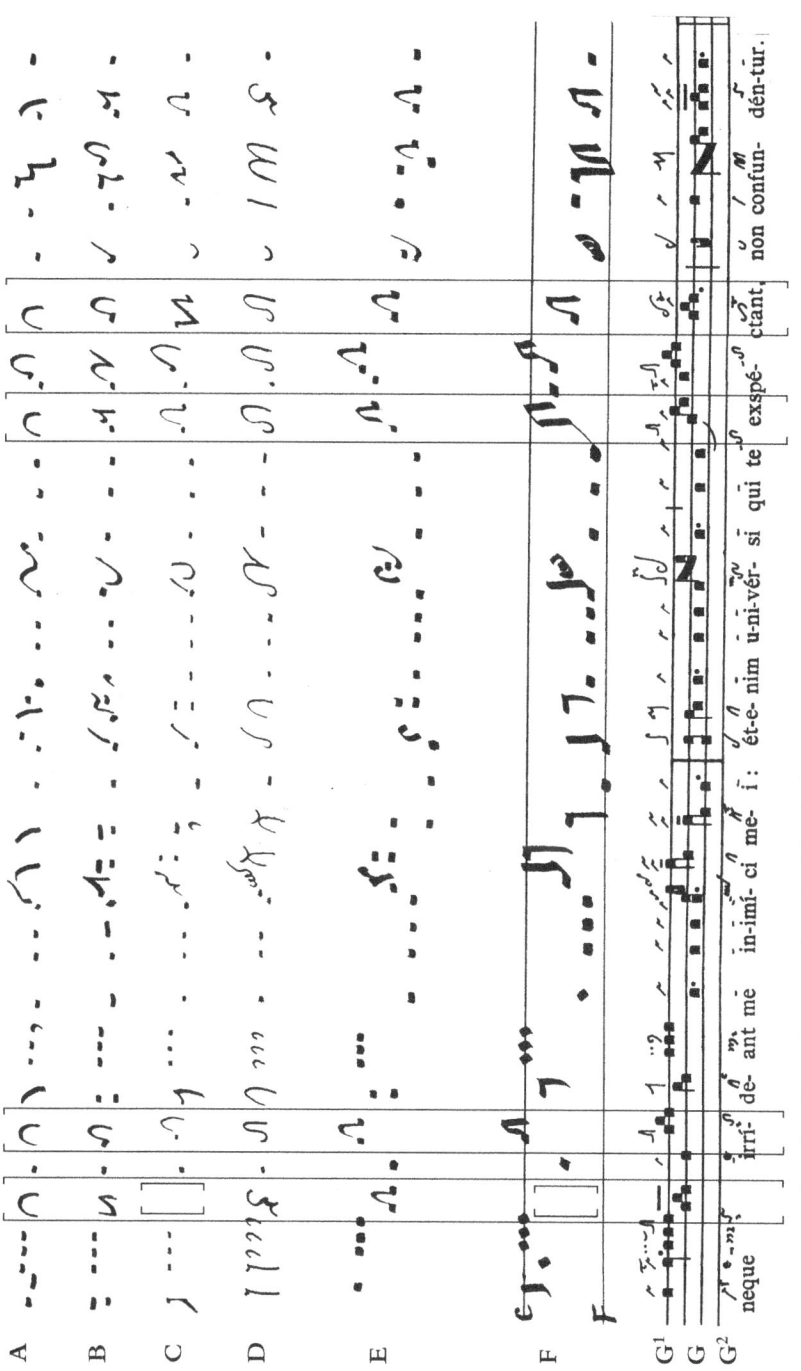

EXAMPLE 3.9. *Ad te levavi* in various notations: A. Paleofrankish (Düsseldorf D 1); B. Bretonic (Angers 91); C. French (Chartres 47); D. St. Gall (St. Gall 339); E. Aquitanian (Paris 903); F. Beneventan (Benevento 34); F. Beneventan (Benevento 34)—and as it appears in the *Graduale triplex*: G¹ (Laon 239); and G² (St. Gall 376)

As the foregoing discussion should have made clear, the treatment of "tone-system, *tonus,* and notation" in Aurelian is so far removed from the treatment of these topics by Boethius, Martianus, and other writers in late Antiquity that a comparison seems almost out of place. Aurelian's work is a practical manual for singing the music of the church.[81] Entirely absent in Aurelian are such staples of the approach of the writers of late Antiquity as the instrumental nomenclature of ancient Greek harmonic theory, the elegant proofs that a tone cannot be divided into two equal parts, the tone-systems consisting of discrete, mathematically defined points on a pitch continuum, the various species of consonance, and the earlier notions of "*tonus, tropus* vel *modus.*"[82] Neither *modus* nor *tropus* is equated with *tonus* in the body of Aurelian's treatise. For him, the concept of *tonus* is closely bound up with melodic formulas, either in the classification of antiphons for the purpose of joining them properly with their verses or in the demonstration of the *toni* by way of intonation formulae. He provides a rich discussion of actual, performed music, with descriptions of chant that are quite striking in their detail and specificity, even though they refer to gestures, rather than to individual pitches. The repertoire he is discussing was clearly fixed in the minds of the singers, if not already preserved in some sort of practical notation.[83] Finally, the notation Aurelian does discuss is described in terms drawn from grammar, with specific use of the nomenclature for prosodic accents, cued to individual syllables of text. Indeed, his language, terminology, and various aspects of his approach point to the discipline of grammar, rather than to that of harmonics, as the true conceptual background for the *Musica disciplina.*

One cannot identify a direct source for the approach to the various topics found in Aurelian, but there is a parallel tradition in the Eastern branch of the Christian church that may shed some light on his work, namely, that of the Greek παπαδική (*papadikē;* pl. *−ai*).[84] The *papadikai* were, like Aurelian's *Musica disciplina,* singers' manuals. They typically convey information about the notation of the chant and about the ἦχοι (*ēchoi*) (for an example, see ex. 3.10).

81. By saying this I do not mean to imply that Aurelian's treatise was written for beginners, an "eigentliches Lehrbuch, das die Kenntnis des Choralgesanges vermitteln will," as Pietsch puts it (*Die Klassifikation der Musik von Boethius bis Ugolino von Orvieto,* 5–6). As Gushee points out ("Questions of Genre in Medieval Treatises on Music," 390), the one thing essential for the readers of Aurelian's work was "prior knowledge of the large repertory of plain-chant and the techniques of psalmody," a knowledge that would be possessed only by singers beyond the elementary stages of training.

82. As Gushee suggests: "Apart from the few insignificant references to intervals in chapters I–VII, there is no attention whatever paid to consideration of a gamut, its derivation from numerical proportions, the monochord as paradigm of the tonal system, the pitch relationships between finals, octave-species and the *toni,* and so forth " ("Questions of Genre in Medieval Treatises on Music," 389).

83. On this question, see Treitler, "Reading and Singing: On the Genesis of Occidental Music-Writing," 151–52; and Levy, "Aurelian's Use of Neumes," esp. 192–94.

84. The *papadikai* generally make up a small, didactic introduction to a book of chants (παπαδικὸν βίβλιον: *papadikon biblion*) for the priest (πάπας: *papas*); hence they are called *papadikē technē* (παπαδικὴ τέχνη). On the *papadikē,* see the articles with that title by Schlötterer, Raasted, and di Salvo, and the discussion in Hannick, "Die Lehrschriften zur byzantinischen Kirchenmusik," 202–7. For a listing of the *papadikai* available in modern editions, see Raasted, "Papadiké"; and Haas, *Byzantinische und slavische Notationen,* 5–6. As Raasted points out, the manuscript tradition for the *papadikē* begins rather late, in the

EXAMPLE 3.10.   Excerpt from the *papadikē* in Rome 300 (reprinted from Tardo, *L'antica melurgia bizantina*, 160)

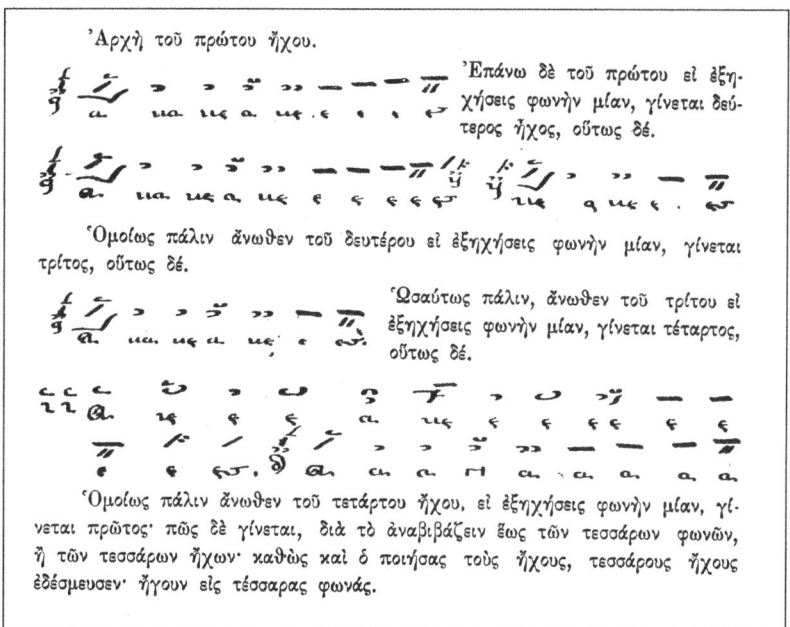

This is part of the description of the *ēchoi* from a *papadikē* in Rome 300.[85] The section just before this one discusses the notation signs (τόνοι [*tonoi*] and πνεύματα [*pneumata*]) and goes on to suggest that it will proceed to show how they function when distributed in the ὀκτὼ ἤχοι (*oktō ēchoi*):

> Those understanding clearly the art of the psaltist know the "power" or "energy" [ἐν-εργίαν] of these, yet we will accordingly demonstrate only a little bit their respective properties—how the *tonoi* with their *pneumata* ought to function in their ebb and flow, just as the teacher clearly taught them.
>
> Beginning of the *protus ēchos* [πρῶτος ἦχος]:

A   να   νε   α   νε   ε   ε   ε   ες

fourteenth and fifteenth centuries. Raasted himself indicates, however, that a number of elements found in these sources are documented much earlier in ninth-century treatises such as the *Musica disciplina* of Aurelian and the *Commemoratio brevis* (Raasted, *Intonation Formulas and Modal Signatures*, 153–61). I am most grateful to Professor Raasted (d. 1995) for his many helpful comments and suggestions on the sections of this essay that treat Byzantine chant and theory.

85. From Tardo, *L'antica melurgia bizantina*, 160–61. The manuscript dates from the fifteenth century. The section dealing with the *ēchoi*—the one reproduced here—is not a fixed part of all the *papadikai* (see Hannick, "Die Lehrschriften zur byzantinischen Kirchenmusik," 202).

If you will sing one sound [φωνή]⁸⁶ above the *protus*, it becomes the *deuterus ēchos*, thus:

A να νε α νε   ε   ε   ε   ες   Νε α   νε   ε   ες

In like manner, if you again sing one sound above the *deuterus*, it becomes the *tritus*, thus:

Νε α νε   ε   ες   Α νε   ε   ε   α νε ε   ε   ε   ε   ε   ε   ες

In like manner again, if you sing one sound above the *tritus*, it becomes the *tetartus*, thus:

A   α   α γι α   α   α   α   α   α να νε α νε   ε   ε   ε   ες

In like manner again, if you sing one sound above the *tetartos ēchos*, it becomes the protus; this comes about by going up through four sounds or four *ēchoi*, just as creating the *ēchoi* drew together four *ēchoi* into four sounds.⁸⁷

Following this is a similar treatment of the plagal *ēchoi* (πλάγιοι ἦχοι [*plagioi ēchoi*]).⁸⁸ Of particular interest here is the virtual equation of ἦχος (*ēchos*) and φωνή (*sound*), which is typical of many of the *papadikai*.⁸⁹ (It should also be pointed out that one of the meanings of the term *ēchos* itself is "sound" or even "tone.")⁹⁰

Echos in these manuals is used to convey a twofold meaning: (1) In conjunction with the intonation formulas (*ēchēmata*), the *ēchoi* have "tonal" significance. Indeed, the *ēchēmata* that demonstrate the *ēchoi* could, in this case, almost be taken to be

86. I have chosen to translate φωνή (*phonē*) quite literally here as "sound," although "step" might be closer to the intended meaning. See Strunk's statement: "As set forth by the author or authors of our principal literary source, the Papadikē, the theoretical starting-tones of the four authentic modes form an ascending series, the theoretical starting-tone of Mode II lying one step above that of Mode I, the theoretical starting-tone of Mode III lying one step above that of Mode II, the theoretical starting-tone of Mode IV lying one step above that of Mode III" (Strunk, "The Tonal System of Byzantine Music," 4). On the further significance of "sound" in relation to "tone," see the discussion of the passages from the *Musica enchiriadis* associated with notes 100–103 here.

87. Tardo, *L'antica melurgia bizantina*, 160–61.

88. Each of the plagal *ēchoi* lies four steps or sounds (φωναί; *phonaí*) lower than the principal *ēchos* of the same ordinal position. The author begins the exposition of the plagal *ēchoi* as follows: "From the *protos ēchos* go down four steps and you will discover its plagal. In like fashion for the *deuteros*, go down four steps and you will find its plagal, [etc.]." Each of the plagal *ēchoi* likewise has its own intonation formula.

89. On this, see Schlötterer, "Die kirchenmusikalische Terminologie der griechischen Kirchenväter," 42–43, 46–47.

90. Indeed, *tonus* is given as the Latin equivalent for *ēchos* by Du Cange in his *Glossarium ad Scriptores mediae & infimae Graecitatis* of 1688, 1: col. 481. Citing Moschopulos's *Lexicon Philostrati*, Du Cange defines *ēchos* as follows: "ἦχος In cantu Ecclesiastico, idem est quod *Tonus* in Latino." In col. 482, he defines ὀκτώηχος as "Octo tonus." See Schlötterer, "Die kirchenmusikalische Terminologie der griechischen Kirchenväter," 42–43.

identical with them.[91] (2) The *ēchoi* are also treated as individual pitches that are located above or below each other in acoustic space and that can be "drawn together" to form a tetrachord. Most of the *papadikai* do not specify the intervallic content of this tetrachord, but Gombosi, Strunk, and others have shown that this fundamental Byzantine tetrachord would have had the structure tone-semitone-tone.[92] Although a concatenation of such tetrachords would form a tone-system, the *papadikai* usually discuss the character of the four principal *ēchoi* and their plagals and suggest that these four may be replicated infinitely up or down.[93] (The presentation of this idea sometimes takes the graphic form of a wheel.)[94]

Thus, the four primary pitches (protus, deuterus, tritus, tetartus) and the character they impart to the melodies built on them become the primary tonal determinant for the *ēchoi*. As a means of categorizing chant, the system of *ēchoi* presented in the *papadikai* was simple and at the same time, through the use of the modulatory signs called φθοραί (*phthorai*, "corruptions"), quite flexible.[95] The very fact that the earliest manuscripts of the *papadikai* date from relatively late (fourteenth and fifteenth centuries) suggests the durability of the theory they contain.[96]

The close kinship between Aurelian's *Musica disciplina* and certain features of the Byzantine *papadikai* should already be apparent. Both are practical manuals for singers. Both teach a system of chant classification whose categories share the same nomenclature and are demonstrated in the same way—by melodic formulas. From what we know about the function of the intonation formulas in the Byzantine

---

91. See the discussion of this in Raasted, *Intonation Formulas and Modal Signatures,* 42–43; and Schlötterer, "Die kirchenmusikalische Terminologie der griechischen Kirchenväter," 42–47. Raasted makes the trenchant observation "it might even be that it is we who, in distinguishing between 'mode' and 'intonation,' violate the Byzantine way of thinking" (43).

92. See Gombosi, "Studien zur Tonartenlehre des frühen Mittelalters," 128–31; and Strunk, "The Tonal System of Byzantine Music," *MQ,* 199–201, and in *Essays on Music in the Byzantine World,* 7–9.

93. The author of the *papadikē* in the Codex Chrysander says: "So it is, even if you descend a hundred steps or again if you ascend as many more" (Fleischer, *Die spätgriechische Tonschrift,* 38).

94. For an example, see Tardo, *L'antica melurgia bizantina,* 259. Tardo offers the "wheel of Koukouzeles," which attempts to relate the ancient Greek *tonoi* to the Byzantine *ēchoi*. A similar example may be found in Raasted, *Intonation Formulas and Modal Signatures,* 51–53.

95. On the *phthorai,* see Fleischer, *Die spätgriechische Tonschrift,* 20; Tillyard, *Handbook of Middle Byzantine Musical Notation,* 36; Wellesz, *A History of Byzantine Music,* 309–10; Raasted, *Intonation Formulas and Modal Signatures,* 44–46; Floros, *Universale Neumenkunde,* 1: 282–300; Haas, *Byzantinische und slavische Notationen,* 39, 51, 83–84; Wolfram, "Fragen der Modulation in der byzantinischen Musik"; and Wolfram, "Die *Phthorai* der Paläobyzantinischen Notationen." The group of eight *ēchoi,* as presented in Rome 300 and elsewhere, is often referred to as the *oktoechos.* From the extensive literature on this topic, see, in particular, Wolfram, "Oktoechos"; Gombosi, "Studien zur Tonartenlehre des frühen Mittelalters," 128–31; Strunk, "The Tonal System of Byzantine Music"; Petrović, "Byzantine and Slavonic Oktoechos until the Fifteenth Century"; Haas, *Byzantinische und slavische Notationen,* 40–56; and Haas, *Mündliche Überlieferung und altrömischer Choral,* 162–69.

96. The same theory of the *ēchoi*—although with their number expanded to ten—is also present in the *Hagiopolites,* by all accounts the earliest of the preserved treatises on Byzantine sacred music. Its primary manuscript, Paris 360, dates from the fourteenth century. See Raasted, ed., "The *Hagiopolites*"; and Hannick, "Die Lehrschriften zur byzantinischen Kirchenmusik," 200–201. Haas (*Mündliche Überlieferung und altrömischer Choral,* 162–69) points out that one should be extremely cautious in "backdating" the system of the Byzantine *oktoechos.* He feels that a full-fledged "system" as such did not yet exist in the ninth century, even though elements of it, according to Western testimony, certainly did.

church, mastery of the *ēchoi* was probably as important for effecting smooth transitions between the recitation of a psalm verse and the following sticheron, hirmos, or troparion as the mastery of the *toni* was important for effecting smooth transitions between the ends of psalm verses and the beginnings of antiphons in the West.[97] As will become apparent, there are yet more parallels between the *papadikai* and the theory found in another important mid- to late ninth-century treatise in the West, the *Musica enchiriadis*.[98]

Even the opening chapter of the *Musica enchiriadis* contains several "echoes" of both Aurelian and the *papadikai*—and of the ancient treatises on grammar as well (ex. 3.11a). Beginning with a paraphrased definition of *vox* from Calcidius's commentary on Plato's *Timaios* (ex. 3.11a, ll. 1–9), this opening chapter presents a tone-system that has as its basis four *phthongi* or "tones," which it calls *soni* (ex. 3.11a, ll. 3–4).[99] It likens these *phthongi* or *soni* to letters, the "elementary and individual elements of speech, from which are composed the syllables that further make up the verbs and nouns that compose the fabric of a complete discourse" (ex. 3.11a,

97. See Strunk, "Intonations and Signatures of the Byzantine Modes," in *Essays on Music in the Byzantine World,* 19–36.

98. Ed. Schmid, *Musica et Scolica enchiriadis*; the *Musica* and its companion treatise, the *Scolica enchiriadis,* are available in English translation in Erickson, *Musica enchiriadis and Scolica enchiriadis*. Scholars have long disagreed on the dating of these two treatises and their relationship to each other. The most recent essays on the question are Torkewitz, "Zur Entstehung der *Musica* und *Scolica enchiriadis*"; and Walter, "Vom Beginn der Musiktheorie und dem Ende der Musik." Both authors focus on the ninth-century fragment of the *Scolica* from Werden, Düsseldorf H. 3, earlier reported on by Hans Schmid in "Die Kölner Handschriften der *Musica enchiriadis*." A new edition of the fragment by Torkewitz has recently appeared (*Das älteste Dokument zur Entstehung der abendländischen Mehrstimmigkeit*). There is a vast literature on the *Musica* and *Scolica enchiriadis,* of which I can cite only a few of the relevant works here. Possible connections of the treatises with Byzantine music and music theory are discussed in Gombosi, "Studien zur Tonartenlehre des frühen Mittelalters–II," 128–31; 22–25; and Richter, "Antike Überlieferungen in der byzantinischen Musiktheorie," 78–79 (rev. and updated in *ActaM,* 194–98). For commentary on the works and their sources, see Phillips, "'Musica' and 'Scolica Enchiriadis': The Literary, Theoretical, and Musical Sources"; Phillips, "Musica enchiriadis"; Gushee, "Questions of Genre in Medieval Treatises on Music," 398–401; Erickson, "Eriugena, Boethius, and the Neoplatonism of *Musica* and *Scolica enchiriadis*"; and Hebborn, *Die Dasia-Notation*.

The treatises play an important role in Ferrari-Barassi, "I modi ecclesiastici," esp. 35–45; as they do in Powers, "Language Models and Musical Analysis." The place of the treatises in Carolingian education is discussed in Smits van Waesberghe, "Die besondere Stellung der *ars musica* im Zeitalter der Karolinger" (originally "La Place exceptionelle de l'Ars musica"); Haas, "Die *Musica enchiriadis* und ihr Umfeld"; and Viret, "Modalité et pédagogique au IXe siècle."

Petra Bockholdt discusses conceptual and terminological problems as they relate to the definition of *tonus* in the *Musica* in her "'Conditio–qualitas–proprietas.' Über die Bestimmung des Tons in der *Musica enchiriadis*." Most recently, Andreas Ostheimer has contributed articles concerning the place of the treatises in ninth-century musical thought ("Orpheus und die Entstehung einer Musiktheorie im 9. Jahrhundert") and the treatment of mode in the first eight chapters of the *Musica* ("Das Modusverständnis in der *Musica enchiriadis*"); Andreas Traub has devoted a separate study to the ninth chapter ("Zum neunten Kapitel der Musica enchiriadis").

99. *Phthongos* (φθόγγος) in Greek can be "any clear, distinct sound," but in treatises on harmonics it has the technical meaning of "musical sound" or even "pitched sound." See Martianus Capella, *De nuptiis Philologiae et Mercurii,* sec. 939: "phthongus dicitur uocis modulatae particula una intentione producta est autem intentio"—"*phthongus* is applied to a particle of modulated voice produced on a single *intentio* [lit. 'stretching,' i.e. of a string]".

EXAMPLE 3.11a.   Beginning of chap. 1 of *Musica enchiriadis* (ed. Schmid, 3–4)

INCIPIT LIBER ENCHIRIADIS DE MUSICA

Sicut vocis articulatae elementariae atque individuae partes sunt litterae, ex quibus compositae syllabae rursus componunt verba et nomina eaque perfectae orationis texture, sic canorae vocis ptongi, qui Latine dicuntur soni, origines sunt et totius musicae continentia in eorum ultimam resolutionem desinit. Ex sonorum
5 copulatione diastemata, porro ex diastematibus concrescunt systemata; soni vero prima sunt fundamenta cantus. Ptongi autem non quicumque dicuntur soni, sed qui legitimis ab invicem spaciis melo sunt apti. Eorum quidem sic et intendendo et remittendo naturaliter ordo continuatur, ut semper quattuor et quattuor eiusdem conditionis sese consequantur. At singuli horum quattuor sic sunt competenti inter
10 se diversitate dissimiles, ut non solum acumine differant et gravitate, sed in ipso acumine et gravitate propriam naturalitatis suae haben qualitatem, quam rursus his singulis ratum ab invicem acuminis et laxionis spacium format.

Exempli gratia hae in ordine ipsorum notae:

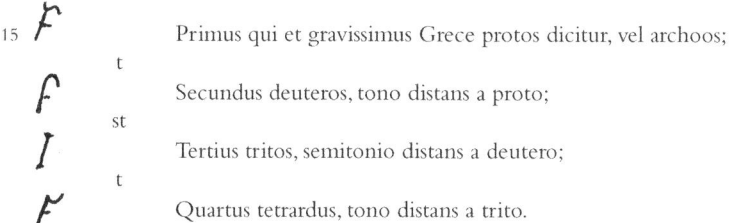

15   Primus qui et gravissimus Grece protos dicitur, vel archoos;

    Secundus deuteros, tono distans a proto;

    Tertius tritos, semitonio distans a deutero;

    Quartus tetrardus, tono distans a trito.
20

Horum continua multiplicatione sonorum infinitas texitur, et tamdiu quaternis quaterni eiusdem conditionis succedunt, donec vel ascendendo vel descendendo deficiant.

---

ll. 1–3).[100] Just as letters are the building blocks of speech, the *soni* are important because "they are first principles, and the content of all music resides in their ultimate resolution" (ex. 3.11a, ll. 4–5). Each of them has its own individual qualities (ex. 3.11a, ll. 9–12): "Each of these four is different via the diversity coincident among them, so that they differ not only in highness and lowness but also have by their natures their own specific quality, which the fixed interval of their height and

100. Cf. the chapters of Donatus's *Ars maior:* (1) *De voce;* (2) *De littera;* (3) *De syllaba;* (4) *De pedibus;* (5) *De tonis;* and (6) *De posituris.* (See chapter 1 here, pp. 40–42) Compare, in turn, the gloss in Paris 10275 (tenth century) on the beginning of Boethius, *De institutione musica* (Book I, chap. 3), which constructs the musical hierarchy *motus, pulsus, sonus, consonantia,* as follows: "Consonantia oratio, sonus pars, pulsus syllaba, motus littera. Quod haec faciunt, in musica haec faciunt, ista in gramatica" (Bernhard and Bower, eds., *Glossa maior in institutionem Boethii,* 1: 109, Gloss 6 on Book I, chap. 3). A later manuscript of Boethius's *Musica,* Paris 16201 (eleventh century), uses this material to gloss the opening of Book I, chap. 8, which treats *sonus:* 1. "*Sonus casus vocis* dicitur, i. exitus vel emissio vel processio de gravi in acutum, vel de acuta in gravem, vel talis vocis terminatio, que sit apta melo. [See the discussion at notes 54–55 in

depth relative to each other produces." The names of these four sounds, the Dasia notational symbols representing them,[101] and their "fixed intervals" in relation to each other are then given (ex. 3.11a, ll. 15–22):

> The first and lowest is called *protos* or *archoos* in Greek; the second, *deuteros,* standing a tone from the first; the third, *tritos,* standing a semitone from the second; the fourth, *tetrardos,* standing a tone from the third.[102] By continuous multiplication, an infinity of these sounds is woven, and they continue succeeding each other, four by four of the same structure, ascending and descending, until they stop.

The nomenclature here is, of course, the same as that in Aurelian and in the Byzantine *papadikai.* The latter's notion of linking together an "infinity" of tetrachords is likewise present here, indicated by simply repeating the four fundamental signs over and over again (ex. 3.11b, "Infinite system"). But out of the possible infinity, an array of eighteen sounds, divided into four tetrachords (*Graves, Finales, Superiores, Excellentes*) plus two additional sounds, has been chosen (see ex. 3.11b, "*Enchiriadis* system"). The four tetrachords are named functionally, according to their relative positions in acoustic space, rather than their position on an instrument: (1) the *Graves,* or "low" tetrachord; (2) the *Finales,* so called because "it is necessary that every melody be ended in one of them";[103] (3) the *Superiores,* or "higher" tetrachord; and (4) the *Excellentes,* "elevated," or "surpassing,"—plus two extra sounds. One can see this system in example 3.11b; it is transcribed in example 3.12.

---

chapter 1 here.] 2. Sonus est materia consonantiarum *a similitudine locutionis.* 3. Sicut in locutione gramatica considerantur littere, sillabe, dictiones et orationes, sic etiam in mus<*ica*> denotantur, 4. quia, quod vo<*ca*>mus literas in gramatica, vocamus simplices voces in musica, sillabas tonos, dictione<*s*> dyatessaron, orationes vero compositas consonantias vel simplicitatem cantus" (Bernhard and Bower, eds., *Glossa maior in institutionem Boethii,* 1: 164, Gloss 3 on Book I, chap. 8, emphasis added). The author of the *Musica enchiriadis* will carry the analogy between grammar and music further in chap. 9, where he says that *cola* and *commata* are the phrases into which chant is divided and which "make distinctions in chant at its ends" ("Particulae sunt sua cantionis cola vel commata, quae suis finibus cantum distingunt"; ed. Schmid, 22). See Atkinson, "Johannes Affligemensis as a Historian of Mode," 4–7; Bielitz, *Musik und Grammatik,* 56–60, 136–37; Treitler, "Reading and Singing: On the Genesis of Occidental Music-Writing," 146–47; Powers, "Language Models and Musical Analysis," 49–50; Caldwell, "From Cantor to Parchment: Linguistic Aspects of Early Western Notation," 219; and Bower, "The Grammatical Model of Musical Understanding in the Middle Ages," esp. 134–40.

101. On the Dasia notation, see Phillips, "'Musica' and 'Scolica enchiriadis': The Literary, Theoretical, and Musical Sources," 163–200; Phillips, "The Dasia Notation and its Manuscript Tradition"; Ferrari-Barassi, "I modi ecclesiastici," 38–41; Hebborn, *Die Dasia-Notation;* and Ostheimer, "Die Niederschrift von Musik mit Dasiazeichen." As mentioned in chapter 1 (p. 42) here, the Dasia sign that forms the basis for this notation is the *nota* for the *aspiratus* in Donatus's *Ars maior* and other treatises on grammar.

102. Note that the intervals *tonus* and *semitonus* are not given quantitative descriptions here. Neither receives any more specific definition until chap. 9 of the treatise, which forms the introduction to its second section, that treating *harmonia,* the symphonies, and organum. There, the interval of the tone is said to be in the sesquioctave proportion (9:8); the author says of the semitone that "it is not the full interval of a tone," and that it is called "limma" or "diesis." See Atkinson, "'Harmonia' and the 'Modi, quos abusive tonos dicimus,'" 492–94.

103. "Terminales sive finales dicuntur, quia in unum aliquem ex his quattuor melos omne finiri necesse est" (beginning of chap. 3, ed. Schmid, 7).

EXAMPLE 3.11b. The "Infinite"
and "*Enchiriadis*" systems from the
Musica enchiriadis (reprinted from
Schmid, ed., 5)

"Infinite"   "*Enchiriadis*"

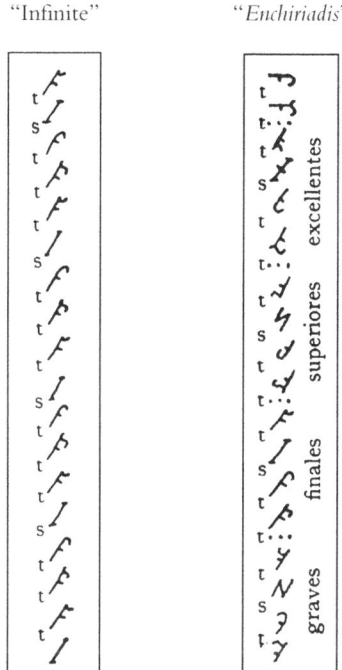

A comparison of the system just described with the ancient Greek tone-system
(see exs. 1.1 and 1.3, respectively) yields important information. It shows that the
system of the *enchiriadis* differs from its ancient Greek "counterpart" in a number of
ways.

- Although both systems are presented vertically, the pitch order of the two
  is inversely related. Whereas the pitches in Boethius's diagrams proceed
  from high to low, as one reads from bottom to top, those in the *Musica
  enchiriadis* proceed from low to high.
- The names of three of the tetrachords in the *Enchiriadis* system reflect
  their positions relative to each other in acoustic space, rather than their
  position on an instrument; the base tetrachord, that of the Finales, derives
  its name from its function in sung music.
- The pitches themselves—protus, deuterus, tritus, tetardus—are named
  with Greek ordinal numbers on the basis of ascending pitch.
- The same four *soni,* with their distinctive qualities, make up every tetrachord—an identity that is reinforced by the fact that the same four Dasia
  signs are used in each tetrachord, distinguished only by being rotated to a

EXAMPLE 3.12.   The *Enchiriadis* system, as presented in *Musica*
and *Scolica enchiriadis*

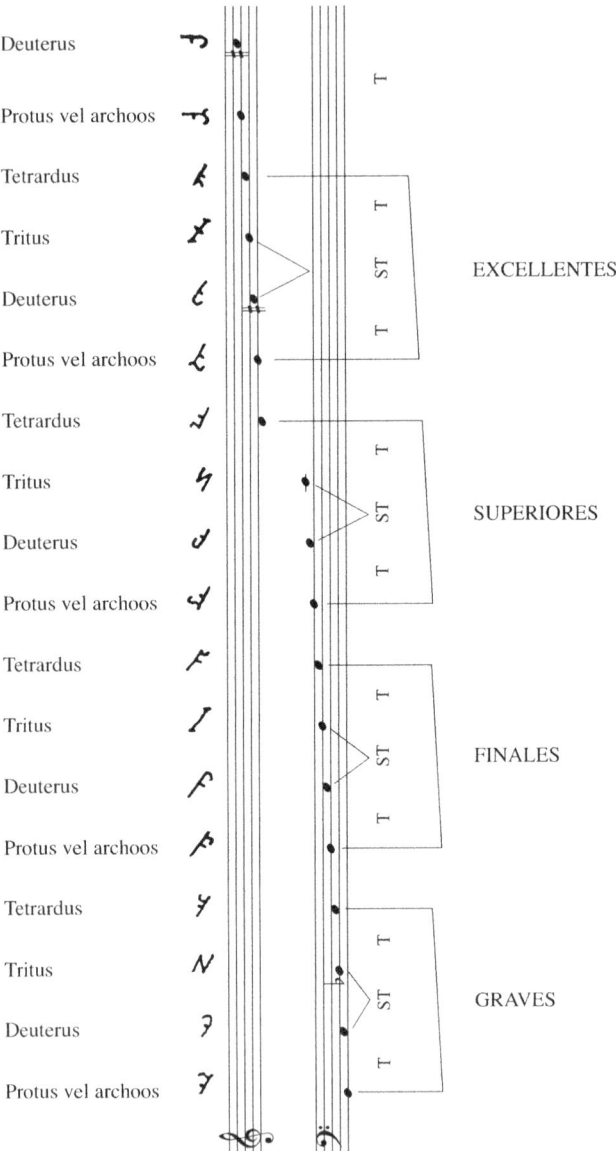

different position in each. Thus, the "system" is in essence a multiplication of a single tetrachord.

- The intervallic content of the tetrachords is T-ST-T, not the ST-T-T of the ancient Greek tetrachords in the diatonic genus.
- The system that results from the concatenation of these tetrachords has, in modern nomenclature, a low G, a low Bᵇ, and a high f♯ not in the Greater Perfect System.[104]
- Every fifth degree of the system is of the same name and quality (e.g., protus/Finales = protus/Superiores). Every eighth note has a different name and quality from the starting note (protus/Finales = tetrardus/Excellentes). In some cases, this results in augmented octaves (e.g., Bᵇ–b♮ between tritus/Graves and deuterus/Excellentes; F–f♯ between tritus/Finales and deuterus/Excellentes).[105]
- The four *soni* that make up each tetrachord have functional importance as finales, being given their distinctive qualities by their intervallic relationship to the semitone in the music immediately surrounding or ending in them. They are thus integral to the definition of the melodic categories called *toni* or *modi,* as the *Musica enchiriadis* itself makes clear.

In conjunction with the naming of the four sounds and their grouping into tetrachords, thereby creating the tone-system I have called the *Enchiriadis* system (exs 3.11b and 3.12), the author says: "The *virtus* ("strength," "character") of these four sounds determines the *potestas* ("energy," "power") of the eight modes, as will be discussed later in its place."[106] Chapter 3 of the *Musica enchiriadis,* which explains the naming of the Finales tetrachord, takes this one step further (ex. 3.13).

EXAMPLE 3.13.   Excerpt from Chapter 3 of the *Musica enchiriadis* (ed. Schmid, 7–8)

> Terminales sive finales dicuntur, quia in unum aliquem ex his quattuor melos omne finiri necesse est. Etenim primi toni melum et subiugalis sui sono 𝄪 archoo regitur et finitur. Secundus tonus cum subiugali suo sono 𝄪 deutero regitur et finitur. Tertius eiusque subiugalis sono 𝄍 trito regitur et finitur. Quartus cum suo subiugali sono 𝄎 tetrardo regitur et finitur. Vocatur autem autentus maior quilibet tonus, plagis minor.

104. As will become apparent below, the protus, deuterus, tritus, and tetrardus of the Finales tetrachord in the *Musica* and *Scolica enchiriadis* become *D, E, F,* and *G,* respectively, in the tone-system of Pseudo-Odo's *Dialogus* (*d, e, f,* and *g* in modern nomenclature). I use modern nomenclature here because the low Bᵇ and the f♯ in *Musica* and *Scolica enchiriadis* are not in Pseudo-Odo's tone-system.

105. These pitches are named in modern nomenclature.

106. "Horum etiam quattuor sonorum virtus octo modorum potestatem creat, ut postea suo loco dicetur" (ed. Schmid, 5). On the implications of this passage, see Atkinson, "'Harmonia' and the 'Modi, quos abusive tonos dicimus'"; and Atkinson, "On the Interpretation of '*Modi, quos abusive tonos dicimus.*'" The latter study appears within the context of a series of essays on medieval hermeneutics.

These [sounds] are called "terminals" or "finals" because it is necessary that all melody be completed in one of these four. Melody of the first *tonus* and its subordinate is governed and completed by the sound archoos F. The second *tonus* with its subordinate is governed and completed by the sound deuteros F. The third and its subordinate are governed and completed by the sound tritos I. The fourth with its subordinate is governed and completed by the sound tetrardos F. The greater *tonus* is called "autentus," the lesser "plagis."

After reemphasizing the importance of determining the *vis, virtus,* or *karacter* of every sound (chap. 6) and providing an exercise that will reinforce this (chap. 7), the author shows, in chapter 8, how all the *toni* are produced from the *vis* of the four *soni* (ex. 3.14):

EXAMPLE 3.14.   The beginning of Chapter 8 of the *Musica enchiriadis* (ed. Schmid, 13–14—diagram reprinted from Schmid)

QUOMODO EX IIII^{or} SONORUM VI OMNES TONI PRODUCANTUR

Demonstrandum nunc, quomodo haec quattuor ptongorum vis modos, quos abusive tonos dicimus, moderetur, et fiat dispositio talis: Sternantur in ordine veluti quaedam cordae e sonorum notis singulis e regione positis procedentes. Sint autem cordae vocum vice, quas eae significent notae. Inter quas chordas exprimatur neuma quaelibet, ut puta huiusmodi:

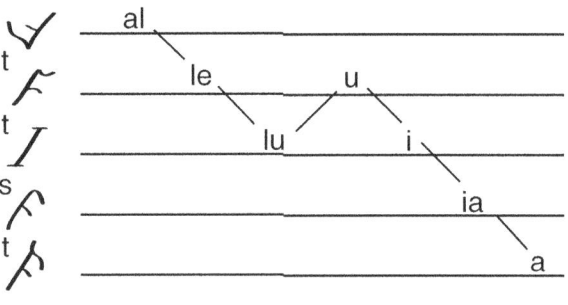

It must now be demonstrated how the *vis* of these four *phthongi* governs the modes, which we wrongly call tones. Let there be such a disposition: Let them [the *soni* or *phthongi*] be arrayed in order as if they were strings, proceeding in a straight line after the individual *notae* of the *soni* have been written. Let these strings be in the place of the sounds that these *notae* signify. Let some melody be copied among these.[107]

107. On the implications of the first sentence of this chapter, see the essays cited in the preceding note.

The author of the *enchiriadis* then has the same melody (*Alleluia*) copied four times, ending successively on the sounds protus, deuterus, tritus, tetrardus. The melodies thus differ from each other in their vertical, or "harmonic" dispositions of tones and semitones (see ex. 3.15):[108]

EXAMPLE 3.15.   The continuation of Chapter 8 of the *Musica enchiriadis* (ed. Schmid, 15–16—diagram reprinted from Schmid)

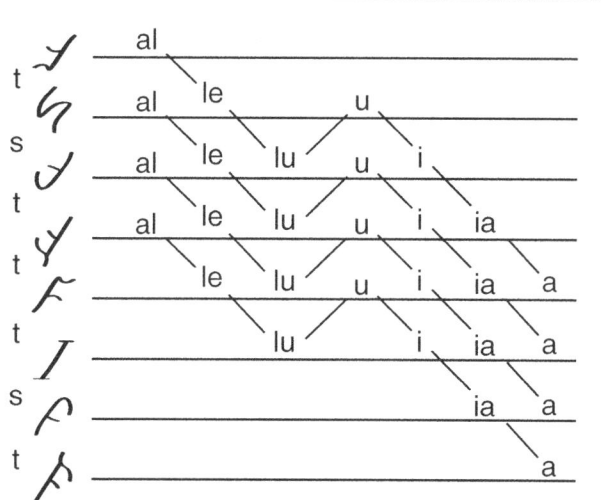

Hae quattuor descriptiunculae, dum solo ab invicem semitonio vel tono id est armonico spacio distant, eo solo a genere in genus singulae transponuntur. Primam dispositionem cum cecineris, poteris dinoscere, quia vis primi soni Ϝ primi toni virtutem creet, qui protus autentus dicitur. Secundam cum cecineris, senties tonum deuterum a sono Ϝ deutero gubernari. Tertiam assumens videbis similiter in sono Ι trito triti toni consistere potestatem. Quartam cum fueris modulatus, intelleges toni tetrardi genus a sono tetrardo Ϝ procedere.

While the four representations are each separated by a tone or a semitone, that is by a harmonic interval, they are singularly transposed from genus to genus. When you have sung the first disposition, you can recognize that the *vis* of the first sound Ϝ creates the *virtus* [character] of the first *tonus*, which is called protus autentus. When you have sung the second, you will perceive the deuterus *tonus* to be governed by the deuterus sound Ϝ. Likewise, considering the third, you will see that the *potestas* of the tritus *tonus* depends on the tritus sound Ι. When you have modulated the fourth, you will know that the genus of the tetrardus *tonus* proceeds from the tetrardus sound Ϝ.

108. A similar procedure for illustrating the relative position of tones and semitones within a given intervallic span is employed in the glosses of the tenth-century manuscript Paris 10275. Here the aim is

Clearly, the *vis, virtus,* or *potestas* of each of the four *soni* is conveyed by the position of the semitone in relation to that final sound as projected in each successive transposition of the melody.

Following this exposition of the "power" of each of the four *soni,* the *Musica enchiriadis* provides four melodies (*modulationes*) to demonstrate each of the primary modes: protus, deuterus, tritus, and tetrardus. The author concludes this chapter by underscoring the importance of these melodies for understanding the character of the *toni* or *modi* and by forging a direct link between them and the intonation formulas (NOANNOEANE, NOEAGIS, etc., ex. 3.16).

EXAMPLE 3.16.   The conclusion of Chapter 8 of the *Musica enchiriadis* (ed. Schmid, 19–20—diagram reprinted from Schmid)

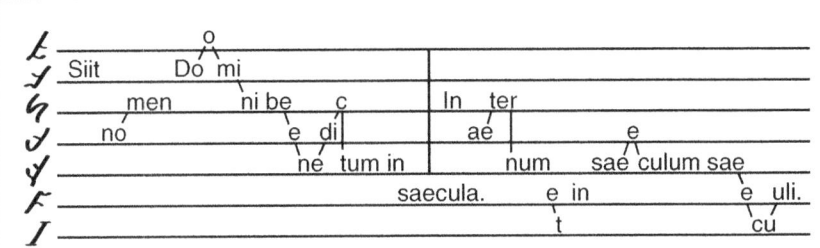

Ad hunc modum consuetis utuntur modulis ad investigandam toni cuiusque vim eadem ratione compositis. Quorum principales quique a suis sonis superioribus ordientes desinunt in finales, minores vero in finalibus et inchoant et consistunt nec superiorem attingunt locum, utpote NOANNOEANE, NOEAGIS et cetera, quae putamus non tam significativa esse verba quam syllabas modulationi attributas.

In this manner they make use of the customary formulas [*moduli*] composed according to the same rationale, for investigating a *tonus* and its character [*vis*]. The four principal ones of these, beginning from the Superiores sounds, end in the Finales; but the lesser ones both begin and end in the Finales, not reaching the place of the Superiores, as for example NOANNOEANE, NOEAGIS, and others, which we take not to be meaningful words, but rather syllables assigned to modulation.

---

to illustrate the species of diatessaron and diapente as presented in Book IV, chap. 14 of Boethius's *De institutione musica.* For the diatessaron, the glossator disposes the three four-note phrases of the melody "Nil suavius—dulcedine—karitatis" over a hexachord with the structure T-T-ST-T-T. For the diapente, the four five-note phrases of the melody "Qui non diligit—fratrem quem videt—invisibilem—non amat Deum" are disposed across an octachord with the structure T-T-T-ST-T-T-ST. The resulting species are the same as those set out in Boethius: for the diatessaron—first: T-T-ST; second: T-ST-T; third: ST-T-T; for the diapente—first: T-T-T-ST; second: T-T-ST-T; third: T-ST-T-T; fourth: ST-T-T-ST. For the diagrams themselves, see Bernhard and Bower, eds., *Glossa maior in institutionem Boethii,* 3: 270 and 274, Glosses 20 and 50 on Book IV, chap. 14.

It should be remembered that Aurelian's Greek had pointed out that the NOEANE formulas contained the *modulationes tonorum*.[109]

In addition to demonstrating the importance of the four *soni* in determining the character of the tones or modes, the *Musica enchiriadis* also explains the difference between authentic and plagal.[110] In the fourth chapter, the author says that any chant can descend to the fifth sound below its final, for example, from the sound archoos or protus in the Finales down to the same sound in the Graves for chants in the first or second mode.[111] After having pointed out that chant could ascend from any final "up to the third sound with the same name" (i.e., a ninth),[112] he goes on to say that authentic and plagal chants are different, in that "there are fewer intervals in ascending with the lesser tones, and an inferior tone occasionally ascends up to the fifth sound from its final, but this is rare."[113] Here we receive some confirmation that Aurelian's statement that the "first are higher, the seconds lower" could be applied literally to the *toni* or *modi*.[114] According to the *enchiriadis* author, the chief difference between authentic and plagal is that while both can descend to a fifth below the final, the plagals can ascend only up to the fifth above their final.

By now, the reader may be asking why the author of the *Musica enchiriadis* claims that the modes are wrongly called tones—but then continues to use the term *tonus* to describe them.[115] Put succinctly, the author refers to the melodic categories as *toni* as long as he is discussing chant, that is, in the first eight chapters. But when he has to discuss polyphony, in the second part of the treatise, he switches to *modus* as a designation for these categories, presumably so that he will have the term *tonus* available to him as an intervallic designation in his discussion of organum (ex. 3.17).[116]

Note that the title of chapter 9 itself makes allusions to differences between what we might call "cantus" theory and the "harmonic" theory necessary for discussing polyphony. The author says he will explain the differences between *phthongoi* and

---

109. See p. 98 here.

110. This occurs in chap. 5, "Quid distet inter Autentos et Minores tonos." The text reads as follows: "Praeterea cum eodem sono autentus quisque tonus, et qui sub ipso est, regantur et finiantur, unde et pro uno habentur tono, in hoc tamen differunt, quod minoribus tonis minora in elevando sunt spatia, et inferior quisque tonus non nisi ad quintum usque sonum a finali suo ascendit, sed et hoc raro" (ed. Schmid, 9).

111. "Simplex et legitimus cantus inferius non descendit quam usque ad sonum quintum a finali suo, in primo dumtaxat tono et secundo ab archoo vel proto finali usque in eundem" (ed. Schmid, 8). Interesting here is that this specification of lower range applies to both authentic and plagal chants.

112. "At vero in acumine a quocumque finali sono usque in tertium eiusdem nominis sonum efferri valet, id est, usque in excellentes" (last sentence in chap. 4, ed. Schmid, 9).

113. "In hoc tamen differunt, quod minoribus tonis minora in elevando sunt spatia, et inferior quisque tonus non nisi ad quintum usque sonum a finali suo ascendit, sed et hoc raro" (last sentence in chap. 5, ed. Schmid, 9).

114. See n. 31 here and the associated discussion.

115. See Atkinson, "'Harmonia' and the 'Modi, quos abusive tonos dicimus,'" 485; and Atkinson, "On the Interpretation of 'Modi, quos abusive tonos dicimus,'" 147–48.

116. It is in this chapter that *tonus* is defined mathematically for the first time, as an interval in the proportion 9:8. See note 102 here and the associated discussion. Erickson, *Musica enchiriadis and Scolica enchiriadis*, 8, points out that despite calling attention to the same "mistaken" use of the term *tonus*, the *Scolica enchiriadis* author continues to use that term interchangeably with *tropus* and *modus* for "mode."

EXAMPLE 3.17. The beginning of Chapter 9 of the *Musica enchiriadis* (ed. Schmid, 20–21; boldface added)

QUID SIT INTER PTONGOS ET SONOS, INTER TONOS ET EPOGDOOS, QUID ETIAM TONI ET MODI SIVE TROPI, PARTICULAE QUOQUE, QUID DIASTEMA ET SISTEMA

(1) Sed his veluti praeexercitaminibus quibusdam ac vilioribus licet iniciis ante cognitis **dehinc faciliori via armonicas prosequimur rationes. Armonia est diversarum vocum apta coadunatio.** In quibus vocibus quia plerumque sonos et ptongos indifferenter accipimus, sonos et ptongos, tonos et epogdoos, quae singulorum sit proprietas, intimandum. Sonus quarumque (5) vocum generale est nomen, sed ptongos dicimus vocis canorae sonos. **Tonus est spacii legitima magnitudo a sono in sonum.** Hocque spacium musicorum sonorum, quia in **sesquioctava proportione est,** Greco nomine dicitur **epogdous. . . . Semitonium non plenum toni intervallum.** Idem interdum limma vel diesis dicitur.
Modi vel tropi sunt species modulationum, de quibus supra dictum est, ut protos autentus (10) **vel plagis, deuteros autentus vel plagis, sive modus Dorius, Frigius, Lidius, et ceteri, qui ex gentium vocabulis sortiti sunt nomina.** Particulae sunt sua cantionis cola vel commata, quae suis finibus cantum distingunt. Sed cola fiunt coeuntibus apte commatibus duobus pluribusve, quamvis interdum est, ubi indiscrete comma sive colon dici potest (etc.).

---

soni; toni and *epogdoi; toni, tropi* and *modi;* and *diastema* and *systema*. At least one of each pair of terms is drawn from harmonic theory. The importance of such theory is explained in the first two sentences, where the author says that having spent time with preliminary exercises, he will now pursue "harmonic theories via an easier path." He then defines *harmonia* itself: "Armonia est diversarum vocum apta coadunatio" ("Harmony is the apt joining together of diverse pitches"). Following this, he provides definitions of various terms, saying that "*tonus* is a fixed magnitude of space from sound to sound"; he goes on to define that "fixed magnitude" as the sesquioctave proportion or epogdous. Finally, he makes the decisive break between "modes, which they also call tropes or tones" (see ex. 3.17, l. 9): "Modi vel tropi sunt species modulationum, de quibus supra dictum est, ut protos autentus vel plagis, deuteros autentus vel plagis, sive modus Dorius, Frigius, Lidius, et ceteri, qui ex gentium vocabulis sortiti sunt nomina." ("Modes or tropes are types of modulation, about which we have spoken above—as, for example protus autentus or plagis, deuterus autentus or plagis, or the modes Dorius, Frigius, Lidius, etc., which are names derived from the names of peoples.") The hand of Boethius is very much in evidence here, but also that of Donatus and other grammarians, as we see in the following sentences ("Particulae sunt sua cantionis cola vel commata, quae suis finibus cantum distingunt," etc.). The parallels between music and grammar, presented already in the first sentence of the treatise and present symbolically in the Dasia notation, carry all the way through its discussion of chant.

Before leaving the *Musica enchiriadis,* we must look at two aspects of what its companion treatise, the *Scolica enchiriadis,* has to say about tone-system. In order to

EXAMPLE 3.18.   *Scolica enchiriadis:*
"normal" pentachord (ed. Schmid,
68—diagram reprinted from Schmid)

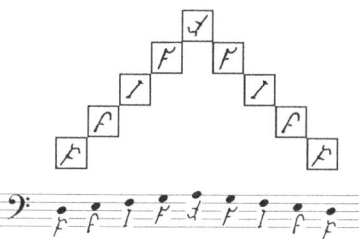

provide the possibility of pitch alteration in the *Enchiriadis* system, the *Scolica* intro-duces a series of *vitia* ("corruptions") that make possible the alteration via semitone of the deuterus and tritus degrees of each tetrachord, yielding—for example—either $E♭$ or $F♯$ in the tetrachord of the Finales.[117] These are derived in a fashion rather similar to mutation in the later system of hexachordal solmization. In order to demonstrate the possibility of $F♯$, for example, the Master tells the Student to sing a tetrachord up and down starting from protus (see ex. 3.18).

Next, the Master repeats the process, but changes the intervals in descent. He says: "I shall sing the same, but, deviating a bit from this order on the second side, I shall join the deuterus sound beneath the tetrardus as if [the latter] were a tritus, thusly [ex. 3.19]."[118] We may explain the latter passage in terms of solmization. By reinterpreting the tetrardus (Sol) as if it were a tritus (Fa), the Master renders the half step immediately below that note as deuterus, or Mi. That Mi—our $F♯$—can thus be accommodated quite easily as one of the *vitia,* as such semitones are pre-sented in the *Scolica enchiriadis.*

That these *vitia* were not simply mistakes but a recognized necessity for accom-modating certain chants is revealed by one of the Master's comments following the examples of *vitia* just provided. He says that the *vitia* are customarily referred to as "limmata" and that through them one mode can be changed to another, or the original mode restored, in chants.[119] In response to the Student's query "Can we ac-tually consider these things to be defects?" the Master says: "Certainly they are de-fects. However, just as barbarisms and solecisms are frequently intermixed as figures

117. The pitches are named here according to modern nomenclature. Treatments of the *vitia* or *ab-sonia* in the *Scolica enchiriadis* are available in Jacobsthal, *Die chromatische Alteration im liturgischen Gesang der abenländischen Kirche,* 269–354; Ferrari-Barassi, "I modi ecclesiastici," 38–40; Möbius, *Das Tonsystem aus der Zeit vor 1000;* and Hebborn, *Die Dasia-Notation,* 277–83. See also Atkinson, "From 'Vitium' to 'Tonus ac-quisitus,'" 192–97.

118. "Dicam et ego hoc idem, dehinc paululum ab hoc ordine declinans in sequenti latere deuterum sonum tetrardo quasi trito subiungam ita" (ed. Schmid, 68).

119. "Limmata ergo haec non plena spacia vocari solent et per ea interdum vel modus a modo trans-fertur vel per eadem restituitur, sicut in cantibus satis observari poterit" (ed. Schmid, 69–70).

EXAMPLE 3.19.   *Scolica enchiriadis:* "normal" pentachord
altered by placing *deuterus* sound immediately beneath
tetrardus in descending, an example of a *vitium* (ed.
Schmid, 68—diagram reprinted from Schmid)

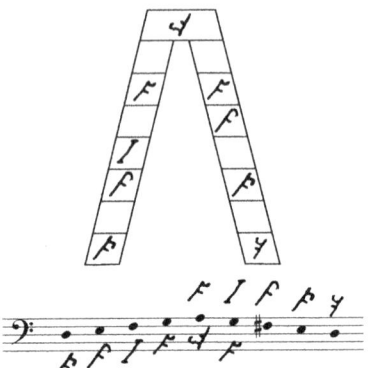

[*figuraliter*] into metric verse, so, too, semitones [*limmata*] are inserted in chants as a result of conscientiousness."[120]

Thus, just as Manuel Chrysaphes would later discuss *phthorai* ["corruptions"] as a way of rationalizing nonsystemic semitones in Byzantine chant,[121] here the *vitia* (also perceived as "corruptions") are used as a method of rationalizing nonsystemic semitones in early Western chant. By making use of these *vitia,* even chants such as the Gradual *Haec dies,* with its implied B^b and E^b, or the Communion *Beatus servus,* with both an F and an $F^{\sharp}$, can be notated in their proper positions, with finals on protus and deuterus, respectively (see ex. 3.20).

Although it might be a bit difficult for us to sing, the notation in this example has the advantage of preserving intact the tonal architecture of the two chants when notated so as to end on their proper finals.[122] More important is that it demonstrates

120. "Vitia nimirum sunt, sed sicut barbarismi et soloecismi metris plerumque figuraliter intermiscentur, ita limmata interdum de industria cantibus inseruntur" (ed. Schmid, 70). Erickson, *Musica enchiriadis and Scolica enchiriadis,* 41, renders *figuraliter* with the phrase "for poetic reasons."

121. Conomos, ed. and transl., *The Treatise of Manuel Chrysaphes.* See particularly ll. 213–523 of the treatise. See also Tillyard, *Handbook of Middle Byzantine Musical Notation,* 36; Wolfram, "Fragen der Modulation in der byzantinischen Musik"; and Wolfram, "Die *Phthorai* der Paläobyzantinischen Notationen." Chrysaphes describes the *phthora* as follows: "A *phthora* is the unexpected destruction of the melody of the mode being chanted and the creation of another melody together with a brief, partial transposition from the mode being chanted to another; then, with the cancellation of the *phthora,* the previous mode is sung in the form that it had beforehand" (Conomos, ed. and transl., *The Treatise of Manuel Chrysaphes,* 49).

122. It is probable in any case that the Dasia notation of the *enchiriadis* treatises was never intended to be a practical notation for musical performance, but rather one that fulfilled theoretical or pedagogical purposes. The author himself seems to suggest as much when he says in chap. 6 that with the aid of the signs, one should be able to "examine" or "decipher" an unknown melody ("quo . . . discant . . . ignotum melum ex nota eorum qualitate et ordine per signa investigare"; ed. Schmid, 10). See Schmid's reply to Martin Vogel's presentation ("Die Entstehung der Kirchentonarten") in a discussion at the 1962 meeting of the Gesellschaft für Musikforschung. (Further on this exchange, see note 34 of chapter 1 here).

Much has been written on this topic; the literature is summarized in Hebborn, *Die Dasia-Notation.* My own view is that the Dasia notation provides a means for representing and rationalizing the *enchiri-*

EXAMPLE 3.20. The Gradual *Haec dies* and the Communion *Beatus servus* as notated in the *Graduale Romanum* (**a**) and at their proper modal levels using *vitia* (**b**)

EXAMPLE 3.21.   Diagram of organum at the octave in Chapter 10 of the *Musica enchiriadis,* (reprinted from Schmid, ed., 27)

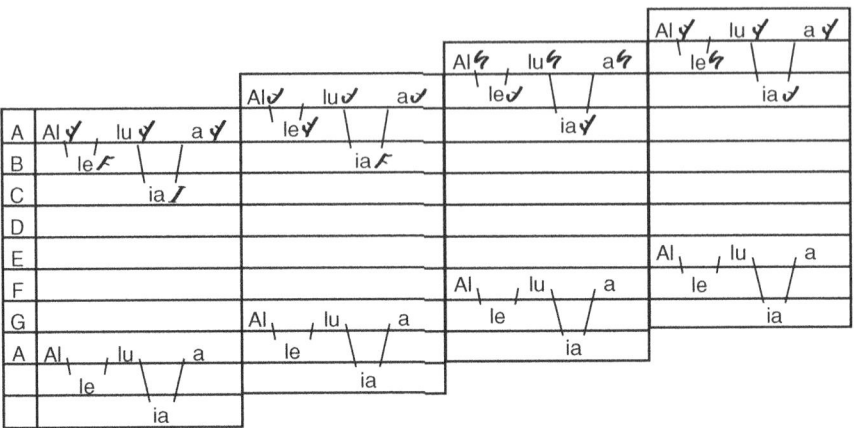

EXAMPLE 3.22.   Diagram demonstrating compound intervals, with the double-octave system represented by A-G, A-G, A (*Musica enchiriadis,* chap. 11, reprinted from Schmid, ed., 29)

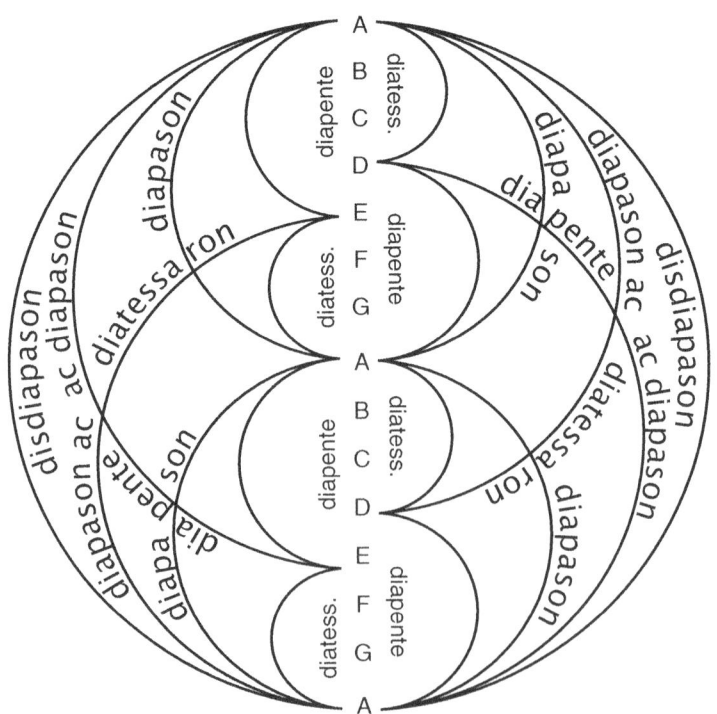

EXAMPLE 3.23.   Diagram of organum at the double octave using the letter array A-G (A-G A) (*Musica enchiriadis*, chap. 11, reprinted from Schmid, ed., 32)

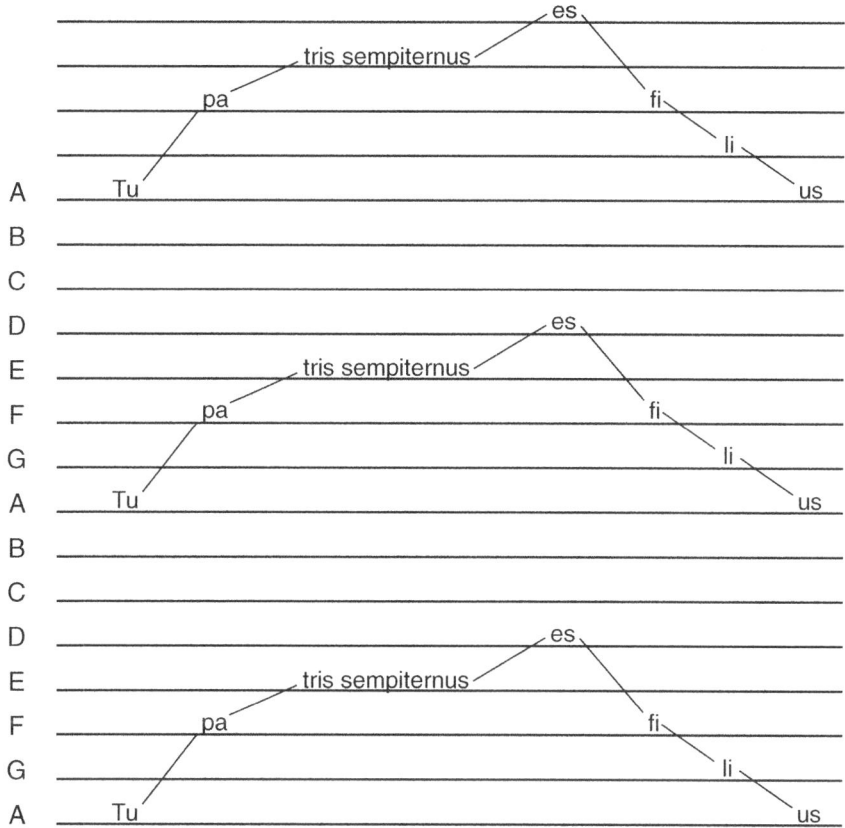

that there was in the ninth century a tonal and notational matrix that was perfectly adequate to accommodate pieces such as *Haec dies, Beatus servus,* and others that had implied accidentals. As will become apparent, that notational matrix—and the tonal system that lay at its foundation—were not the ones that eventually formed the basis for the notation of medieval music. Ironically, the seeds of the alternative system that would become that foundation are likewise present in the *Musica enchiriadis.* (See exs. 3.21–23.)

---

adis tone-system, both in its underlying structure and with its allowed *vitia,* and that that tone-system is fundamentally consonant with the tonal structure of plainchant and was probably conceived to accommodate it. However, although Dasia notation offers a rational, systemic matrix for plainchant, it does not, in itself, provide the chant with a practical notation. Further on this matter, see Atkinson, "From 'Vitium' to 'Tonus acquisitus'"; Phillips, "'Musica' and 'Scolica enchiriadis': The Literary, Theoretical, and Musical Sources," 173–74; Phillips, "The Dasia Notation and Its Manuscript Tradition"; Phillips, "Notationen und Notationslehren," 311–14; and Hebborn, *Die Dasia-Notation,* 47–49. Hebborn's rationale in treating this issue is substantially different from mine or that of Phillips.

When the anonymous author of the *enchiriadis* presents organum at the diapason and bisdiapason, he uses a letter array (A-G, A-G, A) associated with the Greater Perfect System, rather than the Dasia notation with which the *Musica enchiriadis's* own tone-system is presented (see ex. 3.22).[123] Although he notates the *vox principalis* in Dasia notation in the example of organum at the octave (ex. 3.21), he does not employ this notation for the *vox organalis* an octave lower; in the second example, organum at the double octave (ex. 3.23), he dispenses with the Dasia notation entirely. Inasmuch as the *Musica enchiriadis* system contains augmented octaves (between $B^\flat$ and $b^\natural$, F and $f^\sharp$, using modern nomenclature), a shift to the Greater Perfect System was imperative for organum at the octave. The author explains this in chapter 11 as a "miraculous mutation" (*mutatio mirabilis*), saying, in effect, "It's a miracle."[124] Thus, within one and the same treatise, two different tone-systems were operative. One, the *Musica enchiriadis* system itself, was well suited for plainchant; the other, the Greater Perfect System, was better suited for organum at the octave and the fourth.[125]

123. On the array A-G (A-G A), which seems to have been intended to show the relationship between pitches an octave apart, see Santosuosso, *Letter Notations*, 23–25; and Smits van Waesberghe, "Les Origines de la notation alphabétique," 9–11. Santosuosso goes on to point out that some manuscripts of pt. 2 of the *Scolica enchiriadis* present the Boethian A-H-P array, but in ascending order. This is the array used originally by Boethius to determine the octave species for the eighth mode, specifically as a means of demonstrating octave equivalence. See *De institutione musica*, Book IV, chap. 17, where A represents the Nete hyperboleon and P the Proslambanomenos (see ex. 1.9). The earliest sources for the *Scolica*, however, do not present the entire array, but merely the octaves, A, H, and P (with A at the lowest extremity and P at the highest). They can then serve as points of orientation for octave transpositions of the Dasia symbols for the hexachord protus/Finales through deuterus/Superiores.

For Santosuosso's interpretation of the A-H-P array in the second part of the *Scolica enchiriadis*, see her *Letter Notations*, 26–29, and "The a–p System of Letter Notation," 9–11. On the manuscripts of the *Scolica enchiriadis* that present the A-H-P array in ascending order, see the critical apparatus of Schmid's edition (91), and GS 1: 184–85, where reference is also made to the use of the octaves A, H, and P as points of orientation for transposition of the Dasia symbols.

124. "Attendenda quoque in hoc mira ratio, ut quamvis absolute canendo vel in ordine sonos rimando, idem inveniuntur noni ad nonos, non octavi ad octavos, in symphonia tamen non modo diapason, quae octava incedit regione, sed et in bis diapason mutatione mirabili octavi et octavi idem fiunt" (ed. Schmid, 33–34). ("There should be noted in this an amazing relationship. Whether by singing the sounds absolutely or by examining them in order, ninth sounds [compared] to ninths are found to be the same—not eighths to eighths. Nevertheless, not only in the diapason symphony, which occurs at the eighth position, but also in the bisdiapason symphony, by means of a miraculous mutation eighths and eighths become the same.")

125. Calvin Bower pointed this out in a presentation, "The Conflict of Tonal Systems," given on 13 Nov. 1971 during the Annual Meeting of the American Musicological Society, Chapel Hill and Durham, North Carolina. See also Phillips, "'Musica' and 'Scolica enchiriadis': The Literary, Theoretical, and Musical Sources," 173–74; and Phillips, "The Dasia Notation and Its Manuscript Tradition," 166–67. In his discussion of organum at the fourth, the *enchiriadis* author employs neither letter notation nor the implied Greater Perfect System. As a result, he must find a way to avoid the tritone that exists naturally in the *enchiriadis* tone-system between the deuterus in any given tetrachord and the tritus in the next lower tetrachord. His solution is to enjoin the *vox organalis* not to descend below the tetrardus in the next lower tetrachord in any given phrase of organum, thereby producing what is commonly called organum in oblique motion (see *Musica enchiriadis*, chaps. 17–18, ed. Schmid, 47–56). The combined Greater and Lesser Perfect System, as employed by Guido d'Arezzo (using letter notation), obviates this procedure. See Guido d'Arezzo, *Micrologus*, chaps. 18–19, in Babb and Palisca, *Hucbald, Guido, and John on Music*, 77–82.

EXAMPLE 3.24.   Monochord division for the instrumental tone-system *Scolica enchiriadis,*
Part III, diagram after Schmid, ed., 147)

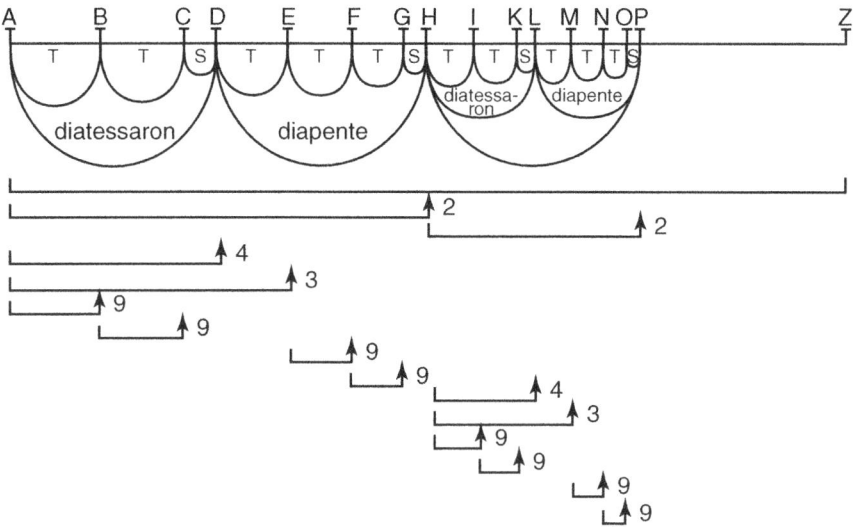

As if two were not enough, yet a third tone-system is presented in the *Scolica enchiriadis,* one that has its roots in instrumental practice, just as the "Dasia" system has its roots in the practice of singing liturgical chant. I refer to the tone-system depicted in example 3.24, a monochord division that appears in the *Scolica enchiriadis, pars tertia.*[126]

The master has just finished explaining to the student that there is a method of dividing the octave that is peculiar to the measurement of pipes or strings, and he has already provided an initial proof of this in an elementary organ-pipe *mensura* ("Atsi mensionum").[127] Then, in a monochord division that is a model of simplicity, he tells the student to take a string, A to Z, and divide it at the midpoint, H, thereby yielding the octave. He then divides the upper section H–Z at its midpoint, P, to give a second octave higher. Then come divisions by a fourth and a third, yielding D Z and E Z, respectively. Subtracting the ninth part of the full string yields a tone from A to B; subtracting another ninth part from the string B Z yields another tone between B and C, and a semitone between C and D. This process of subtracting ninth parts is then continued from E, yielding the rest of the intervals of the

126. Ed. Schmid, 146–47; *GS* 1: 209; also edited in Meyer, *Mensura monochordi,* 203. This monochord division is discussed in Markovits, *Das Tonsystem der abendländischen Musik im frühen Mittelalters,* 44; Meyer, *Mensura monochordi,* lvi–lvii; and Adkins, "The Theory and Practice of the Monochord," 130–35. An English translation appears in Erickson, *Musica enchiriadis and Scolica enchiriadis,* 88–89.

127. Ed. Schmid, 145–46; *GS* 1: 209; Erickson, *Musica enchiriadis and Scolica enchiriadis,* 87–88. The text is also edited in Sachs, *Mensura fistularum,* 1: 54, with German translation on 1: 172; a discussion and commentary on the text may be found at 2: 37–38, 61, 152–54, and 249–51. Noteworthy here is that measuring a fourth (3:4), fifth (2:3), and octave (1:2), and then filling them in with whole tones (8:9), yields the ascending intervallic succession T-T-ST-T-T-T-ST—just as does the monochord division that follows.

lower octave. Repeating the entire process between H Z and H P produces all the intervals of the higher octave. With its letter array A–P, this instrumental scale has the outward appearance of the Greater Perfect System as presented by Boethius, but its internal structure is completely different.[128]

The beauty of this division is that one never has to calculate the semitone. Put another way, one never has to divide the string into any more than nine parts. This would have obvious advantages for anyone actually having to cut pipes for an organ. Reckoning the minor semitone between the hypate and the parhypate hypaton, for example, would require dividing the string into 256 parts and subtracting 13. For this reason, Michael Markovits postulated that this instrumental scale actually came about through the process of organ building, but was then incorporated into treatises on the *Ars musica* and made to represent the principles of *harmonia*.[129]

Although ancient Greek harmonic theory starts to make some inroads into medieval chant theory in the *Musica enchiriadis,* it is perhaps important to emphasize that the theory presented in both Aurelian's *Musica disciplina* and in the *Musica enchiriadis* is, in most respects, different from that presented in Boethius. Boethius treated music as the expression of abstract quantitative relationships. He used musical instruments to demonstrate principles and derive nomenclature, and he defined eight modes by species of octave. By contrast, the theory in the chant treatises— such as Aurelian, the *Musica enchiriadis,* or the *papadikai*—comes from vocal practice. It uses nomenclature for pitches and tetrachords derived from functional relationships in plainchant and from their relative positions in acoustic space; it defines tones or modes by the quality (*vis, virtus, qualitas*) of the final sound governing them; and it illustrates them with intonation formulas or model melodies. At the same time, the very presence of *modus* as the preferred designation for what "we wrongly call tones" in the *Musica enchiriadis* is the leading edge of a terminological shift that would bring with it several shifts that are more concrete as well. Those will be the subject of the following chapters. As will become apparent, the synthesis of ancient Greek harmonic theory with the theory and practice of plainchant will find its most telling expression in the way music is represented in graphic form—that is, in its system of notation.

One of the most important legacies of the Western church in the eighth and ninth centuries is the development of a practical system of notation for its music,[130]

128. This scale and its letter array are discussed briefly in Santosuosso, *Letter Notations,* 29; Phillips, "Notationen und Notationslehren," 321; and Smits van Waesberghe, "Les Origines de la notation alphabétique," 7–9. As mentioned, some manuscripts of the *Scolica* present the ascending A-H-P array at the beginning of pt.2, but without specifying its intervallic content (see note 123 here; Schmid, ed., *Musica et Scolica enchiriadis,* 91; *GS* 1 : 184; and Adkins, "The Theory and Practice of the Monochord," 130–35, where the array is represented as an "instrumental" system).

129. Markovits, *Das Tonsystem der abendländischen Musik im frühen Mittelalter,* 53–62. But cf. Sachs, "Remarks on the Relationship between Pipe-Measurements and Organ-Building"; Sachs, "Die Rolle der Mensura von Monochord, Orgelpfeifen und Glocken in der mittelalterlichen *Ars musica*"; and Sachs, *Mensura fistularum,* 2: 58–77. See also Smits van Waesberghe, ed., *Cymbala: Bells in the Middle Ages,* 23.

130. As mentioned earlier in this chapter (note 70), I employ the term "practical" to distinguish this type of notation from that found in theoretical sources, such as Aurelian and the *Musica* and *Scolica enchiriadis.* Although the scholarly consensus places this development in the period from the late eighth through the ninth centuries, individual scholars differ as to whether it took place closer to the beginning or the

a system of graphic signs that in the tenth and eleventh centuries would come to be called "neumes."[131] Appropriately, the advent of Western musical notation has few rivals as a topic of scholarly investigation.[132] It is not my purpose here to set out yet another theory of the origins and development of musical notation, but rather to ascertain the fundamental features of that notation in its early state, before it comes under the influence of harmonic theory.

I have already discussed, albeit briefly, one of the earliest examples of practical musical notation: the partially neumed *Doxa* that appears in Paris 2291 (see fig. 3.2 and ex. 3.8). As I observed, the Greek text in this manuscript was provided with Paleofrankish neumes, one of several different types of practical notation that make their appearance in the ninth century.[133] Other types that can be documented from that period are of northern French, German, and Spanish provenance.[134] In order to gain some idea of the commanding features of these notations, let us return to the neumations of the Introit *Ad te levavi* given in figure 3.3 and example 3.9.

---

end of that period. Levy dates the origins of musical notation to the later eighth century and postulates a notated archetype ca. 800. Hucke places the advent of notation in the ninth century and the production of a notated cycle of proper chants in the latter part of that century. See the citations in note 2 here for the works in which Levy and Hucke put forth their respective positions on this chronology.

131. I suggested earlier (see note 49 here, and chapter 1, notes 35 and 127 and the discussion attached to them) that the standard Latin term for musical notation from Antiquity onward was *nota*. The original meaning of *neuma* (from Gr. πνεῦμα-, "breath" or "spirit") was "melody" or "melodic phrase" (see Bautier-Regnier, "A propos des sens de *neuma* et de *nota*"; and Hiley, "Neume," in *Western Plainchant*, 345–46). One of the earliest references to *neuma* as a notational sign appears in an anonymous treatise dated to the tenth century that I mentioned above: "De accentibus toni oritur nota que dicitur neuma" (Rome 235, fol. 39; see note 5 here, and Wagner, "Un piccolo trattato," 482). In the eleventh- and twelfth-century didactic tables listing and explaining the notational signs, the signs themselves are most frequently called "neumae," but the term "notae" also appears. See Huglo, "Les Noms des neumes" 57–60; and Bernhard, "Die Überlieferung der Neumennamen": *neuma*, 14, 17–25, 27–28, 30, 33–35, 36–40, 42–44, 47, 51–52, 54, 57, 72–75, 87; *nota*, 14, 33, 45, 46, 48, and 61.

132. Excellent surveys are available in Wagner, *Einführung in die gregorianischen Melodien*, vol. 2, *Neumenkunde*; Suñol, *Introduction à la paléographie musicale grégorienne*; Jammers, *Tafeln zur Neumenschrift*; Stäblein, *Schriftbild der einstimmigen Musik*; Corbin, *Die Neumen*; Hiley, *Western Plainchant*, "Notation," 340–401; Hiley, *NG 2*, "Notation, III, 1: Western Plainchant"; ; Treitler, "Mündliche und schriftliche Überlieferung: Anfänge der musikalischen Notation"; and Phillips, "Notationen." Huglo has provided a valuable survey of research on this subject in "Bilan de 50 années de recherches (1939–1989) sur les notations musicales." Special mention should be made of several studies devoted specifically to the historical and conceptual foundations of music writing in the West: Jammers, "Gedanken und Beobachtungen zur Geschichte der Notenschriften," "Die Entstehung der Neumenschrift"; Hucke, "Die Anfänge der abendländischen Notenschrift," "Choralforschung und Musikwissenschaft," "Gregorianische Fragen"; Levy, "Charlemagne's Archetype of Gregorian Chant," "On the Origin of Neumes," "Gregorian Chant and Oral Transmission," "From Aural to Notational: The Gregorian *Antiphonale Missarum*"; Treitler, "The Early History of Music Writing in the West," "Reading and Singing: On the Genesis of Occidental Music-Writing," "Die Entstehung der abendländischen Notenschrift," "The Beginnings of Music-Writing in the West," "The 'Unwritten' and 'Written Transmission' of Medieval Chant"; Grier, "Adémar de Chabannes"; and Cullin, "Écritures."

133. Hiley's list of ninth-century examples of neumes (*NG 2*, "Notation, III, 1: Western Plainchant," table 4) includes five Paleofrankish sources: Düsseldorf D. 1 (Werden); Paris 2291 (St. Amand); and Valenciennes 148, 150, and 337 (all from St. Amand).

134. Hiley (*NG 2*, "Notation, III, 1: Western Plainchant," table 4) arranges the manuscripts according to notational conventions, as follows: *Breton Notation* (four examples): (1) Valenciennes 407; (2) Ox-

Paleofrankish neumes appear in column A of example 3.9.[135] In the other columns, we see the same piece copied in a variety of other notations: Breton (B, C),[136] St. Gall (D and G²),[137] Laon (G¹),[138] Aquitanian (E),[139] and Beneventan (F).[140] Of the various types of notation represented here, four can be documented in the ninth century: Paleofrankish, Breton, St. Gall, and Laon.[141] The earliest examples of Aquitanian and Beneventan notation date from the tenth century.[142] The neumes in the modern gradual (col. G) that serves here as a control are actually a reproduction of the script that came into use in France in the twelfth century; they are customarily known as "twelfth-century square notation" or simply "square notation."

As one looks at the neumations reproduced here, one first notices that the neumes in all the columns except F and G give no information about the specific pitch content of the melody; only the Beneventan script in column F, with its C and F clefs, along with the modern gradual, provides such information. Second, all the neumations have one or more notes per syllable of text, but beyond that there seems to be a high degree of consistency across the various neumations as to the number of notes, their groupings, and even the graphic shapes representing them within each syllable. Whereas most of the notations provide at best only a sense of the melodic ductus over each syllable of the text, and give little or no information about the pitch relations between syllables, three of them—Aquitanian, Beneventan, and Laon (cols. E, F, G¹)—can be said to reproduce the larger shape of the melody as a whole.[143]

The synoptic transcriptions make clear that one must familiarize oneself with the conventions of each of the notational families in order to reproduce the melodic motion represented. One finds, for example, that the simple upward ascending stroke

---

ford 4.26; (3) Leiden 25—all from Brittany; and (4) New York 115 (from Landévennec). *Early French Notation* (seven exs.): (1) Autun 4 (Flavigny); (2) Autun 28 (Autun); (3) Paris 227 (Vierzon); (4) Paris 11958 (Corbie); (5) Paris 1190 (Senlis); (6) Rome 215 (Fleury); and (7) Tours 184 (1017) (Tours). *French/German Notation* (four examples): (1) Sélestat 1 (1093) (from Northern Italy); (2) Rome 313 (?Tours); (3) Leipzig I.93 (?near Trier); and (4) Vienna 958 (Northeastern France). *German Notation* (ten examples): (1) Berlin 2° 58 (Lorsch); (2) Heidelberg 52 (?Weissenburg); (3–6) Munich 9543, 14314, and 29164/I, and Regensburg 2 (all from Regensburg); (7) Naples 68 (St. Gall); (8) Rome 485 (Lorsch); (9) St. Gall 242 (Southern Germany); and (10) Vienna 3645 (Southern Germany). *Spanish Notation* (three examples): (1) Madrid 10001, and (2) Toledo 2 (both from Toledo); and (3) Paris 8093 (Spain). *Notation from Laon* (four examples): Laon 9, 107, 121, and 266.

135. Column A: Düsseldorf D. 1, tenth century (*Le Graduel romain* II: *Les Sources*, 49).

136. Column B: Angers 91, tenth century (*Le Graduel romain* II: *Les Sources*, 25); Column C: Chartres 47, tenth century (*Les Sources*, 43).

137. Column D: St. Gall 339, tenth century; Column G²: St. Gall 376, eleventh century (*Le Graduel romain* II: *Les Sources*, 131–32), as represented in the *Graduale Triplex*.

138. Column G¹: Laon 239, ca. 930 (*Le Graduel romain* II: *Les Sources*, 57) as represented in the *Graduale Triplex*.

139. Column E: Paris 903, eleventh century (*Le Graduel romain* II: *Les Sources*, 98).

140. Column F: Benevento 34, eleventh/twelfth centuries (*Le Graduel romain* II: *Les Sources*, 32).

141. See the lists in notes 133 and 134 here.

142. See Corbin, *Die Neumen*, 3: 94–95 and 142–43, respectively.

143. Borrowing Treitler's terminology (which he had taken from Charles Peirce), the Aquitanian, Beneventan, and Laon neumations could be described as "iconic," the others "symbolic" (see Treitler, "The Early History of Music Writing").

without preparation, corresponding to the *nota* for the acute accent, signifies a single pitch in most of the neumations, but a two-note ascent in the Paleofrankish.[144] The reverse of the latter grapheme, the simple downward stroke without preparation, corresponding to the *nota* for the grave accent, does not even exist in most of the scripts. In the Paleofrankish, it represents a two-note descent; in the other families of notation, that gesture is represented by a downward stroke with preparation (ⅤＶⅤＶ) or by two *puncti,* one directly over the other.[145] The three-note ascending-descending movement represented by the C (sigma) facing downward in the Paleofrankish script is reproduced in the other neumations by a similar shape with a preparatory stroke (ＶＶＶＶＶＶ).[146] In general, one is struck by the tendency in all the scripts to link together no more than two or three pitches with a single stroke of the pen, even when there are more than that over a single syllable of text. The principle seems to be one of directionality: more than two pitches in the same direction over a single syllable are not linked together; one can link three, or even more than three, pitches together if there is a change of direction after the second and each subsequent one.[147] That this will rarely involve more than four pitches seems self-evident from the style of the music.

Yet another feature that is strikingly consistent among the various neumations is the use of signs conveying nuances of performance. This manifests itself on the very first word, *Ad.* With the exception of the single punctum that appears in Paris 903, all the neumations have a sign for liquescence here. Guido d'Arezzo describes it as follows.

> At many points notes "liquesce," like the liquid letters, so that the interval from one note to another is begun with a smooth glide and does not appear to have a stopping place en route. We put a dot like a blot beneath the liquescent note, as here.[148]

144. See, for example, the single strokes in cols. C and D on the syllable "De-" of *Deus* and on the word *te* in the phrase *in te confido.*

145. See the syllables "-do" of *confido*, "e-" of *erubescam*, "-de-" of irrideant, and "me-" of *mei.*

146. See the syllables "-ri-" in *irrideant* and "ex-" in *exspectant.*

147. See, for example, "-am" of *meam* and "-spec-" of *exspectant.* The "McDonald's" M over "-am" of *meam* in the Paleofrankish is perhaps best seen as two simple signs joined together, as is the pair of descending two-note signs in cols. A and D over the syllable "-fun-" of *confundentur.* One could argue that the reasons for the paucity of multinote linked groups are (1) that this is an Introit in a neumatic style, and (2) that there is a large number of pitch repetitions. However, as a comparison of the facsimile of the Gradual *Universi qui te exspectant* in Düsseldorf D. 1 (fig. 3.3) with its modern counterpart in the *Graduale Romanum* or *Liber usualis* demonstrates, the principle of directional ligation holds true even in melismatic chants.

148. "Liquescunt vero in multis voces more litterarum, ita ut inceptus modus unius ad alteram limpide transiens nec finiri videatur. Porro liquescenti voci punctum quasi maculando supponimus hoc modo" (ed. Smits van Waesberghe, *CSM* 4, 175–76; transl. from Babb and Palisca, *Hucbald, Guido, and John on Music,* 72). On musical liquescence, see Freistedt, *Die liqueszierenden Noten des gregorianischen Chorals;* Hiley, "The Plica and Liquescence"; Göschl, *Semiologische Untersuchungen zum Phänomen der gregorianischen Liqueszenz;* Bielitz, *Zum Bezeichneten der Neumen, insbesondere der Liqueszenz;* and Haug, "Zur Interpretation der Liqueszenzneumen," esp. 99–100. Haug points out that the treatment of musical liquescence parallels that of the *litterae semivocales* or liquid consonants, a discussion of which is part of virtually every work on grammar, including those by Donatus and Martianus Capella. The works of the latter two authors were certainly taught in the Carolingian schools, as Glauche points out (*Schullektüre im Mittelalter,* esp. 15–30) and as may also be seen in the abundant glosses on them. Indeed, particularly detailed

GD   F   Ga   a G
  •
Ad   te   le—va-vi[149]

Even though Guido says that this particular note does not have to be performed as a liquescence, the scribes represented here obviously preferred it to be liquescent. The word "in" in the phrase *in te confido* is likewise given a liquescent sign in columns A, B, D, F, and all three neumations in column G of example 3.9.

Yet another sign for a subtle performance technique that is applied rather consistently in the sources reproduced in example 3.9 is the quilisma (from Gr. κύλισμα -ματα: "rolling"), a note one sees in all the notations but the Beneventan (col. F) over the syllable "-mi-" in the word *inimici*.[150] Its appearance is that of a wavy line or two or three semicircles completed by a stroke upward; it is usually preceded by a single note. As is true here, the complex of three notes usually spans a minor third, although larger intervals are possible.[151] Aurelian of Réôme describes the syllable "can-" of *canticum* in the verse of the Gradual *Exaltabunt sancti* V. *Cantate domino* as being "given forth with a tremulous inflexion"; indeed, that syllable receives a quilisma in most of the early sources.[152] Apart from its being described as "tremulous" by both Aurelian and Hucbald, however, we learn little about its performance from contemporaneous sources.[153]

A final important trait of several of the earliest neumations is the information

---

treatments of liquid consonants may be found in three ninth-century Irish commentaries on Donatus: *Murethach (Muridac), In Donati Artem maiorem*, ed. Holtz; *Ars Lavreshamensis: Expositio in Donatum maiorem*; and *Sedulius Scottus: In Donati Artem maiorem*, the last two ed. Löfstedt. A similarly detailed discussion of liquid consonants appears in the independent *Donatus ortigraphus, Ars grammatica*, ed. Chittenden. See Holtz, "Sur trois commentaires irlandais."

149. The manuscripts vary considerably in the way they illustrate this passage. (See *CSM* 4, 176, apparatus criticus.) Some simply render the melody in the letter notation used throughout the treatise, in some cases placing the *D* beneath the *G*; others supply neumes; some omit indication of the melody completely.

150. The word *quilisma* (pl. *-mata*) itself seems to appear for the first time in the large tonary of Bern of Reichenau (post 1021). Referring to a small group of antiphons that begin on the final of the Protus authentic, he says: "Hae antiphonae licet a finali incipiant, tamen quia per *quilismata*, quae nos *gradatas neumas* dicimus, magis gutturis quam cordarum vel alicuius instrumenti officio modulantur, pocius huius differentiae sono quam principali ipsius autentici promuntur modo" (Rausch, ed., *Die Musiktraktate des Abtes Bern von Reichenau*, 79; *GS* 2: 80; emphasis added). Indeed, the antiphons he cites all have a quilisma in an ascending neume *D-f* in the first phrase, if not always on the first syllable. A bit later in the eleventh century, Aribo mentions the quilisma in his *De musica* (1068–78): "Quod dicit aut *tremulam* habeant, puto intelligendum sic esse. *Tremula* est neuma quam *gradatam* vel *quilisma* dicimus" (ed. Smits van Waesberghe, *CSM* 2, 66; emphasis added).

151. Cardine, "Sémiologie gréorienne," 123, cites the antiphon *Veni sponsa Christi* as an example of the appearance of the quilisma in a three-note group spanning a perfect fourth from *G* to *c*, pointing out the difficulty of placing the quilisma itself. He suggests that it should probably be placed on the *b♮* immediately beneath the *c*.

152. "Modulatione altera, quae fit in 'can[ticum]', flexibilis est modulatio duplicata, quae inflexione tremula emittitur vox" (*Musica disciplina*, chap. 18; ed. Gushee, *CSM* 21, 98). Hiley, *Western Plainchant*, 358, provides comparative transcriptions of the passage. On the sign and its performance, see Vivell, "Das Quilisma"; and Wiesli, *Das Quilisma*.

153. See note 169 here and the associated discussion.

they provide about rhythmic aspects of performance.[154] This information is conveyed in two ways: either intrinsically, by means of graphic modifications to the neumes themselves, or extrinsically, via letters that supplement the neumatic text. Let us consider the second of these possibilities first.

Turning once more to example 3.9, one notices in column G^1, from the manuscript Laon 239, and G^2, from St. Gall 376, the appearance of several letters above or next to individual neumes. In Laon 239, the letter t appears above the first note of the syllable "-que" in *neque* and "-spec-" in *exspectant*, the letter m over the first neume in the syllable "-ver-" of *universi*, and the letter a within the three-note group over the syllable "-tant-" of *expectant*. Although there are no additional letters in the setting of *Ad te levavi* in St. Gall 339 (col. D), a number of them appear in the later manuscript St. Gall 376, whose setting is reproduced in column G^2. Here the letter t appears over "-mam" of *animam*, "me-" in *inimici mei*, and "-tant" of *exspectant;* the letter c appears over the last note of the syllable "me-" of *meus* and "-de-" of *irrideant;* the letter e over the syllable "con-" of *confido,* "-scam" of *erubescam,* "-que" of *neque,* and "ir-" of *irrideant;* the letter s over the syllables "-us" of *meus* and "ne-" of *neque;* and the letter m over "-ver-" of *universi.*

The key to the meaning of these "litterae significativae" is provided in a famous letter written in the late ninth century by Notker Balbulus (ca. 840–912) of St. Gall to a certain Lantpertus, who had apparently asked him to clarify them.[155] Notker goes through the entire alphabet, providing definitions for each letter that incorporate as many words as possible starting with that letter. For example:

L   leuare laetatur. ("L Loves to eLevate.")
M   mediocriter melodiam moderari mendicando memorat.
     ("M [re]Minds one [who is] seeking to Measure the Melody
     Moderately.")
N   notare hoc est noscitare notificat. ("N Notifies that this is to kNow
     how to Notate.")[156]

Although the meanings sometimes seem a bit forced because of the avid use of

---

154. That several of the early neumatic scripts convey information about the temporal flow of the music they represent has, to my knowledge, never been seriously questioned. The sources themselves, however, provide little by way of suggestions as to how to interpret the information they convey. As a result, the question of the rhythmic performance of early monophony has been the subject of many differing interpretations. Corbin, *Die Neumen,* 3: 195–211; and Apel, *Gregorian Chant,* 126–32, provide excellent surveys of the various theories.

155. See von den Steinen, *Notker der Dichter,* 1: 121, 495. Although von den Steinen places the letter among the undatable opuscula of Notker (495), Smits van Waesberghe (*Musiekgeschiedenis der Middeleeuwen,* 2: 773) hypothesizes that it was written between 885 and 890 to Lantpert of Metz. (The link between St. Gall and Metz coincides with the circumstance that the letters are found primarily in the St. Gall and Messine/Lotharingian scripts.) The letter is perhaps most easily accessible in Mocquereau's preface to *Pal. Mus.* 4, where it is not only edited (10–11), but also given in facsimile (plts. B–D) from St. Gall 381 (tenth century). As well as an edition and detailed historical study, Smits van Waesberghe provides facsimiles of all the manuscript sources for the text in the second volume of his *Musiekgeschiedenis der Middeleeuwen.* The most recent critical edition is that by Froger ("L'Épitre de Notker").

156. Froger, "L'Épitre de Notker," 69. My reading is best considered a "singing translation." Other translations are invited.

alliteration, the letters relate to various aspects of notation and performance, in particular to melodic contour and rhythm. One of the most important signs relating to the former is one that occurs quite frequently in St. Gall 376 (ex. 3.9, col. G²), namely *e* (*equaliter*—"equally").[157] Written between neumes, as one can see, it tells the singers to start the subsequent neume at the same pitch on which the preceding one had ended. Other letters pertinent to melodic shape are *a* (*altius*— "higher"), *m* (*mediocriter*—"moderately," "in a mean position") and *s* (*susum* or *sursum*—"upward," "high up").[158] An example of the last named appears over *neque* in both the Laon and St. Gall manuscripts, apparently reminding the singers that the phrase beginning with that word requires an ascent up a fourth from the end of the preceding distinction. Its use earlier, reinforcing the two-note ascent at the end of *meus*, may help to remind the singers that the first note of the next phrase is substantially lower—a major sixth, to be exact, the largest leap of any kind during the piece. The *m* over "-ver-" in *universi* may be there to remind the singers not to ascend as high as *c*, the destination of all the preceding leaps upward from G.[159]

There are three letters that bear directly on rhythm: *a, c,* and *t*. Whereas *a* in Notker's letter pertains to melodic ductus (*altius*—"higher"), at Laon it could apparently have been employed to indicate a lengthening, taking *a* as *augete* ("augment," "lengthen").[160] Its appearance here in Laon 239, in the two-note descent over the syllable "-tant" of *exspectant* at the end of a distinction, is most likely an example of such rhythmic use. The letter *c*, according to Notker, signifies "cito uel celeriter" ("quickly"). As noted, it appears in the St. Gall manuscript over the penultimate syllables "me-" of *meus* and "-de-" of *irrideant*. In both cases, it accompanies a two-note neume traversing only a second. It may tell the singers to "sing through" that neume so as to place emphasis on the final syllable.

The final letter to be discussed here, *t*, is one of the most prominent in all scripts in which the litterae significativae appear. Notker says that "T testifies that it should be drawn out or held."[161] The letter appears in Laon 239 over "-que" in *neque* and "-spec-" in *exspectant*, and in St. Gall 376 over "-mam" of *animam*, "me-" of *mei*, and "-tant" of *exspectant*.[162]

Although Notker's description is clear enough in its own right, the rhythmic significance of *t* seems to receive some corroboration in the way the neumes themselves are written—that is, in what I referred to above as intrinsic information. Taking these in the order of their appearance: the *t* over "-mam" in *animam* seems to receive no confirmation in the scripts in columns A–F. In Laon 239, however, the

---

157. "E ut equaliter sonetur eloquitur" ("E declares that it should be sounded equally"—Froger, "L'Épitre de Notker," 69).

158. The phrases given for A and S are: "A ut altius eleuetur admonet"; "S susum uel sursum scandere sibilat" (Froger, "L'Épitre de Notker," 69–70). The phrase for M is given above.

159. Given its description in Notker's letter ("mediocriter melodiam moderari mendicando memorat"), the *m* could also have rhythmic significance. It has been so interpreted by various scholars, among them Mocquereau (*Pal. mus.* 4: 13–14) and Ménager (*Pal. mus.* 10: 181).

160. Corbin, *Die Neumen*, 3: 201, and Ménager, *Pal. mus.* 10: 181.

161. "T trahere uel tenere debere testatur" (Froger, "L'Épitre de Notker," 70).

162. On the use of *t* and its significance in Laon 239, see Billecocq, "Lettres ajoutées à la notation neumatique," 11–20.

two-note ascent is written not with one penstroke—its normal orthography in Laon and elsewhere[163]—but rather with two, the second of which is elongated. The *t* over "me-" in *mei* receives apparent corroboration in columns B–D and G[1]. The first note of the two-note descent is written as a tractulus, as opposed to the normal punctus, in Angers 91 and Chartres 47. St. Gall 339 and St. Gall 359 render this melodic gesture with a single arched penstroke, consisting of an upward preparation, then a turn downward.[164] The scribes of both these sources, however, add another mark at the top of the arc, a slightly curved horizontal stroke referred to as an *episema* (ἐπίσημα, "a distinguishing mark").[165] Rather than writing the single preparation-plus-downward stroke that is normal for this gesture in Laon 239 (ʻ), the scribe places two separate notes above the syllable. Finally, whereas most of the sources render the three-note ascent-descent over "-tant" in *espectant* with a single penstroke—a downward C (sigma) in the Paleofrankish script and the same shape with preparatory stroke in the others[166]—the Laon scribe writes two notes: an upward stroke with preparation for the first two pitches, then a single stroke for the final one. Between the last two pitches, however, he writes the letter *a,* a sign that in the Laon manuscript is used to signify augmentation.[167]

There are other graphic modifications in the various neumations given here that have been interpreted to have rhythmic significance; outlining these would lie outside the bounds of this study.[168] What we can say with certainty is that (1) the early neumes do contain both intrinsic and extrinsic information regarding the rhythmic flow of the music, and (2) this information is relative, that is, it does not tell us precisely how fast or slow, how long or short, specific notes or groups of notes are to be in performance. In this respect, the information the early neumes provided regarding rhythm is analogous to that they provide about pitch: they do not tell us the precise size of the intervals from one pitch to another or from one neume to another.

In summarizing the characteristics of early notation, we are fortunate to have a direct contemporary of Notker Balbulus as a witness. Writing toward the end of the ninth century, Hucbald of St. Amand (ca. 850–930) makes the following observation.

---

163. This note will be called a "pes" or "podatus" in the neume tables. See Huglo, "Les Noms des neumes," 57–60, and Bernhard, "Die Überlieferung der Neumennamen." 19–30, 32–40, 42, 44–60, 62–63, 67, 71–78, 87–88.

164. This note will be called "clivis" or "clinis" in the neume tables. See Huglo, "Les Noms des neumes," and Bernhard, "Die Überlieferung der Neumennamen," 19–30, 32–40, 42, 44–54, 56, 87, 88.

165. This designation is a formulation of modern scholarship.

166. This note will be called a "torculus" in the neume tables.

167. See Ménager, "Aperçu sur la notation du manuscrit 239 de Laon."

168. In addition to the publications summarized by Corbin and Apel (see note 154 here), I refer the reader in particular to the writings of Eugène Cardine and his students. Cardine's principal work is his *Semiologia gregoriana,* published in French translation as "Sémiologie grégorienne." A list of the publications of Dom Cardine and of his students' dissertations may be found in the Festschrift for Cardine, *Ut mens concordet voci,* ed. Göschl, 488–94. See also the bibliography and discussion of Cardine and his work given in Corbin, *Die Neumen,* 3: 202–8, Göschl, "Der gegenwärtige Stand der semiologischen Forschung," *Beiträge zur Gregorianik* 1 (1985): 43–102, and the items listed under "Paläographie und Aufführungspraxis" and "Gregorianische Semiologie" in the "Bibliographie Gregorianischer Choral," ed. Kohlhase and Pauker, *Beiträge zur Gregorianik* 9/10 (1990): 263–86, and 15/16 (1993): 196–212. Colette provides an excellent *accessus* to semiological research in "La Sémiologie comme voie d'accès à la connaissance de l'interprétation au Moyen Age."

The customary notes are not considered altogether unnecessary, since they are deemed quite useful in showing the slowness or swiftness of the melody, and where the sound demands a tremulous voice, or how these sounds are grouped together or separated from each other, also where they are closed lower or higher by reason of certain letters—things of which these artificial notes can show nothing whatsoever.[169]

The "customary notes" Hucbald is referring to are the signs I have just been discussing—practical, neumatic notation. With his references to rhythm ("slowness or swiftness") and melodic groupings, and to ornamental neumes such as the quilisma ("tremulous voice"), and perhaps liquescents ("closed lower or higher by reason of certain letters"), his remarks could serve as a catalogue of the features of ninth-century neumatic notation. The neumes—especially those from the region of northern France where Hucbald was active—are indeed an indispensable guide to the proper performance of the music they represent.

Hucbald had begun this section of his work by introducing a different kind of notation, one created by placing letters next to strings, claiming that this notation had advantages over the "customary notes." He reinforces his assertion by giving an example, an Alleluia written in neumatic notation (ex. 3.25).

EXAMPLE 3.25.   Alleluia in neumatic notation from Hucbald, *De harmonica institutione* (Brussels 10078/95, fol. 90v; Chartier, ed., *L'Oeuvre musicale d'Hucbald*, 194; Babb and Palisca, *Hucbald, Guido, and John on Music*, 36—reprinted from Babb and Palisca)

Of this example he says:

When you have looked at the first note, which appears to be relatively high, you will be able to perform it easily at any pitch whatsoever. But when you try to join the first note to the second, which you observe is lower, there is no way for you to know by what interval you should do it—that is, whether the second note, as established by the composer, should be distant from the first by one, two, or even three degrees [*puncta*]—unless you happen to get it by ear from someone else.[170]

169. "Hae autem consuetudinariae notae non omnino habentur non necessariae, quippe cum et tarditatem seu celeritatem cantilenae, et ubi tremulam sonus contineat vocem, uel qualiter ipsi soni iungantur in unum uel distinguantur ab inuicem, ubi quoque claudantur inferius uel superius pro ratione quarumdam litterarum, quorum nihil omnino hae artificiales notae valent ostendere, ad modum censentur proficuae" (Chartier, ed., *L'Oeuvre musicale d'Hucbald*, 196; transl. 197; GS 1: 118a; Traub, ed., *Hucbald von Saint-Armand*, 64; Babb and Palisca, *Hucbald, Guido, and John on Music*, 37). Chartier (*L'Oeuvre musicale*, 197) feels that *tremulam vocem* probably refers to a quilisma; *qualiter ipsi soni iungantur* to a pressus; and *ubi claudantur* to a liquescent neume such as a cephalicus or ancus.

170. "Primam enim notulam cum aspexeris quae esse uidetur elatior, proferre eam quocumque uocis casu facile poteris. Secundam uero quam pressiorem adtendis, cum primae copulare quaesieris, quonammodo id facias utrum uidelicet uno uel duobus aut certe tribus ab ea elongari debeat punctis, nisi auditu ab alio recipias, nullatenus, sicut a compositore statuta est, pernoscere potes" (Chartier, ed., *L'Oeuvre musicale d'Hucbald*, 194; GS 1: 117; Traub, *Hucbald von Saint-Armand*, 62; Babb and Palisca,

Hucbald is simply describing one of the other characteristics of ninth-century notation, namely, its lack of diastematy. (He could just as easily have been describing any of the notations in the first four columns of ex. 3.9.) Despite their lack of intervallic specificity, however, he admits that these "customary notes" do have advantages, as demonstrated above—advantages his new "artificial notes" do not offer. Nonetheless, even though they cannot show the nuances of performance the traditional notation conveys, these new, "artificial notes" obviously have virtues the "customary notes" do not. Just what those virtues are and how they are conveyed we shall explore in the next chapter.

Hucbald, Guido, and John on Music, 36). Hucbald had earlier defined musical sound as the "uocis casus **EMMEΛEC** . . . una intensione productus" ("the harmonious falling of the voice . . . on a single pitch"; Chartier, ed., *L'Oeuvre musicale d'Hucbald,* 152; GS 1: 108; Traub, ed., *Hucbald von Saint-Armand,* 34; Babb and Palisca, *Hucbald, Guido, and John on Music,* 21). On Hucbald's use of *punctum,* see chapter 4 here, note 5. My translation of the entire passage is a bit free for the sake of clarity.

PART II

THE SYNTHESIS
OF ANCIENT GREEK THEORY
AND MEDIEVAL PRACTICE

CHAPTER FOUR

HUCBALD OF ST. AMAND
AND REGINO OF PRÜM

As we saw in the preceding chapters, it was during the course of the ninth century that various aspects of ancient Greek harmonic theory, drawn primarily
from Boethius's *De arithmetica* and *De institutione musica* and from Martianus Capella's
De nuptiis Philologiae et Mercurii, began to be commented on and assimilated into medieval musical thought. Chapter 2 of Aurelian's *Musica disciplina* and chapters 9–19 of
the *Musica enchiriadis* include some of the first independent signs of this activity. A
work that makes even greater use of Boethius, and to a lesser extent Martianus
Capella, than did its ninth-century predecessors is the treatise *De harmonica institutione*,
written either around 885 or 893–99 by Hucbald of St. Amand (ca. 850–930).[1]
Hucbald's work represents the first attempt to fuse Boethian theory with chant theory, and it is, in many ways, a remarkable accomplishment. This is perhaps no wonder,
given that three loci of his activity—St. Amand, Auxerre, and Reims—are among the
most important centers for the early transmission of Boethius's *De institutione musica*,
and for Donatus's *Ars grammatica* and Martianus Capella's *De nuptiis Philologiae* as well.[2]

---

1. Ed. in Chartier, *L'Oeuvre musicale d'Hucbald*, 136–212; GS 1: 104–21; and Traub, ed., "Hucbald von
Saint-Amand" (with corrections in Traub, "Nachlese zu Hucbald von Saint-Amand"). The date of
Hucbald's birth is not secure. Weakland ("Hucbald as Musician and Theorist," 68) felt it was ca. 840;
Chartier (*L'Oeuvre musicale d'Hucbald*, 2) is of the opinion that it is closer to 850 than to 840. The date of
his death is 20 June 930. Chartier (*L'Oeuvre musicale d'Hucbald*, 76) believes that the treatise was written
ca. 885 at the monastery of St. Bertin. The later date, 893–99, was suggested by Huglo in "Les Instruments de musique chez Hucbald," 183–84. This would place the composition of the work in Reims during Hucbald's tenure there as teacher, together with Remigius of Auxerre. Emendations to Gerbert's text,
as well as an English translation of the treatise and an introduction to it, are available in Babb and Palisca,
Hucbald, Guido, and John on Music. The treatise is variously titled in its manuscript sources. Gerbert chose
De harmonica institutione, following the manuscript Cesena XXVI. 1 (fifteenth century); the same designation is found in Barcelona 42 (eleventh century). In most of its eleven surviving sources, the work either carries no designation or is called simply *Musica* (Chartier, *L'Oeuvre musicale d'Hucbald*, 46).

2. According to the twelfth-century chronicler Gonthier de St. Amand, Hucbald received his initial
training in St. Amand in Tournai; around 870, he became a student of Heiric at Auxerre, and later a colleague of Remigius of Auxerre, when the two of them were teaching at the cathedral school of Reims
in 893. For the chronicles of Gonthier de St. Amand, see Migne, ed., *PL* 203: cols. 1311–12. On Heiric,
see Ganz, "Heiric d'Auxerre." On Hucbald at Reims, see Chartier, *L'Oeuvre musicale d'Hucbald*, 5–10.

The *Musica disciplina* of Aurelian of Réôme, the *Musica* and *Scolica enchiriadis,* and the works of John Scottus Eriugena must likewise have been known to him.[3]

That Hucbald intended his work for singers, rather than mathematicians, is apparent from the opening sections of his treatise. Rather than defining concepts by means of mathematical proportions or the monochord, Hucbald describes pitches, intervals, and consonances by referring to examples from the repertoire of plainchant. This is true even in his presentation of the intervals of the tone and semitone. Whereas Boethius had presented the whole tone as the musical expression of the sesquioctave proportion, and had then provided a brief mathematical demonstration that it could not be divided into two equal semitones,[4] Hucbald makes no use of mathematics at all. Instead, he says "It is a tone when a pitch is lowered or raised from another pitch, either low or high, by a moderately small interval—a displacement, as it were, by one degree [*unius puncti*]—so that the hearing notices the difference between them quite easily."[5] He completes his demonstration with a reference

---

Boethius's *De institutione musica* is likely to have been accessible to Hucbald. Of the ten ninth-century manuscripts selected by Bower as "control manuscripts" for his translation (*Boethius: Fundamentals of Music,* xl–xliii), nine were copied close to the orbit of Hucbald's activity—that is, in the region of what is now northern France and southern Belgium. St. Amand itself is the probable place of origin for Paris 7201; Reims is also where Paris 13908 was probably written. (This is MS *Q* in Bernhard and Bower, eds., *Glossa maior in institutionem Boethii.* The comments of its second glossator are discussed in chapter 2 here, pp. 79–81).

As to the proximity of Donatus to Hucbald, the commentaries on Donatus by Murethach (dating from ca. 835–40), and Sedulius Scottus (dated ca. 840–50) are among the most important early commentaries on this text, and their provenance can be situated in Auxerre and Liège, respectively (see chapter 2 here, pp. 56–58; see also Holtz, "Sur trois commentaires irlandais"; and Holtz, "Murethach et l'influence de la culture irlandaise à Auxerre."). Moreover, several of the earliest manuscripts of Donatus were copied in this region (see Holtz, *Donat et l'enseignement grammatical,* 377–78, 386–88, 394–95; and Holtz, "L'École d'Auxerre").

Similar circumstances pertain to the transmission of Martianus Capella's *De nuptiis Philologiae et Mercurii* (see Préaux, "Les Manuscrits principaux," 77–80; and Shanzer, "Felix Capella," 66–72; 76–78). Four of the eight earliest sources of Martianus in Teeuwen's stemma (*Harmony and the Music of the Spheres,* 147) are from Auxerre or Reims, and Remigius's commentary on Martianus—one of the most important— may have been written in Reims while he and Hucbald were teaching there (see Lutz, ed., *Remigius of Auxerre: Commentum in Martianum Capellam,* 1: 50–62). Finally, the twelfth-century *Index maior* of the St. Amand library (Paris 1850, fol. 199, ed. Delisle, *Le Cabinet des manuscrits,* 2: 449–58) attributes a manuscript copy of Martianus's work, now lost, to Hucbald (see Phillips, "'Musica' and 'Scolica enchiriadis,'" 40–41; and Chartier, ed., *L'Oeuvre musicale d'Hucbald,* 51).

3. As we have seen, the earliest manuscript of the *Musica disciplina* of Aurelian is Valenciennes 148, which was copied in the late ninth century at St. Amand, or perhaps St. Germain d'Auxerre (see chapter 3 here, note 17). What is, perhaps, the earliest manuscript of the complete text of both the *Musica* and *Scolica enchiriadis*—Valenciennes 337—was also copied at St. Amand, in either the late ninth or early tenth century. See the descriptions of these manuscripts in *RISM* B III[1]; see Gushee, ed., *Aurelianus Reomensis: Musica disciplina, CSM,* 21, 1–30; Schmid, *Musica et Scolica enchiriadis,* vii–xii; and Phillips, "'Musica' and 'Scolica enchiriadis,'" 40–51. On Hucbald's familiarity with John Scottus, see Chartier, ed., *L'Oeuvre d'Hucbald,* 8 and 77–81. The latter connection is particularly important, because John commented on Martianus Capella and Calcidius and, according to Duchez ("Jean Scot Érigène"), may have been the "premier lecteur du 'De institutione musica' de Boèce." Whether he was the "premier lecteur" or not, John was certainly well acquainted with Boethius's *De musica.*

4. Boethius, *De institutione musica,* Book I, chap. 16. See the discussion of this in chapter 1 here, pp. 20–21.

5. "Est ergo tonus cum uox ab alio seu graui seu acuto sono, modico deflectitur aut erigitur interu-

to the antiphon *Ite dicite Iohanni.* Of the semitone, he says (apparently following Martianus Capella) that it "appears to be so called from its containing approximately half a tone."[6] Then, however, he plants himself firmly in the Pythagorean camp by way of Boethius when he continues: "But if this were so, a tone could be divided into two equal parts, whereas proof has been furnished by some of the greatest authorities that this is utterly impossible."[7] He goes on to say that there are two semitones, one major and one minor, and he even provides a simple diagram:[8]

Tonus   Semitonium maius   Semitonium minus

‾‾‾‾‾‾‾‾‾‾‾‾‾‾‾‾‾   ‾‾‾‾‾‾‾‾‾‾‾   ‾‾‾‾‾‾

But despite extensive further description and the provision of two examples from plainchant by way of illustration, Hucbald never attempts to provide even the simple mathematical proof that Boethius had given in Book I, chapter 16 of his work.[9] He does, however, present a method of demonstrating these intervals that at least hints of the precision of instrumental, harmonic theory.

Hucbald says that one can find an example of a semitone between the third and fourth strings of a six-stringed cithara, either ascending or descending.[10] In order to demonstrate this, he maps the incipit of the antiphon *Ecce vere Israhelita* onto a six-line matrix representing the "strings" of the cithara, between each of which the letters *T* (for tone) or *S* (for semitone) are placed in order to indicate the size of the interval in question (ex. 4.1).[11]

---

allo, ueluti unius puncti diremptione, ita ut omnino earum diuisionem facile auditus aduertat . . . et in hac probare poteris antiphona." [An. *Ite dicite*] (Chartier, ed., *L'Oeuvre d'Hucbald*, 154–56; GS 1: 108b; Traub, ed., "Hucbald von Saint-Amand," 36; and Babb and Palisca, *Hucbald, Guido, and John on Music,* 21). Chartier makes the point that Hucbald's use of the term *punctus* here is a direct reference to the diagram of the "instrumental scale" that immediately precedes it in these manuscripts. (See Chartier, ed., *L'Oeuvre d'Hucbald*, 156–57; and Traub, ed., "Hucbald von Saint-Amand," 36, 80, and 88; the latter two pages contain facsimiles of Brussels 10078/95, fol. 86v, and Einsiedeln 169, fol. 118, respectively. Unfortunately, the diagram does not appear in Gerbert's edition of the text or in Babb's translation.) In the diagram, the interval of a whole tone is represented by a single *punctus,* a semitone by two *puncti.*

6. "Semitonivm vero dictum videtur. Quasi medietatem contineat toni" (Chartier, ed., *L'Oeuvre d'Hucbald*, 156; Traub, ed., "Hucbald von Saint-Amand," 38; Babb and Palisca, *Hucbald, Guido, and John on Music,* 22). Martianus had described the semitone as follows: "Hemitonium dicitur quod toni medium tenet" (*De nuptiis,* sec. 930; ed. Cristante, 132; ed. Willis, 357).

7. "Sed si ita esset, tunc in duas aequas partes tonus posset partiri, quod nullatenus fieri posse, diligentiorum probabile reddiderunt ingenia" (Chartier, ed., *L'Oeuvre d'Hucbald*, 156; Traub, ed., "Hucbald von Saint-Amand," 38–39; Babb and Palisca, *Hucbald, Guido, and John on Music,* 22).

8. Chartier, ed., *L'Oeuvre d'Hucbald*, 158; Traub, ed., "Hucbald von Saint-Amand," 38–39, 80 (Brussels 10078/95, fol. 86v), and 88 (Einsiedeln 169, p. 118); Babb and Palisca, *Hucbald, Guido, and John on Music,* 22.

9. See the discussion in chapter 1 here, pp. 20–21.

10. Significantly, in order to illustrate the disposition of the six strings, Hucbald compares them to analogous passages in plainchant. An example containing the semitone in an ascending passage is the phrase *acceperunt ramos* from the antiphon *Cum audisset populus;* the interval is found in a descending passage at the word *Pentecostes* in the antiphon *Hodie completi sunt.* (See Babb and Palisca, *Hucbald, Guido, and John on Music,* 23, for examples in the original notation together with modern transcriptions. See also Huglo, "Les Instruments de musique chez Hucbald," 184–88.

11. On the six-string cithara, as well as the piece itself, see Huglo, "Les Instruments de musique chez Hucbald," 184–88.

EXAMPLE 4.1.   Line diagram representing the six-string cithara in Hucbald, *De harmonica institutione* (Chartier, ed., *L'Oeuvre musicale d'Hucbald*, 160—diagram reprinted from Chartier)

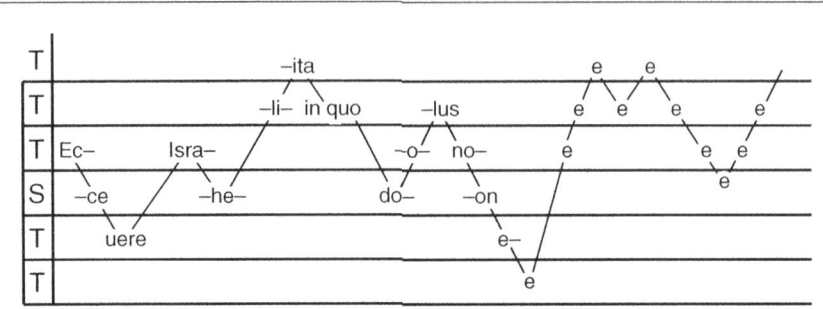

VBICVMQVE ERGO IN QUOLIBET MELO huiusmodi reppereris interuallum quale hic inter sillabas .**ec**. et .**ce**. uel .**ra**. **he**. uel .**do o**. uel .**no**. **on**. semitonium esse non dubites. Vbi uero taliter discrepantes uoces, ut .**li**. **ita**. uel .**ta**. **in**, uel .**lus**. **no**. uel .**ce**. **ue**. uel ultimam .**non**. et primam **est**. uel ipsam primam .**est**. et eius ultimam, tonus sine dubio erit.

As he says:

> Wherever, then, you find in any melody an interval such as here between the syllables "Ec-" and "-ce," or "-ra-" and "-he-," or "do-" "-o-," or "no-" "-on," you should not doubt that it is a semitone. But where you find syllables differing in sound, such as "-li-" "-ita," or "-ta" "in," or "-lus" "no-," or "-ce" "ue-," or the end of "non" and the beginning of "est," or the beginning and end of "est," there, without doubt, will be a tone.[12]

Even if the Boethian proportions are not presented here, one certainly detects the impression of harmonic precision *avant la lettre*.

After introducing the intervals of plainchant, Hucbald follows Boethius in the way he presents the two-octave system, but the initial presentation of this system is made by means of successive intervals, in ascending pitch-order and without any of the Greek instrumental nomenclature or mathematical precision of the earlier author. In his words: "In ascending order, after you first place one extra note, as it were, separating it by a tone from the next one, you then go up through [the pattern] semitone, tone, tone for seven notes. Thereupon, after again inserting a gap [*disiunctio*] of a tone, you proceed through the next seven notes higher in just the same way."[13] The whole series of notes may be indicated by this diagram:

12. Chartier, ed., *L'Oeuvre d'Hucbald*, 160; GS 1: 109; Traub, ed., "Hucbald von Saint-Amand," 40; see Babb and Palisca, *Hucbald, Guido, and John on Music*, 23.

13. "Ut si scandendum fuerit, uno inprimis sono quasi extra posito, quem tono diuidas a sequenti, deinceps per semitonium, tonum et tonum usque ad septem uoces conscendas. Post quas disiunctione

T	ST	T	T	ST	T	T	T	ST	T	T	ST	T	T

[A   B   C   D   E   F   G   a   ♭   c   d   e   f   g   aa][14]

In what might seem like a digression, Hucbald then presents the "instrumental" scale also given in the *Scolica enchiriadis* (see ex. 4.2). Unlike the author of the *Scolica,* however, Hucbald provides neither a mathematical rationale nor a monochord division for this scale. Instead, he describes its structure (in ascending order) and provides an example from chant (part of the offertory *Angelus Domini*) in order to demonstrate it. Again in his words:

> The disposition of such instruments, then, is so planned as to ascend by a tone, tone, and semitone, and then three adjacent tones and a semitone for eight notes; and beginning again from this eighth note, a higher series is measured off by the same steps, in this manner.

EXAMPLE.4.2.   Instrumental tone-system as presented in Hucbald, *De harmonica institutione* (Chartier, ed., *L'Oeuvre musicale d'Hucbald*, 166—diagram reprinted from Chartier)

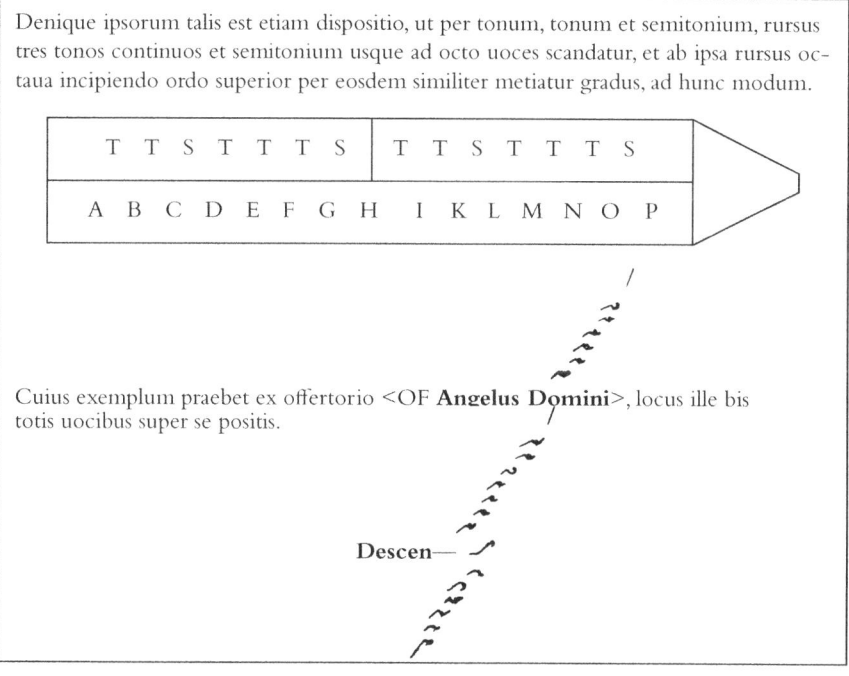

Denique ipsorum talis est etiam dispositio, ut per tonum, tonum et semitonium, rursus tres tonos continuos et semitonium usque ad octo uoces scandatur, et ab ipsa rursus octaua incipiendo ordo superior per eosdem similiter metiatur gradus, ad hunc modum.

T	T	S	T	T	T	S	T	T	S	T	T	T	S
A	B	C	D	E	F	G	H	I	K	L	M	N	O	P

Cuius exemplum praebet ex offertorio <OF **Angelus Domini**>, locus ille bis totis uocibus super se positis.

Descen—

iterum toni admissa, superiores septem uoces eodem modo per omnia decurres" (Chartier, ed., *L'Oeuvre d'Hucbald*, 162; GS 1: 110; Traub, ed., "Hucbald von Saint-Amand," 42; transl. in Babb and Palisca, *Hucbald, Guido, and John on Music*, 24.

14. For Hucbald's diagram, see the sources cited in the preceding note. I have supplied the modern note-equivalents that appear within brackets below the diagram.

An example of this is supplied by the offertory [*Angelus Domini*] at the place [*Descendit*] over which all the notes appear.[15]

As one can see, the diagram shows the letters A-H-P opposite the degrees of the scale, just as in the *Scolica enchiriadis,* although there is no monochord division in Hucbald's treatise.[16] (Significantly, these letters had not been assigned to the Greater Perfect System just given.) Hucbald acknowledges at the outset that this "instrumental" scale is different from the one he had just presented, which he says was derived from Boethius. He justifies its inclusion here, however, by saying that it has been in use for a long time, and that it is particularly appropriate for instruments. He also says that the large number of strings or pipes is present "for the variety of the modes, which are nowadays called tones, such as the Protus authentic and the others,"[17] so that each might have sufficient scope for its range, from whatever note it may start. As we shall see, there may be a concrete reason for the upward extension of range Hucbald mentions.[18]

After presenting both the Greater Perfect System and the instrumental scale, Hucbald explains one of the features common to both and why it is important. The feature in question is the octave equivalence that characterizes both of these scales, a feature that contrasts with the augmented octaves in the Dasia tone-system of the *Musica* and *Scolica enchiriadis.* Of both the scales he has presented, Hucbald says that their upper octaves are like boys' voices, the lower ones like men's, so that when sung together they will blend with an "altogether pleasant and harmonious sweetness" that is called the "consonance of the diapason."[19] Clearly, Hucbald does not want to rely on "miracles" in order to sing organum at the octave![20]

Once the principle of octave equivalence has been set forth, Hucbald then returns to the Greater Perfect System, disposing it now in descending pitch order, with two pairs of conjunct tetrachords separated by a point of disjunction. The tetrachords themselves are disposed T-T-ST descending, just as they would be in Boethius. Hucbald's method of realizing them, however, is to remind his reader that they are like "the first four notes of the [NOEANE] melody of the Protus authentic."[21]

---

15. Chartier, ed., *L'Oeuvre d'Hucbald,* 166; GS 1: 110b–111; Traub, ed., "Hucbald von Saint-Amand," 42–45; Babb and Palisca, *Hucbald, Guido, and John on Music,* 25.

16. On this notation, see Santosuosso, *Letter Notations,* 16–17; Phillips, "Notationen und Notationslehren," 336–38; and Smits van Waesberghe, "Les Origines de la notation alphabétique," 7–9.

17. "[P]ro uarietate modorum, qui toni nunc appellantur, ut est 'autentus protus' et ceteri." Chartier, ed., *L'Oeuvre d'Hucbald,* 164; GS 1: 110b; Traub, ed., "Hucbald von Saint-Amand," 42–43; Babb and Palisca, *Hucbald, Guido, and John on Music,* 25.

18. See notes 36–39 here and the associated discussion.

19. The entire passage reads "Hoc autem tam in hac quam superiori dispositione est attendendum, quod superiores octo voces eaedem sunt, quae et inferiores, excepto quod illae quasi puerilis sunt uocis, hae contra ipsas quasi virilis. Et ideo postquam septimum protuleris sonum, continuo in octavo quasi in nouam prosilies vocem. Itaque prima cum octaua, secunda cum nona; tertia cum decima, et ita per ordinem singulae inferiores cum singulis superioribus pulsae, dulci et concordabili suauitate omnimodis consonabunt, ac si unus, simplexque sit sonus. Et haec talis concordia diapason consonantia appellatur" (Chartier, ed., *L'Oeuvre d'Hucbald,* 166; GS 1: 111a; Traub, ed., "Hucbald von Saint-Amand," 44; Babb and Palisca, *Hucbald, Guido, and John on Music,* 25).

20. See *Musica enchiriadis,* chap. 11 (ed. Schmid, 33–34).

21. "Huius autem cuiusque tetrachordi exemplum, prima e .IIII. uoculae ex melodia autenti proti

EXAMPLE. 4.3.   Greater Perfect System in ascending order as presented by Hucbald in
De harmonica institutione (Brussels 10078/95, fol. 88v; Chartier, ed., *L'Oeuvre musicale
d'Hucbald*, 174; Babb and Palisca, *Hucbald, Guido, and John on Music*, 28—diagram reprinted
from Babb and Palisca)

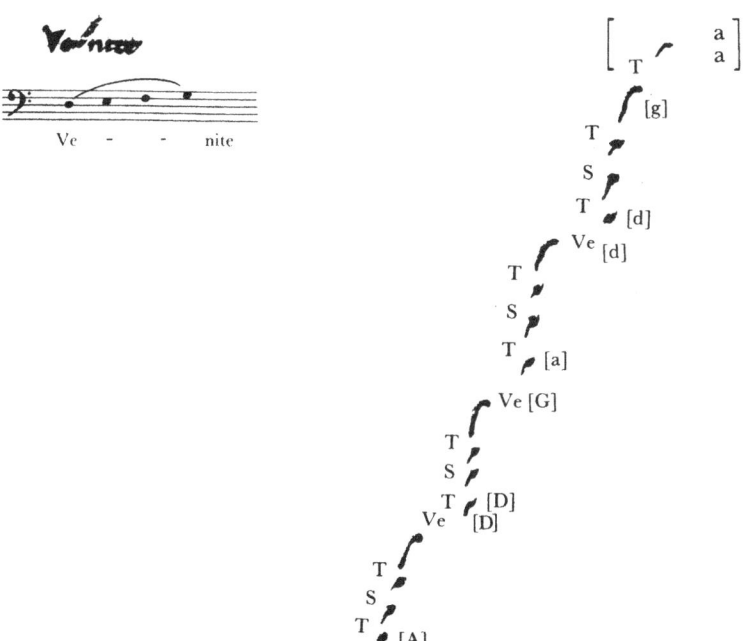

Following this, however, he presents the same system in ascending order "from the
very first note" (i.e., the proslambanomenos, which is represented by *A*), employing "modal" tetrachords with the structure T-ST-T, the same as those found in the
Enchiriadis system (ex. 4.3). The chant phrase that serves as the model for this tetrachord is "Venite" from the invitatorium *Christus natus est*.[22]

When Hucbald demonstrates the insertion of the conjunct tetrachord "that
the theorists call 'synemmenon,'"[23] the tetrachords he uses to illustrate are again
"modal" tetrachords, T-ST-T, rather than the ancient Greek diatonic tetrachord
with the ascending pitch structure ST-T-T. Hence, the point of conjunction must
be, in effect, the lichanos meson, rather than the mese (ex. 4.4).[24] The chant example
illustrating this is the phrase on "David" from the responsory *Nativitas gloriosae*.

monstrabunt" (Chartier, ed., *L'Oeuvre d'Hucbald*, 168; GS 1: 111b; Traub, ed., "Hucbald von Saint-
Amand," 46; Babb and Palisca, *Hucbald, Guido, and John on Music*, 26).

22. Chartier, ed., *L'Oeuvre d'Hucbald*, 174; GS 1: 112b; Traub, ed., "Hucbald von Saint-Amand," 48;
Babb and Palisca, *Hucbald, Guido, and John on Music*, 28.

23. Chartier, ed., *L'Oeuvre d'Hucbald*, 178; GS 1: 113; Traub, ed., "Hucbald von Saint-Amand," 52–53;
Babb and Palisca, *Hucbald, Guido, and John on Music*, 29–30.

24. Hucbald says that the synemmenon tetrachord is located "post septimam superioris ordinis chor-

EXAMPLE 4.4.   Lesser Perfect System in ascending order as presented by Hucbald in *De harmonica institutione* (Brussels 10078/95, fol. 88v; Chartier, ed., *L'Oeuvre musicale d'Hucbald*, 178; Babb and Palisca, *Hucbald, Guido, and John on Music*, 29–30—diagram reprinted from Babb and Palisca)

Da - - vid

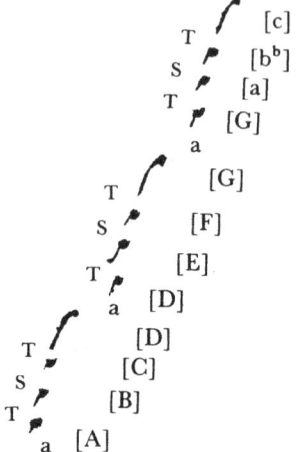

T [c]
S [b♭]
T [a]
[G]
a

T [G]
S [F]
T [E]
a [D]

T [D]
[C]
S
T [B]
a [A]

After having presented both the Greater and Lesser Perfect Systems by means of examples drawn from plainchant, Hucbald then goes on to present the full Greek instrumental nomenclature of pitches and tetrachords in both the Greater Perfect and "synemmenon" systems.[25] These are presented together with his own version of the Alypian notational signs from Boethius (see ex. 4.5, sec. A).[26]

---

dam: ita ut ipsa septima prima sit huius" (after the seventh [pitch] of the above array, so that that seventh [pitch] must be its first). In the array immediately preceding, Hucbald had constructed the system from top to bottom, ending on the proslambanomenos. Thus, the seventh pitch, the lichanos meson (G), rather than the mese (A), would have to be the point of conjunction.

25. This combined system is what several ancient Greek writers refer to as the *ametabolon systema* or Immutable System (see chapter 1 here, note 30).

26. On the use of the Alypian notational signs in Hucbald, see Babb and Palisca, *Hucbald, Guido, and John on Music*, 9–10; Santosuosso, *Letter Notations*, 11–17; Chartier, ed., *L'Oeuvre d'Hucbald*, 67–75; Chartier, "Hucbald de Saint-Amand et la notation musicale," 145–56; Phillips, "Notationen und Notationslehren," 305–11; Smits van Waesberghe, "Les Origines de la notation alphabétique," 9–11; Wingell, "Hucbald," 24–26; Potiron, "Origine de la notation alphabetique"; and Potiron, "La Notation grecque dans 'l'Institution harmonique' d'Hucbald." One should note that the signs appear in a number of manuscripts of the treatise. together with the presentation of the ancient Greek nomenclature for the Greater Perfect System (Chartier, ed., *L'Oeuvre d'Hucbald*, 184; GS 1: 115), and that they are used in subsequent illustrations as well. Their omission from most of the diagrams in Traub, ed., "Hucbald von Saint-Amand," and from Babb and Palisca, *Hucbald, Guido, and John on Music*, is regrettable, but it came about because Brussels 10078/95, which also omits the diagram, served as the base manuscript for the editions in both of the latter sources.

EXAMPLE 4.5. (A) Hucbald's tone-system; and (B) that of Pseudo-Odo (Brussels 10078/95, fol. 91; Chartier, ed., *L'Oeuvre musicale d'Hucbald*, 198; Babb and Palisca, *Hucbald, Guido, and John on Music*, 38—diagram based on that in Babb and Palisca)

		A Hucbald		B Pseudo-Odo
Nete hyperboleon: it has an amplified iota, thus:		Ƴ	$\begin{bmatrix} a \\ a \end{bmatrix}$	a a
Paranete hyperboleon: [has] an amplified Greek Π		ᗺ	[g]	g
Trite hyperboleon: a simple y		⅄	[f]	f
Nete diezeugmenon: a small N		и	[e]	e
Paranete diezeugmenon: a square ω		ᗺ	[d]	d
Trite diezeugmenon: a simple ε		Ɛ	[c]	c
Paramese: a Greek Π lying on its side		▬	[b♮]	♮
Nete synemmenon: the same as the paranete diezeugmenon		ᗺ	[d]	(d)
Paranete synemmenon: the same as the trite diezeugmenon		ᗷ	[c]	(c)
Trite synemmenon: a Greek theta		ᴑ	[b♭]	b
Mese: a simple iota		I	[a]	a
Lichanos meson: a simple M		ᴙ	[G]	G
Parhypate meson: a simple Greek P [rho]		ᖘ	[F]	F
Hypate meson: a simple Greek sigma		ᘓ	[E]	E
Lichanos hypaton: a simple digamma		Ⅎ	[D]	D
Parhypate hypaton: a simple beta		Ⴆ	[C]	C
Hypate hypaton: a simple gamma		Γ	[B]	B
Proslambanomenos: an upright dasia		ⱦ	[A]	A
				Γ

(Finales: G, F, E, D)

Hucbald brings these ancient Greek systems and their notation into congruence with the medieval practice of plainchant in two ways. First, as one can see in example 4.6, he applies the pseudo-Alypian signs to examples of chant written in normal, neumatic notation, thereby mapping the neumes onto an ancient Greek scalar matrix. He claims that this is important because

These musical signs [*notae musicae*, i.e., the modified Alypian signs he has been discussing] were devised so that . . . every melody notated with them, once they have

EXAMPLE 4.6.   Notation using both neumes and letters in Hucbald,
De harmonica institutione (Brussels 10078/95, fol. 90v; Babb and Palisca,
Hucbald, Guido, and John on Music, 36–37—reprinted from Babb and Palisca)

been learned, can be sung even without a teacher. One is scarcely able to attain this
by means of the signs [*notae*] that practice has handed down to us, and that in diverse
regions are given no less diverse shapes, although they are of some help as an aid to
one's memory. For they always lead the reader on an uncertain path.[27]

As observed in chapter 3, what Hucbald refers to as the "signs that practice has
handed down to us, and that in diverse regions are given no less diverse shapes" are
the signs we know as neumes. Indeed, Hucbald's testimony supports the evidence
of surviving manuscript sources that at least some of the various families of neumes,
such as Paleofrankish, Breton, and early French, were already in existence in the
ninth century. As also noted, the earliest neumes are not diastematic, but rather
served as an *aide memoire* to the singers, reminding them of melodic contour along
with other aspects of the chant they were singing—just as Hucbald says. In accord
with this, Hucbald urges that his pseudo-Alypian letters be added to traditional
chant notation in order to secure an adequate *Schriftbild* of the chant:

> Therefore, if these same letters that we accept as musical notes are placed above or near
> the customary ones, one by one, it will clearly be possible to perceive a perfect trac-
> ing [*indago*] of the truth, without any error, since these letters indicate how much
> higher or lower each pitch should be borne, while the customary notes fix more ac-

27. "Hae [notas musicas] ad hanc utilitatem sunt repertae, ut . . . per has omne melos adnotatum,
etiam sine docente, postquam semel cognitae fuerint, ualeat decantari. Quod his notis quas nunc usus
tradidit quaeque pro locorum uarietate diuersis nichilominus deformantur figuris, quamuis ad aliquid
prosint rememorationis subsidium, minime potes contingere. Incerto enim semper uidentem ducunt
uestigio" (Chartier, ed., *L'Oeuvre d'Hucbald*, 194; *GS* 1: 117; Traub, "Hucbald von Saint-Amand," 62; Babb
and Palisca, *Hucbald, Guido, and John on Music*, 36).

curately in the mind the above-mentioned nuances of performance, without which valid melody is not created.[28]

Hucbald accomplished a truly signal development by combining traditional neumes with quasi-Boethian letters to situate the melodies of chant on the scalar matrix of the ancient Greek Greater Perfect and Lesser Perfect Systems.

A second important innovation Hucbald made in the *De harmonica institutione* was to bring not just the melodies but also the melodic classifications of the "four *modi* or *tropi*, that are nowadays called *toni*" into rapport with the ancient Greek tone-system.[29] He explains that the ancient Greek lichanos hypaton (*D*) governs the Protus authentic and its plagal, that is, the first and second (*toni*); the hypate meson (*E*) governs the Deuterus authentic and its plagal, the third and fourth; the parhypate meson (*F*) governs the Tritus authentic and its plagal, the fifth and sixth; and the lichanos meson (*G*) governs the Tetrardus authentic and its plagal, the seventh and eighth.[30] In his words:

> These four [protus, deuterus, tritus, tetrardus] are called Finales, since all things that are sung take their end in them. . . . In the likeness of these, the other tetrachords—one of which is lower, three [!] above—derive their intervals and quality of sound. Consultation of the examples given above will have made all of these things sufficiently clear.[31]

28. "Quapropter si super aut circa has per singulos ptongos eaedem litterulae, quas pro notis musicis accipimus, apponantur, perfecte ac sine ullo errore indaginem ueritatis liquebit inspicere, cum hae quanto elatius quantoue pressius uox quaeque feratur insinuent: illae vero supradictas varietates, sine quibus rata non texitur cantilena, menti certius figant" (Chartier, ed., *L'Oeuvre d'Hucbald*, 196; GS 1: 118; Traub, ed., "Hucbald von Saint-Amand," 64; Babb and Palisca, *Hucbald, Guido, and John on Music*, 37). See chapter 3 here, note 169, for Hucbald's description of the performance nuances conveyed by the "customary notes."

29. See Chartier, ed., *L'Oeuvre d'Hucbald*, 200; GS 1: 119a; Traub, ed., "Hucbald von Saint-Amand," 66; and Babb and Palisca, *Hucbald, Guido, and John on Music*, 38. It is, of course, Boethius who first advances the equation of *modi, tropi, vel toni*. The fact that Hucbald says that the modes or tropes are "nowadays called *toni*" offers yet further evidence that the scheme of classification found in the tonaries and related ninth-century writings was the common one in his day. See chapter 3 here, pp. 86–98.

30. According to Huglo, *Les Tonaires*, 57, Hucbald is the first to provide this numbering scheme for the modes or tones, which will become the standard one in the West. (It is implied in the *Musica enchiriadis*, chap. 4, and it is presented explicitly in the *Commemoratio brevis*.) The Byzantine equivalent numbers first the four ἦχοι, then their plagals (see chapter 3 here, pp. 114–17).

31. "Unde & eaedem finales appellatae, quod finem in ipsis cuncta quae canuntur, accipiunt. . . . Ad quarum exemplar caetera nihilominus tetrachorda, quorum unum inferius, tria superius eminent, spatia vel qualitates deducunt sonorum. Quae omnia sufficiens superioribus exemplorum monstravit adiectio" (Chartier, ed., *L'Oeuvre d'Hucbald*, 200–203; GS 1: 119; Traub, ed., "Hucbald von Saint-Amand," 68; Babb and Palisca, *Hucbald, Guido, and John on Music*, 39). In his reference to "three [tetrachords] above," Hucbald may have had in mind the three ancient Greek tetrachords that would lie above the tetrachord of the Finales in pitch, namely, the synemmenon, the diezeugmenenon, and the hyperboleon. If this is the case, however, he would be contradicting himself. With their ST-T-T structure, the ancient Greek tetrachords do not "derive their intervals and quality of sound" from the tetrachord of the Finales. Given that he refers to one tetrachord below the Finales, one might assume that the reference is to the tetrachord of the Graves as expounded in the *Musica enchiriadis*. In Hucbald's tone-system, however, there are only three pitches beneath the tetrachord of the Finales (see ex. 4.5, sec. A).

With these two gestures, Hucbald forges a link between the "instrumental" Greek theory of Boethius and the "vocal" theory of plainchant and its notation found in the *Musica enchiriadis*.[32] When the definitive scheme of Latin letter notation for plainchant finally does appear in the treatise of Pseudo-Odo in the late tenth or early eleventh century,[33] it preserves the scalar matrix already set out by Hucbald, adding only a gamma at the lower end of the system. Pseudo-Odo's system appears next to Hucbald's in column B of example 4.5. It assumes special importance because Odo applies it directly to the teaching of singing via musical notation and the use of the monochord.[34] As Odo says, he has taught boys to learn several antiphons by themselves "simply with an exemplar written according to the rules."[35] The "exemplar written according to the rules" that Odo had before him must have looked something like Hucbald's notation illustrated in example 4.6, that is, chants written in neumatic notation but with Latin letters added to them.

Inasmuch as Hucbald is our first witness to the direct conjunction of ancient Greek theory and chant notation, it should perhaps come as no surprise that he is also our first witness to the possible necessity of transposing chant, introducing the notion of the *socialitas* ("comradeship") of notes a fifth above the final (the "affinities" or alternative finals).[36] In his words:

> It should be observed in these [examples given above] that—the tetrachord of the synemmenon having been omitted—the notes at a fifth position above each of these four finals are always joined with them in such a bond of similarity that melodies may often be found to close on these notes a fifth above without offending either one's judgment or ear, and that they run their course perfectly within the same mode or trope. Therefore, they hold this *socialitas*.[37]

32. Hucbald never mentions the *Musica* or *Scolica enchiriadis* by name, but various kinds of evidence suggest that he did know the works. Apart from the web of manuscript evidence cited in note 3 here, Nancy Phillips mentions that one of the four extant ninth-century copies of the florilegium containing the passages from Augustine used in the *Scolica* was in the library at St. Amand. Moreover, Valenciennes 293, one of three extant ninth-century copies of Calcidius's commentary on Plato's *Timaeus*, from which the *enchiriadis* treatises clearly borrowed, may have been a personal copy of Hucbald (see Waszink, ed., *Timaeus a Calcidio translatus*, cxxvii; Phillips, "'*Musica*' and '*Scolica enchiriadis*,'" 40; and Chartier, ed., *L'Oeuvre d'Hucbald*, 51; in "Classical and Late Latin Sources," 127–28, however, Phillips calls this assignment of ownership into question).

33. Ed. *GS* 1: 252–64; a new edition is being prepared by Karl-Werner Gümpel. See Huglo, "L'Auteur du 'Dialogue sur la musique' attribué à Odon"; Huglo, *Les Tonaires*, 182–224, 325; Gushee, "Questions of Genre in Medieval Treatises on Music," 404–7; Oesch, *Guido von Arezzo*, 49–63; and Markovits, *Das Tonsystem der abendländischen Musik im frühen Mittelalter*, 17, 25, 29–31, 35, 45, 79, 81, 103. The treatise is discussed in chapter 6 here, pp. 212–19.

34. See the discussion in chapter 6 here, pp. 212–14.

35. "[Q]uam plures antiphonas, non audientes ab aliquo, sed regulari tantummodo descriptione contenti per se discerent." *D. Oddonis Dialogus de musica*, in *GS* 1: 251. My translation is a slightly modified version of that in Strunk, *Source Readings*, 104, and McKinnon, *The Early Christian Period and the Latin Middle Ages*, 89. On Hucbald's desire that singers be able to learn and sing chant without a teacher, see note 27 here.

36. Guido d'Arezzo's term for this is *affinitas* ("affinity"). On the affinities, see Pesce, *The Affinities and Medieval Transposition;* and Pesce, "B-Flat: Transposition or Transformation?"

37. "Illud in his adtendendum, quod synemenon tetrachordo submoto, quinta semper loca his singulis quatuor superiora, quadam sibi conexionis unione iunguntur <uel participant>, adeo, ut pleraque

He expands this by specifying that the lichanos hypaton (*D*) is linked with the mese (*a*), the hypate meson (*E*) with the paramese (♮), the parhypate meson (*F*) with the trite diezeugmenon (*c*), and the lichanos meson (*G*) with the paranete diezeugmenon (*d*).[38] These are the possible alternative finals for each tone, and each is an example of *socialitas*.

Having presented the notion of affinities or alternative finals, Hucbald then extends this notion of *socialitas* to the beginnings of chants:

> To a certain extent, [these four finals] also have a similar relationship with the fourths and, in certain cases, with the fifths below them, although these lower degrees should not be assigned to the end, but to beginnings: the beginnings extend down to these as a [lower] limit. These [beginnings and finals] are: proslambanomenos [*A*] to the lichanos hypaton [*D*]; hypate hypaton [*B*] to the hypate meson [*E*], but this is rare; parhypate hypaton [*C*] to the parhypate meson [*F*]; lichanos hypaton [*D*] to the lichanos meson [*G*]. The last may sometimes descend to the parhypate hypaton [*C*], that is, down to the fifth degree, but for the other finals this is rare.[39]

Hucbald summarizes this discussion by saying that no tone or trope can begin more than a fifth above or below its final, and adding that both *initia* and finals of all chants, whether authentic or plagal, are situated within the ambitus of an octave or a ninth surrounding their respective finals.[40]

Once he has established the theoretical foundation defining *toni vel tropi* by means of both the finals and initial notes of the chants embodying them—thereby creating an implicit link with the practice of psalmody—Hucbald concludes his treatise. He does so by providing for each of the four finals the incipits of chants representing each of the possible eight or [in the case of the Tetrardus] nine begin-

---

etiam in eis quasi regulariter mela inueniantur desinere, nec rationi ob hoc uel sensui quid contraire, et sub eodem modo uel tropo perfecte decurrere. Hanc ergo socialitatem continent (Chartier, ed., *L'Oeuvre d'Hucbald*, 202; *GS* 1: 119, Traub, ed., "Hucbald von Saint-Amand," 68; Babb and Palisca, *Hucbald, Guido, and John on Music*, 39).

38. Chartier, ed., *L'Oeuvre d'Hucbald*, 202; Traub, ed., "Hucbald von Saint-Amand," 68; Babb and Palisca, *Hucbald, Guido, and John on Music*, 39. The last-named relationship, lichanos meson (*G*) with paranete diezeugmenon (*d*), is interesting, in that later authors, such as Guido d'Arezzo, would specifically deny it.

39. "Cum inferioribus quoque quartis et in quibusdam quintis, parem quodammodo obtinent [hae quattuor finales] habitudinem, quamuis non fini sed initiis deputentur: usque ad has enim metam inchoandi declinant. Hae sunt. Proslambanomenos: ad lichanos ypaton. Hypate ypaton: ad hypate meson, sed id raro. Parhypate ypaton: ad parhypate meson. Lichanos ypaton: ad lichanos meson, sed in hoc aliquando usque ad parhypate hypaton descenditur, idest usque ad quintum locum, in ceteris rarissime" (Chartier, ed., *L'Oeuvre d'Hucbald*, 202; Traub, ed., "Hucbald von Saint-Amand," 68; Babb and Palisca, *Hucbald, Guido, and John on Music*, 39).

40. "Omnis omnino tonus uel tropus a finali suo, nec supra quintum superiorem, nec infra quintum inferiorem umquam ordiendi facultatem habebit, sed intra eas octo uoces uel aliquando nouem, partim principales partim laterales, fines uel initia cohibebunt" (Chartier, ed., *L'Oeuvre d'Hucbald*, 202; Traub, ed., "Hucbald von Saint-Amand," 68; Babb and Palisca, *Hucbald, Guido, and John on Music*, 39). The next step, adding internal cadences or *distinctiones* to the factors defining *tonus* or *tropus*, would be taken in a small treatise formerly attributed to Hucbald, *Ecce modorum* (ca. 900), transmitted in the group of treatises associated with the *Musica enchiriadis*. Its anonymous author compares the distinctions of chant with the cola or commata of speech, both units being those that can be sung in a single breath. See Schmid, ed., *Musica et Scolica enchiriadis*, 182–84; and Atkinson, "Modus," *HmT*, sec. V. (I) (3).

ning pitches for authentic and plagal chants ending on each of those finals.[41] What results, in fact, is a kind of tonary, but without the *saeculorum Amen* formulas, or differentiae, that are typical of the genre.[42]

As noted, Hucbald's theory of *socialitas* makes possible the transposition of a chant to a position a fifth above its final without removing it from its mode. But why should it have been necessary to end any chant a fifth above its final, especially given Hucbald's own statement that "everything that is sung takes its end in them"? Apparently, the limitations of the Greater Perfect System as a matrix for the notation of chant were already beginning to be felt, even as they were being introduced. They would be felt even more distinctly in the eleventh century, with the advent of a fully diastematic, practical notation—a notation that was given its impetus in part by Hucbald's ideas.

Hucbald's treatise is in many ways a remarkable synthesis of ancient Greek theory with contemporaneous chant theory and practice. It does not offer the mathematical precision of Boethius or a means (the monochord) of translating mathematical relationships into sound, nor does it define *tonus* or *modus* in terms of species of octave. Nonetheless, it offered a development of far-reaching significance by presenting the diatonic genus of the Greater Perfect System plus the synemmenon tetrachord as a suitable scalar basis for plainchant, and by providing examples of chant notated in a manner that preserved the tonal architecture of that system. There was now a theory of chant that, at least ostensibly, was a viable alternative to the theory presented in Aurelian, the *Musica enchiriadis,* and related treatises. This "new" theory had the advantage of greater clarity of expression and the weight of *auctoritas* on its side, not to mention its potential as the basis for a comprehensive theory of both plainchant and organum.

Both the advantages and some of the disadvantages of the grafting of ancient Greek harmonic theory onto the theory and practice of plainchant—particularly as represented by the double notation advocated by Hucbald—are illustrated in Montpellier 159.[43] This manuscript was copied in the early eleventh century, probably at

41. Hucbald lists possible beginning pitches even when he cannot cite pieces that begin on each of the notes given. The array of beginning pitches in Protus, for example, extends from the mese down to the proslambanomenos, a span of eight notes. Hucbald admits that there are scarcely any chants that begin on either the hypate meson (*E*) or the hypate hypaton (*B♮*). In these cases, he cites an interior phrase from a Protus chant that contains the pitch in question.

42. This had already been pointed out in Potiron, "Les Modes grégoriens," 115; and, more recently, by Huglo (*Les Tonaires,* 58). The six examples of chants provided for Protus authentic and plagal are listed under the first, second, fourth, fifth, and seventh differentiae of the Protus autentus and the single differentia of the Protus plagis in the Metz and Bamberg tonaries (see Lipphardt, ed., *Das karolingische Tonar von Metz,* 69–100). Huglo (*Les Tonaires,* 57) mentions that a later hand added a list of the differentiae, written in Dasia notation, to Hucbald's treatise in the fifteenth-century manuscript Cesena S. XXVI. 1, fol. 173. He feels, however, that the sources for the chants listed in each pair of *toni* were probably manuscripts of the antiphonary and gradual, and not a tonary.

43. Facs. ed. in *Pal. mus.* 8, with an introduction, "Note sur l'antiphonaire digrapte, codex H. 159 de Montpellier," by Beyssac in vol. 7. The contents have been transcribed in Hansen, ed., *H 159 Montpellier.* These works, along with Huglo, "Le Tonaire de Saint-Bénigne de Dijon," Browne, "The a–p System of Letter Notation," and Phillips, "Notationen und Notationslehren," 565–70, form the starting point for current work with this source. M.-N. Colette's study of the manuscript in the CD-ROM *Cantor et Musicus* may well contribute similarly, but unfortunately, I have not been able to consult this work.

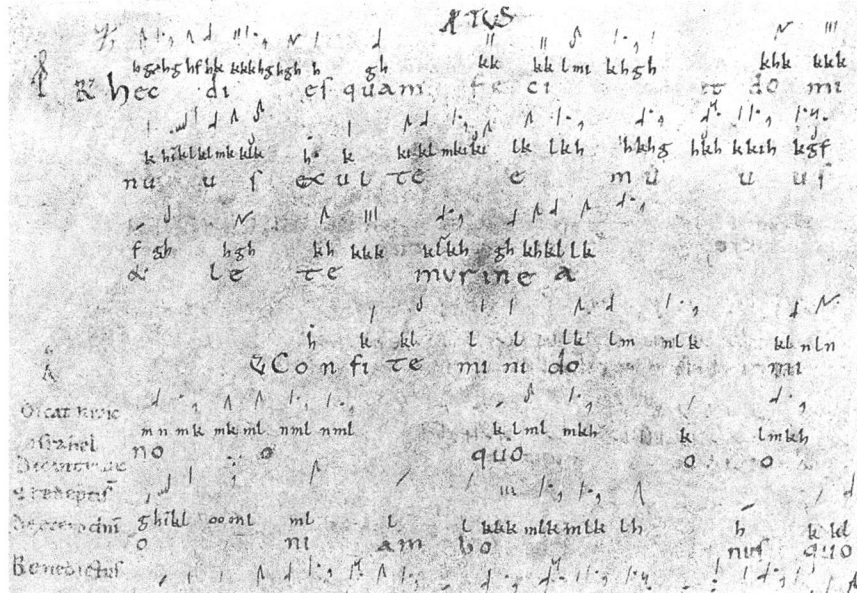

FIGURE 4.1.   *Haec dies* in Montpellier 159, fol. 83v (reproduced with the permission of
the Bibliothèque Interuniversitaire-Section Médicine, Montpellier)

St. Benigne de Dijon, and perhaps during the abbacy of Guillaume de Volpiano.[44] It
is unusual in the fact that the chants of the Mass are arranged within it not according to the liturgical year or in the normal liturgical order, but rather according to the
toni or church modes.[45] Moreover—and directly relevant to the topic at hand—it
transmits its chants not only in their neumatic versions, but also with an alphabetic
notation derived from Boethius. Figures 4.1 and 4.2 present chants from the Dijon
tonary: the Gradual *Haec dies* and the Communion *Beatus servus,* respectively.

   In both examples, one sees above each syllable of the chant two lines of notation—one of letters just above the text, and above that a line of neumes in early
French notation. As Hucbald had suggested, the two types of notation go together,
with the neumes presenting the contour and grouping of the melodic signs above
each syllable, and the letters furnishing precise indications of the relative position
of the pitches in acoustic space. These examples, however, raise two questions:
(1) What system of letters is being utilized? and (2) What type of scale do these letters represent?

44. Guillaume de Volpiano was abbot at St. Bénigne from 990 until his death in 1131. After introducing the Cluniac reform at St. Bénigne, he was invited to reform a number of other Norman monasteries. At least twenty manuscripts exhibiting the a–h–p notation found in Montpellier 159 originated in
the monasteries associated with his reform movement. Hence, although there is no documentary evidence linking him directly to these manuscripts or their notation, the circumstantial evidence for some
sort of connection is quite strong. For further bibliography on Guillaume, see Browne, "The a–p System
of Letter Notation," 14 and n. 34; and Corbin, *Die Neumen,* 102–10.

45. A useful overview of the contents and organization of the manuscript, cued to Hansen's edition,
may be found in Huglo, "Grundlagen und Ansätze der mittelalterlichen Musiktheorie," 98.

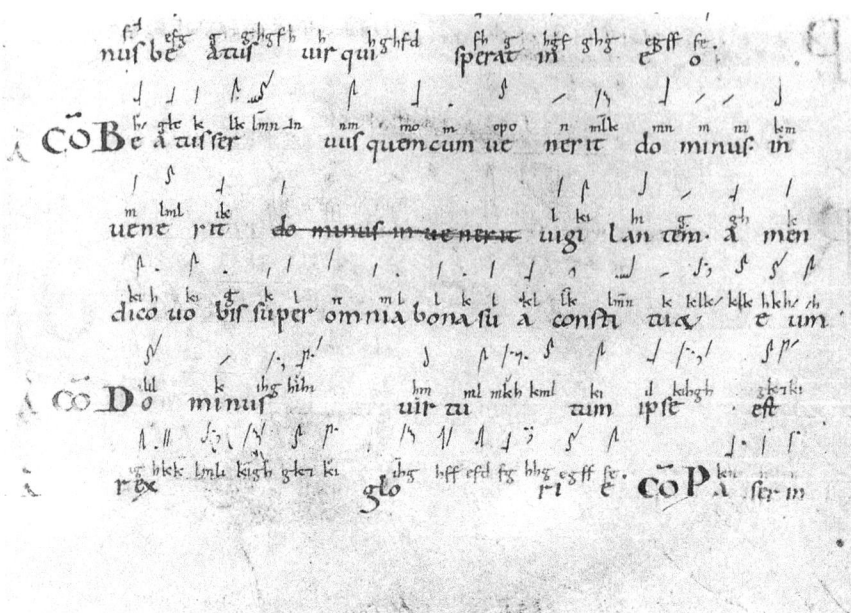

FIGURE 4.2.   *Beatus servus* in Montpellier 159, fol. 29 (reproduced with the permission of the Bibliothèque Interuniversitaire-Section Médicine, Montpellier)

One can respond fairly easily to the first question. Rather than employing the modified Alypian system used by Hucbald, the scribes of Montpellier 159 used the two-octave series a–h–p in the diatonic genus that Boethius had set out for determining the species of the eight modes (Book IV, chap. 17).[46] In addition to the fifteen letters of the diatonic scale, however, the notational array of Montpellier 159 also includes six signs that cannot be found in Boethius: an inclined *i* (/) signifying the pitch *b*♭, along with five additional signs: ⊢, ⊣, ⌐, ⌐, and ⌐. The precise meaning of these additional signs has long been a subject of controversy, but the most compelling line of argument interprets them as quarter-tones, perhaps deriving from the ancient Greek enharmonic genus.[47] Example 4.7 presents the entire series of twenty-one notes. Employing them as a key, one can decipher the notes of the two preceding examples.

46. Hansen (*H 159 Montpellier*, 25*–33*) is of the opinion that six scribes worked on the manuscript, four copying the neumes and two the letter notation. Although the direct source for the a–h–p series is Boethius, *De institutione musica*, Book IV, chap. 17, several manuscripts of Boethius's work employ these letters in place of the A–O–LL sequence in the arithmetic monochord division in Book IV, chaps. 6–12. The a–h–p series also appears in the treatise of Odorannus of Sens (985–1046), a younger contemporary of Guillaume de Volpiano. There it is associated with a complete monochord division in the three genera, but is also used for notating three pieces of music. See Bautier and Gilles, eds., *Odorannus de Sens: Opera omnia*, esp. 198, 202, 210; and Phillips, "Notationen und Notationslehren," 549–72. Some manuscripts associated with Guillaume's reforms (e.g., Paris 10508 and Paris 10509, from St. Evroult and St. Wandrille, respectively) also use these letters in monochord divisions, but no such division appears in Montpellier 159.

47. Gmelch (*Die Viertelstonstufen im Meßtonale von Montpellier*, esp. 14–22, 68–75), Hansen (*H 159 Montpellier*, 43*), Ferreira ("Music at Cluny," 160–282), and Phillips ("Notationen und Notationslehren,"

EXAMPLE 4.7.   Tone-system projected by the alphabetic notation in
Montpellier 159

For *Haec dies* in figure 4.1, the introductory succession of letters is h g i-inclined
h g h f h k. If one projects these on a staff (see ex. 4.7), one recognizes these notes
as part of the scale we know as the combined Greater and Lesser Perfect Systems.
If one reads all the way to the end, however, one discovers that even though the
chant is labeled Protus, implying a finalis on *D,* it has been transposed up a fifth in
Montpellier 159, which results in its final being placed on *a.* Indeed, the chant appears in this transposition in the modern gradual (ex. 4.8). The reason for this would
seem to be the presence of both *E♭* and *B♭* in the introductory phrase of the chant
if it is not transposed, as one can see in example 4.9.

Turning to *Beatus servus* in Figure 4.2, we find an even more striking series of
notes: h is followed immediately by an inclined i, conveying a movement from *a* up
to *b♭.* These two notes are followed by G k k (the notes *G c c*), for the remainder of
the word "Beatus." The following succession, on the word "servus," l k, lmn (i.e., *D
C, D E F*), is followed by a special sign (⌐), then n (*F*), and finally n m (*F E*) in

EXAMPLE 4.8.   *Haec dies* in the *Graduale Romanum,* 203

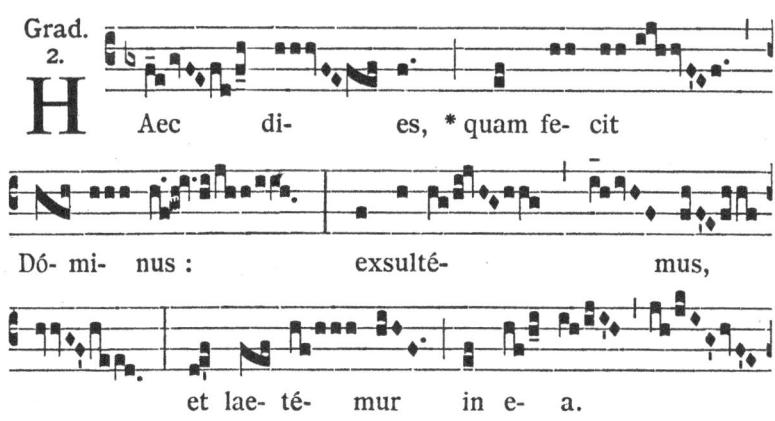

565–68), among others, hold that these signs do indeed represent quarter tones, or at least intervals
smaller than a semitone. Phillips points out that they occur at the precise points where the second diesis
of the enharmonic genus would be located in each of the five tetrachords of the combined Greater and
Lesser Perfect Systems (the ancient Greek Immutable System). Nonetheless, no less a scholar than Jacques
Froger ("Les Prétendus Quarts de ton dans le chant grégorien et les symboles du MS H 159 de Mon-
pellier") is convinced that the signs are not indicators of quarter tones, but serve, rather, as supplementary rhythmic signs.

EXAMPLE 4.9. *Haec dies* (a) and *Beatus servus* (b) notated in their proper modal positions, with finales on protus and deuterus, respectively

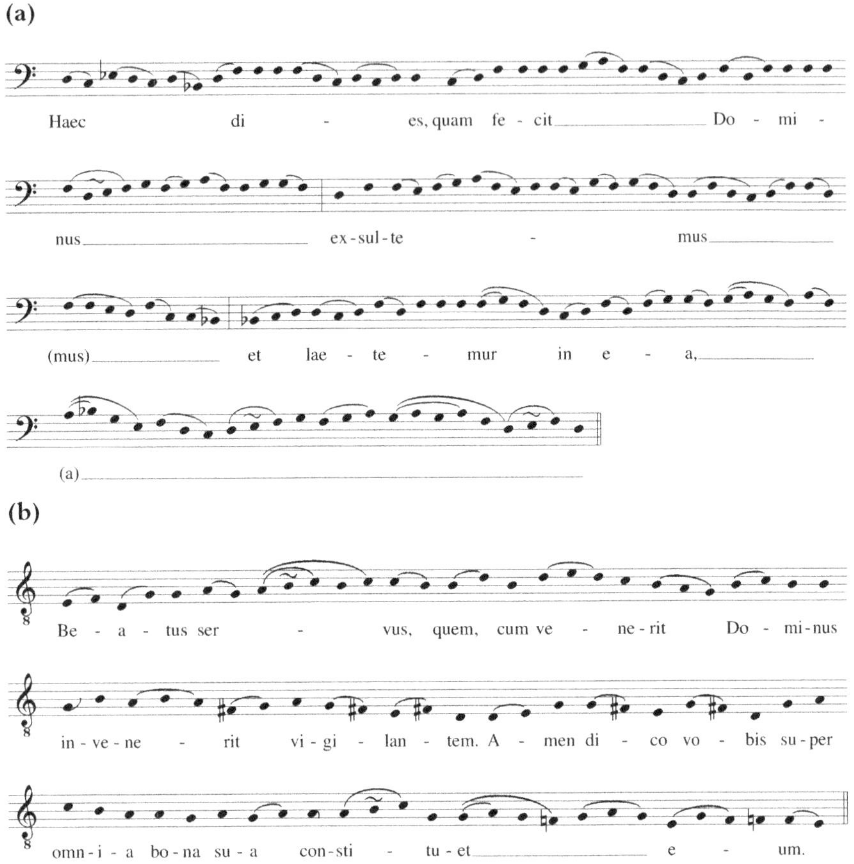

(a)

(b)

order to conclude the word. Dom Pothier thought that this special sign signified an E,[48] and it is so transcribed in the modern gradual (see ex. 4.10). Gmelch, however, in his study of Montpellier 159, suggested that the special sign in this position represented a quarter-tone below the pitch F, and it is so transcribed by Hansen.[49]

Continuing in figure 4.2, one notices two other intriguing sections in this piece: the group of letters on the word *vigilantem* and that on the last word, *eum*. The succession l k i h i g, which can be translated into the pitches d, c, ♭, a, ♮, G, appears over the word *vigilantem*. The letters h k h (a c a), followed by two inclined i's and the letter h ($b♭$, $b♭$, a) are written over the word *eum*. *Beatus servus* is a chant in Deuterus, which should have its finalis on E, as one can see in example 4.9. Like

---

48. Pothier, *Les Mélodies grégoriennes*, 26, as cited in Beyssac, introduction, *Pal. mus.* 7: 12.

49. Hansen, *H 159 Montpellier*, 90, no. 459; Gmelch, *Die Viertelstonstufen im Meßtonale von Montpellier*, 19–22, 48.

EXAMPLE 4.10. *Beatus servus* in the *Graduale Romanum*, [39–40]

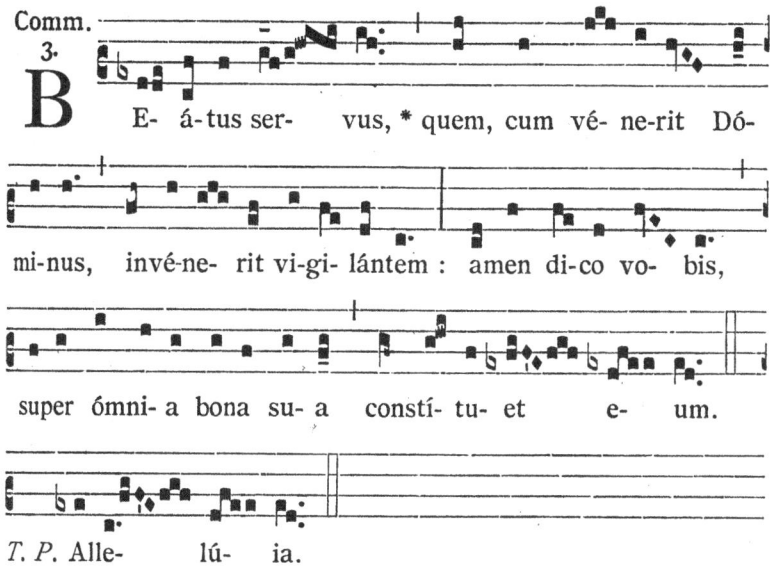

Haec dies, it has also been transposed up to *a,* but only to permit both the *F* and *F♯* of the nontransposed chant to be represented by the inclined i and normal i, respectively.

Although Montpellier 159 does not utilize the modified Alypian alphabetic notation introduced by Hucbald, its scalar matrix is nonetheless the same ancient Greek tone-system transmitted into the Middle Ages by Boethius and taken up in Hucbald's *De harmonica institutione.* Furthermore, Montpellier 159 provides abundant examples demonstrating Hucbald's statement that one will find that "melodies may often be found to close on these notes a fifth above without offending either one's judgment or ear, and that they run their course perfectly within the same mode or trope." In the case of the two chants shown in figures 4.1 and 4.2, *Haec dies* and *Beatus servus,* it was not merely possible, but indeed necessary to transpose them so as to permit their melodic movements to be represented on the combined Greater and Lesser Perfect Systems. We saw earlier that these two chants could easily be situated on the scalar matrix represented by the tone-system of the *Musica enchiriadis* and its *vitia.*[50] (At the same time, it had to be admitted that the Dasia notation that projected that system was not particularly well suited for the singing of chant.) Nonetheless, one wonders what would have happened if the Dasia symbols had been combined with the neumes that were already in use for the notation of chant in the ninth century. As *Haec dies* and *Beatus servus* show, however, the adoption of the ancient Greek tone-system as a scalar matrix for Western chant would

50. See chapter 3 here, pp. 129–33.

create, in certain cases, a rupture between the notation of the chant and its intrinsic tonal or modal structure.

As the discussion above has shown, two rather different kinds of music theory were current in the later ninth century, one deriving its terminology and approach from the practice of singing plainchant—often called *cantus* theory—and the other strongly influenced by ancient Greek harmonic theory as transmitted into the Middle Ages by writers such as Boethius. The dichotomy that obviously existed around 900 is both reflected and acknowledged by Regino of Prüm in his *Epistola de harmonica institutione*.[51]

The opening of the *Epistola* makes clear that Regino intended the work as an introduction to his tonary,[52] and indeed, the work reads like a manual for singers. Regino explains that he wrote it in order to correct the mistakes in psalmody resulting from mistaken identification of the *toni* of the various categories of antiphonal chant; to that end, he distributed the antiphons in their proper *toni* and *divisiones* or *differentiae*.[53] Regino then discusses the *nothae*—antiphons that are difficult to classify because they begin in one tone, are in another in the middle, and are in yet a third at the end.[54] Then he shifts to a description of two different types of music, natural and artificial.[55] Natural music is that "sung in praise of God" with four principal tones: protus, deuterus, tritus, and tetrardus. Artificial music is made up of five tones and two semitones, "which semitones do not fill out a whole tone." In his words:

---

51. Ed. *GS* 1: 230–47, and more recently by Bernhard in *Clavis Gerberti*, 37–73. On Regino himself, see Hüschen, "Regino von Prüm"; on the treatise, its sources, and its influences, see Bernhard, *Studien zur Epistola de armonica institutione des Regino von Prüm*. As Bernhard points out (*Studien*, 12–23), there are two principal versions of the treatise, one that preserves it in the form of a letter addressed to Bishop Rathbod of Trier and another that replaces the opening and closing references to Rathbod with an introduction and conclusion. Even within these groups, however, there are substantial differences. Of the two manuscripts that present the work as a letter, one (Brussels 2751, from the second half of the tenth century) is fairly short, serving as an introduction to Regino's tonary and containing virtually no references to harmonic theory. The other (Leipzig I. 93), the source used for Gerbert's edition, presents a longer version of the text, containing a substantial treatment of harmonic theory. The passages presented here may all be found in the shorter version of the *Epistola*, the one preserved in the Brussels manuscript.

52. The tonary itself is printed in facsimile in *CS* 2: 3–53. As pointed out above, there are questions regarding the authenticity of the tonary and its relationship to the *Epistola*. See chapter 3 here, note 11.

53. "2. Cum frequenter in aecclesia vestrae diocesis chorus psallentium psalmorum melodiam confusis resonaret vocibus propter dissonantiam *toni*, et pro huiuscemodi re vestram venerationem sepe commotam vidissem, arripui antiphonarium, et eum a principio usque in finem per ordinem diligenter revolvens, antiphonas, quas in illo adnotatas repperi, propriis, ut reor, distribui *tonis*. 3. *Divisiones* etiam *tonorum*, id est *differentias*, quae in extrema syllaba in versu solent fieri, ut decens et conveniens fiat concinentia, sicut a maioribus nobis traditae sunt, et sicut ipsa armonicae disciplinae experientia nos instruit, distinctis ordinibus inserere curavi" (Bernhard, *Clavis Gerberti*, 39; see *GS* 1: 230–31; emphasis added).

54. "Sunt namque quaedam antiphonae, quas nothas, id est degeneres et non legitimas, appellamus, quae ab uno tono incipiunt, alterius sunt in medio, et in tertio finiuntur" (*GS* 1: 231a; Bernhard, *Clavis Gerberti*, 40). On the *nothae*, see Atkinson, "The *Parapteres: Nothi* or Not?" and Atkinson, "Parapter," in *HmT*.

55. On this dichotomy, see Bower, "Natural and Artificial Music"; and Bernhard, *Studien zur Epistola de armonica institutione des Regino von Prüm*, 46–54.

There are found in natural music—that is, in song that is modulated in divine praise—four principal tones, which are called thus by their Greek names: *authenticus protus, authenticus deuterus, authenticus tritus, authenticus tetrardus*. From these sources flow the other four, which are called: *plaga proti, plaga deuteri, plaga triti, plaga tetrardi.*[56]

He then provides a more extensive description:

In artificial music there are five tones and two semitones, which semitones, however, do not fill out a whole tone: indeed they are not able to be divided into equal parts. One is larger, the other smaller, and for that reason they do not assume equal sections. These five tones with two semitones stand together in the three consonances of musical perfection, the diapente, the diatessaron, and the diapason. Whereas from the four tones of natural music the other four arise, just as streams flow from their sources and the branches of a tree grow from its trunk. . . . None of this is true for artificial music. There, no tone begets another tone of itself, nor does one tone precede another in authority, but all are distributed in equal divisions, that is, in sesquioctave proportions, except for the semitones.

It should also be noted that in natural music all eight tones are integral and perfect, although they differ among themselves in authority; none receives a semitone, nor a *diesis* nor an *apotome,* nor a *tristemoria* [*sic*] nor a *tetrastemoria* [*sic*].[57] It is into these parts that the tone of artificial music is divided.[58]

A more vivid depiction of the contrasts between *cantus* theory and harmonic theory could hardly be imagined! But just as one can see clearly where Regino's heart is, he also shows us where his mind is: "From this disagreement it is apparent that those often-discussed eight, which are called *toni,* should not be called *toni,* but

56. "Inveniuntur vero in naturali musica, id est, in cantilena, quae in divinis laudibus modulatur, quattuor principales toni, qui ita graeco vocabulo nuncupantur: authenthicus protus, authenthicus deuterus, authenthicus tritus, authenthicus tetrarcus. Ex quorum fontibus alii quattuor manant, qui ita vocantur: plaga proti, plaga deuteri, plaga triti, plaga thetrarchi" (Bernhard, *Clavis Gerberti*, 42; GS 1: 232).

57. As Bernhard points out (*Studien zur Epistola de armonica institutione des Regino von Prüm*, 46), Regino should not be taken here to be saying that the church modes—the *toni* of the *cantus* tradition—do not make use of semitones, but rather that the subdivisions of the whole tone are not mathematically defined. The terms *diesis* and *apotome,* the quarter tone and greater semitone, respectively, are discussed at length in Boethius's *De institutione musica.* The *tritemoria* and *tetartemoria,* a third tone and a quarter tone, respectively, are discussed in Book IX, sec. 930 of Martianus Capella, *De nuptiis Philologiae et Mercurii.* Important here is that all of these terms are characteristic of harmonic theory, and not of *cantus* theory.

58. "2. Toni vero artificialis musicae sunt quinque et duo semitonia, quae tamen semitonia integrum non implent tonum; non enim in aequis partibus dividi possunt. 3. Est denique unum maius et alterum minus, ac idcirco aequas non recipiunt sectiones. 4. Constant autem hi quinque toni cum duobus semitoniis in tribus consonantiis musicae perfectionis, videlicet in diapente, diatessaron et diapason. 5. Item ex quatuor principalibus tonis naturalis musicae alii quatuor oriuntur, et veluti a fontibus rivuli manant, et a radice arboris rami procedunt, . . . 6. Nihil horum fit in artificiali musica; nam neque tonus alium tonum ex se gignit, neque unus ex illis alium autoritate praecellit, sed omnes inter se aequis dimensionibus partiuntur, scilicet sesquioctava proportione, exceptis semitoniis." 7. "Illud etiam attendendum, quod in naturali musica omnes octo toni integri sunt atque perfecti, quamvis auctoritate inter se differant, nullumque recipiant semitonium, nec diesin, nec apotomen, aut tristemoria, aut tetrastemoria: siquidem in his partibus tonus artificialis musicae dividitur" (Bernhard, *Clavis Gerberti*, 43; GS 1: 232).

modi or *differentiae* or *tropi,* of the consonances of musical modulation."[59] By urging that the *toni* be called "*modi* or *differentiae* or *tropi,*" Regino seems to be advocating the use of Boethius's terminology for melodic categorization and not that of *cantus* theory, despite his seeming disdain for the theoretical foundation on which the terminology was based.[60]

Even if Regino was a somewhat reluctant observer of the shift from tones defined by "qualities" of sounds to modes determined by proportionate relationships of mathematical "quantities," that shift was already ineluctably under way. It was being paralleled contemporaneously with Regino, and would be expanded substantially a bit later in the tenth century, by the work that has come down to us under the title *Alia musica,* and it is to that extraordinary document that we turn our attention in chapter 5.

59. "8. Ex hac itaque dissonantia apparet, quod illi sepe dicti octo, qui dicuntur toni, non tam toni dicendi sunt, quam modi vel differentiae seu tropi consonantiarum musicae modulationis" (Bernhard, *Clavis Gerberti,* 44; GS 1: 232). See the reference in the *Musica enchiriadis,* chap. 8, to the "modos, quos abusive tonos dicimus" (ed. Schmid, 13), and in Hucbald to the "four *modi* or *tropi,* that are nowadays called *toni*" (Chartier, ed., *L'Oeuvre d'Hucbald,* 200; GS 1: 119a; Traub, ed., "Hucbald von Saint-Amand," 66; Babb and Palisca, *Hucbald, Guido, and John on Music,* 38).

60. See Bernhard, *Studien zur Epistola de armonica institutione des Regino von Prüm,* 46–47. I would have to admit that "disdain" may be in the eye of the reader. If Regino was indeed responsible for the long version of the treatise found in Leipzig I. 93 and edited in both *GS* 1 and *Clavis Gerberti,* one can hardly argue that he had anything but admiration for ancient Greek harmonics. The bulk of the long version of the treatise is pure harmonic theory, consisting for the most part of borrowings from Boethius, with a scattering of items from Macrobius, Fulgentius, and Remigius's commentary on Martianus Capella (see the list of sources in Bernhard, *Studien,* 39–42).

CHAPTER FIVE

ALIA MUSICA

O ne of the most complex and perplexing of all medieval writings on music, *Alia musica* is actually a core treatise with succeeding layers of commentary on it, the commentators themselves drawing their material from various sources.[1] Among the many questions that still surround the *Alia musica* are those of authorship and date. Wilhelm Mühlmann, one of the first scholars to deal with the *Alia musica* in depth, posited five different authors for the work, whose final redaction he placed in the tenth century, the presumed date of the earliest surviving manuscript.[2] In his edition of 1965, Jacques Chailley divided the *Alia* into three different "treatises" (table 5.1).[3]

The first of these, which could date from the end of the ninth century, is that

1. Ed. Chailley, *Alia musica.* The *Alia musica* was published originally in GS 1: 125b–147b, as edited from a now-lost manuscript, Strasbourg 926, and from Munich 14272. An edition and translation based on Gerbert's edition and the Munich manuscript is in Heard, "*Alia musica,*" 119–229. For a list of sources not consulted by Chailley, along with additional bibliography, see Bernhard, *Clavis Gerberti,* 16–17. For emendations to Chailley's text, see Bernhard, ed., *Anonymi saeculi decimi et undecimi tractatus de musica "Dulce ingenium musicae,"* 1–2, along with the critical apparatus to the two versions of the treatise; and Gümpel, "Musica cum Rhetorica: Die Handschrift Ripoll 42," 281. See also Gümpel, "Die 'Nova expositio' der Handschrift Ripoll 42: Text und Kommentar," 129–43.

2. Mühlmann, *Die "Alia musica,"* 47–48. The earliest extant manuscript is Munich 14272 (from St. Emmeram), which, according to Bischoff ("Literarisches und künstlerisches Leben in St. Emmeram," 80–82) and Huglo and Meyer (*RISM,* B III³, 110–13), was copied in France in the early eleventh century, probably by the monk Hartwic of St. Emmeram during his studies with Fulbert of Chartres (1007–29). The revised dating for Munich 14272 pushes the terminus ante quem for the origin of the complete treatise into the later tenth or even early eleventh century, as suggested by Phillips ("Notationen und Notationslehren," 343). I should mention here that, according to Chartier (*L'Oeuvre musicale d'Hucbald,* 114, 319), Strasbourg 926, the manuscript used by Gerbert—a paper manuscript, according to Gerbert—probably dated from the fifteenth century. Chartier points out that the order of treatises in this source concords almost exactly with that in the fifteenth-century manuscript Cesena XXVI. 1. He feels that both manuscripts base their readings on an eleventh-century source related to Barcelona 42.

3. Chailley, *Alia musica,* 12–27. One hesitates to call these "treatises"—Chailley's *traités*—in the sense of formal, systematic essays or books. Nonetheless, I have adopted Chailley's nomenclature for ease of discussion.

TABLE 5.1.   Contents of *Alia musica* (a conflation of Mühlmann and Chailley)

The order is that in Chailley, *Alia musica*; § numbers are from Chailley; M numbers are sections in Mühlmann, *Die "Alia musica"*; Roman numerals designate Mühlmann's five authors in chronological order. Indentations are a supplementary indication of Mühlmann's chronological layers: farther to the right = later.

First Quidam

A. Presentation of the Eight *Toni*

§§181–187, 180 [M24. III]   [Appears independently in Karlsruhe 504]

B. Symbolic Considerations

§§154–156 [M22a. III]   "Praemissus Expositor" [Not in Karlsruhe 504]

Principal Treatise

A. Harmonic theory derived from Boethius

1.	§§1–12 [M1. II]	[De medietate harmonica] (Boethius, De arithmetica)
2.	§§13–20 [M2. I]	Octave species as modi (Boethius De musica)
3.	§§21–29 [M3a/c.V]	Commentary from Boethius De musica

(§§26–27 [M3b. II: Descriptions of intonation formulae for 1st and 2nd tropi])

B. Commentary on the First Quidam

1.	§§30–36 [M4a. III]	Exposition of First Tonus
2.	§§37–40 [M4b.V]	Commentary on Exposition
1.	§§45–48 [M6a. III]	Exposition of Second Tonus
2.	§§49–53 [M6b.V]	Commentary on Exposition
1.	§§58–60 [M8a. III]	Exposition of Third Tonus
2.	§§61–76 [M8b.V]	Commentary on Exposition
1.	§§77–83 [M9–10a. III]	Exposition of Fourth Tonus
2.	§§84–89 [M10b.V]	Commentary on Exposition
1.	§§99–100 [M13a. III]	Exposition of Fifth Tonus
2.	§§101–107 [M13b.V]	Commentary on Exposition
1.	§§112–113 [M15a. III]	Exposition of Sixth Tonus
2.	§§114–121 [M15b.V]	Commentary on Exposition
1.	§§126–128 [M17a. IV]	Exposition of Seventh and Eighth Tonus
2.	§§129–132 [M17b.V]	Commentary on Exposition

C. Commentary on the "Symbolic Considerations" of First Quidam (*Praemissus expositor*)

2.	§§157–160 [M22a. IV]	"Tonus expositor"
3.	§§161–170 [M22b/c. IV/V]	Reworker's additional material

D. Tabular Summary

§§171–79, 188 [M23. IV]; §188 [M24. III] "Tonus expositor"

Nova expositio

Litterae designantes directim nervos secundum Boetium (Paris 7212, Paris 7211, and Barcelona 42)★

A. Description of 8 *Toni*

§§41–44 [M5.Tonary.V]	First Tropus
§§54–57 [M7.Tonary.V]	Second Tropus
§§90–94 [M11.Tonary.V]	Third Tropus
§§95–98 [M12.Tonary.V]	Fourth Tropus
§§108–111 [M14.Tonary.V]	Fifth Tropus
§§122–125 [M16.Tonary.V]	Sixth Tropus
§§146–149 [M20.Tonary.V]	Seventh Tropus
§§150–53 [M21.Tonary.V]	Eighth Tropus

B. Discussion of Modal Octaves

§§133–42 [M18. II]	Modal Octaves
	§§143–45 [M19.V] Commentator on Modal Octave

which Chailley calls the "Premier Quidam."[4] It is followed in his edition by the one he calls the "Traité Principal."[5] The third consists of a tonary—called *Nova expositio* in the manuscript sources—plus some additional material he feels was composed by the same author, a person to whom he also attributes the compilation of the entire work. According to Chailley, the *Traité Principal* and the *Nova expositio* probably date from the early tenth century.[6]

In presenting the various treatises of *Alia musica* in the order in which they were presumably composed, Chailley's edition took an important step toward an understanding of the work.[7] At the same time, its very organization presents a kind of barrier to that understanding, since it does not represent the work as it appears in any manuscript source; in the manuscripts containing the complete *Alia musica,* it appears consistently as it does in Gerbert's edition. The work as a whole was thus composed (in the sense of *com-ponere*) and read in this form in the Middle Ages. A modern reader should be able to do the same.[8]

Table 5.2. provides a list of the twelve extant manuscripts known to contain the *Alia musica* in whole or in part. Only four of these were available to Mühlmann, Chailley, and Heard—or five, if one counts Strasbourg 926, the manuscript (now lost) Gerbert used for his edition. It is important to point out that according to Bernhard Bischoff, the earliest manuscript of the treatise, Munich 14272, was copied in the eleventh century (ca. 1007–29), and not in the tenth century as earlier scholars had assumed.[9] Nancy Phillips thus suggests that the *Alia musica* did not receive its final form until sometime in the late tenth century, if not the early eleventh.[10]

There are several features of table 5.2 that are of special interest. One is that the treatise of the "First Quidam" and the tonary that is labeled *Nova expositio* in the *Alia musica* both enjoyed an independent transmission in the Middle Ages. The First Quidam appears by itself in Karlsruhe 504; the tonary appears independently in Barcelona 42, Paris 8663, Bruges 532, and Prague 26. It is also striking that parts of what Chailley calls the *Traité Principal* were likewise transmitted independently. I

4. This treatise on the eight *toni*, which I shall refer to as the First Quidam, is the most unified of the three. It appears at the end of *Alia musica* in the form in which the complete work is transmitted in most of its sources, Munich 14272, Paris 7211, Paris 7212, Cesena XXVI. 1, and Strasbourg 926, the manuscript Gerbert used for his edition. It was also copied as an independent treatise in Karlsruhe 504, fol. 34, a manuscript compiled in St. Michelsberg in Bamberg in the eleventh to twelfth centuries (see Huglo and Meyer, *RISM* B III³, 63–65, and Meyer, "Aus der Werkstatt des Kompilators").

5. The Principal Treatise, as I shall call it, consists of at least three layers: (1) an exposition of harmonic theory derived from Boethius (sec. A); (2) an "exposition" of the treatise of the First Quidam (secs. B and C); and (3) a tabular summary of the numeric proportions characteristic of each of the church modes.

6. I agree with Chailley (*Alia musica,* 59–60) that the First Quidam is anterior to Hucbald's *De harmonica institutione*, and that the Principal Treatise and *Nova expositio* are posterior to it. Since Hucbald's work has been dated to the period 885–99 (see chapter 4 here, note 1), the last two parts of *Alia musica* would accordingly have to date from no earlier than the last decade of the ninth century.

7. By way of justifying his organization of the work, Chailley says: "Le problème soulevé trouve une solution beaucoup plus simple, et parfaitement satisfaisante; en lisant le traité tel qu'il est écrit" (Chailley, *Alia musica,* 12).

8. This was also the view of Heard, and one of the reasons he chose to edit the work as it appears in the Munich manuscript (Heard, "Alia musica," 17).

9. Bischoff, "Literarisches und künstlerisches Leben in St. Emmeram," 80–82.

10. Phillips, "Notationen und Notationslehren," 343.

TABLE 5.2.   *Alia musica:* Manuscript sources

Complete Treatise

★Munich 14272 (eleventh century, St. Emmeram), fol. 175–181 (also consulted by Gerbert)
★Paris 7211 (late eleventh century, St. Pierre de Luxeil), fol. 54–71
★Paris 7212 (early twelfth century, Bourgogne), fol. 39v–50v
Cesena XXVI. 1 (1425–50, based on an 11th-century[?] model from Lorraine), fol.
   179v–194 (consulted by Gerbert)
Strasbourg 926 (fifteenth century[?]; Gerbert's primary source, now lost)

Sections

Barcelona 42 (ca. 1018–46), fol. 65v–68v (*Nova expositio* Tonary [complete])
Barcelona 42 (ca. 1018–46), fol. 68v–69 (Principal Treatise: §§1–2a; *Nova expositio* Tonary,
   §§122–25, §§150–153)
Bruges 532 (thirteenth century), fol. 3–4 (*Nova expositio* Tonary [complete])
Florence 565 (late eleventh century, Florence, Santa Maria Novella), fol. 76v–77 (Principal
   Treatise, §§173–80)
Florence 652 (thirteenth century; unknown provenance), fol. 83v–85 (Principal Treatise,
   §§173–80)
★Karlsruhe 504 (eleventh–twelfth centuries, Bamberg or St. Gall), fol. 34r–v (First Quidam:
   §§181–87, §180)
Madrid 9088 (early eleventh century, northern Italy), fol. 124–25 (Principal Treatise,
   §§13–20)
Paris 8663 (early eleventh century, Fleury-sur-Loire): 51 (*Nova expositio* Tonary [complete])
Prague 26 (ca. 1100, region of Liège), fol. 17v–8v (Principal Treatise, §§134–41; §162a;
   §§166–68; §170; *Nova expositio,* Tonary [complete])

   ★Consulted by Mühlmann, Chailley, and Heard

refer here to §§13–20 (table 5.1: Principal Treatise, sec. A.2), the section presenting
the Boethian octave species as *modi,* a section that appears by itself in Madrid 9088.
A condensed version of §§173–80 (table 5.1: Principal Treatise, sec. D), those presenting a prose summary of the proportional bases of the eight church modes, also
appears separately in two manuscripts, Florence 565 and Florence 652. Although
one cannot rule out the possibility that all of these were extracted from the *Alia musica* as a whole, it would seem more likely that at least some were circulating independently or as parts of small *libelli* before being combined in the late tenth or early
eleventh century into the complete work we know as the *Alia musica.* On the other
hand, Prague 26, dating from around 1100, contains both the *Nova expositio* tonary
and parts of the Principal Treatise. In this case, we can be reasonably certain, I believe, that the compiler had the complete *Alia musica* before him, and not just one
or more of its constituent parts.

   But what, one might ask, does all of this have to tell us about the composition
of the *Alia musica* itself? I believe that one of the first things it suggests is that we
should revisit Chailley's hypothesis as to the composition of the treatise. He believed
that the person who compiled the work as a whole was the author of the tonary,
that is, the *Nova expositio,* and that he added some of his own material to the Principal Treatise in the course of putting the whole work together. If that were so, however, how can one explain the contemporaneous, independent transmission of the

tonary by itself without any additional material? To that reservation I would add several more, all of which have to do with internal inconsistencies within the Principal Treatise and between it and the *Nova expositio.*[11]

My own work with *Alia musica* in its various textual and manuscript states has led me to the conclusion that there are five different conceptual "layers" of the treatise, and that there were at least four authors or commentators involved in the creation of the work. Table 5.3 presents these in a revised table of contents for the *Alia musica* that incorporates the ideas of Mühlmann, Chailley, and Heard with my own.[12]

In this table, the form of the work is that appearing in the manuscripts and in Gerbert's edition, including the headings I feel were placed there by the compiler of the work as a whole. The reader will notice that the table has four levels of indentation indicating the contributions of the various authors or commentators, whom I have designated with the Greek letters α, β, γ, and δ. I agree with Chailley that the treatise on the *toni* or church modes by the First Quidam, called the "Praemissus expositor" in the manuscripts, was probably the first to be composed, perhaps even in the late ninth century. It was followed not long afterward by an exposition and expansion of the First Quidam's work, drawing on harmonic theory from Boethius, that makes up the first layer of the Principal Treatise. This was written by a man designated as the "Expositor" in the headings, whom I have labeled β in table 5.3. The *Nova expositio,* composed by a person referred to as "Quidam" (my Author γ), originated independently, almost certainly after the treatise of Hucbald and its concluding tonary. These three tracts were then combined in the later tenth or early eleventh century by an author I have designated δ, who not only put them together, but added his own material to what the Expositor had already written. I would characterize the four authors as follows.

Author α, the First Quidam (§§181–87, 180) or "Praemissus expositor." This section is transmitted independently of the remainder of *Alia musica* in Karlsruhe 504, albeit in a slightly more developed state.[13] The author uses *tonus* as designation for melodic category, and numbers the *toni* with Latin ordinals (*primus, secundus,* etc.). His approach is related to that of Aurelianus Reomensis in that he describes each *tonus* by means of characteristic intervals, which are presented both mathematically and verbally (e.g., "IX ad XII, . . . quae proportio sesquitertia dicitur . . . et facit

---

11. To cite but one example, three of the eight intonation formulas exemplifying the church modes in the Principal Treatise differ from those found in the *Nova expositio*—a phenomenon rather difficult to explain if the author of the *Nova expositio* was in fact responsible for composing the entire treatise.

12. It also incorporates, at least indirectly, the findings of Cynthia Cyrus. In her presentation "Errors and Improvements: Changing Ideas of Mode in the *Alia musica*," which she delivered at the national meeting of the American Musicological Society, Pittsburgh, 6 November 1992, Cyrus also posited a fourth author, whom she designated the "New Trope Author." The sections of the Principal Treatise she attributed to the New Trope Author are among those I have attributed to my Author δ, in table 5.3 and below.

13. To the version of the First Quidam in the central corpus (Chailley's GMP), Karlsruhe 504 adds for each *tonus* the Byzantine designations (*protos autentos,* etc.), which are also translated into Latin (e.g., *auctoritas prima*); an intonation formula for each (NONANEANE, NOEAGIS, etc.); and the sets of lettered terms of the *tetraktys* identifying each *tonus* as found in Munich 14272, fol. 180v–181 (Chailley, *Alia musica,* 173–74, §171. The ancient Greek ethnic names appear to be a later addition to the Munich manuscript; they do not appear in the two Paris sources).

TABLE 5.3.   Revised table of contents for *Alia musica* (a conflation of Mühlmann, Chailley, Heard and Atkinson)

The layout of this table follows that of table 5.1, but with the following changes: The order is that the various manuscripts and GS 1. The abbreviations *PQ*, *TP*, and *NE* designate Chailley's three authors: *PQ = Premier Quidam; TP = Traité principal; NE = Nova expositio*. My own provisional designations for the various authors/commentators and their implied order are given in Greek letters. My relative chronology is indicated by way of indentation, with the latest sources appearing farther to right. Unbracketed headings are those given in GS 1 and in the various manuscripts.

[A. Harmonic theory derived from Boethius]

1.   *TP* §§1–12 [M1. II] {β}   [*De medietate harmonica*] (Boethius, *De arithmetica*)
2.   *TP* §§13–20 [M2. I] {β}   Octave species as *modi* (Boethius, *De musica*)
3.   *TP* §§21–29 [M3a.V] {β}   Consonances and proportions (Boethius, *De musica*
         TP §§26–27 [M3b. II: Descriptions of intonation formulae for first and second *tropi*] {δ

[B. Exposition and expansion of the First Quidam]

1.   *TP* §§30–38 [M4a. III] {β}   Exposition of First *Tonus*
2.   *TP* §§39–40 [M4b.V] {δ}   Commentary on Exposition

ITEM CUIUSDAM DE EADEM RE NOVA EXPOSITIO

      NE §§41–44 [M5. Tonarius.V] {γ}   *Nova expositio*: First *Tropus*

DE SECUNDO TONO SEQUITUR IN EADEM EXPOSITIONE

1.   *TP* §§45–52 [M6a. III] {β}   Exposition of Second *Tonus*
2.   *TP* §53 [M6b.V] {δ}   Commentary on Exposition

ITEM DE SECUNDO TONO NOVA CUIUSDAM EXPOSITIO

      NE §§54–57 [M7. Tonarius.V] {γ}   *Nova expositio*: Second *Tropus*

SEQUITUR TONORUM EXPOSITOR DE TERTIO TONO

1.   *TP* §§58–67 [M8a. III] {β}   Exposition of Third *Tonus*
2.   *TP* §§68–76 [M8b.V] {δ}   Commentary on Exposition

DE QUARTO TONO

1.   *TP* §§77–86 [M9–10a. III] {β}   Exposition of Fourth *Tonus*
2.   *TP* §§87–89 [M10b.V] {δ}   Commentary on Exposition

ITEM DE TERTIO & QUARTO TONO NOVA CUIUSDAM EXPOSITIO

      NE §§90–94 [M11. Tonarius.V] {γ}   *Nova expositio*: Third *Tropus*
      NE §§95–98 [M12. Tonarius.V] {γ}   *Nova expositio*: Fourth *Tropus*

SEQUITUR EXPOSITOR DE QUINTO TONO

1.   *TP* §§99–102 [M13a. III] {β}   Exposition of Fifth *Tonus*
2.   *TP* §§103–7 [M13b.V] {δ}   Commentary on Exposition

ITEM DE QUINTO TONO NOVA CUISDAM EXPOSITIO

      NE §§108–11 [M14. Tonarius.V] {γ}   *Nova expositio*: Fifth *Tropus*

SEQUITUR IDEM EXPOSITOR DE SEXTO TONO

1.   *TP* §§112–18 [M15a. III] {β}   Exposition of Sixth *Tonus*
2.   *TP* §§119–21 [M15b.V] {δ}   Commentary on Exposition

ITEM DE SEXTO TONO NOVA CUIUSDAM EXPOSITIO

      NE §§122–25 [M16. Tonarius.V] {γ}   *Nova expositio*: Sixth *Tropus*

SEQUITUR EXPOSITOR DE SEPTIMO TONO

TP §§126–28 [M17a. IV] {β}	Exposition of Seventh and Eighth *Tonus*
TP §§129–32 [M17b.V] {δ}	Commentary on Exposition
TP §§133–42 [M18. II] {δ}	Presentation of Octave *Tropi*
TP §143–45 [M19.V] {δ}	Presentation of Eighth *Tropus*

ITEM DE SEPTIMO ET OCTAVO TONO NOVA CUIUSDAM EXPOSITIO

NE §§146–49 [M20.Tonarius.V] {γ}	*Nova expositio*: Seventh *Tropus*
NE §§150–53 [M21.Tonarius.V] {γ}	*Nova expositio*: Eighth *Tropus*

[**C.** Symbolic Considerations]

SEQUITUR PRAEMISSUS EXPOSITOR

PQ §§154–56 [M22a. III] {α}	"Praemissus Expositor" (Chailley's "First Quidam")
TP §§157–67 [M22b. IV] {β}	"Tonus expositor"
TP §§168–70 [M22c.V] {δ}	Compiler's additional material

[**D.** Tabular Summary:]

TP §§171–80 [M23. IV] {β}	"Tonus expositor"

[**E.** Prose Summary of the Eight *toni*]

ITEM EXPOSITIO EORUNDEM TONORUM

Q §§181–88 [M24. III] {α}	Chailley's "First Quidam"

diatessaron"); moreover, he uses three of the four chants cited by Aurelian as representative of their respective *toni*.[14] One finds here a close correlation of musical examples with those in early tonaries, such as Metz or the tonary of Regino von Prüm.[15] This author also contributed the section Chailley calls "symbolic considerations," which I have labeled C.1 in the Principal Treatise.[16]

Author β, the "Exposifor". He contributed two main parts in my opinion, starting with the Principal Treatise, section A (§§1–29, excepting §§26–27). As mentioned, paragraphs 13–20 of this section are also transmitted independently of the *Alia musica* as a whole, appearing in Madrid 9088. These may have been the "kernel" that was then expanded by Author β. He presents harmonic theory derived from Boethius's *De arithmetica* and *De musica*, probably introduced in order to provide a rationale for the intervallic ratios in the First Quidam. It is in this section that the diatonic scale is segmented progressively to yield *species*, which Author β equates with *modi*, and which are given *ancient* Greek ethnic names (Dorian, Phrygian, etc.).

14. See ex. 3.4.

15. On this, see Huglo, *Les Tonaires*, 58–59. Although no single model has thus far surfaced, the bulk of the examples in the First Quidam can also be found in the Metz tonary or in the tonary of Regino.

16. Chailley, *Alia musica*, 95–98, §§154–56. Chailley points out that this section is known only through its citation by the author of the Principal Treatise, who refers to its author as "Praemissus expositor," the designation he normally uses for the First Quidam. Mühlmann takes this to be by his Author III, whom he calls the "Theorist of the Six Tones" (Mühlmann, *Die "Alia musica,"* 47–48).

Following Boethius, this author uses ancient Greek instrumental nomenclature (*mese, paramese,* etc.) to designate pitches.

The main contribution of Author β can be found in the Principal Treatise, the sections marked B.1 in table 5.3, the exposition and expansion of the First Quidam. Here, the "Expositor" paraphrases the text of the First Quidam, preferring the term *tonus,* but substituting ancient Greek ethnic names for the First Quidam's Latin ordinals (e.g., "primus tonus, quem dorium dicimus"). He uses ancient Greek instrumental nomenclature to name the pitches and expands even further the proportional theory already found in the First Quidam, without, however, enhancing it substantially.

Author γ, Nova expositio (Tonary). As mentioned, this is transmitted independently of the *Alia musica* in four sources (see table 5.2). In the manuscripts of the complete treatise, each section of the *Nova expositio* carries a heading with the phrase *nova cuiusdam expositio* ("a new exposition by a certain author"), which I take as one indication that they were written by someone other than the composer/compiler of the complete treatise. The author of the *Nova expositio* uses the term *tropus* as a generic name for the church modes, which he names individually by means of numbers (*primus, secundus,* etc.). He also provides an intonation formula for each of them (NOANNOEANE, NOEAGIS, etc.), which he calls *forma.* (Surprisingly, he does not employ the Byzantine designations Protus, Deuterus, etc.) This author describes each *tropus* in terms of its *differentia,* by which he means the concluding note of the *saeculorum Amen* formula, and the *locum,* or first note of the family of antiphons associated with each. He labels specific pitches by means of letters derived from the second division of the monochord in Boethius's *De institutione musica* (Book IV, chaps. 6–12).[17]

Author δ, the compiler of the final version of the work. This author provided commentary on the Exposition of the First Quidam (Principal Treatise, sec. B.2) and the treatment of the octave tropes (Principal Treatise, sec. C). He probably added the concluding paragraphs to sec. D, "Symbolic Considerations." Following the *Nova expositio,* this author prefers the term *tropus* for the church modes, to which he gives ancient Greek ethnic names (Dorian, Phrygian, etc.), but he equates these for the first time with the Byzantine ordinal designations Protus autentus and plagis, Deuterus autentus and plagis, etc.). He, too, employs intonation formulas (NOANNOEANE, etc.), but differs from the *Nova expositio* in those for the third, sixth, and seventh church modes, presumably introducing those sung in his own monastery instead.[18] Author δ uses ancient Greek instrumental nomenclature and Boethian letter notation. He applies *species* both to the determination of mode and the analysis of chant and includes a discussion of the synemmenon tetrachord and its

17. The *Nova expositio* resembles the tonary at the end of Hucbald's *De harmonica institutione* in several ways: both use the term *tropus*; both provide catalogues of antiphon incipits for each church mode; both designate these by means of letters derived directly or indirectly from Boethius. Hucbald, however, does employ the Byzantine designations for the church modes (e.g., Protus autentus, plagis). The intonation formulas (NONEANE, etc.) are present as examples in his treatise but are not provided as descriptors in the tonary.

18. See Chailley, *Alia musica,* 62; and Bailey, *The Intonation Formulas of Western Chant,* 50–51, 55–56.

implications for chant. Finally, this author was probably the person responsible for the headings that introduce each section in the manuscripts.

The scenario I suggest for the composition of the *Alia musica* should be considered provisional. I believe, however, not only that it fits the manuscript evidence better than the usual model but also that it provides a better framework than we have had before for understanding the importance and implications of the treatise within the medieval theoretical tradition. I shall now examine the parts of the *Alia musica* in the light of its relationship to that tradition. As we shall see, all three treatises show the influence of Boethius,[19] but the First Quidam and the tonary of the *Nova expositio* are linked much more closely to the *cantus* tradition than is the Principal Treatise. I shall therefore discuss them in that order.

The reader will recall that in the second chapter of his *Musica disciplina,* Aurelian of Réôme classified four chants simultaneously as examples of the four Pythagorean consonances and the four principal *toni* of the *cantus* tradition.[20] As he said, one could find the octave in a chant of the Protus autentus, *Inclina Domine;* the diatessaron in one of the Deuterus autentus, *Confessio et pulchritudo;* the diapente in *Circumdederunt me,* in Tritus autentus; and the tone in *Puer natus est nobis,* a chant in Tetrardus autentus. Establishing a strong link with Aurelian's work, the First Quidam chooses the last three of these chants and their identifying intervals as the principal examples of their respective *toni* in his own treatment.[21]

As we shall begin to see in examples 5.1 and 5.2, the First Quidam expands the treatment of Aurelian in three directions.[22] First, he provides examples from the chant repertoire for both the authentic and plagal church modes, not just for the authentics. Second, he goes further than Aurelian in furnishing a mathematical basis for the characteristic intervals of the *toni.* Third, he gives examples of these intervals drawn not just from the beginning of each chant, as Aurelian had done, but also from interior phrases.

As an example of the First Quidam's approach, let us consider his treatment of the first church mode or *tonus primus* (ex. 5.1). It is significant, I believe, that the designation employed here is *tonus* primus, rather than *modus* primus, despite the fact that the author seems to be trying to put his description on a mathematical basis that would be typical of harmonic theory based on Boethius.[23] The terminology

19. A direct link with both Boethius's *De institutione musica* and the glosses on it is present in Munich 14272. In the upper margin of fol. 178, it contains the same gloss on Boethius Book IV, chap. 16 that is found in Munich 14523 (see ex. 2.27). Both manuscripts are from St. Emmeram; both also contain Boethius's *De musica* itself.

20. See ex. 3.2 and the discussion associated with it.

21. See Chailley, *Alia musica,* 88, 92, and 93–94.

22. I should mention here that I am discussing the text of the First Quidam as it was known to the remaining author/commentators of the *Alia musica,* that is, without the intonation formulas and Byzantine terminology for the church modes that were added to the version in Karlsruhe 504. That additional material appears in brackets in ex. 5.1.

23. The First Quidam's numbering of the eight *toni* is also of note: it is the same as that found in the *Commemoratio brevis* and in Hucbald's *De harmonica institutione* (see chapter 4 here, note 30). This Western numbering scheme was clearly well established by the late ninth century.

EXAMPLE 5.1. Description of the *tonus primus* by the First Quidam (*Alia musica*, ed. Chailley, 85, §181)

---

a) Tonus primus [NONANOEANE, qui graece dicitur autentos protos, id est auctoritas prima, A 12, C 6, B 8, D 9.] b) 6 ad 12 18 sunt, qui sunt ter 6, quae proportio dupla diapason dicitur. c) Item 8 ad 12 20 sunt, quae proportio sesquialtera dicitur ad 12, ideo quia 12 habet 8 in se et alteram ejus partem, id est 4, et facit diapente. d) Item 9 ad 12 21 sunt, quae proportio sesquitertia* dicitur ad 12, quia 12 habet 9 in se et ejus tertiam partem, id est 3, et facit diatessaron, id est ter 7 qui sunt 21. e) Omnis igitur primus tonus aut ter 6 habet in dupla proportione diapason, ut est *Rorate celi desuper*, aut quater 5, id est 2 de 8 et 3 de 12 in sesquialtera proportione qui faciunt diapente, quod est 20, ut est *et nubes pluant justum, aperiatur*, aut ter 7, id est 3 de 9 ad 4 de 12 in sesquitertia proportione, qui faciunt diatessaron, ut est *terra et germinet Salvatorem*. f) Item Introitum *Gaudete in Domino semper*, et *Justus es Domine*; similiter antiphonae *Urbs fortitudinis nostrae Sion, Johannes autem cum audisset in vinculis opera Christi, Traditor* [-86-] *autem dedit eis.* g) Et hoc videndum, quod saepe evenit, ut bis aut ter aut totum etiam in antiphonis, aut quocumque cantu primi toni fit, aut per 6 et 12 quod est diapason, aut per 5 aut 10 quod est diapente, aut per 7 totum quod est diatessaron, decurrit; h) ut *Urbs fortitudinis; Johannes autem* diapente. [from Karlsruhe 504] *Ed.: sesquialtera

---

here establishes a further link with the treatise of Aurelian and others in the *cantus* tradition.[24] In contradistinction to Aurelian, however, the First Quidam does not restrict himself to naming a single proportion and its corresponding interval as being characteristic for Protus autentus. Instead, he presents a Pythagorean *tetraktys* 12, 6, 8, 9,[25] implying that all of the Pythagorean consonances can be found in the chants of this *tonus*. Then, rather than contenting himself with a simple intervallic presentation using the numbers just given, the author describes the proportions as sums of their terms, which can also be multiplied or divided (see ex. 5.1). I translate the first four sentences:

> (a) The first tone [is] (b) six plus 12, which gives 18, which is three times six, which duple proportion is called the octave. (c) Further, 8 plus 12 yields 20, which proportion is called sesquialtera in relation to 12, because 12 contains in itself 8 and its other part, that is 4, which makes the diapente. (d) Further, 9 plus 12 equals 21, which proportion is named sesquitertia in relationship to 12, because 12 contains in itself 9 plus its third part, that is 3, which makes the diatessaron, that is, 3 times 7, which equals 21.

Although the expression of the proportions as both ratios and sums is a bit unusual, the text as it stands certainly makes sense.[26]

---

24. As pointed out, the early tonaries, the treatise of Aurelian, the *Musica* and *Scolica enchiriadis*, the *Commemoratio brevis*, Hucbald, and Regino all employ *tonus* as their principal designation for melodic category.

25. A *tetraktys* is simply a formal ordering of four items. The best-known Pythagorean *tetraktys* is probably that of the decad, 1, 2, 3, 4.

26. If one takes addition and comparison as two different operations starting from the first number of each pair, most of the relationships can be explained: 6 + 12 = 18; 6:12 = proportio dupla = diapa-

EXAMPLE 5.2. *Rorate caeli desuper* from the *Graduale Romanum*, as described by First Quidam of *Alia musica* (octave, diapente, and diatessaron bracketed)

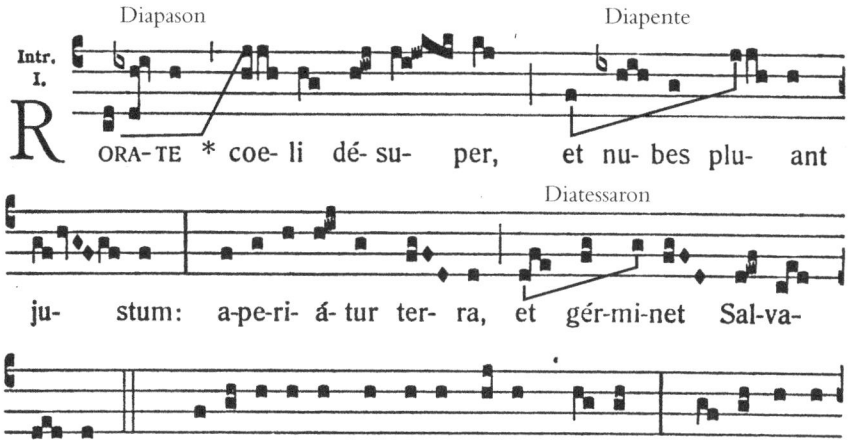

If the mathematical procedures of the First Quidam might seem a bit suspect, his knowledge of the chant repertoire is not. He provides an intervallic analysis of the sections of the Introit *Rorate caeli* that is strikingly perceptive, using an approach that is almost prophetic of analyses to come.[27] (See exs. 5.1 and 5.2.) He says in example 5.1, sentence (e) that all the examples of chant in the first church mode can exhibit the duple proportion or octave, as in the phrase *Rorate caeli;* or the proportion sesquialtera or diapente, as in the phrase *et nubes pluant iustum;* or the proportion sesquitertia or diatessaron, as in the phrase *et germinet Salvatorem.* As the transcription of the chant in example 5.2 shows, the author is well aware of the intervallic structure of the different parts of *Rorate caeli,* surpassing even Aurelian in this regard.[28]

The traits just noted in the First Quidam's discussion of the first *tonus* are likewise true for the rest of his treatise, which presents a discussion of the remaining church modes and consonances that identify them. Each of these is given a discrete set of proportions that result from simple multiplication of the terms of the first *tetraktys,* 12, 6, 8, 9 (table 5.4). As one can see, not all of the consonances are represented in all the *toni.* The fourth *tonus,* for example, has only the diatessaron; the fifth and sixth have only the diapente, since there is not a diatessaron above the final.

---

son; $8 + 12 = 20$, $8{:}12 =$ proportio sesquialtera $=$ diapente; $9 + 12 = 21$; $9{:}12 =$ proportio sesquitertia $=$ diatessaron. For discussion of the mathematical procedures in the *Alia musica,* see Heard, "Alia musica," 53–62; and Mühlmann, *Die "Alia musica."* 16–17, 21–26, 30–31, 39–41.

27. I am thinking here of some of the analyses by Johannes Cotto/Affligemensis or by the Cistercian theorists.

28. In the example, I have bracketed the initial appearances of the intervals in question, but one could mark their presence in other places, as well. For example: the opening phrase, *Rorate caeli desuper,* begins on C and ends on *c* an octave higher; the second phrase, *et nubes . . . aperiatur,* has the ambitus of a fifth, F–*c;* in the phrase *terra . . . salvatorem* the fourth, D–G, appears on the word *terra* and then serves as the framing interval for the remainder of the phrase.

TABLE 5.4. Summary of numerical terms of consonances characteristic for each tonus (based on §171 in Chailley, ed., *Alia musica*, 173–74)

Tonus	Terms				Characteristic Consonances		
	12 (a)*	6 (c)	8 (b)	9 (d)			
Tonus primus	12	18 (6x3)	16 (8x2)	18 (9x2)	Diapason (12:6)	Diapente (12:8)	Diatessaron (12:9)
Tonus secundus	12	24 (6x4)	24 (8x3)	18 (9x2)		Diapente (12:18)	Diatessaron (12:16)
Tonus tertius	12	18 (6x3)	24 (8x3)	18 (9x2)	Diapason (12:24)	Diapente (12:18)	
Tonus quartus	24 (12x2)	24 (6x4)	24 (8x3)	36 (9x4)			Diatessaron (24:18)
Tonus quintus	36 (12x3)	36 (6x6)	24 (8x3)	36 (9x4)		Diapente (36:24)	
Tonus sextus	24 (12x2)	36 (6x6)	24 (8x3)	36 (9x4)		Diapente (36:24)	
Tonus septimus	24 (12x2)	18 (6x3)	24 (8x4)	18 (9x2)			Diatessaron (24:18)
Item de eodem	36 (12x3)	24 (6x4)	24 (8x3)	36 (9x4)		Diapente (36:24)	
Item propria et consonantia diapason	48 (12x4)	48 (6x8)	48 (8x6)		Diapason (48:96)		
Tonus octavus	24 (12x2)	18 (6x3)	24 (8x3)	18 (9x2)			Diatessaron (24:18)
Item ex eodem	36 (12x3)	24 (6x4)	24 (8x3)	36 (9x4)		Diapente (36:24)	

*The letters a–d in parentheses are those assigned to the numbers 12, 6, 8, and 9, respectively, in §171 of the edition.

EXAMPLE 5.3.   The intervals of the diapason and diapente in chants of the sixth tonus

Fortunately, the same perceptivity regarding chant structure noted in the discussion of *Rorate caeli* distinguishes the rest of the First Quidam's treatise as well. In cases in which the numerical terms for a specific consonance have not been given, he will nonetheless provide that consonance if it is necessary in order to describe the chants in that particular church mode. A case in point is the sixth *tonus*, which he says is identified by both the diapason and the diapente, even though the numerical terms provide only the diapente.[29] Among his examples, the introits *Omnes gentes* and *Os justi* and the antiphons *O admirabile commercium* and *Virgo hodie fidelis* exhibit both the octave and the fifth, as one can see in example 5.3.[30]

29. §186. (d): "Totus iste tonus aut per diapason consonantiam, id est 6 ad 12, aut per diapente, id est denarium, mensurabitur" (Chailley, *Alia musica*, 92–93).

30. Ibid.

EXAMPLE 5.4.   Two series of letters that appear in the *Nova expositio* of *Alia musica* (**P** = Glosses in Paris 7212, Paris 7211, and Barcelona 42; **NE** = *Nova expositio*; **O** = Letter notation in Pseudo-Odo; **kk** and **ll** from Bernhard, ed., *Dulce ingenium musicae*, 14–26)

P:	A	B	C	F	H	-	M	O	Q	X	Y	CC	DD	FF	NN	II	
NE:	a	b	c	e	♭	i	m	o	q	x	y	cc	dd	ff	nn		
															kk	**ll**	(NE in *Dulce ingenium*)
O:	A	B	C	D	E	F	G	a	b	♭	c	d	e	f	g	aa	

Just as is true of the work of the First Quidam, the third "treatise" of the *Alia musica*, the tonary that forms the heart of the *Nova expositio*, reflects an extensive knowledge of the chant repertoire on the part of its author, whom I have labeled γ in table 5.3. It is related conceptually to Aurelian's *Musica disciplina* and more concretely to the last section of Hucbald's *De harmonica institutione* by virtue of its providing a range of chant incipits for each church mode, for which this author's term is *tropus* (see ex. 5.5). The subject expounded here is the relationship between the *differentiae* of the psalm tones and the various incipits of antiphons—called *loca* (positions)—that can be sung with each. The author makes use of the alphabetic notation presented in the second monochord division of Boethius to express the relationships he describes.[31]

There are, in fact, two series of letters in the manuscript tradition for the *Nova expositio*. The "standard" series is the one appearing in Gerbert's edition and in Munich 14272; a second series appears in the marginal glosses in three other manuscripts preserving the treatise: Paris 7211 (eleventh century), Paris 7212 (twelfth century), and Barcelona 42 (ca. 1018–46).[32] Both series of letters, together with their modern equivalents (drawn from the treatise of Pseudo-Odo), are given in example 5.4. As one can see here, the two series preserve the architecture of the ancient Greek Greater and Lesser Perfect Systems in the diatonic genus. (We have already encountered the "Paris" series as a gloss in the tenth-century manuscript, Paris 8674, fol. 111v, where it immediately follows Remigius's commentary on Martianus Capella.)[33]

Utilizing these letters, the author of the *Nova expositio* devises a functional system of chant classification based on the *differentia* of each psalm tone—in this case, the concluding pitch—and the incipits or starting pitches of each chant. We can follow his description in example 5.5.[34]

31. This division, with pitches designated by the letters A through O to LL, is presented in Boethius, Book IV, chaps. 6–12. As pointed out by Phillips ("Notationen und Notationslehren," 549–64), the discrepancies between the letters in the *Nova expositio* and those in Boethius can be traced to variants in the manuscript transmission of Boethius's text.

32. See Chailley, *Alia musica*, 180–82. See Phillips, "Notationen und Notationslehren," however, for a more reliable discussion of these two series. I have added the last two sets of letters, kk and ll, as they appear in the principal manuscripts of the treatise *Dulce ingenium* (Bernhard, ed., *Anonymi saeculi decimi et undecimi tractatus de musica "Dulce ingenium musicae,"* 14–26).

33. See figure 2.5 and chapter 2 here, note 75.

34. In the table at the bottom of ex. 5.5, I have given for each chant the *differentia* and *locum* indicated for it in the *Nova expositio* (NE), followed by the same information as derived from easily accessible practical sources. In the translation that follows in the text here, I have provided modern pitch names in square brackets.

EXAMPLE 5.5. *Alia musica, Nova expositio*: Description of the *differentiae* and *loca* in the first church mode (ed. Chailley, 183, §41, with emendations from Bernhard, *Dulce ingenium musicae*, 1, 20-21, followed by the same information gleaned from practical sources

A prima quoque specie diapason, quae est mese, id est o, inchoatur primus tropus: finiturque in diapente remissum, quod est e, et haec est forma NOANNOEANE: habet autem 5 differentias et 9 loca in nocturnis. b) Est namque prima differentia in o quae habet duo [loca]: primum in se: *Veniet Dominus*; secundum in i enarmonio remisso: *Apertis thesauris suis.* c) Secunda vero differentia in m lichanos meson, quae habet tria loca: in se: *Canite tuba.* Diatessaron remissum in e: *Ecce nomen Domini*, diapente remissum in c: *In tempesta nocte.* d) Tertia differentia in i quae habet unum locum: se, diatessaron scilicet remissum in c: *O beatum pontificem.* e) Quarta differentia est in H quae habet unum locum: in se: *Inclinans se Iesus.* f) Quinta differentia est in e quae habet duo loca: se, *Euge serve bone*, sesquioctavum remissum in C: *Sint lumbi vestri.* g) Concluditurque hujus tropi forma intra integrum diapente, h) et singulae chordae singulas retinent differentias, et prima differentia duo habet loca, secunda tria, tertia unum, quarta unum, quinta duo. i) Unde constat, ut hic tropus quinque habeat differentias, et novem loca in nocturnis.

Chant	Differentia (NE)	Locum (NE)	Differentia (actual)★	Note of incipit★
1.Veniet Dominus	*a*	*a*	*a* (AM)	*a* (AM)
1.Apertis thesauris suis	*F*	*F*	*G/a* (AM)	*f* (AM)
2. Canite tuba	*G*	*E*	*G* (MMMA)	*E* (MMMA)
2. Ecce nomen Domini	*D*	*D*	*F/G* (AM)	*D* (AM)
2. In tempesta nocte	*G*	*C*	*G* (WA)	*C* (WA)
3. O beatum pontificem	*F*	*C*	*F* (LA)	*C* (LA)
4. Inclinans se Iesus (Inclinavit se Iesus)	*E*	*E*	*G/F* (MMMA/WA)	*D/C* (MMMA/WA)
5. Euge serve bone	*D*	*D*	*D* (AM)	*D* (AM)
5. Sint lumbi vestri	*D*	*C*	*D (F?)* (WA)	*C* (WA)

★Sources
AM = Antiphonale Monasticum
LA = Lucca Antiphonale
WA = Worcester Antiphonale
MMMA = Monumenta Monodica Medii Aevi, V/1

(a) The first trope begins with the first species of octave, which is the mese, o [*a*], and finishes at the fifth below, which is e [*D*], and this is its *forma*: NOANNOEANE.[35] There are five *differentiae* and nine *loca* [positions] in the antiphons of the Nocturnes. (b) The first *differentia* is o [*a*], which has two positions or *loca*. The first [position] is in itself, that is, o [*a*]: *Veniet Dominus*. The second [position] is on the i enharmonic below [*F*]: *Apertis thesauris suis*. (c) The second *differentia* is on m, the lichanos meson [*G*], which has three positions or *loca*: in itself, [*G*]: *Canite tuba;* a fourth below, on e [*D*]: as in *Ecce nomen domini;* and a fifth below, on c [*C*], as in *In tempesta nocte*. (d) The third differentia is on i [*F*], which has a single position [*locum*], in itself but the fourth below [*C*], as in *O beatum pontificem*. (e) The fourth *differentia* is on H [*E*] and has a single position or place, in itself: *Inclinans se Iesus*.[36] (f) The fifth *differentia* is on e [*D*], and has two positions: in itself, as *Euge serve bone* and the sesquioctave below, c [*C*], as in *Sint lumbi vestri*. (g) The *forma* of this trope is encompassed within an integral diapente, (h) and each of the notes [*chordae*] has its *differentia*. The first *differentia* has two positions, the second three, the third one, the fourth one, the fifth two. (i) One can therefore confirm that this trope has five *differentiae* and nine positions in the antiphons of the Nocturns.

There are some discrepancies between the musical descriptions of the *Nova expositio* and the characteristics of the antiphons as they are transmitted in chant collections—either contemporaneous or contemporary. Nonetheless, it is clear that the author of this treatise had a very clear image of the chants themselves and how they could be used to exemplify the church modes in a verbal tonary. In effect, the author of the *Nova expositio* systematizes further the approach Hucbald takes at the conclusion of his *De harmonica institutione*.

Indeed, the author goes even further than Hucbald in grafting ancient Greek ideas onto the inchoate medieval theory of the church modes. But he is not the only contributor to the *Alia musica* to have surpassed Hucbald in this manner. The author of section A of the Principal Treatise—the one I have designated Author β— does so as well (ex. 5.6).[37]

35. The use of the term *forma* here is noteworthy. As its appearances here and elsewhere in the *Nova expositio* demonstrate, it can stand as a designation for "intonation formula" (e.g., NOANNOEANE, as here) or for species (e.g., for the second church mode, "Concluditur autem ejus *forma* intra diapente, quod est ab m [*G*] ad c [*C*]"; Chailley, *Alia musica*, 186, §54). What may be its earliest usage within the Western music-theoretical tradition is its appearance in the glosses on Martianus Capella formerly attributed to Martin of Laon (see Teeuwen, *Harmony and the Music of the Spheres*, 492), and it is used there as an equivalent for *tropus*. In Leiden 36, fol. 120v, for example, it appears in a marginal gloss opposite sec. 931, numbering the eighteen sounds in the fifteen tropes: "Tropus est *forma* vocis." In Besançon 594 and Leiden 48, the gloss simply reads "Tropus forma." That the glossator understands *forma* to mean "species" is suggested by a further gloss, based on a mistaken reading of the text. For Martianus's ΥΛΙΚΟΝ in sec. 936, the glossator reads ΥΛΙΚΟΝ (interpreting it as derived from εἶδος, = Lat. *species, forma*), then explains: "Yda forma. ΥΛΙΚΟΝ formabile" (Teeuwen, *Harmony and the Music of the Spheres*, 499).

36. The incipit is given as *Inclinavit se Jesus* in Bruges 532 and in Prague 26 (see Bernhard, ed., *Anonymi saeculi decimi et undecimi tractatus de musica "Dulce ingenium musicae,"* 20–21), as well as in most of the practical sources I have been able to consult. Chailley, *Alia musica*, 184, emends the letter H (*E*) for the differentia to m (*G*), despite the fact that no such alternative is given in the critical apparatus. Given the fact that the author says that there is a *differentia* on each degree of the diapente a-D, I have maintained the reading given in the manuscripts. It is likewise the reading retained in Bernhard, ed., *Anonymi saeculi decimi et undecimi tractatus de musica "Dulce ingenium musicae,"* 21, 39, and Gümpel, "Die 'Nova expositio' der Handschrift Ripoll 42: Text und Kommentar," 130.

37. For my assignment of the sections of the *Alia musica* to various authors and compilers, see table

EXAMPLE 5.6. *Alia musica*, Principal Treatise, Introduction of *tropi vel modi* (ed. Chailley, 105, §13)

> a) His praemissis, ad 8 troporum, quos Latini modos nuncupant, dispositionem veni-amus. b) Primoque sciendum quod tropus de graeco in latinum conversio dicitur, idcirco quod, excepta sua proprietate, alter in alterum convertitur. c) Toni vero ideo dicuntur quod, exceptis semitoniis, ipsi omnium troporum communis mensura sint. d) Modi etiam dicti sunt, eo quod unusquisque troporum proprium modum teneat nec mensuram excedat.

This author (β) begins his treatment by presenting a discussion "de harmonica consideratione" according to Boethius, encompassing a discourse on the Boethian consonances and the two principal types of means, the harmonic (e.g., 6:8:12) and arithmetic (e.g., 6:9:12).[38] Having established this mathematical basis for his discussion, Author β then moves to a presentation of the eight "tropes, which the Latins call modes." As one can see in example 5.6, he explains: that the Greek "tropus" is called "conversio" because one is converted into another (Sentence b)[39]; that *toni* are the common measure of all the tropes (Sentence c)[40]; and that *modi* are so called because they do not exceed their range (*modus*) or measure (*mensura*, Sentence d).[41]

Following this, in the section given in example 5.7, Author β sets out the designation of the modes or tropes in which he equates *modi* with species of diapason, thereby betraying a fundamental misunderstanding of the way the species had been used in Boethius.[42] He says that the first mode, the Hypodorian, is of the first spe-

5.3. Mühlmann, *Die "Alia musica,"* 43–44, suggests that sec. A.3 is the work of a later author, his Author V. While I feel that §§26 and 27 are indeed the work of a later author, whom I have designated δ, I do not see substantial differences of treatment in the remainder of secs. A.1–3.

38. This discussion is drawn from Boethius, *De arithmetica*, Book II, chaps. 48–49, 54. In the harmonic mean, the ratio of the differences between terms is equal to the ratio of the outer terms to each other (e.g., in 6:8:12, the differences, 2 and 4, are related to each other in the same 1:2 ratio as are the outer terms). In the arithmetic mean, the differences between terms are equal.

39. This is the earliest appearance of this definition I have found. See Atkinson, "Modus," *HmT*, sec. V. (I) (IV). It will later appear in Treatise 11, chap. 1 of the *Lucidarium* of Marchetto of Padova (ed. Herlinger, 370–71; *GS* 3: 101a). It may derive from Remigius of Auxerre's commentary on sec. 966 of Martianus Capella's *De nuptiis Philologiae et Mercurii*: "ETIAM TROPI id est conversiones vocum, DICUNTUR" (Lutz, ed., *Remigius of Auxerre: Commentum in Martianum Capellam,* 351; Dick, ed., *Martianus Capella: De nuptiis Philologiae et Mercurii*, 515, l. 13).

40. As noted in chapter 2 here, a statement similar to this first appears in glosses to both Martianus Capella and Boethius (see exs. 2.18–20). Its source is probably Boethius, *De arithmetica*, Book II, chap. 54: "tonus vocatur, quae omnium musicorum sonorum mensura communis est" (ed. Friedlein, 171–72).

41. The fundamental meaning of *modus* is, of course, "measure," translated variously as "size," "length," "circumference," "boundary," or "limit." The idea of *modus* as measure in this sense seems to be documented earliest in Quintilian's *Institutio oratoria* (ca. 93–95 C.E.); see Atkinson, "Modus," *HmT*, sec. I. (V) and (VI). Following its use with that meaning here, the term *modus* was taken into a number of subsequent treatises on music, perhaps most notably into the *Lucidarium* of Marchetto of Padova (see the discussion in the epilogue here, at note 42).

42. One should recall that Boethius presented the octave species as a means of identifying the mode of each of the respective transpositions of the system, rather than equating the species with the modes

EXAMPLE 5.7. *Alia musica*, Principal Treatise, equation of modes with octave species (ed. Chailley, 107, §15)

---

a) Erit ergo primus modus omnium gravissimus videlicet hypodorius ex prima specie diapason, et terminatur eo qui meses dicitur, medio nervo. b) Secundum modum hypophrygium secunda species diapason efficit, quae in paramesen finitur. c) Tertium modum hypolydium tertia species diapason determinat in eum quem vocant triten diezeugmenon nervum. c) Quartum modum dorium quarta species diapason reddit, quae finit in paranete diezeugmenon. e) Quintus modus phrygius quinta specie diapason finitur, cui nete diezeugmenon nervus est ultimus. f) Sextum nihilominus modum lydium sexta species diapason exerit, cui trite hyperbolaeon est finis. g) Septimum quoque modum mixolydium septima species diapason informat, quam paranete hyperbolaeon determinat.

---

cies of diapason, and ends on the mese (*a*), the middle string; the second mode, the Hypophrygian, is produced by the second species of diapason and ends on the paramese (♭); the third, the Hypolydian, is the third diapason species and ends on the trite diezeugmenon (*c*), and so on. He concludes by saying that the seventh species of diapason, which ends on the paranete hyperboleon, forms the seventh mode, the Mixolydian.

Since, however, he can justify only seven modes on the basis of the seven discrete species of octave—as one can see in example 5.7—he then (incorrectly) invokes Ptolemy, by way of Boethius, to explain that the Hypermixolydian had been added as an eighth mode, one that is informed by the properties of both the second and third modes (ex. 5.8).

I translate:

> Thus, because a single duple proportion (i.e., a diapason) consisting of eight pitches does not receive more species [than the seven just enumerated]—inasmuch as every consonance admits one pitch more than [the number of its] species—Ptolemy added an eighth, Hypermixolydian, mode, which he formed with properties of the second and third mode.[43]

---

per se (see chapter 1 here, pp. 19, 21–25). As we shall see, Author β of the Principal Treatise does set out the species themselves by reading downward in pitch—just as Boethius had—but the modes and their corresponding species are nonetheless reversed (see table 5.5).

43. See Chailley, *Alia musica*, 22–25. I must confess that—along with Chailley—I am not sure why Author β says that the eighth mode is that which "secundi ac tertii modi proprietatibus informavit." The answer may lie in §156, a passage Chailley attributes to the First Quidam. In it, the author is naming the intervals and their proportions characteristic for each of the *toni*. At the end, in a passage that both Chailley and Gerbert feel is corrupted, the writer speaks of the eighth tone as exhibiting the diapason consonance "with the duple and triple" ("et dupla diapason in octavo tono, una cum duplo et triplo"). Elsewhere, the authors of both the Principal Treatise and the *Nova expositio*, following the confirmed text of the First Quidam, say that the eighth church mode combines the diatessaron and diapente of the fourth and fifth *toni* (see Chailley, *Alia musica*, 94, §180; 163, §130; 173–74, §171). One is led to suspect some sort of corruption of the text as the explanation for the odd position Author β takes with respect to the eighth mode.

This eighth mode, which would presumably extend from the mese (a) up to the nete hyperboleon (aa) in the nomenclature of the Principal Treatise, would have the same species as the first, but placed an octave higher.[44] It is important to note, however, that Author β does not define this mode in terms of its species; he merely says that it was "formed with properties of the second and third mode."

The sort of problems that this creates can be seen in a section following shortly thereafter (ex. 5.9). In §20, the same author (β) wants to relate the species of the modes to their positions relative to each other in tonal space. He says correctly that since the lichanos hypaton of the Hypodorian mode (D) is the proslambanomenos of the Dorian (D), and the mese of the Dorian (d) is the paranete diezeugmenon of the Hypodorian (d), the mese of the Dorian is higher than that of the Hypodorian (a) by a diatessaron consonance.[45] The same relationships characterize the Phrygian and Hypophrygian and the Lydian and the Hypolydian. They do not apply to the remaining pair, however, "for the Mixolydian and the Hypermixolydian are distant from each other by a tone." Originating as a commentary on Boethius, Book IV, chapter 17, this description would work well in conjunction with Boethius's wing diagram of the modes.[46] Given the obvious sophistication of this description, however, one wonders why its author did not notice the lack of symmetry between the first three pairs of modes and the last pair.

The sections of the Principal Treatise written by Author β and presented in examples 5.7–9 are important not just because the author defines the modes by means of octave species obtained via successive segmentations of the diatonic scale. Also important is the fact that Author β designates the species as *modi*, the Latin translation of τρόποι and the preferred designation of Boethius for the transposition scales, as is his choice of the ancient Greek ethnic names, Dorian, Phrygian, and so on, for the modes.

After having defined the modes by means of species of octave, Author β turns to the definition of the species of diatessaron and diapente, as one can see in examples 5.10 and 5.11. One notes with interest that he defines each species according to the position occupied by the semitone(s), merely situating the species on a tone-system without reference to specific pitches. In example 5.10, the first species of diatessaron has the semitone in the third position, the second species in the second position, and the third species in the first position.[47] In example 5.11, three species of diapente are created by adding a tone to those of the diatessaron, starting with the nete

---

44. See exs. 1.8 and 1.9, and the text associated with them. Boethius had said: "There still remains then HP (mese to proslambanomenos [a to A in modern nomenclature]), which has been added so that the whole series might be filled out. This then is the eighth mode, which Ptolemy incorporated at the top." See ex. 5.12 and table 5.5 and the discussion connected with them.

45. I should point out as a corrective to the translation in McKinnon, *The Early Christian Period and the Latin Middle Ages*, 88, that the author here is dealing with the dynamic nomenclature of the modes, not the thetic.

46. See Chailley, *Alia musica*, 111.

47. If one takes the nete diezeugmenon as the initium, as suggested in §18, the species read correctly downward: (1) nete diezeugmenon to paramese (T-T-ST); (2) paranete diezeugmenon to mese (T-ST-T); and (3) trite diezeugmenon to lichanos meson (ST-T-T).

EXAMPLE 5.8. *Alia musica*, Principal Treatise: the eighth mode (ed. Chailley, 107, §16)

> Verum, quia unus duplus, hoc est una diapason, octo vocibus pollens, plures species
> non recipit, quandoquidem omnis symphonia unam vocem pluresque species admittit,
> b) octavum modum hypermixolydium Ptolomaeus adjecit, quem secundi ac tertii modi
> proprietatibus informavit.

EXAMPLE 5.9. *Alia musica*, Principal Treatise: differences between the hypo- and normal
forms of each modus (ed. Chailley, 111, §20)

> Ceterum, ut ad ipsas species diapason redeamus, quoniam lichanos hypaton hypodorii
> est proslambanomenos dorii, meses dorii, quae est paranete diezeugmenon hypodorii,
> integra consonantia diatessaron acutior est a mese ejusdem hypodorii. b) Similiter
> differentia est inter phrygium et hypophrygium, lydium quoque et hypolydium, nam
> mixolydius ab hypermixolydio tantum distat tono.

EXAMPLE 5.10.   *Alia musica*, Principal Treatise: species of diatessaron (ed. Chailley, 108, §17)

> Denique prima species diatessaron tertio loco habet semitonium, secunda species
> secundo, tertia species primo, b) semperque sive per disjunctum sive per conjunctum
> tetrachordum quartis locis eadem species redit.

EXAMPLE 5.11.   *Alia musica*, Principal Treatise: species of diapente (ed. Chailley, 109, §18)

> a) Quintis locis non tamen semper diapente sibi invicem succedit. b) Unde constat
> quod tres species diatessaron tres prima species diapente, uno tono adjecto, constituunt.
> c) Quarta vero species semitonio terminatur, et prima a nete diezeugmenon sumit
> initium.

EXAMPLE 5.12.   *Alia musica*, Principal Treatise: species of octave (ed. Chailley, 110, §19)

> a) Restat ut proprietates specierum diapason investigemus. b) Prima itaque species
> tertio et sexto loco utitur semitonio, c) secunda quarto et septimo, d) tertia primo et
> quinto, e) quarta secundo et sexto, f) quinta tertio et septimo, g) sexta primo et quarto,
> h) septima secundo et quinto, i) octava sicut et prima tertio et sexto.

diezeugmenon; the fourth species is made up of three whole tones followed by a semitone.[48]

As one can see in example 5.12, Author β does not form the species of octave from the juxtaposition of fourths and fifths, as later writers will do, but rather by describing the position of the semitones.

I translate, starting with Sentence (b) of the example:

> The first species utilizes the semitone in the third and sixth position; the second in the fourth and seventh positions; the third in the first and fifth positions; the fourth in the second and sixth positions; the fifth in the third and seventh positions; the sixth in the first and fourth; the seventh in the second and fifth; and the eighth and first in the first and sixth positions.

As the diagrams in Chailley's edition make clear, the species are set out in descending pitch succession, but starting with the mese and progressing upward; hence, they do correspond to the order of species and modes given earlier in §15 (see ex. 5.7). They do not, however, correspond to the species and their modal equivalents given in Boethius, as is shown by table 5.5.[49] Since the author had already declared that the eighth mode was not defined via a new species of octave, but rather by traits common to the second and third mode [*sic*], it should not be surprising that he describes the eighth and the first in the same way here.

After what is obviously a fairly sophisticated treatment of Boethian harmonic theory on the part of Author β, one would expect an equally sophisticated application of Boethian ideas to the incipient theory of the church modes in the next layer of the treatise, an exposition on the tonal theory of the First Quidam. Surprisingly, the ideas presented in section A of the treatise have little effect on the exposition in section B.[50] In essence, Author β provides a slightly expanded rephrasing of the text of the First Quidam, using, for the most part, the earlier author's vocabulary, mathematical demonstrations, and musical examples, while providing some additional matter of his own. He takes us through the church modes in order, usually referring to them as *toni,* and occasionally—but inconsistently—supplying the ancient Greek ethnic names.[51] In only one instance—his discussion of the third *tonus* in §58—does he employ the Byzantine terminology of the *octoechos,* but this is merely a paraphrase of the only passage in which the First Quidam had done the same.[52] Author

---

48. Again, reading downward from the nete diezeugmenon: (1) nete diezeugmenon to mese (T-T-ST-T); (2) paranete diezeugmenon to lichanos meson (T-ST-T-T); (3) trite diezeugmenon to parhypate meson (ST-T-T-T); and (4) paramese to hypate meson (T-T-T-ST).

49. See also ex. 1.7, and the discussion associated with it.

50. In my Revised Table of Contents (table 5.3, sec. C of the Principal Treatise), I follow Mühlmann in describing this author as "Tonus expositor."

51. In §31, he says that the first *tonus* is called Dorius; in §48, he makes the statement "Nam hypodorius in dorium transit si suam diapason excesserit"; in §82, he equates the fourth *tonus* with the Hypophrygium mode: "Tonus quartus, quem nos hypophrygium dicimus"; in §99, we read "Tonus quintus, quem nos lydium dicimus"; in §126: "Tonus septimus, quem nos mixolydium dicimus"; and in §127: "ex quarti et quinti toni proportionibus mixolydium fieri." If this commentator is responsible for the addition of the Greek ethnic names to the tabular summary, §§171–80, then one can add these instances to those just given.

52. In his discussion of the third *tonus* in §58, Author β makes the statement "Tertius tonus duo a

TABLE 5.5. Comparison of octave species in Boethius and in the Principal Treatise (Author β) of the *Alia musica* (semitones in boldface)

Boethius		Mode	Alia musica	
1. NHyperb—Mese:	T–T–**ST**–T–T–**ST**–T	Hypodorian	1. Mese – Prosl:	T–T–**ST**–T–T–**ST**–T
2. PnHyperb—LM:	T–**ST**–T–T–**ST**–T–T	Hypophrygian	2. Pm – HHypat:	T–T–**ST**–T–T–T–**ST**
3. THyperb—PhM:	**ST**–T–T–**ST**–T–T–T	Hypolydian	3. TDz—PhHypat:	**ST**–T–T–**ST**–T–T–T
4. NDz—HM:	T–T–**ST**–T–T–T–**ST**	Dorian	4. PnDz—LHypat:	T–**ST**–T–T–T–**ST**–T
5. PnDz—LHypat:	T–**ST**–T–T–T–**ST**–T	Phrygian	5. NDz—HM:	T–T–**ST**–T–T–T–**ST**
6. TDz—PhHypat:	**ST**–T–T–T–**ST**–T–T	Lydian	6. THyperb—PhM:	**ST**–T–T–**ST**–T–T–T
7. Pm—HHypat:	T–T–T–**ST**–T–T–**ST**	Mixolydian	7. PnHyperb—LM:	T–**ST**–T–T–**ST**–T–T
8. [H (Mese)—P (Pr):	T–T–**ST**–T–T–**ST**–T]	[Hypermixolydian]	8. Nhyperb—Mese:	T–T–**ST**–T–T–**ST**–T]

The determination of the species for Boethius's eighth mode, the Hypermixolydian, is from *De institutione musica* IV.17. Cf. Exs. 1.7–9 above, and the discussion associated with them.

β does not employ the intonation formulae as a means of identifying the church modes, nor does he apply the species in any significant way to the analysis of chant. This changes, however, in the work of Author δ.

As mentioned in the discussion of the revised table of contents in table 5.3, Author δ employs the term *tropus* for the church modes, to which he gives the ancient Greek ethnic names. As we shall see, he is the first author—indeed, probably the first one ever—to equate these with the Byzantine names for the church modes, which he also identifies by means of intonation formulas (NOEANE, etc.). Not the least of his accomplishments is the solution of the problem of the eighth mode (ex. 5.13).

Author β, the "Expositor of the First Quidam," had said nothing specific about the eighth mode, perhaps because the First Quidam had said only "Tonum octavum require supra."[53] The *Nova expositio* characterizes the eighth *tropus* by saying "From the seventh species of octave, which is m [G], where the seventh [intonation formula] ends, the eighth [intonation formula] begins; it finishes here where it begins."[54] This concords well with the shape of the typical intonation formula of the eighth church mode (see ex. 5.13), but it has nothing to do with the species of octave characteristic for the eighth mode.

Author δ goes into even more detail in the Principal Treatise in describing the intonation formula of the eighth church mode, saying "Where the intonation formula of this [seventh] trope, which is NOEOEANE, ends, the intonation formula of the eighth trope, which is NOEAGIS, begins [moving] through a diatessaron above, from which it immediately returns."[55] As can be seen in example 5.13, this is a perfect description of the typical intonation formula for the eighth church mode.

Author δ is not content to leave the problem there, however. After the statement just quoted, he continues by saying that the eighth church mode does not differ from the seventh except in its name, the Hypermixolydian, which is so called because it transcends the Mixolydian, and which, according to Ptolemy, occupied an eighth octave species higher than the others.[56] That Ptolemy's putative classification

---

habet, unum propter mensuram autenti deuteri, et alterum propter plagam ejus." This is, however, simply a rephrasing of the only instance in which the Byzantine terminology appears in what seems to be the earliest state of the treatise of the First Quidam (cf. §183 of Chailley's edition with the same passage in GS 1: 146b). It is worth noting that the ancient Greek ethnic names Phrygian and Hypophrygian do not appear in this paragraph.

53. Chailley, *Alia musica*, 195, §188. Chailley correctly points out that the manuscripts of the complete *Alia musica* limit themselves to this text for the eighth *tonus*. At this spot in its treatment of the eight *toni*, however, Karlsruhe 504 provides an alternate text for the eighth *tonus*—namely, the one that appears in the *Alia* manuscripts as §180 in the tabular summary of the tones that concludes the Principal Treatise (see the Revised Table of Contents in table 5.3). Contradicting the *Alia* manuscripts, Chailley has inserted §180 from Karlsruhe 504 after §187 in his edition, offering it as the treatment of the eighth *tonus* by the First Quidam. The *Alia* manuscripts would suggest that §188 is what the First Quidam actually wrote.

54. §150. "A septima specie diapason, quae est m, ubi finitur septimus, inchoatur octavus; ibi finitur ubi inchoatur" (Chailley, *Alia musica* , 194).

55. §130. "Ubi autem melodia hujus tropi, quae est NOEOEANE, desinit, melodia octavi tropi, quae est NOEAGIS, per diatessaron intensum incipit, quod statim remittit" (Chailley, *Alia musica*, 163).

56. "Hypermixolydius sane dicitur, quod mixolydium transcendit, qui juxta Ptolomaeum octavam speciem diapason, omnibus reliquis, acutiorem percurrit" (Chailley, *Alia musica*, 163).

EXAMPLE 5.13.   Intonation formulas
for the eighth church mode (Bailey, *The
Intonation Formulas of Western Chant*, 57)

does not obtain for the chant repertoire and its theory, however, is clear from his concluding statement: "Moreover, chants of the eighth church mode move within the fourth species of octave in the manner of the *subjugalis* [i.e., plagal]."[57]

The rationale for this statement is delivered immediately thereafter.[58] Author δ describes the pitches that Hucbald had set forth as alternative finals (*a*, ♭, *c*, *d*) as being those "to which the synemmenae are proximate and situated at their sides."[59] As he says, these four notes "provide the beginning, from the upper end, for the first four species of diapason and for the melodies [intonation formulas] of the four tropes."[60] When he names these pitches and expands his explanation of their function, however, it is clear that they are not the mese, paramese, trite diezeugmenon, and paranete diezeugmenon we might expect, but rather the protus, deuterus, tritus, and tetrardus of *cantus* theory:

> The first of these tropes, or even of sounds, is called "Protus" in Greek, the second "Deuterus," the third "Tritus," and the fourth "Tetrardus," which differ individually from their finals below by a pentachord, that is a diapente. Above, however, they need a tetrachord, which is a diatessaron, so that each one may hold its own species of octave, through which it may run freely up and down in its movement.[61]

In language reminiscent of the *Musica enchiriadis,* Author δ continues:

> The Dorian is governed primarily by the protus, the Phrygian likewise by the deuterus, the Lydian by the tritus, the Mixolydian by the tetrardus. In certain chants of each plagal, they share in a way by reaching these sounds [i.e., the cofinals]. Hence the plagal of the Protus may reach the protus, the plagal of the Deuterus the deuterus, the plagal of the Tritus the tritus, that of the Tetrardus the tetrardus. And it is appropriate that this can be perceived in antiphons of the gradual.[62]

57. §132. "Porro cantilenae octavi tropi more subjugalium infra quartam speciem diapason decurrunt" (Chailley, *Alia musica*, 164).

58. Chailley, *Alia musica*, 196–204, §§133–45.

59. Hucbald presents the mese, paramese, trite diezeugmenon, and paranete diezeugmenon as alternative finals, saying that they exhibit *socialitas* with their respective finals (Chartier, ed., *L'Oeuvre d'Hucbald*, 202; GS 1: 119, Traub, ed., "Hucbald von Saint-Amand," 68; Babb and Palisca, *Hucbald, Guido, and John on Music,* 45–46). He does not, however, place these pitches in a tetrachord. See the discussion in chapter 4 here, pp. 160–61.

60. §133. "Sunt autem a mese superius quatuor chordae, quibus synemmenae sunt proximae et e latere vicinae, quae dant ab excellentiori parte exordium quatuor primis speciebus diapason, atque melodiis quatuor troporum" (Chailley, *Alia musica*, 196). Chailley rightly points out (196) that this contorted description was necessary because these four notes—the mese, paramese, trite diezeugmenon, and paranete diezeugmenon—do not make up a tetrachord in the ancient Greek system. As the passage makes clear, however, the names of these pitches and their functions derive primarily from *cantus* theory, rather than ancient Greek harmonic theory. The *Musica enchiriadis* has the same pitches in a tetrachord of their own. They are the protus, deuterus, tritus, and tetrardus of the tetrachord of the Superiores (see *Musica enchiriadis*, chaps. 1–4, ed. Schmid, 3–9).

61. §134. "Quorum videlicet troporum, sive etiam sonorum, primus graeca lingua dicitur protus, secundus deuterus, tertius tritus, quartus tetrardus, qui singuli a suis finalibus deorsum pentachordo, quod est diapente, differunt. Superius vero tetrachordum, quod est diatessaron, requirunt, ut unusquisque suam speciem diapason teneat, per quam evagando sursum ac deorsum libere currat" (Chailley, *Alia musica*, 196–97).

62. §135. "Dorius maxime proto regitur, similiter phrygius deutero, lydius trito, mixolydius tetrardo.

Putting this in different terms: the range of plagal chants can extend up to the cofinal of each of the principal *toni;* hence, the plagals may share the identity of the authentics by sharing the range between final and cofinal.

Having established a conceptual basis for considering both the octave species and the finals as determinants of the church modes, Author δ then sets out a theoretical framework that allows him to accomplish this goal (exs. 5.14 and 5.15). He says that there are four *metae* (boundary markers or limits) of the species of the principal modes Dorian, Phrygian, Lydian, and Mixolydian—four *superiores,* o, x, y, cc (*a,* ♭, *c, d*), and four *inferiores,* e, h, i, m (*D, E, F,* and *G*).[63] The *superiores* provide the upper terminus for the Hypodorian, Hypophrygian, Hypolydian, and Hypermixolydian species;[64] the *inferiores* provide the lower terminus for the Dorian, Phrygian, Lydian, and Mixolydian and hence are called *finales.* Any chant moving within the species of the Hypodorian is Hypodorian, and if it ascends above that, it is Dorian; any moving within the species of Hypophrygian is Hypophrygian, and ascending higher is Phrygian; and so on with the rest of the species, "including the Hypermixolydian."[65] Author δ keeps the name Ptolemy had ostensibly given the eighth mode, but he treats the mode itself as the plagal or *subjugalis* of the seventh.

The keystone in the theoretical edifice rationalizing this solution is set in §140, in which Author δ articulates a principle regarding the distinction between authentic and plagal that would prove to be quite far-reaching (ex. 5.16). I translate: "Each principal mode will always have a diapente below its mean pitch and a diatessaron above, as if 8 were between 6 and 12. Each *subjugalis* will have a diapente above its final pitch and a diatessaron below, as if 9 were between 6 and 12."

Here, Author δ draws on the discussion of means in section A.1 of the Principal Treatise.[66] Its author (β) had said that the proportion 6:8:12 was an example of the harmonic mean, 6:9:12 an example of an arithmetic mean. Converting this into string lengths, the proportion 6:8:12 would divide the octave into a diapente below (8:12 equals 2:3, a diapente) and a diatessaron above (6:8 equals 3:4, a diatessaron), placing the mean pitch a fifth above the final in the authentic modes. The proportion 6:9:12 would place the diatessaron below (9:12 equals 4:3, a diatessaron), the diapente above (6:9 equals 2:3, a diapente), making the mean pitch identical with the final in the plagal modes.

Quos sonos in quibusdam cantilenis suae plagae quodammodo tangendo libant, ut plaga proti tangat protum, deuteri deuterum, triti tritum, tetrardi tetrardum. Et id fas est experiri in gradalibus antiphonis" (Chailley, *Alia musica,* 197). See *Musica enchiriadis,* chap. 8 (ed. Schmid, 13–20). Here the *toni* are likewise equated to the four finals, which also serve as *affines* or "cofinals" in later nomenclature, and impart to each of their respective *toni* its characteristic *vis* or *qualitas.* See the discussion in chapter 3, pp. 123–26.

63. Note again the conceptual and terminological parallels with the *Musica enchiriadis,* in which the four principal pitches, protus, deuterus, tritus, and tetrardus, are the same in all four tetrachords, Graves, Finales, Superiores, and Excellentes.

64. Note that the Hypermixolydian species is now the fourth octave species.

65. Chailley, *Alia musica,* 200, places sentence (d) of §139 within parentheses, saying that it seems to be an interpolated gloss. I would point out that the sentence is part of the running text in Munich 14272, fol. 179v, and in Strasbourg 926, the manuscript used by Gerbert (GS 1: 139b).

66. Chailley, *Alia musica,* §§1–12. See note 38 above and the discussion associated with it .

EXAMPLE 5.14. *Alia musica*, Principal Treatise (ed. Chailley, 198-200, §§137-39)

---

§137 a) Quarum videlicet specierum metas principalium troporum superius et inferius observantium prima dorii est, secunda phrygii, tertia lydii, quarta mixolydii; . . .

§138 a) Sunt igitur quatuor superiores, id est o, x, y, cc; et quatuor inferiores, id est e, h, i, m. b) Et superiores quidem excellentiori parte finiunt, hypodorium, hypophrygium, hypolydium, hypermixolydium. c) Inferiores vero finiunt ex graviore parte, dorium, phrygium, lydium, mixolydium, unde et finales dictae sunt.

§139 a) Quapropter modulatio cantilenae infra speciem hypodorii decurrens sua est, superius ascendens dorii est. b) Eodem modo infra speciem hypophrygii sua est, superius ascendens phrygii est. c) Infra quoque speciem hypolydii sua est, superius ascendens lydii est. d) Et de hypermixolydio similiter intelligendum est.

EXAMPLE 5.15. The octave species and their upper and lower boundaries, according to Author δ of the *Alia musica*

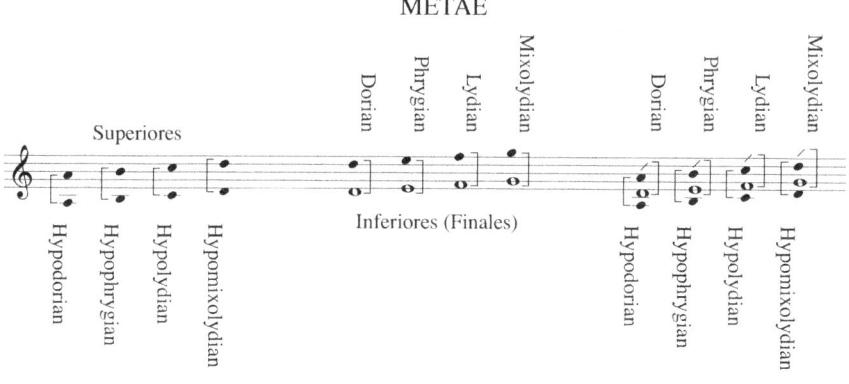

EXAMPLE 5.16. Harmonic and arithmetic means as determinants of authentic and plagal (*Alia musica*, ed., Chailley, 200-201, §140)

---

c) Et semper unusquisque principalis tropus inferius habet diapente a media chorda, superius diatessaron, ac si 8 sint inter 6 et 12. d) Subjugalis vero unusquisque tropus a finali chorda superius habet diapente, inferius vero diatessaron, ac si 9 sint inter 6 et 12.

EXAMPLE 5.17.   Analysis of the neuma for the first church mode via species of diatessaron and diapente (*Alia musica*, ed. Chailley, 116, §26)

> Itaque melodiam primi tropi, quae est NONANOEANE, 8 et 12 videntur claudere; sed eidem clausulae, quae constat diapente, quidam addunt tonum, ut prius in eadem melodia resonat prima species diatessaron, deinde secunda, ut postmodum intendatur tertia; ad extremum ex ordine remittatur ab 8 ad 12 prima species diapente.

Having outlined a theory of mean pitches as the primary determinant of the distinctions between authentic and plagal, Author δ can now say: "The eighth church mode holds the same species of diapason as the first, but they differ in that the former has the mean pitch m [G, its final] as the 'guardian' of its character, the latter, the mean pitch o [a, a fifth above its final] under the name of Protus."[67] In this way, he confirms and clarifies what he had said earlier—namely, that "chants of the

EXAMPLE 5.18.   Successive species of diatessaron and the first species of diapente in the intonation formula of the first church mode (Bailey, *The Intonation Formulas of Western Chant*, 48)

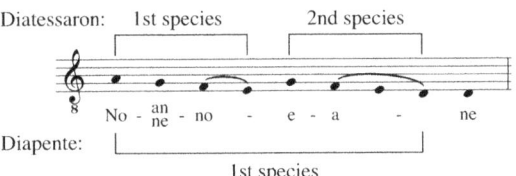

Hypothetical downward extension yielding third species of diatessaron

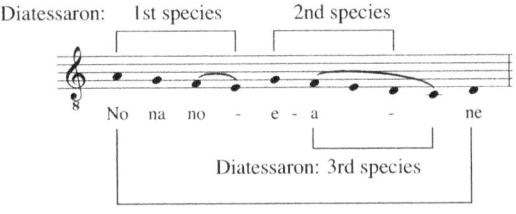

1st species of Diapente

67. §143. "Tandem octavus tropus tenet eamdem speciem diapason quam et primus; tamen eo differt quod ille habet m mediam chordam suae qualitatis custodem: hic vero o sub proti nomine" (Chailley, *Alia musica*, 202). As Author δ had pointed out in §138, the mean pitch m [G] is one of the lower *metae* called *finales*, that for the Mixolydian, which is "governed by the Tetrardus" (§135); the mean pitch o [a] is one of the *metae superiores*, forming the upper boundary for the Hypodorian and located a pentachord above the *finalis* of the Dorian, both of which are "governed by the Protus."

eighth church mode move within the fourth species of octave in the manner of the *subjugalis.*"[68]

With this, the problem of the eighth mode had effectively been solved. Moreover, Author δ's defining the distinction between authentic and plagal as that between harmonic and arithmetic divisions of the octave is one that would become a central determinant of mode for such Renaissance writers as Gaffurius and Glareanus.[69]

Effecting a rapprochement between the ancient Greek modes and the Byzantine-influenced church modes; providing a solution to the problem of the eighth mode that arose as a result; and defining authentic and plagal church modes via harmonic and arithmetic means—all of these are signal contributions to the history of medieval music theory. They would have been enough in themselves to mark Author δ as one of the finest music-theoretical minds of the early Middle Ages. Yet another development can be attributed to this author, however, that is just as forward-looking as the ones I have already discussed. I refer to his analysis of chant according to *species*—not just of octaves, but of fourths and fifths—a type of analysis that would go on to become a hallmark of the theory of Marchetto da Padova, and later that of Johannes Tinctoris.[70]

Author δ begins the process of species analysis by inserting two examples of such analysis into the discussion of consonances and their proportions in section A.3 of the Principal Treatise (exs. 5.17 and 5.18). He says that the numbers 8 and 12 (2:3, a diapente) encompass the intonation formula of the first trope, NONANOEANE. "But to that same clausula, which constitutes a diapente," he says, "certain ones add a tone, so that in that same melody the first species of diatessaron sounds first, then the second, and afterward the third may be set out. From 8 to 12 the first species of diapente will be rendered between the extremes in order." Indeed, this process works perfectly well using the species of diatessaron and diapente that were provided in section A.2, a few paragraphs earlier.

The same is true of the description of the intonation formula of the second church mode that follows, NOEAGIS, which, according to Author δ includes two species of the diatessaron consonance (exs. 5.19 and 5.20). The two species in question here are the second and third in the scheme given by Author β.

Author δ returns to species analysis in his discussion of the sixth church mode (exs. 5.21 and 5.22). After setting out the characteristics of this mode, he then describes several chants exemplifying it, using species to illustrate his analysis. He says of the Alleluia *Omnes gentes,* for example, that "it touches the mese in ascending, and afterward, in descending, returns via the third species of diatessaron." A comparison of the description in example 5.21 with the transcription of *Omnes gentes* in example 5.22 reveals that Author δ's description of the chant is indeed accurate.[71]

---

68. §132. "Porro cantilenae octavi tropi more subjugalium infra quartam speciem diapason decurrunt" (Chailley, *Alia musica,* 164).

69. On this, see my article "Modus," *HmT,* sec.V. (III) (4).

70. I would submit that the framework for this kind of analysis had already been provided by the intervallic analyses of *Rorate caeli* and other chants given by the First Quidam (see exs. 5.1 and 5.2). It is but a small step from pointing out the consonant intervals framing a specific phrase of chant to discussing the species of consonance displayed by those intervals.

71. The text here implies that *Omnes gentes* is sung to the same melody as the intonation formula

EXAMPLE 5.19. Analysis of the intonation formula of the second church mode by way of two species of the diatessaron (*Alia musica*, ed. Chailley, 117, §27)

Hinc incipit melodia secundi tropi, quae est NOEAGIS, et non ad 8 sed ad 9 pertingit, sicut omnes cantilenae ejusdem tropi. Clauduntur enim duabus diatessaron consonantiis.

EXAMPLE 5.20.   Two successive species of diatessaron in the intonation formula of the second church mode (Bailey, *The Intonation Formulas of Western Chant*, 49)

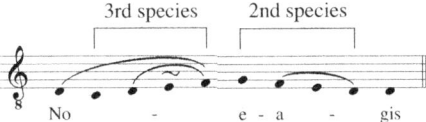

EXAMPLE 5.21. Author δ's discussion of the sixth church mode (*Alia musica*, ed. Chailley, 160, §121)

Alleluia etiam *Omnes gentes* ejusdem tropi melodia, quae est AANNES, intonando retinet. Siquidem ipsa melodia ascendendo mesen tangit, ac postea tertiam speciem diatessaron descendendo remittit.

EXAMPLE 5.22.   Incipit of the Alleluia *Omnes gentes*, with initial ascent to mese [*a*], followed by descent from *b*♭ in the third species of diatessaron (ST-T- T) (*Alia musica*, ed. Chailley, 161)

As the examples just examined suggest, Author δ's use of species of fourths and fifths to describe chant adds yet another component of harmonic theory to the growing analytical instrumentarium of *cantus* theory, an innovation that was a harbinger of several later developments. What neither Author δ nor any of the other contributors to the *Alia musica* does, however, is define the octave species of the various church modes themselves as concatenations of species of fourths and fifths. The next chapter will begin by tracing this development from a small treatise that first appears among works attributed to Hucbald (d. 930) through the interpolated version of the *Prologus in tonarium* of Bern of Reichenau (d. 1048).

---

for the sixth church mode, AANNES, but none of the intonation formulas given in Bailey, *The Intonation Formulas of Western Chant*, 55, seems to match this description.

CHAPTER SIX

PSEUDO-BERNELINUS,
BERN OF REICHENAU, PSEUDO-ODO,
AND GUIDO D'AREZZO

As explained in chapter 5, Author δ of the *Alia musica* made a significant contribution to the theory of the church modes in distinguishing authentic from plagal modes via differences in their octave species. He made a further contribution to this theory in describing plainchant by means of species of fourths and fifths. Given the potency of this approach as an analytical tool, it should come as no surprise that the church modes themselves would soon be defined as a concatenation of species of fourths and fifths. The fullest early presentation of this aspect of species theory may be found in the interpolated version of the *Prologus in tonarium* of Bern of Reichenau (d. 1048). Its most concise statement, however, and perhaps its earliest, may be found in the treatise *Prima species,* originally published in two different versions by Martin Gerbert. It first appears among works attributed to Hucbald of St. Amand (GS 1: 122a–b), and later in an expanded version attributed to a certain Bernelinus (GS 1: 313a–314a).[1] The latter attribution was challenged in 1979 by Joseph Smits van Waesberghe, who wanted to assign the work to Gerbert d'Aurillac, later Pope Sylvester II (d. 1003), but this attribution has been effectively disproved by Jane Warburton.[2] In view of these conflicting attributions, I shall refer to the author of this treatise as "Pseudo-Bernelinus."

1. The first version of *Prima species* was printed by Gerbert (GS 1: 122a–b) from Strasbourg 926 and Cesena XXVI. 1, among the texts attributed to Hucbald; the second version (GS 1: 313a–314a) was taken from the manuscript Rome 1661, which contains the notation, in a later hand: " BERNELINI Abacus, musica, Arithmetica & Geometria" (see GS 1: 312–13). In both versions, it immediately follows a brief monochord division with the heading *Cita et vera divisio monochordi;* hence it is often referred to under this name. On the relationships between these texts and their manuscript sources, see Bernhard, *Clavis Gerberti,* 13, 77–81. The earliest manuscript preserving this treatise would appear to be Chartres 130, now dated to the eleventh century, but parts of which may have been copied much earlier (*RISM* B III¹, 84–85). (The manuscript was severely damaged 26 June 1944.) That *Prima species* dates from no later than the early eleventh century is suggested by the fact that it forms the basis for the species theory in the part of the *Prologus in tonarium* (post 1021) that can legitimately be attributed to Bern of Reichenau. On this, see Warburton, "Questions of Attribution and Chronology in Three Medieval Texts on Species Theory," 231–35.

2. See Smits van Waesberghe, ed., *Bernonis Augiensis Abbatis De arte disputationes traditae,* pt. B, 45–47.

202

Pseudo-Bernelinus's method is both simple and direct. He first sets out the three species of diatessaron, then adds a tone above or below each of them to construct the species of diapente (ex. 6.1):

EXAMPLE 6.1.   *Prima species:* Description of species of diatessaron and diapente (*GS* 1: 313a; Bernhard, *Clavis Gerberti*, 80)

Prima species diatessaron constat ex tono, semitonio et tono. 2. Secunda ex duobus tonis et semitonio. 3. Tertia ex semitonio et duobus tonis. 4. Prima species diapente constat ex prima specie diatessaron adiecto tono superius. 5. Secunda ex secunda diatessaron adiecto tono superius. 6. Tertia ex tertia diatessaron adiecto tono inferius. 7. Quarta ex prima specie diatessaron adiecto tono inferius.

The first species of diatessaron consists of tone, semitone, and tone; the second of two tones and a semitone; the third of a semitone and two tones. The first species of diapente consists of the first species of diatessaron with a tone added above; the second [consists] of the second [species of] diatessaron with a tone added above; the third [consists] of the third [species of] diatessaron with a tone added below; the fourth [consists] of the first species of diatessaron with a tone added below.

Then Pseudo-Bernelinus joins these species with each other to construct the church modes. As Warburton points out, the species of consonance are not mapped onto a tone-system of any kind, but are presented as pure successions of intervals; indeed, one does not even know whether to read them in ascending or descending order. It is only when they are combined with each other to create the church modes that one can deduce the structure of both the species themselves and the tone-system than underlies them (ex. 6.2):

Protus [authentic] consists of the first species of diapente, with the first species of diatessaron above; its subjugalis consists of the same species of diapente, with the same species of diatessaron below. Deuterus [authentic] consists of the second species of diapente and the second species of diatessaron above; its subjugalis [consists] of the same species of diapente and the same species of diatessaron below. Tritus [authentic] consists of the third species of diapente and the third species of diatessaron; its subjugalis [consists] of the same species of diapente and the same species of diatessaron below. Tetrardus [authentic] consists of the fourth species of diapente and the first species of diatessaron above; its subjugalis [consists] of the same species of diapente and the same species of diatessaron below.

As one sees here, Pseudo-Bernelinus does not situate the church modes on specific degrees of a scale. By comparing them with their counterparts in Hucbald and *Alia musica*, however, one finds that they are completely congruent with the implied intervallic structure of the eight church modes as presented by Author δ of the *Alia musica*. One major difference between *Alia musica* and *Prima species*, though, is that

---

Warburton's refutation appears in "Questions of Attribution and Chronology in Three Medieval Texts on Species Theory," 225–29, 234–35.

EXAMPLE 6.2.   *Prima species:* Description of church modes as combinations of species of diatessaron and diapente (GS 1: 313a; Bernhard, *Clavis Gerberti*, 80; diagram after Warburton, "Questions of Attribution," 229)

8. Protus constat ex prima specie diapente et prima specie diatessaron superius.
9. Subiugalis eius ex eadem specie diapente, et eadem specie diatessaron inferius.
10. Deuterus constat ex secunda specie diapente et secunda specie diatessaron superius.
11. Subiugalis eius ex eadem specie diapente et eadem specie diatessaron inferius.
12. Tritus constat ex tertia specie diapente et tertia specie diatessaron superius.
13. Subiugalis eius ex eadem specie diapente et eadem specie diatessaron inferius.
14. Tetrardus constat ex quarta specie diapente et eadem specie diatessaron superius.
15. Subiugalis eius ex eadem specie diapente et eadem specie diatessaron inferius.

Protus	Deuterus	Tritus	Tetrardus
T S T	T T S	S T T	T S T
T T S T (auth)	T T T S (auth)	S T T T (auth)	T S T T (auth)
(plagal)	(plagal)	(plagal)	(plagal)
T S T	T T S	S T T	T S T

Prima species makes no attempt to describe the modes in terms of octave species, thereby avoiding the most substantial problem Author δ had to solve.

When the species theory first expounded in the *Prima species* is picked up by Bern of Reichenau in his *Prologus in tonarium* (post 1021), it undergoes several transformations.[3] In his own presentation of this material, Bern anchors the species to specific pitches, using ancient Greek string names (ex. 6.3).

As one can see, a problem arises immediately in the succession of species of diatessaron. Bern's first species, of tone, semitone, and tone, begins on the lichanos meson (G) and finishes on the lichanos hypaton (D); his second species, of two

3. The *Prologus in tonarium* was edited in GS 2: 62–79, and more recently in Rausch, ed., *Die Musiktraktate des Abtes Bern von Reichenau*. Subsequent citations will be to Rausch's edition. As Hans Oesch has already demonstrated in *Berno und Hermann von Reichenau als Musiktheoretiker*, 84–91, the *Prologus* as it was transmitted was subjected to a substantial measure of interpolation. The interpolations were edited separately in Smits van Waesberghe, ed., *Bernonis Augiensis Abbatis De arte disputationes traditae*. Three further studies by Rausch are relevant here: "Beobachtungen zum Kurztonar des Bern von Reichenau"; "Bern von Reichenau und sein Einfluß auf die Musiktheorie"; and "Neue Quellen zur Rezeption des *Prologus in tonarium* des Bern von Reichenau."

EXAMPLE 6.3.   Bern of Reichenau, *Prologus in tonarium:* Presentation of species of diatessaron and diapente (GS 2: 67; Rausch, ed., *Die Musiktraktate des Abtes Bern von Reichenau*, 41–42. Following Warburton, "Questions of Attribution," 232, the passages of text from *Prima species* appear in italics, and the modern equivalents for the ancient Greek string names provided are set within brackets).

---

[6]Ergo *prima species diatessaron constat ex tono, semitonio et tono,* exordium sumens a lichanos meson [G] et finiens in lichanos ypaton [D]; [7]cui si adieceris tonum superius, oritur tibi prima species dyapente. [8]*Secunda* species *ex duobus tonis et semitonio,* incipiens a mese [a] et finiens in ypate meson [E]; [9]cui si adieceris tonum superius, erit secunda species dyapente. [10]*Tertia ex semitonio et duobus tonis,* incipiens a trite dyezeugmenon [c] et finiens in lichanos meson [G]; [11]cui adhibendus est tonum inferius, ut fiat tertia species dyapente. [12]*Quarta* species diapente constat *ex prima specie dyatessaron, adiecto tono inferius,* [13]non quidem per eiusdem nominis cordam, sed altius idest a paranete dyezeugmenon [d] incipiens, ac sic per tonum semitonium et tonum in meson [a] descendit, assumtoque inferius tono, quartam speciem dyapente perficit.

---

tones followed by a semitone, starts on the mese (*a*) and ends on the hypate meson (*E*).[4] Because the third species would be a tritone were it to begin on the paramese (the next pitch in order after the mese), Bern skips to the trite diezeugmenon (*c*) to begin the third species. Forming the first three species of diapente is not problematic for him, since (following the *Prima species*) the first two species of diapente are created by adding a tone above, and the second two by adding a tone below the species of diatessaron. He does run into a problem with the fourth species, however. Here, Bern has to transpose the first species of diatessaron from its original position, the lichanos meson (*G*), to the paranete diezeugmenon (*d*). As he says (ex. 6.3, Sentences 12–13):

> *The fourth* [species of diapente] *consists of the first species of diatessaron with a tone added below,* not through the string of the same name, but higher, that is, beginning from the paranete diezeugmenon [*d*]; and thus it descends through tone, semitone, and tone to the mese [*a*], and with a tone added below [*G*] completes the fourth species of diapente.

One can represent Bern's presentation of the species of diatessaron and diapente as in example 6.4.

Immediately following his presentation of the species of fourths and fifths, Bern presents the species of octave (ex. 6.5). As was true of Author β's presentation of the species in section A.2 of the Principal Treatise in the *Alia musica*, Bern's species of octave have nothing to do with his species of fourths and fifths. Fortunately, Bern does not try to equate his species of octave with the church modes, as Author β of

---

4. We should recall that the *Alia musica* had begun its species of diatessaron and diapente from the nete diezeugmenon, *e*, and had proceeded downward both in placing their starting pitches and in projecting their successions of intervals (see exs. 5.10 and 5.11 and the associated discussion). This yielded the diatessaron species T-T-ST, T-ST-T, and ST-T-T.

EXAMPLE 6.4.   Species of diatessaron and diapente as presented by Bern of Reichenau, *Prologus in tonarium* (*GS* 2: 67; Rausch, ed., *Die Musiktraktate des Abtes Bern von Reichenau*, 41–42; after Warburton, "Questions of Attribution," 232)

Species of diatessaron			Species of diapente			
1st	2nd	3rd	1st	2nd	3rd	4th
(G)	(a)	(c)	(a)	(b)	(c)	(d)
T	T	S	T	T	S	T
S	T	T	T	T	S	S
T	S	T	S	T	T	T
(D)	(E)	(G)	T	S	T	T
			(D)	(E)	(F)	(G)

the *Alia musica* had done with the ancient Greek modes. His presentation is none-theless complicated by the fact that he cannot use the species of diatessaron and diapente in the systemic positions he had originally assigned them (ex. 6.6).

As he did for his presentation of the species of fourth and fifth, Bern follows *Prima species* in his presentation of the *toni*, adding his own commentary to what the earlier author had written. It is perhaps symptomatic, though, that the only church modes for which he provides pitch indications are the first and second, and even here he must modify his original exposition. In defining the relative positions of the diatessaron and diapente in the first church mode, he places the first species of diatessaron in the position to which he had transposed it (to the paranete diezeugmenon [*d*]) in order to create the fourth species of diapente (see Sentences 12 and 13 of ex. 6.3); in the second church mode this species is transposed down an octave to the lichanos hypaton (*D*). Starting with Bern's own words (ex. 6.6, Sentence 3):

> The first tone has the freedom of ascending in a diapente from its final, that is from the lichanos hypaton [*D*] up to the mese [*a*], and from the mese up to the paranete diezeugmenon [*d*], that is the first species of diatessaron. The second tone, which is called its plagal, ascends in the same diapente; but it descends through the same spe-

EXAMPLE 6.5.   The species of octave as presented by Bern of Reichenau, *Prologus in tonarium* (*GS* 2: 67; Rausch, ed., *Die Musiktraktate des Abtes Bern von Reichenau*, 42; after Warburton, "Questions of Attribution," 233)

[14]Dyapason vero species facile est pervidere. [15]Si enim a proslambanomenos [*A*] incoeperis, usque in mese [*a*] prima species erit; sicque semper semitonio vel tono altius per ordinem repetendo septimae speciei finis in paranete yperboleon [*g*] erit.

(The species of diapason are easy to discern. If indeed you begin from the proslambanomenos [*A*], the first species will extend to the mese [*a*]; and thus always repeating by a semitone or tone higher there will be seven species ending at the paranete hyperboleon [*g*].)

EXAMPLE 6.6.   The eight church modes as presented by Bern of Reichenau, *Prologus in tonarium* (GS 2: 69–70; Rausch, ed., *Die Musiktraktate des Abtes Bern von Reichenau*, 44–46. Following Warburton, "Questions of Attribution," 232–33, the passages of text from *Prima species* appear in italics, and the modern equivalents for the ancient Greek string names provided are set within brackets).

---

[1]*Protus constat ex prima specie diapente, et prima specie diatessaron superius.* [2]*Subiugalis eius ex eadem specie diapente, et eadem specie diatessaron inferius.* Quod autem dico, tale est: [3]Primus tonus a suo finali idest licanos ypaton [D] habet licentiam ascendendi in dyapente hoc est in mese [a], a mese in paranete dyezeugmenon [d], quod est prima species dyatessaron, constans ex tono, semitonio et tono. [4]Secundus vero tonus, qui dicitur eius subiugalis, in eandem dyapente ascendit; sed descendit per eandem speciem dyatessaron inferius per tonum semitonium ac tonum, a licanos ypaton in proslambanomenos; . . . [8]*Deuterus constat ex secunda specie dyapente, et secunda specie diatessaron superius.* [9]*Subiugalis eius ex eadem specie diapente, et [eadem] specie diatessaron inferius.* [10]Ex superiori sermone potes et istud comprehendere. [11]*Tritus constat ex tertia specie dyapente et tertia specie diatessaron superius.* [12]*Subiugalis eius ex eadem specie diapente et eadem specie diatessaron inferius.* [13]*Tetrardus constat ex quarta specie diapente, et prima specie diatessaron superius.* [14]*Subiugalis eius ex eadem specie diapente, et eadem specie diatessaron inferius.* [15]Omnis tonus subiugalis eandem habet dyapente et diatesseron quam autenticus eius. [16]Differunt autem in hoc, quod autenticus dyatesseron habet supra dyapente, subiugalis infra.

---

cies of diatessaron below from the lichanos hypaton [D] to the proslambanomenos [A], through tone and semitone and tone.[5]

Given the rather cumbersome nature of this process, it is perhaps no wonder that Bern does not continue describing the church modes as conjunctions of his own species of fourths and fifths.[6] Instead, he simply defers to the abstract presentation of the *Prima species* (see ex. 6.6, Sentences 8–14). He then concludes his presentation on the modes (Sentences 15–16) by saying that every plagal has the same diapente and diatessaron as the corresponding authentic, and that they differ in that the authentic modes have the diatessaron above the diapente, while the plagals have it below. Bern's presentation of the church modes can be diagrammed as shown in example 6.7.

As we have just seen, Bern's own generation of the church modes from the species of diatessaron and diapente is flawed by his initial choices of the degrees of the Greater Perfect System on which to place them. A later eleventh-century author, therefore, took it upon himself to correct this.[7] His source was apparently another eleventh-century treatise with the incipit *Duo semisphæria.*[8]

---

5. Translation from Warburton, "Questions of Attribution and Chronology in Three Medieval Texts on Species Theory," 233.

6. As Warburton points out ("Questions of Attribution and Chronology in Three Medieval Texts on Species Theory," 233), the only church modes that can be constructed from Bern's species of diatessaron and diapente are those of Tetrardus, with the fourth species of diapente and the first species of diatessaron.

7. Rausch is of the opinion that Frutolf of Michelsberg (d. 1103) was responsible for these interpolations in Bern's text (see Rausch, *Die Musiktraktate des Abtes Bern von Reichenau*, 117–27). His opinion is shared by Hochadel, "Zur Stellung des pseudo-bernonischen Traktats *De mensurando monochordo*," 43–44, 68.

8. *Duo semisphæria* was assigned to "Anonymous I" by Gerbert, who edited it from a now-lost twelfth-

EXAMPLE 6.7.   Bern of Reichenau's presentation of the church modes as concatenations of fourths and fifths (after Warburton, "Questions of Attribution," 232)

Basing its discussion on a monochord division that yields the diatonic scales A— H M N O P Q R S (with ♮) and A—H I K L P Q R S (with ♭), the *Duo semi-sphæria* treats the three genera of the ancient Greek tone-system; the five tetrachords, including the synemmenon; the Pythagorean consonances; the species; and the church modes and their ranges.[9] It presents a much more developed theory than that in the original version of Bern's *Prologus*. Using this treatise as a basis, a later eleventh-century author, perhaps Frutolf of Michelsberg, added a number of interpolations to the original text of the *Prologus*.[10]

---

century manuscript from St. Blasien (GS 1: 330–38). It has been reedited by Smits van Waesberghe from the sole surviving source, the twelfth-century manuscript Vienna 51, fol. 52v–55. Smits van Waesberghe follows the attribution in Vienna 51 in ascribing the tract to Bern himself (see *Bernonis Augiensis Abbatis De arte disputationes traditae*. pt: A, *Bernonis Augiensis de mensurando monochordo*, 7–8, 10–17). Alexander Rausch holds that *Duo semisphæria* is a compilation of material from the *Breviarium* of Frutolf of Michelsberg, along with the interpolations he claims Frutolf made in Bern's *Prologus*. He dates the *Duo semisphæria* from "vor oder um 1100" ("before or around 1100"; 127). Jane Warburton, however, feels that *Duo semisphæria* was written by a younger contemporary of Bern, and that its material was then incorporated into the interpolated version of Bern's *Prologus* ("Questions of Attribution and Chronology in Three Medieval Texts on Species Theory," 234–35). Her opinion is supported by Hochadel, "Zur Stellung des pseudo-bernonischen Traktats De mensurando monochordo"; see, in particular, his stemma on p. 68. The monochord division of the treatise, "A dextro semispherio," has been edited by Meyer in *Mensura monochordi*, 56–57, and Smits van Waesberghe, *De musico-paedagogico et theoretico Guidone Aretino eiusque vita et moribus*, 166, no. 21; it is discussed in Adkins, "The Theory and Practice of the Monochord," 123–24. See Bernhard, *Clavis Gerberti*, 85.

9. This particular type of letter notation is found in no other treatise. See Phillips, "Notationen und Notationslehren," 557–59; and Hochadel, "Zur Stellung des pseudo-bernonischen Traktats De mensurando monochordo," 49.

10. As mentioned in note 8 here, Rausch feels that *Duo semisphæria* is later than the interpolated ver-

EXAMPLE 6.8a   Interpolated version of Bern of Reichenau's *Prologus in tonarium* (after Warburton, "Questions of Attribution." 234). Interpolator's determination of species of diatessaton and diapente

Species of diatessaron			Species of diapente			
1st	2nd	3rd	1st	2nd	3rd	4th
D	E	F	a	♭	c	d
T ↑	T ↑	S ↑	(T)↑	(T)↑	(S)↑	(T)↑
S	T	T	(T)	(T)	(T)	(S)
T	S	T	(S)	(T)	(T)	(T)
A	B	C	(T)	(S)	(T)	(T)
			D	E	F	G

The interpolator's first intervention occurs immediately after Bern's presentation of the species of diatessaron, diapente, and diapason (exs. 6.3–5). In response, the interpolator comments that "this is the disposition of the species of consonances according to certain older theorists [*veteres*]. More discriminating modern theorists [*moderni diligentiores*] agree to some extent with them in everything as regards the diapente and the diapason, but they assign a different beginning and order to the diatessaron in its species."[11] He points out that since an octave consists of a fifth plus a fourth, and since the first species of octave extends from *A* to *a*, it is "incongruous" that the tetrachord of the graves, extending from the lichanos hypaton (*D*) down to the proslambanomenos (*A*), should have been excluded from the reckoning of the species. The interpolator, now following *Duo semisphæria* almost verbatim, except for the names of the pitches, then proceeds to set out the species of diatessaron (ex. 6.8a). The first species starts from *A* and extends *upward* to *D* (T-ST-T);

sion of Bern's *Prologus*; Warburton and Hochadel place it earlier. Although this is not the place for a detailed analysis of the chronology of these two tracts, at least two points speak in favor of the anteriority of *Duo semisphæria*. First, the language the *Prologus* interpolator uses as he introduces material from *Duo semisphæria* strongly suggests that his own work is later than the material he is introducing. Second, the letter-notation used in *Duo semisphæria* is derived from Boethius (see Smits van Waesberghe, *De musico-paedagogico et theoretico Guidone Aretino eiusque vita et moribus*, 166, no. 21b; Smits van Waesberghe, ed., *Bernonis Augiensis Abbatis De arte disputationes traditae*, pt. A, 58; Markovits, *Das Tonsystem der abendländischen Musik im frühen Mittelalter*, 34, 43; and Phillips, "Notationen und Notationslehren," 557, 559). The letter notation used by the *Prologus* interpolator, on the other hand, is the more modern Γ-G-g, with ♭ and ♮ usually attributed to Pseudo-Odo (ca. 1000). Frutolf of Michelsberg uses the latter notation, in expanded form, in his *Breviarium* (see Vivell, ed., *Frutolfi Breviarium de musica et Tonarius*, 45–51.). This could be another index for his putative role as the interpolator of Bern's *Prologus* (see Rausch, ed., *Die Musiktraktate des Abtes Bern von Reichenau*, 117–27). On this, see also Hochadel, "Zur Stellung des pseudo-bernonischen Traktats *De mensurando monochordo*," 43–44, 48–59, 68.

11.   "Et haec quidem dispositio specierum in consonantiis secundum veteres quosdam est. Sed moderni diligentiores in omnibus in diapente & diapason eis aliquatenus consentiunt; diatessaron vero in speciebus et aliud exordium & ordinem tribuunt" (*GS* 2: 67). The translation is that of Warburton, "Questions of Attribution and Chronology in Three Medieval Texts on Species Theory," 234.

the second extends from *B* up to *E* (ST-T-T); and the third from *C* up to *F* (T-T-ST). Finally, the interpolator points out that these species will always appear in series of four letters except between the parhypate meson (*F*) and the paramese (♮), and between the trite synemmenon (♭) and the nete diezeugmenon (*e*).

The interpolator follows the same procedure for the species of diapente, reading the first upward from *D* (*D E F G a*), the second upward from *E* (*E F G A* ♮), and so on.[12] After pointing out the locations of diminished fifths among them, the interpolator concludes by setting out the seven species of diapason. He notes that if one constructs an octave from the mese (*a*) through the paramese (♮) and trite diezeugmenon (*c*) to the nete hyperboleon (*aa*), it will not differ from the first.

As mentioned, neither Bern nor his interpolator equates the octave species with modes, as Author β of *Alia musica* had done. But after he has discussed the species themselves, the interpolator says: "Thus, the diapason has seven species, one less than [it has] pitches, among which the eight modes are variously positioned, which the following discussion should clarify."[13] He relates that there were originally only seven modes based on species of octave, but "Ptolemy had added an eighth mode in addition, which we know Boethius transmitted in his *Musica*."[14] He then says that he will explain this "according to ecclesiastical usage" (*secundum ecclesiasticum usum*). And this he does.

The interpolator provides a textbook description of the "eight modes, which we wrongly call tones," explaining that there are four that are called "authentic" or "magister," designated Protus, Deuterus, Tritus, and Tetrardus—or first, second, third, and fourth—and that there are another four in a lower position that are called "plagis" or "lateralis."[15] He then names four pitches, "*D E F G*, which are the lichanos hypaton, hypate meson, parhypate meson, and lichanos meson," that are called finals because all regular chants end in one of them.[16] Every chant of the first or second *modus* is ended in *D*, of the third or fourth *modus* in *E*, of the fifth or sixth *modus* in *F*, of the seventh or eighth *modus* in *G*. He concludes this discussion: "But because we have discussed the names and finals of these [modes], we must now explain the limits of their ascent and descent."[17]

At this point, something rather remarkable happens. Having set the stage for a discussion of the conjoining of species to create the modes, the interpolator simply yields the floor to Bern's presentation of this topic (as given in exs. 6.6 and 6.7). The

---

12. The species of diapente are in fact the same as Bern's. Bern had derived them from his species of diatessaron, naming them from top down, using the ancient Greek string names. See exs. 6.3 and 6.4.

13. "Sic igitur diapason septem habet species: una minus quam voces, in quibus octo modorum diversa fit positio, quod sequens expediet ratio" (*GS* 2: 68b). My translation of the third clause is a bit free. A more literal rendering would be "among which the placement of the eight modes is made diverse."

14. "Septem vero tantum modos secundum diapason species primum fuisse, sed Ptolomaeum octavum superaddidisse, Boetium in musica scimus tradidisse" (*GS* 2: 68b). The use of *superaddo*, "to add in addition," rather than Boethius's *superadnecto*, "to join at the top," is a felicitous, and probably purposive, substitution.

15. *GS* 2: 68b–69a.

16. *GS* 2: 69a.

17. "Sed quia nomina & finales eorum diximus, intensionis & remissionis limites aperiamus" (*GS* 2: 69a).

EXAMPLE 6.8b.   Interpolated version of Bern of Reichenau's *Prologus in tonarium* (after Warburton, "Questions of Attribution," 234). Presentation of the church modes as concatenations of fourths and fifths

Protus		Deuterus		Tritus		Tetrardus	
d							
T		T		S		T	
S		T		T		S	
T		S		T		T	
a	auth	b	auth	c	auth	d	auth
T		T		S		T	
T		T		T		S	
S		T		T		T	
T		S		T		T	
D	plagal	E	plagal	F	plagal	G	plagal
T		T		S		T	
S		T		T		S	
T		S		T		T	
A		B		C		D	

reader will recall that the bulk of this had been quoted from *Prima species*, because Bern's faulty positioning of the species of diatessaron prevented their use in creating the modes. Now that the species themselves have been repositioned—voilà!—Bern's original treatment makes perfectly good sense. Like the contemporaneous authors of liturgical tropes, who could make the Old Testament text of an Introit proper to a Christian feast day by providing a newly composed introduction and interpolations to it, the interpolator of Bern's *Prologus* gives new meaning to Bern's own words (and to those of the *Prima species*).[18] As a result, the modes could now be rationalized perfectly well as concatenations of species of fourths and fifths. A diagram of this "new" derivation of the modes appears in example 6.8b.

Rationalizing the tones or modes as conjunctions of species of diatessaron and diapente, rather than species of octave, made it possible for the first time to distinguish clearly among the eight modes on a systemic basis. With this, the implications held by Boethius's *De institutione musica* for the theory of mode and tone-system in the Middle Ages were well on the way to being fully realized.

Going hand in hand with the combination of Boethian mathematics and chant theory was the reintroduction of the monochord as a means of converting mathematical abstraction into sounding musical reality. Concomitant with all of these developments in the tenth century came the rise of diastematic musical notation—a precise graphic representation of tones analogous to the precise determination of pitch relationships made possible by the monochord. But along with the "gains" made possible by the advent of a nearly complete fusion of Boethian and chant theory, there were some "losses" as well. Both gains and losses are well demonstrated

---

18. On this process, see Stäblein, "Zum Verständnis des 'klassischen' Tropus."

by the *Dialogus de musica* of the early eleventh-century Lombard Anonymous better known to most of us as "Pseudo-Odo."[19]

Pseudo-Odo begins his treatise with a division of the monochord, but one substantially different from either of those of Boethius (ex. 6.9).[20] Unlike Boethius, who began his monochord division by dividing the string (AB) into four segments locating the proslambanomenos (A), the lichanos hypaton (C), the mese (D), and the nete hyperboleon (E), Pseudo-Odo begins his division by assigning the letter gamma to the lowest note, then shortening the string by one-ninth to yield the first step, which he calls *A*. A similar procedure yields the next step, *B*.

EXAMPLE 6.9.   Division of the monochord in Pseudo-Odo, *Dialogus de musica* (GS 1: 253)

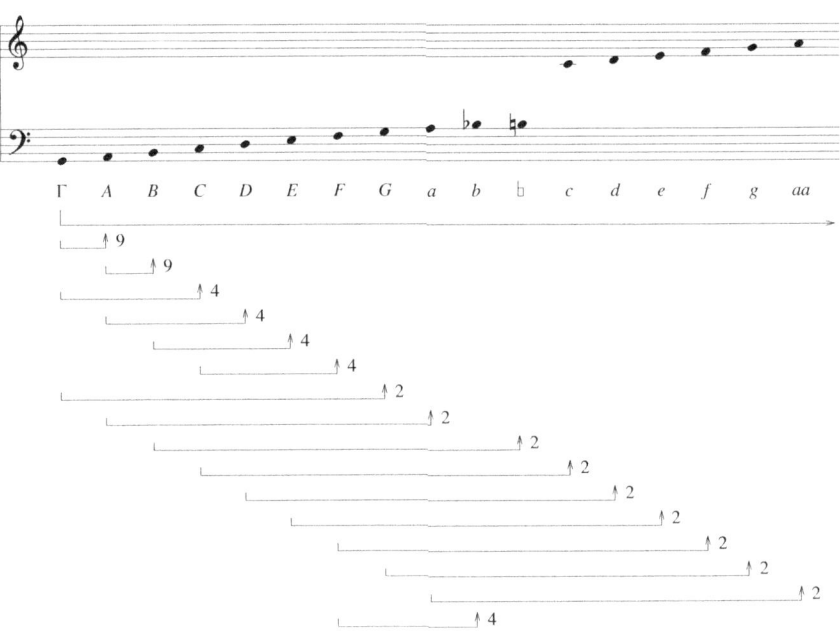

19. GS 1: 252–64. The manuscript sources for the treatise are listed in Bernhard, *Clavis Gerberti*, 74. A promised new edition by K.-W. Gümpel has not yet appeared. On the authorship of the treatise, formerly ascribed to Odo of Cluny (ca. 878–942), see Huglo, "L'Auteur du 'Dialogue sur la musique' attribué à Odon," "Der Prolog des Odo zugeschriebenen 'Dialogus de Musica,'" and *Les Tonaires*, 221–24. Huglo feels that the treatise was written in the early eleventh century (before 1026) by a Benedictine monk working in the diocese of Milan; hence the alternative authorial designation "Lombard Anonymous."

20. On the monochord division, see Meyer, *Mensura monochordi*, xli–xliii, 93–97, 259–60; Markovits, *Das Tonsystem der abendländischen Musik im frühen Mittelalter*, 46; Smits van Waesberghe, *De musicopaedagogico et theoretico Guidone Aretino eiusque vita et moribus*, 172, no. 38; Adkins, "The Theory and Practice of the Monochord," 140–48; and Wantzloeben, *Das Monochord*, 69–76.

EXAMPLE 6.10.   Tone-System of
Pseudo-Odo, *Dialogus de musica*
(GS 1: 253)

Fifteenth Step	*aa*	
Fourteenth Step	*g*	
Thirteenth Step	*f*	
Twelfth Step	*e*	
Eleventh Step	*d*	
Tenth Step	*c*	
Second Ninth Step	♮	
First Ninth Step	*b*	
Eighth Step	*a*	
Seventh Step	*G*	
Sixth Step	*F*	
Fifth Step	*E*	
Fourth Step	*D*	
Third Step	*C*	
Second Step	*B*	
First Step	*A*	
First Step	Γ	

The following step, *C*, is derived by shortening the full string by one-fourth; the next steps, *D, E,* and *F,* are derived by performing the same operation starting from *A, B,* and *C,* respectively. After this, the series of notes *G, a,* ♮, *c, d, e, f, g, aa* is derived by bisecting the string from each original letter name. The division is completed by shortening the string by one-fourth from *F* to yield a second ninth step, the round *b.* The tone-system that results from this appears in example 6.10.

Note that the system begins with a note one step below the former proslam-banomenos, a note given the designation Γ (gamma), presumably because it is an octave below G. (Pseudo-Odo even says that the gamma is "by many not under-stood.") The entire system is presented in upward succession, rather than the down-ward procession of Boethius, with the individual pitches designated by Latin letters that repeat after the seventh degree and thus designate octave equivalency.[21] The upper limit of the system is the *aa* corresponding to the nete hyperboleon, lying two octaves above the old proslambanomenos and numbered as the fifteenth step. The other striking feature of the system is the presence of two ninth steps, the first rep-resenting *b*♭ (*b-rotundum*), and the second *b*♮ (*b-quadratum*). Thus, this system preserves the tonal architecture of the ancient Greek two-octave system transmitted by Boethius, but differs from it in adding the low Γ and in using ascending letter no-tation repeating after the seventh letter, G. It is this system, with several notes added at the top, which would become the standard one for Western music until well into the Renaissance.

After presenting the system itself via its monochord derivation, Pseudo-Odo de-votes the bulk of the remainder of his treatise to presentation of the modes, to which he refers by their Byzantine names (Protus, Deuterus, Tritus, and Tetrardus) in both authentic and plagal forms, placing their finals on the degrees *D, E, F,* and *G* of his tone-system. Particularly important in his treatment are (1) the introduction of the *conjunctiones vocum* into the theory of mode; (2) an integration of *b*♭ into that theory; and (3) defining the role of starting pitch and tessitura in determining the mode of a given chant.

The six *conjunctiones vocum* are the intervals, from semitone through perfect fifth (but excluding the tritone), that can be used both ascending and descending in plain-chant. One understands the importance of this when one reads the beginning of the treatise's section on mode. In a formulation that several subsequent authors would take over, Pseudo-Odo says that "a tone or mode is a rule that judges every melody according to its final," and adds that unless one knows the final, one cannot know where the melody should begin or what its range should be.[22] When his student asks how the final can affect the beginning, the Master says that every beginning ought to begin on or concord with the final in one of the six "consonances" (*conjunctiones*) he has already mentioned. He also says that *distinctiones* (intermediate pauses or ca-

21. On the origins of this notation, which seems first to have appeared in the late tenth century in northern Italy in the complex of treatises associated with Pseudo-Odo, see Huglo, "L'Auteur du 'Dia-logue sur la musique' attribué à Odon," and *Les Tonaires*, 182–224. Phillips, "Notationen und Notations-lehren," 572–76, provides an excellent summary. The earliest version seems to be that in the tonary as-cribed to "Abbot Odo" (late tenth–early eleventh century), the preface to which is printed in *GS* 1: 248–49a. It uses lower-case letters only, makes no distinction between *b* and *b*♭, and exhibits no low gamma. In contradistinction to the horizontal lines of letters in Montpellier 159 (see figs. 4.1 and 4.2), the letters in the tonary are copied "diastematically" ("heighted") above the chant texts (see Huglo, "L'Auteur du 'Dialogue sur la musique' attribué à Odon," 151–63, and *Les Tonaires*, 182–213 and 219–21.)

22. "Tonus vel modus est regula, quae de omni cantu in fine diiudicat. Nam nisi scieris finem, non poteris cognoscere, ubi incipi, vel quantum elevari vel deponi debeat cantus" (*GS* 1: 257). See Steglich, ed., *Die "Quaestiones in musica,"* 34; Bragard, ed., *Jacobi Leodiensis Speculum musicae, CSM* 3:VI, xxxvi, 90. Cserba, ed., *Hieronymous de Moravia. O. P.:Tractatus de musica,* 154, has "Tropus . . . est regula, quae de omni cantu in fine dijudicat."

dences) should be made according to one of these six intervals from the final, because "a chant belongs most to that mode in which most of its distinctions lie."[23]

As mentioned, Pseudo-Odo places the four finals on the pitches designated *D*,
E, *F*, and *G* in his tone-system. Indeed, he says that "some consider that there are
four modes," since every regular chant ends on one of the four finals.[24] He himself
numbers the modes from 1 to 8, with Protus authentus and plagis designated modes
1 and 2; Deuterus authentus and plagis designated modes 3 and 4, and so on. Regarding ambitus, he says that authentic chants can ascend up to an octave above the
final and descend one sound below it (in his diagrams each mode has an ambitus of
ten degrees); plagal chants can ascend up to the fifth or sixth degree above the final
and descend as far as a fifth below it (the largest allowable *conjunctio vocum*).[25]

Although his general remarks on mode do not go substantially beyond those of
earlier authors, Pseudo-Odo's discussion of individual modes does bring new insights.
For each mode he provides a diagram indicating its range and *forma* (sequence of tones
and semitones; the term "species" does not appear, and oddly, "forma" itself plays no
significant role in the discussions). He indicates possible initial pitches by citing specific chants exemplifying them, and he says whether they are frequent or rare.

Pseudo-Odo's presentation of the first church mode can serve as an example of
his method. In answer to the student's dutiful request that he teach him about the
modes that follow, the Master gives the description given in example 6.11.

> The first *tonus* ends in the fourth pitch [*D*] and proceeds to the eleventh, in which
> there is the same letter *d*, via tones and semitones thusly: After the final there follows
> a tone, then a semitone, and two tones and again a semitone, and two tones. It descends
> from the final to the third pitch [*C*] by one tone in this manner:[26]

Forma

toni I. C. tonus D. tonus E. semi. F. tonus G. tonus a. semi. b. ♮. semi. c. tonus d.

> Certain people wish to make a decachord, to which they add one pitch, the sec-
> ond, *B*. But this is not in use [to the extent] that the first mode might descend to it.

23. "Omne principium secundum praedictas sex consonantias suo fini concordare debet. Nulla vox
potest incipere cantum, nisi ipsa vel finalis fit, vel consonet finali per aliquam de sex consonantiis. . . .
Distinctiones quoque, id est loca, in quibus repausamus in cantu, & in quibus cantum dividimus, in eis-
dem vocibus debere finiri in unoquoque modo, in quibus possunt incipi cantus eius modi, manifestum
est. . . . Ad eum denique modum magis cantus pertinet, ad quem suae distinctiones amplius currunt"
(*GS* 1: 257). The earliest discussion I have found of *distinctiones* as codeterminants of the *tonus* of a chant
is in "Ecce modorum" (ca. 900), a small treatise transmitted in the group associated with the *Musica
enchiriadis*: "Primus tropus habet tetrachorda III, mese, paramese, hypate meson, scilicet usque nete
diezeugmenon, *distinctiones* lichanos meson, hypate meson, lichanos hypaton, et parhypate hypaton secundum quosdam" (Schmid, ed., *Musica et Scolica enchiriadis*, 182; emphasis added).

24. "M. Quatuor esse modos quidam putant. D. Quare? M. Quia omnis regularis cantus in quatuor
monochordi vocibus finiri potest" (*GS* 1: 258b). Cf. Smits van Waesberghe, ed., *De numero tonorum litterae
Episcopi A. ad Coepiscopum E. missae ac Commentum super tonos Episcopi E.* (ad 1000), 26–27.

25. The discussions of the specific modes, including for each a diagram of their respective intervallic succession or *forma*, can be found in *GS* 1: 259b–63. Unfortunately, this is a part of the treatise that
was not translated in either edition of Strunk's *Source Readings in Music History*.

26. Note that in the diagram of the *Forma toni I* that follows, both ♭ and ♮ occur, although the sequence of intervals given in the text accounts only for the former of the two. On this, see the discussion
of *b♭* below.

A chant of the same mode begins on *C*, as *O beatum pontificem*; often on *D*, in which case the beginning concords with the end, as in *Ecce nomen Domini*. It can also begin on *E*, but rarely, as in *Gaudete in Domino*; on *F*, as in *Ipsi soli*; on *G*, also, as in *Canite tuba*; and even on *a*, as in *Veniet Dominus*.

EXAMPLE 6.11.   Pseudo-Odo's presentation of the first *tonus* (GS 1: 259)

Primus tonus finitur in voce quarta, proceditque in undecimam, in qua est eadem littera d. per tonos et semitonia ita: post finem primo tonus occurrit, deinde semitonium,
et duo toni ac iterum semitonium, et duo toni: deponitur vero a fine ad vocem tertiam
tono uno, hoc modo:*

Forma
toni I. **C.** tonus **D.** tonus **E.** semi. **F.** tonus **G.** tonus **a.** semi. **b. ♭.** semi. **c.** tonus **d**

Quidam autem decachordum volunt facere, adiiciuntque vocem unam, secundam B.
Sed non est in usu, ut ad eam primus deponatur modus. Incipit autem cantus eiusdem
modi in C. ut: *O beatum pontificem*: saepius in D. quando principium cum fine concordat, ut: *Ecce nomen Domini*. In E. quoque, sed raro, ut: *Gaudete in Domino*; in F. ut: *Ipsi
soli*. in G. quoque, ut: *Canite tuba*, in a. etiam, ut: *Veniet Dominus*.

*Pitch names in the diagram appear in boldface.

Similar descriptions follow for the remaining seven *toni* or *modi*, the preferred term being "modi."

Indeed, the use of both terms—*toni* and *modi*—by the Master may have had a didactic purpose. Earlier in the treatise, when the topic of melodic classification is first
introduced, he has made the statement appearing in example 6.12.

EXAMPLE 6.12.   Pseudo-Odo's distinction between *tonus* and *modus* (GS 1: 256a)

Modos autem dico de omnibus octo tonis et modis omnium cantuum, qui in formulis
per ordinem fiunt, ne si tonos dixeris, dubitatio fiat, an de tonis formularum, an de
tonis, qui novenaria facti sunt dispositione et divisione, dicatur.

I say "modus" with reference to all eight of the tones or modes of chant that are given
in order in the formulas [the NOEANE or "Primum quaerite" formulas we have seen in
the tonaries], because if one says "tonus" there is doubt as to whether one is speaking
of the tones of the formulas or about the tones in the ninefold disposition and division [of the monochord].

By employing both terms in reference to what he had called the "tones of the formulas," the Master subtly underscores the necessity of clarity concerning their use.
Perhaps more important, he reminds us of the distinction between *cantus* theory and
ancient Greek harmonic theory—the same distinction made by Regino of Prüm

in his contrast between the eight tones of natural music and the five tones and two semitones of artificial music.[27]

Two of the most innovative features of Pseudo-Odo's treatise pertain to the use of b and to the question of ambitus or range. The role of b here is rather surprising: it is a fixed part of both the second and fifth modes, and by implication a part of the first and sixth modes as well (see GS 1: 259–62). When b is present, these four modes will be based on the "instrumental" scale of Hucbald—our major mode—situated on F.[28]

With regard to range or ambitus, Pseudo-Odo first clarifies the need for the low gamma in his tone-system: he says *expressis verbis* that that pitch is necessary to accommodate several chants in Protus plagal.[29] Perhaps even more important are his remarks on classifying chants with nonstandard ranges (in which the range "misceatur" between authentic and plagal). In such cases, starting pitch and tessitura are the deciding factors. For example, he points out that many chants in Protus do not descend to the lowest three notes (Γ, A, B), nor do they ascend to the tenth or eleventh notes (c and d); hence doubt arises as to whether they are in the first or second tone.[30] His solution: If they do not ascend to the eighth and ninth tones (a and b), they should be assigned to the second mode. Since the eighth and ninth notes are common to both modes, however, what does one do if a chant does make use of them? His answer:

> If it should linger on these [pitches] or repeat them three or four times, or if it should begin on the eighth [a], it will be of the first [mode]; but if it should begin among the lower [pitches] and ascend to these only rarely in comparison with the number of notes in the antiphon, it will be of the second mode.[31]

This is an important expansion and refinement of the role played by ambitus in defining mode, and one that would be taken over by many later authors—most tellingly Marchetto of Padova.[32]

As the preceding discussion should have made clear, Pseudo-Odo's treatise is a significant milestone in the adaptation of ancient Greek harmonic principles to the theory of chant. Thanks to his monochord division, the mathematically determined intervals of a scale combining the Greater and Lesser Perfect Systems with an added

---

27. See the discussion in conjunction with chapter 4, notes 55–59 here. It should be recalled here that the tones in artificial music are in the sesquioctave proportion, the result of a ninefold division.

28. In fact, the diagrams of the *formae* for these four modes, e.g., that given in ex. 6.11, all include both ♭ and ♮. With the ♭, the two modes on F would then "sound" major; those on D would "sound" like our relative minor.

29. "Deponitur vero a fine tono & semitonio & tono usque ad primam A aliquando autem, sed raro, & alio tono usque ad gamma" (GS 1: 259b).

30. "Sunt autem horum plurimi cantus, qui ad Γ. & primam A. & secundam B. non deponuntur, ad decimam vel undecimam non elevantur, de quibus dubium est, an primi, an secundi sint toni" (GS 1: 260).

31. "Si diu in eis permaneat, sive tertio vel quarto eas repercutiat, aut si in octava [a] incipiat, modi erit primi. Sin autem in inferioribus incipiat, & secundum quantitatem antiphonae rarissime ad illas ascendat, secundi erit modi" (GS 1: 260a).

32. Marchetto da Padova, *Lucidarium*, 11.2.20–35 (ed. Herlinger, *The Lucidarium of Marchetto of Padua*, 378–91; GS 3: 101b–103b).

EXAMPLE 6.13.   *Domine, qui operati sunt* from the Worcester Antiphoner (A) transposed to c; (B) untransposed on F; (C) transposed to G

low gamma could easily be converted into sound and taught to students by means of a new letter notation. His introduction of the *conjunctiones vocum*, *b*♭, and a refined treatment of ambitus made it possible to describe and classify chant more precisely than ever before. At the same time, though, we find that the greater precision and specificity of Pseudo-Odo's treatment of tone-system, mode, and notation led to problems of chant classification that had not been present in earlier *cantus* theory. These problems surface in the sixth chapter of the *Dialogus*.

In demonstrating the effect the placement of tones and semitones has on mode, Pseudo-Odo mentions several chants that require pitches "not in the system" when given their proper modal position. One of these is the sixth-mode antiphon *Domine qui operati sunt* (ex. 6.13). Pseudo-Odo says that "if you begin, as many attempt to, on *F*, in the sixth mode, it will not depart from that mode until the semitone, at *in tabernaculo tuo*, on one syllable."[33] As Strunk shows (ex. 6.13B), *Domine, qui operati sunt* would have an *E*♭ immediately below the final on the syllable "-na-" of *in tabernaculo tuo* if sung at its proper modal level on *F*.[34] The offending *E*♭, of course, is not a part of the tone-system laid out at the beginning of the treatise. Pseudo-Odo's first response to this is to leave the problematic note alone: "Since it is thus in use, and sounds well, it ought not to be emended."[35] An alternative, he suggests, is to transpose the chant to *G* and sing it in the eighth mode (ex. 6.13C).[36] The problem with this solution is that the opening melodic formula of *Domine, qui operati sunt* is typ-

33. "Si eam incipias in sexto modo, ut multi probant, in F. littera, non discrepabit ab eo modo, usque ad semitonium, quod est in tabernaculo tuo, in una syllaba" (*GS* 1: 256a). Translation from Strunk, *Source Readings in Music History*, 111; McKinnon, *The Early Christian Period and the Latin Middle Ages*, 96.

34. Strunk, *Source Readings in Music History*, 111; McKinnon, *The Early Christian Period and the Latin Middle Ages*, 96.

35. "Sed quia in usu ita est, & bene sonat, emendari non debet" (*GS* 1: 256b); Strunk, *Source Readings in Music History*, 111; McKinnon, *The Early Christian Period and the Latin Middle Ages*, 96.

36. "Incipe itaque eam in G. littera, hoc est, in octavo modo, & regulariter in eo stare probabis" (*GS* 1: 256b); Strunk, *Source Readings in Music History*, 111; McKinnon, *The Early Christian Period and the Latin Middle Ages*, 96.

ical of the sixth mode, not the eighth. Thus, he suggests, "some begin *Domine* as in *Amen dico vobis*"—whose opening is typical of the eighth mode.[37] The result of this would have been a hybrid melody bearing little resemblance to the original.[38]

Regardless of which of the proposed solutions one adopts, one is confronted with difficulties on attempting to map *Domine, qui operati sunt* with its proper modal final onto Pseudo-Odo's extended ancient Greek system. That this was not an isolated problem is suggested by the comments Pseudo-Odo makes after his discussion of *Domine*. He says that in such a case one should try all the modes to see if the problematic melody might not stand in one or another of them without emendation. "But," he concludes, "if it suits no mode, let it be emended according to the one with which it least disagrees."[39]

What Pseudo-Odo says, in essence, is that if a chant does not fit the system, then the notes of the chant—widely presumed to have been divinely inspired—should be changed.[40] It seems not to have occurred to him that perhaps the system itself ought to be changed. Obviously, the attempt to apply Boethian mathematical precision to the body of chant and the habits of singers, both of which had developed over the course of centuries, could not be completely successful. There were, in fact, a number of problematic chants that lay at the very heart of the repertoire—chants that "suggested one tone at the beginning, another in the middle, and yet another at their end" (Regino), or that contained notes not in the system.[41] Without the flexible tone-system and method of classification offered by the chant treatises, such as the *Musica enchiriadis*, the only solutions for such pieces were (1) to transpose them, or (2) to "emend" them according to the mode with which they least disagreed. Theory that had originally been conceived as a method of classifying and rationalizing plainchant now became a Procrustean bed that forced modifications in the very melodies it was supposed to help preserve.

Means for modifying the system were not yet available in the late tenth or early eleventh centuries. The seeds for further change, however, were sown by a slightly later writer, and one of the most influential of the Middle Ages, Guido d'Arezzo.

The Greek two-octave system plus low Γ presented by Pseudo-Odo is the standard one for Guido in all of his works, but it plays an especially prominent role in two

37. "Unde quidam incipiunt *Domine* sicut *Amen dico vobis*" (GS 1: 256b); Strunk, *Source Readings in Music History*, 111; McKinnon, *The Early Christian Period and the Latin Middle Ages*, 96.

38. See Strunk, *Source Readings in Music History*, 112; McKinnon, *The Early Christian Period and the Latin Middle Ages*, 96, for a reconstruction.

39. "Quodsi nulli tono placet, secundum eum tonum emendetur, in quo minus dissonat" (GS 1: 256b; Strunk, *Source Readings in Music History*, 111; McKinnon, *The Early Christian Period and the Latin Middle Ages*, 96).

40. See the prologue here, p. 3

41. Regino says "Sunt namque quaedam antiphonae, quas nothas, id est degeneres et non legitimas, appellamus, quae ab uno tono incipiunt, alterius sunt in medio, et in tertio finiuntur" (GS 1: 231a; Bernhard, *Clavis Gerberti*, 40). On these *nothae,* "degenerate and illegitimate" according to Regino, but nonetheless a fixed part of the early repertoire, see Atkinson, "The *Parapteres: Nothae* or Not?" and "Parapter." See also chapter 4 here, notes 51–54 and associated discussion.

EXAMPLE 6.14.   Comparison of the *Enchiriadis* tone-System (A) with that of Guido d'Arezzo (B). Brackets indicate flexible degrees.

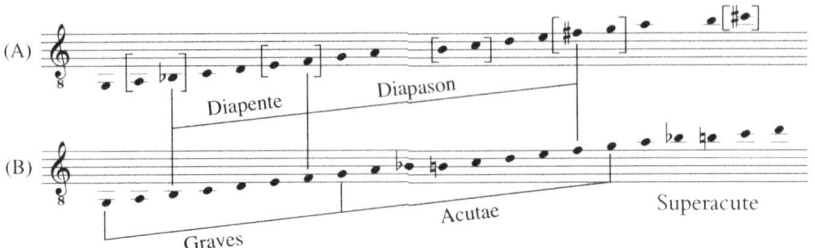

of them, the *Micrologus* (ca. 1026–28)[42] and the *Epistola de ignoto cantu* (ca. 1032).[43] It is also the system that is presented in the first codification of the principles of diastematic, staff notation in his *Prologus in antiphonarium* (ca. 1030).[44]

Guido begins his *Micrologus* by setting out the notes of the system, which one may see in the lower staff of example 6.14; then he provides two different monochord divisions for deriving them.[45] Like Pseudo-Odo before him, Guido starts with gamma, "added by the moderns." This is followed by the series *A* through *G*, which, along with gamma, Guido calls the "Graves." The next octave, *a* through *g*, including both "hard" and "soft" *b* (*b-quadratum* and *b-rotundum*, respectively), he calls the "Acutae." Above these, however, he adds five notes (*aa bb ♭ ♮ cc dd*) called "Superacutae." His system thus has twenty-one degrees, rather than the fifteen numbered degrees of Pseudo-Odo.[46]

42. Ed. *GS* 2: 2–24; Smits van Waesberghe, ed., *Guido Aretinus, CSM* 4. English translation with commentary in Babb and Palisca, *Hucbald, Guido, and John on Music*, 48–83; French translation in Colette, *Gui d'Arezzo, Micrologus*.

43. Ed. *GS* 2: 43–50, and together with translation into English in Pesce, *Guido d'Arezzo's Regule rithmice, Prologus in antiphonarium, and Epistola ad Michahelem*, 438–531. Partial English translation in Strunk, *Source Readings in Music History*, 121–25; McKinnon, *The Early Christian Period and the Latin Middle Ages*, 104–8.

44. Ed. *GS* 2: 34–37; Smits van Waesberghe, *Tres tractatuli Guidonis Aretini. Guidonis Prologus in antiphonarium;* and (with English translation) in Pesce, *Guido d'Arezzo's Regule rithmice, Prologus in antiphonarium, and Epistola ad Michahelem*, 406–35. Another English translation in Strunk, *Source Readings in Music History*, 117–20, and McKinnon, *The Early Christian Period and the Latin Middle Ages*, 101–4.

45. Ed. Smits van Waesberghe, *CSM* 4, 93–102. On these monochord divisions, see Sachs, "Musikalische Elementarlehre im Mittelalter," 158–60; and Markovits, *Das Tonsystem der abendländischen Musik im frühen Mittelalter*, 48. See also Brockett, "Comparison of the Five Monochords of Guido of Arezzo," 29–42; Meyer, *Mensura monochordi*, xli–xlix, 106–7, 154–55, 260, 265; Smits van Waesberghe, *De musicopaedagogico et theoretico Guidone Aretino eiusque vita et moribus*, 172–73, no. 39; 174, no. 43; Adkins, "The Theory and Practice of the Monochord," 148–50; and Wantzloeben, *Das Monochord*, 76–79. The Vivell Anonymous points out that the second of the two divisions is incomplete ("Micros graece, brevis latine"). See Vivell, ed., *Commentarius anonymus in Micrologum Guidonis Aretini*, 10; and Smits van Waesberghe, ed., *Expositiones in Micrologum*, 104. A number of the manuscripts of the treatise provide different solutions for it; see Meyer, "La Tradition du *Micrologus* de Guy d'Arezzo," 5–14.

46. Smits van Waesberghe, ed., *CSM* 4, 93–95; and Babb and Palisca, *Hucbald, Guido, and John on Music*, 61–62.

But at the same time he takes over the tone-system and nomenclature introduced for it by Pseudo-Odo, Guido shows his awareness—and misunderstanding—of the tone-system presented in the *Musica enchiriadis* (Ex. 6.14a) when he says:

> Some people nowadays incautiously employ only four symbols [the four Dasia symbols for protus, deuterus, tritus, tetrardus]. They indicate every fifth sound always by the same symbol, though it is true beyond a doubt that some notes disagree completely with those a fifth away, and that no note agrees perfectly with its fifth. For no note agrees perfectly with any other except its octave.[47]

As noted earlier, every fifth note in the *Enchiriadis* system is in fact the same in both name and quality; the octaves, by contrast, are not. As shown in example 6.14, Guido's comments actually pertain to *his* system, with its octave equivalence, and not to the *Enchiriadis* system with its equivalence at the fifth. This point becomes especially telling because of the importance of Guido's work in yet another aspect of chant, his application of the principles of the ancient Greek tone-system to the system of practical notation using neumes.[48]

One of the most distinctive features of Guido's work is his own application of species theory to the concept of mode (although not employing the term *species* itself as did Author δ of the *Alia musica*). It is his notion of *modi vocum*, or "species of degrees."[49] It first appears in the *Micrologus* (ca. 1025/26), and again in the *Epistola* (ca. 1032). In both works, Guido begins as described above, by setting out a tone-system derived via division of the monochord. The six *modi conjunctionum* ("types of conjunctions") or *motus vocum* ("movements of pitches")—his equivalent to Pseudo-Odo's six *conjunctiones vocum*—follow immediately in both works, as does a discussion of octave equivalence, which serves as preparation for the discussion of the *modi vocum*.[50] The progression as it appears in the *Epistola* is as follows.

Guido first says that pitches can be joined to each other in six *modi*: tone, semitone, ditone, semiditone, diatessaron, and diapente. He has already discussed the tone and semitone earlier, and says that the ditone is when there are two tones between pitches, as for example between the third and fifth degrees of the scale (*C* and *E*). In his de-

---

47. "Moderni quidam nimis incaute quattuor tantum signa posuerint, quintum et quintum videlicet sonum eodem ubique charactere figurantes, cum indubitanter verum sit perfecte concordet. Nulla enim vox cum altera praeter octavam perfecte concordat" (Smits van Waesberghe, ed., *CSM* 4, 112–13; Babb and Palisca, *Hucbald, Guido, and John on Music,* 62). See Smits van Waesberghe, *Guidonis Aretini Regulae rhythmicae,* 101 (in apparatus criticus); and Pesce, *Guido d'Arezzo's Regule rithmice,* ll. 71–75, 344–45, "De notis Enchiriadis," where Guido can be seen to include the Dasia signs themselves. ("Miror quatuor fecisse quosdam signa vocibus, quasi quinte sint eedem, quarum quedam dissonant. Quedam quamvis sint affines, non perfecte consonant"; "I am astonished that some have made four symbols for the pitches, as if they are the same at the fifth, of which some differ. Some, however much they are related, do not agree perfectly"; translation by Pesce.)

48. See the discussion below, pp. 228–30.

49. My translation of this phrase derives in part from the usage found in two commentaries on Guido's *Micrologus,* the *Liber specierum* and *Micros graece, brevis Latine* (both ed. Smits van Waesberghe, *Expositiones in Micrologum Guidonis Aretini*), and in part from Harold Powers's translation of it as "mode of degrees" in "Mode," 388. It refers to the configuration of tones and semitones (*species*) surrounding each pitch (*vox*) treated as a degree of the scale, hence "species of degrees."

50. Meyer points out ("La Tradition du *Micrologus* de Guy d'Arezzo," 14–18) that a number of manuscripts add additional intervals to the six Guido takes over from Pseudo-Odo.

scriptions of the other three *modi*, all involving both tones and semitones, he gives examples of the disposition of intervals between the boundary pitches (ex. 6.15).

EXAMPLE 6.15.   Guido's presentation of the *modi vocum* in the "Epistola ad Michaelem" (Pesce, ed., Guido d'Arezzo's *Epistola ad michahelem*, 486–88, lines 208–14; GS 2: 46b–47a)

Semiditonus autem dicitur, quia minor est ditono, cum inter reliquas duas voces est unus tonus et unum semitonium D t. E s. F. Diatessaron autem dicitur de quatuor, cum inter aliquam vocem et quartam a se duo sunt toni et unum semitonium D t. E s. F t. G. Diapente dicitur de quinque, cum inter aliquam vocem et quintam a se tres sunt toni et unum semitonium D t. E s. F t. G t. a

---

A semiditone is so called because the ditone is smaller when between any two pitches there is one tone and one semitone *D* t. *E* s. *F*. A diatessaron is called "of four," since between some pitch and that a fourth from it there are two tones and one semitone *D* t. *E* s. *F* t. *G*. A diapente is called "of five," since between some pitch and that a fifth from it there are three tones and one semitone *D* t. *E* s. *F* t. *G* t. *a*.[51]

He recognizes implicitly that there are several different ways of arranging the tones and semitones within a larger interval (minor third to perfect fifth), and conversely, that each pitch or degree of the scale will be the locus of one specific disposition of intervals (*species*) between boundary pitches on either side of it. Although there is perfect correspondence of degrees only at the diapason (as he later acknowledges), one finds that three pairs of degrees within the octave are linked by "affinities," while the seventh degree, G, is not.[52] There are thus four *modi vocum*, as Guido calls them (called "species vocum" by two of his commentators),[53] each being defined by the disposition of intervals immediately above and below it—in *depositione* and *elevatione*, as he puts it (ex. 6.16).[54]

EXAMPLE 6.16.   The affinities within the *modi vocum*, as presented in Guido's "Epistola ad Michaelem" (Pesce, ed., *Epistola*, 490–94, lines 225–38; GS 2: 47)

Omnes autem voces in tantum sunt similes et faciunt similes sonos et concordes neumas, in quantum similiter elevantur vel deponuntur secundum depositionem tonorum et semitoniorum; utputa prima vox et quarta similes et unius modi dicuntur, quia utraque in depositione tonum, in elevatione vero habent tonum et semitonium et duos tonos. Atque hec est prima similitudo in vocibus, id est, primus modus. Secundus modus est in secunda et quinta; habent enim utraque in depositione duos tonos, in elevatione semitonium et duos tonos. Tercius modus est in tertia et sexta; ambe enim semitonio et duobus tonis descendunt, duobus vero tonis ascendunt. Sola vero septima quartum modum facit, que in depositione unum tonum et semitonium et duos tonos, in elevatione vero duos habet tonos et semitonium.

---

51. Translation from Pesce, *Guido d'Arezzo's Regule rithmice*, 487, 489.

52. For Guido's presentation of the theory of affinities, see below, pp. 226–27.

53. *Liber specierum* and *Micros graece, brevis Latine*, ed. Smits van Waesberghe, *Expositiones in Micrologum Guidonis Aretini*, 31–35 and 114–19, respectively.

54. As Pesce points out, Guido uses the phrase *similitudo in vocibus* as the equivalent of *modus vocum* in the *Epistola* (see the quotation from the *Epistola* in ex. 6.16).

But all pitches are similar and make similar sounds and neumes that agree to the extent that they are raised or lowered similarly according to the arrangement of tones and semitones; for instance, the first pitch [*A*] and the fourth [*D*] are called similar and of one mode, because they both have a tone in descent, but a tone, a semitone, and two tones in ascent. And this is the first likeness in pitches, that is, the first mode. The second mode is on the second [*B*] and on the fifth [*E*]; for they both have two tones in descent, a semitone and two tones in ascent. The third mode is on the third [*C*] and on the sixth [*F*]; for they both descend by a semitone and two tones, but ascend by two tones. Only the seventh [*G*] forms the fourth mode, which has one tone, a semitone, and two tones in descent, but two tones and a semitone in ascent.[55]

Following this prose description, Guido demonstrates the way the four *modi* differ from each other by copying out a simple melody four times, once on each of the four finals (cf. *Musica enchiriadis*, chap. 7, and ex. 6.17).[56] The *modi vocum* are thus what might be described as the species of hexachord or octave surrounding each degree of the scale.[57] They will play an important role in shaping Guido's approach to yet another type of *modus*, namely, the one that functions as a melodic category.[58]

EXAMPLE 6.17.   Melodic demonstration of the *modi vocum* (*GS* 2: 47)

| D F G G G G G a F e D |
| *Tu Patris sempiternus es Filius.* |
| E G a a a a a ♭ G F E |
| *Tu Patris sempiternus es Filius.* |
| F a ♭ ♭ ♭♭ ♭c a G F |
| *Tu Patris sempiternus es Filius.* |
| G ♭ c c c cc c d ♭a G |
| *Tu Patris sempiternus es Filius.* |

One of the features associated with the *modi vocum* that will be especially telling for melodic classification is what Guido refers to as "transformatio"—the notion that the use of *b♭* can transform a chant based on one *modus vocum* into another.[59] For example, with *b♭*, the *modus vocum* on G will sound as if it is protus, rather than tetrardus (ex. 6.18):

55. Translation.from Pesce, *Guido d'Arezzo's Regule rithmice*, 491–95.

56. *GS* 2: 47; Pesce, *Guido d'Arezzo's Regule rithmice*, 496.

57. In the *Micrologus*, the fourth *modus vocum*, that on G, is described only by its position within a diapente (*F-c*) (see Smits van Waesberghe, ed., *CSM* 4, 118; and Babb and Palisca, *Hucbald, Guido, and John on Music*, 63).

58. The concept of *modus vocum* is taken up by several subsequent theorists, among them Hermannus Contractus and Wilhelm of Hirsau. For an overview, see Pesce, *The Affinities and Medieval Transposition*, chaps. 2–3.

59. See Pesce, "B-Flat: Transposition or Transformation?"

EXAMPLE 6.18.   *Transformatio* as discussed in Guido's *Micrologus* (*CSM* 4, 124–25)

> In eodem vero cantu maxime .b. molli utimur, in quo .F.f. amplius continuatur gravis
> vel acuta, ubi et quandam confusionem et *transformationem* videtur facere, ut .G. sonet
> protum, .a. deuterum, cum ipsa .b. sonet tritum (emphasis added).

We use *b♭* mostly in that chant in which *F* or *f* recurs rather extensively, either low or
high, where it seems to create a certain confusion; it seems to effect a *transformatio*, so
that *G* sounds as protus and *a* as deuterus, whereas *b♭* itself sounds as tritus.[60]

Later he says that if one "compels" the melody of one *modus* (*vocum*) to be received
by another, it will be transformed:"As for those [pitches] in which no resemblance is
evident, or which are of different *modi* [*vocum*], no one of them will accept the melody
of another. But if you force it to receive one, it will transform."[61] The idea of *transformatio* and the terminology expressing it are taken up by several later writers, starting
with Guido's commentators, the *Liber argumentorum* (1050–1100) and the "Micros
graece, brevis latine" (1070–1100); it ultimately becomes the basis for a categorical
distinction of its own in the use of *modus* as a term for melodic classification.[62]

According to one of Guido's commentators, the theory of *modus vocum* is an important foundation for the theory of *modus* as melodic category. He introduces
Guido's theory of mode by saying "Having set out the species of pitches of which
chant is composed, now he will give the modes of chant, that is, the finals, according to which the entire chant should be directed and controlled."[63] The anonymous
commentator's equation of *modi* with *finales* is in fact an important part of Guido's
treatment. Following Pseudo-Odo, Guido assigns great importance to the finalis in
determining the mode of a chant, saying that only after a chant is finished can one
recognize what has gone before:

> Furthermore, when we hear someone sing, we do not know what mode his first note
> is in, since we do not know whether tones, semitones, or other intervals will follow.
> But when the chant has ended we know clearly from the preceding notes the mode
> of the last one. . . . Thus the last note is the one we are better aware of.[64]

Guido reinforces the importance of the finalis by pointing out that it is on the finalis
that most distinctions are made ("Additur quoque et illud quod accurati cantus in

---

60. My translation is based on that of Babb and Palisca, *Hucbald, Guido, and John on Music,* 64.

61. "In quibus [voces] vero nulla similitudo monstrata est vel quae diversorum modorum sunt, altera alterius neumam cantumque non recipit; quod si compellas recipere, transformabit" (Smits van
Waesberghe, ed., *CSM* 4, 131). Again my translation is based on that of Babb and Palisca, *Hucbald, Guido,
and John on Music,* 65. In that translation, *transformabit* is rendered as "it will change its sound."

62. For more on this, see Atkinson, "Modus," *HmT*, sec.V. (I) (9).

63. "Dispositis vero speciebus vocum ex quibus cantus componitur, nunc dabit modos cantus, finales
scilicet, secundum quas totus cantus regatur et moderetur" (Smits van Waesberghe, ed., *Expositiones in
Micrologum,* 114; Vivell, ed., *Commentarius anonymus in Micrologum Guidonis Aretini,* 20).

64. "Praeterea cum aliquem cantare audimus, primam eius vocem cuius modi sit, ignoramus, quia
utrum toni, semitonia reliquaeve species sequantur, nescimus. Finito vero cantu ultimae vocis modum ex
praeteritis aperte cognoscimus. . . . Itaque finalis vox est quam melius intuemur" (Smits van Waesberghe,
ed., *CSM* 4, 144; the translation follows Babb and Palisca, *Hucbald, Guido, and John on Music,* 67).

finalem vocem maxime distinctiones mittunt").[65] As the treatment here suggests, both the distinctions and the beginnings of chants are important determinants of mode.

In order to explain this, Guido refers to the *neumae* that had been invented for "discerning the mode in chant" ("Primum quaerite regnum Dei," "Secundum autem," etc.). As his explanation makes clear, these are particularly useful for determining the mode in chants sung with psalm tones. Commenting on the *neuma* "Primum quaerite regnum Dei," he says: "As soon as we have seen that this *neuma* accords with the end of an antiphon, there is no need to doubt that it is of the authentic Protus; and similarly with the other modes."[66]

The passage immediately following this, however, renders Guido's treatment of the *neumae* somewhat ambiguous, in that it almost suggests that the *neumae* themselves have the features of psalm tones or, more specifically, the *differentiae* of psalm tones. Just after the sentence quoted above, he says:

> Most helpful for this are the verses of the responsories of nocturns, the psalms of the offices, and all the chants that are prescribed in the formulas of the modes. . . . Here [i.e., in the verses] one can foresee on what notes of the particular modes chants less often or more often begin, and on what notes they do so least.[67]

Indeed, in the discussion that ensues, Guido specifies the levels at which chants can begin. But rather than relating this to the *neumae*, he is actually referring to the reciting tones, the first notes in the *differentiae*, of their respective psalm tones:

> Thus in plagal modes it is by no means permissible either for the beginnings or endings of distinctions to rise to the fifth degree [above the final], although one may very rarely rise to the fourth [degree]. In authentic modes, however, except the Deuterus, it is most unsuitable to rise in these beginnings and endings of phrases to the sixth degree. Yet those of the plagal of the Protus and the plagal of the Tritus go as high as the third, and those of the plagal of the Deuterus and the plagal of the Tetrardus go as high as the fourth.[68]

The Vivell Anonymous clarifies this, as one can see in example 6.19, saying that the verses show the highest point at which a distinction can begin or end, a point no higher than the *saeculorum Amen* and tenor of the psalm (the language the Vivell Anonymous took directly from Guido appears in small capitals in the passage that follows):

---

65. Smits van Waesberghe, ed., *CSM* 4, 144; Babb and Palisca, *Hucbald, Guido, and John on Music*, 67.

66. "Mox enim ut cum fine alicuius antiphonae hanc neumam bene viderimus convenire, quod autenti proti sit non opus est dubitare; sic et de reliquis" (Smits van Waesberghe, ed., *CSM* 4, 154–55; Babb and Palisca, *Hucbald, Guido, and John on Music,* 68; cf. Regino, in *GS* 1: 256a).

67. "Ad hoc etiam plurimum valent et versus nocturnalium responsoriorum et psalmi officiorum et omnia quae in modorum formulis praescribuntur. . . . Ibi enim praevidetur quibus in vocibus singulorum modorum cantus rarius saepiusve incipiant et in quibus minime id fiat" (Smits van Waesberghe, ed., *CSM* 4, 154; Babb and Palisca, *Hucbald, Guido, and John on Music,* 68).

68. "Ut in plagis quidem minime licet vel principia vel fines distinctionum ad quintas intendere, cum ad quartas perraro soleat evenire. In autentis vero, praeter deuterum, eadem principia et fines distinctionum minime licet ad sextas intendere; plagae autem proti vel triti ad tertias intendunt, et plagae siquidem deuteri vel tetrardi ad quartas intendunt" (Smits van Waesberghe, ed., *CSM* 4, 154–55; Babb and Palisca, *Hucbald, Guido, and John on Music,* 68–69).

EXAMPLE 6.19.   Commentary by the Vivell Anonymous on the role of the *neumae* as discussed by Guido (Vivell, ed., *Commentarius anonymous*, 46; Smits van Waesberghe, ed., *Expositiones in Micrologum Guidonis Aretini*, 142–43)

> IBI ENIM, id est in illis formulis, sicut in "Saeculorum amen" videmus IN QUIBUS VOCIBUS SINGULORUM MODORUM CANTUS SAEPIUS RARIUSVE INCIPIANT, ET IN QUIBUS ID, scilicet inceptio, MINIME fiat. 29) Ibi enim altius potest omnis cantus tam plagalis quam authentus super finalem incipere, vel etiam incipere et finire quaelibet distinctio in cantu, 30) ubi ascendit "Saeculorum amen," et tenor totius psalmi aptati alicui modo authento vel plagali, 31) et ideo in ipsis videtur ubi non ascendat principium et finis distinctionis, quia non ascendit altius quam "Saeculorum amen," et tenor ipsius psalmi.

HERE INDEED, that is, in these formulas, just as we see in *saeculorum Amen*, ONE CAN FORESEE ON WHAT NOTES OF THE PARTICULAR MODES CHANTS LESS OFTEN OR MORE OFTEN BEGIN, AND ON WHAT NOTES THEY DO SO, that is begin, LEAST. Here indeed every sort of chant, either plagal or authentic, is able to begin, or even any distinction is able to begin or end, at the height to which the *saeculorum Amen* and the tenor of the entire psalm connected with any authentic or plagal mode ascends above the finalis. And therefore in these distinctions and ends it can be seen where the beginning cannot ascend, because it cannot ascend higher than the *saeculorum Amen* and the tenor of the psalm itself.

Thus, both the *neumae* and the *differentiae* work in conjunction with each other in defining the starting pitches and distinctions of chants in each mode.

As was true of Pseudo-Odo, Guido follows his discussion of the *initia* and *distinctiones* with a treatment of the ambitus of the modes. He says that except for the Tritus, authentic chants scarcely go more than one pitch below their final, and they can ascend to a ninth or even a tenth above it. The normal ambitus of plagal modes is a fifth above and below the finalis, but they can ascend up to a sixth above. What is particularly intriguing, though, in Guido's discussion of ambitus is his pointing out that transposition is sometimes necessary so that the plagal chants of the Protus, Deuterus, and Tritus may end on high *a*, ♭, and *c*, respectively ("Plagae vero proti, deuteri et triti aliquando in a.♭.c. acutas necessario finiuntur").[69] The question is why should plagal chants be singled out as candidates for transposition? The explanation, I would submit, is found in Guido's discussion of the affinities in chapters 7 and 8 of the *Micrologus*.

The starting point for Guido's treatment of *affinitas* was apparently the principle of *socialitas* already introduced in the treatise of Hucbald. Guido provides a diagram to show that three of the four finals, *D*, *E* and *F*, have affinities a fourth below and a fifth above themselves (ex. 6.20).

69. (Smits van Waesberghe, ed., *CSM* 4, 156). Commenting on this passage, the Vivell Anonymous ("Micros graece, brevis latine") says that transposition can be either whole or partial. As an example of the former he cites the Gradual *Haec dies*, transposed from *D* to *a*; as an example of the latter, the Alleluia *Iudicabunt* (Vivell, ed., *Commentarius anonymous in Micrologum Guidonis Aretini*, 48; Smits van Waesberghe, ed., *Expositiones in Micrologum Guidonis Aretini*, 144–45).

EXAMPLE 6.20.   Diagram of the affinities from Guido, *Micrologus*, chap. 7 (*CSM* 4, 119)

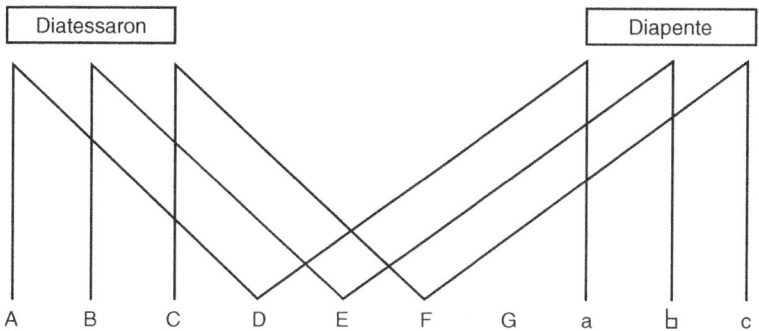

He then shows how one can employ these affinities in order to accommodate specific intervallic patterns of plainchant. One of his examples is particularly striking in that it shows his awareness of a *B♭* in the *graves* that was not part of his standard tone-system (ex. 6.21):

EXAMPLE 6.21.   Guido's demonstration of the necessity for partial transposition, *Micrologus*, chap. 8 (cf. *CSM* 4, 125–26)

If it is the kind of melody that . . . going down after *D E F* wants two whole tones [i.e., *D* to *C* and *C* to *B♭* in the *graves*], then instead of *D E F* use *a ♭ c*, which are of the same mode and have the perfectly regular descents and ascents just mentioned.[70]

Here, rather than transposing the entire melody, Guido introduces the technique of partial transposition. As he says, a melodic phrase with the pitches *D E F D C B♭* within a longer melody would have to be notated *a ♭ c a G F,* leaving the rest of the melody notated at its proper modal level. It should be emphasized that this is a matter of notation, not performance; the singers would sing such as melody as they always had sung it.[71] Medieval scribes, however, would make extensive use of both whole and partial transposition when confronted with the problem of notating nonsystemic pitches.[72]

70. "Si talis est neuma, quae post .D.E.F. . . . in depositione vult duos tonos, pro .D.E.F. assume .a. ♭.c. quae eiusdem sunt modi et praedictas depositiones et elevationes regulariter habent" (Smits van Waesberghe, ed., *CSM* 4, 125–26; Babb and Palisca, *Hucbald, Guido, and John on Music*, 64). On this passage, see also Pesce, "B-Flat: Transposition or Transformation?" 338–39.

71. The transmission of the Sanctus prosula *Laudes deo ore pio* is a particularly clear and fascinating example of this, but one that shows that the partially transposed version could take on a life of its own (see Atkinson, "Music as 'Mistress of the Words'").

72. The investigation of transposition as a means of notating melodies containing pitches not in the

Armed with this information, one can deduce the reason for the greater necessity for transposition of plagal chants: they are the ones that are most likely to use the low $B^{\flat}$ that was not a part of either Pseudo-Odo's or Guido's Greek-derived tone-system.

As seen in the preceding discussion, in his *Micrologus* (ca. 1026–28) Guido uses the monochord to set out the Pseudo-Odonian tone-system, employing letters of the alphabet both for the monochord division itself and as a means of notating chant. In using letters as chant notation he was following a procedure that had been used in theoretical works at least as far back as Hucbald and the *Alia musica*. In his *Prologus in antiphonarium* (1030), however, Guido takes one step further that is seemingly small, but whose implications are truly gigantic. In that work, he explains that he has copied an antiphonary using a new method of notation so that "any intelligent and studious person may learn the chant by means of it; after he has thoroughly learned a part of it through a master, he will unhesitatingly understand the rest of it by himself without one."[73] Guido's new notational method, clearly intended for practical use, is a combination of elements drawn from the line diagrams found in theoretical works with the "signs [*notae*] that custom has handed down to us, and that in diverse regions are given no less diverse shapes," as Hucbald had described conventional neumes.[74]

---

medieval tone-system has a long scholarly tradition of its own, beginning with Jacobsthal, *Die chromatische Alteration im liturgischen Gesang der abendländischen Kirche* (1897), and continuing with such works such as Kessler, *Über die leiterfremden Tonstufen im gregorianischen Gesang* (1922); Bomm, *Der Wechsel der Modalitätsbestimmug* (1929); and Delalande, "L'Insuffisance du système d'écriture guidonien" (1950). The topic has been the focus of renewed interest in recent years. See, in particular, Stuart, "Melodic Corrections in an Eleventh-Century Gradual" (1979); Frasch, "Notation as a Guide to Modality" (1986); Pesce, *The Affinities and Medieval Transposition* (1987); Atkinson, "From 'Vitium' to 'Tonus acquisitus'" (1990); Praßl, "Chromatische Veränderungen von Choralmelodien in Theorie und Praxis" (1992); Karp, "The Offertory *In die solemnitatis*" (1995); Karp, *Aspects of Orality and Formularity in Gregorian Chant* (1998); Ferreira, "Music at Cluny: The Tradition of Gregorian Chant for the Proper of the Mass" (1997); Hankeln, *Die Offertoriums-Prosuln der Aquitanischen Handschriften* (1999); Fischer, "Die Notation von Stücken mit chromatisch alterierten Tönen" (2000); Pfisterer, *Cantilena Romana: Untersuchungen zur Überlieferung des gregorianischen Chorals* (2002); and Maloy, "The Roles of Notation in Frutolf of Michelsberg's Tonary" (2002).

73. In his words: "Taliter etenim Deo auxiliante hoc antiphonarium notare disposui, ut per eum leviter aliquis sensatus et studiosus cantum discat, et postquam partem eius bene per magistrum cognoverit, reliqua per se sine magistro indubitanter agnoscat" (Smits van Waesberghe, ed., *Guidonis Aretini Prologus in antiphonarium*, 67–68; Pesce, *Guido d'Arezzo's Regule rithmice*, 414–16; translation from Strunk, *Source Readings in Music History*, 119; McKinnon, *The Early Christian Period and the Latin Middle Ages*, 102).

74. See the line diagrams found in glosses to Martianus Capella (fig. 2.4 here), in the *Musica* and *Scolica enchiriadis* (exs. 3.14–16), or in Hucbald's *De harmonica institutione* (ex. 4.1). Like Hucbald, Guido also recognizes the utility of the "customary" neumes. At the end of the *Prologus* he says "How pitches are liquescent, and whether they sound connectedly or separately, or slowly, tremulously, or suddenly, or how a song is divided into phrases; and whether a pitch is lower, or higher, or in unison with the preceding [pitch], is shown by an easy argument to be present in the very shape of the neumes, if they are arranged diligently [*ex industria componantur*], as they ought to be" (transl. Pesce, *Guido d'Arezzo's Regule rithmice*, 435). Guido's saying that the neumes should be properly constructed (*ex industria componantur*) reminds one of the phrase in the *Scolica enchiriadis* in which the Master says that *vitia* are inserted into chants as a result of conscientiousness (*de industria cantibus inseruntur*; see chapter 3 here, note 120). Both authors are urging adherence to "best practices."

Guido first explains the underlying principle, a system of lines and spaces articulating a tonal matrix in acoustic space:

> The notes are so arranged that each sound, however often it may be repeated in a melody, is found always in its own row. And in order that you may better distinguish these rows, lines are drawn close together, and some rows of sounds occur on the lines themselves, others in the intervening intervals or spaces. All the sounds on one line or in one space sound alike.[75]

He then quantifies the musical space so articulated by assigning to each line or space a scale degree derived via the monochord.

> In order that you may also understand to which lines or spaces each sound belongs, certain letters of the monochord are written at the beginning of the lines or spaces and the lines are also gone over in colors, thereby indicating that in the whole antiphonary and in every melody those lines or spaces which have one and the same letter or color, however many they may be, sound alike throughout.[76]

With this simple step, the fusing of the ancient Greek Immutable System (*ametabolon systema*) with the tonal matrix of medieval music and its embodiment in practical notation was complete.[77] There was now available to the West a practical method of notating music that was fully diastematic, whose intervals represented precise numerical ratios that could be converted directly into sound via the monochord.[78] That notation, however, preserved a systemic architecture based on the

---

75. "Ita igitur disponuntur voces ut unusquisque sonus, quantumlibet in cantu repetatur, in uno semper et suo ordine inveniatur. Quos ordines ut melius possis discernere, spissae ducuntur lineae, et quidam ordines vocum in ipsis fiunt lineis, quidam vero inter lineas in medio intervallo et spatio linearum. Quanticumque ergo soni in una linea vel in uno sunt spatio, omnes similiter sonant" (Smits van Waesberghe, ed., *Guidonis Aretini Prologus in antiphonarium*, 67–68; Pesce, *Guido d'Arezzo's Regule rithmice*, 418; transl. from Strunk, *Source Readings in Music History*, 119; McKinnon, *The Early Christian Period and the Latin Middle Ages*, 102). It should be pointed out that the line diagrams in earlier theoretical works had typically placed degrees of the scale on lines, leaving the spaces free for text or intervallic designations, but had not placed them successively on both, as Guido does. His method thus resulted in a substantial saving of space and hence of parchment.

76. "Ut autem et illud intelligas, quantae lineae vel spatia unum habent sonum, quibusdam lineis vel spatiis quaedam litterae de monochordo praefiguntur atque etiam colores superducuntur. Unde datur intelligi, quia in toto antiphonario et in omni cantu quantaecumque lineae vel spatia unam eandemque habent litteram vel eundem colorem, ita per omnia similiter sonant" (see the editions and translations cited in the preceding note). Phillips ("Notationen und Notationslehren," 582–83) points out that both the *Musica* and *Scolica enchiriadis* mention the use of color in line diagrams, and an early gloss to the *Scolica* specifies that the colors for the Finales should be red (protus), green (deuterus), gold (tritus), and black (tetrardus). For an extensive treatment of Guido's notation, including a provisional catalogue of manuscripts containing it, see Smits van Waesberghe, "The Musical Notation of Guido of Arezzo." In his *Musikerziehung*, plt. 51 (p. 111; discussion on p. 110), Smits van Waesberghe reproduces in color facsimile an early example of Guidonian notation from the eleventh-century manuscript Munich 9921, fol. 54v.

77. The *ametabolon systema*, or Immutable System, was the eighteen-note system constructed by adding the synemmenon tetrachord to the Greater Perfect System. See chapter 1 here, note 30, and the discussion associated with it.

78. The famous picture of Guido and Bishop Theodaldus, the dedicatee of the *Micrologus*, in Vienna 51, fol. 35v, shows Guido manipulating a monochord, on whose side is inscribed the Pseudo-Odonian/ Guidonian tone-system, Γ-A-a. It would be hard to imagine a more appropriate representation of Guido's theories. Because this picture also encapsulates in a most vivid way so much of what the "critical nexus" in the title of this book is about, I have chosen to reproduce it on the cover.

mathematical principles of ancient Greek harmonic theory and the instruments with which it was demonstrated, rather than upon the flexible melodic shapes of the plainchant sung in the Western church. The implications that this would hold for medieval music and its theory would be far-reaching: as the discussions of transposition and methods for "correcting the mistakes" of singers found in virtually every subsequent theorist's work show, any chant—such as *Domine qui operati sunt*—that made use of scale degrees not in the tone-system became a problem.[79]

EXCURSUS

One of the new devices Guido developed to teach the "standard" tone-system proved to be an important tool for expanding it. This device, presented in his *Epistola de ignoto cantu*, was the system of solmization, using the syllables of the hymn *Ut queant laxis* as symbols of the pitches in a hexachord formed by adding one note at each end of the tetrachord of the Finales.[80] As shown in example 6.22, each phrase of the hymn starts on a successively higher degree of the scale, matching the syllables Ut, Re, Mi, Fa, Sol, and La with the notes *C, D, E, F, G,* and *a* of the system.

In conjunction with Guido's theory of the affinities, the system of hexachords would quickly become an important tool for teaching the system itself and for teaching the important technique of transposition. Coupled with another device, the so-called Guidonian hand,[81] the theory of hexachords quickly expanded to encompass the entire system and to make necessary the intercalation of an additional note, *ee*, at the top. By the twelfth century, the standard system could be diagrammed as an interlocked array of seven hexachords, all with the same intervallic structure, but with different names (ex. 6.23).

The natural hexachord was that on *C*. The "durum" hexachord had a ♮ as the syllable Mi, the "molle" hexachord a ♭ as the syllable Fa. Each pitch in the system

79. Guido's establishment of the combined Greater and Lesser Perfect Systems as standard in his works also made an impact on his treatment of polyphony. Whereas the *Musica* and *Scolica enchiriadis* had to introduce a system change in order to rationalize parallel organum at the octave, and had to introduce oblique motion in order to avoid the tritone in organum at the fourth, parallel organum—at both of these intervals—is unproblematic for Guido. (See chaps. 18 and 19 of his work and chaps. 10 and 13 of the *Musica enchiriadis*; see chapter 3 here, notes 123–26, and the associated discussion). Organum at the fifth, the only interval at which parallel organum was unproblematic in the *enchiriadis* treatises, is expressly forbidden by Guido (*semitonium et diapente non admittimus*, Smits van Waesberghe, ed., *CSM* 4, 201). Although he, too, says that the organal voice should not descend below the tritus (=tetrardus in the Dasia tone-system) in approaching a cadence, his proscription was not made in order to avoid the tritone; rather, Guido seems to advocate the rule for aesthetic reasons.

80. *GS* 2: 45a; Pesce, *Guido d'Arezzo's Regule rithmice*, 466; Strunk, *Source Readings in Music History*, 124; McKinnon, *The Early Christian Period and the Latin Middle Ages*, 106. On solmization and the hexachord, see Allaire, *The Theory of Hexachords*; Bent, "Musica recta and musica ficta"; Bent, "Diatonic Ficta"; and Berger, *Musica Ficta*. On the formation of the hexachord and its importance as a conceptual mechanism, see Crocker, "Hermann's Major Sixth."

81. The "Guidonian" hand does not appear in any of the authentic works of Guido, but it may derive from his teaching. It is based on the ancient practice of using the hand for didactic purposes, particularly the teaching of arithmetic. See Smits van Waesberghe, *Musikerziehung*, 23–24 and plts. 57–84; Russell, "A Poetic Key to a Pre-Guidonian Hand and the Echemata"; Berger, "The Hand and the Art of Memory"; and Berger, *Musica Ficta*, 2–55.

EXAMPLE 6.22.   "Ut queant laxis," as
presented in Guido, *Epistola de ignoto cantu*
(Smits van Waesberghe, *Musikerziehung*, 112)

could then be precisely located with from one to three hexachordal syllables (e.g.:
Γ-ut, C-fa-ut, G-sol-re-ut). In order to move from one hexachord to another, the
singer simply substituted the syllable in the target hexachord corresponding to the
same position or *locus* in the home tetrachord in a process known as "mutation."
This process itself was facilitated by use of the "Guidonian" hand, on which the
pitches of the entire tone-system could be located, each with its appropriate hexachordal syllables (fig. 6.1). Thus, the system itself came to be referred to as "the

EXAMPLE 6.23.   Hexachords of the "standard" system (Smits van Waesberghe,
Musikerziehung, 117)

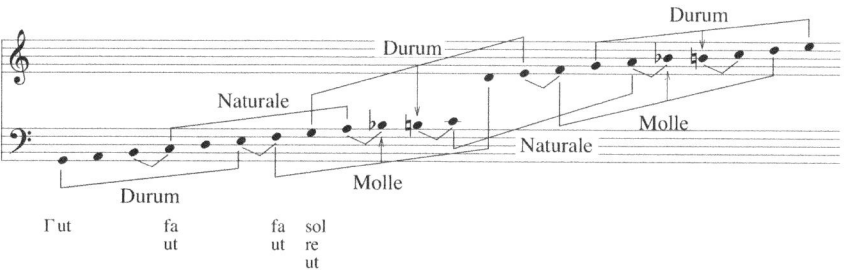

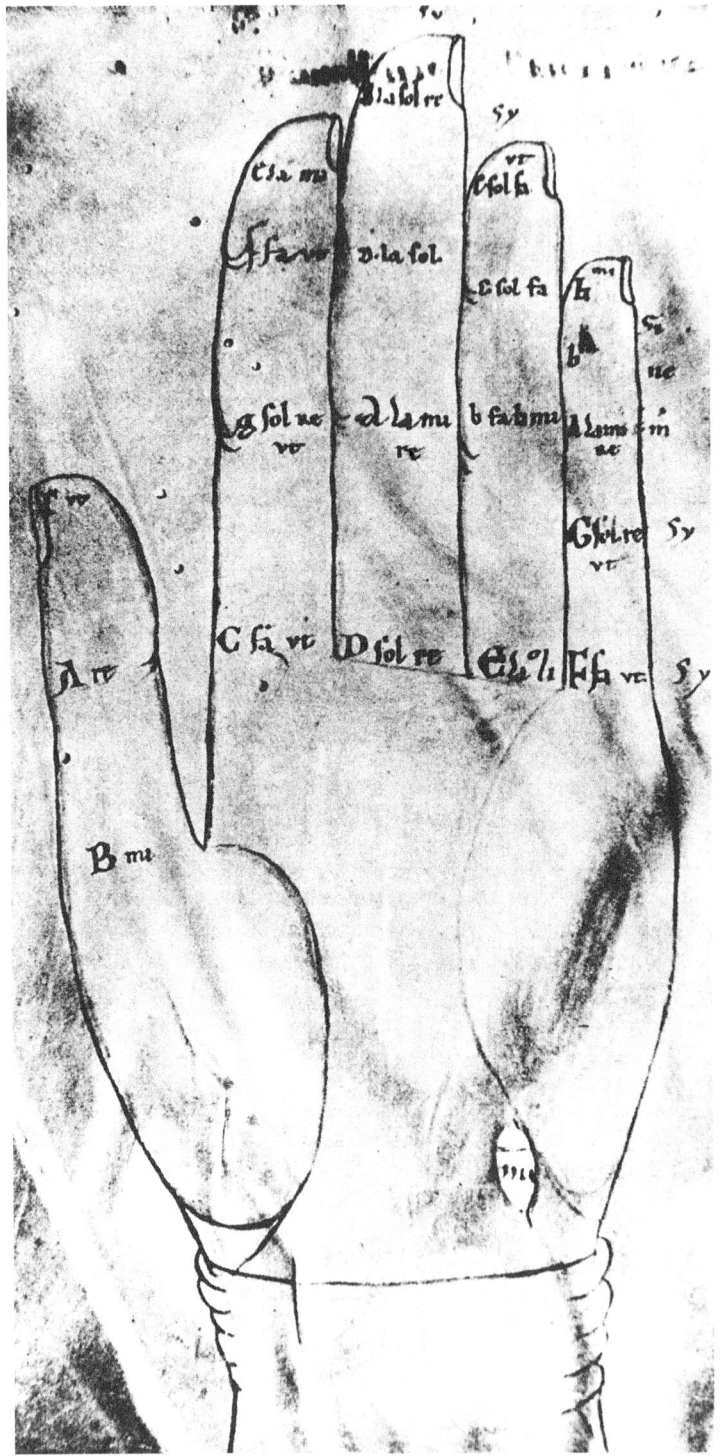

FIGURE 6.1. The "Guidonian" hand in Rochester ML92 1200, fol. 93v (reproduced by courtesy of the Sibley Music Library Eastman School of Music, University of Rochester)

hand." Notes lying outside the system would be referred to as lying "outside the hand."[82]

Let me conclude this chapter by mentioning one further innovation in the *Micrologus*. There Guido concludes his discussion of the church modes with what may well be the first description of the modes on the basis of musical style. He says, for example, that the authentic Deuterus is characterized by intermittent leaps; the plagal of the Tritus is "delightful"; "garrulousness" is the identifying trait of the authentic Tetrardus, "sweetness" that of the plagal Tetrardus, and so forth.[83] Guido's descriptions of modal traits may have been inspired by the characterizations of the ancient Greek modes in Boethius and other writers, but they do not represent a slavish copying of earlier characteristics. Although they offer little concrete information in themselves, these brief descriptions became the starting point for subsequent characterizations that would offer more telling information about the modes as melodic categories.[84] Especially important in this respect is the treatise of a certain Johannes (ca. 1100), who provides a new set of descriptions for the church modes that go beyond Guido's in providing hints of genuine musical qualities.[85] His work, drawing as it does on that of Guido and several other authors I have discussed, will form an appropriate beginning for the epilogue of this study.

82. See Berger, *Musica Ficta*, 12–55, for a discussion and survey of sources.

83. "Unus autenti deuteri fractis saltibus delectetur, alius plagae triti eligat voluptatem, uni tetrardi autenti garrulitas magis placet, alter eiusdem plagae suavitatem probat; sic et de reliquis" (Smits van Waesberghe, ed., *CSM* 4, 159).

84. See *Frutolf of Michaelsberg: Breviarium de musica et tonarius*, ed. Vivell, 104; Smits van Waesberghe, ed., *Johannes Affligemensis: De musica cum tonario, CSM* 1: 109; *Guidonis Augensis Regulae de arte musica*, ed. C. Maître, 164–65, and *CS* 2: 169b; Robert-Tissot, ed., *Johannes Aegidius de Zamora, CSM* 20, 100–104; Pseudo-Johannes de Muris, *Summa musicae, GS* 3: 235, and ed. Page, 195–98; Adam von Fulda, *Musica, GS* 3: 356.

85. This author, known variously as Johannes Cotto or Johannes Affligemensis, says that "slow and ceremonious peregrinations" characterize the first *modus*; "severe and almost haughty prancing" the third; a "sudden fall to the final" the fifth; and "spectacular leaps" the seventh ("Alios namque morosa et curialis vagatio primi delectat, alios rauca secundi gravitas capit, alios severa et quasi indignans tertii persultatio iuvat, alios adulatorius quarti sonus attrahit, alii modesta quinti petulantia ac subitaneo ad finalem casu moventur, alii lacrimosa sexti voce mulcentur, alii mimicos septimi saltus libenter audiunt, alii decentem et quasi matronalem octavi canorem diligunt" (Smits van Waesberghe, ed., *CSM* 1: 109).

EPILOGUE

Chapter 6 concluded with a discussion of treatises by Pseudo-Odo and Guido d'Arezzo that were distinguished by their use of a tone-system that began on a low gamma ("gamma-ut" in Guidonian terms) and that included only one accidental, the $b^\flat$ in the middle of the scale. Described in another way, this was the ancient Greek *ametabolon systema*, extended downward to low Γ by Pseudo-Odo and upward to *dd* by Guido. That scale had been set out in both treatises via one or more monochord divisions; it enabled the reader to translate the mathematical proportions of the scale into sounding reality. In Guido's *Prologus in antiphonarium,* the scale itself was linked directly to a system of practical musical notation that preserved its tonal architecture. With its system of clefs and lines that rendered the intervals of the music in precisely measured tones and semitones, musical notation in the West, as we have seen, became fully diastematic for the first time.

As the discussion of Pseudo-Odo and Guido intimated, however, the tone-system presented in their treatises, firmly rooted, as it was, in Greek Antiquity, was in fact *not* ideally suited for the notation of the repertoire of plainchant. (To use later terminology, there were in the chant repertoire several notes lying "outside the hand.") Ironically, the fact that a portion of the chant repertoire would not easily fit any fixed tone-system had been obvious even to the author of the *Scolica enchiriadis* in the ninth century. His response to the situation, as we saw earlier, was the set of *vitia* that made possible alterations in the intervallic structure of the fundamental tone-system he used. By making use of the *vitia* one could accommodate an $E^\flat$ below the final of F in a chant such as *Domine, qui operati sunt,* to use Pseudo-Odo's example, or both an $E^\flat$ and a low $B^\flat$, as in *Haec dies,* quite easily. (It should be remembered that the low gamma that Pseudo-Odo had to add to the system in order to permit the notation of Protus plagal chants was already an integral part of the tone system presented in the *Musica enchiriadis.*) This kind of flexibility, however, was not present in the extended Greek Greater and Lesser Perfect Systems presented by Pseudo-Odo that became the standard tone-system for both the theory and notation of Western music in the eleventh century. As later authors such as Bern of Reichenau and Johannes Cotto make especially clear, the incongruities between the flexibility inherent in the body of plainchant itself and the relative inflexibility of the ancient Greek system as a notational matrix came increasingly to be perceived as a problem that had to be solved. As a consequence, later authors developed their own solutions to the difficulties of rationalizing and notating problematic melodies.

I should like to conclude this study by looking at three different approaches to this problem, those of Johannes (dictus Cotto vel Affligemensis), Marchetto da Padova, and the first treatise in the Berkeley manuscript ("Quoniam in antelapsis temporibus"). The three are linked together by the fact that they all respond to the problem as it is manifested in the Communion *Beatus servus*. Hence, that chant will serve as a kind of "rondo theme" for this chapter.

Beatus servus is a demonstrably early chant, appearing as the Communion for the feast of St. Silvester in all but two graduals in the *Antiphonale Missarum Sextuplex*.[1] (It is lacking only in the Monza and Rheinau graduals.) The earliest tonaries are unanimous in classifying the chant in the Deuterus authentic mode, and they provide no indication that it was in any way unusual. Discussion of *Beatus servus* is conspicuously absent in ninth- and tenth-century music treatises, such as the *Musica disciplina* of Aurelian, the *Musica* and *Scolica enchiriadis*, the *De harmonica institutione* of Hucbald, or any of the treatises of the *Alia musica*. (The only reference to the Communion in the *Alia musica* is a single listing of it among chants in Deuterus authentus.) Furthermore, *Beatus servus* is not included by Regino of Prüm among those irregular chants he calls "nothae," nor does it appear in any of the ninth- and tenth-century treatises discussing the *parapteres* or *medii toni*.[2]

It is in the ninth chapter of the *Prologus in tonarium* of Bern of Reichenau, which dates from the first half of the eleventh century, that we find for the first time an extensive discussion of the necessity of transposing certain kinds of chants.[3] The third and fourth modes, in particular, offer several examples of these problematic chants. As one can see in example E.1, Bern says of the fourth-mode antiphons *Factus sum, O mors ero, Syon renovaberis, Syon noli*, and *Vade iam* "If you wish to begin these antiphons in the third place from the final, that is, from the lichanos meson [G], you will fail in singing [them] because you will not find the semitone where it ought to be." He concludes the paragraph by saying "The same defect of the neumes will appear in the communion *Beatus servus*, which is in the third mode, unless it be transposed from the hypate meson [E] to the mese [a]." I have provided a version of *Beatus servus*, "transposed from the hypate meson [E] to the mese [a]," immediately below Bern's text.

I believe it is no accident that *Beatus servus* and many chants like it were perceived as problematic for the first time in the eleventh century. As a glance at example E.2 will show, there is nothing particularly unusual about the melodic duc-

---

1. Hesbert, ed., *Antiphonale missarum sextuplex*, 16b, pp. 22–23. In addition to the Mass for Pope Silvester, 16b, the chant appears in Masses 129b (Simplicius et Soc.), 139 (S. Eusebius), 141 (Laurentius), 142b (Agapitus), 158 (Marcus), 166 (Clementis), 171 (Nat. Pont.), and 171 *ter* (Nat. Pont.).

2. A list of the chants so classified appears in Atkinson, "The *Parapteres: Nothi* or Not?" 34–37.

3. Ed. *GS* 2: 74a–76b (where it is numbered as chap. 11); and Rausch, ed., *Die Musiktraktate des Abtes Bern von Reichenau*, 55–61. See chapter 4 here, figs. 4.1 and 4.2, and chapter 6 here, notes 69–72, and the associated discussion.

EXAMPLE E.1.   Bern of Reichenau, *Prologus in Tonarium*, chap. 9 (Rausch, ed.,
Die Musiktraktate des Abtes Bern von Reichenau, 57–59)

> Ut enim hoc clarius elucescat, ex quarto tono ponamus haec sub exemplo: *A. Factus
> sum, A. O mors ero, A. Syon renovaberis, A. Syon noli, A. Vade iam.* Si has antiphonas tertio a
> finali loco idest a lychanos meson incipere volueris, in modulando deficis, dum semito-
> nium, ubi esse debuit, minime repperis . . .
> Idem neumarum defectus in illa communione *Beatus servus,* quae est tertii toni, prove-
> niet, nisi ab ypate meson [*E*] transposita in mese [*a*] fuerit.

tus of either the intonation or the final cadence of the chant that would prevent it
from being classified in the Deuterus authentus by Aurelian or Regino. It is only in
the middle of the chant, at the words *invenerit vigilantem. Amen dico vobis,* that one
encounters a "problem." The interval that had been a semitone above the final is
now a full tone. If one tries to notate it at its proper modal position on the scale set
out by Pseudo-Odo, Guido, Bern, or the manuscript Montpellier 159, one will indeed "not find the semitone where it ought to be"—just as Bern suggests.

We have already seen what Bern's solution to this problem was. He says that

EXAMPLE E.2.   *Beatus servus* in its proper modal position

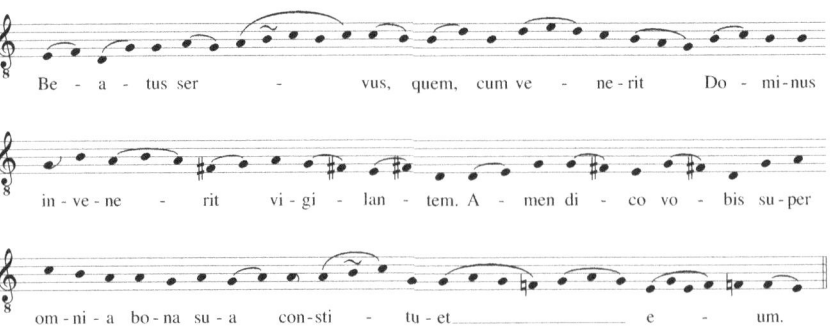

one should transpose the chant from the hypate meson (*E*) to the mese (*a*). As was shown in chapter 4, the same solution was adopted for the manuscript Montpellier 159, which could notate the transposed *F* and *F♯*, respectively, as I and I inclined (i.e., *b* and *b♭*). Let us now see what other solutions were offered by post-tenth-century authors.

Writing about 1100, Johannes Cotto/Affligemensis (whom I shall designate hereafter simply as "John)" offered not one but several alternative solutions for the notation of *Beatus servus*.[4] John employs the same tone-system as does Guido, extending from gamma up to *dd*. Moreover, he also takes over Guido's second monochord division as a means of converting the structure of the scale itself into sound.[5] The importance of both the scale and monochord division is emphasized by the very first sentence of the treatise, which is a virtual paraphrase of the first sentence of Guido's *Micrologus*:

> First we enjoin him who wishes to prepare himself for training in music that he zealously master the letters of the monochord and the syllables written above them, and not stop this task before he has them by memory.[6]

As this passage also suggests, the syllables of the hexachords, which are firmly linked to the diatonic scale, are likewise an important element of the definition of the scale itself.

Parallels with the *Micrologus* are not limited to the first sentence. Indeed, in its treatment of tone-system, mode, and notation, John's treatise is heavily indebted to Guido and, to a lesser extent, to Pseudo-Odo. The ranges, *initia*, and *distinctiones* of the *modi* for John are essentially the same as Guido's, as is his presentation of the *affines* for Protus (*D-a*), Deuterus (*E-♮*), and Tritus (*F-c*). His discussion of tessitura as a guide to ambiguous chants, moreover, is drawn directly from Pseudo-Odo. In another parallel with Pseudo-Odo, John points out the necessity of having the low gamma in order to accommodate passages from chants in the second mode, such as *Spiritum veritatis*, from the antiphon *O rex gloriae*.[7]

John does go beyond his predecessors, however, in three areas. First, in accord with the new hermeneutic methods and interests of the high Middle Ages, he is one of the earliest writers to attempt an etymological and historical treatment of the

---

4. For an edition of John's *De musica*, see Smits van Waesberghe, ed., *Johannes dictus Cotto vel Affligemensis: De musica cum tonario*. Huglo, "L'Auteur du traité de musique dedié à Fulgence d'Affligem," has shown that the author was probably from southern Germany, since he shows intimate familiarity with the chant dialect of Reichenau and St. Gall and such innovations as the didactic verses of Hermannus Contractus, found among writings from those two centers. The work was written, however, at the request of Fulgentius, abbot of Afflighem from 1098, and was completed before his death in 1122. See also the discussion and bibliography in Palisca's introduction to the treatise in Babb and Palisca, *Hucbald, Guido, and John on Music*, 87–100.

5. See chapter 6 here, note 45, for information on this monochord division.

6. "Primum hoc illi, qui se ad musicae disciplinam aptare desiderat, iniungimus, uti litteras monochordi cum syllabis suprascriptis firmare studeat, nec antequam eas memoriter teneat, ab hoc opere desistat" (*De musica*, chap. 1, ed. Smits van Waesberghe, 49; transl. Babb and Palisca, *Hucbald, Guido, and John on Music*, 103).

7. *De musica*, chap. 5, ed. Smits van Waesberghe, 60; transl. Babb and Palisca, *Hucbald, Guido, and John on Music*, 107–8.

term *modus*. In a misguided attempt at etymology that several subsequent authors would nonetheless take up, he derives the term *modus* from *moderando* or *modulando*, because chant is governed (*moderatur*) or composed (*modulatur*) through them.[8] He then says "Those things that we name 'modes' or 'tropes,' the Greeks call 'phthongi.'"[9] This seems to hark back to the *Musica enchiriadis*, where the four *soni* governing the tones or modes were designated with the Greek term *phthongi*, but John gives no further explanation.[10] He then discusses the similarities between the *toni* of plainchant and the *toni* or accents of prosody as discussed by Donatus, pointing out that the chant modes move among the hexachords of the graves, finales, and acuti, each of which corresponds to one of the *varietates* of prosodic accent (*gravis, circumflexus, acutus*) and to one of the *distinctiones* (*colon, comma, periodus*).[11] Having recognized this, he also acknowledges—for the first time since the ninth century— that "modes are not altogether wrongly called tones."[12] John then proceeds to give a short course in the history of the modes, saying that there were at first four, and that they were later divided into eight, with an authentic and a plagal mode built on each of four finals, protus, deuterus, tritus, and tetrardus.[13]

A second innovation of John's treatise is that he integrates the psalm-tone tenor fully into the theory of mode.[14] This occurs in chapter 11 of his treatise, "On the Tenors of the Modes and their Finals."[15] He points out that the tenor is the first note of the *seculorum Amen*, that these tenors occur on four different degrees (*F, a, c,* and *d*), and that there can be three church modes holding one tenor (e.g., *a* as the tenor for first, fourth, and sixth).[16] In conjunction with his discussion of the tenors,

8. "Modi a moderando sive modulando vocati sunt, quia videlicet per eos cantus moderatur id est regitur, vel modulatur id est componitur" (*De musica*, chap. 10, ed. Smits van Waesberghe, 77). See the so-called Schneider Anonymous (second half of the twelfth century), discussed in Schneider, "Primum tractatum huius voluminis de symphonia," in *Geschichte der Mehrstimmigkeit*, 107; *De musica* of Jerome of Moravia (second half of the thirteenth century), ed. Cserba, 152; and Jacques de Liège, *Speculum musicae* (ca. 1325), *CSM* 3, Book VI, chap. 35, p. 87. On the relationships between John's treatise and those of several later writers, see Smits van Waesberghe, "Some Music Treatises and their Interrelation." On his treatment of the term *modus*, see Atkinson, "Modus," *HmT,* sec. V. (I) (1).

9. "Quos autem nos modos vel tropos nominamus, Graeci phtongos vocant" (*De musica*, chap. 10, ed. Smits van Waesberghe, 77).

10. On this, see Atkinson, "Modus," *HmT,* sec. V. (I) (1).

11. "Vel certe toni dicuntur ad similitudinem tonorum, quos Donatus distinctiones vocat; sicut enim in prosa tres considerantur distinctiones, quae et pausationes appellari possunt, scilicet colon id est membrum, comma incisio, periodus clausura sive circuitus, ita et in cantu" (*De musica*, chap. 10, ed. Smits van Waesberghe, 79). See Reckow, "Aspekte der Ausbildung einer lateinischen musikalischen Fachsprache im Mittelalter," 615; Atkinson, "*Tònus* in the Carolingian Era"; and the discussion in chapter 3 here, pp. 102–13.

12. On this, see chapter 3 here, pp. 124–27; and Atkinson, "Modus," *HmT,* sec. V. (I) (1). John's words are echoed by Jacques de Liège, *Speculum musicae*, ed. in *CSM* 3, Book VI, chap. 35, p. 87.

13. On this first medieval history of the church modes, see Atkinson, "Johannes Affligemensis as a Historian of Mode."

14. As the discussion of tonaries in chapter 3 here shows, this had been implicit in *cantus* theory since the early ninth century, if not earlier.

15. "De tenoribus modorum et finalibus eorum" (*De musica,* chap. 11, ed. Smits van Waesberghe, 77). Interesting from a terminological standpoint is that John then uses *tonus,* or even *tropus,* to refer to the church modes.

16. See Schneider Anonymous, ed. Schneider, in *Geschichte der Mehrstimmigkeit*, 110; Jacques de Liège, *Speculum musicae*, ed. *CSM* 3, Book VI, chap. 79, p. 225; and the *Tractatus de natura et distinctione octo tonorum musice,* ed. in *CS* 2: 450.

John presents in order the starting tones for the psalm tones and the model melodies ("Primum quaerite regnum Dei," etc.), and he concludes with the identifying letters (a, or first; e, or second; i, or third; etc.) found in certain medieval manuscripts as designations of mode.[17]

As mentioned at the end of chapter 6, a third area where John presents important new information is in his discussions of the character of the modes. He provides a new set of descriptions for the *modi* that, in some instances, give hints of genuine musical qualities. He says, for example, that "slow and ceremonious peregrinations" characterize the first mode; "severe and almost haughty prancing" the third; a "sudden fall to the final" the fifth; and "spectacular leaps" the seventh.[18] Several later authors either copy or paraphrase John's descriptions, illustrating them with appropriate examples from the chant repertoire.[19]

The preceding discussion shows that John's treatment of the modes is a kind of summary of modal theory and practice to his time, even going so far as to provide a history and etymology for *modus*. The fact that his technical descriptions of the modes do not surpass anything found in earlier theorists, along with his statement that the *modi* had "not altogether incorrectly" been labeled *toni*, actually signals the end of what might be called the "classic" phase of the theory of the church modes.

For the concerns inherent in this study, however, perhaps the most important aspect of John's treatise is his commentary on individual chants. In these he shows himself to be not only an astute observer of the practices of his time but also well aware of the commentaries of several of his predecessors—particularly those of Pseudo-Odo and Guido.

An example of that awareness is John's commentary on the classification of chants according to their accepted ranges (chap. 12). For him, the authentic modes can ascend an octave above their finals, and "by license" a ninth or tenth, and can descend to the subfinalis; the plagals ascend a fifth or sixth above their finals and a fourth or fifth below. Realizing that there are certain chants that do not correspond

17. These letters, found in several manuscripts from St. Gall and southern Germany (among them the "Hartker Codex," St. Gall 390–91), are also discussed by the Schneider Anonymous, ed. Schneider, *Geschichte der Mehrstimmigkeit*, 108; and Jacques de Liège, *Speculum musicae*, ed. *CSM* 3, Book VI, chap. 82, p. 230. See also Wagner, *Einführung in die gregorianischen Melodien*, vol. 2, *Neumenkunde*, 248.

18. "Alios namque morosa et curialis vagatio primi delectat, alios rauca secundi gravitas capit, alios severa et quasi indignans tertii persultatio iuvat, alios adulatorius quarti sonus attrahit, alii modesta quinti petulantia ac subitaneo ad finalem casu moventur, alii lacrimosa sexti voce mulcentur, alii mimicos septimi saltus libenter audiunt, alii decentem et quasi matronalem octavi canorem diligunt" (ed. Smits van Waesberghe, 109; transl. in Babb and Palisca, *Hucbald, Guido, and John on Music*, 133). See the paraphrased versions in Schneider Anonymous, ed. Schneider, *Geschichte der Mehrstimmigkeit*, 109; the *Summa musicae*, attributed to Johannes de Muris, ed., *GS* 3: 235–37, ed. Page, 195–97); and the *Cantuagium* of Heinrich Eger von Kalkar, ed. Hüschen, 47–48. See also Johannes Aegidius de Zamora, *Ars musica*, chap. 15, ed. Robert-Tissot, *CSM* 20, 100–104; Jacques de Liège, *Speculum musicae*, chap. 6, ed. *CSM* 3, 214–16; and *Cujusdam Carthusiensis monachi tractatus de musica*, chap. 8, ed. *CS* 2: 448.

19. In his paraphrase of John's descriptions (see the preceding note), Heinrich Eger mentions *O pastor aeterne* and *Gloria tibi trinitas* as examples of the characteristics of the first mode; for the third mode, he names *Angelus domini*; for the fifth, he mentions the Marian antiphon *Alma redemptoris mater;* as examples of the "spectacular leaps" of the seventh mode, he gives the antiphons *In civitate domini* and *Assumpta est Maria* (*Cantuagium*, ed. Hüschen, 47–48).

EXAMPLE E.3.   *Deus omnium exauditor est* in John, *De musica*, chap. 12 (Babb and Palisca, *Hucbald, Guido, and John on Music*, 123)

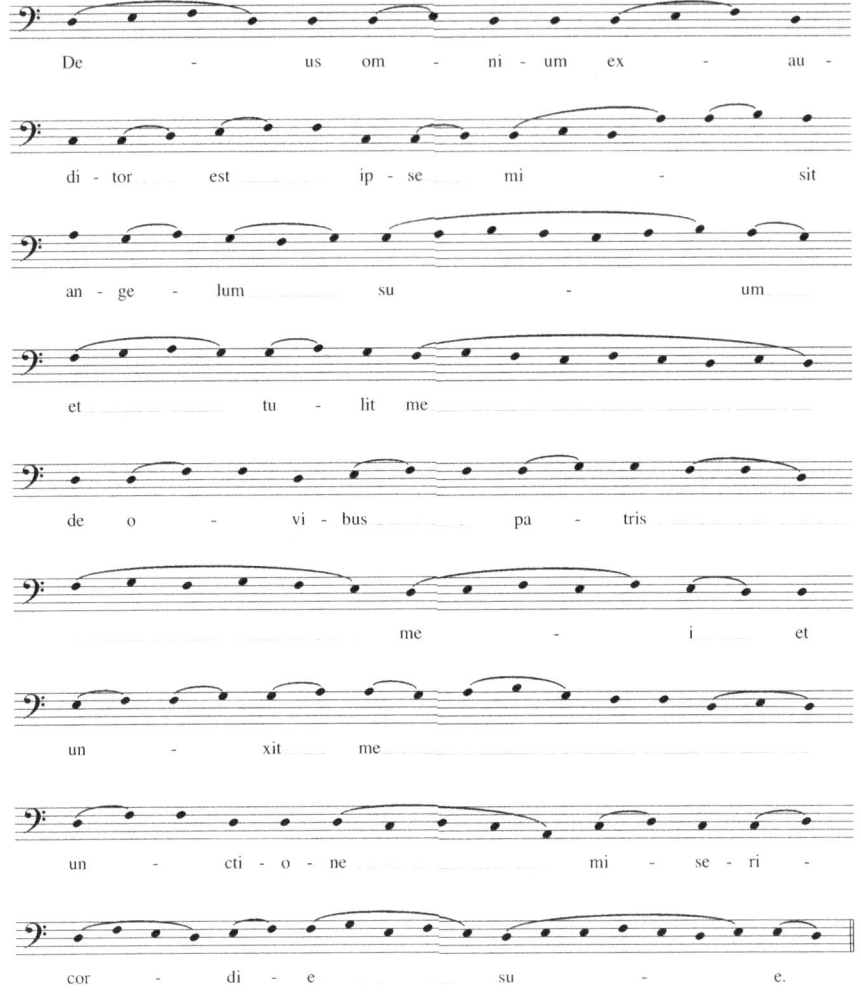

to his descriptions, John invokes Pseudo-Odo's "rule of tessitura" in order to make a distinction between authentic and plagal.

John mentions that "Odo, who was most experienced in this art" had said that "a chant that ascends to a fifth above the final and touches it three or four times should be assigned to the authentic." Although Pseudo-Odo had not given examples of this, John provides two of them, one of which is the Protus respond *Deus omnium exauditor est* (ex. E.3). He says that despite the fact that it descends to low *A* on the word "unctione," it should be assigned to the authentic, rather than plagal,

EXAMPLE E.4.   The antiphon *Magnum hereditatis mysterium* transposed in order to avoid low B♭ in John, *De musica*, chap. 14 (Babb and Palisca, *Hucbald, Guido, and John on Music*, 128)

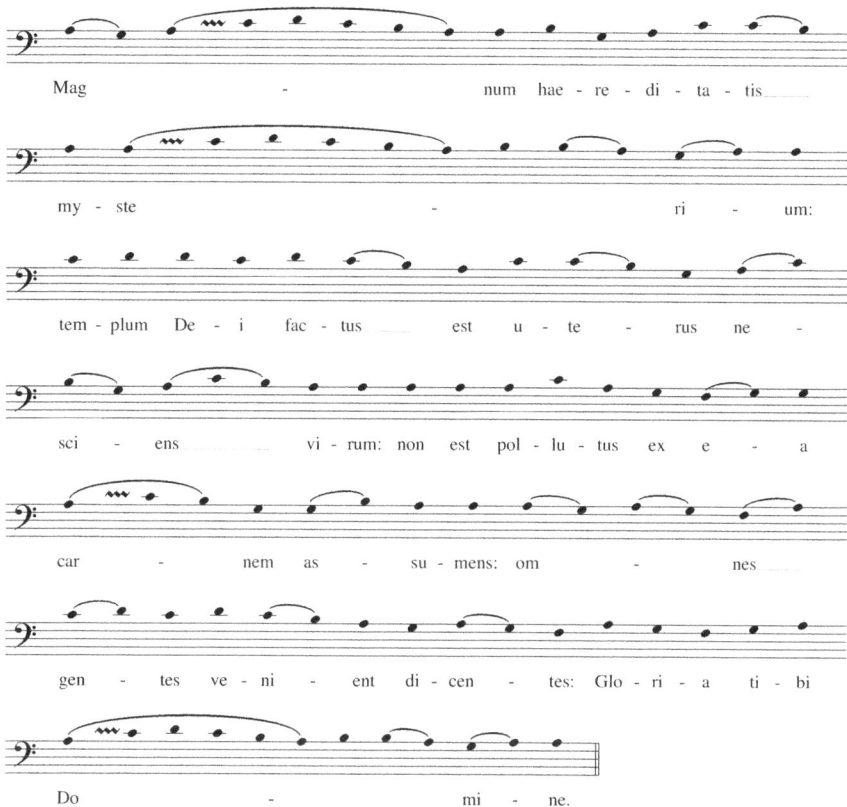

because it "moves about rather frequently among the higher notes" ("in superioribus frequentius versatur").[20]

In the course of my examination of Hucbald (ca. 900), I explained that certain chants might need to be ended on their alternative finals, or *socialitates*. Guido d'Arezzo, writing about one hundred years later, provided a thorough rationale for this subject in his treatment of the *affinitates*. John, too, addresses the problem in his fourteenth chapter, *Quid faciendum sit de cantu qui in proprio cursu deficit* ("What should be done concerning chant that is defective in its proper course"—see ex. E.4).[21]

He begins his discussion by referring to two examples, *Gaudendum est nobis* and *Magnum hereditatis mysterium*, about which he offers the following statement:

> The antiphon *Gaudendum est nobis*, although it is in the Protus, cannot be sung in its natural location because in certain places it demands, according to some, a whole tone

20. *De musica*, ed. Smits van Waesberghe, 92–93.
21. *De musica*, ed. Smits van Waesberghe, 101–3.

below parhypate hypaton, that is, low *C*, which is not there. Yet if begun on the mese, that is, *a*, it proceeds to this same *a* at the end without going astray. Thus, too, the antiphon *Magnum hereditatis mysterium*.[22]

As may be observed in example E. 4, the transposed *Magnum hereditatis mysterium* contains *F*'s, which would become *B*-flats—a whole tone beneath the parhypate hypaton—if the chant were transposed back down to a final on *D*.

Interestingly enough, John goes even farther than had Guido in blaming singers for the "defects" found in such chants. In John's chapter 15, *Quod stultorum ignorantia saepe cantum depravet* (How the ignorance of fools often corrupts the chant), he first says "We are not sure whether the fact that these and other such chants cannot be sung in their proper course results from the fault of singers or whether they were thus issued by composers in the first place." He seems to decide against the singers, however, when in the next sentence he says "we do know most assuredly that a chant is oftentimes distorted by the ignorance of men, so that we could now enumerate many corrupted ones."[23] Ultimately, whether it be the fault of composer or singer, John's solution for a "corrupted" chant is either to transpose or to emend it so that it can be sung to the monochord.[24]

In chapter 21, *Quid utilitatis afferant neumae a Guidone inventae* (Of what use the neumes are that Guido invented),[25] John points out that where the chant is written with ordinary neumes, the intervals cannot be ascertained, and many errors can creep in as a result. Guidonian neumes, however, "indicate all the intervals unambiguously" ("omnia intervalla distincte demonstrent").[26] His example for both the problem and its solutions is the Communion *Beatus servus*.

As pointed out in chapter 3, and as shown again in example E.2, if it is notated at its proper pitch level on *E*, *Beatus servus* requires the use of both *F*-naturals and *F*-sharps. John provides three different solutions to the notation of the chant using Guidonian neumes. Two of them involve the technique of partial transposition, as it is presented in chapter 8 of Guido's *Micrologus*.[27] The first of these, taken from the

---

22. "Antiphona ista *Gaudendum est nobis*, cum sit proti, in loco suo cantari non potest, quia in quibusdam locis sub parhypate hypaton id est .C. gravi secundum quosdam tonum requirit, qui ibi non est, ceterum in mese id est .a. incepta absque errore ad eandem .a. in fine deducitur. Similiter et ista antiphona *Magnum hereditatis mysterium*" (*De musica*, chap. 14, ed. Smith van Waesberghe, 102; transl. Babb and Palisca, *Hucbald, Guido, and John on Music*, 127–28).

23. "Quod autem illa et alia istiusmodi in proprio cursu cantari nequeunt, utrum ex cantorum vitio processerit, an sic a modulante primum prolata fuerint, incertum habemus. Ceterum hoc certissime novimus, quod per quorundam ignorantiam multoties cantus depravatur, quemadmodum iam plures habemus depravatos quam enumerare possimus" (*De musica*, chap. 14, ed. Smits van Waesberghe, 104; transl. Babb and Palisca, *Hucbald, Guido, and John on Music*, 129–30).

24. The case for this is made most strongly in chap. 22, "On rejecting corrupt usage," where John urges that doing so will create an agreement that will be pleasing to God. The chapter concludes with a discussion of the antiphon *Facti sumus*, which, in his view, cannot be "sung to the monochord" with the differentia that is customarily joined to it: "Haec enim adeo perversa est, ut cum saeculorum amen quod ei adaptari solet in monochordo, nullatenus cantari valeat" (*De musica*, ed. Smits van Waesberghe, 155; transl. Babb and Palisca, *Hucbald, Guido, and John on Music*, 158). The Cistercians would eventually make John's view of the corruption of chant official policy (see the excursus below, pp. 244–45).

25. *De musica*, ed. Smits van Waesberghe, 133–41.

26. *De musica*, ed. Smits van Waesberghe, 133; transl. Babb and Palisca, *Hucbald, Guido, and John on Music*, p. 147.

27. See chapter 6 here, pp. 227–28.

EXAMPLE E.5. *Beatus servus* in Pistoia 121, fol. 86v (John's first solution)

Hunc autem quidam sic corrigunt, quod *Dominus* a trite diezeugmenon in mese cadere faciunt, et *invenerit* in parhypate meson incipiunt et *super omnia* in lichanos meson.

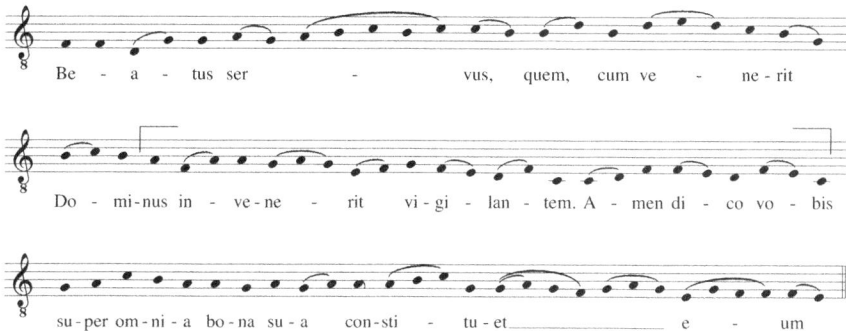

manuscript Pistoia 121, appears in example E.5 along with John's description. In his words: "Some correct it thus: they make *Dominus* fall from the trite diezeugmenon [c] to the mese [a], and they begin *invenerit* on the parhypate meson [F] and *super omnia* on the lichanos meson [G]." A comparison of examples E.5 and E.2 shows that this method of correction causes the phrase *invenerit vigilantem. Amen, dico vobis* to be transposed downward by one step. Thus, the half step from F♯ to G is rendered in notation by the pitches E and F. Once the problematic F-sharps are out of the way, the piece continues at its original pitch level, starting at the phrase *super omnia*.

The second method of emendation John describes is illustrated by the version of *Beatus servus* in Graz 807, which appears in example E.6. Again in John's words:

EXAMPLE E.6. *Beatus servus* in Graz 807, fol. 22 (John's second solution)

Alii autem ita emendant quod *invenerit* iuxta usum incipiunt, et penultimam eius in mese inchoantes in lichanos meson emittunt, et ultimam in hypate meson incipientes in parhypate meson exire faciunt, *super omnia* secundum priores corrigunt.

EXAMPLE E.7.   *Beatus servus* in Padua 47, fol. 36v (John's third solution)

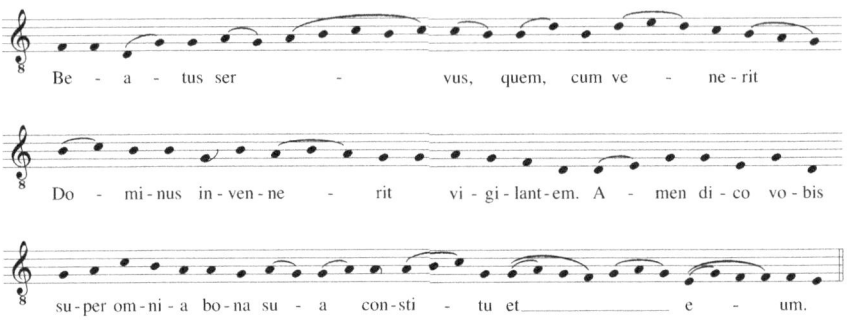

Mihi autem facilior correctio videtur, si ultima syllaba *invenerit* in lichanos meson per unisonum cantetur, quod et Guarino et Stephano in musica subtilibus placet.

Be - a - tus ser - vus, quem, cum ve - ne - rit

Do - mi - nus in - ven - ne - rit vi - gi - lant - em. A - men di - co vo - bis

su - per om - ni - a bo - na su - a con - sti - tu et _____ e - um.

Others so emend it that they begin *invenerit* as is the custom, but after beginning its penultimate [neume] on the mese [*a*] they end it on the lichanos meson [G]. Beginning its final [neume] [over "-rit" of *invenerit*] on the hypate meson [E], they make it end on the parhypate meson [F]. Then they correct *super omnia* in the same way as do the former.

Here, too, partial transposition downward by a step is the solution to notating the offending semitone.

As his third method of treating the semitone between F♯ and G, John offers perhaps the most drastic solution of all: simply leave it out (see ex. E.7). John says "It seems to me an easier correction if the last syllable of *invenerit* is sung to a unison on the lichanos meson [G], as pleases both Guarinus and Stephanus, who are musically discriminating." As example E.7 demonstrates, John's third method was employed in some practical sources. The version of *Beatus servus* in Padua 47 has two G's for the last syllable of *invenerit*, but it goes even beyond John's favored solution. It leaves the entire melody untransposed, but uses only F-naturals throughout—no F-sharps at all!—thereby obliterating one of the most distinctive features of the chant.[28] As the version of *Beatus servus* in Padua 47 shows, Pseudo-Odo's recommendation that "if it suits no mode, let it be emended according to the one with which it least disagrees" was taken quite literally by at least one medieval scribe or his master.

28. I should mention that despite the advocacy of such an approach by John and his "discriminating friends," Padua 47 is the only one of the practical sources I have seen that adopts this solution to the problem.

AN EXCURSUS ON THE CISTERCIAN REFORM
OF CHANT

That not just scribes and theorists but also theologians felt it necessary to emend the chant is made clear to us by a movement nearly contemporaneous with John, namely, the Cistercian reform of chant.[29] Until recently, it was rather common to criticize the early Cistercians for their revision—some would say distortion—of the "perfection" of Gregorian chant. Thanks to modern editions of several of the primary sources documenting the Cistercian reform, together with a number of studies of the reform itself, we are now able to view the Cistercians in a new light—one that shows them to have been among the most perceptive critics and analysts of plainchant in the twelfth and thirteenth centuries.[30] Chief among the Cistercian innovations were (1) the introduction of a new terminology for describing chant; (2) more precise characterizations of the musical traits of each mode than had been available theretofore; (3) a strict application of the principles of range and melodic ductus; and, concomitant with that, (4) a condemnation of the chants that did not follow these rules, together with the suggestion that they should be corrected in accord with them.[31]

A thorough consideration of the Cistercian reforms, of course, lies beyond the scope of this study. But it would also be out of place, for the factors motivating the Cistercians to emend the chant were rather different from those I have reported here.[32] The wide and excellent literature on the Cistercian reforms, to which I have alluded above, will surely facilitate continuing study of the nature of the Cistercian emendation of chant and of the underlying causes for it.[33]

———————

Let us now return to the "mainstream" of what might be called the "post-Boethian" phase of developments in the domain of tone-system, mode, and notation. I have

29. On the Cistercian reforms, associated most notably with Bernard of Clairvaux (1090–1152), see, in particular, Maître, *La Réforme cistercienne du plain-chant;* Sweeney, "The Musical Treatise Formerly Attributed to John Wylde and the Cistercian Chant Reform"; Veroli, "La revisione cisterciense del canto liturgico"; and Waddell, "The Origin and Early Evolution of the Cistercian Antiphonary." The classic study in this area is Marosszécki, "Les Origines du chant cistercien."

30. The principal documents of the reform are the prologue (*Bernardus humilis Abbas Clarevallis*) and preface (*Cantum quem Cisterciensis ordinis*) to the Cistercian antiphonal of 1147, along with the *Regule de arte musica,* a treatise by Guy d'Eu (Guido Augensis), who may well have written the preface, and a tonary, the *Tonale sancti Bernardi.* All are available in *PL* 182: cols. 1121–66. The prologue and preface have been edited by Guentner in *CSM* 24, and the *Regule* is available in a new edition by Maître (*La Réforme cistercienne du plain-chant*). The *Tonale* is available in *GS* 2: 265–67. In addition, a treatise and tonary attributed to John Wylde, *Musica manualis cum tonale* (post 1220), have been edited by Sweeney in *CSM* 28. Fuller, "An Anonymous Treatise dictus de Sancto Martiale," places the so-called St. Martial Organum Treatise within the tradition of Cistercian theory.

31. See Atkinson, "Modus," *HmT,* sec.V (II) (a–d), and review of *La Réforme cistercienne du plain-chant* by Claire Maître.

32. On the underlying reasons for the Cistercian reform, see, in particular, the history of the first and second reforms given by Maître in *La Réforme cistercienne,* 35–64.

33. In addition to the works cited in notes 29 and 30 here, the central literature on the Cistercian reform includes the facsimiles of the Cistercian temporale and sanctorale in Paris 1411 and Paris 1412,

already explained that both Bern of Reichenau and John Cotto offered rather extensive discussions concerning the notation of "problematic chants." Several of the chants John mentions, and indeed several of the same solutions to their notation, are used as examples of problematical chants in the *Lucidarium* of Marchetto da Padova, written around 1317–18.[34] At the same time, Marchetto follows in the tradition of the *Alia musica* and Bern of Reichenau in his application of species theory to the definition of mode, and in the level of refinement he brings to bear on it.

A strong link with *Alia musica* is established at the very beginning of Marchetto's treatment of the "*toni,* which are properly called *modi,*" in treatise 11 of his work.[35] Marchetto first cites Boethius in explaining that "a *tonus, tropus,* or *modus* is a system of pitches, disposed in all their orders, differing in highness or lowness."[36] He continues by saying that tropes are so called "because they are converted, that is, because one changes to another, as in mixed and mingled modes, for the Greek *tropos* is *conversio* in Latin."[37] This statement traces its lineage back to Author β of *Alia musica,* who said that "the Greek 'tropus' is called 'conversio' because one is converted into another."[38] The same author also said that "*modi* are so called because each of the *tropi* should maintain its own range [*modus*] and should not exceed its measure."[39] As I will show, this definition will play an important role in Marchetto's own treatment of the church modes.

Marchetto completes his introduction to the church modes by providing a brief history of them.[40] He says that there were originally four "modes, tropes, or tones" called Protus, Deuterus, Tritus, and Tetrardus, but because of the "incommodiousness" (*inconvenientia*) of their ascent and descent (up to a tenth above their finals, and down to a sixth below), the four were subdivided into eight, four authentic and four plagal. He names the normal finals, but then says that because of *accidentia* that occur in these modes, cofinals (*confinales*) had to be added.[41]

To begin his own treatment of mode, which he now designates *tonus,* Marchetto

---

ed. by Maître, and the extensive transcriptions and commentaries in Veroli, La revisione cisterciense del canto liturgico" and "La revisione musicale bernardina e il graduale cisterciense."

34. Ed. in GS 3: 65–121; and in Herlinger, *The Lucidarium of Marchetto of Padua.*

35. *Lucidarium,* ed. and transl. Herlinger, 370–518; GS 3: 101–17.

36. "Tonus, tropus, sive modus, secundum dicta Boetii, est constitutio vocum in totis vocum ordinibus, differens acumine ac etiam gravitate" (*Lucidarium,* Treatise 11, chap. 1, sec. 1, ed. Herlinger, 370–71; GS 3: 101. See Boethius, *De institutione musica,* Book IV, chap. 15). My translation is a slightly modified version of Herlinger's.

37. "Tropi [dicuntur] cum convertuntur, puta cum unus in alium transit, ut est mixtus vel commixtus, nam tropus grece, latine conversion" (*Lucidarium,* Treatise 11, chap. 1, sec. 6, ed. Herlinger, 370–71; GS 3: 101).

38. "Tropus de graeco in latinum conversio dicitur, idcirco quod, . . . alter in alterum convertitur" (*Alia musica,* ed. Chailley, 105, §13). See ex. 5.6 and the discussion associated with it. As mentioned there, the *Alia musica* marks the earliest appearance of this definition I have found.

39. "Modi etiam dicti sunt, eo quod unusquisque troporum proprium modum teneat nec mensuram excedat" (*Alia musica,* ed. Chailley, 105, §13).

40. *Lucidarium,* Treatise 11, chap. 2, secs. 1–19, ed. Herlinger, 372–77; GS 3: 101.

41. As Herlinger points out (*Lucidarium,* 377), it is clear that in Marchetto's view, the *accidentia* that caused certain chants to be transposed were chromatic inflections.

EXAMPLE E.8. Examples of *tonus perfectus* in Marchetto da Padova, *Lucidarium*, Treatise 11, chap. 2, secs. 21–25 (ed. Herlinger, 378–80)

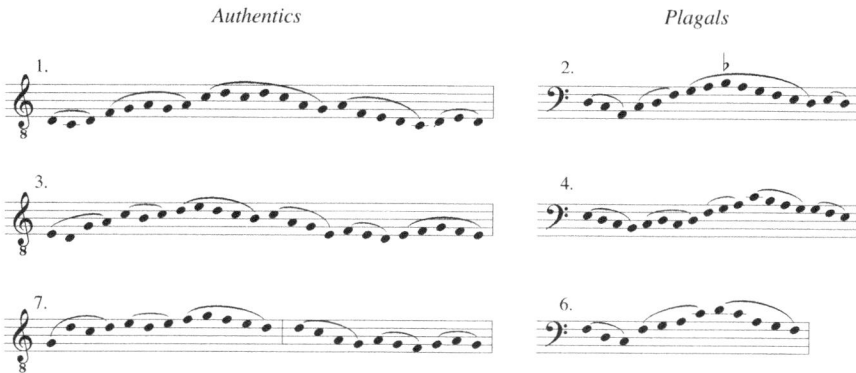

EXAMPLE E.9. Definition and examples of *tonus imperfectus* in Marchetto da Padova, *Lucidarium*, Treatise 11, chap. 2, sec. 26 (ed. Herlinger, 382)

> Tonus vero imperfectus, sive sit auctenticus sive sit plagalis, dicitur ille qui non implet modum suum, aut supra aut infra, modo superius declarato, ut hic:

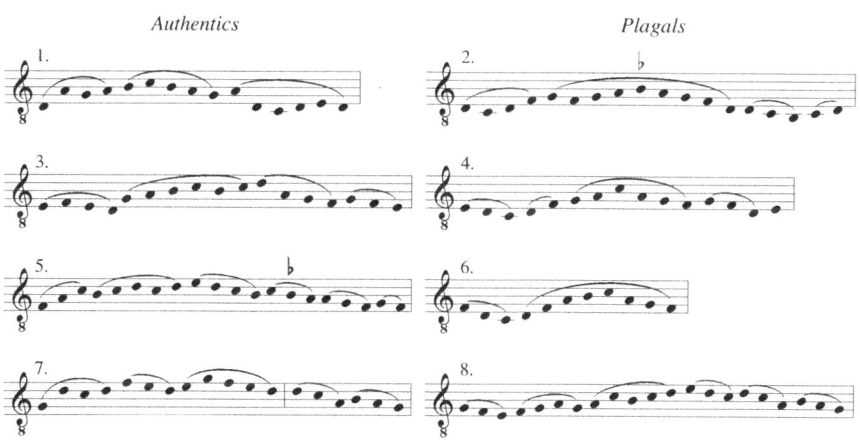

EXAMPLE E.10. Examples of *tonus mixtus* in Marchetto da Padova, *Lucidarium*, Treatise 11, chap. 2, secs. 31–33 (ed. Herlinger, 386–88)

> Tonus mixtus dicitur ille, si auctenticus est, qui plus quam unum tonum descendit a fine suo, tangens aliquid de sui plagalis descensu, ut hic:

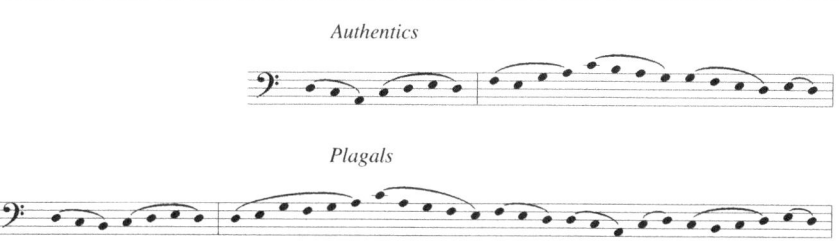

EXAMPLE E.11.   *Sint lumbi vestri*, cited in Marchetto da Padova,
Lucidarium, Treatise 11, chap. 3, Sects. 1–6 (ed. Herlinger, 390–92)

Sint   lumbi   vestri precin   ti   Vigilate   ergo

sets out five categories: perfect, imperfect, plusquamperfect, mixed, and mingled.[42]
These *toni* are then defined on the basis of *modus*— that is, range or ambitus—echoing Author δ's final definition of *modus* in the *Alia musica* (see above). Of the first
category, for example, he says: "That *tonus* is called perfect which fills its range
(*modus*) both above and below [the final]."[43] For the authentic tones or modes,
"filling its range" means ascending an octave above the final and descending a tone
below it; for the plagals, it implies ascending to the sixth above the final and the
fourth below.[44] (Illustrations of these are given in ex. E.8.)

Imperfect tones, in either authentic or plagal, are those that do not fill out their
range. Marchetto's description, as well as illustrations of the first four imperfect
tones, are given in example E.9. The tones called plusquamperfectus are authentics
that ascend beyond an octave and plagals that descend below a fourth from their respective finals. The *toni mixti* are authentics that descend more than one whole tone
beneath their finals and plagals that ascend beyond a sixth above their finals (ex.
E.10). He says that there are other categories as well, but that they are based on features other than range and thus will be discussed later.

After having described the "standard operating procedures" for the tones or
modes, Marchetto starts to introduce his own refinements on these procedures in
his chapter 3, basing them primarily on the employment of species. He justifies this
by saying that some chants do not fill out their proper ranges and hence are am-

EXAMPLE E.12.   Species in the formation of the modes
in Marchetto da Padova, *Lucidarium*, Treatise 11, chap. 4,
secs. 1–4 (ed. Herlinger, 394–96)

> Primus tonus formatur ex prima specie dyapente, que
> est a D gravi ad a acutum, et ex prima specie dyates-
> saron superius . . . ut hic:

42. In Latin: *perfectus, imperfectus, plusquamperfectus, mixtus,* and *commixtus.* See *Lucidarium*, Treatise 11,
chap. 2, sec. 20, ed. Herlinger, 378; GS 3: 102. Herlinger's translation of *modus* as "measure" picks up the
second attribute of *modus* as defined by the *Alia musica*'s Author β, namely: "nec mensuram excedat" (see
ex. 5.6 and the associated discussion).

43. "Tonus perfectus dicitur ille qui implet modum suum supra et infra" (*Lucidarium*, Treatise 11,
chap. 2, sec. 21, ed. Herlinger, 378; GS 3: 102).

44. See *Lucidarium*, Treatise 11, chap. 2, secs. 21–25, ed. Herlinger, 378–81; GS 3: 101–2.

EXAMPLE E.13.   Chant ductus requiring that it be sung with *b quadratum* in Marchetto da Padova, *Lucidarium*, Treatise 11, chap. 4, secs. 13–14 (ed. Herlinger, 398–400)

biguous, and that there are still others that have the low range of the plagal, but are still categorized as authentic. His example for this is the responsory *Sint lumbi vestri* (see ex. E.11)—but only later will he make clear to us how this particular responsory exemplifies the refinements he is introducing.

Having thus piqued our interest, Marchetto finally launches his discussion of the tones or modes based on species; he begins it in chapter 4 of treatise 11. His initial descriptions are so straightforward that they could have been taken from the treatise *Duo semisphæria* or from the interpolated version of the *Prologus in tonarium* of Bern of Reichenau.[45] He says, as one can see in example E.12, that "The first mode is formed of the first species of diapente, which runs from low *D* to high *a*, and the first species of the diatessaron above . . . as here."

Marchetto responds to the question whether the first mode should be sung with *b rotundum* or *b quadratum* with a series of answers. First, he suggests, it should be sung with *b quadratum* if it uses its full range above the final, because otherwise the presence of *b rotundum* would alter the species of the upper diatessaron. If, however, a chant in first mode does not ascend to the octave above the final, Marchetto offers two further possibilities. If it ascends only to the sixth degree—that is, to the *b* itself—then one should sing *b♭*. In this case, the mode would be said to be "commixtus" with the sixth mode. If the chant ascends to *b* several times, however, and then moves on up to *c* before descending, then the *b* will be sung as *b♮*, as in example E.13. If the chant ascends to *b*, then descends to *F* before ascending to high *c*, the *b* should be *rotundum*.

Clearly, Marchetto's description of modal traits as presented here is based on that of Pseudo-Odo, but it provides a greater level of detail and a more complete rationale. Marchetto then nods in the direction of Guido d'Arezzo by saying that the first mode and its plagal, or indeed any mode and its plagal, can be "ended in any location on the hand where the species that form them can be set in the proper order above and below the final."[46] He points out, however, that it should be necessary to end a chant on its cofinal only because of some sort of *accidens* (anomaly), and he further adds that in such cases the mode must be considered "irregular."[47] Follow-

45. See chapter 6 here, pp. 210–11.

46. "Sed notandum est quod primus tonus et subiugalis eius possunt terminari in quolibet loco manus ubi species que ipsos formant superius et inferius possunt proprie ordinari, et idemque dicimus de quolibet alio tono, tam auctentico quam etiam subiugali, ut de ipsis inferius ostendetur" (*Lucidarium*, Treatise 11, chap. 4, secs. 17–18, ed. Herlinger, 400–402.)

47. See *Lucidarium*, Treatise 11, chap. 4, secs. 25–30, ed. Herlinger, 404–7; *GS* 3: 105. Marchetto's example for this is the second-mode gradual, *Nimis honorati*. If it were notated on its proper final, *D*, it would have both a low *B♭* and an *E♭* above the final; these notes would become *F* and *b♭*, respectively, were this gradual to be notated on its cofinal, *a*.

EXAMPLE E.14.   Examples of species of diatessaron and diapente in Marchetto da Padova, *Lucidarium*, Treatise 11, chap. 4, secs. 212-30 (ed. Herlinger, 488-509)

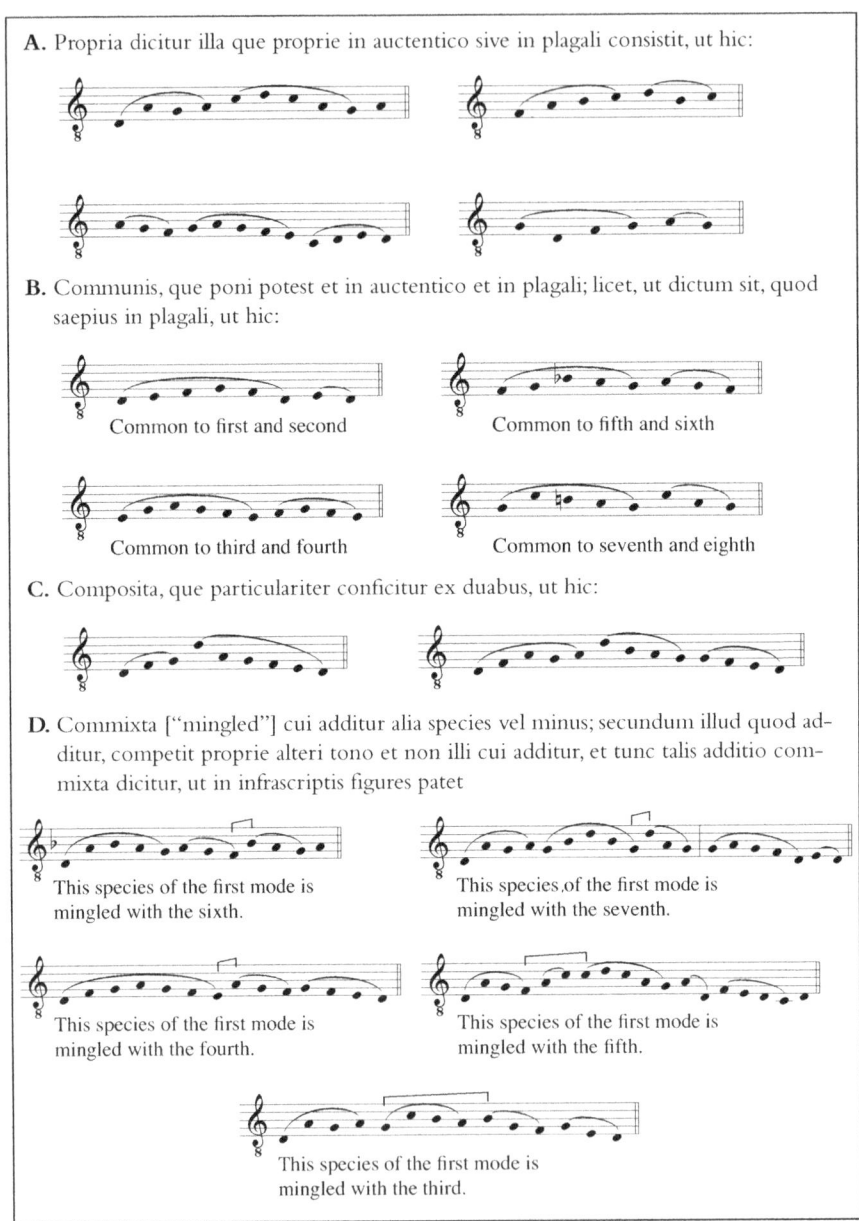

A. Propria dicitur illa que proprie in auctentico sive in plagali consistit, ut hic:

B. Communis, que poni potest et in auctentico et in plagali; licet, ut dictum sit, quod saepius in plagali, ut hic:

Common to first and second

Common to fifth and sixth

Common to third and fourth

Common to seventh and eighth

C. Composita, que particulariter conficitur ex duabus, ut hic:

D. Commixta ["mingled"] cui additur alia species vel minus; secundum illud quod additur, competit proprie alteri tono et non illi cui additur, et tunc talis additio commixta dicitur, ut in infrascriptis figures patet

This species of the first mode is mingled with the sixth.

This species of the first mode is mingled with the seventh.

This species of the first mode is mingled with the fourth.

This species of the first mode is mingled with the fifth.

This species of the first mode is mingled with the third.

ing a discussion of irregular chants, Marchetto concludes his remarks on the first mode with a listing and description of the possible *initia* for this mode and a consideration of the chants exemplifying each. Similar discussions of the remaining modes follow, but without the level of detail given here.

Marchetto concludes his discussion of the *toni* or *modi* with a thoroughgoing

EXAMPLE E.15.   Second, seventh, and eighth *interruptiones* in Marchetto da Padova, *Lucidarium*, Treatise 11, chap. 4, secs. 234–48 (ed. Herlinger, 510–517)

A. Secunda interruptio fit ex tono et dyatessaron, ut hic:

Hec semper in quarto; in ceteris, commixta.

B. Septima ex semiditono et duobus tonis, ut hic:

Hec species in primo et in octavo, et aliquando in sexto; si vero locetur in A gravi, in secundo.

C. Octava [interruptio], que fit ex uno intervallo; ut hic:

Hec autem species semper in primo; aliquando autem in quarto.

Sed notandum est quod species dyapente que fit ex uno intervallo, quecunque sit illa, est tante auctoritatis quod si in uno cantu bis vel ter repercussa fuerit, quantumcunque talis cantus descendat, etiamsi non ascendat ultra dyapente a fine, talis cantus auctenticus dicitur, ut est Responsorium *Sint lumbi vestri* et similes.

---

treatment of the species of diatessaron and diapente and their effect on the character of the modes,[48] and a similar discussion of what he calls *interruptiones*, likewise considering their effects on modal character and definition.[49] Although it owes something to his predecessors, such as Author δ of the *Alia musica* and Bern of Reichenau, Marchetto's presentation of species theory is far more detailed and refined than those of the earlier theorists.

Building on a foundation laid by Guido d'Arezzo and his commentators, Marchetto divides the species into fifteen different types: initial or terminal; proper or common; simple or composite; aggregate or segregate; apposite, preposite, or supposite; continuous, mingled, intense, or relaxed.[50] Example E.14 presents four of

---

48. *Lucidarium*, Treatise 11, chap. 4, secs. 212–30; ed. Herlinger, 488–509.

49. *Lucidarium*, Treatise 11, chap. 4, secs. 231–50; ed. Herlinger, 509–19. Herlinger translates the term *interruptiones* as "intermediations."

50. The terms in Latin are *principalis, terminalis; propria, communis; simplex, composita; aggregata, disgregata; apposita, preposita, supposita; continua, commixta; intensa*, and *remissa* (*Lucidarium*, Treatise 11, chap. 4, sec.

these types that are particularly important here. The defining feature of "proper" species, as shown in example E.14a, is that they belong to a specific authentic or plagal mode. Example E.14b, by contrast, presents "common" species that can be placed either in an authentic or a plagal mode, although they are more often found in the plagal. As Marchetto says in example E.14c, "That is called 'composite' which is made up of two species." Particularly important are those species labeled *commixta* or "mingled" (ex. E.14d) because they allow the analysis of melodic features that are typical of differing modes.[51]

A similar level of detail permeates Marchetto's presentation of "interruptions," or typical melodic gestures in the various modes. The second, seventh, and eighth of these appear in example E.15. The second "interruption" (ex. E.15a) reveals clearly the proximity of *interruptiones* to the categories of species. Consisting of a tone and a diatessaron, this interruption is typically found in the fourth mode; in other modes, it is considered to be "mingled." Of the seventh interruption (ex. E.15b) Marchetto says that it consists of a semiditone and two whole tones. It is placed in the first and eighth modes, and sometimes in the sixth, but, if it is built on a low *A*, it can be part of the second mode. "The eighth [*interruptio*]," in his words, "is that formed of a single interval, as here [ex. E.15c]. This species always appears in the first [mode] and sometimes in the fourth." He then underscores the force of this particular type of interruption:

> The species of the diapente that is formed of a single interval is of such authority that if it occurs in a melody two or three times, no matter how far the melody descends—even if it does not ascend beyond a diapente from the final—that melody is called authentic, as are the Responsory *Sint lumbi vestri* and the like.

Now that the mystery of *Sint lumbi vestri* has been resolved, let us see how Marchetto handles the problem of *Beatus servus*.

Marchetto treats *Beatus servus* in his chapter on the importance of cofinals as endings for anomalous chants. His description is so concise and perceptive that I can do no better than to let him speak for himself. (The original text appears in example E.16; the translation, a modified version of that by Jan Herlinger, follows it.)[52]

214; ed. Herlinger, 488–89). As Herlinger points out (497–99), Guido himself seems to have been the first to employ the adjectives *appositus, prepositus, suppositus,* and *commixtus,* along with others, such as *laxationis, interpositus, augmentus, detrimentus,* and *mixtus.* They appear in his descriptions of melodic movements (*motus vocum*) in chap. 15 of the *Micrologus.* Guido adds, however, that these categories can also be applied to *neumae* and *distinctiones.* In addition, the mid-eleventh-century treatise *De modorum formulis* (ed. Brockett, *CSM* 37; *GS* 2: 37–41; and *CS* 2: 78–81), earlier attributed to Guido himself, applies these categories to the relationship between *differentia* and antiphon incipit. And the late eleventh-century *Liber specierum* applies them to *distinctiones* (see Smits van Waesberghe, *Expositiones in Micrologum,* 51–52). From such applications, it was but a short step to Marchetto's application of these categories to species. Further on this issue, see Atkinson, "Modus," *HmT,* sec. V. (I) (9).

51. In Herlinger's translation: "That is called 'mingled' to which is added another [diapente or diatessaron] species or less. According to the nature of the addition, it properly belongs to a mode other than that to which it is added; in that case the mode of the addition is said to be mingled, as is manifest in the following figures" (*Lucidarium,* Treatise 11, chap. 4, sec. 227; ed. Herlinger, 500–501).

52. *Lucidarium,* Treatise 11, chap. 4, secs. 36–47, ed. Herlinger, 409–17.

EXAMPLE E.16.   Treatment of *Beatus servus* in Marchetto da Padova, *Lucidarium*, Treatise 11, chap. 4, secs. 36–48 (ed. Herlinger, 408–16)

Sunt namque nonnulli cantus, qui neque in finali neque in confinali finiri possunt propter aliqua inconvenientia accidentia in ipsis cadentia, ut est communio: *Beatus servus*, et similes.

Nam si in finali propria terminatur, tunc oportet, quod fiat semiditonus descendendo ab a. acuto ad F. grave in eo loco, ubi dicitur *invenerit* a syllaba *ne* ad syllabam *rit*. Praeterea illae species diatessaron, quae sunt ab *invenerit* usque ad *dico vobis*, sunt in figura primae speciei diatessaron, et earum prolatio sonat tertiam speciem diatessaron. Nam in omni loco, ubi descendimus de G. gravi in F. grave, naturaliter coinclinamus ad semitonium proferendum, ut hic de ambobus accidentibus praedictis possumus probabiliter experiri:

In ve - ne - rit vi - gi - lan - tem   a - men dico vo - bis

Si autem in confinali debeat terminare, tunc oportet, quod fiat semitonium ascendendo ab f. acuto ad g. acutum in eo loco ubi dicitur *servus*, in *ser* syllabam, ut hic patet:

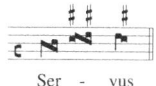

Ser - vus

et in pluribus aliis locis, quod quidem semitonium non est ibi naturaliter.

Praeterea primum inconveniens, quod erat a *ne* syllaba ad syllabam *rit*, scilicet ab a. acuto ad F. grave, nunc ab e. acuto ad c. acutum similiter invenitur. Item aliud, scilicet de speciebus dyatessaron, ut hic clarissime demonstratur:

In ve - ne - rit vi - gi - lan-tem   a - men di - co vo - bis

Et hiis rationibus dicimus, quod quilibet tonus potest terminare in quolibet loco manus, ubi eius species possunt proprie reperiri;

Debemus enim locare hanc communionem *Beatus servus* in a. acuto, principium et finem cantando per b rotundum, medium autem eius et distinctionem per [♮] quadrum, et in eodem loco etiam terminatur, ut hic:

Bea - tus servus   constituet eum

There are some melodies that can be ended neither on their finals nor on their cofinals on account of some incommodious anomalies occurring in them, as in the Communion *Beatus servus* and the like.

If *Beatus servus* were ended on its proper final, a semiditone would be made in descending from *a acutus* to *F gravis* in that place where *invenerit* is sung, from the syllable "-ne-" to the syllable "-rit."

Moreover, the species of diatessaron from *invenerit* to *dico vobis* would be notated as the first species of the diatessaron, yet would sound as the third species of the diatessaron, for in every place where we descended from *G gravis* to *F gravis* we would be naturally inclined to sing a semitone. We can put both anomalies to the test here:

In - ve-ne - rit   vi - gi - lan - tem   a - men di - co vo - bis

If *Beatus servus* had to end on its cofinal (i.e., ♭) it would be necessary that a semitone be made in ascending from *f acutus* to *g acutus* in that place where *servus* is sung, on the syllable "ser-," as is manifest here:

Ser   -   vus

and in many other places where there is by nature no semitone.

Moreover, the first incommodius difficulty, from the syllable "-ne-" to the syllable "-rit," that is, from *a acutus* to *F gravis,* would now be found from high *e acutus* to *c acutus* in similar fashion, and the second, concerning the species of the diatessaron, would likewise remain, as demonstrated very clearly here:

In - ve-ne - rit   vi - gi - lan - tem   a - men di - co vo - bis

For these reasons we say that any mode may end in any location on the hand where its species can properly be found.

We must locate this Communion, *Beatus servus,* on *a acutus,* singing its beginning and its end with round *b* and its middle and its internal phrase endings with square *b,* and end it in the same location where it began, as is manifest here:

Be - a - tus ser   -   vus   con - sti - tu - et   e - um

Marchetto's solution to the problem of nonsystemic accidentals in *Beatus servus* is thus the same one we saw earlier in Montpellier 159: transposition up to *a,* with the use of both ♭ and ♮.[53] He concludes his discussion of the chant by saying that it is an example of a *tonus acquisitus,* because its species are "acquired" through use of the square and round *b,* and because it is ended on a location other than its proper final.

53. See chapter 4 here, pp. 162–68.

EXAMPLE E.17.   The hand "secundum usum" in the first treatise of the Berkeley manuscript ("Quoniam in antelapsis temporibus") (ed. Ellsworth, 40)

e'							la
d'						la	sol
c'						sol	fa
♮'							mi
b'						fa	
a'					la	mi	re
g					sol	re	ut
f					fa	ut	
e				la	mi		
d			la	sol	re		
c			sol	fa	ut		
♮				mi			
b			fa				
a		la	mi	re			
G		sol	re	ut			
F		fa	ut				
E	la	mi					
D	sol	re					
C	fa	ut					
B	mi						
A	re						
Γ	ut						

One particularly important matter seems clear from Marchetto's discussion of *Beatus servus*. Even the most sophisticated of post-Boethian species analysis was not sufficient to allow *Beatus servus* and other pieces like it to be accommodated at its proper modal level in the post-Boethian tone-system of Western plainchant. Indeed, not until later in the fourteenth century would music theory provide a theoretical mechanism that would enable the full rationalization and notation of chant. What was needed was a tone-system that would allow chants to be notated at their proper modal level and that would accommodate any succession of intervals. One of the earliest systems to allow this—if not the earliest altogether—is that presented in the first treatise in the Berkeley manuscript ("Quoniam in antelapsis temporibus"), written around 1375.[54]

The anonymous author of this treatise begins by presenting the notes of the sys-

54. Ellsworth, ed. and transl., *The Berkeley Manuscript*. An even earlier treatise presenting a "chromatically" expanded system is the *De legitimis ordinibus pentachordorum et tetrachordorum* of Theinred of Dover, probably dating from the twelfth century. Theinred's tone-system includes both B and B♭, E and E♭, F and F♯, ♮, and b. On this treatise and its tone-system, see Snyder, "The *De legitimis ordinibus pentachordorum et tetrachordorum* of Theinred of Dover"; and Snyder, "A Road Not Taken: Theinred of Dover's Theory of Species." For a recent discussion of the Berkeley manuscript and its importance in the study of "irregu-

EXAMPLE E.18.   Description of the *coniuncta* in the first treatise of the Berkeley manuscript (ed. Ellsworth, 50–52)

Est enim coniuncta quedam acquisita canendi actualis attribucio in qua licet facere de tono semitonum, et e converso. Vel aliter: coniuncta est alicuius proprietatis seu deduccionis de loco proprio ad alienum locum secundum sub vel supra intellectualis transposicio. Pro cuius evidencia notandum est, quod omnis coniuncta aut signatur per ♭ aut ♯ in locis inusitatis positum. Item ubicumque ponitur signum ♭ debet deprimi sonus verus illius articuli per unum maius semitonum, et dici fa. Et ubi signum ♯ ponitur, sonus illius articuli debet per maius semitonum elevari, et dici ibidem mi.

---

tem by means of the hand, using Guidonian solmization syllables to locate the individual pitches (gamma-ut, *A*-re, *B*-mi, etc. up to *ee*-la).[55] One of the interesting features here is that the author adds a note below gamma, *F*-ut, which makes possible a fa on *B* (= *B*♭).[56] He then lists the seven hexachords on the hand "secundum usum": gamma-ut, *C*-fa-ut, *F*-fa-ut, *G*-sol-re-ut, *C*-sol-fa-ut, *F*-fa-ut altus, and *G*-sol-re-ut altus (see ex. E.17). Following a fairly straightforward discussion of intervals, clefs, and the process of mutation, he introduces the theory of *coniunctae*.

Although the term *coniuncta* had been a part of medieval theory for centuries, having been introduced originally with reference to the *synemmenon*, or conjunct tetrachord,[57] the author of the Berkeley treatise uses it to permit the chromatic alteration of virtually any note of the tone-system in order to capture the intervallic structure of plainchant. They had been invented, in his words, "so that a chant formerly called irregular could be brought into regularity by them."[58] He then goes on to describe the *coniuncta* and its function (ex. E.18):

> A *coniuncta* is the attribute, realized in actual singing, of permitting one to make a semitone out of a tone and conversely. Or rather, a *coniuncta* is the mental transposition of any property or hexachord from its own location to another location above or below. As evidence of this, it must be noted that every *coniuncta* is signed by ♭ or ♯, placed in an unusual location. Also, wherever the sign ♭ is placed, the true sound of that joint ought to be lowered by a major semitone and called fa. And where the sign ♯ is placed, the sound of that joint ought to be raised by a major semitone and called mi.[59]

---

lar" chants, see Karp, *Aspects of Orality and Formularity in Gregorian Chant*, 181–223, and his article "The Offertory *In die solemnitatis.*" See also Pfisterer, *Cantilena Romana: Untersuchungen zur Überlieferung des gregorianischen Chorals,* 19–25.

55. Ellsworth ed., 32–47.

56. Ellsworth ed., 34–35.

57. Martianus Capella, for example, uses the genitive plural *coniunctarum*, the literal translation of *synemmenon* into Latin, as the designation for the *synemmenon* tetrachord. See Ellsworth, "The Origin of the *Coniuncta*: A Reappraisal," and Seay, "The Fifteenth-Century *Coniuncta*: A Preliminary Study."

58. "Et propterea invente fuerunt ipse coniuncte ut cantus antedictus irregularis per eas ad regularitatem quodammodo duci posset" (ed. Ellsworth, 50). Here one should recall the words of the Master in the *Scolica enchiriadis*, who said that semitones had been introduced into chant "as a result of conscientiousness [*industria*]" (see chapter 3 here, note 120 and the associated discussion).

59. Ed. Ellsworth, 50–52. Note the rationalization of the accidental via "mental transposition" of the hexachord so as to place the semitone on the proper degree. On this, see Bent, "Musica recta and Musica ficta," 79–81.

EXAMPLE E.19.   Tone-system of the first treatise in the Berkeley manuscript (ed. Ellsworth, 50–52). *Coniunctae* are designated by the letter c.

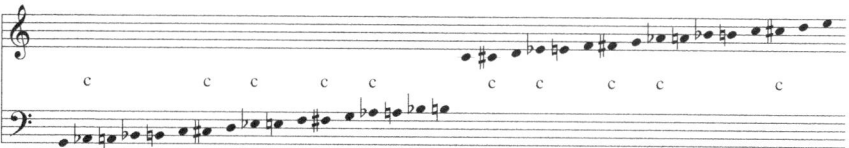

He then goes on to say that whereas some musicians set the number of these *coniunctae* at seven and others at eight or more, he numbers ten of them.

One of the most fascinating aspects of the Berkeley author's discussion of *coniunctae* occurs early on in the treatise. He says that according to "common custom," the first *coniuncta* would be placed between *A* and *B graves*, that is, a low *B♭*. He refuses to consider this a *coniuncta* because for him it is normal, occurring, as it does, in the Responsories *Sancta et immaculata* and *Emendemus in melius* and "in diversis aliis cantibus"; it is rationalized via the hexachord on *F-ut graves*.[60] Thus, for him the first *coniuncta* is between gamma and *A graves* (*A♭*). The entire group of ten *coniunctae* consists of *A♭, C♯, E♭, F♯, a♭, c♯, e♭, f♯, aa♭*, and *cc♯* (or *dd♭*).[61] The complete tone-system, including the *coniunctae*, appears in example E.19.

For each one of the *coniunctae*, the Berkeley author supplies examples drawn from the repertoire of Gregorian chant. In many cases, they are the same chants that had been singled out ever since the eleventh century as "problem" chants. The chant used as an illustration of the *coniuncta* between *F* and *G graves* (*F♯*), for example, is the Communion *Beatus servus*, already mentioned, as we have seen, by Bern of Reichenau, John Cotto, Marchetto da Padova, and others as a problematic piece.[62] Thanks to the use of the *coniuncta*, the passage at "invenerit vigilantem" containing the *F*-sharps can be accommodated quite easily, and the chant as a whole can be notated at its proper modal level (see exs. E.20 and E.21).

With the first treatise in the Berkeley manuscript, the theory of tone-system and mode and its implications for the notation of medieval chant comes full circle. As noted earlier, the tone-system of the *Musica* and *Scolica enchiriadis*, with its disjunct, modal tetrachords (T-ST-T) and the alterations made possible by the *vitia*, could accommodate a wide array of varying intervallic structures in plainchant—including those of *Beatus servus*. Most of the distinctive features of that system were suppressed, however, in favor of the ancient Greek Greater and Lesser Perfect Systems as presented in Boethius, and adapted for use in plainchant by theorists such as Hucbald and Pseudo-Odo. Indeed, the combined two-octave or Immutable System of the ancient Greeks, with the addition of the low Γ, became the standard tone-system for Western chant in the eleventh century. The system of diastematic notation that likewise crystallized in the eleventh century preserved the tonal architecture of this tone-system. The disadvantage it presented was the fact that it had only

60. Ed. Ellsworth, 54–55.
61. Ed. Ellsworth, 52–67.
62. See the discussion above and Atkinson, "From 'Vitium' to 'Tonus acquisitus.'"

EXAMPLE E.20.   "Invenerit vigilantem" from the Communion *Beatus servus* in the first
treatise of the Berkeley manuscript (ed. Ellsworth, 58).

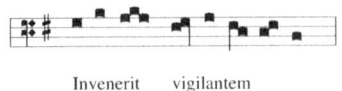

Invenerit   vigilantem

EXAMPLE E.21.   *Beatus servus* notated as indicated by the Berkeley manuscript.

Be - a - tus ser - vus, quem, cum ve - ne-rit   Do - mi-nus

in - ve - ne - rit   vi - gi - lan - tem. A - men di - co vo - bis su - per

om - ni - a bo - na su - a   con - sti - tu - et_____   e - um.

one flexible degree, the *b-quadratum* or *b-rotundum* in the middle of the system. Thus,
many chants with an unusual intervallic structure had to be transposed to their
cofinals or to other pitch levels in order to be accommodated in the system and on
the staff. Only with the advent of the theory of *coniunctae* in the fourteenth century
could the "standard system" be made flexible enough to accommodate these chants
at the levels of their proper finals. But by that time, the combined weight of theory
and practice was too great to overcome. For the most part, plainchant continued to
be copied in the standard system, using transposition and ♭ or ♮ to accommodate
problematical chants. Only when the theory and practice of polyphony began to
make full use of the *coniunctae,* and when the ancient Greek genera were "rediscov-
ered" in the sixteenth century, could the standard tone-system become the fully
chromatic structure we know today.

BIBLIOGRAPHY

Abbreviations

ActaM   *Acta musicologica*
AfMw   *Archiv für Musikwissenschaft*
CAO   *Corpus antiphonalium Officii.* Rerum ecclesiasticarum documenta, Series Maior: Fontes 7. Edited by René-Jean Hesbert. 6 vols. Rome: Herder, 1963.
CCCM   *Corpus Christianorum. Continuatio mediaevalis.* Turnhout: Brepols, 1966–.
CS   *Scriptorum de musica medii aevi nova series.* Edited by Edmond de Coussemaker. 4 vols. Paris: A. Durand, 1864–76.
CSM   *Corpus scriptorum de musica.* Rome: American Institute of Musicology, 1950–.
CTC   *Catalogus translationum et commentariorum.* Mediaeval and Renaissance Latin Translations and Commentaries. Annotated Lists and Guides. Edited by Paul Oskar Kristeller, F. E. Cranz, et al. Washington, D.C: Catholic University of America Press, 1960–.
DACL   *Dictionnaire d'archéologie chrétienne et de liturgie.* Edited by Fernand Cabrol, Henri Leclercq, and Henri Marrou. 15 vols. in 30 fascicles. Paris: Letouzey et Ané 1907–53.
DMA   *Divitiae musicae artis.* Edited by Joseph Smits van Waesberghe. Buren, Netherlands: Fritz Knuf, 1975–.
EG   *Études grégoriennes*
EMH   *Early Music History*
GdMth   *Geschichte der Musiktheorie.* Darmstadt: Wissenschaftliche Buchgesellschaft, 1985–.
GR   *Graduale Romanum.* Solesmes: Abbey of St.-Pierre, 1974.
GS   *Scriptores ecclesiastici de musica sacra potissimum.* Edited by Martin Gerbert. 3 vols. St. Blasien, Typis S. Blasiensis, 1784; repr., Milan: Bollettino bibliografico musicale, 1931.
HmT   *Handwörterbuch der musikalischen Terminologie.* Edited by Hans Heinrich Eggebrecht. Wiesbaden: Steiner Verlag, 1972–2005.
JAMS   *Journal of the American Musicological Society*
JM   *Journal of Musicology*
JPMMS   *Journal of the Plainsong and Medieval Music Society*
KmJb   *Kirchenmusikalisches Jahrbuch*

LmL   *Lexicon musicum Latinum medii aevi.* Edited by Michael Bernhard. Munich:Verlag der Bayerischen Akademie der Wissenschaften in Kommission bei der C. H. Beck'schen Verlagsbuchhandlung, 1992–.

MD   *Musica disciplina*

Mf   *Die Musikforschung*

MGG   *Die Musik in Geschichte und Gegenwart.* Edited by Friedrich Blume. 17 vols. Kassel: Bärenreiter, 1949–86.

MGG 2   *Die Musik in Geschichte und Gegenwart. Zweite neubearbeitete Ausgabe.* Edited by Ludwig Finscher. Kassel: Bärenreiter, 1994–.

MGH   *Monumenta Germaniae historica*

MQ   *The Musical Quarterly*

NG   *The New Grove Dictionary of Music and Musicians.* Edited by Stanley Sadie. 20 vols. London: Macmillan, 1980.

NG 2   *The New Grove Dictionary of Music and Musicians.* Rev. ed. Edited by Stanley Sadie. 27 vols. London: Macmillan, 2001.

Pal. mus.   *Paléographie musicale: Les Principaux Manuscrits du chant grégorien, ambrosien, mozarabe, gallican.* Solesmes, 1889–.

PL   *Patrologiae cursus completus sive bibliotheca universalis, integra, uniformis, commoda, oeconomica omnium ss. patrum, doctorum scriptorumque ecclesiasticorum qui ab aevo apostolico ad usque Innocentii III tempora floruerunt . . . Series latina.* 221 vols. Edited by J. P. Migne. Paris, 1844–64.

RB   *Revue bénédictine*

RdM   *Revue de musicologie*

RG   *Revue grégorienne*

RISM   *Répertoire international des sources musicales*

Manuscripts Cited
(Arranged by city, library, and numerical portion of call number)

Angers, Bibliothèque Municipale, 91 (83)
Autun, Bibliothèque Municipale, S 4 (olim 5)
Autun, Bibliothèque Municipale, S 28 (olim 24)
Autun, Bibliothèque Municipale, S 46 (olim 40B)
Bamberg, Staats- und Universitätsbibliothek, Msc. Class. 39
Barcelona, Arxiu de la Corona d'Aragó, Ripoll 42
Benevento, Biblioteca Capitolare, VI.34
Berlin, Staatsbibliothek: Preussischer Kulturbesitz, theol. lat. 2° 58
Bern, Burgerbibliothek, 36
Bern, Burgerbibliothek, 56b
Bern, Burgerbibliothek, 101
Bern, Burgerbibliothek, 331
Besançon, Bibliothèque Municipale, 594
Boulogne-sur-Mer (St. Omer), Bibliothèque Municipale, 666
Bruges, Stadsbibliotheek, 532
Brussels, Bibliothèque Royale, 2750/65
Brussels, Bibliothèque Royale, 10078/95
Cesena, Biblioteca Comunale Malatestiana, *Pluteus* S. XXVI. 1
Chartres, Bibliothèque Municipale, 47
Chartres, Bibliothèque Municipale, 130
Chicago, Newberry Library, F. 9

Cologne, Dombibliothek, 166

Douai, Bibliothèque Municipale, 6

Douai, Bibliothèque Municipale, 246

Düsseldorf, Universitäts- und Landesbibliothek, D. 1

Düsseldorf, Universitäts- und Landesbibliothek, D. 2

Düsseldorf, Universitäts- und Landesbibliothek, D. 3

Düsseldorf, Universitäts- und Landesbibliothek, H. 3

Einsiedeln, Benediktinerkloster, Musikbibliothek, 121

Einsiedeln, Benediktinerkloster, Musikbibliothek, 169 (468)

Einsiedeln, Benediktinerkloster, Musikbibliothek, 298

Einsiedeln, Benediktinerkloster, Musikbibliothek, 358

Florence, Biblioteca Nazionale Centrale, Conventi soppressi, F.III.565

Florence, Biblioteca Riccardiana, Fr. 652

Graz, Universitätsbibliothek, 807

Heidelberg, Universitätsbibliothek, Pal. lat. 52

Karlsruhe, Badische Landesbibliothek, Aug. perg. 73

Karlsruhe, Badische Landesbibliothek, K. 504

Laon, Bibliothèque Municipale, 9

Laon, Bibliothèque Municipale, 107

Laon, Bibliothèque Municipale, 121

Laon, Bibliothèque Municipale, 239

Laon, Bibliothèque Municipale, 266

Leiden, Universiteitsbibliotheek, B. P. L. 25

Leiden, Universiteitsbibliotheek, B. P. L. 28

Leiden, Universiteitsbibliotheek, B. P. L. 36

Leiden, Universiteitsbibliotheek, Voss. Lat F. 48

Leiden, Universiteitsbibliotheek, Voss. lat. F. 74

Leiden, Universiteitsbibliotheek, Voss. lat. F. 82

Leiden, Universiteitsbibliotheek, BPL 88

Leiden, Universiteitsbibliotheek, BPL 122

Leipzig, Städtische Bibliotheken, Rep. I. 93

Leipzig, Universitätsbibliothek, 169

Leipzig, Universitätsbibliothek, 1493

London, British Library, Harley 2685

Lucca, Biblioteca Capitolare, 601

Madrid, Biblioteca Nacional, 9088

Madrid, Biblioteca Nacional, 10001

Metz, Bibliothèques Médiathèques de Metz/Collections patrimoniales, 351

Metz, Bibliothèques Médiathèques de Metz/Collections patrimoniales, 494

Milan, Biblioteca Ambrosiana, C 128 inf.

Montpellier, Bibliothèque Interuniversitaire-Section Médecine, H 159

Munich, Bayerische Staatsbibliothek, clm 6250

Munich, Bayerische Staatsbibliothek, clm 6275

Munich, Bayerische Staatsbibliothek, clm 6361

Munich, Bayerische Staatsbibliothek, clm 9543

Munich, Bayerische Staatsbibliothek, clm 9921

Munich, Bayerische Staatsbibliothek, clm 14272

Munich, Bayerische Staatsbibliothek, clm 14314

Munich, Bayerische Staatsbibliothek, clm 14523

Munich, Bayerische Staatsbibliothek, clm 14729

Munich, Bayerische Staatsbibliothek, clm 18478
Munich, Bayerische Staatsbibliothek, clm 18480
Munich, Bayerische Staatsbibliothek, clm 29164/I
Naples, Biblioteca Nazionale "Vittorio Emanuele III," IV. G. 68
New York, New York Public Library, 115
Orléans, Bibliothèque de la Ville, 293B
Oxford, Bodleian Library, Auct. T.2.19
Oxford, Bodleian Library, Auct. F.4.26
Oxford, Bodleian Library, Canonici misc. 212
Padua, Biblioteca Capitolare, 47
Paris, Bibliothèque de l'Arsenal, 227
Paris, Bibliothèque nationale de France, f. gr. 360
Paris, Bibliothèque nationale de France, f. lat. 903
Paris, Bibliothèque nationale de France, f. lat. 1118
Paris, Bibliothèque nationale de France, f. lat. 1190
Paris, Bibliothèque nationale de France, f. lat. 1411
Paris, Bibliothèque nationale de France, f. lat. 1412
Paris, Bibliothèque nationale de France, n. a. lat. 1618
Paris, Bibliothèque nationale de France, n. a. lat. 1620
Paris, Bibliothèque nationale de France, f. lat. 1850
Paris, Bibliothèque nationale de France, f. lat. 2291
Paris, Bibliothèque nationale de France, n. a. lat. 2554
Paris, Bibliothèque nationale de France, f. lat. 2717
Paris, Bibliothèque nationale de France, f. lat. 4995
Paris, Bibliothèque nationale de France, f. lat. 7200
Paris, Bibliothèque nationale de France, f. lat. 7201
Paris, Bibliothèque nationale de France, f. lat. 7211
Paris, Bibliothèque nationale de France, f. lat. 7212
Paris, Bibliothèque nationale de France, f. lat. 7297
Paris, Bibliothèque nationale de France, f. lat. 7490
Paris, Bibliothèque nationale de France, f. lat. 7583–85
Paris, Bibliothèque nationale de France, f. lat. 7670
Paris, Bibliothèque nationale de France, f. lat. 7671
Paris, Bibliothèque nationale de France, f. lat. 7972
Paris, Bibliothèque nationale de France, f. lat. 8093
Paris, Bibliothèque nationale de France, f. lat. 8663
Paris, Bibliothèque nationale de France, f. lat. 8669
Paris, Bibliothèque nationale de France, f. lat. 8670
Paris, Bibliothèque nationale de France, f. lat. 8671
Paris, Bibliothèque nationale de France, f. lat. 8674
Paris, Bibliothèque nationale de France, f. lat. 8675
Paris, Bibliothèque nationale de France, f. lat. 9430
Paris, Bibliothèque nationale de France, f. lat. 10275
Paris, Bibliothèque nationale de France, f. lat. 10508
Paris, Bibliothèque nationale de France, f. lat. 10509
Paris, Bibliothèque nationale de France, f. lat. 11958
Paris, Bibliothèque nationale de France, f. lat. 12960
Paris, Bibliothèque nationale de France, f. lat. 13025
Paris, Bibliothèque nationale de France, f. lat. 13159
Paris, Bibliothèque nationale de France, f. lat. 13908

Paris, Bibliothèque nationale de France, f. lat. 14753
Paris, Bibliothèque nationale de France, f. lat. 14754
Paris, Bibliothèque nationale de France, f. lat. 15614
Paris, Bibliothèque nationale de France, f. lat. 16201
Paris, Bibliothèque nationale de France, f. lat. 17305
Paris, Bibliothèque nationale de France, f. lat. 17306
Paris, Bibliothèque nationale de France, f. lat. 17436
Paris, Bibliothèque Sainte-Geneviève, 1190
Pistoia, Biblioteca Capitolare, 121
Prague, Národní knihovna České Republiky, CZ, XIX.C.26
Regensburg, Bischöfliche Zentralbibliothek, Proske-Musikbibliothek, Cim. 2
Reims, Bibliothèque Municipale, 213
Reims, Bibliothèque Municipale, 426
Rochester, Sibley Music Library, Vault ML92 1200
Rome, Biblioteca Apostolica Vaticana, Reg. lat. 215
Rome, Biblioteca Apostolica Vaticana, lat. 235
Rome, Biblioteca Apostolica Vaticana, Barberini gr. 300
Rome, Biblioteca Apostolica Vaticana, Ottob. lat. 313
Rome, Biblioteca Apostolica Vaticana, Pal. lat. 485
Rome, Biblioteca Apostolica Vaticana, Reg. lat. 1005
Rome, Biblioteca Apostolica Vaticana, Reg. lat. 1638
Rome, Biblioteca Apostolica Vaticana, Reg. lat. 1661
St. Gall, Stiftsbibliothek, 231
St. Gall, Stiftsbibliothek, 237
St. Gall, Stiftsbibliothek, 242
St. Gall, Stiftsbibliothek, 339
St. Gall, Stiftsbibliothek, 359
St. Gall, Stiftsbibliothek, 376
St. Gall, Stiftsbibliothek, 381
St. Gall, Stiftsbibliothek, 390–91
Schaffhausen, Stadtbibliothek, 108
Sélestat, Bibliothèque Municipale, 1 (1093)
Stockholm, Kungliga Biblioteket, Sveriges Nationalbibliotek. A 136
Strasbourg, Séminaire Protestant 926 (anc. B.I.24)
Toledo, Museo de San Vicente, Fr. 2
Tours, Bibliothèque Municipale, 184 (1017)
Valenciennes, Bibliothèque Municipale, 107
Valenciennes, Bibliothèque Municipale, 148
Valenciennes, Bibliothèque Municipale, 150
Valenciennes, Bibliothèque Municipale, 293
Valenciennes, Bibliothèque Municipale, 294
Valenciennes, Bibliothèque Municipale, 337
Valenciennes, Bibliothèque Municipale, 399
Valenciennes, Bibliothèque Municipale, 407
Vienna, Österreichische Nationalbibliothek, 51
Vienna, Österreichische Nationalbibliothek, 958
Vienna, Österreichische Nationalbibliothek, 2269
Vienna, Österreichische Nationalbibliothek, 3222
Vienna, Österreichische Nationalbibliothek, Ser. nova 3645
Worcester, Cathedral Library, F. 160

Modern Editions and Studies That Contain Them

Andrieu, Michel, ed. *Les Ordines romani du haut moyen âge.* 5 vols. Spicilegium sacrum Lo-
vaniense. Études et documents: Fascicles 11, 23, 24, 28, 29. Gembloux, 1931–61.

Anon. *Admonitio generalis* (789). In *MGH, leges* II, vol. 1, *Capitularia regum Francorum,* edited
by Alfred Boretius, no. 22, pp. 52–62. Hannover: Impensis Bibliopolii Hahniani,
1881.

Anon. *Commemoratio brevis.* In *Musica et Scolica enchiriadis una cum aliquibus tractatulis adiuncti,*
edited by Hans Schmid, 157–78. Veröffentlichungen der Musikhistorischen Kommis-
sion 3. Munich: Bayerische Akademie der Wissenschaften, 1981.

Anon. *Cujusdam Carthusiensis monachi tractatus de musica.* CS 2: 434–83.

Anon. [Pseudo-Bernelinus]. "Prima species diatessaron." GS 1: 122a–b, 313a–314a.

Anon. [Pseudo-Odo]. *Dialogus de musica.* GS 1: 252–64.

Anon. [Pseudo-Odo]. *Musicae artis disciplina.* GS 1: 265–83.

Anon. "Duo semisphæria, quas magadas vocant." GS 1: 331–38.

Anon. *Inchiriadon Uchubaldi Francigenae.* In *Musica et Scolica enchiriadis una cum aliquibus tractatulis adiuncti,* edited by Hans Schmid, 187–213. Veröffentlichungen der Musikhistorischen
Kommission 3. Munich: Bayerische Akademie der Wissenschaften, 1981.

Bailey, Terence. *The Intonation Formulas of Western Chant.* Toronto: Pontifical Institute of Medieval Studies, 1974.

———, ed. and transl. *Commemoratio brevis de tonis et psalmis modulandis.* Ottawa Medieval
Texts and Studies 4. Ottawa: University of Ottawa Press, 1979.

———. "*De modis musicis*: A New Edition and Translation." *KmJb* 61/62 (1977/78): 47–60.

Bautier, Robert-Henri, and Monique Gilles, eds. *Odorannus de Sens—Opera omnia.* Sources
d'histoire médiévale 4. Paris: Éditions du Centre national de la recherche scientifique,
1972.

Bern Augiensis. *Prologus in tonarium.* GS 2: 62–79.

Bernhard, Michael, ed. *Anonymi saeculi decimi et undecimi tractatus de musica "Dulce ingenium musicae."* Veröffentlichungen der Musikhistorischen Kommission 6. Munich: Bayerische
Akademie der Wissenschaften, 1987.

———. *Clavis Coussemakeri.* In *Quellen und Forschungen zur Musiktheorie des Mittelalters,* vol. 1.
Veröffentlichungen der Musikhistorischen Kommission 8. Munich: Bayerische Akademie der Wissenschaften, 1990.

———. *Clavis Gerberti: Eine Revision von Martin Gerberts Scriptores ecclesiastici de musica sacra
potissimum (St. Blasien, 1784).* Veröffentlichungen der Musikhistorischen Kommission 7.
Munich: Bayerische Akademie der Wissenschaften, 1989.

Bernhard, Michael, and Calvin Bower, eds. *Glossa maior in institutionem musicam Boethii.* Veröffentlichungen der Musikhistorischen Kommission 9–11. Munich: Bayerische Akademie der Wissenschaften, 1993–96.

Boretius, Alfred, ed. *MGH, leges* II, vol. 1, *Capitularia regum Francorum.* Hannover: Impensis
Bibliopolii Hahniani, 1881.

Bragard, Roger, ed. *Jacobi Leodiensis Speculum musicae.* CSM 3, [1973].

Brockett, Clyde, ed. *Anonymi De modorum formulis et tonarius.* CSM 37, 1997.

Burnet, Ioannes, ed. ΙΠΠΙΑΣ ΜΕΙΖΩΝ [*Greater Hippias*]. In *Platonis opera,* 3: 281–304.
Scriptorvm classicorvm bibliotheca Oxoniensis, 1901; repr., Oxford: Clarendon Press,
1977.

———. ΦΙΛΗΒΟΣ [*Philebos*]. In *Platonis opera,* 2: 57–149. Scriptorvm classicorvm bibliotheca Oxoniensis, 1901; repr., Oxford: Clarendon Press, 1977.

Chailley, Jacques, ed. *Alia musica: Traité de musique du IXe siècle. Édition critique commentée avec
une introduction sur l'origine de la nomenclature modale pseudo-greque au moyen-âge.* Publica-

tions de l'Institut de Musicologie de l'Université de Paris 6. Paris: Centre de documentation universitaire, 1965.

Chartier, Yves, ed. and transl. "La *Musica* d'Hucbald de Saint-Amand (traité de musique du IXe siècle). Introduction, établissement du texte, traduction et commentaire." Ph.D. diss., Université de Paris, 1973.

———. *L'Œuvre musicale d'Hucbald de Saint-Amand. Les Compositions et le traité de musique.* Cahiers d'études médiévales (Cahier spécial no. 5). Montreal: Éditions Bellarmin, 1995.

Chittenden, John, ed. *Donatus ortigraphus, Ars grammatica. CCCM* 40D, 1982.

Christ, Guilelmus, ed. *Aristotelis De arte poetica liber.* Bibliotheca scriptorum Graecorum et Romanorum Teubneriana. Leipzig: Teubner, 1882.

Conomos, Dmitri, ed., transl., and comm. *The Treatise of Manuel Chrysaphes, the Lampadarios: On the Theory of the Art of Chanting and on Certain Erroneous Views That Some Hold about It (Mount Athos, Iviron Monastery MS 1120 [July, 1458]).* Monumenta musicae Byzantinae, Corpus scriptorum de re musica 2. Vienna: Verlag der Österreichischen Akademie der Wissenschaften, 1985.

Cristante, Lucio. *Martiani Capellae De nuptiis Philologiae et Mercurii liber IX.* Medioevo e Umanesimo 64. Padua: Editrice Antenore, 1987.

Cserba, Simon, ed. *Hieronymus de Moravia, O. P.: Tractatus de musica.* Freiburger Studien zur Musikwissenschaft. Veröffentlichungen des Musikwissenschaftlichen Instituts der Universität Freiburg CH. Regensburg: Pustet, 1935.

Da Rios, Rosetta, ed. *Aristoxeni Elementa Harmonica.* Scriptores Graeci et Latini Consilio Academiae Lynceorum Editi. Rome: Typis Publicae Officinae Polygraphicae, 1954.

Dick, Adolf, ed. *Martianus Capella.* Bibliotheca scriptorum Graecorum et Romanorum Teubneriana. Leipzig: Teubner, 1925.

Dick, Adolf, ed., with addenda by J. Préaux. *Martianus Capella.* Bibliotheca scriptorum Graecorum et Romanorum Teubneriana. Stuttgart: Teubner, 1969.

Du Cange, Charles du Fresne. *Glossarium ad scriptores mediae et infimae Latinitatis.* 10 vols. 1883–87; repr., Graz: Akademische Druck- u. Verlagsanstalt, 1954.

Duchez, Marie-Elizabeth, and Michel Huglo, eds. *"Odorannus Senonensis" (ca. 975–ca. 1046): Liber opusculorum.* In *Odorannus de Sens: Opera omnia.* Textes édités, traduits et annotés par R.-H. Bautier et M. Gilles. Sources d'histoire médiévale 4. Paris: Éditions du Centre national de la recherche scientifique, 1972.

Dümmler, Ernst, ed. *MGH, Epistolarum,* vol. IV, *Karolini aevi,* vol. 2. Berlin: Weidmann, 1895.

Düring, Ingemar, ed. *Die Harmonielehre des Klaudios Ptolemaios.* Göteborgs Högskolas Årsskrift 36, 1930, 1. Göteborg: Elanders Boktryckeri Aktiebolag, 1930.

Ellsworth, Oliver, ed. *The Berkeley Manuscript: University of California Music Library, MS. 744 (olim Phillips 4450).* Greek and Latin Music Theory. Lincoln: University of Nebraska Press, 1984.

Eyssenhardt, Franz Rudolf, ed. *De nuptiis Philologiae et Mercurii.* Bibliotheca scriptorum Graecorum et Romanorum Teubneriana. Leipzig: Teubner, 1866.

Finaert, Guy, and F.-J. Thonnard, eds. *De musica libri sex.* In *Œuvres de Saint Augustin,* ser. 1, *Opuscules 7, Dialogues philosophiques 4, La Musique.* Bruges: Desclée, de Brouwer, 1947.

Fordyce, P. J., ed. *P. Vergili Maronis Aeneidos libri VII–VIII with a Commentary.* Glasgow: Oxford University Press, 1977.

Friedlein, Gottfried, ed. *Anicii Manlii Torquati Severini Boetii De institutione arithmetica, libri duo; De institutione musica libri quinque.* Leipzig, 1867; repr., Frankfurt: Minerva, 1966.

Le Graduel romain. Vol. 2. *Les sources.* Édition critique. Solesmes: Abbaye St.-Pierre, 1957.

Gümpel, Karl-Werner, ed. "Die 'Nova expositio' der Handschrift Ripoll 42: Text und Kommentar." In *Miscellània litúrgica catalana,* 15: 125–86. Barcelona: Institut d'Estudis Catalans, 2007.

Guentner, Francis, ed. *Epistola S. Bernardi de revisione cantus Cisterciensis et Tractatus scriptus ab auctore incerto Cisterciense cantum quem Cisterciensis Ordinis ecclesiae cantare.* CSM 24, 1974.

Gushee, Lawrence, ed. *Aurelianus Reomensis: Musica disciplina.* CSM 21, 1975.

Hansen, Finn Egeland, ed. *H 159 Montpellier. Tonary of St. Bénigne of Dijon.* Copenhagen: Dan Fog Musikforlag, 1974.

Hanssens, Jean-Michael, ed. *Amalarii episcopi opera liturgica omnia.* Studi e testi 138–40. Vatican City: Biblioteca Apostolica Vaticana, 1948–50.

Heard, Edmund Brooks. "*Alia musica:* A Chapter in the History of Music Theory." Ph.D. diss., University of Wisconsin, 1966.

Herlinger, Jan, ed. *The Lucidarium of Marchetto of Padua: A Critical Edition, Translation, and Commentary.* Chicago: University of Chicago Press, 1985.

Hesbert, René-Jean, ed. *Antiphonale missarum sextuplex.* Brussels: Vromant, 1935.

Hilberg, Isidorvs, ed. *Sancti Evsebii Hieronymi epistvlae.* Corpus scriptorum ecclesiasticorum Latinorum 54. Vienna: Tempsky, 1910.

Hiller, Eduard, ed. *Theonis Smyrnaei philosophi Platonici Expositio rervm mathematicarvm ad legendvm Platonem vtilivm.* Bibliotheca scriptorum Graecorum et Romanorum Teubneriana. Leipzig: 1878; repr., Leipzig: Teubner, 1995.

Holtz, Louis, ed. *Donat et la tradition de l'enseignement grammatical. Étude sur l'Ars Donati et sa diffusion (IVe–IXe siècle) et édition critique.* Documents, études et repertoires publiés par l'Institut de recherche et d'histoire des textes. Paris: Éditions du Centre national de la recherche scientifique, 1981.

———. *Murethach In Donati Artem maiorem.* Grammatici hibernici Carolini aevi. CCCM 40, 1977.

Hüschen, Heinrich, ed. *Das Cantuagium des Heinrich Eger von Kalkar, 1328–1408.* Beiträge zur Rheinischen Musikgeschichte 2. Cologne: Staufen-Verlag, 1952.

Jan, Karl von, ed. [ΚΛΕΟΝΕΙΔΟΥ] Εἰσαγωγὴ ἁρμονική. In *Musici scriptores Graeci,* 179–207. Leipzig: Teubner, 1895; repr., Hildesheim: Georg Olms, 1962.

———. *Musici scriptores Graeci.* Leipzig: Teubner, 1895; repr., Hildesheim: Georg Olms, 1962.

Jonkers, G. H., ed. ΜΑΝΟΥΗΛ ΒΡΥΕΝΝΙΟΥ ΑΡΜΟΝΙΚΑ. *The Harmonics of Manuel Byennius.* Groningen: Wolters-Noordhoff, 1970.

Karoli epistola de litteris colendis (780–800). In *MGH, leges* II, vol. 1, *Capitularia regum Francorum,* edited by Alfred Boretius, no. 29, pp. 78–79. Hannover: Impensis Bibliopolii Hahniani, 1881.

Keil, Heinrich, ed. *Grammatici latini.* 8 vols. Leipzig: Teubner, 1870; repr., Hildesheim: Georg Olms, 1961.

Kneepkens, C. H., and H. F. Reijnders, eds. *Magister Siguinis "Ars lectoria": Un Art de lecture à haute voix du onzième siècle.* Leiden: Brill, 1979.

Lindsay, Wallace M., ed. *Isidori Hispalensis episcopi Etymologiarum sive originum libri XX.* Scriptorum classicorum bibliotheca Oxoniensis. Oxford: Clarendon Press, 1911.

Lipphardt, Walther, ed. *Der karolingische Tonar von Metz.* Liturgiewissenschaftliche Quellen und Forschungen 43. Münster: Aschendorff, 1965.

Löfstedt, Bengt, ed. *Ars Lavreshamensis: Expositio in Donatvm maiorem.* Grammatici hibernici Carolini aevi. CCCM 40A, 1977.

———. *Sedulius Scottus In Donati Artem maiorem.* Grammatici hibernici Carolini aevi. CCCM 40B, 1977.

Lowe, E[lias] A[very], ed. *Codices latini antiquiores: A Palaeographical Guide to Latin Manuscripts prior to the Ninth Century.* Oxford: Clarendon Press, 1972.

Lutz, Cora, ed. *Dunchad: Glossae in Martianum.* Philological Monographs 12. Lancaster, Pa.: American Philological Association, 1944.

———. *Johannis Scotti Annotationes in Marcianum.* Cambridge, Mass.: Medieval Academy of America, 1939.

———. *Remigii Autissiodorensis Commentum in Martianum Capellam.* Leiden: Brill, 1962.

Maître, Claire, ed. *Guidonis Augensis Regulae de arte musica. La Réforme cistercienne du plain-chant: Étude d'un traité théorique.* Cîteaux: Studia et Documenta 6. Brecht, Belgium: Abdij Nazareth, 1995. Also in *CS* 2: 150–92.

———. *Un Antiphonaire cistercien pour le sanctoral. XIIe siècle. Paris, Bibliothèque nationale de France, nouvelles acquisitions latines 1412.* Paris: Éditions du C.T.H.S., 1999.

———. *Un Antiphonaire cistercien pour le temporal. XIIe siècle.* Paris, Bibliothèque nationale de France, nouvelles acquisitions latines 1411. Poitiers: Maison des sciences de l'homme et de la société de Poitiers, 1998.

Marius Servius Honoratus. *Commentarius in Artem Donati.* In *Grammatici Latini,* edited by Heinrich Keil, 4: 403–48. Leipzig: Teubner, 1870; repr., Hildesheim: Georg Olms, 1961.

Meibom, Marcus, ed. *Antiquae musicae auctores septem Graece et Latine.* 2 vols. Monuments of Music and Music Literature in Facsimile 51. New York: Broude, 1977. (Facsimile of 1652 Amsterdam ed.)

Meyer, Christian. *Mensura monochordi: La Division du monocorde (IXe–XVe siècles).* Publications de la Société française de musicologie, ser. 12, vol. 15. Paris: Société française de musicologie, 1996.

Mynors, Robert A. B., ed. *Cassiodori Senatoris Institutiones.* Oxford: Clarendon Press, 1937.

Najock, Dietmar, ed. *Anonyma de musica scripta Bellermanniana.* Bibliotheca scriptorum Graecorum et Romanorum Teubneriana. Leipzig: Teubner, 1975.

Page, Christopher, ed. and trans. *The "Summa musice": A Thirteenth-Century Manual for Singers.* Cambridge Musical Texts and Monographs. Cambridge: Cambridge University Press, 1991.

Pesce, Dolores, ed. and trans. *Guido D'Arezzo's "Regule rithmice," "Prologus in antiphonarium," and "Epistola ad michahelem": A Critical Text and Translation with an Introduction, Annotations, Indices, and New Manuscript Inventories.* Wissenschaftliche Abhandlungen/Musicological Studies 73. Ottawa: Institute of Mediaeval Music, 1999.

Pöhlmann, Egert, ed. *Denkmäler altgriechischer Musik: Sammlung, Übertragung und Erläuterung aller Fragmente und Fälschungen.* Nuremberg: Hans Carl, 1970.

Raasted, Jørgen, ed. "The *Hagiopolites:* A Byzantine Treatise on Musical Theory. Preliminary Edition by Jørgen Raasted." *Cahiers de l'Institut du moyen-âge Grec et Latin* 45 (1983): 1–99.

Radermacher, Ludwig, ed. *Marci Fabi Quintiliani Institutionis oratoriae libri XII.* Bibliotheca scriptorum Graecorum et Romanorum Teubneriana. Leipzig: Teubner, 1907.

Rausch, Alexander, ed. *Die Musiktraktate des Abtes Bern von Reichenau: Edition und Interpretation.* Musica mediaevalis Europae occidentalis 5. Tutzing: Hans Schneider, 1999.

Sachs, Klaus-Jürgen, ed. *Mensura fistularum: Die Mensurierung der Orgelpfeifen im Mittelalter,* vol. 1. Edition der Texte. Schriftenreihe der Walcker-Stiftung für Orgelwissenschaftliche Forschung 1. Murrhardt, Germany: Musikwissenschaftliche Verlags-Gesellschaft, 1970.

Schmid, Hans, ed. *Musica et Scolica enchiriadis una cum aliquibus tractatulis adiuncti.* Veröffentlichungen der Musikhistorischen Kommission 3. Munich: Bayerische Akademie der Wissenschaften, 1981.

Schneider, Marius, ed. "Primum tractatum huius voluminis de symphonia" [Anonymous Schneider; London Anonymous]. In *Geschichte der Mehrstimmigkeit,* 106–18. Tutzing: Schneider, 1969.

Sergius. *Explanationes Artis Donati.* In *Grammatici Latini,* edited by Heinrich Keil, 4: 486–565. Leipzig: Teubner, 1870; repr., Hildesheim: Georg Olms, 1961.

Smits van Waesberghe, Joseph, ed. *Bernonis Augiensis Abbatis De arte disputationes traditae*. *DMA*, ser. A, vols. 6a and 6b, 1978–79.

———. *Cymbala: Bells in the Middle Ages*. Musicological Studies and Documents 1. Rome: American Institute of Musicology, 1951.

———. *De numero tonorum litterae Episcopi A. ad Coepiscopum E. Missae ac Commentum super tonos Episcopi E. (ad 1000)*. *DMA*, ser. A, vol. 1, 1975.

———. *Expositiones in Micrologum Guidonis Aretini*. Musicologica medii aevi 1. Amsterdam: North-Holland, 1957.

———. *Guido Aretinus: Micrologus*. CSM 4, Nijmegen, Netherlands, 1955.

———. *Guidonis Aretini Prologus in antiphonarium*. *DMA*, ser. A, vol. 3, 1975.

———. *Guidonis Aretini Regulae rhythmicae*. *DMA*, ser. A, vol. 4, 1985.

———. *Johannes dictus Cotto vel Affligemensis: De musica cum tonario*. CSM 1, 1950.

———. *Micros graece, brevis latine* (also known as Vivell Anonymous: *Commentarius anonymus in Micrologum Guidonis Aretini*). In *Expositiones in Micrologum Guidonis Aretini*, 95–172. Musicologica medii aevi 1. Amsterdam: North-Holland, 1957.

Solomon, Jon, ed. and transl. "Clenonides: ΕΙΣΑΓΩΓΗ ΑΡΜΟΝΙΚΗ. Critical Edition, Translation, and Commentary." Ph.D. diss., University of North Carolina, 1980.

Steglich, Rudolph, ed. *Die "Quaestiones in musica." Ein Choraltraktat des zentralen Mittelalters und ihr mutmaßlicher Verfasser Rudolf von St. Trond*. Publikationen der Internationalen Musikgesellschaft, Beihefte, Zweite Folge 10. Leipzig: Breitkopf und Härtel, 1911.

Sweeney, Cecily, ed. *Johannis Wylde: Musica manualis cum tonale*. CSM 28, 1982.

Robert-Tissot, Michel, ed. *Johannes Aegidius de Zamora: Ars musica*. CSM 20, 1974.

Torkewitz, Dieter. *Das älteste Dokument zur Entstehung der abendländischen Mehrstimmigkeit: Eine Handschrift aus Werden an der Ruhr. Das Düsseldorfer Fragment*. Stuttgart: Steiner Verlag, 1999.

Traub, Andreas, ed. and trans. "Hucbald von Saint-Amand, *De harmonica institutione*." *Beiträge zur Gregorianik* 7 (1989): 3–101. Corrections in his "Nachlese zu Hucbald von Saint-Amand," *Beiträge zur Gregorianik* 30 (2000): 57–60.

Uhlig, Gustav, ed. *Dionysii Thracis Ars grammatica et Scholia in Dionysii Thracis Artem grammaticam*. In *Grammatici Graeci*, vol. 1, nos. 1 and 3. Leipzig: Teubner, 1883–1901.

Vancamp, Bruno, ed. *Hippias maior; Hippias minor/Platon*. Stuttgart: Steiner Verlag, 1996.

Vivell, P. Coelestin, ed. *Commentarius anonymus in Micrologum Guidonis Aretini*. Akademie der Wissenschaften in Wien, Philosophisch-historische Klasse, Sitzungsberichte, vol. 185, 5th study. Vienna: Hölder, 1917.

———. *Frutolfi Breviarium de musica et Tonarius*. Akademie der Wissenschaften in Wien, Philosophisch-historische Klasse, Sitzungsberichte, vol. 188, 2nd study. Vienna: Hölder, 1919.

Waeltner, Ernst Ludwig, ed. and trans. *Die Lehre von Organum bis zur Mitte des 11. Jahrhunderts*. Münchner Veröffentlichungen zur Musikgeschichte 13. Tutzing: Hans Schneider, 1975.

Wagner, Peter, ed. *De tonis* (Rome, Biblioteca Vaticana, Pal. lat. 235). In "Un piccolo trattato sul canto ecclesiastico in un manoscritto del secolo x–xi." *Rassegna gregoriana* 3 (1904): 481–84.

Waszink, J. H., ed. *Timaeus a Calcidio translatus commentarioque instructus*. Plato Latinus 4. Leiden: Brill, 1962.

Willis, James, ed. *Martianus Capella*. Bibliotheca scriptorum Graecorum et Romanorum Teubneriana. Leipzig: Teubner, 1983.

Winnington-Ingram, Reginald Pepys, ed. *Aristidis Quintiliani: De musica libri tres*. Bibliotheca scriptorum Graecorum et Romanorum Teubneriana. Leipzig: Teubner, 1963.

Wolfram, Gerda, and Christian Hannick. *Die Erotapokriseis des Pseudo-Johannes Damaskenos zum Kirchengesang.* Monumenta musicae Byzantinae, Corpus scriptorum de re musica 5. Vienna: Verlag der Österreichischen Akademie der Wissenschaften, 1997.

————. *Gabriel Hieromonachos: Abhandlung über den Kirchengesang.* Monumenta musicae Byzantinae, Corpus scriptorum de re musica 1. Vienna: Verlag der Österreichischen Akademie der Wissenschaften, 1985.

Zimpel, Detlev, ed. *Hrabanus Maurus: De institutione clericorum libri tres.* Freiburger Beiträge zur mittelalterlichen Geschichte 7. Frankfurt: Peter Lang, 1996.

Translations and Studies

Adkins, Cecil. "The Technique of the Monochord." *ActaM* 39 (1967): 34–43.

————. "The Theory and Practice of the Monochord." Ph.D. diss., University of Iowa, 1963.

Alberi, M. "Alcuin, the Aachen Palace School of Charlemagne, and the Carolingian Renaissance." *History Today* 39 (1989): 34–41.

Allaire, Gaston. *The Theory of Hexachords, Solmization and the Modal System: A Practical Application.* Musicological Studies and Documents 24. Rome: American Institute of Musicology, 1972.

Allen, W. Sidney. *Accent and Rhythm: Prosodic Features of Latin and Greek: A Study in Theory and Reconstruction.* Cambridge Studies in Linguistics 12. Cambridge: Cambridge University Press, 1973.

————. *Vox Latina: A Guide to the Pronunciation of Classical Latin.* Cambridge: Cambridge University Press, 1978.

Anderson, Warren D. *Music and Musicians in Ancient Greece.* Ithaca, N.Y.: Cornell University Press, 1994.

Apel, Willi. *Gregorian Chant.* Bloomington: Indiana University Press, 1958.

Appel, Margarete. *Terminologie in den mittelalterlichen Musiktraktaten. Ein Beitrag zur musikalischen Elementarlehre des Mittelalters.* Bottrop i. W.: Buch- und Kunstdruckerei Postberg, 1935. (Inaugural-Dissertation, Friedrich-Wilhelms-Universität zu Berlin)

Arlt, Wulf. "Akpekte der musikalischen Paläographie." In *Palaeographie der Musik,* vol. 1, pt. 1, *Die einstimmige Musik des Mittelalters,* edited by Wulf Arlt, 1–48. Cologne: Arno Volk Verlag, 1979.

————. "Anschaulichkeit und analytischer Charakter: Kriterien der Beschreibung und Analyse früher Neumenschriften." In *Musicologie médiévale. Notations et séquences. Actes de la Table ronde du C. N. R. S. à l'Institut de recherche et d'histoire des textes, 1982,* edited by Michel Huglo, 29–55. Paris: Éditions du Centre national de la recherche scientifique, 1987.

Atkinson, Charles M. "*De accentibus toni oritur nota quae dicitur neuma:* Prosodic Accents, the Accent Theory, and the Paleofrankish Script." In *Essays on Medieval Music in Honor of David G. Hughes,* edited by Graeme M. Boone, 17–42. Isham Library Papers 4. Cambridge, Mass.: Harvard University Department of Music, 1995.

————. "The *Doxa,* the *Pisteuo,* and the *ellinici fratres:* Some Anomalies in the Transmission of the Chants of the 'Missa graeca.'" *JM* 7 (1989): 81–106.

————. "From 'Vitium' to 'Tonus acquisitus': On the Evolution of the Notational Matrix of Medieval Chant." In *IMS Study Group Cantus Planus: Papers Read at the Third Meeting, Tihany, Hungary, 19–24 September 1988,* edited by László Dobszay et al., 181–98. Budapest: Hungarian Academy of Sciences, Institute for Musicology, 1990.

————. "Further Thoughts on the Origin of the *Missa graeca.*" In *"De musica et cantu": Studien zur Geschichte der Kirchenmusik und der Oper: Helmut Hucke zum 60. Geburtstag,* edited by Peter Kahn and Ann-Katrin Heimer, 75–94. Hochschule für Musik und Darstellende Kunst, Frankfurt am Main: Musikwissenschaftliche Publikationen 2. Hildesheim: Georg Olms, 1993.

————. "Glosses on Music and Grammar and the Advent of Music Writing in the West." In *Western Plainchant in the First Millennium: Studies in the Medieval Liturgy and Its Music in Honor of James McKinnon*, edited by Sean Gallagher et al., 199–215. Aldershot, England: Ashgate, 2003.

————. "'Harmonia' and the 'Modi, quos abusive tonos dicimus.'" In *Atti del XIV Congresso della Società Internazionale di Musicologia, Bologna, 27 agosto–10 settembre 1987*, edited by Lorenzo Bianconi et al., 3: 485–500. Turin: EDT, 1990.

————. "Johannes Affligemensis as a Historian of Mode." In *Laborare fratres in unum. Festschrift László Dobszay zum 60. Geburtstag*, edited by David Hiley and Janka Szendrei, 1–10. Spolia Berolinensia 7. Hildesheim: Georg Olms, 1995.

————. "Martianus Capella 935 and Its Carolingian Commentaries." *JM* 17 (1999): 498–519.

————. "Modus." *HmT*, 1996.

————. "Music as 'Mistress of the Words': *Laudes deo ore pio*." In *Liturgische Tropen: Referate zweier Colloquien des Corpus Troporum in München (1983) und Canterbury (1984)*, edited by Gabriel Silagi, 67–82. Münchener Beiträge zur Mediävistik und Renaissance-Forschung 36. Munich: Arbeo-Gesellschaft, 1985.

————. "*O amnos tu theu*: The Greek Agnus Dei in the Roman Liturgy from the Eighth to the Eleventh Century." *KmJb* 65 (1981): 7–30.

————. "On the Interpretation of '*Modi, quos abusive tonos dicimus.*'" In *Hermeneutics and Medieval Culture*, edited by Patrick Gallacher and Helen Damico, 147–61. Albany: State University of New York Press, 1989.

————. "Parapter." *HmT*, 1979.

————. "The *Parapteres*: A Perspective on Changes in the Concept of *Tonus* in the Ninth and Tenth Centuries." In *Proceedings of the Twelfth Congress of the International Musicological Society, Berkeley, 1977*, edited by Daniel Heartz and Bonnie Wade, 504–8. Kassel: Bärenreiter, 1981.

————. "The *Parapteres*: *Nothi* or Not?" *MQ* 68 (1982): 32–59.

————. Review of *La Réforme cistercienne du plain-chant. Étude d'un traité théorique*, by Claire Maître; *Un Antiphonaire cistercien pour le sanctoral. XIIe siècle*, edited by Claire Maître; *Un Antiphonaire cistercien pour le temporal. XIIe siècle*, edited by Claire Maître. *Cahiers de civilisation médiévale* 44 (2001): 192–94.

————. "Das Tonsystem des Chorals im Spiegel mittelalterlicher Musiktraktate." In *Die Lehre vom einstimmigen liturgischen Gesang*, edited by Thomas Ertelt and Frieder Zaminer, 103–33. GdMth 4, 2000.

————. "Tonos/tonus." *HmT*, 2005.

————. "*Tonus* in the Carolingian Era: A Terminological *Spannungsfeld*." In *Musiktheorie im Mittelalter, Symposionsbericht: München, 23–27 Juli 2000. Quellen und Studien zur Musiktheorie des Mittelalters*, edited by Michael Bernhard, 3: 19–46. Munich: Bayerische Akademie der Wissenschaften, 2001

————. "Zur Entstehung und Überlieferung der 'Missa graeca.'" *AfMw* 39 (1982): 113–45.

Babb, Warren, and Claude Palisca. *Hucbald, Guido, and John on Music*. Music Theory Translation Series. New Haven, Conn.: Yale University Press, 1980.

Barker, Andrew. *Greek Musical Writings*. Vol. 1. *The Musician and His Art*. Cambridge: Cambridge University Press, 1984.

————. *Greek Musical Writings*. Vol. 2. *Harmonic and Acoustic Theory*. Cambridge: Cambridge University Press, 1989.

Bautier-Regnier, Anne-Marie. "A propos des sens de *neuma* et de *nota* en latin médiévale." *Revue belge de musicologie* 18 (1964): 1–9.

Bent, Margaret. "Diatonic Ficta." *EMH* 4 (1984): 1–48.

————. "Musica recta and Musica ficta." *MD* 26 (1972): 73–100.

Berger, Christian. "Modus II: 14. und 15. Jahrhundert." *MGG 2,* Sachteil [Subjects] 6 (1997), cols. 413–16.

Berger, Karol. "The Hand and the Art of Memory." *MD* 35 (1981): 117–21.

————. *Musica ficta: Theories of Accidental Inflections in Vocal Polyphony from Marchetto da Padova to Gioseffo Zarlino.* Cambridge: Cambridge University Press, 1987.

Bernhard, Michael. "Didaktische Verse zur Musiktheorie des Mittelalters." In *IMS Study Group Cantus Planus: Papers Read at the Third Meeting, Tihany, Hungary, 19–24 September 1988,* edited by László Dobszay et al., 227–36. Budapest: Hungarian Academy of Sciences, 1990.

————. "Das musikalische Fachschriftum im lateinischen Mittelalter." In *Rezeption des antiken Fachs im Mittelalter,* edited by Frieder Zaminer, 37–103. GdMth 3, 1990.

————. *Studien zur Epistola de armonica institutione des Regino von Prüm.* Veröffentlichungen der Musikhistorischen Kommission 5. Munich: Bayerische Akademie der Wissenschaften, 1979.

————. "Textkritisches zu Aurelianus Reomensis." *MD* 40 (1986): 49–61.

————. "Traditionen im mittelalterlichen Tonsystem." In *Altes im Neuen: Festschrift Theodor Göllner zum 65. Geburtstag,* edited by Bernd Edelman and Manfred Hermann Schmid, 11–23. Münchner Veröffentlichungen zur Musikgeschichte 51. Tutzing: Hans Schneider, 1995.

————. "Die Überlieferung der Neumennamen im lateinischen Mittelalter." In *Quellen und Studien zur Musiktheorie des Mittelalters,* edited by Michael Bernhard, 2: 13–91. Veröffentlichungen der Musikhistorischen Kommission 13. Munich: Bayerische Akademie der Wissenschaften, 1997.

————. "Überlieferung und Fortleben der antiken lateinischen Musiktheorie im Mittelalter." In *Rezeption des antiken Fachs im Mittelalter,* edited by Frieder Zaminer, 7–35. GdMth 3, 1990.

————. *Wortkonkordanz zu Anicius Manlius Severinus Boethius, "De institutione musica."* Veröffentlichungen der Musikhistorischen Kommission 4. Munich: Bayerische Akademie der Wissenschaften, 1979.

————. "Zur Rezeption der musiktheoretischen Werke des Hermannus Contractus." In *Beiträge zur Musik, Musiktheorie und Liturgie der Abtei Reichenau. Bericht über die Tagung Heiligenkreuz 6.–8. Dez. 1999,* edited by Walter Pass and Alexander Rausch, 99–126. Musica Mediaevalis Europae Occidentalis 8. Tutzing: Hans Schneider, 2001.

————. "Zwei bayerische Exzerpte der 'Epistola de armonica institutione' des Regino von Prüm." *Musik in Bayern* 17 (1978): 57–60.

Berschin, Walter. *Biographie und Epochenstil im lateinischen Mittelalter.* Vol. 3. *Karolingische Biographie 750–920 nach Christus.* Quellen und Untersuchungen zur lateinischen Philologie des Mittelalters 10. Stuttgart: Anton Hiersemann, 1991.

————. *Griechisch-Lateinisches Mittelalter von Hieronymus zu Nikolaus von Kues.* Bern: Francke, 1980. Translated by Jerold C. Frakes as *Greek Letters and the Latin Middle Ages: From Jerome to Nicholas of Cusa.* Washington, D.C.: Catholic University of America Press, 1988.

Beyssac, Gabriel. "Note sur l'antiphonaire tonale digrapte, codex H. 159 de Montpellier." *Pal. mus.* 7 (1901–5): 9–18.

Bielitz, Mathias. *Hexachord und Semantik: Miszellen zu neueren Vorstellungen über Musik vor Josquin.* Neckargemünd, Germany: Männeles Verlag, 1998.

————. *Musik und Grammatik.* Beiträge zur Musikforschung 4. Munich: Emil Katzbichler, 1977.

————. *Die Neumen in Otfrids Evangelien-Harmonie. Zum Verhältnis von geistlicher und weltlicher Musik des frühen Mittelalters, sowie zur Entstehung der raumanalogen Notenschrift.* Heidelberger Bibliotheksschriften 39. Heidelberg: Universitätsbibliothek Heidelberg, 1989.

————. *Zum Bezeichneten der Neumen, insbesondere der Liqueszenz: Ein Hypothesenansatz zum Verhältnis von Musik und Sprache, zur diatonischen Rationalität, zur Bewegungs- und Raum-Analogie, zur Entstehung der Neumenschrift und zur Rezeption des Gregorianischen Chorals in Benevent.* Neckargemünd, Germany: Männeles Verlag, 1998.

Billecocq, Marie-Claire. "Lettres ajoutées à la notation neumatique du codex 239 de Laon." *EG* 17 (1978): 7–144.

Bischoff, Bernhard. "Elementarunterricht und Probationes Pennae in der ersten Hälfte des Mittelalters." In *Classical and Medieval Studies in Honor of Edward Kennard Rand,* edited by Leslie Weber Jones, 9–20. New York: published by the editor, 1938. Also in Bernhard Bischoff, *Mittelalterliche Studien: Ausgewählte Aufsätze zur Schriftkunde und Literaturgeschichte,* 1:74–87. Stuttgart: Anton Hiersemann, 1966.

————. "Literarisches und künstlerisches Leben in St. Emmeram (Regensburg) während des frühen Mittelalters." *Studien und Mitteilungen zur Geschichte des Benediktiner-Ordens und seiner Zweige* 51 (1933): 102–42. Also in Bernhard Bischoff, *Mittelalterliche Studien: Ausgewählte Aufsätze zur Schriftkunde und Literaturgeschichte,* 2:77–115. Stuttgart: Anton Hiersemann, 1967.

————. *Die südostdeutschen Schreibschulen und Bibliotheken in der Karolingerzeit.* Vol. 1. *Die Bayrischen Diözesen.* 3rd ed. Wiesbaden: Harrassowitz, 1974.

————. *Die südostdeutschen Schreibschulen und Bibliotheken in der Karolingerzeit.* Vol. 2. *Die vorwiegend österreichischen Diözesen.* 3rd ed. Wiesbaden: Harrassowitz, 1980.

Bishop, Terence A. M. "Autographa of John the Scot." In *Jean Scot Érigène et l'histoire de la philosophie: Colloques internationaux du C.N.R.S. 561,* edited by R. Roques, 47–58. Paris: Éditions du Centre national de la recherche scientifique, 1977.

Bockholdt, Petra. "'Conditio—qualitas—proprietas.' Über die Bestimmung des Tons in der *Musica enchiriadis.*" *Musiktheorie* 12 (1997): 119–24.

Bomm, Urbanus. *Der Wechsel der Modalitätsbestimmung in der Tradition der Meßgesänge im 9. bis 13. Jahrhundert.* Einsiedeln: Benziger, 1929; repr., Hildesheim: Georg Olms, 1975.

Bower, Calvin. *Anicius Manlius Severinus Boethius: Fundamentals of Music.* Music Theory Translation Series. New Haven, Conn.: Yale University Press, 1989.

————. "Boethius and Nichomachus: An Essay Concerning the Sources of *De Institutione Musica.*" *Vivarium* 16 (1978): 1–45.

————. "Boethius' *De institutione musica:* A Handlist of Manuscripts." *Scriptorium* 42 (1988): 205–51.

————. "Boethius' The Principles of Music." Ph.D. diss., George Peabody College for Teachers, 1967.

————. "The Grammatical Model of Musical Understanding in the Middle Ages." In *Hermeneutics and Medieval Culture,* edited by Patrick Gallacher and Helen Damico, 133–45. Albany: State University of New York Press, 1989.

————. "The Modes of Boethius." *JM* 3 (1984): 252–64.

————. "Natural and Artificial Music: The Origins and Development of an Aesthetic Concept." *MD* 25 (1971): 17–33.

————. "The Role of Boethius' *De institutione musica* in the Speculative Tradition of Western Musical Thought." In *Boethius and the Liberal Arts: A Collection of Essays,* edited by Michael Masi, 157–74. Utah Studies in Literature and Linguistics 18. Las Vegas: P. Lang, 1981.

————. "The Transmission of Ancient Music Theory into the Middle Ages." In *The Cambridge History of Western Music Theory,* edited by Thomas Christensen, 136–67. Cambridge: Cambridge University Press, 2002.

————. "Die Wechselwirkung von *philosophia, mathematica* und *musica* in der karolingischen Rezeption der 'Institutio musica' von Boethius." In *Musik und die Geschichte der Philoso-*

phie und Naturwissenschaften im Mittelalter, edited by Frank Hentschel, 163–83. Studien und Texte zur Geistesgeschichte des Mittelalters 62. Leiden: Brill, 1998.

Bower, Calvin, and Michael Bernhard. *Glossa maior in institutionem musicam Boethii.* Veröffentlichungen der Musikhistorischen Kommission 9. Munich: Bayerische Akademie der Wissenschaften, 1993–.

Boyle, Leonard. "The Friars and Reading in Public." In *Le Vocabulaire des écoles des mendiants au moyen âge. Actes du colloque, Porto (Portugal), 11–12 octobre 1996,* edited by Maria Candida Pacheco, 8–15. CIVICIMA. Études sur le vocabulaire intellectual du moyen âge 9. Turnhout: Brepols, 1999.

———. "Tonic Accent, Codicology, and Literacy." In *The Centre and Its Compass: Studies in Medieval Literature in Honor of Professor John Leyerle,* edited by Robert A. Taylor et al., 1–10. Medieval Institute Publications. Kalamazoo: Western Michigan University, 1993.

———. *"Vox paginae": An Oral Dimension of Texts.* Unione internazionale degli istituti di archeologia, storia e storia dell'arte in Roma, Conferenze 16. Rome: Unione internazionale degli istituti di archeologia, storia e storia dell'arte in Roma, 1999.

Brambach, Wilhelm. *Das Tonsystem und die Tonarten des christlichen Abendlandes im Mittelalter, ihre Beziehungen zur griechisch-römischen Musik und ihre Entwicklung bis auf die Schule Guidos von Arezzo.* Leipzig: Teubner, 1881.

Brockett, Clyde. "Comparison of the Five Monochords of Guido of Arezzo." *Current Musicology* 32 (1981): 29–42.

———. "Noeane and Neuma. A Theoretical and Musical Equation." In *Report of the Eleventh Congress of the International Musicological Society, Copenhagen 1972,* edited by Henrik Glahn et al., 1: 301–8. Copenhagen: Wilhelm Hansen, 1974.

———. *"Saeculorum Amen* and *Differentia:* Practical versus Theoretical Tradition." *MD* 30 (1976): 13–36.

Browne, Alma Colk [see also Santosuosso, Alma Colk Browne]. "The a–p System of Letter Notation." *MD* 35 (1981): 5–54.

Brunhölzl, Franz. "Der Bildungsauftrag der Hofschule." In *Karl der Große: Lebenswerk und Nachleben,* vol. 2, *Das geistige Leben,* edited by Bernhard Bischoff, 28–41. Düsseldorf: L. Schwann, 1965.

———. *Geschichte der lateinischen Literatur des Mittelalters.* Vol. 1. *Von Cassiodor bis zum Ausklang der karolingischen Erneuerung.* Munich: Fink, 1975.

Bullough, Donald. *Carolingian Renewal: Sources and Heritage.* Manchester, England: Manchester University Press, 1991.

———. *"Europae Pater:* Charlemagne and His Achievement in the Light of Recent Scholarship." *English Historical Review* 85 (1970): 59–105.

Burkert, Walter. *Weisheit und Wissenschaft: Studien zu Pythagoras, Philolaus und Platon.* Erlanger Beiträge zur Sprach- und Kunstwissenschaft 10. Nuremberg: Hans Carl, 1962. Translated by Edwin L. Minar as *Lore and Science in Ancient Pythagoreanism.* Cambridge, Mass.: Harvard University Press, 1972.

Caldwell, John. "From Cantor to Parchment: Linguistic Aspects of Early Western Notation." *Musica antiqua Europae orientalis* 8/1, 219–31. Bydgoszcz, Poland: Philharmonia Pomorska im. Ignacego Paderewskiego, 1988.

Cappuyns, Maieul. "Martianus Capella." In *Dictionnaire d'histoire et de géographie ecclésiastique,* vol. 11, col. 843. Paris: Letouzey et Ané, 1949.

Cardine, Eugene. "Sémiologie grégorienne." *EG* 11 (1970): 1–158. Originally published as *Semiologia gregoriana.* Rome: Pontificio Istituto de Musica Sacra, 1968.

Chartier, Yves. "Hucbald de Saint-Amand et la notation musicale." In *Musicologie médiévale. Notations et séquences. Actes de la Table ronde du C.N.R.S. à l'Institut de recherche et d'histoire des textes, 1982*, edited by Michel Huglo, 145–56. Paris: Éditions du Centre national de la recherche scientifique, 1987.

Cohen, David. "Notes, Scales and Modes in the Earlier Middle Ages." In *The Cambridge History of Western Music Theory*, edited by Thomas Christensen, 307–63. Cambridge: Cambridge University Press, 2002.

Colette, Marie-Noël. *Analyse du manuscrit Montpellier H 159, "tonaire de Dijon, XIe s."* Introduction and notes to *Cantor et Musicus* (CD ROM). Montpellier: Bibliothèque Interuniversitaire de Montpellier, 2000.

———. "Des introïts témoins de psalmodie archaïque." In *Requirentes modos musicos. Mélanges offerts à Dom Jean Claire*, edited by Daniel Saulnier, with the assistance of Micheline Albert, 165–78. Solesmes: Abbaye de St.-Pierre, 1995.

———. *Gui d'Arezzo, Micrologus, traduction française, en collaboration avec J. C. Jolivet.* Paris: Institut de pédagogie musicale et chorégraphique, 1993.

———. "La Sémiologie comme voie d'accès à la connaissance de l'interprétation au moyen âge." In *Musicologie médiévale. Notations et séquences. Actes de la Table ronde du C.N.R.S. à l'Institut de recherche et d'histoire des textes, 1982*, edited by Michel Huglo, 121–28. Paris: Éditions du Centre national de la recherche scientifique, 1987.

Contreni, John. *Carolingian Learning. Masters and Manuscripts.* Aldershot, England: Ashgate, 1992.

———. "The Carolingian Renaissance: Education and Literary Culture." In *The New Cambridge Medieval History*, vol. 2, *c. 700–c. 900*, edited by Rosamond McKitterick, 709–57. Cambridge: Cambridge University Press, 1995.

———. *The Cathedral School of Laon from 850 to 930: Its Manuscripts and Masters.* Münchener Beiträge zur Mediävistik und Renaissance-Forschung 29. Munich: Arbeo-Gesellschaft, 1978.

———. "Inharmonious Harmony: Education in the Carolingian World," *Annals of Scholarship* 1 (1980): 81–96.

———. "A Note on the Attribution of a Martianus Capella Commentary to Martinus Laudunensis (Martinus Scotus), 'Martianus Capella. Addenda et corrigenda.'" *CTC*, 3 (1976): 451–52.

Corbin, Solange. "Neumatic Notations, I–IV." *NG* 13: 128–44.

———. *Die Neumen.* In *Palaeographie der Musik*, vol. 1, pt. 3, edited by Wulf Arlt. Cologne: Arno Volk Verlag, 1977.

———. "The Neumes of the Martianus Capella Manuscripts." In *Essays on Opera and English Music in Honor of Sir Jack Westrup*, edited by F. W. Sternfeld et al., 1–7. Oxford: Clarendon Press, 1975.

———. "Les Notations neumatiques à l'époque carolingienne." *Revue d'histoire de l'église de France* 38/39 (1952): 225–32.

———. "Les Représentations de neumes dans les livres peints au neuvième siècle." *EG* 1 (1954): 169–71.

———, ed. *Répertoire des manuscrits médiévaux contenant des notations musicales.* 3 vols. Paris: Éditions du Centre national de la recherche scientifique, 1965–74.

———. "Valeur et sens de la notation alphabétique à Jumièges et en Normandie." In *Jumièges: Congrès scientifique du XIIIe centenaire*, 2: 913–24. Rouen: Lecerf, 1955.

Crocker, Richard. "Frankish Music Theory." In *New Oxford History of Music*, 2: 278–83. 2nd ed. Oxford: Clarendon Press, 1990.

———. "Hermann's Major Sixth." *JAMS* 25 (1972): 19–37.

———. "Medieval Chant." In *New Oxford History of Music*, 2: 256–64. 2nd ed. Oxford: Clarendon Press, 1990.

Cullin, Olivier. "Écritures (Noter la musique I)." In *Laborintus: Essais sur la musique au moyen âge*, 17–46. Paris: Fayard, 2004.

DeJong, M. B. "From *Scolastici* to *Scioli*: Alcuin and the Formation of an Intellectual Elite." In *Alcuin of York: Scholar at the Carolingian Court. Proceedings of the Third Germania Latina Conference, University of Groningen, May, 1995*, edited by L. A. J. R. Houwen and A. A. McDonald, 45–58. Mediaevalia Groningana 22. Groningen: Forsten, 1998.

Delalande, P. Dominique. "L'Insuffisance du système d'écriture guidonien, ou l'existence de plusieurs notes mobiles dans le système grégorien." In *Atti del congresso internazionale di musica sacra, Roma 1950*, edited by Higini Anglès, 202–6. Tournai: Desclée, 1952.

Delisle, Léopold. *Le Cabinet des manuscrits de la Bibliothèque Impériale: Étude sur la formation de ce dépôt comprenant les éléments d'histoire de la calligraphie, de la miniature, de la reliure, et du commerce des livres à Paris avant l'invention de l'imprimerie*. 4 vols. Paris: Imprimerie impériale, 1868–81.

———. *Mémoire sur d'anciens sacramentaires*. Mémoires de l'Institut national de France, Académie des inscriptions et belles-lettres 32. Paris: Imprimerie nationale, 1886.

Deshusses, Jean. "Chronologie des grands sacramentaires de Saint-Amand." *RB* 87 (1977): 230–37.

———. "Encore les sacramentaires de Saint-Amand." *RB* 89 (1979): 310–12.

Duchez, Marie-Elisabeth. "Description grammaticale et description arithmétique des phénomènes musicaux: Le Tournant du IXe siècle." In *Sprache und Erkenntnis im Mittelalter: Akten des VI. Internationalen Kongresses für mittelalterliche Philosophie der Société internationale pour l'étude de la philosophie médiévale, 29. August–3. September 1977 in Bonn*, edited by Jan P. Beckmann et al., 561–79. Miscellanea Mediaevalia 13/2. Berlin: de Gruyter, 1981.

———. "Des neumes à la portée: Elaboration et organisation rationnelles de la discontinuité musicale et de sa représentation graphique, de la formule mélodique à l'échelle monocordale." *Revue de musique des universités canadiennes* 4 (1983): 22–65. Short version in *Musicologie médiévale. Notations et séquences. Actes de la Table ronde du C.N.R.S. à l'Institut de recherche et d'histoire des textes, 1982*, edited by Michel Huglo, 57–60. Paris: Éditions du Centre national de la recherche scientifique, 1987.

———. "Jean Scot Érigène, premier lecteur du 'De institutione musica' de Boèce?" In *Eriugena: Studien zu seinen Quellen. Vorträge des 3. Internationalen Eriugena-Colloquiums Freiburg im Breisgau, 1979*, edited by Werner Beierwaltes, 165–87. Abhandlungen der Heidelberger Akademie der Wissenschaften, Philosophisch-historische Klasse, 1980. Heidelberg: Carl Winter Universitätsverlag, 1980.

———. "La Représentation de la musique: Information d'action et expression structurelle dans la représentation de la musique occidentale traditionnelle." In *Actes du XVIIIe Congrès des sociétés de philosophie de langue française, Strasbourg, Juillet 1980*, 177–82. Strasbourg: Association des publications près des Universités de Strasbourg. Paris: Vrin, 1982.

———. "La Représentation spatio-verticale du caractère musical grave-aigu et l'élaboration de la notion de hauteur de son dans la conscience musicale occidentale." *ActaM* 51 (1979): 54–73.

———. "Le Savoir théorico-musical carolingien dans les commentaires de Martianus Capella. La Tradition érigénienne." In *Giovanni Scoto nel suo tempo: L'organizzazione del sapere en età carolingia. Atti del XXIV convegno storico internazionale, Todi, 11–14 ottobre 1987*, 553–92. Spoleto: Centro italiano di studi sull'alto medioevo, 1989.

Duckett, Eleanor. *Alcuin, Friend of Charlemagne: His World and His Work*. Hamden, Conn.: Archon Books, 1965.

Dyer, Joseph. "The Monastic Origins of Western Music Theory." In *IMS Study Group Cantus Planus: Papers Read at the Third Meeting, Tihany, Hungary, 19–24 September 1988*, edited by

László Dobszay et al., 199–225. Budapest: Hungarian Academy of Sciences, Institute for Musicology, 1990.

Ellsworth, Oliver. "The Origin of the *Coniuncta:* A Reappraisal." *Journal of Music Theory* 17 (1973): 86–109.

Erickson, Raymond. "Eriugena, Boethius and the Neoplatonism of *Musica* and *Scolica enchiriadis.*" In *Musical Humanism and Its Legacy: Essays in Honor of Claude V. Palisca,* edited by Nancy Kovaleff Baker and Barbara Hanning, 53–78. Festschrift Series 11. Stuyvesant, N.Y.: Pendragon Press, 1992.

———. *Musica enchiriadis and Scolica enchiriadis.* Music Theory Translation Series. New Haven, Conn.: Yale University Press, 1995.

Ferrari-Barassi, Elena. "I modi ecclesiastici nei trattati musicali dell'età carolingia." *Studi musicali* 4 (1975): 3–56.

Ferreira, Manuel Pedro R. "Music at Cluny: The Tradition of Gregorian Chant for the Proper of the Mass: Melodic Variants and Microtonal Nuances." Ph.D. diss., Princeton University, 1997.

Fischer, Rupert. "Die Notation von Stücken mit chromatisch alterierten Tönen—Schwierigkeiten der melodischen Restitution." *Beiträge zur Gregorianik* 29 (2000): 43–78.

Fisher, Scott Alden. "*Tonos* and Its Relatives: A Word Study." Ph.D. diss., Ohio State University, 1989.

Fleischer, Oskar. *Die spätgriechische Tonschrift.* Neumen-Studien 3. Berlin: G. Reimer, 1904.

Floros, Constantin. *Universale Neumenkunde.* 3 vols. Kassel: Bärenreiter, 1970.

Frasch, Cheryl Crawford. "Notation as a Guide to Modality in the Offertories of Paris, Bibliothèque nationale, lat. 903." Ph.D. diss., Ohio State University, 1986.

Freistedt, Heinrich. *Die liqueszierenden Noten des gregorianischen Chorals.* Freiburg, Switzerland: Sankt Paulus-Druckerei, 1929.

Froger, Jacques. "L'Epitre de Notker sur les 'lettres significatives': Édition critique." *EG* 5 (1962): 23–71.

———. "Les Prétendus Quarts de ton dans le chant grégorien et les symboles du MS H 159 de Montpellier." *EG* 17 (1978): 145–79.

Fuller, Sarah. "An Anonymous Treatise dictus de Sancto Martiale." *MD* 71 (1977): 5–30.

Ganshof, François Louis. "Alcuin's Revision of the Bible." In *The Carolingians and the Frankish Monarchy,* translated by Janet Sondheimer, 28–40. Ithaca, N.Y.: Cornell University Press, 1971.

———. "The Use of the Written Word in Charlemagne's Administration." In *The Carolingians and the Frankish Monarchy,* translated by Janet Sondheimer, 125–42. Ithaca, N.Y.: Cornell University Press, 1971.

Ganz, David. "Book Production and the Spread of Caroline Minuscule." In *The New Cambridge Medieval History,* vol. 2, *c. 700–c. 900,* edited by Rosamond McKitterick, 786–808. Cambridge: Cambridge University Press, 1995.

———. *Corbie in the Carolingian Renaissance.* Beihefte der Francia 20. Sigmaringen, Germany: Thorbecke, 1990.

———. "Heiric d'Auxerre, glossateur du *Liber glossarum.*" In *L'École carolingienne d'Auxerre. De Murethach à Remy 830–908,* edited by D. Iogna-Prat et al., 297–305. Paris: Beauchesne, 1991.

———. "Theology and the Organisation of Thought." In *The New Cambridge Medieval History,* vol. 2, *c. 700–c. 900,* edited by Rosamond McKitterick, 758–85. Cambridge: Cambridge University Press, 1995.

Gastoué, Amedée. "Über die acht Töne." *KmJb* 25 (1930): 25–30.

Gevaert, François Auguste. *Histoire et théorie de la musique de l'antiquité.* 2 vols. Gand, Belgium: Annoot-Braeckman, 1875–81.

————. *La Mélopée antique dans les chants de l'église latine*. Gand, Belgium: A. Hoste, 1895–96.

Gibson, Margaret T., and Jane L. Nelson, eds. *Charles the Bald: Court and Kingdom*. Rev. ed. Aldershot, England: Ashgate, 1990.

Glauche, Günther. *Schullektüre im Mittelalter*. Münchener Beiträge zur Mediävistik und Renaissance-Forschung 5. Munich: Arbeo-Gesellschaft, 1970.

Gmelch, Joseph. *Die Viertelstonstufen im Meßtonale von Montpellier*. Veröffentlichungen der Gregorianischen Akademie zu Freiburg (Schweiz) 6. Eichstätt, Germany: Ph. Brönnersche Buchdruckerei (P. Seitz), 1911.

Göschl, Johannes Berchmans. "Der gegenwärtige Stand der semiologischen Forschung," *Beiträge zur Gregorianik* 1 (1985): 43–102.

————. *Semiologische Untersuchungen zum Phänomen der gregorianischen Liqueszenz: Der isolierte dreistufige Epiphonus praepunctis, ein Sonderproblem der Liqueszenzforschung*. 2 vols. Forschungen zur älteren Musikgeschichte 3. Vienna: Verband der wissenschaftlichen Gesellschaften Österreichs, 1980.

————, ed. *Ut mens concordet voci: Festschrift Eugène Cardine zum 75. Geburtstag*. St. Ottilien, Germany: EOS-Verlag, 1980.

Gombosi, Otto. "Studien zur Tonartenlehre des frühen Mittelalters–I." *ActaM* 10 (1938): 149–74; II: *ActaM* 11 (1939): 28–39, 128–35; *ActaM* 12 (1940): 21–29; III: *ActaM* 12 (1940): 29–52.

Grebe, Sabine. "Die Musiktheorie des Martianus Capella: Eine Betrachtung der in 9,921–935 benutzten Quellen." *International Journal of Musicology* 2 (1993): 23–60.

Grier, James. "Adémar de Chabannes, Carolingian Musical Practices, and the *Nota Romana*." *JAMS* 56 (2003): 43–98.

Gümpel, Karl-Werner. "Musica cum Rhetorica: Die Handschrift Ripoll 42." *AfMw* 42 (1977): 260–86.

Gushee, Lawrence. "The *Musica Disciplina* of Aurelian of Réôme, a Critical Text and Commentary." Ph.D. diss., Yale University, 1963.

————. "Questions of Genre in Medieval Treatises on Music." In *Gattungen der Music in Einzeldarstellungen: Gedenkschrift Leo Schrade*, edited by Wulf Arlt et al., 365–433. Bern: Francke Verlag, 1973.

Gysin, Hans-Peter. *Studien zum Vokabular der Musiktheorie im Mittelalter*. Amsterdam: Frits Knuf, 1958. (Ph.D. diss., Universität Basel)

Haas, Max. *Byzantinische und slavische Notationen*. Cologne: Arno Volk Verlag, 1973.

————. "Modus als Skala—Modus als Modellmelodie. Ein Problem musikalischer Überlieferung in der Zeit vor den ersten notierten Quellen." In *Palaeobyzantine Notations. A Reconsideration of the Source Material*, edited by Jørgen Raasted and Christian Troelsgård, 11–32. Hernen, Netherlands: A. A. Bredius Foundation, 1995.

————. *Mündliche Überlieferung und altrömischer Choral: Historische und analytische computergestützte Untersuchungen*. Bern: Lang, 1996.

————. "Die *Musica enchiriadis* und ihr Umfeld: Elementare Musiklehre als Propaedeutik zur Philosophie." In *Musik und die Geschichte der Philosophie und Naturwissenschaften im Mittelalter*, edited by Frank Hentschel, 210–26. Studien und Texte zur Geistesgeschichte des Mittelalters 62. Leiden: Brill, 1998.

————. "Notation IV: Neumen." *MGG 2*, Sachteil [Subjects] 7 (1997), cols. 296–317; 418–19.

Haggh, Barbara. "Aurelian's Library." In *IMS Study Group Cantus Planus: Papers Read at the Ninth Meeting, Esztergom and Visegrád, 1998*, edited by László Dobszay et al., 271–300. Budapest: Hungarian Academy of Sciences, Institute for Musicology, 2001.

————. "Traktat 'Musica disciplina' Aureliana Reomensis. Proweniencja i datowanie." *Muzyka: Kwartalnik Instytutu Sztuki Polskiej Akademii Nauk* 45 (2000): 25–79 (summary in English 78–79).

Handschin, Jacques."Eine alte Neumenschrift." *ActaM* 22 (1950): 69–97.

―――. "Die Musikanschauung des Johannes Scotus (Eriugena)." *Deutsche Vierteljahresschrift für Literaturwissenschaft und Geistesgeschichte* 5 (1927): 316–41.

―――. "Zu 'Eine alte Neumenschrift.'" *ActaM* 25 (1953): 87–88.

Hankeln, Roman. *Die Offertoriums-Prosuln der Aquitanischen Handschriften: Voruntersuchung zur Edition des aquitanischen Offertoriumscorpus und seiner Erweiterungen.* Regensburger Studien zur Musikgeschichte 2. Tutzing: Hans Schneider, 1999.

―――. "Tonar." *MGG 2*, Sachteil [Subjects] 9 (1998), cols. 629–37.

Hannick, Christian. "Die Lehrschriften zur byzantinischen Kirchenmusik." In *Die hochsprachliche profane Literatur der Byzantiner*, edited by Herbert Hunger, 2: 196–218. Byzantinisches Handbuch im Rahmen des Handbuchs der Altertumswissenschaft, pt. 5, vol. 2. Munich: Beck, 1978.

Haug, Andreas. "Zur Interpretation der Liqueszenzneumen." *AfMw* 50 (1993): 85–100.

Hebborn, Barbara. *Die Dasia-Notation.* Orpheus Schriftenreihe zu Grundfragen der Musik 79. Bonn: Orpheus-Verlag, 1995.

Henderson, Isobel. "Ancient Greek Music." *New Oxford History of Music* 1: 336–403.

Hildebrandt, M. M. *The External School in Carolingian Society.* Leiden: Brill, 1992.

Hiley, David. "Modus I: Das frühe Mittelalter." *MGG 2*, Sachteil [Subjects] 6 (1997), cols. 397–413.

―――. "Notation III, 1: Western, Plainchant." *NG 2*, 18: 344–54.

―――. "The Plica and Liquescence." In *Gordon Athol Anderson (1929–1981) in Memoriam*, edited by Luther Dittmer, 379–91. Musicological Studies 49. Ottawa: Institute of Medieval Music, 1984.

―――. *Western Plainchant: A Handbook.* Oxford: Clarendon Press, 1993.

Hochadel, Matthias. "Zur Stellung des pseudo-bernonischen Traktats *De mensurando monochordo* und seinem Verhältnis zu Frutolfs *Breviarium*." In *Beiträge zur Musik, Musiktheorie und Liturgie der Abtei Reichenau. Bericht über die Tagung Heiligenkreuz 6.–8. Dez. 1999*, edited by Walter Pass and Alexander Rausch, 41–68. Musica Mediaevalis Europae Occidentalis 8. Tutzing: Hans Schneider, 2001.

Hoffmann-Axthelm, Dagmar. "Tenor." *HmT*, 1973.

Holtz, Louis. "L'École d'Auxerre." In *L'École carolingienne d'Auxerre. De Murethach à Remy 830–908*, edited by D. Iogna-Prat et al., 131–46. Paris: Beauchesne, 1991.

―――. "Murethach et l'influence de la culture irlandaise à Auxerre." In *L'École carolingienne d'Auxerre. De Murethach à Remy 830–908*, edited by D. Iogna-Prat et al., 147–56. Paris: Beauchesne, 1991.

―――. "Sur trois commentaires irlandais de l'*Art majeur* de Donat au IXe siècle." *Revue d'histoire des textes* 2 (1972): 45–72.

Hourlier, Jacques. "Le Domaine de la notation messine." *RG* 30 (1951): 96–113, 150–58.

Hourlier, Jacques, and Michel Huglo. "La Notation paléofranque." *EG* 2 (1957): 212–19.

Hucke, Helmut. "Die Anfänge der abendländischen Notenschrift." In *Festschrift Rudolf Elvers zum 60. Geburtstag*, edited by Ernst Hettrich and Hans Schneider, 271–88. Tutzing: Hans Schneider, 1985.

―――. "Die Cheironomie und die Entstehung der Neumenschrift." *Mf* 32 (1979): 1–16.

―――. "Choralforschung und Musikwissenschaft." In *Das musikalische Kunstwerk. Geschichte—Ästhetik—Theorie. Festschrift Carl Dahlhaus zum 60. Geburtstag*, edited by H. Danuser et al., 131–41. Laaber, Germany: Laaber Verlag, 1988.

―――. "Die Einführung des Gregorianischen Gesangs im Frankenreich." *Römische Quartalschrift* 49 (1954): 172–87.

―――. "Die Entstehung der Überlieferung von einer musikalischen Tätigkeit Gregors des Grossen." *Mf* 8 (1955): 259–64.

―――. "Gregorianische Fragen." *Mf* 41 (1988): 304–30.

————. "Die Herkunft der Kirchentonarten und die fränkische Überlieferung des Gregorianischen Gesangs." In *Gesellschaft für Musikforschung: Bericht über den internationalen musikwissenschaftlichen Kongreß Berlin 1974,* edited by Helmut Kühn and Peter Nitsche, 257–60. Kassel: Bärenreiter, 1977.

————. "Karolingische Renaissance und Gregorianischer Gesang," *Mf* 28 (1975): 4–18.

————. "Towards a New Historical View of Gregorian Chant." *JAMS* 33 (1980): 437–67.

————. "Der Übergang von mündlicher zu schriftlicher Musiküberlieferung im Mittelalter." In *Proceedings of the Twelfth Congress of the International Musicological Society, Berkeley 1977,* edited by Daniel Heartz and Bonnie Wade, 180–91. Kassel: Bärenreiter, 1981.

Hüschen, Heinrich. "Regino von Prüm, Historiker, Kirchenrechtler und Musiktheoretiker." In *Festschrift Karl Gustav Fellerer zum 60. Geburtstag,* edited by Heinrich Hüschen, 205–23. Regensburg: G. Bosse, 1962.

Hughes, David. "Evidence for the Traditional View of the Transmission of Gregorian Chant." *JAMS* 40 (1987): 377–404.

————. "The Implications of Variants for Chant Transmission." In *"De musica et cantu": Studien zur Geschichte der Kirchenmusik und der Oper: Helmut Hucke zum 60. Geburtstag,* edited by Peter Kahn and Ann-Katrin Heimer, 65–73. Hochschule für Musik und Darstellende Kunst, Frankfurt am Main, Musikwissenschaftliche Publikationen 2. Hildesheim: Georg Olms, 1993.

Huglo, Michel. "L'Auteur du Dialogue sur la musique attribué à Odon" *RdM* 55 (1969): 119–71. Reprinted in *The Garland Library of the History of Western Music,* edited by Ellen Rosand, 1: 95–148. New York: Garland Press, 1985.

————. "L'Auteur du traité de musique dedié à Fulgence d'Affligem." *Revue belge de musicologie* 31 (1977): 5–19. Reprinted in *La Théorie de la musique antique et médiévale,* no. 10. Variorum Collected Studies Series CS822. Aldershot, England: Ashgate, 2005.

————. "Bibliographie des éditions et études relatives à la théorie musicale du moyen âge (1972–1987)." *ActaM* 40 (1988): 229–72.

————. "Bilan de 50 années de recherches (1939–1989) sur les notations musicales de 850 à 1300." *ActaM* 62 (1990): 224–59.

————. "La Chironomie médiévale." *RdM* 49 (1963): 155–71.

————. "Comparaison de la terminologie modale en orient et en occident." In *Report of the Eleventh Congress of the International Musicological Society, Copenhagen 1972,* edited by Henrik Glahn et al., 2: 758–61. Copenhagen: Wilhelm Hansen, 1974.

————. "Le Développement du vocabulaire de l'*Ars musica* à l'époque carolingienne." *Latomus* 34 (1975): 131–51.

————. "Les Formules d'intonations 'noeane noeagis' en Orient et en Occident." In *Aspects de la musique liturgique au moyen âge: Actes de colloques de Royaumont de 1986, 1987, 1988,* edited by Christian Meyer, 43–53. Paris: Éditions Créaphis, 1991.

————. "Gerbert, théoricien de la musique, vu de l'an 2000." *Cahiers de civilisation médiévale* 43 (2000): 143–60. Reprinted in *La Théorie de la musique antique et médiévale,* no. 7. Variorum Collected Studies Series CS822. Aldershot, England: Ashgate, 2005.

————. "Grundlagen und Ansätze der mittelalterlichen Musiktheorie von der Spätantike bis zur ottonischen Zeit." In *Die Lehre vom einstimmigen liturgischen Gesang,* edited by Thomas Ertelt and Frieder Zaminer, 18–102. GdMth 4, 2000.

————. "Les Instruments de musique chez Hucbald." *Mélanges à la mémoire d'André Boutemy,* ed. Guy Cambier, 173–96. Collection Latomus 145. Brussels: Latomus, 1976. Reprinted in *La Théorie de la musique antique et médiévale,* no. 6. Variorum Collected Studies Series CS822. Aldershot, England: Ashgate, 2005.

————. "L'Introduction en occident des formules byzantines d'intonation." *Studies in Eastern Chant* 3 (1973): 81–90.

————. "Die Musica Isidori nach den Handschriften des deutschen Sprachgebietes mit

Berücksichtigung der Handschrift Wien, ÖNB 683." In *Mittelalterliche Musiktheorie in Zentraleuropa*, edited by Walter Pass and Alexander Rausch, 79–86. Musica mediaevalis Europae occidentalis 4. Tutzing: Hans Schneider, 1998.

———. "Les Noms des neumes et leur origine." *EG* 1 (1954): 53–67. Reprinted in *La Théorie de la musique antique et médiévale*, no. 17. Variorum Collected Studies Series CS822. Aldershot, England: Ashgate, 2005.

———. "Un Nouveau Manuscrit du Dialogue sur la musique du Pseudo-Odon (Troyes, Bibl. mun. 2142)." *Revue d'histoire des textes* 9 (1979): 299–314. Reprinted in *La Théorie de la musique antique et médiévale*, no. 9. Variorum Collected Studies Series, CS822. Aldershot, England: Ashgate, 2005.

———. "Odo." *NG* 13: 503–4.

———. "Der Prolog des Odo zugeschriebenen 'Dialogus de Musica.'" *AfMw* 28 (1971): 134–46. Reprinted in *La Théorie de la musique antique et médiévale*, no. 8. Variorum Collected Studies Series, CS822. Aldershot: Ashgate, 2005.

———. "La Réception de Calcidius et des *Commentarii* de Macrobe à l'époque carolingienne." *Scriptorium* 44 (1990): 3–20. Reprinted in *La Théorie de la musique antique et médiévale*, 4. Variorum Collected Studies Series, CS822. Aldershot: Ashgate, 2005.

———. "Relations et influences réciproques entre musique de l'Orient grec et musique occidentale." In *The Proceedings of the Thirteenth International Congress of Byzantine Studies, Oxford 1966*, edited by J. M. Hussey et al., 267–80. Oxford: Oxford University Press, 1967. Reprinted in *Les Anciens Répertoires de plain-chant*, no. 15. Variorum Collected Studies Series, CS804. Aldershot, England: Ashgate, 2005.

———. "Römisch-fränkische Liturgie." In *Geschichte der katholischen Kirchenmusik*, vol. 1, *Von den Anfängen bis zum Tridentinum*, edited by Karl Gustav Fellerer, 233–44. Kassel: Bärenreiter, 1972.

———. "Le Tonaire de Saint-Bénigne de Dijon." *ActaM* 4 (1956): 7–18.

———. "Un Tonaire du graduel de la fin du VIIIe siècle (Paris, B.N. lat. 15139)." *RG* 31 (1952): 176–86, 224–33.

———. *Les Tonaires. Inventaire, analyse, comparaison*. Paris: Société française de musicologie, 1971.

———. "Tonary." *NG* 19: 55–59.

———. "Tradition orale et tradition écrite dans la transmission des mélodies grégoriennes." In *Studien zur Tradition in der Musik: Kurt von Fischer zum 60. Geburtstag*, edited by Hans Heinrich Eggebrecht and Max Lütolf, 31–42. Munich: E. Katzbichler, 1973.

———. "Un Troisième Témoin du tonaire carolingien." *ActaM* 40 (1968): 22–28.

Huglo, Michel, and J. Hourlier. "La Notation paléofranque." *EG* 2 (1957): 212–19.

Huglo, Michel, and Christian Meyer. *The Theory of Music. Manuscripts from the Carolingian Era up to c.1500 in the Federal Republic of Germany (D-brd)*. RISM B III³. Munich: Henle, 1986.

Iogna-Prat, Dominique, Colette Jeudy, and Guy Lobrichon, eds. *L'École carolingienne d'Auxerre. De Murethach à Remy 830–908*. Paris: Beauchesne, 1991.

Jacobsthal, Gustav. *Die chromatische Alteration im liturgischen Gesang der abendländischen Kirche.* Berlin: Springer, 1897.

Jammers, Ewald. "Die Entstehung der Neumenschrift." In *Schrift, Ordnung, Gestalt: Gesammelte Aufsätze zur älteren Musikgeschichte*, 1: 70–87. Neue Heidelberger Studien zur Musikwissenschaft. Bern: Francke Verlag, 1969.

———. *Die Essener Neumenhandschriften der Landes- und Stadtbibliothek Düsseldorf.* Veröffentlichungen der Landes- und Stadtbibliothek Düsseldorf 1. Ratingen, Germany: Aloys Henn Verlag, 1952.

———. "Gedanken und Beobachtungen zur Geschichte der Notenschriften." In *Festschrift für Walter Wiora zum 30. Dezember 1966,* edited by Ludwig Finscher and Christoph Mahling, 196–204. Kassel: Bärenreiter, 1967.

———. *Der gregorianische Rhythmus: Antiphonale Studien (mit einer Übertragung der Introitus- und Offiziumsantiphonen des 1. Tones).* Sammlung musikwissenschaftlicher Abhandlungen 25. Zurich: Heitz, 1937.

———. *Musik in Byzanz, im päpstlichen Rom und im Frankenreich: Der Choral als Musik der Textaussprache.* Abhundlungen der Heidelberger Akademie der Wissenschaften, Philosophisch-historische Klasse, 1. Heidelberg: Carl Winter Universitätsverlag, 1962.

———. "Die Paläofränkische Neumenschrift." *Scriptorium* 7, 2 (1953): 235–58.

———. *Tafeln zur Neumenschrift.* Tutzing: Hans Schneider, 1965.

Jammers, Ewald, H. Schmid, R. Schlötterer, and E. Waeltner. "Byzantinisches in der karolingischen Musik." In *Berichte zum XI. Internationalen Byzantinisten-Kongreß, München 1958,* 1–29. Munich: Beck, 1958.

Jeauneau, Éduoard. "Les Écoles de Laon et d'Auxerre au IXe siècle." In *La scuola nell'occidente latino dell'alto medioevo,* 2: 459–522. Settimane di studio dell Centro italiano di studi sull'alto medioevo 19. Spoleto: Presso la sede del Centro, 1972.

Jeffery, Peter. "The Oldest Sources of the *Graduale:* A Preliminary Checklist of Manuscripts Copied before about 900 A.D." *JM* 2 (1983): 316–21.

Jeudy, C. "L'Œuvre de Remi d'Auxerre: État de la question." In *L'École carolingienne d'Auxerre. De Murethach à Remy 830–908,* edited by D. Iogna-Prat et al., 373–97. Paris: Beauchesne, 1991.

Kaczynski, Bernice M. *Greek in the Carolingian Age: The St. Gall Manuscripts.* Speculum Anniversary Monographs 13. Cambridge, Mass.: Medieval Academy of America, 1988.

Karp, Theodore. *Aspects of Orality and Formularity in Gregorian Chant.* Evanston, Ill.: Northwestern University Press, 1998.

———. "The Offertory *In die sollemnitatis.*" In *Laborare fratres in unum. Festschrift László Dobszay zum 60. Geburtstag,* edited by David Hiley and Janka Szendrei, 151–65. Spolia Berolinensia 7. Hildesheim: Georg Olms, 1995.

Kent, Roland G., trans. *Varro: On the Latin Language.* 2 vols. Loeb Classical Library, Latin Authors. Cambridge, Mass.: Harvard University Press, 1938.

Kessler, Ernst. *Über die leiterfremden Tonstufen im gregorianischen Gesang. Zur Geschichte des mittelalterlichen Tonsystems.* Veröffentlichungen der gregorianischen Akademie zu Freiburg in der Schweiz 10. Dornbirn, Austria: Vorarlberger Verlagsanstalt, 1922.

Klaper, Michael. "Die musikalische Überlieferung aus dem Kloster Reichenau im 11. Jahrhundert und die kompositorische Tätigkeit des Abtes Bern (1008–1048)." In *Beiträge zur Musik, Musiktheorie und Liturgie der Abtei Reichenau. Bericht über die Tagung Heiligenkreuz 6.–8. Dez. 1999,* edited by Walter Pass and Alexander Rausch, 1–40. Musica mediaevalis Europae occidentalis 8. Tutzing: Hans Schneider, 2001.

———. *Die Musikgeschichte der Abtei Reichenau im 10. und 11. Jahrhundert: Ein Versuch.* Beihefte zum Archiv für Musikwissenschaft 52. [Wiesbaden]: Steiner Verlag, 2003.

Klauser, Theodor. "Die liturgischen Austauschbeziehungen zwischen der römischen und der fränkisch-deutschen Kirche vom achten bis zum elften Jahrhundert." *Historisches Jahrbuch, im Auftrage der Görres-Gesellschaft* 53 (1933): 169–89.

Kohlhase, Thomas, with Günther Michael Pauker, eds. "Bibliographie Gregorianischer Choral." *Beiträge zur Gregorianik* 1 (1985): 3–400; 9/10 (1990): 3–410; and 15/16 (1993): 3–484.

Kohlhäufl, Josef. "Die Tironischen Noten im Codex Laon 239." *Beiträge zur Gregorianik* 27 (1999): 21–32.

Kristeller, Paul Oskar, ed. *Catalogus translationum et commentariorum: Mediaeval and Renaissance Latin Translations and Commentaries.* 2nd ed. Washington, D.C.: Catholic University of America Press, 1971. An addendum has been edited by F. E. Cranz (1975).

Kunz, Lukas. "Die Tonartenlehre des Boethius." *KmJb* 31 (1936): 5–24.

———. "Ursprung und textliche Bedeutung der Tonartensilben Noeane, Noeagis." *KmJb* 30 (1935): 5–22.

Labowsky, Lotte. "A New Version of Scotus Eriugena's Commentary on Martianus Capella." *Mediaeval and Renaissance Studies* 1 (1941–43): 187–93.

Laistner, Max Ludwig Wolfram. *Thought and Letters in Western Europe, a.d. 500 to 900.* New York: Dial Press, 1931. Rev. ed., Ithaca, N.Y.: Cornell University Press, 1966.

Laum, Bernhard. *Das alexandrinische Akzentuationssystem, unter Zugrundelegung der theoretischen Lehren der Grammatiker und mit Heranziehung der praktischen Verwendung in den Papyri.* Studien zur Geschichte und Kultur des Altertums 4. Paderborn: Ferdinand Schöningh, 1928.

Lehmann, Paul. *Mittelalterliche Bibliothekskataloge Deutschlands und der Schweiz.* Munich: Beck, 1918.

Leonardi, Claudio. "I Codici di Marziano Capella." *Aevum* 33 (1959): 443–89; 34 (1960): 1–99; 411–524.

———. "I commenti altomedievali ai classici pagani: da Severino Boezio a Remigio d'Auxerre." In *La cultura antica nell'occidente latino dal 7 all' 11 secolo,* 459–508. Settimane di studio del Centro italiano di studi sull'alto medioevo 22. Spoleto: Presso la sede del Centro, 1975.

———. "Glosse eriugeniane a Marziano Capella in un codice Leidense." In *Jean Scot Érigène et l'histoire de la philosophie: Colloques internationaux du C.N.R.S. 561,* edited by René Roques, 171–82. Paris: Éditions du Centre national de la recherche scientifique, 1977.

Levy, Kenneth. "Aurelian's Use of Neumes." In *Gregorian Chant and the Carolingians,* 187–94. Princeton, N.J.: Princeton University Press, 1998.

———. "A Carolingian Visual Model." In *Gregorian Chant and the Carolingians,* 214–62. Princeton, N.J.: Princeton University Press, 1998.

———. "Charlemagne's Archetype of Gregorian Chant." In *Gregorian Chant and the Carolingians,* 82–108. Princeton, N.J.: Princeton University Press, 1998.

———. "From Aural to Notational: The Gregorian *Antiphonale Missarum.*" *EG* 28 (2000): 5–19.

———. *Gregorian Chant and the Carolingians.* Princeton, N.J.: Princeton University Press, 1998.

———. "Gregorian Chant and Oral Transmission." In *Essays on Music in Honor of David G. Hughes,* edited by Graeme M. Boone, 277–86. Isham Library Papers 4. Cambridge, Mass.: Harvard University Department of Music, 1995.

———. "On the Origin of Neumes." *EMH* 7 (1987): 59–90. Reprinted in *Gregorian Chant and the Carolingians,* 109–40. Princeton, N.J.: Princeton University Press, 1998.

———. "Plainchant before Neumes." In *Gregorian Chant and the Carolingians,* 195–213. Princeton, N.J.: Princeton University Press, 1998.

Lindsay, Wallace M. *The Latin Language: An Historical Account of Latin Sounds, Stems, and Flexions.* Oxford: Clarendon Press, 1894.

Lutz, Cora. "Martianus Capella." *CTC,* 2 (1971) 367–75; "Addenda et corrigenda," *CTC,* 3 (1976): 449–51, and *CTC,* 6 (1986): 185–86.

Maas, Martha, and Jane Snyder. *Stringed Instruments of Ancient Greece.* New Haven, Conn.: Yale University Press, 1989.

Machabey, Armand. *La Notation musicale.* Paris: Presses universitaires de France, 1952.

———. "De Ptolémée aux Carolingiens." *Quadrivium* 6 (1964): 37–56.

McKinnon, James. *The Early Christian Period and the Latin Middle Ages.* In *Source Readings in Music History,* edited by Oliver Strunk, Rev. ed. edited by Leo Treitler, 113–280. New York: Norton, 1998.

McKitterick, Rosamond. *Books, Scribes, and Learning in the Frankish Kingdoms, Sixth to Ninth Centuries.* Aldershot, England: Ashgate, 1994.

———. *The Frankish Church and the Carolingian Reforms, 789–895.* London: Royal Historical Society, 1977.

———, ed. *Carolingian Culture: Emulation and Innovation.* Cambridge: Cambridge University Press, 1994.

———. Review of *Carolingian Chant and the Carolingians,* by Kenneth Levy. In *EMH* 19 (2000): 279–301.

Maître, Claire. "La Modalité archaïque dans le répertoire d'Autun." In *Requirentes modos musicos. Mélanges offerts à Dom Jean Claire,* edited by Daniel Saulnier, with the assistance of Micheline Albert, 179–91. Solesmes: Abbaye de St.-Pierre, 1995.

———. "La Psalmodie dans les textes de la réforme cistercienne." In *IMS Study Group Cantus Planus: Papers Read at the Fourth Meeting, Pécs, Hungary, 3–8 September 1990,* edited by László Dobszay et al., 87–98. Budapest: Hungarian Academy of Sciences, 1992.

———. *La Réforme cistercienne du plain-chant: Étude d'un traité théorique [Regulae de arte musica].* Cîteaux: Studia et Documenta 6. Brecht, Belgium: Abdij Nazareth, 1995.

Maloy, Rebecca. "The Roles of Notation in Frutolf of Michelsberg's Tonary." *JM* 19 (2002): 641–93.

Manitius, Max. *Geschichte der lateinischen Literatur des Mittelalters.* Vol. 1. *Handbuch der klassischen Altertumswissenschaft.* Munich: Beck, 1911.

Markovits, Michael. *Das Tonsystem der abendländischen Musik im frühen Mittelalter.* Publikationen der Schweizerischen Musikforschenden Gesellschaft 30. Stuttgart: Paul Haupt, 1977.

Marosszéki, Solutor R. "Les Origines du chant cistercien: Recherches sur les réformes du plain-chant cistercien au XIIe siècle." *Analecta Sacri ordinis Cisterciensis* 8 (1952): 1–179.

Masi, Michael. *Boethian Number Theory: A Translation of the "De institutione arithmetica."* Studies in Classical Antiquity 6. Amsterdam: Rodopi, 1983.

Mathiesen, Thomas. *Apollo's Lyre: Greek Music and Music Theory in Antiquity and the Middle Ages.* Lincoln: University of Nebraska Press, 2000.

———. *Aristides Quintilianus on Music in Three Books.* Music Theory Translation Series. New Haven, Conn.: Yale University Press, 1983.

———. "Greece," pt. 1, "Ancient." *NG* 2, 10: 327–48.

———. *Greek Views of Music.* In *Source Readings in Music History,* edited by Oliver Strunk, Rev. ed. edited by Leo Treitler, 3–112. New York: Norton, 1998.

———. "*Harmonia* and *Ethos* in Ancient Greek Music." *JM* 3 (1984): 94–103.

———. "Problems of Terminology in Ancient Greek Theory: ΆΡΜΟΝΊΑ." In *Festival Essays for Pauline Alderman,* edited by Burton Karson, 3–17. Provo, Utah: Brigham Young University Press, 1976.

Ménager, Amand. "Aperçu sur la notation du manuscrit 239 de Laon. Sa concordance avec les 'codices' rythmiques sangalliens." *Pal. mus.* 10 (1909): 177–211.

Merkley, Paul. *Italian Tonaries.* Musicological Studies 48. Ottawa: Institute of Medieval Music, 1988.

———. *Modal Assignment in Northern Tonaries.* Musicological Studies 56. Ottawa: Institute of Medieval Music, 1992.

———. "Tonaries and Melodic Families of Antiphons." *JPMMS* 11 (1988): 13–24.

———. "The Transmission of Italian Tonaries." *Studies in Music from the University of Western Ontario* (1985): 51–74.

Meyer, Christian. "Aus der Werkstatt des Kompilators. Bemerkungen über zwei musiktheoretische Schriften des 11. Jahrhunderts." In *Quellen und Studien zur Musiktheorie des Mittelalters,* edited by Michael Bernhard, 2: 1–12. Veröffentlichungen der Musikhistorischen Kommission 13. Munich: Bayerische Akademie der Wissenschaften, 1997.

————."Métaphore instrumentale et présentation du système acoustique à l'époch carolingienne." In *Musik und die Geschichte der Philosophie und Naturwissenschaften im Mittelalter,* edited by Frank Hentschel, 141–49. Studien und Texte zur Geistesgeschichte des Mittelalters 62. Leiden: Brill, 1998.

————."Die Tonartenlehre im Mittelalter." In *Die Lehre vom einstimmigen liturgischen Gesang,* edited by Thomas Ertelt and Frieder Zaminer, 135–216. *GdMth* 4. Darmstadt: Wissenschaftliche Buchgesellschaft, 2000.

————."La Tradition du *Micrologus* de Guy d'Arezzo. Une Contribution à l'histoire du texte." *RdM* 83 (1997): 5–31.

Meyer, Christian, and Michel Huglo. *The Theory of Music. Manuscripts from the Carolingian Era up to c.1500 in the Federal Republic of Germany (D-brd). RISM* B III³. Munich: Henle, 1986.

Michaelides, Solon. *The Music of Ancient Greece.* London: Faber, 1978.

Mierow, Charles C., trans. *The Letters of St. Jerome.* With introduction and notes by Thomas Comerford Lawler. Vol. 1. *Letters 1–22.* Ancient Christian Writers 33. New York: Newman Press, 1963.

Mocquereau, André. "Le Manuscrit 121 de la bibliothèque d'Einsiedeln: Lettres et signes romaniens." *Pal. mus.* 4 (1894): 7–24; plates B–D.

Möbius, Gerhard. *Das Tonsystem aus der Zeit vor 1000.* Bonn: Gerd Wasmund, 1963.

Möller, Hartmut. "*De octo tonibus*: Ein europäisch-amerikanisches Verwirrspiel und seine Klärung." In *IMS Study Group Cantus Planus: Papers Read at the Sixth Meeting, Eger, Hungary, 1993,* edited by László Dobszay, 697–710. Budapest: Hungarian Academy of Sciences, 1995.

————."Deutsche Neumenschriften außerhalb St. Gallens." In *"De Musica et cantu": Studien zur Geschichte der Kirchenmusik und der Oper: Helmut Hucke zum 60. Geburtstag,* edited by Peter Cahn und Ann-Katrin Heimer, 225–42. Hochschule für Musik und Darstellende Kunst, Frankfurt am Main, Musikwissenschaftliche Publikationen 2. Hildesheim: Georg Olms, 1993.

————."Institutionen, Musikleben, Musiktheorie." In *Neues Handbuch der Musikwissenschaft,* vol. 2, *Die Musik des Mittelalters,* edited by Hartmut Möller and Rudolf Stephan, 129–99. Laaber, Germany: Laaber Verlag, 1991.

————."Die Prosula 'Psalle modulamina' (Mü 9543) und ihre musikhistorische Bedeutung." In *La tradizione dei tropi liturgici. Atti dei convegni sui tropi liturgici Parigi (15–19 ottobre 1985), Perugia (2–5 settembre 1987),* edited by Claudio Leonardi and Enrico Menesto, 279–96. Spoleto: Centro italiano di studi sull'alto medioevo, 1990.

————."Der Tonarius Bernonis: Rätsel um Gerberts Ausgabe." In *IMS Study Group Cantus Planus: Papers Read at the Fourth Meeting, Pécs, Hungary, 3–8 September 1990,* edited by László Dobszay et al., 69–86. Budapest: Hungarian Academy of Sciences, 1992.

————."Zur Frage der musikgeschichtlichen Bedeutung der Akademie Karls des Grossen: Die Musica Albini." In *Akademie und Musik: Festschrift für Werner Braun zum 65. Geburtstag,* edited by W. Frobenius et al., 269–88. Saarbrücker Studien zur Musikwissenschaft 4. Saarbrücken: Saarbrücker Druckerei und Verlag, 1992.

Mühlmann, Wilhelm. *Die "Alia musica" (Gerbert, Scriptores I): Quellenfrage, Umfang, Inhalt und Stammbaum.* Leipzig: O. Brandstetter, 1914.

Münxelhaus, Barbara. *Pythagoras Musicus. Zur Rezeption der pythagoreischen Musiktheorie als quadrivialer Wissenschaft im lateinischen Mittelalter.* Orpheus Schriftenreihe zu Grundfragen der Musik 19. Bonn: Verlag für systematische Musikwissenschaft, 1976.

Najock, Dietmar. *Drei anonyme griechische Traktate uber die Musik: Eine kommentierte Neuausgabe des Bellermannschen Anonymus.* Göttinger musikwissenschaftliche Arbeiten 2. Kassel: Bärenreiter, 1972.

Netzer, Henri. *L'Introduction de la messe romaine en France sous les Carolingiens*. Paris: Alphonse Picard, 1910.

Niemöller, Klaus Wolfgang. "Die Musik im Weltbild des Johannes Scotus Eriugena." In *Musik und die Geschichte der Philosophie und Naturwissenschaften im Mittelalter*, edited by Frank Hentschel, 293–304. Studien und Texte zur Geistesgeschichte des Mittelalters 62. Leiden: Brill, 1998.

Nowacki, Edward. "Chant Research at the Turn of the Century and the Analytical Programme of Helmut Hucke." *Plainsong and Medieval Music* 7 (1999): 47–72.

Ochsenbein, Peter. "Die St. Galler Klosterschule." In *Das Kloster St. Gallen im Mittelalter*, edited by Peter Ochsenbein, 95–108. Darmstadt: Wissenschaftliche Buchgesellschaft, 1999.

Oesch, Hans. *Berno und Hermann von Reichenau als Musiktheoretiker*. Publikationen der Schweizerischen Musikforschenden Gesellschaft 9. Bern: Haupt, 1961.

———. *Guido von Arezzo*. Publikationen der Schweizerischen Musikforschenden Gesellschaft 4. Bern: Franke, 1954.

Ostheimer, Andreas. "Das Modusverständnis in der *Musica enchiriadis*. Zu den Kapiteln vor der Organallehre." *Beiträge zur Gregorianik* 28 (2000): 35–50.

———. "Die Niederschrift von Musik mit Dasiazeichen. Untersuchungen zur praktischen Anwendung eines 'theoretischen' Schriftsystems." *Beiträge zur Gregorianik* 28 (2000): 51–72.

———. "Orpheus und die Entstehung einer Musiktheorie im 9. Jahrhundert." *Mittellateinisches Jahrbuch* 33 (1998): 19–35.

Pesce, Dolores. *The Affinities and Medieval Transposition*. Bloomington: Indiana University Press, 1987.

———. "B-Flat: Transposition or Transformation?" *JM* 4 (1986): 330–49.

Petrović, Danica. "Byzantine and Slavonic Oktoechos until the Fifteenth Century." In *Musica antiqua Europae orientalis*, 4: 175–90. Bydgoszcz, Poland: Philharmonia Pomorska im. Ignacego Paderewskiego, 1975.

Pfisterer, Andreas. *Cantilena Romana: Untersuchungen zur Überlieferung des gregorianischen Chorals*. Beiträge zur Geschichte der Kirchenmusik 11. Paderborn: Ferdinand Schöningh, 2002.

Phillips, Nancy. "Classical and Late Latin Sources for Ninth-Century Treatises on Music." In *Music Theory and Its Sources: Antiquity and the Midde Ages*, edited by André Barbera, 100–135. Notre Dame, Ind.: University of Notre Dame Press, 1990.

———. "The Dasia Notation and Its Manuscript Tradition." In *Musicologie médiévale. Notations et séquences. Actes de la Table ronde du C.N.R.S. à l'Institut de recherche et d'histoire des textes, 1982*, edited by Michel Huglo, 157–73. Paris: Éditions du Centre national de la recherche scientifique, 1987.

———. "'Musica' and 'Scolica Enchiriadis.' The Literary, Theoretical and Musical Sources." Ph.D. diss., New York University, 1984.

———. "Musica enchiriadis." *MGG 2*, Sachteil [Subjects] 6 (1997), cols. 654–62.

———. "Notationen und Notationslehren von Boethius bis zum 12. Jahrhundert." In *Die Lehre vom einstimmigen liturgischen Gesang*, edited by Thomas Ertelt und Frieder Zaminer, 293–623. GdMth 4, 2000.

Pietzsch, Gerhard. *Die Klassifikation der Musik von Boethius bis Ugolino von Orvieto*. Studien zur Geschichte der Musiktheorie im Mittelalter 1. Halle: Niemeyer, 1929.

Pizzani, Ubaldo. "Studi sulle fonti del 'De Institutione Musica' di Boezio." *Sacris erudiri* 16 (1965): 5–164.

Ponte, Joseph. "Aureliani Reomensis *Musica Disciplina*: A Revised Text, Translation, and Commentary." Ph.D. diss., Brandeis University, 1961.

Potiron, Henri. "Les Modes grégoriens selon les premiers théoriciens du moyen âge." *EG* 5 (1962): 109–18.

———. "La Notation grecque dans 'l'Institution harmonique' d'Hucbald." *EG* 2 (1957): 37–50, and *EG* 5 (1962): 115.

———. "Origine de la notation alphabetique." *RG* 31 (1952): 234–39.

Pouderoijen, Kees. "Die melodische Gestalt der Communio *Videns Dominus.*" In *Cantando praedicare: Godehard Joppich zum 60. Geburtstag,* edited by Stefan Klöckner, 129–55. Special issue, *Beiträge zur Gregorianik* 13/14. Regensburg: Gustav Bosse, 1992.

Powers, Harold. "Language Models and Musical Analysis." *Ethnomusicology* 24 (1980): 1–60.

———. "Mode." *NG* 12: 376–450.

Praßl, Franz Karl. "Chromatische Veränderungen von Choralmelodien in Theorie und Praxis." In *Cantando praedicare: Godehard Joppich zum 60. Geburtstag,* edited by Stefan Klöckner, 157–68. Special issue, *Beiträge zur Gregorianik* 13/14. Regensburg: Gustav Bosse, 1992.

Préaux, Jean G. "Le Commentaire de Martin de Laon sur l'oeuvre de Martianus Capella." *Latomus* 12 (1953): 437–59.

———. "Deux manuscrits gantois de Martianus Capella." *Scriptorium* 13 (1959): 15–21.

———. "Les Formes et la signification de la pédagogie des arts libéraux latins au milieu de 9e siècle. L'Enseignement palatin de Jean Scot Érigène." In *Arts libéraux et philosophie au moyen âge (Actes du quatrième congrès international de philosophie médiévale, Université de Montréal, Montréal, Canada, 27 août—2 semptembre 1967),* 47–64. Montreal: Institut d'études médiévales, 1969.

———. "Jean Scot et Martin de Laon en face du *De Nuptiis* de Martianus Capella." In *Jean Scot Érigène et l'histoire de la philosophie: Colloques internationaux du C.N.R.S. 561,* edited by R. Roques, 161–70. Paris: Éditions du Centre national de la recherche scientifique, 1977.

———. "Les Manuscrits principaux du 'De nuptiis Philologiae et Mercurii' de Martianus Capella." In *Lettres latines du moyen âge et de la renaissance,* edited by Guy Cambier et al., 76–128. Collection Latomus 158. Brussels: Latomus, 1978.

Raasted, Jørgen. *Intonation Formulas and Modal Signatures in Byzantine Musical Manuscripts.* Monumenta musicae Byzantinae, Subsidia 7. Copenhagen: Munksgaard, 1966.

———. "The 'laetantis adverbia' of Aurelian's Greek Informant." In *Aspects de la musique liturgique au moyen âge: Actes de colloques de Royaumont de 1986, 1987, 1988,* edited by Christian Meyer, 55–66. Paris: Éditions Créaphis, 1991.

———. "Papadiké." *NG* 14: 166–67.

Rankin, Susan. "Carolingian Music." In *Carolingian Culture. Emulation and Innovation,* edited by Rosamond McKitterick, 274–316. Cambridge: Cambridge University Press, 1994.

Rausch, Alexander. "Beobachtungen zum Kurztonar des Bern von Reichenau." In *IMS Study Group Cantus Planus: Papers Read at the Seventh Meeting, Sopron, Hungary, 1995,* edited by László Dobszay, 473–80. Budapest: Hungarian Academy of Sciences, 1998.

———. "Bern von Reichenau und sein Einfluß auf die Musiktheorie." In *Mittelalterliche Musiktheorie in Zentraleuropa,* edited by Walter Pass and Alexander Rausch, 133–50. Musica Mediaevalis Europae Occidentalis 4. Tutzing: Hans Schneider, 1998.

———. "Neue Quellen zur Rezeption des *Prologus in tonarium* des Bern von Reichenau." In *Beiträge zur Musik, Musiktheorie und Liturgie der Abtei Reichenau. Bericht über die Tagung Heiligenkreuz 6.–8. Dez. 1999,* edited by Walter Pass and Alexander Rausch, 69–98. Musica Mediaevalis Europae Occidentalis 8. Tutzing: Hans Schneider, 2001.

Reckow, Fritz. "Aspekte der Ausbildung einer lateinischen musikalischen Fachsprache im Mittelalter." In *Report of the Eleventh Congress of the International Musicological Society, Copenhagen, 1972,* edited by Henrik Glahn et al., 2: 612–17. Copenhagen: Wilhelm Hansen, 1974.

———. "Organum-Begriff und frühe Mehrstimmigkeit. Zugleich ein Beitrag zur Bedeutung des 'Instrumentalen' in der spätantiken und mittelalterlichen Musiktheorie." *Forum Musicologicum,* Basler Studien zur Musikgeschichte 1: 31–167. Bern: Francke Verlag, 1975.

Riché, Pierre. *Écoles et enseignement dans le haut moyen âge: Fin du Ve siècle–milieu du XIe siècle.* Paris: Picard, 1989.

Richter, Lukas. "Antike Überlieferungen in der byzantinischen Musiktheorie." *Deutsches Jahrbuch der Musikwissenschaft* 6 (1962): 75–115. Revised, updated version in *ActaM* 70 (1998): 133–208.

Riou, Y.-F. "Chronologie et provenance des manuscrits classiques latins neumés." *Revue d'histoire des textes* 21 (1991): 77–113.

Russell, Tilden. "A Poetic Key to a Pre-Guidonian Hand and the Echemata." *JAMS* 34 (1981): 109–18.

Sachs, Klaus-Jürgen. *Mensura fistularum: Die Mensurierung der Orgelpfeifen im Mittelalter.* Vol. 1. *Edition der Texte.* Schriftenreihe der Walcker-Stiftung für Orgelwissenschaftliche Forschung 2. Murrhardt: Musikwissenschaftliche Verlags-Gesellschaft, 1970.

———. *Mensura fistularum: Die Mensurierung der Orgelpfeifen im Mittelalter.* Vol. 2. *Studien zur Tradition und Kommentar der Texte.* Schriftenreihe der Walcker-Stiftung für Orgelwissenschaftliche Forschung 2. Murrhardt: Musikwissenschaftliche Verlags-Gesellschaft, 1980.

———. "Musikalische Elementarlehre im Mittelalter." In *Rezeption des antiken Fachs im Mittelalter,* edited by Frieder Zaminer, 105–61. GdMth 3, 1990.

———. "Musiktheorie, B. Antike und Mittelalter." *MGG 2,* Sachteil [Subjects] 6 (1997), cols. 1718–25.

———. "Remarks on the Relationship between Pipe-Measurements and Organ-Building in the Middle Ages." *Organ Yearbook* 4 (1973): 87–100.

———. "Die Rolle der Mensura von Monochord, Orgelpfeifen und Glocken in der mittelalterlichen Ars musica." In *Mensura. Mass, Zahl, Zahlensymbolik im Mittelalter,* edited by Albert Zimmermann, 459–75. Miscellanea mediaevalia 16. Berlin: de Gruyter, 1984.

Salvo, Bartolomeo di. "Papadiké." *Riemann Musiklexikon.* Sachteil [Subjects], col. 700. Mainz: Schott, 1967.

Santosuosso, Alma Colk Browne [see also Browne, Alma Colk]. *Letter Notations in the Middle Ages.* Ottawa: Institute of Mediaeval Music, 1989.

———. "Music in Bede's *De temporum ratione:* An Eleventh-Century Addition to MS London, British Library, Cotton Vespasian B.VI." *Scriptorium* 43 (1989): 255–59.

———. *Paris, Bibliothèque nationale fonds latin 7211: Analysis, Inventory, and Text.* Ottawa: Institute of Mediaeval Music, 1991.

Saulnier, Daniel. "La Mise par écrit du répertoire romano-franc." In *Requirentes modos musicos. Mélanges offerts à Dom Jean Claire,* edited by Daniel Saulnier, with the assistance of Micheline Albert, 237–48. Solesmes: Abbaye de St.-Pierre, 1995.

Schlötterer, Reinhold. "Die kirchenmusikalische Terminologie der griechischen Kirchenväter." Ph.D. diss., Universität München, 1953.

———. "Papadiké." *MGG* 10 (1962), col. 729.

Schlötterer, Reinhold, E. Jammers, H. Schmid, and E. Waeltner. "Byzantinisches in der karolingischen Musik." In *Berichte zum XI. Internationalen Byzantinisten-Kongreß, München 1958,* 1–29. Munich: Beck, 1958.

Schmid, Hans. "Die Kölner Handschriften der *Musica enchiriadis.*" In *Internationale Musikwissenschaftliche Gesellschaft: Bericht über den siebenten internationalen musikwissenschaftlichen Kongress Köln 1958,* edited by Gerald Abraham et al., 262–64. Kassel: Bärenreiter, 1959.

Schoell, Fridericus. *De accentu linguae Latinae.* In *Acta Societatis philologiae Lipsiensis,* vol. 6, edited by Fridericvs Ritschelivs. Leipzig: in aedibvs B. G. Teubneri, 1876.

Schrimpf, Gandolf. "Zur Frage der Authentizität unserer Texte von Johannes Scottus' Annotationes in Martianum." In *The Mind of Eriugena,* edited by J. J. O'Meara and L. Bieler, 125–39. Dublin: Irish University Press, 1973.

Seay, Albert. "The Fifteenth-Century *Coniuncta:* A Preliminary Study." In *Aspects of Medieval and Renaissance Music: A Birthday Offering to Gustave Reese,* edited by Jan LaRue, 723–37. New York: Norton, 1966.

Serbat, Guy. *Les Structures du Latin.* Paris: A. and J. Picard, 1975.

Shanzer, Danuta. "Felix Capella: minus sensus quam nominis pecudalis." *Classical Philology* 81 (1986): 62–81.

———. *A Philosophical and Literary Commentary on Martianus Capella's "De nuptiis Philologiae et Mercurii," Book 1.* Berkeley: University of California Press, 1986.

———. "Review of W. H. Stahl and R. Johnson, *Martianus Capella and the Seven Liberal Arts.*" *Beiträge zur Geschichte der deutschen Sprache und Literatur* 104 (1982): 110–17.

Smits van Waesberghe, Joseph. "Die besondere Stellung der *ars musica* im Zeitalter der Karolinger." In *Dia-pason. De omnibus. Ausgewählte Aufsätze von Joseph Smits van Waesberghe,* edited by C. J. Maas and M. U. Schouten-Glass, 48–70. Buren, Netherlands: Frits Knuf, 1976. Originally published as "La Place exceptionelle de l'Ars musica dans le développement des sciences au siècle des Carolingiens," *RG* 31 (1952): 81–104.

———. *De musico-paedagogico et theoretico Guidone Aretino eiusque vita et moribus.* Florence: Leo Olschki, 1953.

———. "The Musical Notation of Guido of Arezzo." *MD* 5 (1951): 15–53.

———. *Musiekgeschiedenis der Middeleeuwen.* 2 vols. Tilburg: W. Bergmans, 1936–42.

———. *Musikerziehung.* In *Musikgeschichte in Bildern,* vol. 3, *Musik des Mittelalters und der Renaissance,* pt. 3. Leipzig: VEB Deutscher Verlag für Musik, 1969.

———. "Les Origines de la notation alphabétique au moyen âge." *Anuario musical* 12 (1957): 3–14.

———. "Some Music Treatises and Their Interrelation: A School of Liège c. 1050–1200?" *MD* 3 (1949): 25–32.

Smits van Waesberghe, Joseph, with Peter Fischer and Christian Maas. *The Theory of Music from the Carolingian Era up to 1400. RISM* B III¹ Munich: Henle, 1961.

Snyder, John. "The *De legitimis ordinibus pentachordorum et tetrachordorum* of Theinred of Dover." Ph.D. diss., Indiana University, 1982.

———. "A Road Not Taken: Theinred of Dover's Theory of Species." *Journal of the Royal Musical Association* 115 (1990): 145–81.

Sowa, Heinrich. *Quellen zur Transformation der Antiphonen.* Tonar- und Rhythmusstudien. Kassel: Bärenreiter, 1935.

Stäblein, Bruno. "Der altrömische Gesang." In *Monumenta monodica medii aevi,* vol. 2, *Die Gesänge des altrömischen Graduale, Vat. lat. 5319,* edited by Bruno Stäblein and Margareta Landwehr-Melnicki, 1★–164★. Kassel: Bärenreiter, 1970.

———. "Psalm, B.: Lateinischer Psalmgesang." *MGG* 10 (1962), cols. 1676–90.

———. *Schriftbild der einstimmigen Musik. Musikgeschichte in Bildern.* Vol. 3. *Musik des Mittelalters und der Renaissance,* pt. 4. Leipzig: VEB Deutscher Verlag für Musik, 1975.

———. "Zum Verständnis des 'klassischen' Tropus," *ActaM* 35 (1963): 84–95.

Stahl, William. *Martianus Capella and the Seven Liberal Arts.* 2 vols. New York: Columbia University Press, 1971–77.

Steinen, Wolfram von den. *Notker der Dichter und seine geistige Welt.* Bern: Francke Verlag, 1948.

Strunk, Oliver. "Intonations and Signatures of the Byzantine Modes." *MQ* 31 (1945): 339–55. Reprinted in *Essays on Music in the Byzantine World,* edited by Kenneth Levy, 19–36. New York: Norton, 1977.

————. *Source Readings in Music History: From Classical Antiquity through the Romantic Era.* New York: Norton, 1950.

————. "The Tonal System of Byzantine Music." *MQ* 28 (1942): 190–204. Reprinted in *Essays on Music in the Byzantine World,* edited by Kenneth Levy, 3–18. New York: Norton, 1977.

Stuart, Nicholas. "Melodic Corrections in an Eleventh-Century Gradual (Paris, B.N. lat. 903)." *JPMMS* 2 (1979): 1–10.

Sullivan, Blair. "Grammar and Harmony: The Written Representation of Musical Sound in Carolingian Treatises." Ph.D. diss., University of California, Los Angeles, 1994.

Suñol, Grégoire Marie. *Introduction à la paléographie musicale grégorienne.* Tournai: Desclée, 1935.

Sweeney, Cecily. "The Musical Treatise Formerly Attributed to John Wylde and the Cistercian Chant Reform." Ph.D. diss., University of California, Los Angeles, 1972.

Tardo, Lorenzo. *L'antica melurgia bizantina.* Grottaferrata, Italy: Scuola Tip. Italo Orientale "S. Nilo," 1938.

Teeuwen, Mariken. *Harmony and the Music of the Spheres: The "Ars Musica" in Ninth-Century Commentaries on Martianus Capella.* Mittellateinische Studien und Texte 30. Leiden: Brill, 2002.

Tillyard, Henry J. W. *Handbook of Middle Byzantine Musical Notation.* Monumenta musicae Byzantinae, Subsidia 1. Copenhagen: Munksgaard, 1935.

Thompson, Edward Maunde. *An Introduction to Greek and Latin Paleography.* Oxford: Clarendon Press, 1912.

Torkewitz, Dieter. "Zur Entstehung der *Musica* und *Scolica Enchiriadis.*" *ActaM* 69 (1997): 156–81.

Traub, Andreas. "Zum neunten Kapitel der Musica enchiriadis." In *Cantando praedicare: Godehard Joppich zum 60. Geburtstag,* edited by Stefan Klöckner, 211–17. Special issue, *Beiträge zur Gregorianik* 13/14 (1992). Regensburg: Gustav Bosse, 1992.

Treitler, Leo. "The Beginnings of Music-Writing in the West: Historical and Semiotic Aspects." *Language and Communication* 9 (1989): 93–211.

————. "The Early History of Music Writing in the West." *JAMS* 35 (1982): 237–79. Reprinted in *With Voice and Pen: Coming to Know Medieval Song and How It Was Made,* 317–64. Oxford: Oxford University Press, 2003.

————. "Die Entstehung der abendländischen Notenschrift." *Mf* 37 (1984): 259–67.

————. "Homer and Gregory: The Transmission of Epic Poetry and Plainchant." *MQ* 60 (1974): 333–72. Reprinted in *With Voice and Pen: Coming to Know Medieval Song and How It Was Made,* 131–85. Oxford: Oxford University Press, 2003.

————. "Mündliche und schriftliche Überlieferung: Anfänge der musikalischen Notation." In *Neues Handbuch der Musikwissenschaft,* vol. 2, *Die Musik des Mittelalters,* edited by Hartmut Möller and Rudolf Stephan, 54–93. Laaber, Germany: Laaber Verlag, 1991.

————. "Reading and Singing: On the Genesis of Occidental Music-Writing." *EMH* 4 (1984): 135–208. Reprinted in *With Voice and Pen: Coming to Know Medieval Song and How It Was Made,* 365–428. Oxford: Oxford University Press, 2003.

————. "The 'Unwritten' and 'Written Transmission' of Medieval Chant and the Start-up of Musical Notation." *JM* 10 (1992): 131–91.

————. *With Voice and Pen: Coming to Know Medieval Song and How It Was Made.* Oxford: Oxford University Press, 2003.

Veroli, Cristiano. "La revisione cisterciense del canto liturgico: Un compromesso tra rinnovamento e conservazione." *Rivista internazionale di musica sacra* 15 (1994): 88–155.

————. "La revisione musicale bernardina e il graduale cisterciense." *Analecta cisterciensa* 47 (1991): 3–141; 48 (1992): 3–104; 49 (1993): 147–256.

Viret, Jacques. "Modalité et pédagogique au IXe siècle: Le Quaternaire Modal selon la *Musica enchiriadis.*" In *Requirentes modos musicos. Mélanges offerts à Dom Jean Claire,* edited by Daniel Saulnier, with the assistance of Micheline Albert, 211–34. Solesmes: Abbaye de St.-Pierre, 1995.

Vivell, Coelestin. "Das Quilisma." *Gregorianische Rundschau* 4 (1905): 81–84; 5 (1906): 21–24.

Vogel, Cyrille. "Les Échanges liturgiques entre Rome et les pays francs jusqu'à l'époque de Charlemagne." *Le Chiese nei regni dell'Europa occidentale e i loro rapporti con Roma fino all' 800.* Settimane di studio del Centro italiano di studi sull'alto medioevo 7 (1960): 1: 185–295.

———. "La Réforme cultuelle sous Pépin le Bref et sous Charlemagne (deuxième moitié du VIIIe siècle et premier quart du IXe siècle)." In *Beiträge zur Geschichte der Kultur des frühen Mittelalters: Die karolingische Renaissance,* edited by Erna Patzelt, 171–242. Graz: Akademische Druck- und Verlags-Anstalt, 1965.

———. "La Réforme liturgique sous Charlemagne." In *Karl der Große: Lebenswerk und Nachleben,* vol. 2, edited by Bernhard Bischoff, 217–32. Düsseldorf: Schwann, 1965.

Vogel, Martin. "Boetius und die Herkunft der modernen Tonbuchstaben." *KmJb* 46 (1962): 1–19.

———. "Die Entstehung der Kirchentonarten." In *Gesellschaft für Musikforschung, Kongreßbericht Kassel, 1962,* edited by Georg Reichert and Martin Just, 101–6. Kassel: Bärenreiter, 1963.

Waddell, Chrysogenos. "The Origin and Early Evolution of the Cistercian Antiphonary: Reflections on Two Cistercian Chant Reforms." In *The Cistercian Spirit: A Symposium in Memory of Thomas Merton,* edited by M. Basil Pennington, 190–223. Cistercian Studies 3. Shannon: Irish University Press, 1970.

Waeltner, Ernst Ludwig. "Die Methode terminologischer Untersuchungen frühmittelalterlicher Musiktraktate dargestellt an einem Beispiel des Aurelianus Reomensis (Musica disciplina, Cap. X: De authentu proto)." In *Medium aevum vivum: Festschrift für Walter Bulst,* edited by Robert Jauss and Dieter Schaller, 48–60. Heidelberg: Carl Winter Universitätsverlag, 1960.

———. "Die 'Musica disciplina' des Aurelianus Reomensis." In *Internationale Musikwissenschaftliche Gesellschaft: Bericht über den siebenten Internationalen Musikwissenschaftlichen Kongress Köln 1958,* edited by Gerald Abraham et al., 293–95. Kassel: Bärenreiter, 1959.

———. "*Organicum melos.* Zur Musikanschauung des Iohannes Scottus (Eriugena)." Veröffentlichungen der musikhistorischen Kommission 1. Munich: Bayerische Akademie der Wissenschaften, 1977.

Waeltner, Ernst Ludwig, H. Schmid, E. Jammers, and R. Schlötterer. "Byzantinisches in der karolingischen Musik." In *Berichte zum XI. Internationalen Byzantinisten-Kongreß, München 1958,* 1–29. Munich: Beck, 1958.

Wagner, Peter. *Einführung in die gregorianischen Melodien.* Vol. 2. *Neumenkunde.* 2nd ed. Freiburg, Switzerland: Universitäts-Buchhandlung, 1912.

———. *Einführung in die gregorianischen Melodien.* Vol. 3. *Gregorianische Formenlehre.* Freiburg, Switzerland: Universitäts-Buchhandlung, 1921.

Wallach, Leopold. *Alcuin and Charlemagne.* Studies in Carolingian History and Literature. Ithaca, N.Y.: Cornell University Press, 1959.

Walter, Michael. *Grundlagen der Musik des Mittelalters. Schrift—Zeit—Raum.* Stuttgart: J. B. Metzler, 1994.

———. "Vom Beginn der Musiktheorie und dem Ende der Musik: Über die Aktualität des Mittelalters in der Musikgeschichte." *ActaM* 70 (1998): 209–28.

Wantzloeben, Sigfrid. *Das Monochord als Instrument und als System.* Halle: Max Niemeyer, 1911.

Warburton, Jane. "Questions of Attribution and Chronology in Three Medieval Texts on Species Theory." *Music Theory Spectrum* 22 (2000): 225–35.

Weakland, Rembert. "Hucbald as Musician and Theorist." *MQ* 42 (1956): 66–84.

Wegner, Max. *Griechenland. Musikgeschichte in Bildern*, vol. 2, pt. 4, edited by Heinrich Besseler and Marius Schneider. Leipzig: VEB Deutscher Verlag für Musik, 1963.

Wellesz, Egon. *A History of Byzantine Music and Hymnography.* Oxford: Clarendon Press, 1961.

West, Martin L. *Ancient Greek Music.* Oxford: Oxford University Press, 1992.

White, Alison. "Boethius in the Medieval Quadrivium." In *Boethius: His Life, Thought and Influence*, edited by Margaret Gibson, 162–205. Oxford: Clarendon Press, 1981.

Wiesli, Walter. *Das Quilisma im Codex 359 der Stiftsbibliothek St. Gallen, erhellt durch das Zeugnis der Codices Einsiedeln 121, Bamberg lit. 6, Laon 239 and Chartres 47: Eine paläographisch-semiologische Studie.* Immensee, Germany: Missionshaus Bethlehem, 1966.

Wille, Günther. *Musica romana: Die Bedeutung der Musik im Leben der Römer.* Amsterdam: P. Schippers, 1967.

Willis, James. "Martianus und die mittelalterliche Schulbildung." *Das Altertum* 19 (1973): 164–74.

Wilmart, André. "Expositio missae." *DACL* 5.1 (1922): 1014–27.

Wingell, Richard. "Hucbald of St. Amans [sic] and Carolingian Music Theory." In *Festival Essays for Pauline Alderman*, edited by Burton L. Karson, 19–26. Provo, Utah: Brigham Young University Press, 1976.

Winnington-Ingram, Reginald Pepys. "Greece, Ancient." *NG* 7: 659–72.

Wolfram, Gerda. "Fragen der Modulation in der byzantinischen Musik." In *IMS Study Group Cantus Planus: Papers Read at the Fourth Meeting, Pécs, Hungary, 3–8 September 1990*, edited by László Dobszay et al., 221–30. Budapest: Hungarian Academy of Sciences, 1992.

———. "Notation III: Byzantinische und altslawische Notation." *MGG 2*, Sachteil [Subjects] 7 (1997), cols. 289–96; 417–18.

———. "Oktoechos." *MGG 2*, Sachteil [Subjects] 7 (1997), cols. 613–16.

———. "Die *Phthorai* der paläobyzantinischen Notationen." In *Palaeobyzantine Notations: A Reconsideration of the Source Material*, edited by Jørgen Raasted and Christian Troelsgård, 119–30. Hernen, Netherlands: A. A. Bredius Foundation, 1995.

Zaminer, Frieder. "Introduction" to *Geschichte der Musiktheorie*, vol. 3, *Rezeption des antiken Fachs im Mittelalter*, edited by Frieder Zaminer, 1–6. Darmstadt: Wissenschaftliche Buchgesellschaft, 1990.

———. "Theoretische Elemente in der frühmittelalterlichen Musikaufzeichnung." In *Notenschrift und Aufführung. Symposion zur Jahrestagung der Gesellschaft für Musikforschung, 1977*, edited by Theodor Göllner, 41–54. Münchner Veröffentlichungen zur Musikgeschichte 30. Munich: Hans Schneider, 1980.

———. "Über Grammatica und Musica." In *Gesellschaft für Musikforschung, Kongreß-Bericht 1974*, edited by Hellmut Kühn and Peter Nitsche, 255–57. Kassel: Bärenreiter, 1980.

INDEX OF CHANTS AND
MANUSCRIPTS CITED

Chants

Angelus Domini (Off.), 153–4, 239 n. 19
Ad te levavi (Intr.), 110–3, 137–43
Alma redemptoris mater (Ant.), 239 n. 19
Amen dico vobis (Ant.), 219
Apertis thesauris suis (Ant.), 185
Assumpta est Maria (Ant.), 239 n. 19
Astiterunt reges terre (Ant.), 68 n. 58

Beatus servus (Comm.), 163–7, 226 n. 69, 234–5,
   131, 235–7, 242–44, 252–5,
   257–8

Canite tuba (Ant.), 185, 216
Christus natis est (Invit.), 155
Circumdederunt me (Intr.), 94
Confessio et pulchritudo (Intr.), 94
Cum audisset populus (Ant.), 151 n. 10

Deus omnium exauditor est (Resp.), 240–41
Domine, qui operati sunt (Ant.), 218, 230
Doxa in ipsistis theo, 107–9

Ecce nomen Domini (Ant.), 185, 216
Ecce nomen Domini (Intr.), 87 n. 9
Ecce vere Israhelita (Ant.), 151
Erue a framea (Resp.), 103–6
Etenim sederunt principes (Intr.), 91
Euge serve bone (Ant.), 185
Exaltabunt sancti (Grad.), 140
Exclamaverunt ad te (Ant.), 107 n. 67
Exsurge quare (Intr.), 91

Facti sumus (Ant.), 242 n. 24

Gaudeamus omnes in Domino (Intr.), 91
Gaudendum est nobis (Ant.), 241–2

Gaudete in Domino (Intr.), 91, 99–101, 180, 216
Gloria patri (lesser doxology), 87 n. 9, 103–4
Gloria in excelsis, 107–9
Gloria tibi trinitas (Ant.), 239 n. 19

Haec dies (Grad.), 130–1, 133, 163, 165–7, 226
   n. 69, 234
Hodie completi sunt (Ant.), 151 n. 10

In civitate Domini (Ant.), 239 n. 19
In die solemnitatis (Off.), 255–6 n. 54
In tempesta nocte (Ant.), 185
Inclina Domine (Intr.), 91, 94
Inclinans se Iesus (Ant.), 185
Inclinavit se Iesus (Ant.), 185
Ipsi soli (Ant.), 216
Ite dicite Iohanni (Ant.), 151
Iustus es Domine (Intr.), 91, 99–101, 180

Johannes autem (Intr.), 180

Laudes Deo, ore pio (Sanctus prosula), 227 n. 71
Lex Domini (Intr.), 91

Magnum hereditatis mysterium (Ant.), 241–2
Meditatio cordis mei (Intr.), 91
Misereris omnium Domine (Intr.), 91

Nativitas gloriosae (Resp.), 155

O admirabile commercium (Ant.), 183
O beatum pontificem (Intr.), 185, 216
O pastor aeterne (Ant.), 239 n. 19
O rex gloriae (Ant.), 237
Omnes gentes (All.), 199
Omnes gentes (Intr.), 183
Os justi (Intr.), 183
De ore leonis (Resp.), 103–6

Puer natus est nobis (Intr.), 94

Rorate caeli (Intr.), 91, 180

Sint lumbi vestri (Ant.), 185, 248, 252
Statuit ei Dominus (Intr.), 91
Suscepimus Deus (Intr.), 91, 99–101

Tunc praecepit eos omnes (Intr.), 77–8

Urbs fortitudinis (Intr.), 180
Ut queant laxis (Hymn), 230–1
Universi qui te expectant (Grad.), 111, 139 n. 147

Veni sponsa Christi (Ant.), 140 n. 151
Veniet Dominus (Ant.), 185, 216
Virgo hodie fidelis (Ant.), 183

Manuscripts

Angers, Bibliothèque Municipale, 91 (83): 112–3, 138 n. 136, 143
Autun, Bibliothèque Municipale, S 4 (olim 5): 138 n. 134
Autun, Bibliothèque Municipale, S 28 (olim 24): 138 n. 134
Autun, Bibliothèque Municipale, S 46 (olim 40B): 80–1

Bamberg, Staats- und Universitätsbibliothek, Msc. Class. 39: 34 n. 96, 35–6, 61–2
Barcelona, Arxiu de la Corona d'Aragó, Ripoll 42: 149 n. 1, 171 n. 2, 172–4, 184
Benevento, Biblioteca Capitolare, VI.34: 112–3, 138 n. 140
Berlin, Staatsbibliothek: Preussischer Kulturbesitz, theol. lat. 2° 58: 138 n. 134
Bern, Burgerbibliothek, 36: 53 n. 18
Bern, Burgerbibliothek, 56b: 35, 37, 61, 63, 69
Bern, Burgerbibliothek, 101: 53 n. 18
Bern, Burgerbibliothek, 331: 69 n. 63
Besançon, Bibliothèque Municipale, 594: 66, 67 n. 56, 69, 76–77, 186 n. 35
Boulogne-sur-Mer (St. Omer), Bibliothèque Municipale, 666: 110 n. 78,
Bruges, Stadsbibliotheek, 532: 173–4, 186 n. 36
Brussels, Bibliothèque Royale, 2750/65: 87 n. 8, 88–92, 100–1
Brussels, Bibliothèque Royale, 10078/95: 144, 155–8

Cesena, Biblioteca Comunale Malatestiana, *Pluteus* S. XXVI. 1: 149 n. 1, 171 n. 2, 173 n. 4, 174, 202 n. 1

Chartres, Bibliothèque Municipale, 47: 112–3, 138 n. 136, 143
Chartres, Bibliothèque Municipale, 130: 202 n. 1
Chicago, Newberry Library, F. 9: 94 n. 22
Cologne, Dombibliothek, 166: 9

Douai, Bibliothèque Municipale, 6: 110 n. 78
Douai, Bibliothèque Municipale, 246: 110 n. 78
Düsseldorf, Universitäts- und Landesbibliothek, D. 1: 110–3, 137 n. 133, 138 n. 135, 139 n. 147
Düsseldorf, Universitäts- und Landesbibliothek, D. 2: 110 n. 78
Düsseldorf, Universitäts- und Landesbibliothek, D. 3: 110 n. 78
Düsseldorf, Universitäts- und Landesbibliothek, H. 3: 118 n. 98

Einsiedeln, Benediktinerkloster, Musikbibliothek, 121: 140 n. 152
Einsiedeln, Benediktinerkloster, Musikbibliothek, 169 (468): 68 n. 58, 110 n. 78, 151 nn. 5, 8
Einsiedeln, Benediktinerkloster, Musikbibliothek, 298: 67 n. 58
Einsiedeln, Benediktinerkloster, Musikbibliothek, 358: 67 n. 58

Florence, Biblioteca Nazionale Centrale, Conventi soppressi, F.III.565: 174
Florence, Biblioteca Riccardiana, Fr. 652: 174

Graz, Universitätsbibliothek, 807: 243–4

Heidelberg, Universitätsbibliothek, Pal. lat. 52: 138 n. 134, 58 n. 33, 61 n. 40, 65 n. 47

Karlsruhe, Badische Landesbibliothek, Aug. perg. 73: 34 n. 96
Karlsruhe, Badische Landesbibliothek, K. 504: 172–5, 178 n. 22, 180, 53 n. 193

Laon, Bibliothèque Municipale, 9: 138 n. 134
Laon, Bibliothèque Municipale, 107: 138 n. 134
Laon, Bibliothèque Municipale, 121: 138 n. 134
Laon, Bibliothèque Municipale, 239: 112–3, 138 n. 138, 141–3
Laon, Bibliothèque Municipale, 266: 138 n. 134
Leiden, Universiteitsbibliotheek, B. P. L. 25: 138 n. 134
Leiden, Universiteitsbibliotheek, B. P. L. 28: 110 n. 78
Leiden, Universiteitsbibliotheek, B. P. L. 36: 59–60, 64, 76–77, 186 n. 35
Leiden, Universiteitsbibliotheek, Voss. Lat F. 48: 59–60, 66, 76–77, 186 n. 35

Leiden, Universiteitsbibliotheek,Voss. lat. F. 74: 53 n. 18

Leiden, Universiteitsbibliotheek,Voss. lat. F. 82: 53 n. 18

Leiden, Universiteitsbibliotheek, BPL 88: 59–60, 69 n. 63, 70

Leiden, Universiteitsbibliotheek, BPL 122: 53 n. 18

Leipzig, Städtische Bibliotheken, Rep. I. 93: 138 n. 134, 168 n. 51, 170 n. 60

Leipzig, Universitätsbibliothek, 169: 88 n. 11

Leipzig, Universitätsbibliothek, 1493: 81

London, British Library, Harley 2685: 35–6

Lucca, Biblioteca Capitolare, 601: 105–6

Madrid, Biblioteca Nacional, 9088: 174–5, 177

Madrid, Biblioteca Nacional, 10001: 138 n. 134

Metz, Bibliothèques Médiathèques de Metz/Collections patrimoniales, 351: 86 n. 5; 88 n. 10, 100

Metz, Bibliothèques Médiathèques de Metz/Collections patrimoniales, 494: 94 n. 23

Milan, Biblioteca Ambrosiana, C 128 inf.: 80

Montpellier, Bibliothèque Interuniversitaire-Section Médecine, H 159: 94 n. 23, 162–7, 214 n. 21, 236, 254

Munich, Bayerische Staatsbibliothek, clm 6250: 53 n. 18

Munich, Bayerische Staatsbibliothek, clm 6275: 53 n. 18

Munich, Bayerische Staatsbibliothek, clm 6361: 79, 81

Munich, Bayerische Staatsbibliothek, clm 9543: 138 n. 134

Munich, Bayerische Staatsbibliothek, clm 9921: 229 n. 76

Munich, Bayerische Staatsbibliothek, clm 14272: 80–3, 171 nn. 1–2, 173–4, 179 n. 19, 184, 196 n. 65

Munich, Bayerische Staatsbibliothek, clm 14314: 138 n. 134

Munich, Bayerische Staatsbibliothek, clm 14523: 83–4, 179 n. 19

Munich, Bayerische Staatsbibliothek, clm 14729: 72

Munich, Bayerische Staatsbibliothek, clm 18478: 79, 81

Munich, Bayerische Staatsbibliothek, clm 18480: 81

Munich, Bayerische Staatsbibliothek, clm 29164/I: 138 n. 134

Naples, Biblioteca Nazionale "Vittorio Emanuele III," IV.G. 68: 138 n. 134

New York, New York Public Library, 115: 138 n. 134

Orléans, Bibliothèque de la Ville, 293B: 79–81

Oxford, Bodleian Library, Auct. T.2.19: 69 n. 63

Oxford, Bodleian Library, Auct. F.4.26: 138 n. 134

Oxford, Bodleian Library, Canonici misc. 212: 102 n. 50

Padua, Biblioteca Capitolare, 47: 244

Paris, Bibliothèque de l'Arsenal, 227: 138 n. 134

Paris, Bibliothèque nationale de France, f. gr. 360: 117 n. 96

Paris, Bibliothèque nationale de France, f. lat. 903: 112–3, 138 n. 139, 139

Paris, Bibliothèque nationale de France, f. lat. 1118: 103 n. 55, 108–9

Paris, Bibliothèque nationale de France, f. lat. 1190: 138 n. 134

Paris, Bibliothèque nationale de France, f. lat. 1411: 245–6 n. 33

Paris, Bibliothèque nationale de France, f. lat. 1412: 245–6 n. 33

Paris, Bibliothèque nationale de France, n. a. lat. 1618: 110 n. 78

Paris, Bibliothèque nationale de France, n. a. lat. 1620: 119 n. 100

Paris, Bibliothèque nationale de France, f. lat. 1850: 150 n. 2

Paris, Bibliothèque nationale de France, f. lat. 2291: 107–11, 137

Paris, Bibliothèque nationale de France, f. lat. 2664: 81

Paris, Bibliothèque nationale de France, f. lat. 2717: 110 n. 78

Paris, Bibliothèque nationale de France, f. lat. 4995: 92–3 n. 15

Paris, Bibliothèque nationale de France, f. lat. 7200: 79–81

Paris, Bibliothèque nationale de France, f. lat. 7201: 150 n. 3

Paris, Bibliothèque nationale de France, f. lat. 7211: 74, 102 n. 51, 172–4, 184

Paris, Bibliothèque nationale de France, f. lat. 7212: 74, 172–4, 184

Paris, Bibliothèque nationale de France, f. lat. 7297: 80–1, 94 n. 22

Paris, Bibliothèque nationale de France, f. lat. 7490: 55

Paris, Bibliothèque nationale de France, f. lat. 7583–85: 53 n. 18

Paris, Bibliothèque nationale de France, f. lat. 7670: 53 n. 18

Paris, Bibliothèque nationale de France, f. lat. 7671: 53 n. 18

Paris, Bibliothèque nationale de France, f. lat. 7972: 110 n. 78

Paris, Bibliothèque nationale de France, f. lat.
8093: 138 n. 134
Paris, Bibliothèque nationale de France, f. lat.
8663: 173–4
Paris, Bibliothèque nationale de France, f. lat.
8669: 64
Paris, Bibliothèque nationale de France, f. lat.
8670: 35–7
Paris, Bibliothèque nationale de France, f. lat.
8671: 67 n. 56, 76–7
Paris, Bibliothèque nationale de France, f. lat.
8674: 62 n. 43, 75, 184
Paris, Bibliothèque nationale de France, f. lat.
8675: 69 n. 63
Paris, Bibliothèque nationale de France, f. lat.
10275: 79, 119 n. 100, 125 n. 108
Paris, Bibliothèque nationale de France, f. lat.
10508: 100, 164 n. 46
Paris, Bibliothèque nationale de France, f. lat.
10509: 164 n. 46
Paris, Bibliothèque nationale de France, f. lat.
11958: 138 n. 134
Paris, Bibliothèque nationale de France, f. lat.
12960: 69 n. 63, 71 n. 67
Paris, Bibliothèque nationale de France, f. lat.
13025: 54–5
Paris, Bibliothèque nationale de France, f. lat.
13159: 86 n. 5
Paris, Bibliothèque nationale de France, f. lat.
13908: 79–83, 150 n. 2
Paris, Bibliothèque nationale de France, f. lat.
14753: 34–5
Paris, Bibliothèque nationale de France, f. lat.
14754: 64–5, 71
Paris, Bibliothèque nationale de France, f. lat.
15614: 110 n. 78
Paris, Bibliothèque nationale de France, f. lat.
16201: 110 n. 78
Paris, Bibliothèque nationale de France, f. lat.
17305: 110 n. 78
Paris, Bibliothèque nationale de France, f. lat.
17306: 110 n. 78
Paris, Bibliothèque nationale de France, f. lat.
17436: 86 n. 2
Paris, Bibliothèque Sainte-Geneviève, 1190: 138
n. 134
Pistoia, Biblioteca Capitolare, 121: 242–3
Prague, Národní knihovna České Republiky,
CZ, XIX.C.26: 173–4, 186 n. 36

Regensburg, Bischöfliche Zentralbibliothek,
Proske-Musikbibliothek, Cim. 2: 138 n. 134
Reims, Bibliothèque Municipale, 213: 107
n. 69
Reims, Bibliothèque Municipale, 426: 53 n. 18

Rochester, Sibley Music Library, Vault ML92
1200: 232
Rome, Biblioteca Apostolica Vaticana, Reg. lat.
215: 138 n. 134
Rome, Biblioteca Apostolica Vaticana, lat. 235: 87
n. 5, 137 n. 131
Rome, Biblioteca Apostolica Vaticana, Barberini
gr. 300: 115–7
Rome, Biblioteca Apostolica Vaticana, Ottob. lat.
313: 138 n. 134
Rome, Biblioteca Apostolica Vaticana, Pal. lat.
485: 138 n. 134
Rome, Biblioteca Apostolica Vaticana, Reg. lat.
1005: 80–1
Rome, Biblioteca Apostolica Vaticana, Reg. lat.
1638: 80–1, 94 n. 22
Rome, Biblioteca Apostolica Vaticana, Reg. lat.
1661: 202 n. 1

St. Gall, Stiftsbibliothek, 231: 53 n. 18
St. Gall, Stiftsbibliothek, 237: 53 n. 18
St. Gall, Stiftsbibliothek, 242: 138 n. 134
St. Gall, Stiftsbibliothek, 339: 112–3, 138 n. 137,
141, 143
St. Gall, Stiftsbibliothek, 359: 143
St. Gall, Stiftsbibliothek, 376: 112–3, 138 n. 137,
141–2
St. Gall, Stiftsbibliothek, 381: 141 n. 155
St. Gall, Stiftsbibliothek, 390–91: 105–6, 239 n. 17
Schaffhausen, Stadtbibliothek, 108: 81
Sélestat, Bibliothèque Municipale, 1 (1093): 138
n. 134
Stockholm, Kungliga Biblioteket, Sveriges
Nationalbibliotek. A 136: 107 n. 29
Strasbourg, Séminaire Protestant 926 (anc.
B.I.24): 171 nn. 1–2, 173–4, 196 n. 65,
202 n. 1

Toledo, Museo de San Vicente, Fr. 2: 138 n. 134
Tours, Bibliothèque Municipale, 184 (1017): 138
n. 134

Valenciennes, Bibliothèque Municipale, 107: 110
n. 78
Valenciennes, Bibliothèque Municipale, 148: 93
n. 17, 94 n. 22, 99 n. 38, 101–2, 105–7, 110 n.
78, 137 n. 133, 150 n. 3
Valenciennes, Bibliothèque Municipale, 150: 137
n. 133
Valenciennes, Bibliothèque Municipale, 293: 160
n. 32
Valenciennes, Bibliothèque Municipale, 294: 110
n. 78
Valenciennes, Bibliothèque Municipale, 337: 19
n. 44, 110 n. 78, 137 n. 133, 150 n. 3

Valenciennes, Bibliothèque Municipale, 399: 110
   n. 78
Valenciennes, Bibliothèque Municipale, 407: 137
   n. 134
Vienna, Österreichische Nationalbibliothek, 51:
   208 n. 8, 229 n. 78
Vienna, Österreichische Nationalbibliothek, 958:
   138 n. 134

Vienna, Österreichische Nationalbibliothek,
   2269: 81
Vienna, Österreichische Nationalbibliothek,
   3222: 69 n. 63
Vienna, Österreichische Nationalbibliothek, Ser.
   nova 3645: 138 n. 134

Worcester, Cathedral Library, F. 160: 105–6

GENERAL INDEX

accent (*accentus*), 39–46, 54–65, 84, 92, 94 n. 18,
    96–7, 100–14, 137 n. 131, 139, 238
  acute, 20, 41, 43, 46, 55–9, 61–5, 102–6,
    108–11, 119 n. 100, 139, 238
  circumflex (also *inflexus*), 41–6, 55–64, 102–10,
    238
  grave, 20, 29, 41–6, 54–66, 104–10, 119 n. 100,
    139, 238
  See also tone, prosody
Adkins, Cecil, 10 n. 22, 18 n. 41, 125 n. 126, 136
    n. 128, 208 n. 8, 212 n. 20, 220 n. 45
Admonitio generalis, 49–50. *See also* Alcuin of York;
    Charlemagne
Aeneid. See Vergil
affinities, 160–1, 196 n. 62, 221–3, 226–8
Alberi, M., 49 n. 1
Alcuin of York, 49 nn. 1–2, 50 nn. 4–5, 52, 53
    n. 17, 96
Alia musica, 20 n. 49, 73–4, 76, 83 n. 89, 94, 170,
    171–202, 204–6, 210, 221, 228, 235, 246,
    251
Allaire, Gaston, 230 n. 80
Allen, W. Sidney, 44–5
Alypius, 8, 16–7, 26, 31, 42, 73 n. 70, 156–8, 164,
    167
anima, De. See Aristotle
Annotationes in Martianum. See John Scottus
    Eriugena
Anpassungsgesetz. See Wagner, Peter
Antiphonale missarum sextuplex, 85–6, 235
Apel, Willi, 14 n. 154, 143 n. 168
architectura, De. See Vitruvius
argiletum (argiloetum), 44, 61–4
Aristides Quintilianus, 7, 11 nn. 25–6, 20 n. 48,
    25–7, 28 n. 80, 30–3, 38–9, 73 n. 70
Aristotle, 7–8
Arixtoxenos, 8 n. 16, 28 n. 80, 30, 46

armonia (ἁρμονία). *See harmonia*
Ars grammatica. See Dionysios of Thrace; Donatus
    ortigraphus
Ars lavreshamensis, 42 n. 128, 53 n. 18, 54 n. 24,
    56–57, 140 n. 148
Ars maior. See Donatus
Ars musica. See Johannes Aegidius de Zamora,
arte disputationes traditae, De. See Bern of Reich-
    enau
artificial music (Regino of Prüm), 168–9
Augustine of Hippo, 7–9, 160 n. 32
Aurelian of Réôme (Aurelianus Reomensis), 40,
    87 nn. 5, 7; 93–115, 117–20, 127, 136,
    140, 149–50, 162, 175, 177, 179–81, 184,
    235–6
automela, 93 n. 16

Babb, Warren, 68 n. 58, 134 n. 125, 140 n. 148,
    144–62, 195 n. 59, 219–30, 237–44
Bacchius Geron, 13 n. 30
Bailey, Terence, 87 nn. 5, 7; 178 n. 18, 194,
    198–200
Barker, Andrew, 7 nn. 4–6, 7 n. 11, 8 nn. 13–6, 11
    nn. 25–7, 23 n. 61, 24 n. 63, 25 n. 64, 26
    nn. 73, 76; 28 n. 80, 30 nn. 86–8, 38
    n. 106, 73 n. 70
Bautier-Regnier, Anne-Marie, 101 n. 49, 102
    n. 50, 137 n. 131, 164–46,
Bellermann Anonymous III, 16 n. 36
Bent, Margaret, 230 n. 80, 256 n. 59
Berger, Christian, 230 nn. 80–1, 233 n. 82
Berger, Karol, 230 nn. 80–1, 231 n. 81
Bern of Reichenau, 5, 140 n. 150, 201–2, 204–11,
    234–6, 246, 249, 257. *See also Prologus in*
    tonarium
Bernard of Clairvaux, 245 n. 29
Bernardus humilis Abbas Clarevallis, 245 n. 30

297

Bernhard, Michael, 8–10, 15 n. 34, 20 n. 50, 27
    n. 70, 38 nn. 104–5, 54 n. 22, 66 n. 53, 68
    n. 98, 70 n. 64, 78–84, 88 n. 11, 93 n. 17,
    94 nn. 22–3, 119 n. 100, 120 n. 100, 126
    n. 108, 137 n. 131, 143 nn. 163–4, 150
    n. 2, 168 nn. 51–5, 169 nn. 56–8, 170
    nn. 59–60, 171 n. 1, 173, 184–5, 186 n. 36,
    202 n. 1, 203–4, 208 n. 8, 212 n. 19, 219
    n. 41
Berschin, Walter, 8 n. 17, 38 n. 103, 82 n. 87, 86
    n. 3
Beyssac, Gabriel, 162 n. 43, 166 n. 48
Bielitz, Mathias, 45 n. 141, 58 n. 33, 61 n. 40, 65
    n. 47, 103 n. 56, 120 n. 100, 139 n. 148
Bischoff, Bernhard, 35, 52 n. 15, 70 n. 64, 171
    n. 2, 173
Bishop, Terence A. M., 70 n. 64
Billecocq, Marie-Claire, 142 n. 162
bis-diapason (double-octave), 111, 21–22, 132–4,
    152, 164
Bockholdt, Petra, 118 n. 98
Boethius, 9, 10–31, 42, 46–7, 51, 53–4, 65–68, 71,
    75–84, 94–5, 98, 114, 118–121, 126, 128,
    134, 136, 149–52, 154–6, 159 n. 29, 160,
    162, 164, 167–8, 169 n. 56, 170, 172–9,
    184, 187–92, 209–12, 214, 233, 245–6, 257
Bohn, Peter, 106 n. 65
Bomm, Urbanus, 228 n. 72
Bower, Calvin, 4 n. 3, 10–25, 54 n. 22, 66 n. 53, 67
    n. 58, 78–84, 94 n. 22, 119–20 n. 100, 126
    n. 108, 134 n. 125, 150 n. 2, 168 n. 55
Boyle, Leonard, 45–6 n. 143
Bullough, Donald, 49 n. 1, 50 n. 5
Brambach, Wilhelm, 4 n. 3
Breviarium de musica et tonarius. See Frutolf of
    Michelsberg
Brockett, Clyde, 87 nn. 7–8, 220 n. 45, 251–2
    n. 50
Brunhölzl, Franz, 49 n. 1, 52 nn. 12–6, 53 n. 17
Bryennius, Manuel, 24 n. 63
Burkert, Walter, 8 n. 15

Calcidius, 9, 118, 150 n. 3, 160 n. 32
Caldwell, John, 120 n. 100
cantilena, 59–60, 68–69, 144 n. 169, 159 n. 28, 169
    n. 56, 195 n. 57, 196 n. 62, 197, 199 n. 68,
    200, 228 n. 70, 255–6 n. 54. See also
    melody
Cantum quem Cisterciensis ordinis, 245 n. 31
Cappuyns, Maieul., 10 n. 19
Cardine, Eugène, 140 n. 151, 143 n. 168
Carolingians, 4 n. 3, 5, 29–30, 38 n. 103, 46
    n. 143, 49–84, 85–6, 93, 101, 108, 111, 118
    n. 98, 139 n. 148
Cassiodorus, 9, 38–41, 46, 49, 84, 96, 103 n. 58

Censorinus, 9, 30 n. 85
Chailley, Jacques, 20 n. 49, 74, 83 n. 89, 94 n. 21,
    171–201, 246 nn. 38–9
chant (cantus) 3, 138, 195
    chromatic alterations in, 129–30, 221–2 n. 72,
        230, 234–6, 241–4, 246 n. 41, 253–8
    classification of, 3, 114–118, 120, 123–26, 128,
        159, 170, 175, 180 n. 24, 214, 216, 224, 233
    emendation of, 3, 218–19, 228 n. 72, 242–45
    transposition of, 160–62, 165–7, 218–9, 226–8,
        230, 235–6, 241–4, 249, 253–4
    notation of, 136–45, 157–9, 162–8, 212–4,
        227–30, 234–37, 241–5, 252–4, 256–8
    See also melody
chant theory (cantus theory) 127, 136, 149, 162,
    168–70, 179–86, 191–201, 211, 216, 218,
    221–8, 238 n. 14
Charlemagne, 49–53, 85, 98, 137
Chartier, Yves, 68 n. 58, 144–5, 149–62, 170 n. 59,
    171 n. 2, 195 n. 59
Chrysaphes, Manuel, 130
Cita et vera divisio monochordi, 202
Cleonides, 8 n. 14, 11 n. 27, 13 n. 30, 21 n. 54, 26
Colette, Marie-Noël, 143 n. 168, 162 n. 43, 220
    n. 42
Commemoratio brevis, 87 nn. 5, 7; 115 n. 84, 159
    n. 30, 179 n. 23, 180 n. 24
Commentarius in artem Donati. See Marius Servius
    Honoratus
Commentarius anonymus in Micrologum Guidonis
    Aretini (Vivell Anonymous), 220 n.45, 221
    n. 49, 222 n. 53, 226
Commentary on Cicero's Somnium Scipionis. See
    Macrobius; Favonius Eulogius
Commentum artis Donati. See Pompeius
Commentum in Martianum Capellam. See
    Remigius of Auxerre
commixtio, 249–52
conjunctiones vocum, 214–5, 218, 221–2. See also
    motus vocum (modi conjunctionum)
Conomos, Dmitri, 130 n.121
consonance, 11, 15–6, 19 n. 44, 20–4, 39, 76,
    81–3, 94, 114, 150, 154, 169–70, 176,
    179–83, 187, 188–9, 199, 203, 208–9, 214
    Pythagorean, 11, 20, 76, 78, 94, 169–70, 182,
    208
Contreni, John, 49 n. 1, 49–50 n. 3, 51 n. 7, 60
    n. 39, 66 n. 52, 69 n. 62
Corbin, Solange, 101 n.46, 105 n. 62, 110 n. 79,
    137 n. 132, 138 n. 142, 141 n. 154, 142
    n. 160, 143 n. 168, 163 n. 44
Cristante, Lucio, 25 n. 66, 26 nn. 71–2, 74–5, 27
    nn. 78, 80; 34, 151 n. 6
Crocker, Richard. 230 n. 80
Cserba, Simon, 214 n. 22, 238 n. 8

Cujusdam Carthusiensis monachi tractatus de musica, 239 n. 18
Cullin, Olivier, 137 n. 132
Cyrus, Cynthia, 175 n. 12

DeJong, M. B., 49 n. 1, 51 n. 12
Delalande, P. Dominique, 228 n. 72
Delisle, Léopold, 86 n. 4, 150 n. 2
Deshusses, Jean, 108 n. 69
Dialogus de musica 3, 123 n. 104, 160 n. 35, 212–19. *See also* Pseudo-Odo
diapason (octave), 11, 13, 19–22, 24–31, 34–36, 39, 71, 74, 76, 94–5, 123, 132, 134–6, 154, 161–2, 169, 172, 174, 176–93, 195–99, 206–11, 220, 222–3, 239, 246–8
  species of, 11 n. 27, 15–6, 18, 19, 21–5, 27–9, 65, 68, 73–6, 81–2, 114 n. 82, 126 n. 108, 134 n. 123, 136, 162, 164, 172–7, 186–202, 205, 207, 209–10, 223
diapente (fifth), 94, 136, 189
  species of, 11, 15–6, 18, 19, 126 n. 108, 189–91, 198–9, 201–211, 248–52
diastema (διάστημα), 27, 39, 109–10, 119, 128, 145, 158, 162, 211, 214 n. 21, 220, 229, 234. *See also* interval
diatessaron (fourth), 94, 135–36
  species of, 11, 15–6, 18, 19, 126 n. 108, 189–91, 198–211, 248–54
De die natali. See Censorinus
differentia, 20 n. 47, 39, 87–93, 96–101, 140 n. 150, 162, 168, 170, 178, 184–6, 190, 225–6, 238–9, 242 n. 24, 251–2 n. 50
Diogenes of Babylonia, 40 n. 118, 41 n.122
Dionysios of Thrace, 40 n. 118, 41 n. 120
Disciplinarum libri IX. See Varro
Disputatio de vera philosophia. See Alcuin of York
dissonantia, 168 n. 53, 170 n. 59, 221 n. 47
distinctiones, 42, 120 n. 100, 142, 161 n. 40, 214–5, 224–6, 237–8, 251–2 n. 50, 253–4
Donati Artem maiorem, In. See Murethach; Sedulius Scottus
Donatus, 39–46, 49, 53–8, 60–61, 84, 94 n. 18, 103, 119 n. 100, 120 n. 101, 128, 139–40 n. 148, 149, 150 n. 2, 238
Donatus ortigraphus, 53 n. 18, 140 n. 148
Duchez, Marie-Elizabeth, 4 n. 4, 53–4, 61 n. 40, 65 n. 47, 78, 150 n. 3
Dulce ingenium, 9, 171 n. 1, 184–5, 186 n. 36
Duo semisphaeria, 207–11, 249
Dyer, Joseph, 52 n. 11
dynamic pitch nomenclature, 22–3 n. 61, 25, 31, 189 n. 45

Ecce modorum, 215 n. 23
ēchēmata (ἠχήματα). *See* intonation formulas

ēchos (ἦχος), 114–8, 191
Eisagoge harmonice (Εἰσαγωγὴ ἁρμονική, *Harmonic Introduction*). *See* Cleonides; Gaudentios
Eisagoge musicae (Εἰσαγωγὴ μουσική, *Introduction to music*). *See* Alypius
Elementa harmonica. See Aristoxenos
Ellsworth, Oliver, 255–8
Epistola ad Eustochium. See Jerome
Epistola ad Michaelem (*Epistola ad Michahelem*). *See* Guido d'Arezzo
Epistola de harmonica institutione. See Regino of Prüm
Epistola de ignoto cantu. See Epistola ad Michaelem; Guido d'Arezzo
Epistola de litteris colendis, 50–1. *See also* Alcuin of York; Charlemagne
Erickson, Raymond, 118 n. 98, 127 n. 116, 130 n. 120, 135 n. 126
Etymologiae. See Isidore of Seville
EUOUAE. *See differentia*
Explanationes Artis Donati. See Sergius
Expositio rervm mathematicarvm ad legendvm Platonem vtilivm ("Exposition of the Mathematics Useful for Reading Plato"). *See* Theon of Smyrna
Expositiones in Micrologum Guidonis Aretini, 220 n. 45, 221 n. 49, 222 n. 53, 224 n. 63, 226 n. 69, 251–2 n. 50. *See also Commentarius anonymus in Micrologum Guidonis Aretini*; *Micros graece, brevis latine*
Expositiones missae, 86

Favonius Eulogius, 9
Ferrari-Barassi, Elena, 118 n. 98, 120 n. 101, 129 n. 117
Ferreira, Manuel Pedro R., 164 n. 47, 228 n. 72
Fischer, Rupert, 228 n. 72
Fleischer, Oskar, 117 nn. 93–5
Floros, Constantin, 117 n. 95
forma, 178, 185–6, 215–7. *See also* species
Fragmentum Censorini. See Censorinus
Franks. *See* Carolingians
Frasch, Cheryl, 228 n. 72
Freistedt, Heinrich, 139 n. 148
Froger, Jacques, 141 nn. 155–6, 142 nn. 157–61, 165 n. 47
Frutolf of Michelsberg, 207 n. 7, 208–11, 228 n. 72, 233 n. 84
Fulgentius, 9, 170 n. 60
Fulgentius, abbot of Afflighem, 237 n. 4
Fuller, Sarah, 245 n. 30

Ganshof, François Louis, 50 n. 4, 51–2
Ganz, David, 149 n. 2

Gaudentios, 8 n. 14, 16 n. 36, 39
Gerbert d'Aurillac (Pope Sylvester II), 202
Gevaert, François Auguste, 34, 92
Glareanus, Heinrich, 5, 199
Glauche, Günther, 49 n. 1, 51 n. 7, 138 n. 148
Glossa maior in institutionem Boethii, 10 n. 20, 54
    n. 22, 66 n. 53, 68 n. 58, 78–84, 94, 119–20
    n. 100, 126 n. 108, 150 n. 2
Gmelch, Joseph, 164 n. 47, 166
Göschl, Johannes, 139 n. 148, 143 n. 168
Gombosi, Otto, 4 n. 3, 117, 118 n. 98
Gonthier of St. Amand, 149 n. 2
grammar, 7, 8, 39–46, 49–65, 103–11, 114, 118,
    120 n. 100, 128, 139 n. 148. *See also* ac-
    cent, prosody, tone
grammarian. *See* grammar
Grebe, Sabine, 10 n. 19, 25 n. 68, 30 n. 85
Grier, James, 50 n. 3, 137 n. 132
Gümpel, Karl-Werner, 160 n. 33, 171 n. 1, 186
    n. 36, 212 n. 19
Guido Augensis (Guy d'Eu), 233 n. 84, 245 n. 30
Guido d'Arezzo, 5, 9, 18 n. 43, 93, 134 n. 125,
    139–40, 160 n. 36, 161 n. 38, 219–34, 237,
    239, 241–2, 249, 252 n. 50, 255–6
Guidonian hand, 230–33
Guillaume de Volpiano, 163, 164 n. 46
Gushee, Lawrence, 10 n. 21, 87 n. 5, 93–106, 114
    nn. 81–2, 118 n. 98, 149 n. 3, 160 n. 33

Haas, Max, 86 n. 3, 93 n. 16, 114 n. 84, 117
    nn. 95–6, 118 n. 98
Haggh, Barbara, 93 n. 17
Handschin, Jacques, 101 n. 46, 105–13
Hankeln, Roman, 86 n. 5, 228 n. 72
Hannick, Christian, 114 n. 84, 115 n. 85, 117
    n. 96
Hansen, Finn Egeland, 162 n. 43, 163 n. 45, 164
    nn. 46–7, 166
harmonia (ἁρμονία), 4 n. 4, 8, 10, 25, 26 n. 69, 39,
    40 n. 112, 53, 65, 97, 120 n. 102, 123
    n. 106, 128, 136
harmonica institutione, De. *See* Hucbald of St.
    Amand
Harmonica introductio (Εἰσαγωγὴ ἁρμονική). *See*
    Cleonides; Gaudentios
harmonic theory, 7–40, 46, 54, 65–84, 94, 114,
    118 n. 99, 125–7, 128, 132–7, 145, 151–9,
    167–70, 172–73, 175–8, 187–201, 212–4,
    216, 219–28, 230
Harmonika. *See* Bryennius; Ptolemy
Hartwic of St. Emmeram, 171 n. 2
Haug, Andreas, 139 n. 148
Heard, Edmund Brooks, 171–82
Hebborn, Barbara, 118 n. 98, 120 n. 101, 129
    n. 117, 130 n. 122, 133 n. 122

Heinrich Eger von Kalkar, 239 nn. 18–9
Heiric of Auxerre, 149 n. 2
Herlinger, Jan, 187 n. 39, 217 n. 32, 245–54
Hermannus Contractus, 223 n. 58, 237 n. 4
hexachord, 108 n. 127, 129, 134 n. 123, 223,
    230–33, 237–8, 255–7
Hieronymous de Moravia, 214 n. 22, 237 n. 8
Hildebrandt, M. M., 49 n. 1
Hiley, David, 50 n. 3, 85 n. 1, 86 n. 4, 86 n. 3, 87
    n. 8, 92 n. 14, 137 nn. 131–4, 139–40
    nn. 148, 152
Hippias maior (*Greater Hippias*). *See* Plato
Hochadel, Matthias, 207 n. 7, 208 nn. 8–9, 209
    n. 10
Hoffman-Axthelm, Dagmar, 41 nn. 119, 121
Holford-Strevens, Leofranc, 60 n. 35
Holtz, Louis, 39–42, 49 n. 1, 53 nn. 17–8, 20; 54
    nn. 24, 27; 55–7, 140 n. 148, 150 n. 2
Homer, 7
Hourlier, Jacques, 86 n. 2, 101 n. 46, 110 nn. 78,
    80
Hrabanus Maurus, 52 n. 14
Hucbald of St. Amand, 5, 9, 68 n. 58, 73, 134
    n. 125, 139 n. 148, 140, 143–5, 149–64,
    167, 170 n. 59, 171 nn. 2–3, 173 n. 6, 175,
    178 n. 17, 179 n. 23, 180 n. 24, 184–6,
    195, 201–3, 217, 220 nn. 42, 46; 226, 228,
    235, 241, 257–8
Hucke, Helmut, 85 n. 1, 86 n. 2, 137 nn. 130,
    132
Hüschen, Heinrich, 168 n. 51, 239 nn. 18–9
Huglo, Michel, 4 n. 3, 38 n. 195, 53 n. 18, 85 n. 1,
    86 n. 5, 87 nn. 6–8, 88 n. 11, 101 n. 46,
    110 nn. 78, 80; 137 n. 132, 143 nn. 163–4,
    149 n. 1, 151 nn. 10–11, 159 n. 30, 160
    n. 33, 162 nn. 42–3, 163 n. 45, 171 n. 2,
    173 n. 4, 177 n. 15, 212 n. 19, 214 n. 21,
    237 n. 4

Iliad. *See* Homer
institutione arithmetica libri duo, De. *See* Boethius
institutione clericorum libri tres, De. *See* Hrabanus
    Maurus
institutione musica libri quinque, De. *See* Boethius
Institutio oratoria. *See* Quintilianus
Institutiones. *See* Cassiodorus
intentio, 22 n. 59, 27, 51 n. 7, 118 n. 99. *See also*
    phthongus; tasis
interval, 7, 8 n. 17, 9, 19, 21–2, 26–8, 34, 39, 68,
    70, 71 n. 67, 76, 78–9, 92, 94, 109, 114
    n. 82, 117, 119–25, 127–9, 132, 135–6,
    139–40, 143–5, 150–2, 159, 165 n. 47,
    175–7, 179–83, 189, 199 n. 70, 203–5,
    214–5, 217, 221 n. 50, 222–4, 227, 229–30,
    234, 236, 242, 250–2, 255–8

as part of harmonic theory, 7, 8 n. 17, 9, 18,
    21–2, 26, 34, 39, 70, 76, 78–9, 94, 119–20,
    125, 127–8, 150–1
as characteristic of mode, 94–5, 175–77,
    179–83
as component of species, 19, 27–8, 68, 117,
    119–20, 123, 125, 129, 132, 159, 203, 215
    n. 25, 217, 222, 251–2
as component of melody, 92, 94, 127, 139–40,
    144, 150–2, 214, 224, 227, 236, 255–8
as component of notation, 109, 139–40,
    143–44, 165 n. 47, 229–30, 234, 236,
    242–3, 255–8
in monochord division, 16–18, 135–36, 212–4,
    219–20
See also diastema; species; tone
interruptio, 252
intonation formulas (ἠχήματα, ēchēmata), 87–90,
    92, 98, 102, 114–18, 126, 136, 172, 175
    nn. 11, 13; 176, 178, 179 n. 22, 186 n. 35,
    193–95, 197–201, 230 n. 81
Introductio artis musicae (Εἰσαγωγὴ τεχνῆς
    μουσικῆς). See Bacchius Geron
Isidore of Seville, 9, 10 n. 18, 38–44, 46, 49, 53,
    56, 58, 84, 94 n. 18, 96–7, 103

Jacobi Leodensis (Jacques de Liège), 214 n. 22,
    237 n. 8, 238 nn. 12, 16; 239 nn. 17–8
Jacobsthal, Gustav, 4 n. 3, 129 n. 117, 228 n. 72,
Jammers, Ewald, 106, 110 n. 80, 137 n. 132, 101
    n. 46
Jeauneau, Éduoard, 49 n. 1
Jeffery, Peter, 85 n. 2
Jerome (Sanctus Eusebius Hieronymus), 6
Jerome of Moravia. See Hieronymous de
    Moravia
Johannes Aegidius de Zamora, 233 n. 84, 239
    n. 18
John the Deacon, 85 n. 3
John Scottus Eriugena, 9, 29, 38, 53 n. 18, 65,
    67–71, 73, 76–8, 83–4, 150

Karp, Theodore, 228 n. 72, 255–6 n. 54
Kaczynski, Bernice, 38 n. 103, 82 n. 87
Kessler, Ernst, 228 n. 72
Klauser, Theodore, 85 n. 1
Kunz, Lukas, 24 n. 63, 87 n. 7

Labowski, Lotte, 69 n. 63
Lantpert of Metz, 142 n. 155
Laum, Bernhard, 7 n. 7
Laws. See Plato
Lehmann, Paul, 53 n. 17
Leonardi, Claudio, 35 nn. 98–100, 38 n. 102, 53
    n. 18, 54 n. 22, 60 nn. 34, 36, 38–9; 64

nn. 44–5, 66 nn. 52–3, 69 nn. 61–3, 70
    n. 64
Levy, Kenneth, 4 n. 3, 50 n. 3, 85–6 n. 2, 93 n. 16,
    101 n. 47, 103 n. 57, 105 n. 62, 114 n. 83,
    137 nn. 130–2
legitimis ordinibus pentachordorum et tetrachordorum,
    De. See Theinred of Dover
Liber argumentorum, 224. See also Commentarius
    anonymus in Micrologum Guidonis Aretini;
    Expositiones in Micrologum Guidonis
    Aretini
Liber specierum, 221 n. 49, 222 n. 53. See also
    Guido d'Arezzo
Life of Gregory the Great (Vita Gregorii magni).
    See John the Deacon
Life of the Emperor Charles the Great (Vita impera-
    toris Caroli magni). See Notker Balbulus
Lindsay, Wallace M., 9, 38 n. 105, 39 n. 112, 40
    n. 115, 43 nn. 130–2, 44–5, 56 n. 28, 97
lingua Latina, De. See Varro
Lipphardt, Walter, 86 n. 5, 88 n. 10, 162 n. 42
liquescence, 139–40, 144, 228 n. 74
litterae significativae, 140–2
Lombard Anonymous. See Pseudo-Odo
Lucidarium. See Marchetto da Padova
Lutz, Cora, 16 n. 70, 29, 38 nn. 100, 102; 53 n. 18,
    60 n. 39, 62 n. 43, 65 n. 48, 66 n. 52, 67–8,
    69 nn. 61–3; 71, 75 n. 75, 77, 150 n. 2, 187
    n. 39

McKinnon, James, 3 n. 1, 39 nn. 104–6, 40 n. 112,
    86 n. 3, 160 n. 35, 189 n. 45, 218 nn. 33–6,
    219 nn. 37–9, 220 nn. 43–4, 228 n. 73, 229
    n. 75, 230 n. 80
McKitterick, Rosamond, 85 n. 1, 86 n. 2, 103
    n. 57
Macrobius, 9, 170 n. 60
Maître, Claire, 245 n. 29, 245 n. 31
Maloy, Rebecca, 228 n. 72
Marchetto da Padova, 187 nn. 39, 41; 199, 217,
    235, 245–54
Marius Servius Honoratus, 45 n. 139, 56 n. 28
Markovits, Michael, 4 n. 3, 18 n. 43, 135 n. 126,
    136, 160 n. 31, 209 n. 10, 212 n. 20, 220
    n. 45
Marosszécki, Solutor R., 245 n. 29
Martianus Capella, 8–10, 25–38, 39 n. 107, 40,
    42–6, 49, 51, 53–79, 84, 103 n. 55, 108,
    114, 118 n. 99, 139 n. 148, 149–51, 169
    n. 57, 170 n. 60, 184, 186 n. 35, 187
    nn. 39–40; 228 n. 74, 256 n. 57
Mathiesen, Thomas, 6 n. 2, 7 nn. 5–7, 11; 8 n. 14,
    11 nn. 25–7, 16 n. 36, 21 n. 54, 26 nn. 73,
    76–7; 28 n. 80, 30–33, 38 n. 106, 39
    n. 110, 73 n. 70

means (arithmetic, harmonic), 20, 187, 196–9
μέγεθος φωνῆς (megethos phonēs), 21, 26, 28
    n. 80. *See also* diastema; interval
Melampous, 40 n. 118
melodic classification. *See* chant, classification of
melody (*melodia, melos*), 3, 7, 66–67, 69 n. 58, 103,
    120, 130 nn. 121–22, 137 n. 131, 138, 140
    n. 149, 152, 158 n. 27, 159–60, 167, 170,
    199–200, 227
    and prosodic accents, 43–44, 58–9, 65–67,
        103–13, 199–200
    as determinant of mode, 83, 87 nn. 7–8, 92–93,
        98, 100, 114, 120, 123–27, 136, 195,
        218–19, 223, 151–52
    of psalm-tone, 99, 102–104, 168 n. 53
    notation of, 136–45, 157–58, 163–68, 227–30,
        235–36
    "paradigms of," 94 n. 18
    shape of, 140 n. 152, 224, 227, 230, 234–36,
        242–45, 249–52
    See also chant; model melodies
Ménager, Amand, 142 n. 159–60, 143 n. 167
mensura, 76–9
    as component of mode, 187, 193 n. 52, 246
        n. 39; 248 n. 42
    of monochord, organ pipes, 4 n. 3, 10 n. 22, 16
        n. 39, 18 n. 43, 135, 136 n. 129
mensurando monochordo, De, 207 n. 7, 208 n. 8, 209
        n. 10. *See also* Bern of Reichenau
Merkley, Paul, 86 n. 5, 88 n. 11, 92–3
Metaphysics. See Aristotle
Meyer, Christian, 10 n. 22, 18 n. 43, 71 n. 68, 73
        n. 72, 135 n. 126, 171 n. 2, 173 n. 4, 208
        n. 8, 212 n. 20, 220 n. 45, 221 n. 50
Micrologus. See Guido d'Arezzo
Micros graece, brevis latine, 220 n. 45, 221 n. 49, 222
        n. 53, 224, 226 n. 69. *See also Commentar-
        ius anonymus in Micrologum Guidonis
        Aretini*
Mitologiae. See Fulgentius
Mocquereau, André, 141 n. 155, 142 n. 159
mode (*modus*), 3–6, 8, 10–11, 14, 16–25, 28–31,
        33–9, 46, 49, 65–71, 73–8, 81–85, 93, 96,
        116–18, 120, 123–30, 134 n. 23, 136, 154,
        159 n. 30, 160, 162–4, 167, 169–70, 173–5,
        177–211, 214–7, 218–27, 233, 238–9,
        245–54, 257–8
    as interval, 27 n. 80, 68 n. 58, 221–3, 246–8
    definition of, 21, 67–8, 187, 214, 237–8, 246
    description of, 19–25, 28–38, 69–70, 73–6,
        83–4, 97, 114–17, 124–7, 136, 179–82,
        185–89, 191, 193–9, 203–11, 215–7,
        222–3, 225–6, 233, 238–9, 246
    determination of, 3, 83, 86–94, 98–101, 114,
        124–26, 159, 161–2, 179–82, 185–99,

206–8, 210–11, 214–5, 218–9, 223–6,
    246–52
    wing diagram of, 23, 29, 31, 33, 38, 71–3, 78
        n. 78, 83–4, 189
    See also tone; trope
model melodies, 93 n. 16, 126, 136, 216, 225–6,
    238–9. *See also* neume, as model melody;
    Primum quaerite
modorum formulis, De, 251–2 n. 50
modulatio (melody) 21 n. 57, 22, 44 n. 144, 59–60,
    66–67, 94 n. 18, 98, 104, 126, 128, 140
    n. 142, 170, 194, 197
modulatio tonorum (Aurelian of Réôme), 35, 127
Möbius, Gerhard, 129 n. 117
Möller, Hartmut, 49 nn. 1–2, 96 n. 28,
monochord, 10, 11 n. 25, 15, 18–9, 46, 82, 114
    n. 82, 135, 136 nn. 128–9; 150, 153–4, 160,
    162, 164 n. 46, 178, 184, 202 n. 1, 207 n. 7,
    208, 209 n. 10, 211–7, 220–1, 228–9, 234,
    237, 242
motus vocum (*modi coniunctionum*), 221, 251–2
    n. 50. *See also conjunctiones vocum*
Mühlmann, Wilhelm, 171–91
Murethach, 42, 53 n. 18, 54 nn. 24–6; 56–8, 140
    n. 148, 150 n. 2
Musica disciplina. See Aurelian of Réôme
Musica enchiriadis, 9, 73, 87 n. 5, 116 n. 86, 118–36,
    149–50, 154–6, 159 nn. 30–1; 160–61,
    167, 170 n. 59, 180 n. 24, 195–6, 215
    n. 23, 219–23, 228 n. 74, 229 n. 76, 230
    n. 79, 234–5, 238, 257
musica libri sex, De. See Augustine
musica libri tres, De. See Aristides Quintilianus
Musica manualis cum tonale. See Wylde, John
musician (*musicus,* μουσικός), 3, 7, 40, 92, 149
    n. 1, 162 n. 43, 256

natural music (Regino of Prüm), 168–9
Netzer, Henri, 85 n. 1
neume (*neuma,* πνεῦμα), 4 n. 1, 45 n. 141, 53
    n. 19, 58 n. 33, 61 n. 40, 64, 65 n. 47, 85–6
    n. 2, 93 n. 16, 99, 101 nn. 46–7, 102 n. 51,
    105–10, 114 n. 83, 117 n. 95, 136–45,
    157–9, 163–4, 167, 198, 221, 223, 225, 228,
    235, 239 n. 17, 242–4
    as model melody, 87 n. 7, 225–6, 251–2 n. 50
    See also notation, musical, practical
Nichomachus, 10 n. 21, 24 n. 63
NOEANE melodies (NOEAGIS, NONANEANE, etc.),
    87, 92, 98, 102, 104, 114–8, 126–7,
    136–45, 154, 158, 172, 175–80, 185–6,
    193–5, 197–200, 216. *See also* intonation
    formulas
nota, 4 n. 4, 12 n. 28, 15–6, 16 n. 35, 41–2, 42
    n. 124, 44, 46, 49, 50 n. 3, 54–56, 61–5, 78

n. 78, 101–6, 107 n. 67, 108, 119, 124, 130
n. 122, 137 n. 131, 139, 144, 157–8, 228
n. 73. *See also* chant, notation of; notation
notation, musical, 4–5, 8, 12 n. 28, 15–7, 49, 65,
74–5, 78, 81–3, 85–86, 88, 93, 101, 105–13,
133–45, 156–9, 162–8, 178, 184, 208–9,
212, 214, 218, 220, 227–9, 230 n. 79,
234–7, 241–5, 252–4, 256–8
Dasia, 118 n. 98, 119–26, 129–35, 154, 162
n. 42, 167, 221, 230 n. 79
letter, 15–16, 74–5, 78 n. 78, 81–3, 133–6,
154–6, 178, 184, 208 n. 9, 209 n. 10, 214,
218, 227
used in treatises, 16, 46, 74–5, 78 n. 78, 81–3,
101–2, 105–13, 133–6, 156–9, 178, 184,
202 n. 1, 208 n. 9, 209 n. 10, 214, 218, 220,
227, 257
practical, 85–86 n. 2, 86 n. 4, 88, 93, 99, 100
n. 40, 101, 105–6, 112–3, 136–45, 157–9,
162–8, 221, 227–30, 234–7, 241–5, 252–4,
256–8
Aquitanian, 102, 112–3, 138–9
Beneventan, 112–3, 138, 140
Breton, 112–3, 137–8, 143, 158
French, 112–3, 137–8, 158
Laon, 112–3, 138, 141–3
Paleofrankish, 99, 101–5, 106–13, 137–9,
143, 158
St. Gall, 105–6, 112–3, 138, 141–3, 239 n. 17
See also chant, notation of; *nota*
Notker Balbulus, 85–6, 141–3
nothae, 98 n. 34, 168, 219 n. 41, 235
Nova expositio. See Alia musica
De numero tonorum litterae Episcopi A. ad Coepis-
copum E., 215 n. 24
De nuptiis Philologiae et Mercurii. See Martianus
Capella

Ochsenbein, Peter, 49 n. 1,
Odyssey. See Homer
Oesch, Hans, 160 n. 33, 204 n. 3
oktō ēchoi (ὀκτὼ ἦχοι). *See echos*
Ordines romani, 86
Ostheimer, Andreas, 118 n. 98, 120 n. 101

Palisca, Claude, 68 n. 58, 134 n. 125, 139 n. 148,
144–62, 195 n. 59, 219–30, 237–44
papadikē (παπαδική), 115–8, 120, 136
papadikon biblion. See papadikē
parapteres, 98 n. 34, 168, 219 n. 41, 235. *See also*
nothae
Paulinus of Aquileia, 52
Pepin III, 85
Pesce, Dolores, 160 n. 36, 220 nn. 43–4, 221 n. 47,

222–4, 227 n. 70, 228 n. 72, 229 n. 75, 230
n. 80,
Peter of Pisa, 52
Petrović, Danica, 117 n. 95
Περὶ μουσικῆς (*De musica*). *See* Aristides Quintilianus
Pfisterer, *Andreas*, 228 n. 72, 255–6 n. 54
Philebos. See Plato
Phillips, Nancy, 118 n. 98, 120 n. 101, 133 n. 122,
134 n. 125, 136 n. 128, 137 n. 132, 150
n. 2, 154 n. 16, 156 n. 26, 160 n. 32, 162
n. 43, 164 nn. 46–7, 171 n. 2, 173, 184
nn. 31–2, 208 n. 9, 209 n. 10, 214 n. 21,
229 n. 76
phthongus (φθόγγος), 21, 26–7, 118, 124, 127, 238
phthorai (φθοραί), 117, 130
Pietsch, Gerhard, 114 n. 81
Pizzani, Ubaldo, 10 n. 21, 24 n. 63
Plato, 7–9, 13 n. 30, 118, 160 n. 32
πνεῦμα. *See* neume
Pöhlmann, Egert, 7 n. 3
Poetica. See Aristotle
Politics. See Aristotle
Pompeius, 45 n. 139
Ponte, Joseph, 93 n. 17, 94 n. 18, 99 nn. 36–7, 100,
103 nn. 55–9
positurae, 42–4
Potiron, Henri, 156 n. 26, 162 n. 42,
Powers, Harold, 4 n. 3, 73 n. 72, 118 n. 98, 120
n. 100, 221 n. 49
Praßl, Franz Karl, 228 n. 72
Préaux, Jean, 29, 56 n. 28, 60 n. 39, 61 n. 41, 70,
150 n. 2
Prima species, 202–7, 211. *See also* Pseudo-Berneli-
nus
Primum quaerite, 87 n. 7, 88 n. 11, 216, 225, 238–9,
242 n. 23
Primum tractatum huius voluminis de symphonia. See
Schneider Anonymous
Prologus in antiphonarium. See Guido d'Arezzo
Prologus in tonarium. See Bern of Reichenau
prosody (prosodia, προσῳδία), 7, 41–6, 55–65,
103–14, 238
prosomoia, 93 n. 16
psalm-tone, 87 nn. 5, 8; 92, 99, 101–4, 184–6,
225–6, 238–9
Pseudo-Bernelinus, 5, 203–7. *See also Prima species*
Pseudo-Johannes de Muris, 233 n. 84, 239 n. 18
Pseudo-Martin of Laon, 53 n. 18, 60, 65–71,
76–7, 186 n. 35
Pseudo-Odo, 3–5, 83, 88 n. 12, 123 n. 104, 157,
160, 184, 209 n. 11, 212–21, 224, 226, 228,
229 n. 78, 234, 236–7, 239, 244, 249,
257–8
Pseudo-Plutarch, 8 n. 14

Ptolemy, 10–11, 13 n. 29, 23–5, 46, 188, 193, 196, 210

Pythagoras, 8 n. 15, 11, 71, 78, 94, 151, 179–80, 208

quarter-tones, 164–66

Quaestiones in musica, 214 n. 22

quilisma, 140, 144

Quintilianus, 7 n. 9, 9, 41 n. 120, 187 n. 41

Raasted, Jørgen, 87 n. 7, 93 n. 17, 98 n. 35, 114 n. 84, 117 nn. 91–6

Rathbod of Trier, Bishop, 168 n. 51

Rausch, Alexander, 140 n. 150, 204–11, 235–6

Reckow, Fritz, 11 n. 24, 238 n. 11

Regino of Prüm, 5, 9, 86–7 n. 5, 87 n. 7, 88–92, 94, 98, 101, 149, 168–70, 177, 180 n. 24, 216, 219, 225 n. 66, 235–6

regula, 3, 50, 94 n. 18, 98 n. 33, 160 n. 35, 214 n. 22, 220 nn. 43–4, 221 n. 47, 222 n. 51, 223 nn. 55–6, 228 nn. 73–4, 229 n. 75, 230 n. 80, 233 n. 84, 245 n. 30

Regulae de arte musica. See Guido Augensis (Guy d'Eu)

Regulae rhythmicae (Regule rithmice). See Guido d'Arezzo

Remigius of Auxerre, 9, 29, 35, 37, 53 n. 18, 62, 65, 67–9, 71, 73, 75–8, 84, 149–50 nn 1–2, 170 n. 60, 184, 187 n. 39

Republic. See Plato

Riché, Pierre, 49 n. 1, 51 n. 10, 52 n. 16

Richter, Lukas, 118 n. 98

Sachs, Klaus-Jürgen, 4 n. 3, 16 nn. 39–40, 18 n. 42, 135 n. 127, 136 n. 129, 220 n. 45

saeculorum Amen. See differentia

Santosuosso, Alma Colk Browne, 134 n. 123, 136 n. 128, 154 n. 16, 156 n. 26, 162 n. 43, 163 n. 44

scale. *See* tone-system

Schlötterer, Reinhold, 114 n. 84, 116 nn. 89–90

Schmid, Hans, 15 n. 34, 87 n. 5, 118–36, 136 n. 128, 150 n. 3, 154 n. 20, 161 n. 40, 170 n. 59, 195 n. 60, 196 n. 62, 215 n. 23

Schneider Anonymous, 238 nn. 8, 16; 239 nn. 17, 18

Schrimpf, Gandolf, 70 n. 64

Scolica enchiriadis, 87 n. 5, 118 n. 98, 120 n. 101, 122–3, 127 n. 116, 129–31, 135–6, 150, 153–4, 160 n. 33, 161 n. 40, 215 n. 23, 228 n. 74, 229 n. 76, 230 n. 79, 234–5, 256 n. 58, 257

Sedulius Scottus, 42, 53 n. 18, 54 nn. 23–4, 56–8, 140 n. 148, 150 n. 2

seminarium musices (Martianus Capella), 43, 58–60, 84

semitone, 3, 16 n. 34, 20–22, 26, 30–32, 38–9, 68 n. 58, 70–71, 76–81, 82–4, 87 n. 4, 120, 123, 125–6, 129–30, 135, 150–58, 165 n. 47, 168–9, 189–92, 199–200, 203–7, 212–6, 218, 221–2, 234–6, 241–3, 253–4, 256–7

Sergius, 56 n. 28.

sesquialtera, 20, 79, 135, 180–1. *See also* diapente (fifth)

sesquioctave (*epogdous*), 20–1, 79, 95, 120 n. 102, 128, 150, 169, 185–6, 217 n. 27. *See also* tone

sesquitertia, 20, 79, 135, 175, 180–1. *See also* diatessaron (fourth)

Shanzer, Danuta, 10 n. 19, 150 n. 2

Smits van Waesberghe, Joseph, 18 n. 42, 74 n. 74, 118 n. 98, 134 n. 123, 136 nn. 128–9, 139 n. 148, 140 n. 150, 141 n. 155, 154 n. 16, 156 n. 26, 202, 204 n. 3, 208 n. 8, 209 n. 10, 212 n. 20, 215 n. 24, 219–33, 237–44, 252 n. 50

Snyder, John, 255 n. 54

Somnium Scipionis. See Cicero, Macrobius (commentary on), Favonius Eulogius (commentary on)

sound (*sonus*, φωνή), 20 n. 47, 21, 26–8, 43, 43 n. 131, 44, 44 n. 136, 46, 54–5, 57, 61, 64, 65 n. 49, 66, 66 nn. 51–53, 67, 67 n. 56, 67 n. 58, 68, 68 n. 58, 70–1, 76, 77, 79, 96 n. 26, 97–8, 115–9, 120 n. 100, 121, 123–7, 127 nn. 110–11, 128, 134 n. 124, 140 n. 150, 144 n. 169, 150 n. 5, 152 n. 13, 154 n. 19, 159 n. 31, 187 n. 40, 195 n. 61, 196 n. 62, 222, 229 n. 75, 233 n. 85, 238, 239 n. 18, 256 n. 59. *See also phthongus*, tone, *vox*

species, 11, 15–6, 18–9, 27, 65, 68, 74, 81, 83, 114, 117, 128, 178, 193, 199, 202–4, 208, 215, 221, 224, 246, 248–54

   definition of, 19 n. 44

   of degrees (*modus vocum*), 221–4

   See also diapason (octave); diapente (fifth); diatessaron (fourth)

Speculum musicae. See Jacobi Leodensis (Jacques de Liège)

Stäblein, Bruno, 5 n. 5, 85 n. 1, 87 n. 8, 101 n. 46, 110 n. 80, 137 n. 132, 211 n. 18

Stahl, William, 10 n. 19, 25–30, 34, 66 n. 54

Steinen, Wolfram von den, 141 n. 155

Stephen II, Pope, 85

Strunk, Oliver, 87 n. 7, 116 n. 86, 117, 118 n. 97, 160 n. 35, 215 n. 25, 218, 219 nn. 37–9,

220 nn. 41, 44; 228 n. 73, 229 n. 75, 231
    n. 80
Stuart, Nicholas, 228 n. 72
Sullivan, Blair, 42 n. 126, 46 n. 145
Summa musicae. See Pseudo-Johannes de Muris
Suñol, Grégoire Marie, 137 n. 132
Sweeney, Cecily, 245 n. 29
systema. See tone-system

tasis, 21, 27. *See also phthongus*
Teeuwen, Mariken, 53–4, 60 nn. 34, 36, 38–9; 65
    nn. 49–50, 66 nn. 51–2, 55; 67 n. 56, 69
    n. 62, 70 n. 66, 73 nn. 68–9, 76–8, 150
    n. 2, 186 n. 35
Τέχνη περὶ φωνῆς. *See* Diogenes of Babylonia
tenor, 39, 41, 43, 54–7, 93, 94 n. 18, 96–7, 103–4,
    225–6, 238–9. *See also* accent; tone
Theinred of Dover, 255 n. 54
Theodaldus, Bishop, 229 n. 78
Theodulf of Orléans, 52
Theon of Smyrna, 13 n. 50
thetic pitch nomenclature, 22–3, 25, 27, 189 n. 45
Thrasyllus. See Theon of Smyrna
Tillyard, Henry J. W., 117 n. 95, 130 n. 121
Timaeus. See Plato
Timaeus a Calcidio translatus. See Calcidius
Tinctoris, Johannes, 199
Tonale sancti Bernardi, 245 n. 30
tonary, 86–94, 96, 98, 100–1, 159 n. 29, 162, 214
    n. 21, 216, 228 n. 72, 233 n. 84, 235–7, 238
    n. 14, 245 n. 30
    Alia musica (*Nova expositio*), 172–9, 184–6
    of Bern of Reichenau, 140 n. 150, 204–11,
        249
    Dijon (Montpellier 159), 162–7, 214
    Metz, 87 n. 5, 88, 94 n. 23, 100, 162 n. 42, 177
    of Regino of Prüm, 88–92, 101, 168–70
    St. Riquier, 86 n. 2, 87 nn. 5, 7; 88
tone (*tonus*, τόνος)
    as accent, 39–46, 54–65, 85, 94 n. 18, 96–7, 103,
        238
    as melodic classification, 3 n. 1, 4–6, 8, 19–22,
        26, 30–2, 38–40, 46, 70–71, 73, 83–7,
        94–101, 114, 123–4, 127–8, 154, 159–62,
        168–70, 175–7, 180–1, 188, 193 n. 53,
        206–11, 214–9, 238–9, 246–54
    as pitch (*tasis*, τάσις, *vox*), 28–29, 66 n. 54, 70,
        87 n. 7, 108, 116, 118
    as Psalm-tone, 86–7
    as interval, 3, 16 n. 34, 20–22, 26, 32, 34, 39,
        70–71, 76–80, 82–4, 94–6, 114, 117, 120,
        123, 125, 127–8, 135, 150–58, 168–9, 179,
        189–92, 199–200, 203–7, 212–6, 218,
        221–2, 234–6, 241–3, 247–8, 252, 255–56
    definition of, 8 n. 17, 20–21, 26, 39–41, 44,

54–60, 70–71, 76–7, 79, 94 n. 18, 95– 7, 98
    n. 33, 116 n. 90, 118 n. 98, 123–4, 127
    n. 116, 128, 150, 214, 246–8
    division of, 16 n. 34, 20, 26, 77–8, 114, 136,
        150–1, 169
    tonus commixtus, imperfectus, perfectus, mixtus,
        plusquamperfectus, 246–8
    See also accent; mode; trope
tone-system (*systema*, σύστημα, scale), 4–6, 8,
    10–5, 18–19, 21, 27, 39, 46, 49, 65, 68,
    80–81, 93, 114, 117–8, 120–4, 129–30,
    132–6, 152–7, 164–7, 184, 187 n. 42, 189,
    195 n. 60, 203, 208, 212–4, 217–23,
    226–34, 237, 255–8
tonis, De, 64 n. 46, 87 n. 5, 137 n. 131. *See also* Vat-
    ican Anonymous; Wagner, Peter
tonus acquisitus, 129 n. 117, 133 n. 122, 228 n. 72,
    254, 257 n. 62
τόπος τῆς φωνῆς (*topos tēs phōnēs*; "position" or
    "region of the voice"), 21. *See also* mode;
    tone; trope; transposition scales
Torkewitz, Dieter, 118 n. 98
Tractatus de musica. See Hieronymous de Moravia
Tractatus de natura et distinctione octo tonorum musice
    transformatio, 238 n. 16
transformatio, 223–24
transposition scales, 21, 39–40, 189. *See also* mode,
    tone, trope.
Traub, Andreas, 118 n. 98, 144–45, 149–62, 170
    n. 59, 195 n. 59
Treitler, Leo, 3 n. 2, 4 n. 3, 50 n. 5, 101 n. 45, 105
    n. 62, 106 n. 65, 109, 114 n. 83, 120
    n. 100, 137 n. 132, 138 n. 143
tritone (*tritonus*), 134 n. 125, 135, 205, 214, 230
    n. 79
trope (*tropus*, τρόπος), 8, 19–22, 26, 28–38, 39
    n. 107, 46, 51, 65–76, 78 n. 78, 84–5, 114,
    127–8, 159–62, 167, 170, 172, 175–78,
    184–200, 211, 214–5, 237–8, 246
τρόπος συστηματικός (*tropos systēmatikos*:
    "systemic trope"), 20, 26, 34, 69–71, 78
    n. 78. *See also* trope

Varro, 9, 25 n. 68, 30 n. 85, 45, 62 n. 43
Vergil, 62 n. 43
Veroli, Cristiano, 245 n. 29, 245 n. 33
Viret, Jacques, 118 n. 98
vitia, 129–33
Vitruvius, 9
Vivell Anonymous. See Commentarius anonymus in
    Micrologum Guidonis Aretini
Vivell, Coelestin, 140 n. 152, 209 n. 10, 220 n. 45,
    224 n. 63, 225–6, 233 n. 84
Vogel, Cyrille, 84 n. 1
Vogel, Martin, 15 nn. 33–4, 130 n. 122

vox, 9, 44–6
  as mode, 233 n. 85, 239 n. 18
  as pitch, 12 n. 28, 20 n. 51, 21, 22 n. 59, 24, 28
       n. 80, 46, 66, 128, 139 n. 148, 154 n. 19,
       186 n. 35, 190, 215 nn. 23–4; 216, 221
       nn. 47, 49; 222, 224 nn. 61, 64; 225 n. 67,
       226, 229 n. 75
  as utterance, 43 n. 144, 58–9
  as voice, speech, 39–40, 43 n. 134, 58–9, 66–7,
       96–7, 99, 103–4, 118–9, 134, 140 n. 152,
       143 n. 168, 144 n. 169, 168 n. 53
  See also tone as pitch

Waddell, Chrysogenos, 245 n. 29
Waeltner, Ernst Ludwig, 93 n. 17, 93–4 n. 18, 100
       n. 36, 105–6
Wagner, Peter, 64 n. 46, 87 n. 5, 92, 101, 106, 137
       n. 131, 239 n. 17
Wallach, Leopold, 50 n. 5

Walter, Michael, 85 n. 1, 86 n. 3, 110 n. 77, 118 n. 98
Wantzloeben, Sigfrid, 10 n. 22, 212 n. 20, 220
       n. 45
Warburton, Jane, 202–11
Waszink, J. H., 9, 160 n. 32
Weakland, Rembert, 149 n. 1
Wellesz, Egon, 117 n. 95
West, Martin L., 7 n. 2
Wiesli, Walter, 140 n. 152
Wilhelm of Hirsau, 223 n. 58
Wille, Günther, 8 n. 17, 34
Willis, James, 10 n. 19, 26–30, 34, 43–4, 58–77
Wingell, Richard, 156 n. 26
Wolfram, Gerda, 117 n. 95, 130 n. 121
Wylde, John, 245 n. 30

Zaminer, Frieder, 7–8, 46 n. 144
Zamora, Johannes Aegidius de, 233 n. 84,
       239 n. 18

50077746R00181